P9-CRX-977

1&2 SAMUEL

Smyth & Helwys Bible Commentary: 1 & 2 Samuel

Publication Staff

Publisher and President
Cecil P. Staton

Executive Vice-President
David Cassady

Vice-President, Editorial
Lex Horton

Senior Editor
Mark K. McElroy

Book Editor
P. Keith Gammons

Art Director and Book Designer
Jim Burt

Assistant Editors
Kelley Land, Erin Smith

Smyth & Helwys Publishing, Inc.
6316 Peake Road
Macon, Georgia 31210-3960
1-800-747-3016
© 2001 by Smyth & Helwys Publishing
All rights reserved.
Printed in the United States of America.

Library of Congress Cataloging-in-Publication Data

Cartledge, Tony W.
1 & 2 Samuel / Tony Cartledge
p. cm. — (Smyth & Helwys Bible Commentary, 7)
Includes bibliographical references and index.
ISBN 1-57312-064-2
1. Bible. O.T. Samuel—Commentaries. I. Title: 1 and 2 Samuel.
II. Title: First and Second Samuel. III. Title. IV. Series.

BS1325.3 .C375 2001
222'.4077—dc21

Library of Congress Control Number: 2001049158

SMYTH & HELWYS BIBLE COMMENTARY

1&2 SAMUEL

TONY W. CARTLEDGE

With best wishes to all who study
at Mars Hill —

Tony W. Cartledge

7/2/02

SMYTH&HELWYS
PUBLISHING, INCORPORATED · MACON, GEORGIA

PROJECT EDITOR
R. SCOTT NASH
Mercer University
Macon, Georgia

OLD TESTAMENT
GENERAL EDITOR
SAMUEL E. BALENTINE
Baptist Theological Seminary
at Richmond, Virginia

NEW TESTAMENT
GENERAL EDITOR
R. ALAN CULPEPPER
McAfee School of Theology
Mercer University
Atlanta, Georgia

AREA
OLD TESTAMENT EDITORS
MARK E. BIDDLE
Baptist Theological Seminary
at Richmond, Virginia

AREA
NEW TESTAMENT EDITORS
R. SCOTT NASH
Mercer University
Macon, Georgia

KANDY QUEEN-SUTHERLAND
Stetson University
Deland, Florida

RICHARD B. VINSON
Baptist Theological Seminary
at Richmond, Virginia

KENNETH G. HOGLUND
Wake Forest University
Winston-Salem, North Carolina

ART EDITOR
HEIDI J. HORNIK
Baylor University
Waco, Texas

ADVANCE PRAISE

Tony Cartledge has produced a commentary on 1 and 2 Samuel that is readable by any interested and educated person, with or without theological training. The commentary is informed by, but not bound to the results of critical scholarship. It does not hide from problematic texts, but judges them by the later revelation in Jesus. It is a worthy addition to the series.

—*Paul L. Redditt, Ph. D.*
Chair, Department of Religion
Georgetown College

The new Smyth and Helwys Bible Commentary, *1 & 2 Samuel,* is a refreshing and engaging study of the stories of a crucial time in the life of the ancestors of our faith, the early days of kingship in ancient Israel. Out of these stories arose Israel's concept of Messiah, a deliverer who would restore for the people a golden age of glory. Tony Cartledge combines an outstanding scholarly treatment of a text that comes from a very different time and place in the history of humankind with insightful applications to the twenty-first-century world. *1 & 2 Samuel* is an excellent companion volume to its Bible Commentary Series predecessor, *1 & 2 Kings.* It is one of the most thorough and readable treatments of these often-neglected books that I have read to date, and it will be a necessary addition to libraries and studies and a valuable classroom tool.

—*Nancy L. deClaissé-Walford*
Associate Professor of Old Testament and Biblical Languages,
McAfee School of Theology
Managing Editor, Review and Expositor

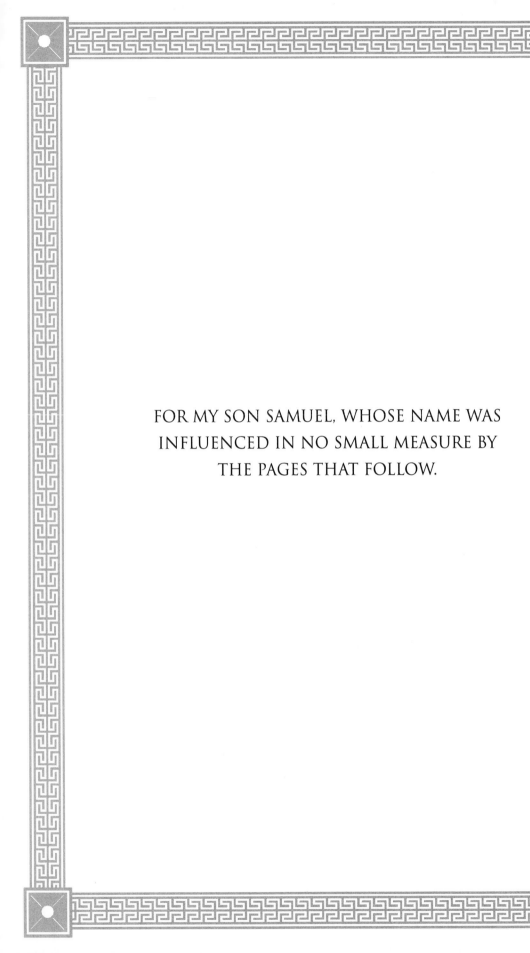

FOR MY SON SAMUEL, WHOSE NAME WAS
INFLUENCED IN NO SMALL MEASURE BY
THE PAGES THAT FOLLOW.

CONTENTS

2 SAMUEL

ABBREVIATIONS USED IN THIS COMMENTARY

Books of the Old Testament, Apocrypha, and New Testament are generally abbreviated in the Sidebars, parenthetical references, and notes according to the following system.

The Old Testament

Genesis	Gen
Exodus	Exod
Leviticus	Lev
Numbers	Num
Deuteronomy	Deut
Joshua	Josh
Judges	Judg
Ruth	Ruth
1–2 Samuel	1–2 Sam
1–2 Kings	1–2 Kgs
1–2 Chronicles	1–2 Chr
Ezra	Ezra
Nehemiah	Neh
Esther	Esth
Job	Job
Psalm (Psalms)	Ps (Pss)
Proverbs	Prov
Ecclesiastes	Eccl
or Qoheleth	Qoh
Song of Solomon	Song
or Song of Songs	Song
or Canticles	Cant
Isaiah	Isa
Jeremiah	Jer
Lamentations	Lam
Ezekiel	Ezek
Daniel	Dan
Hosea	Hos
Joel	Joel
Amos	Amos
Obadiah	Obad
Jonah	Jonah
Micah	Mic

Nahum	Nah
Habakkuk	Hab
Zephaniah	Zeph
Haggai	Hag
Zechariah	Zech
Malachi	Mal

The Apocrypha

1–2 Esdras	1–2 Esdr
Tobit	Tob
Judith	Jdt
Additions to Esther	Add Esth
Wisdom of Solomon	Wis
Ecclesiasticus or the Wisdom of Jesus Son of Sirach	Sir
Baruch	Bar
Epistle (or Letter) of Jeremiah	Ep Jer
Prayer of Azariah and the Song of the Three	Pr Azar
Daniel and Susanna	Sus
Daniel, Bel, and the Dragon	Bel
Prayer of Manasseh	Pr Man
1–2 Maccabees	1–2 Macc

The New Testament

Matthew	Matt
Mark	Mark
Luke	Luke
John	John
Acts	Acts
Romans	Rom
1–2 Corinthians	1–2 Cor
Galatians	Gal
Ephesians	Eph
Philippians	Phil
Colossians	Col
1–2 Thessalonians	1–2 Thess
1–2 Timothy	1–2 Tim
Titus	Titus
Philemon	Phlm
Hebrews	Heb
James	Jas
1–2 Peter	1–2 Pet
1–2–3 John	1–2–3 John
Jude	Jude
Revelation	Rev

Other commonly used abbreviations include:

BC	Before Christ
(also commonly referred to as BCE = Before the Common Era)	
AD	*Anno Domini* ("in the year of the Lord")
(also commonly referred to as CE = the Common Era)	
v.	verse
vv.	verses
C.	century
c.	*circa* (around "that time")
cf.	*confer* (compare)
ch.	chapter
chs.	chapters
d.	died
ed.	edition or edited by or editor
eds.	editors
e.g.	*exempli gratia* (for example)
et al.	*et alii* (and others)
f./ff.	and the following one(s)
gen. ed.	general editor
ibid.	*ibidem* (in the same place)
i.e.	*id est* (that is)
LCL	Loeb Classical Library
lit.	literally
n.d.	no date
rev. and exp. ed.	revised and expanded edition
sg.	singular
trans.	translated by or translator(s)
vol(s).	volume(s)

Additional written works cited by abbreviations include:

AB	Anchor Bible
AN	Ark Narrative
ANET	*Ancient Near Eastern Texts*
Ant.	*Jewish Antiquities*
BA	*Biblical Archaeologist*
BAR	*Biblical Archaeology Review*
BASOR	*Bulletin of the American Schools of Oriental Research*
BBC	Broadman Bible Commentary
BHS	*Biblia Hebraica Stuttgartensia*
BI	*Biblical Illustrator*
BRev	*Bible Review*
BWANT	Beitrage zur Wissenschaft vom Neuen Testament
BZAW	Beiträge zur Zeitschrift für die alttestamentliche Wissenschaft

CBQ	*Catholic Biblical Quarterly*
CC	Communicators Commentary
Civ.	*Civitas = City of God*
DH	Deuteronomistic History
Dtr	Deuteronomist
4QSam[a]	Dead Sea Scroll fragment of Samuel from Cave 4
HDR	History of David's Rise
HUCA	*Hebrew Union College Annual*
IBC	Interpretation: A Bible Commentary for Teaching and Preaching
ICC	International Critical Commentary
IDB	*Interpreters Dictionary of the Bible*
ISBE	*International Standard Bible Encyclopedia*
JB	Jerusalem Bible
JBL	*Journal of Biblical Literature*
JCS	*Journal of Cuneiform Studies*
JHNES	Johns Hopkins Near Eastern Studies
JPS	Jewish Publication Society
JSOT	*Journal for the Study of the Old Testament*
KJV	King James Version
LXX	Septuagint = Greek Translation of Hebrew Bible
MDB	*Mercer Dictionary of the Bible*
MT	Masoretic Text
NASB	New American Standard Bible
NEB	New English Bible
NICOT	New International Commentary on the Old Testament
NIV	New International Version
OTL	Old Testament Library
RSV	Revised Standard Version
SN	Succession Narrative
TDNT	*Theological Dictionary of the New Testament*
TEV	Today's English Version
TNK	Tanak = Hebrew Bible
VT	*Vetus Testamentum*
VTSup	Supplements to Vetus Testamentum
WBC	Word Biblical Commentary
ZAW	*Zeitschrift für die alttestamentliche Wissenschaft*

AUTHOR'S PREFACE

The publisher's gracious invitation to tackle a volume on 1 and 2 Samuel for the new *Smyth & Helwys Bible Commentary* series was a welcome opportunity.

My love of the Hebrew Scriptures runs deep, and the rich narrative of the Deuteronomistic History remains fresh with every reading. The characters of Samuel and Saul, David and Jonathan, Abigail and Bathsheba, Solomon and his brothers reveal the same flashes of nobility, the same lapses into cowardice, the same persistent ambiguities that still endow (or afflict) the human family. The time spent with them has been joyful labor.

The commentary that follows is based on the New Revised Standard Version of the Bible, which is the source of most citations of Scripture. Where quotations vary from the NRSV, they reflect my own translation.

I am grateful to my immediate editor, Sam Balentine, and to the two assistant editors, Jeff Rogers and Ken Hoglund, who read and re-read the manuscript behind this book. Their many helpful suggestions are in no way responsible for any shortcomings that blemish the work. I am grateful for the careful work by the Smyth & Helwys production team: Lex Horton, Keith Gammons, Kelley Land, Erin Smith, and Jim Burt. Thanks also to Heidi J. Hornik for her art commentary.

This volume owes much to Ken Vandergriff, a far better Old Testament scholar than I, who provided invaluable assistance in the research and development of various aspects of the book, especially in the boxed materials. Alison Bailey, my able assistant, provided ongoing encouragement and cheerful support, especially in preparing the indexes. They have both earned my deep gratitude.

My wife Jan has been remarkably patient with me during the many hours and days stolen from our family time for the sake of this project. For this, and for the many other ways she supports, enriches, and blesses my life, I am forever indebted.

Tony W. Cartledge

SERIES PREFACE

The *Smyth & Helwys Bible Commentary* is a visually stimulating and user-friendly series that is as close to multimedia in print as possible. Written by accomplished scholars with all students of Scripture in mind, the primary goal of the *Smyth & Helwys Bible Commentary* is to make available serious, credible biblical scholarship in an accessible and less intimidating format.

Far too many Bible commentaries fall short of bridging the gap between the insights of biblical scholars and the needs of students of God's written word. In an unprecedented way, the *Smyth & Helwys Bible Commentary* brings insightful commentary to bear on the lives of contemporary Christians. Using a multimedia format, the volumes employ a stunning array of art, photographs, maps, and drawings to illustrate the truths of the Bible for a visual generation of believers.

The *Smyth & Helwys Bible Commentary* is built upon the idea that meaningful Bible study can occur when the insights of contemporary biblical scholars blend with sensitivity to the needs of lifelong students of Scripture. Some persons within local faith communities, however, struggle with potentially informative biblical scholarship for several reasons. Oftentimes, such scholarship is cast in technical language easily grasped by other scholars, but not by the general reader. For example, lengthy, technical discussions on every detail of a particular scriptural text can hinder the quest for a clear grasp of the whole. Also, the format for presenting scholarly insights has often been confusing to the general reader, rendering the work less than helpful. Unfortunately, responses to the hurdles of reading extensive commentaries have led some publishers to produce works for a general readership that merely skim the surface of the rich resources of biblical scholarship. This commentary series incorporates works of fine art in an accurate and scholarly manner, yet the format remains "user-friendly." An important facet is the presentation and explanation of images of art, which interpret the biblical material or illustrate how the biblical material has been understood and interpreted in the past. A visual generation of believers deserves a commentary series that contains not only the all-important textual commentary on Scripture, but images, photographs, maps, works of fine art, and drawings that bring the text to life.

The *Smyth & Helwys Bible Commentary* makes serious, credible biblical scholarship more accessible to a wider audience. Writers and editors alike present information in ways that encourage readers to gain a better understanding of the Bible. The editorial board has worked to develop a format that is useful and usable, informative and pleasing to the eye. Our writers are reputable scholars who participate in the community of faith and sense a calling to communicate the results of their scholarship to their faith community.

The *Smyth & Helwys Bible Commentary* addresses Christians and the larger church. While both respect for and sensitivity to the needs and contributions of other faith communities are reflected in the work of the series authors, the authors speak primarily to Christians. Thus the reader can note a confessional tone throughout the volumes. No particular "confession of faith" guides the authors, and diverse perspectives are observed in the various volumes. Each writer, though, brings to the biblical text the best scholarly tools available and expresses the results of their studies in commentary and visuals that assist readers seeking a word from the Lord for the church.

To accomplish this goal, writers in this series have drawn from numerous streams in the rich tradition of biblical interpretation. The basic focus is the biblical text itself, and considerable attention is given to the wording and structure of texts. Each particular text, however, is also considered in the light of the entire canon of Christian Scriptures. Beyond this, attention is given to the cultural context of the biblical writings. Information from archaeology, ancient history, geography, comparative literature, history of religions, politics, sociology, and even economics is used to illuminate the culture of the people who produced the Bible. In addition, the writers have drawn from the history of interpretation, not only as it is found in traditional commentary on the Bible but also in literature, theater, church history, and the visual arts. Finally, the *Commentary* on Scripture is joined with *Connections* to the world of the contemporary church. Here again, the writers draw on scholarship in many fields as well as relevant issues in the popular culture.

This wealth of information might easily overwhelm a reader if not presented in a "user-friendly" format. Thus the heavier discussions of detail and the treatments of other helpful topics are presented in special-interest boxes, or Sidebars, clearly connected to the passages under discussion so as not to interrupt the flow of the basic interpretation. The result is a commentary on Scripture that focuses on the theological significance of a text while also offering the reader a rich array of additional information related to the text and its interpretation.

An accompanying CD-ROM offers powerful searching and research tools. The commentary text, Sidebars, and visuals are all reproduced on a CD that is fully indexed and searchable. Pairing a text version with a digital resource is a distinctive feature of the *Smyth & Helwys Bible Commentary.*

Combining credible biblical scholarship, user-friendly study features, and sensitivity to the needs of a visually oriented generation of believers creates a unique and unprecedented type of commentary series. With insight from many of today's finest biblical scholars and a stunning visual format, it is our hope that the *Smyth & Helwys Bible Commentary* will be a welcome addition to the personal libraries of all students of Scripture.

The Editors

HOW TO USE
THIS COMMENTARY

The *Smyth & Helwys Bible Commentary* is written by accomplished biblical scholars with a wide array of readers in mind. Whether engaged in the study of Scripture in a church setting or in a college or seminary classroom, all students of the Bible will find a number of useful features throughout the commentary that are helpful for interpreting the Bible.

Basic Design of the Volumes

Each volume features an Introduction to a particular book of the Bible, providing a brief guide to information that is necessary for reading and interpreting the text: the historical setting, literary design, and theological significance. Each Introduction also includes a comprehensive outline of the particular book under study.

Each chapter of the commentary investigates the text according to logical divisions in a particular book of the Bible. Sometimes these divisions follow the traditional chapter segmentation, while at other times the textual units consist of sections of chapters or portions of more than one chapter. The divisions reflect the literary structure of a book and offer a guide for selecting passages that are useful in preaching and teaching.

An accompanying CD-ROM offers powerful searching and research tools. The commentary text, Sidebars, and visuals are all reproduced on a CD that is fully indexed and searchable. Pairing a text version with a digital resource also allows unprecedented flexibility and freedom for the reader. Carry the text version to locations you most enjoy doing research while knowing that the CD offers a portable alternative for travel from the office, church, classroom, and your home.

Commentary and Connections

As each chapter explores a textual unit, the discussion centers around two basic sections: *Commentary* and *Connections*. The analysis of a passage, including the details of its language, the history reflected in the text, and the literary forms found in the text, are the main focus of the *Commentary* section. The primary concern of the *Commentary* section is to explore the theological issues presented by the Scripture passage. *Connections* presents potential applications of the insights provided in the *Commentary* section. The *Connections* portion of each chapter considers what issues are relevant for teaching and suggests useful methods and resources. *Connections* also identifies themes suitable for sermon planning and suggests helpful approaches for preaching on the Scripture text.

Sidebars

The *Smyth & Helwys Bible Commentary* provides a unique hyperlink format that quickly guides the reader to additional insights. Since other more technical or supplementary information is vital for understanding a text and its implications, the volumes feature distinctive Sidebars, or special-interest boxes, that provide a wealth of information on such matters as:

- Historical information (such as chronological charts, lists of kings or rulers, maps, descriptions of monetary systems, descriptions of special groups, descriptions of archaeological sites or geographical settings).

- Graphic outlines of literary structure (including such items as poetry, chiasm, repetition, epistolary form).

- Definition or brief discussions of technical or theological terms and issues.

- Insightful quotations that are not integrated into the running text but are relevant to the passage under discussion.

- Notes on the history of interpretation (Augustine on the Good Samaritan, Luther on James, Stendahl on Romans, etc.).

- Line drawings, photographs, and other illustrations relevant for understanding the historical context or interpretive significance of the text.

- Presentation and discussion of works of fine art that have interpreted a Scripture passage.

Each Sidebar is printed in color and is referenced at the appropriate place in the *Commentary* or *Connections* section with a color-coded title that directs the reader to the relevant Sidebar. In addition, helpful icons appear in the Sidebars, which provide the reader with visual cues to the type of material that is explained in each Sidebar. Throughout the commentary, these four distinct hyperlinks provide useful links in an easily recognizable design.

Alpha & Omega Language

This icon identifies the information as a language-based tool that offers further exploration of the Scripture selection. This could include syntactical information, word studies, popular or additional uses of the word(s) in question, additional contexts in which the term appears, and the history of the term's translation. All non-English terms are transliterated into the appropriate English characters.

Culture/Context

This icon introduces further comment on contextual or cultural details that shed light on the Scripture selection. Describing the place and time to which a Scripture passage refers is often vital to the task of biblical interpretation. Sidebar items introduced with this icon could include geographical, historical, political, social, topographical, or economic information. Here, the reader may find an excerpt of an ancient text or inscription that sheds light on the text. Or one may find a description of some element of ancient religion such as Baalism in Canaan or the Hero cult in the Mystery Religions of the Greco-Roman world.

Interpretation

Sidebars that appear under this icon serve a general interpretive function in terms of both historical and contemporary renderings. Under this heading, the reader might find a selection from classic or contemporary literature that illuminates the Scripture text or a significant quotation from a famous sermon that addresses the passage. Insights are drawn from various sources, including literature, worship, theater, church history, and sociology.

Additional Resources Study

Here, the reader finds a convenient list of useful resources for further investigation of the selected Scripture text, including books, journals, websites, special collections, organizations, and societies. Specialized discussions of works not often associated with biblical studies may also appear here.

Additional Features

Each volume also includes a basic Bibliography on the biblical book under study. Other bibliographies on selected issues are often included that point the reader to other helpful resources.

Notes at the end of each chapter provide full documentation of sources used and contain additional discussions of related matters.

Abbreviations used in each volume are explained in a list of abbreviations found after the Table of Contents.

Readers of the *Smyth & Helwys Bible Commentary* can regularly visit the Internet support site for news, information, updates, and enhancements to the series at <**www.helwys.com/commentary**>.

Several thorough indexes enable the reader to locate information quickly. These indexes include:

• An *Index of Sidebars* groups content from the special-interest boxes by category (maps, fine art, photographs, drawings, etc.).

• An *Index of Scriptures* lists citations to particular biblical texts.

• An *Index of Topics* lists alphabetically the major subjects, names, topics, and locations referenced or discussed in the volume.

• An *Index of Modern Authors* organizes contemporary authors whose works are cited in the volume.

INTRODUCTION

The religious and literary heritage of both Christians and Jews is greatly indebted to the books of 1 and 2 Samuel, for they describe events that are central to both faiths, preserving traditions that influence the remainder of the Hebrew and Christian Bibles.

In these two books that once were one, we watch the life of Samuel, from cradle to grave and even beyond. Given by God to a faithful and prayerful woman, Samuel became prophet and priest, maker and advisor of kings. Here we find Saul, the tall lad who took the crown reluctantly but then found himself consumed by the desire to retain it. In these books we meet darkly powerful heroes such as Joab and Abner, along with sinister enemies, from the Philistine giant Goliath to the Israelite prince Absalom. There is palace intrigue and internal revolt, romance and rape, hope and loss, and hope again.

Towering above all others who haunt the ancient tome is David: innocent musician, valiant warrior, creative king—a man after God's own heart with a dark spot on his soul. Other historical books in the Hebrew Bible reveal the many ways in which Israel tried to find its way back to the life it knew—or thought it knew—under David. Every book of Hebrew prophecy reflects or interprets the Davidic covenant, its aftermath, and its future. The Psalms relive the highs and the lows of Israel's life, often with reference to David. Even the Christian Scriptures are built on the foundation of these books of Samuel, as they speak of fulfilled prophecy and a messianic Son of David.

There are many questions to ask as we approach this strategic slice of the biblical record. How do the books of Samuel fit into their context within the canon of Scripture? How did these traditions come to be written and shaped into their present form? Where do the events related here fit into the larger picture of Israelite and ancient Near Eastern history? As words of Scripture, held by believers to be inspired by God, how do these books impact our theology and practice as we seek to follow the same God whose calling so influenced the lives of Samuel and Saul and David? The following paragraphs provide a brief introduction to our present understanding of these issues.

CANONICAL CONTEXT

Jewish readers divide the Hebrew Scriptures (for Christians, the "Old Testament") into three parts, collectively referred to by the acronym TNK or *Tanakh*: the *Torah* (Law), the *Nevi'im* (Prophets), and the *Ketubim* (Writings). [The *Tanakh*] The *Nevi'im* are further subdivided into the "Former Prophets" (historical books with continuing impact) and the "Latter Prophets" (mostly first-person accounts of the literary prophets).

The books of Samuel fall into the category of "Former Prophets," and there are prophets to be found there: the anonymous "man of God" (1 Sam 2:27-36), Samuel himself (1 Sam 3; 8:10-18; 9:6-10:8; among others), Gad (1 Sam 22:5; 2 Sam 24:13-14), and Nathan (2 Sam 7; 12). Even Saul's brief forays among ecstatic holy men led to a proverb connecting him with the prophets (1 Sam 10:9-13; 19:22-24), and David himself was called a prophet in later traditions (2 Chr 29:25).

From the perspective of historical criticism, the books of Samuel cannot be understood apart from some appreciation for their setting within a larger block of text commonly known as the Deuteronomistic History. [Historical Criticism] [Deuteronomistic History] This significant section of the Hebrew Bible (equivalent to the "Former Prophets": Joshua through 2 Kings, with the exception of Ruth) is written or edited so that it reflects a firm footing within the theological presuppositions of the book of Deuteronomy. Thus themes such as the importance of obeying the Deuteronomic law and avoiding apostasy are predominant, as is the rigid system of expected rewards or punishments for those who do or do not adhere to the law.

The *Tanakh*

AΩ The word *Tanakh* (or *Tanak*) is an acronym for Torah, Nevi'im, and Kethuvim, the three major sections of the Hebrew Bible. *Torah*, a familiar term, designates the first five books of the Bible: Genesis, Exodus, Leviticus, Numbers, and Deuteronomy.

The section called *Nevi'im*, a word that means "prophets," includes some books, which are primarily historical, that include characters or events that came to be regarded as prophetic (Joshua, Judges, 1–2 Samuel, 1–2 Kings). These are often called the "Former Prophets." The writings of the literary prophets fall into the category of "Latter Prophets" (Isaiah, Jeremiah, Ezekiel, Hosea, Joel, Amos, Obadiah, Jonah, Micah, Nahum, Habakkuk, Zephaniah, Haggai, Zechariah, Malachi).

The final section, called the *Kethuvim*, which means "writings," contains an amalgam of miscellaneous writings ranging from poetry to wisdom literature to hero stories and historical archives (Psalms, Proverbs, Job, The Song of Solomon, Ruth, Lamentations, Ecclesiastes, Esther, Daniel, Ezra, Nehemiah, 1–2 Chronicles).

Since the Hebrew Bible is arranged according to this system, the books follow a different order than in Christian Bibles: Genesis is still first, but many other books are found in divergent places, and 1–2 Chronicles appear as the last books of the Hebrew Bible.

Historical Criticism

There are several branches of biblical criticism (textual, historical, literary, and canonical, for example). In each case, the word "criticism" is used with its original meaning (from the Greek verb *krinō*), which is "to judge" or "to discern" in making evaluations. Thus the word "criticism" does not imply caustic disparagement of the text, but careful discrimination in its study.

Historical criticism recognizes that each individual part of the Scripture arose in a particular historical setting, and it may have been combined with other traditions and edited within other historical settings. Historical criticism seeks to discover not only the original setting of a text but also the literary history of its development and final incorporation into the canon.

Deuteronomistic History

Since the publication of Martin Noth's *Überlieferungsgeschichtliche Studien* in 1943, many biblical scholars have adopted his view that Joshua to Kings (with the exception of Ruth) forms a unified literary work. Noth argued that this history was promulgated in the exilic period to explain why the people of God, who had been promised possession of the promised land and a Davidic kingship *forever*, were now deprived of both. In Noth's view, there was a single author of the Deuteronomistic History (DH), whom he called "the Deuteronomist" (Dtr).

This editor is seen more as a compiler than a writer, incorporating earlier traditions—both oral and written—into his work. The Deuteronomist's creativity is seen in his skillful editing of narratives covering Israel's history from the 13th century BC settlement in Palestine to the destruction of Jerusalem in 587 BC in order to justify his interpretation of the exile.

Noth's concept, though widely adopted, has been challenged on several grounds. For example, Noth argued that the DH had a negative purpose only: to show the history of unfaithfulness that led to the exile of Israel. Subsequent scholars see a more positive purpose. Hans Walter Wolff, for example, sees an implication of hope in the repetition of the word *shub* ("to return" or "to repent"; see Deut 4:25-31; 20:1-10; 1 Sam 7:3; 1 Kgs 8:33, 35, 47, 48; 2 Kgs 17:13; 23:25). As God had restored the ancestors when they "returned" to faithfulness, perhaps God would do the same for the exiles if they did the same. Likewise, Gerhard von Rad found in God's covenant with David (2 Sam 7) and its frequent reiteration in the books of Kings the implication that God would not utterly forsake his people (1 Kgs 8:20, 25; 9:5; 11:5, 13, 32, 36; 15:4; 2 Kgs 2:4; 8:19; 19:34; 20:6).

Noth held that the DH was the work of a single author who publicized his work shortly after 560 BC (the date of the release of King Jehoiachin from the Babylonian prison, which is the last date mentioned in the DH), but before 538 BC (the date of Cyrus' edict ending the exile, an event not mentioned in the DH). Many scholars now argue for at least two editions of the DH, belonging to the preexilic and exilic periods.

For further reading, consult Terence E. Fretheim, *Deuteronomistic History* (Nashville: Abingdon, 1983); Steven L. McKenzie, "Deuteronomistic History," *The Anchor Bible Dictionary*, ed. David Noel Freedman, 6 vols. (New York: Doubleday & Co., 1992; and the discussion of Walter Brueggemann and Hans Walter Wolff in *The Vitality of Old Testament Traditions*, 2d ed. (Atlanta: John Knox, 1982). An English translation of Noth's original work is available as *The Deuteronomistic History*, 2d ed., JSOT Supplement Series No. 15 (Sheffield: Sheffield Academic Press, 1991).

These principles are illustrated abundantly in the books of Samuel: Saul is blessed and successful so long as he remains open to the spirit of God (1 Sam 11) but is afflicted with an evil spirit when he disobeys Samuel's strict command (1 Sam 15; 16:14). As Saul falls, obedient David experiences a rapid rise to power, replete with evidence of divine blessing (see especially 2 Sam 7). Following his adulterous and murderous behavior in the Bathsheba/Uriah affair, however, David's personal and political life are beset by one calamity after another (2 Sam 12–21).

The surprising thing about 1 and 2 Samuel is that the Deuteronomistic hand is so subdued, especially as compared to the preceding book of Judges and the following books of 1 and 2 Kings. The Judges sagas employ a standardized vocabulary and are carefully organized in a series of cycles in which Israel repeatedly falls into apostasy and judgment before repenting and experiencing deliverance through the agency of a divinely appointed "judge" (see [Israel's "Judges"]). The editorial shaping of the material and the inclusion of characteristic interpretive comments are unmistakable.

In the books of 1 and 2 Kings, the editors' influence is particularly evident in the evaluative comments given to the reigns of both Israelite and Judean kings. These pass judgment in no uncertain terms as to whether the king in question did good or evil in terms of obedience to the Deuteronomistic law (e. g., 2 Kgs 3:1-3; 8:16-18).

Apparently, the length and the focus of the underlying source materials in Samuel were such that the editors saw little need for additional interpretive comment. Thus the editors' influence, with a few exceptions, appears to be limited to the selection and arrangement of their primary sources.

LITERARY DEVELOPMENT

1. *Authorship and development.* An ancient tradition preserved in 1 Chronicles holds that Samuel was the primary author of the scroll that bears his name, with supplementary information about the period following his death being supplied by the prophets Nathan and Gad (see 1 Chr 29:29-30). [1 Chronicles 29:29-30]

Careful study, however, has provided abundant evidence that the issue of authorship is much more complicated. There are, for example, many duplicate and sometimes variant traditions regarding similar events, especially in 1 Samuel. For example, Eli is twice warned that his priestly dynasty will fall (1 Sam 2:27-36; 3:11-14). Likewise, when the issue of kingship is broached, one account is highly antagonistic (7:1–8:22), while another approaches kingship as a means of divine deliverance (9–11). There are two accounts of Saul's public acclamation as king (10:17-24; 11:15) and two stories of his rejection (13:14; 15:23). David is introduced to Saul and becomes his personal musician and close aide in 16:14-23, but in the very next chapter the young man who offers to combat Goliath is unknown to Saul. When David flees from Saul, he is twice betrayed by the Ziphites (23:19-28; 26:1-5). And, on two occasions, he has the opportunity to kill Saul, but refrains (24:1-22; 26:6-25). Saul's death is also related in two versions (1 Sam 31; 2 Sam 1).

Some scholars have attempted to assign these dual traditions to the J (Yahwistic) and E (Elohistic) sources commonly known from

1 Chronicles 29:29-30

Now the acts of King David, from first to last, are written in the records of the seer Samuel, and in the records of the prophet Nathan, and in the records of the seer Gad, with accounts of all his rule and his might and of the events that befell him and Israel and all the kingdoms of the earth.

Pentateuchal studies. Others have spoken of an early (promonarchical) and late (antimonarchical) source. There appear, however, to be even more sources involved. Some of these appear to be brief, such as Hannah's song (1 Sam 2:1-10), a poem that shows signs of great antiquity. Other traditions may have been excerpted from longer sources, such as a presumed compilation of traditions about the ark of the covenant (the "Ark Narrative" [AN], 1 Sam 4–6; 2 Sam 6).

Scholars are largely agreed on the preexistence of at least two considerably longer units that can be regarded as cohesive narratives with their own distinguishing characteristics. The first of these is often called the "History of David's Rise" (HDR). This unit begins with 1 Samuel 16:14 and continues through 2 Samuel 5:10, though some commentators contend that it continues through 2 Samuel 6. The second large unit details the intra-family struggle to determine who would succeed King David on the throne. Generally dubbed "The Succession Narrative" [SN], it extends from 2 Samuel 9–20, where it is interrupted by a series of appendices (2 Sam 21–24), then continues in 1 Kings 1–2.

These and other traditions were collected and adapted over a period of time that may have stretched for many years. Some scholars assign various rescensions of the book to a series of Deuteronomistic editors who sequentially added historical, prophetic, and legal perspectives to the work. Others perceive this complex tracing of tradition as more imaginative than substantive. Many scholars locate the Deuteronomistic editors within prophetic circles of the northern kingdom, for the principles espoused have much in common with northern literary prophets, such as Hosea. Most agree that the Succession Narrative (which has more of a southern perspective) seems to have been inserted as a whole after the remaining corpus had already reached its final form.

The extensive debate concerning the development of these books reveals how difficult it is to reach definite conclusions, and this commentary will attempt to stay in touch with differing aspects of the debate rather than espousing any particular view. Any of the approaches suggested should be seen as guidelines for thinking, not categorical truths.

What does seem clear is that 1 and 2 Samuel were not written down by one person at one time. The books are a carefully edited composite of earlier oral and written traditions. Though some source materials may have been composed during the monarchical period, the final form of 1 and 2 Samuel was almost certainly shaped during the exile as a part of the larger Deuteronomistic corpus.

2. *Canonical shaping.* The books of Samuel began as a single volume. The division of the Samuel scroll into 1 and 2 Samuel originated with the Septuagint (LXX), which labeled the resulting books as "1 and 2 Kingdoms" or "1 and 2 Reigns" (with 1 and 2 Kings being called "3 and 4 Kingdoms/Reigns"). The division was not incorporated into the Hebrew Bible until the fifteenth century AD.

The distinction of Samuel from the preceding and following books, however, is much earlier. Scholars have long questioned why the account of David's death in 1 Kings 1–2 was separated from the books of Samuel. The life of every other main character in the books of Samuel is resolved by death, and one would expect that a work so devoted to the life of David would conclude with his death as well. Yet the account of David's final days and his muddled choice of a successor is found in 1 Kings 1–2.

Perhaps it was thought that these chapters belonged more to the account of Solomon's reign since the story of his accession to the throne is closely intertwined with the account of David's demise. Since both Samuel and Kings probably reached their final form within the larger Deuteronomistic history at about the same time, the editors had no reason to think that readers of Samuel would be left hanging.

3. *Parallels.* Readers familiar with the Hebrew Bible know that many of the traditions found in 1 and 2 Samuel are duplicated in the books of 1 and 2 Chronicles, but with important differences. [Samuel and the Chronicler] The differences grow in part from the apparent use of some variant source materials and in part from the differing perspective of the editors. The Deuteronomists found it important to paint a full portrait of Israel's life, preserving both positive and negative information. This is most evident in the life of David. His human foibles are disheartening, but illustrative of the editors' tendentious ambitions.

The Deuteronomists speak glowingly of David as a man after God's own heart and one to whom God promised an everlasting dynasty, but they are also candid about less flattering features of David's personality. They do not hesitate to recount David's sin in the Bathsheba/Uriah affair and the damage it inflicted on his personal life and public rule. The Chronicler, however, writing during the postexilic period, seems to treat David's life and rule as an icon

---

Samuel and the Chronicler

Any intensive study of the books of Samuel must consider the comparative contribution of the books of Chronicles. The DH is the older record, probably reaching its final form around 550 BC. Although there is wide disagreement concerning a precise date, the Chronicler's history seems to have emerged some two to three centuries later, during the postexilic period.

While the Deuteronomist(s) addressed a people in exile and sought to explain their predicament, the Chronicler's audience was a restored but politically insignificant postexilic Jewish community. Having neither king nor national independence, it had restructured itself as a religious community. One aim of the Chronicler was to show the continuity of the postexilic religious institutions with those of the formative period. By so doing, he explained the relevance of those institutions for his generation and legitimized them by linking them to their origins in the authoritative past.

Thus the Chronicler retained only that information from 1–2 Samuel and 1–2 Kings that suited his purpose. For example, most of Saul's story is omitted by the Chronicler (1 Chr 9:35–10:14); only his death is recounted. It is clear that the writer was familiar with the larger story, however, as revealed by his summary evaluation of Saul's reign, which refers to Saul's unfaithfulness and his consultation of a medium instead of Yahweh (1 Chr 10:13-14).

The Chronicler also omits the DH's narrative about Samuel, as well as the inauguration of the monarchy, choosing instead to focus on David, who was Yahweh's chosen king and Israel's ideal king. The Chronicler rearranges some of the material in 1–2 Samuel, and omits most of the Succession Narrative (2 Sam 9–20; 1 Kgs 1–2), thus eliminating any mention of the moral and ethical debacles in David's personal life. He then adds a considerable amount of material related to David's provision for Israel's religious institutions. Although the DH knows David as a "man after God's own heart," it also reveals the dark places in David's persona. In the Chronicles, however, David's sins are absent, and he lives up to his reputation as the ideal king. David is Israel's great warrior and founder of Israel's religious institutions, a model for imitation in faith and practice.

---

for imitation. David is portrayed as the founder of many important institutions that had come to the fore in the postexilic community, and the ongoing legitimacy of these religious institutions was tied to Israel's memories of the consummate king. Thus the Chronicler's version of the story is so pro-Davidic that the hero's faults are glossed over.

4. *Text.* The Hebrew text of 1–2 Samuel has been poorly preserved. The oldest complete text of the Hebrew Bible is called the Masoretic Text (MT), based on a family of manuscripts prepared and annotated by Jewish scholars called "Masoretes." These scholars were committed to preserving the text, explaining discrepancies, and adding vowel points and accent marks to show how the text was pronounced during their lifetime.

Unfortunately, the text of 1–2 Samuel seems to have suffered greatly in the process of transmission. Many passages are very difficult to read; others are impossible. In these cases, the text must be reconstructed with help from other ancient documents. The most important of these is the Septuagint (LXX), an early translation of the Hebrew Bible into Greek (probably third century BC). The LXX was preserved in different circles and was constantly undergoing revision, so some versions are more helpful than others. The most valuable of the Greek texts for our purposes is a major uncial (written in capital letters only) preserved in the Vatican and designated as LXX[B]. [Ancient Manuscripts] It appears to be less affected by revision and thus closer to the earliest Greek translation.

A second comparative document of great importance is a Samuel scroll discovered among the ancient texts recovered from the caves of Khirbet Qumran, commonly called the "Dead Sea Scrolls." [The Dead Sea Scrolls] Three of these scrolls contain portions of Samuel. Two are fragmentary and offer little substantive information, but another (4QSam[a]) contains parts from 47 of the 57 original columns. This text probably dates to the first century BC, making it more than a thousand years older than the MT. Surprisingly, 4QSam[a] lies closer to the Hebrew text underlying the LXX than to the MT. This has necessitated a reevaluation of the relationship between the MT, LXX, and the ancient documents upon which they were based.

After the exile, some Jews remained in Babylon, while others returned to Palestine, and yet others settled in Egypt and other places. Following Frank Moore Cross, many scholars accept a view that the texts preserved in these different locales diverged over time so that there developed Babylonian, Palestinian, Egyptian, and perhaps other "text types" of the Hebrew text. The Palestinian or Egyptian text types may have been the exemplar for the LXX, while the Babylonian text type could underlie today's MT. The work of the Chronicler also seems to reflect a dependence on a text type that has more in common with the LXX and 4QSam[a] than with the MT.

Since the LXX may reflect readings from a Hebrew original that is older than the MT, some writers, notably Kyle McCarter, tend to favor the LXX reading to the MT. Other ancient sources, such as the Aramaic Targums and the Syriac translation, are sometimes helpful, but the LXX and 4QSam[a] are both essential for any careful interpretation of 1 and 2 Samuel.

Dead Sea Scrolls

Discovered in Qumran in 1947, the most famous leather rolls are the Dead Sea Scrolls. The previous medium used by the Egyptians and the Classical Mediterranean world was the papyrus roll. Egyptians used the leather roll as early at the 24th century BC. The leather roll has been the medium of choice for the Jewish tradition despite that they are thicker and have a more awkward form than papyrus. The Dead Sea Scrolls are very accessible to the public through its international sponsor, Project Judaica Foundation

Dead Sea Scrolls. 3rd century BC–AD 86. Leather rolls. Qumran.(Credit: Scott Nash)

**Maximalist and Minimalist
Interpretations of Biblical History**

Scholarly views on the historical credibility of the Old Testament range from "maximalist" to "minimalist."

Minimalist scholars, heirs of the Alt-Noth school of interpretation, argue that scientific historiography cannot simply accept the Old Testament at face value, and consequently they are not confident of the historical trustworthiness of the biblical narratives.

The maximalists, rising mainly from the Albright–Bright circle, believe that the Old Testament documents are more trustworthy. While acknowledging various discrepancies and problems, these scholars presume that the historical narratives of the Old Testament may be used to reconstruct the history of ancient Israel.

Minimalists argue that the biblical accounts were often written long after the actual events—often centuries later—resulting in their diminished value as historical witnesses. In their view, such documents must always reflect the bias of the author or editor—the self-identity or self-understanding of Israel in the time of the narrative's final composition—rather than the time of the events. Thus the purpose of the narratives was entirely theological, not historiographical, giving reliable evidence only for what was believed during the period in which it was written.

Positions on subjects such as this are not necessarily mutually exclusive, however. Maximalists may agree with the date of the final product, as well as the didactic aims of the editors, while also insisting that earlier and historically valid sources were used in the composition. Thus, maximalists may admit the possibility of bias in the biblical narrative, but believe that modern critical methods of interpretation can identify earlier strata of tradition in a text and separate it out from later elements of bias, thus allowing the interpreter to reconstruct a more accurate picture of historical events.

Historical Setting

Many of the events in 1–2 Samuel are so miraculous that some consider them mythical. Some scholars presume that the biblical accounts offer valid historical data, while others doubt the historicity even of such characters as David. [Maximalist and Minimalist Interpretations of Biblical History]

In regard to the period encompassed by the books of Samuel, minimalists see the Saul–David–Solomon narratives as mythic legends, representing later Israel's need to couch her national origins in terms of a golden age with heroic ancestors. Thus David, an innocent shepherd, is transformed by the storytellers into a conquering national hero. In contrast, maximalists believe that these biblical narratives preserve genuine factual memories, while acknowledging that the actual events may have been obscured by the long process of telling and retelling the stories before they achieved their final written form.

Some minimalists are unconvinced that the united monarchy described in 1–2 Samuel and 1 Kings 1–11 ever existed. As evidence, they insist that archaeologists have failed to uncover any epigraphic (ancient written sources) evidence from the period of the united monarchy. This silence seems quite strange if, as the Old Testament tells it, Israel's empire under David and Solomon stretched from the Mediterranean to the Euphrates.

The recent publication of an Aramaic inscription from Tell Dan threatens this view, however. The discoverers, Avraham Biran and

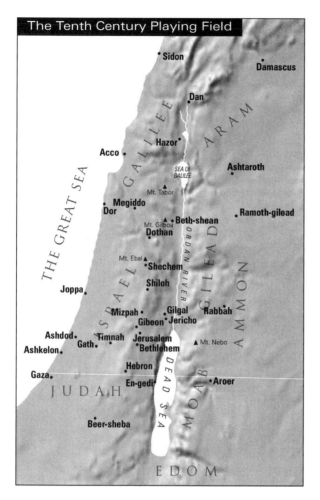

The Tenth Century Playing Field

J. Naveh, contend that the inscription contains a series of letters that should be translated as "House of David" (*bytdwd*). Maximalists have championed this inscription as a historical validation of the united monarchy. Some minimalists have challenged the authenticity of the find, while others have proposed different translations, reading *bytdwd* as a place name or proposing that *dwd* was the name of a god worshiped in Dan or perhaps the name of some public official whose house was in Dan.

This writer takes the position that a historical basis underlies the books of 1–2 Samuel, while acknowledging that "what really happened" may be irretrievably buried beneath centuries of literary accretions. In any case, there is no question that the stories involved take place within a certain historical context. The period described in 1–2 Samuel covers just over a century, beginning with Samuel's birth (probably in the 1070s BC) and ending just before David's death, often dated at 961 BC. This was a fortuitous time for the growth and development of small states in the Levant, as both Egypt and Mesopotamia, the traditional power brokers of the region, were experiencing periods of internal unrest and external weakness.

Egypt had claimed a measure of control over Palestine for nearly four hundred years, but a period of profligate spending on monumental buildings left the economy in a shambles, and a series of ineffective leaders was unable to right the country's financial affairs or to deal with the waves of sea peoples who were invading the northeastern coast. As the Tanite Dynasty took over the ship of state in 1065 BC, Egypt was foundering on the shoals of internal dissent and incapable of retaining control of the eastern lands it once held.

The Mesopotamians were also limited during this period. Tiglath-Pileser I (1116–1078 BC) led a brief Assyrian resurgence, but his descendants were less effective and unable to maintain control over the western territories he had gained. Neither Assyria nor Babylonia would have much influence on affairs in Palestine for another two hundred years.

The absence of the traditional superpowers from the fray did not leave the playing field without obstacles for Israel. Smaller kingdoms and strong tribal groups arose to fill the vacuum. [The Tenth Century Playing Field] The Israelite people themselves lived as interlopers in a land that was already occupied by a heterogenous group of peoples generally referred to as Canaanites, whose power base was centered in fortified city-states such as Hazor, Taanach, Acco, and Megiddo. The Jebusites who controlled Jerusalem can be thought of as a subset of the Canaanite peoples. Weaker tribal units such as the Gibeonites also occupied significant tracts of arable land.

Eastern tribal units or nations, such as the Ammonites (Judg 11:1-40; 1 Sam 11) and Moabites (Judg 3:12-30, with whom were associated the Midianites, Judg 6–7), had grown strong and sought to expand into surrounding territories. From the north, the Aramean states around Damascus worked to extend their influence, leading to armed conflict with the emerging state of Israel (2 Sam 8:3-12; 10:6-19).

The Israelite nation faced its strongest competition from the west, however, as the same sea peoples who had proven so distracting to Egypt traveled north along the Mediterranean coast and settled in a broad, fertile area just to the west of Judah, the southernmost territory occupied by the Israelites. The biblical name for this powerful people is "Philistines." With their power focused in a tight cluster of five cooperating city-states, the military minded and technologically advanced Philistines gradually pushed further and further eastward from their coastal power base, leading to a series of bloody and largely successful conflicts with Israel (Judg 3:31; 13:1-15:20; 1 Sam 4-6). Their advance drove a wedge between the northern and southern tribes of Israel, as Philistine military domination extended all the way to Beth-shan, hard by the Jordan River. First Samuel 7:7-14 suggests that Samuel led Israel to a short period of respite from the Philistines, but Saul found them still occupying much of the hill country when he took office (1 Sam 13:1–14:46). Only through David's leadership was Israel able to force the Philistines back into the coastal plain (1 Sam 17; 23:1-5; 28-31; 2 Sam 5:17-25; 8:1).

Israel's lack of a central government and standing military left the people vulnerable to well-organized enemies such as the Philistines, whose monarchical system supported the development of superior armaments and a powerful standing army. Thus political and military factors led to a natural evolution of Israel's emerging identity. Perceptive elements of the population pressed for the development of a centralized government, headed by a king "like the other nations" (1 Sam 8:5, 20). Those who supported the theocratic ideal that functioned during the period of the judges opposed such a move, while others saw the development of kingship not as a threat to divine authority, but as a gift of God. The negative and positive examples set by Saul and David reveal that both groups had legitimate fears and hopes.

This historical milieu of contrasting forces became the crucible in which Israel was forged, not as a people, but as a political entity. Through this experience, Israel was challenged to trust that Yahweh was sufficient to see them through the period of crisis and into the hopeful future beyond.

Historiography in the Ancient Near East

Historians of the ancient world worked on the basis of differing assumptions than modern Western history writers. Modern historians rely on comfirmable details from comparative materials to assure factual accuracy. Therefore, modern history writing includes no place for miraculous events or acts of God because they cannot be empirically confirmed. Revisionists may continue to use history as a guise for promoting particular agendas, but typical modern historians seek to approach history objectively, without letting personal bias influence their account of what has happened in the past.

Biblical historians seem to have been far less concerned with factual details and chronological sequences than modern writers. When writing was still a novelty and literacy the province of a privileged few, history was compiled from oral traditions drawn from tribal lore or etymological place names rather than comparative documents. Great credence was given to oral traditions, even when different strands of tradition preserved accounts of the past in variant ways. Rather than harmonizing disagreements or choosing one version over the other, historians sometimes incorporated both traditions into their writing.

Biblical historians, like their counterparts in other ancient lands, commonly interjected the miraculous as an explanation for significant events. Indeed, the concept of a history that did not include acts of God would have made little sense to biblical historians, who wrote from a consistently theological perspective.

The historians of ancient Israel, furthermore, carried all of their subjective beliefs into their work, because they wrote to promote a particular theological point of view. Their interest in writing and their historical judgments are clearly slanted in Israel's favor and toward the ideal of obedience to Yahweh. Other nations appear most often as unrighteous enemies of Israel, or find mention in the background of Israel's activities. Kings of Israel are judged, not by their military, economic, or cultural achievements, but by their faithfulness to the law as the historians understood it.

Readers who are cognizant of the different perspectives underlying ancient and modern history writing are better prepared to confront the truth embodied in the biblical text without feeling threatened if it does not hold to the same standards of historical precision that are common to the modern world.

Interpretation: Reading the Text as Story and as History

Ancient historical narratives such as 1 and 2 Samuel are patently tendentious yet also purport to record Israel's history. [Historiography in the Ancient Near East] Individual stories and the text as a whole are literary creations, yet both grow out of a very real historical situation. Thus the interpreter must approach the texts on at least two levels: as *story* and as *history*. The preceding section has dealt with some of the historical issues and limitations associated with 1 and 2 Samuel. Depending on one's approach, the reader will put more or less trust in the historical veracity of the materials but must make some attempt to understand the text, at least within its historical context.

The story element of the narratives is the level on which the reader meets the text. A student of archaeology or ancient Near Eastern history might doubt the factual basis of a particular passage, in all or in part. Nevertheless, the narrative communicates its intended lesson through the medium of the story with little concern for the historical skepticism of future readers.

Thus, while the commentary that follows will make some effort to make the reader aware of historical issues—at least where something substantive can be said—the interpretation of the text will be based on the story *as it is presented*. For example, many scholars have questioned the historical roots of the David and Goliath story (1 Sam 17). Other persons besides David were credited with the same or similar feats (see 2 Sam 21:19; 1 Chr 20:5). Some may assign it purely legendary status. Yet the importance of the story to Israel and the way it is employed in the narrative is largely independent of such consideration. The commentary will give a brief synopsis of historical questions and will make use of pertinent insights gained from archaeological and historical studies. The primary focus, however, will be on understanding the narrative as the storyteller tells it, tracing the ways in which the traditions have impacted Israel's faith and life, and searching for meaning that may speak to the modern world as well.

Theological Significance

Several themes are prominent in the books of Samuel. Foremost among them is the traditional Deuteronomistic mantra that blessings follow the righteous, while punishment awaits the wicked. [The Deuteronomistic Dichotomy] Eli's family loses control of the priesthood because his sons were evil and he did not control them (1 Sam 2:27-36; 3:10-14). Samuel attempted to appoint his own sons as judges over Israel, but they were also wicked, leading to the elders'

The Deuteronomistic Dichotomy

The cutting edge of Deuteronomistic theology is amply illustrated by these quotations from Deuteronomy 28:1-3, 15-16, each of which introduce a long series of specific blessings or curses:

> If you will only obey the LORD your God, by diligently observing all his commandments that I am commanding you today, the LORD your God will set you high above all the nations of the earth; all these blessings shall come upon you and overtake you, if you obey the LORD your God:
>> Blessed shall you be in the city, and blessed shall you be in the field. . . .
>> But if you will not obey the LORD your God by diligently observing all his commandments and decrees, which I am commanding you today, then all these curses shall come upon you and overtake you:
>> Cursed shall you be in the city, and cursed shall you be in the field. . .

rejection of Samuel's leadership in favor of a king, an innovation that was regarded in 1 Samuel 8 as a great evil. Saul's rise and fall were tied to his adherence to and abandonment of the law (as revealed to him by Samuel; see for example 1 Sam 15:17-19). Likewise, David's fortunes rose as he followed Yahweh, but sank quickly after the Bathsheba affair (2 Sam 12). Thus the Deuteronomistic dichotomy of blessing for obedience and punishment for sin pervades the book.

Something else enters the picture, however, something that hints of gospel. David commits crimes that are worthy of death, but he does not die. His sin is transferred to another, who dies in his place (2 Sam 12:13-14). David's sin is egregious, but God does not cut him off. His rule will be diminished, but his dynasty remains intact. He suffers from private and public shame, but still Yahweh gives him victory over his enemies, including those from his own house. Thus there is an element of grace that occasionally bubbles through the Deuteronomistic porridge of crime and punishment. Even in sin, even in darkness, there is hope. There is a future.

In the books of Samuel, Israel is constantly in crisis: the crisis of kingship, the crisis of the Philistine threat, the crisis of the lost ark, the crisis of faulty leadership. Yet, in times of crisis, lessons for life emerge. The loss of the ark becomes a lesson in trusting Yahweh's power. The failures of Saul become a lesson for David. The failures of David speak to future generations.

Individuals also face times of crisis. Young Samuel hears the voice of God. Young David hears the taunts of Goliath. A more mature David is caught between Saul and the Philistines. A much older David flees from the insurgency led by his own son. In these times of crisis, faith emerges. Samuel answers God's call. David trusts in Yahweh's sufficiency. Israel in exile and all readers hence learn from these examples that God can still be trusted. Faith can emerge in the midst of crisis so that no day is dark enough to eclipse the light of God's future.

Outline

Students of 1–2 Samuel rarely perceive the structure of the book in identical ways. The following outline is one way of looking at the text and will serve as the organizing principle for the remainder of the book:

I. Samuel: Prophet, Priest, and Maker of Kings (1 Sam 1:1–12:25)
  A. The Rise of Samuel (1:1–4:1a)
    1. Hannah's Vow and Samuel's Birth (1:1-20)
    2. Samuel's Dedication and Hannah's Song (1:21–2:11)
      a. Hannah's gift to God (1:21-28; 2:11)
      b. Hannah's song of praise (2:1-10)
    3. Eli's Failure and Samuel's Favor (2:12-26)
      a. Eli's worthless sons (2:12-17, 22-25)
      b. Hannah's worthy son (2:18-21, 26)
    4. Eli's Fall and Samuel's Call (2:27–4:1a)
      a. The Man of God (2:27-36)
      b. The Boy of God (3:1–4:1a)
  B. The Ark of God (4:1b–7:1)
    1. Philistine Victories and the Loss of the Ark (4:1b-22)
      a. Losing the battle (4:1b-11)
      b. Losing the "glory" (4:12-22)
    2. The Hand of God and the Hands of Dagon (5:1-12)
    3. The Return of the Ark and a Mixed Reception (6:1–7:1)
      a. The Philistines return the ark (6:1-12)
      b. The Israelites rejoice and mourn (6:13–7:1)
  C. Israel Repents and the Philistines Fall (7:2-17)
    1. Samuel calls Israel to repent at Mizpah (7:2-6)
    2. Renascent Israel routs the Philistines (7:7-14)
    3. Samuel's circuit: the final judge (7:15-17)
  D. The Question of Kingship (8:1–12:25)
    1. The People's Request and Samuel's Warning (8:1-22)
      a. Samuel's sons are wanting (8:1-3)
      b. Israel's elders want a king (8:4-6a)
      c. Samuel sounds a warning (8:6b-18)
      d. A king like other nations (8:19-22)
    2. Saul's Search and a Secret Anointing (9:1–10:16)
      a. Saul in search of his father's donkeys (9:1-4)

1. David Deals with a Famine and the Philistines (21:1-22)
   a. The slaughter of the Saulides (21:1-14)
   b. The exploits of David's men (21:15-22)
2. David's Psalm of Praise (22:1-51)
3. David's Last Words (23:1-7)
4. David's Mighty Men (23:8-39)
5. David's Mistake and God's Judgment (24:1-25)

The Samuel Narratives in Literature

The narratives in the books of Samuel have proved to be "classics" in the sense that they frame the human condition in such a profound way that generations of listeners and readers have found their own foibles, questions, and aspirations mirrored in the story. As popular imagination is drawn to such stories, they are told and retold, updated, deciphered, wondered over, and altered in various ways. The David story in particular, with its themes of greatness and tragedy, of virtue and shame, of war and peace, of family scandal and political intrigue, has inspired numerous retellings.

Any retelling is also a remaking of the story, as each reader filters the biblical material through his or her own presuppositions, concerns, and perceptions. The story becomes a lens through which the reader's own concerns are focused, an opportunity for articulating present concerns. Novelists, poets, and playwrights have exploited a rich variety of themes from the Samuel materials.

In the pre-Renaissance period, David appeared in literature as a *type*—a pattern or prototype that foreshadows a later reality. David appears most often as a type of Christ, as the archetypal penitent, and as the model king.

Several of the early church fathers (including Origen, Athanasius, and Augustine) spoke of David as a type of Christ. For example, Augustine argued that "David first reigned in the earthly Jerusalem as a shadow of that which was to come."[1]

During the Middle Ages, David was most commonly seen as a penitent sinner. His piety was magnified, and the overtly sexual features of his sin were diminished. Some medieval descriptions of David's penitence were extreme. The fifteenth century writer William Caxton asserted that David had himself buried up to his waist, remaining "tyl he felte the wormes crepe in his flesshe. This was a great penaunce and a token of grete repentaunce."

The typology of David as a model king is also found in numerous illustrated manuscripts of the Middle Ages, where his coronation is frequently depicted. Some note that elements of the

King Arthur legend reflect influence from David's story: Early in his life, Arthur slew the giant of Mont St. Michel; he was known as a brilliant king who was crippled by sin (though not adultery); he endured and overcame the rebellion of his own son (Mordred); and he was eventually restored by God's grace. In David's story as well as Arthur's, both medieval and modern readers better comprehend how human frailty can diminish even the best of political leaders.

In the political struggles of seventeenth century England, the Davidic archetype was used by both sides in the Puritan–Royalist conflict. Andrew Marvell supported Oliver Cromwell's legitimacy by depicting him as the good Davidic king, while John Dryden supported Stuart rule by appealing to the same Davidic model.

The Renaissance and post-Renaissance periods witnessed an explosion of literature based on the Samuel narratives. Many were uninspired paraphrases of the biblical narrative but still contributed to a movement away from typology toward new avenues of interpretation.

The rise of humanism in art and literature during the late Middle Ages focused attention on the human physical form and on human nature as worthy of study and admiration. The sculpture of these periods, notably the Davids of Donatello, Verocchio, and Michelangelo, celebrated his physical prowess and beauty. [Michelangelo's *David*] Literature also celebrated the human David. In Michael Drayton's poem *David and Goliah* (1630), for example, David's physical form gives "true lawes to perfect Symmetry" (l. 72). David's handsomeness was such that the bees and wasps "have with his beauties often bin beguild," thinking they have seen roses or lilies (ll. 61-66).

The twentieth century has produced several distinguished treatments of the Samuel materials. D. H. Lawrence's play *David* (1926) treated the transitioning fortunes of Saul and David (1 Sam 15–20). Passionately religious, but not at all an orthodox Christian, Lawrence believed that Christianity's greatness had passed and, as he wrote in his 1923 essay "Books," "a new venture towards God" must be started. In *David*, Jonathan is the character who embodies that new venture.

William Faulkner's *Absalom, Absalom!* (1936), although telling the story of a disintegrating southern family in the mid-1800s, drew inspiration from the

Michelangelo's *David*

The most famous image in our world of the figure of David is this colossal sculpture by Michelangelo. The contemplative David sees Goliath in the distance and concentrates on the action about to happen. The strain of this event is seen only in the muscles of his neck and his knitted brow. His body is depicted in the relaxed position known as contrapposto that was used in 5th century Classic Greek sculpture.

Michelangelo (1475–1564). *David*. 1502-04. Marble. 14'1".Museo di Accademia del Disegno, Florence, Italy. (Credit: Planet Art)

David–Amnon–Absalom episode. It is considered by many to be "the great southern novel." The main characters—Thomas Sutpen, the family patriarch and dynasty-builder, and his two sons, Henry Sutpen and Charles Bon—are modeled after David, Amnon, and Absalom. Henry kills Charles to prevent Bon's marriage to Henry's sister, Judith. Since Bon is part African American, Faulkner has introduced miscegenation into the biblical story of incest and thereby directed attention to that most characteristic southern plague, racism.

Alan Paton also drew inspiration from the David–Absalom story for his renowned novel of South Africa, *Cry, the Beloved Country* (1948). Central character Stephen Kumalo has a son named Absalom who rejects his family, commits murder, and eventually is hanged. The story presents the anguished Kumalo's efforts to find his son, during which he has a moving encounter with the father of one of Absalom's victims.

Literary theorists of the late twentieth century have become sensitive to the role ideology plays in shaping texts. Biblical scholars, using the tool of ideological criticism, have investigated how pro-David, anti-Saul ideology shaped the biblical presentation in the books of Samuel. East German novelist Stefan Heym has used his novel *The King David Report* (1973) to argue that one-party, highly centralized states—such as that of both David and East Germany—tend to produce revisionist histories that promote the ruling regime.

At least two inferences may be drawn from this brief survey of the Samuel narratives in literature and from the many other references in the following commentary. The materials are uncommonly rich in suggestive themes, and readers continually "remake" the biblical stories to address modern-day concerns.

The use of the Samuel narratives in literature is far more voluminous than could be treated here. The best resources for studying this material are: David Lyle Jeffrey, ed., *A Dictionary of Biblical Tradition in English Literature* (Grand Rapids: Eerdmans, 1992); and Raymond-Jean Frontain and Jan Wojcik, eds., *The David Myth in Western Literature* (Purdue University Press, 1980).

NOTE

[1.] Augustine, *Civ.* XVII. 14.

1 SAMUEL

HANNAH'S VOW
AND SAMUEL'S BIRTH

1:1-20

Part One: Samuel—Prophet, Priest, and Maker of Kings, 1 Samuel 1:1–12:25

This commentary treats the text of 1 and 2 Samuel in three sections, each based on the main character who is, at least overtly, in control. As the book begins, the priest Eli serves as an obvious foil for *Samuel*, who is the true power in chapters 1–12. Samuel's presence is felt beyond that point, but in chapter 12 he officially gives over leadership to *Saul*. Saul's rule extends until his death in 1 Samuel 31, even though David emerges as a much more popular character. Second Samuel begins with a reminder of Saul's death and the account of *David's* rapid rise to kingship, and David remains the focal character for the remainder of the book.

Many scholars have analyzed the early chapters of Samuel in great detail, with divergent results. Most will agree that there are subsources present, such as "the biography of Samuel" (chs. 1–3) and "the history of the ark" (chs. 4–6), but opinions vary when it comes to the shape of the larger structure. Some literary analysts see a tight unit in chapters 1–7, while others see the first twelve or fifteen chapters as a cohesive whole.

The account of Samuel's rise to prominence in Israel (1:1–4:1a) is a carefully wrought narrative. It contains elements of history and biography, and the story of Samuel's birth is similar to an annunciation type scene, but the author's main concern is to offer a *theological history*. Likewise, the stories surrounding the ark of God (4:1b–7:2) are more concerned with God's demonstration of his power through the ark than with its appearance or location. The question of kingship, first raised in 8:1–12:25, is not so much about Israel's first human king, but about the nation's rejection of God as king.

As every other part of the Deuteronomistic History, these stories are unashamedly tendentious. This is no "politically correct" document, but a one-sided attempt to show that God is the only true king and that obeying God is the only wise course. Those who accept God's rule and follow his way will prosper, while those who rebuff God's claims will fall. This is the overall theme of 1 and 2 Samuel, told in a myriad of minor plots that hammer home the authors' primary concern: *God is king; it is best to obey!*

COMMENTARY

Most of 1 and 2 Samuel is written in a freely flowing narrative style; the first chapter is no exception. In a literary sense, the chapter falls rather neatly into two parts, as vv. 1-20 recount the circumstances leading up to Samuel's birth and vv. 21-28 describe the events that follow. Thematically, the chapter has four movements, detailing Hannah's need (vv. 1-8), Hannah's bargain with God (vv. 9-18), God's answer (vv. 19-20), and Hannah's fulfillment of her promise (vv. 21-28).

The purpose of this chapter is to relay the story of Samuel's birth in such a way as to emphasize the magnitude of Samuel's personage and the significant role he will play in Hebrew history. [Birth Stories] Several characteristics of the story underscore Samuel's importance, beginning with his introduction at the very beginning of the book. Other emphatic elements include the similarity of this story to earlier narratives about patriarchal wives who had difficulty becoming pregnant, the extensive attention paid to Samuel's mother Hannah, and the insistence that Samuel was born as a result of Hannah's vow and God's response. Though Hannah's vow involves a conversation with God and Eli offers an ambiguous semi-oracle in response, it is Hannah who shows the initiative.

Birth Stories

Some of the most important characters in Israel's history are introduced through an "annunciation type scene," and some scholars use this term to describe the account of Samuel's birth. However, in a true annunciation type scene, the birth of a child is predicted through an impressive encounter with God, usually mediated by an angel. For example, three divine representatives appeared to Abraham by the oaks of Mamre and predicted the birth of Isaac (Gen 18:1-15). Similarly, a single "man of God" majestically appeared to Manoah's unnamed wife—and later to Manoah—to foretell Samson's birth and to give instructions about his upbringing (Judg 13:2-23).

The point of an annunciation story is to emphasize the importance of the child who is about to be born: Isaac, Samson, John, Jesus. While Samuel is no doubt a significant person, the story of his birth lacks the visionary quality of most typical annunciation scenes. There is no angel to announce the birth. Rather, Hannah approaches God through prayer and the making of a vow. Nor does the word of assurance come through an impressive supernatural messenger, but through an old and deaf priest named Eli.

1. *One Man and Two Women.* There once was a man, so the Bible says—a certain man from the village of Ramathaim, of the Zuphite family who lived in the hill country of Ephraim, and his name was Elkanah. (see [Map of Central Hill Country]) While this typical introduction leads the reader to believe that this story is about a man, it is not. The story is about a woman who will soon give birth to a son who becomes the focus of the story. Elkanah is only in the story because this woman is his wife. Or, to be more specific, she is one of his two wives. (see [Was It Bigamy?])

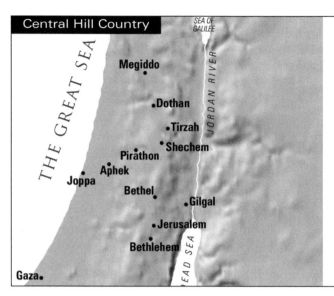

Central Hill Country

Map of Central Hill Country

AΩ Elkanah's home is called Ramathaim (the "double-height") only in v. 1. The LXX calls it *harmathaim*, and it is clearly in Ephraim, probably equivalent to the New Testament town of Arimathea (Matt 27:57). Elsewhere, Elkanah is said to have lived in Ramah (v. 19; 2:11), probably the Benjaminite town of er-Ram, later cited as Samuel's home (7:17; 8:4; 15:34; etc.). This may reflect multiple source traditions that are not fully harmonized by the narrator.

The woman's name was Hannah, and "Hannah" means "grace," but the woman's difficult life betrayed her pleasant name. We are told that Hannah was the most miserable of women; her rival wife had several children, but Hannah had none.

Elkanah had married Hannah for love, so the rabbis say, and our text insists that his love persisted even though she was thought to be barren (v. 5). According to the law, Elkanah could have divorced Hannah on grounds of infertility, but he did not choose to do so. Still, in the ancient world it was every man's duty and desire to beget male children. Sons were needed to perpetuate his family name, to inherit his land, and to carry on his business. As a result, the greatest thing his wife could do for him was to bear at least one son, and preferably more. By the same token, the worst thing she could do was fail. [Divorce]

For women of the ancient world, then, one's honor and reputation were measured by the number of sons produced. Ancient Israelites seem never to have considered that the male partner might be infertile, and they certainly had no idea that the gender of a child

Was It Bigamy?

Monogamy seems to have predominated in ancient Israel, but the taking of a second wife was acceptable under certain circumstances, such as the first wife's failure to produce children. For example, Abraham took Hagar when Sarah was past child-bearing age (Gen 16:1-6), with unhappy results. Jacob married two women as a result of his uncle Laban's manipulations (Gen 29:15-35), but also had children by his wives' "handmaids" when Rachel and Leah experienced periods of infertility (Gen 30:1-13).

Divorce

Rules concerning divorce were quite lax in the ancient world (for men, at least). According to Deut 24:1, a man could divorce his wife if for any reason he found her objectionable. Some rabbis (such as Hillel) interpreted this very loosely, while others insisted that only adultery constituted sufficient grounds (Shammai). In a culture that prized the production of sons over all other female virtues, childlessness may have been a common cause for divorce.

is actually determined by the father's genetic contribution of an X or Y chromosome. Laying the "blame" for childlessness on the woman alone was an unjust and unfortunate fact of life for women in Hannah's world. The reality of these factors serves only to augment Hannah's impressive accomplishments. Her resourceful approach to obtaining God's help in overcoming her barrenness—and her faithfulness to the promise involved—makes Hannah one of the great heroines of the Old Testament.

There came a day when Elkanah accepted Hannah's infertility, but not his own. The text does not reveal the circumstances surrounding Elkanah's decision to pursue other options for having children, though there are many possibilities. Perhaps Elkanah was growing older or experiencing pressure from parents or friends. The rabbis claim that Hannah herself suggested that he marry another. In any case, Elkanah did in fact take a second wife, whose name was Peninnah. [Multiple Marriages] Some interpreters think her name meant "luxuriant hair," while others argue for something like "ruby," "pearl," or even "prolific." The narrator is silent concerning Peninnah's motivation for entering this complicated marriage that was no more fair to her than it was to Hannah. The marriage is an accomplished fact when the story begins.

Multiple Marriages

Elkanah's secondary marriage to Peninnah is different from the arrangement that Abraham and Sarah entered into with Hagar (Gen 16). There, Hagar, who was a servant, actually served as a surrogate mother for Sarah. The intent was for Sarah to adopt Hagar's child from birth and raise him as her own (Gen 16:2). Once she became pregnant, however, Hagar no longer wished to be used in this way, and much unhappiness ensued (cf. Gen 29–30).

There is no hint of this surrogate arrangement, however, in the story of Elkanah's dual marriage. Peninnah is never described as a servant, and her children are clearly *her* children, not Hannah's. Indeed, this fact lies at the heart of Hannah's grief. Both Hannah and Peninnah have full status as wives and full claim to their own children. The triangular relationship, however, also brought with it a full measure of strife.

In one sense, Elkanah's second marriage was successful. Peninnah did in fact produce children, including sons. Yet Hannah remained his first and favorite wife, even though she was no longer the most important wife. The text suggests that Peninnah salved her wounded self-esteem by criticizing her rival at every opportunity, adding substantially to Hannah's misery.

2. *A Sad Celebration.* Family tensions grew so severe that even the annual fall festival at Shiloh brought Hannah no joy, but only increased her grief. The fall festival was a celebrative time when pilgrims gathered at Shiloh to pay their tithes from the harvest and to offer sacrifices of thanks to "Yahweh of Hosts." [Yahweh of Hosts] This divine title is significant, for the motif of God as a warrior who does battle on Israel's behalf appears frequently in 1 and 2 Samuel.

In the course of worship, it was customary that part of the thanksgiving offering be burned on the altar as an offering to

Yahweh of Hosts

AΩ This ancient divine title appears here for the first time in the Bible, the first of five times in 1 Samuel. "Yahweh of Hosts" conjures the mental image of a militaristic God standing at the head of a mighty army composed of the hosts of heaven (angels). "Yahweh" is regarded as the personal name for God in the Hebrew Bible. The only real clue to its meaning is found in Exodus 3:13-16, which seems to tie its origin to the Hebrew verb of being, *hāyah*. ("I am that I am" is *ehyeh asher ehyeh*.) The original Hebrew text was written without vowel points, so we cannot be certain how the divine name *yhwh* was vocalized. Some scholars are content to call it the "Tetragrammaton" for its four letters, while others see it as a war cry (like *yahoo!*). The most common conjecture is that *yhwh* should be read as *yahweh*, the causative verb form of *hyh* ("He who causes to be"). Some writers regard the compound title "Yahweh of Hosts" as a borrowed term from Canaanite worship, for "He who creates the (heavenly) armies" was an early epithet for Baal. Although the word for "hosts" (*ṣebāʾôt*) is normally used to describe an army, a few translators read it as an abstract plural intended to intensify the divine majesty, resulting in "the LORD Almighty" (NIV).

Yahweh and that a part of it be kept by the priests to provide for their support, but most of it was returned to the family. The law required that all sacrifices be consumed within two days, so the festival was a time of major feasting and much joy. [Sacrificial Meals]

But there was little joy for Hannah (v. 8), who seemed to have felt alienated by her infertility and isolated by her grief. Specifically, there was something about Elkanah's carving of the sacrificial meal that exacerbated the conflict and added to Hannah's sorrow. Unfortunately, a clear understanding of Elkanah's actions falls victim to an obscure Hebrew text. It is apparent that Elkanah would first give a number of portions to Peninnah—one for herself, and

Sacrificial Meals

 By the time Israel's sacrificial system was fully codified, sacrifices could be offered only in Jerusalem (Deut 12:13-14); but in early times, sacrifices could be offered at family altars or local shrines, such as the temple at Shiloh.

"Burnt offerings" were completely burned on the altar. Though sometimes having expiatory significance (Lev 9:7; 14:20; Job 1:5; 42:8), the burnt offering more commonly played a role in petitions (1 Sam 13:12), public worship (Num 28–29), votive or voluntary offerings (Lev 22:18), and rites of purification (Lev 12:6, 8; 16:24).

The most common sacrifice was called the *šᵉlamîm* offering, translated variously as "peace offering," "communion offering," or the like. These offerings, which could be offered corporately or individually, functioned to establish or to maintain good relations with God. Although the text uses a generic term for sacrifice, the circumstances of 1 Samuel 1 suggest that Elkanah offered a *šᵉlamîm* offering, for it was commonly given in the payment of votive and freewill offerings. First Samuel 1:21 specifically connects at least one of Elkanah's annual trips to the payment of his vows.

With *šᵉlamîm* offerings, the blood, the visceral fat, and the fat tail of the sheep were burned on the altar to God, since blood and fat were thought to be life-giving (Lev 3:16-17; 7:22-26; 17:11, 14). The priest was given a forequarter as his rightful portion (Lev 7:28-34; 10:14-15), and the worshiper was allowed to keep the rest. Portions returned to the worshiper were to be eaten within two days, with the remainder to be burned on the third day (Lev 7:16-17; 22:18-23).

For a concise description of other Israelite sacrifices, see Tony W. Cartledge, "Sacrifice," *MDB*, eds. Roger A. Bullard, Joel F. Drinkard Jr., Walter Harrelson, and Edgar V. McKnight (Macon GA: Mercer University Press, 1990), 783-84.

Interpreting ʾappāyîmn

AΩ The singular form of the word is *ʾaph*, and it can carry the extended sense of "face" or "brow" (Gen 3:19). In Hebrew, paired facial characteristics (eyes, ears, nostrils) conventionally appear in the dual form. Some scholars through the years have suggested that the text is corrupt and have offered other readings based on conjectured textual emendations. Samuel R. Driver suggested "he used to give one portion, *howbeit* he loved Hannah," but this proposal is weak because the text clearly suggests that Elkanah showed some favoritism to Hannah. Taking a view similar to the Targums (ancient Aramaic translations), others have proposed "one *choice* portion," assuming that *ʾappāyîmn* is somehow related to *pîmâ*, "fat." Kyle McCarter conjectures a corruption from the word *kᵉpîm*, which means "proportionate to," suggesting that Elkanah gave Hannah one portion that was as great as Peninnah's portions combined, thus inciting Peninnah's rancor.

Such linguistic feats are unnecessary, however. The received text makes sense if we simply regard "a portion of two faces" as a means of emphasizing greater quantity: either "enough for two" or "double size."

It is instructive to compare Deut 21:15-17, a legal regulation directed to a man who had two wives, whose oldest son was descended of the less favored wife. The law required him to honor the oldest son as firstborn (even if he preferred a son of his favorite wife) by designating a double portion of the inheritance to him. In this text, the words "double portion" are derived from the Hebrew *pîšᵉnayîm*, "a mouth of two." The word for mouth, like the term for face, could bear the connotation of a part or portion; thus "a mouth of two" is a "double portion."

Samuel R. Driver, *Notes on the Hebrew Text and the Topography of the Book of Samuel*, (2d ed.; Oxford: Clarendon Press, 1913).

P. Kyle McCarter, *I Samuel* (AB 8; Garden City: Doubleday, 1980), 52.

---

one for each of her children (v. 4). What he gave to Hannah, however, is less certain.

A literal reading of the MT reads: "And to Hannah he gave one portion of two faces, because it was Hannah he loved, and Yahweh had closed up her womb." This awkward reading derives from the word *ʾappāyîmn*, which appears to be a dual form of the word for "nostril" or "nose." [Interpreting *ʾappāyîmn*] In this context, it appears that *ʾappāyîmn* suggests "one portion of two faces" (or even "noses"), implying a larger portion than normal, perhaps even a "double portion" (as NRSV). It was Elkanah's small way of expressing a special measure of love to Hannah. Unfortunately, his efforts were lost on Hannah and enraged her rival Peninnah.

Reference to the legal requirements of Deuteronomy 21:15-17 (see [Eating and Drinking]) assists us in translating the text and also points to an ironic aspect of the story. The law insists that Elkanah favor Peninnah's son, as firstborn, by designating a double portion of the inheritance to him, but in the ceremonial moment of their sacrificial meal, Elkanah gives a double portion to Hannah, who has no sons at all.

This painful distribution of the sacrificial meal was not a singular incident, but "went on year after year" (v. 7). Peninnah's persistent taunting would upset heartbroken Hannah so deeply that she could not even eat the food that Elkanah provided in such abundance. Hannah's grief was obvious, but her husband was unable to comfort her. The storyteller takes delight in describing Elkanah's obtuseness by suggesting that his solicitation was limited to bumbling questions, such as "Hannah, why are you weeping? Hannah, why don't you eat? Hannah, why are you so downhearted? *Don't I mean more to you than ten sons?*" (v. 8). Hannah's silence shouts.

3. *A Desperate Bargain.* The narrator uses a variety of Hebrew expressions to describe and to underscore Hannah's misery. She was provoked severely and irritated by her rival (v. 6) so that she wept and would not eat (v. 7). She was brokenhearted (v. 8), miserable (lit., "afflicted," v. 11), and sorrowful in spirit (NRSV: "deeply troubled," v. 15). [Utilizing Affliction] There came a day, however, when Hannah had absorbed all of the misery she could take. She left while the others were eating and drinking, and ran in tears to the very door of the temple in *Shiloh.* [Shiloh] "*In bitterness of soul,*" the narrator says (v. 10), Hannah wept much and poured out her heart to the LORD—and she offered to make a desperate bargain with God.

Utilizing Affliction

There may be a theological motive behind this literary device of piling up synonyms for "affliction." The DH probably reached its final form during the Babylonian exile, the darkest days of Hebrew history. The exiled Israelites were brokenhearted, miserable, and afflicted in Babylon, where they wept for the loss of Zion (Ps 137:1).

Deut 26:7 recalls how the Israelites were saved from their affliction under the Egyptians because they called out to Yahweh, while Deut 28:3 predicts even greater afflictions if Israel should fail to remain obedient.

Demonstrating how brokenhearted Hannah turned to Yahweh and found deliverance would effectively serve the authors' apologetic purpose of urging Israel to return to God and cry out for salvation.

Shiloh

AΩ The ruins of Shiloh are usually associated with the modern village of Khirbet Seilun, a site located in the hill country of Ephraim, 18–20 miles north-northeast of Jerusalem. Although it enjoyed a brief fluorescence as an established cultic center in late pre-monarchic times, archaeological studies suggest that it was not a very important city either before or after that period.

The temple in Shiloh may have been a temporary affair, a sturdy tent surrounded by a courtyard, bearing an altar for sacrifices. The term "house of Yahweh" (*bêt yhwh*, 1:7) could refer either to a tent-shrine or a permanent temple, and 2 Sam 7:6 insists that the ark of God never resided in a permanent structure prior to Solomon's temple (see also Pss 78:60 and 132:7). However, the Shiloh temple is called the "temple of Yahweh" (*hêkal yhwh*) in 1 Sam 1:9 and 3:3. This term is ordinarily used of a permanent sanctuary. If the Shiloh temple was a tent, it may have been similar to these modern Bedouin homes.

1 Samuel 1:10—Hannah's prayer was a bitter but hopeful cry for help.

Julius Schnoor von Carolsfeld. *Hannah's Prayer.* 19th century. Woodcut. *Das Buch der Bucher in Bilden.* (Credit: Dover Pictorial Archive Series)

Hannah is described throughout as a pious woman, and one last resort often favored by the downtrodden and desperate was the making of a sacred vow to Yahweh. Hannah boldly asked the LORD to supply her greatest need—and she promised with all her heart that if only God would grant her prayer, she would give to him the most precious thing she had. Hannah did not yet have this most precious possession—this she asked for, and this she promised to return. [Vows]

"O LORD God Almighty," she prayed, "if you will only look upon your servant's misery and remember me, and not forget your servant but give her a son, then I will give him to the LORD for all the days of his life, and no razor will ever be used on his head" (v. 11). Hannah's promise that "no razor will ever be used on his head" has led many writers to assume that Hannah's son would be a nazirite, but this goes beyond the evidence. [Was Samuel a Nazirite?] Whether Hannah intended for Samuel to be known as a nazirite is secondary to her obvious desire that the child be marked as one who was dedicated to God.

Vows

Vow-making in the Old Testament, as well as in the entire ancient Near East, was not equivalent to the modern, Western notion of vows. Modern readers think of a vow as a sacred and unconditional promise, but in the Old Testament (and the ancient Near East as a whole), vows were always *conditional promises* made at the initiative of the worshiper. Vows were one of the few means by which any person could approach God directly without the medium of a priest or public ceremony, though vows were often made (and always paid) in the public arena.

Vows were sometimes made as a matter of course (such as Elkanah's annual vows in 1 Sam 1:21), but the most memorable vows arose in times of distress. The Old Testament often refers to vow-making and has extensive regulations for the practice (Lev 27; Num 6; 30), but it

contains the text of only five narrative vows: those made by Jacob (Gen 28:20-22), Israel (Num 21:2), Jephthah (Judg 11:30-31), Hannah (1 Sam 1:11), and Absalom (2 Sam 15:8).

Vow accounts are always prayers, and they follow a typical pattern: "If you will do thus and so for me, then I will do thus and so for you." By making the vow, the worshiper enters into a binding relationship with God, calling upon him for a certain blessing and promising specific actions or gifts in return. This gives added force to the distressed person's petition, who has now done everything possible in search of divine favor.

For more information on vows, see Cartledge, *Vows in the Hebrew Bible and the Ancient Near East* (Sheffield: JSOT Press, 1992); or "Vows," *ISBE.* Ed. G.W. Bromiley. 4 vols. (Grand Rapids: Eerdmans, 1979-1988), 4: 998-99.

The formalized vow in v.11 is, of course, the narrator's depiction of Hannah's vow. With only a little imagination, one might envision Hannah standing at the temple door and praying in more lengthy and more heated fashion: "Oh God, please give me a son. That's all I want from you, all I will ever ask from you. I've been your faithful servant all my life, but I think you have forgotten me. Oh God, remember me! Oh, God, have mercy on my misery! Oh God, don't forget me! Oh God, please just grant me a son! One son. That's all I ask. God, give me a son—just for a while—and I will give him back to you. I will dedicate him to your service. I will see to it that he never cuts his hair, so that all will know he is dedicated to you. Oh God, don't forget me! Oh God, have mercy! Oh God. . . ."

When the aged priest Eli finally took notice of Hannah, he assumed that she was intoxicated. [Eli] The text does not tell us if Hannah expected to meet the priest or if her prayer was intended for God's ears only. Indeed, the narrator tells us that Eli's faculties were so impaired that he could not hear what Hannah said. Something about her appearance or her actions led Eli to conclude that she was besotted, like so many others who used the feast as an excuse for excess.

Eli's first response was less than pastoral: "How long will you make a drunken spectacle of yourself? Put away your wine!" (v. 14). Hannah, however, would not be so easily dismissed. Her persistence

Was Samuel a Nazirite?

Persons making a nazirite vow in its classic form were bound by three conditions. For a specified period of time, they pledged that they would not cut their hair or shave their beard, imbibe any alcoholic beverage, or become "unclean" by touching the dead (see Num 6). All three prohibitions may not have been required in early periods, however.

While scholars traditionally have seen the nazirite vow as an unconditional, pious pledge to God, after the order of a modern monastic vow, nazirite vows could be just as conditional as any other (see Cartledge, "Were Nazirite Vows Unconditional?" *CBQ* 51 [Jul 1989]: 409-22; and in a less technical treatment, "The Nazirites," *BI* 19 [Oct–Dec 1992]: 54-58).

Our understanding of early nazirites is uncertain, and the institution certainly evolved with the passing of time. According to the MT, Hannah promised only that Samuel would never cut his hair (1:21). Later nazirites pledged to abstain from cutting their hair, drinking wine, or touching the dead, but only for a limited time. Samuel's commitment included fewer conditions, but a life-long commitment.

McCarter uses evidence from the Septuagint (an ancient Greek translation) and 4QSam^a (one of the Dead Sea Scrolls) to argue that v. 11 originally included a prohibition against wine and strong drink and that v. 22 specifically used the word "nazirite." These variant readings could reflect later attempts to harmonize the vow with typical nazirite practice, however, so the argument is inconclusive. It is more likely that the nazirite elements would be added to the text than that a later editor would delete them, so the MT is preferred.

P. Kyle McCarter, *I Samuel* (AB 8; Garden City: Doubleday, 1980), 49-50, 53.

Eli

We know little about Eli's descent or how it is that he came to be priest at Shiloh. The Old Testament does not mention anything about his ancestry other than one reference in 2:27-28, which connects him to the line of Aaron. In competing, though much later, traditions, Josephus assigns Eli to the Aaronide family of Ithamar (*Ant.* 5.11.5), while 2 Esdras puts him in the rival house of Eleazar (1:2-3). Ithamar and Eleazar were two of Aaron's sons (Exod 28:1).

The writers of 1 Samuel are less concerned with Eli's rise than with his fall (along with other Aaronides), and the ultimate ascension of the Zadokite priesthood. Eli's bumbling interaction with Hannah sets the stage for a more extensive description of his incompetence in later chapters.

Blessing or Oracle?

At different times in Israel's history, prophetic and priestly functions seemed to overlap. The pronouncing of a divine oracle about the future is generally thought of as a prophetic task, while the expression of a hopeful blessing is more in the purview of the priests (Num 6:22-27). Samuel, Eli's successor, was widely regarded as a "seer" who made authoritative predictions about the future. This seems to assign to Samuel a *dual* role, however, rather than an *expanded* one. For example, Samuel honored Saul at a sacrificial feast (1 Sam 9:22-24) but took him out of the hearing of others before declaring the word of God to him (1 Sam 9:27).

Some persons became so large in Israel's memory that their spoken blessings were accorded the power of fulfillment, as though they had been oracles of God (Isaac, Gen 27:1-40; Joseph, Gen 49:1-28). Eli, however, does not share this powerful persona. The text presents him as a doddering old priest who recognizes when God speaks to others (1 Sam 3:8) but must receive the word of God from traveling prophets (1 Sam 2:28-36) or even his own apprentice (1 Sam 3:10-18). The reader, then, should recognize Eli's comforting words to Hannah as a wish for God's blessing, rather than an oracular assurance of divine intervention.

---

was as strong as her grief. "No, my lord, I am a woman deeply troubled; I have drunk neither wine nor strong drink, but I have been pouring out my soul before the LORD. Do not regard your servant as a worthless woman, for I have been speaking out of my great anxiety and vexation all this time" (vv. 15-16). "Worthless woman" is, literally, "a daughter of Belial." The Hebrew word *Belial* means "worthlessness," but it was also regarded as a proper name, later attributed to Satan (2 Cor 6:15). Although Eli had not used the term, Hannah assumed that he had judged her as a wicked woman, perhaps even a follower of other gods. Pious Hannah's sharp and somewhat presumptuous response led Eli to understand that she was a righteous woman, inebriated only by her grief.

When Eli realized the truth of Hannah's pain, he responded as best he could. He could not claim to have the word of the LORD, for "the word of the LORD was rare in those days" (1 Sam 3:1). He could not make the woman a promise, but he made her a wish. Very carefully he said, "Go in peace; the God of Israel grant you the petition you have asked of him." When Eli said this, he used a verb form that can be interpreted in either of two ways. He probably intended to say "*May* God grant your wish," but Hannah could have understood his words to mean "God *will* grant your wish." Some scholars assume that Israelite priests often responded to worshipers' prayers with a prophetic "oracle," thought to be a word from God about the future. Thus, some interpreters refer to Eli's response as an oracle. His words, however, seem to be a simple blessing, though the obliqueness of his language allows for variant interpretations. [Blessing or Oracle?]

Samuel's Name

AΩ Much ink has been spilled in an attempt to explain Hannah's comment about Samuel's name. Since the word for "asked" and the name "Saul" are the same (šaûl), many commentators have assumed that an ancient legend about Saul's name has become confused with the Samuel traditions. This is unnecessary speculation, however.

Hannah *asked for* Samuel by a vow, with the result that God *heard* her prayer and answered her. Old Aramaic and Punic votive texts found on ancient stele (commemorative markers) often ended with a characteristic line: kšmᶜ ql', "because he heard his voice." The votive inscriptions were commissioned and erected as a testimony to the deity because the postulant had made a vow to the god and was *heard* (šmᶜ). When the qal passive participle of the Hebrew verb "to hear" (šamûᶜ) is combined with the common divine appellative, ʾēl, the resulting combination (šamûᶜēl) could easily contract to form šamûʾēl, the Hebrew form of the name "Samuel," meaning "heard of God." The first vowel would shorten when it became the antepenult (second from the last syllable), and the conjunction of the two gutturals would naturally elide into a single consonant (the letters ᶜ [ayin] and ʾ [aleph] were not voiced).

In the light of grammatical evidence and the extrabiblical texts which routinely connect divine "hearing" with the fulfillment of votive requests, this proposal seems quite reasonable, and it obviates at least one rationale for attributing Samuel's birth story to Saul.

Tony W. Cartledge, *Vows in the Hebrew Bible and the Ancient Near East*, JSOT Supplement Series, 147 (Sheffield: JSOT Press, 1992), ch. 3.

Whatever his intention, Eli's words became a remarkable gift to Hannah, a heartening assurance that God had heard her prayer, an audible wish that all her dreams would come true. The combination of her own fervent prayer and the old priest's blessing was such that Hannah seems to have experienced a resurgence of *hope*. She believed that God's final word had not yet been spoken.

Hannah's renewed sense of hope brought about a remarkable change in her demeanor. The text says, "Then she went her way and ate something, and her face was no longer downcast" (v. 18). For the exegete, it is essential to notice that Hannah's prayer had not yet been answered. Indeed, Hannah had no positive assurance that it *would* be answered. But she had a newly found hope, and she believed that God had heard her plea. Hannah had placed her future squarely in God's hands, and her heart was at peace.

We can only imagine Elkanah's surprise when Hannah dried her tears, ate her supper, and smiled once again. The text implies that there was a new joy in Hannah's smile, and perhaps a new spark in her sexual relationship with Elkanah. In short order, the narrator declares that God did "remember" Hannah, who in her prayer had described herself as a forgotten handmaid. She quickly conceived, and in due time she gave birth to a son. The narrator has so skillfully built the level of suspense that when the child is born, it is almost anticlimactic. The real focus of the narrative is on Hannah's vow and her resultant sense of peace; the final appearance of Samuel serves as a denouement to the first episode (his birth) and as a transition leading to the second (his dedication).

The reader is surprised when Hannah gives the child his name, for it would have been more culturally acceptable for Elkanah, as the father, to choose the name. Hannah called her son Samuel—

šᵉmûʾēl—saying, "because I asked the LORD for him"(1:20). [Samuel's Name] Hannah had asked, and the LORD had heard. *Šᵉmûʾēl* means "heard by God." By this significant name, young Samuel's life would always be linked to his mother's vow.

CONNECTIONS

Hannah's story teaches important lessons about trust and hope. Hannah, like all people, experienced periods of deep disappointment in life. Hannah lived in a culture that defined the value of women by their fecundity, but she had no children after many years of marriage. Like other women of her day, Hannah had looked forward to bearing children and enjoying a satisfying marriage, but this "normal" woman's role had been denied to her, and her dreams remained unfulfilled. As a result, for many years Hannah led a miserable life.

Hannah was not ashamed to mourn her childlessness nor the loss of her husband's full attention. This willingness to confront her troubles and to vent her feelings was a sign of Hannah's healthy emotional life. Yet, Hannah's determination not to be defeated by the circumstances and the obstacles of life also speaks of her strong spiritual sense.

Even as Hannah grieved over her misfortune, there came a day when she determined that she would not spend the rest of her life this way. While worshiping at the temple, Hannah came to an understanding with God. She would turn it over to him. If God granted her a son, she would give him back to God and be satisfied to visit him in his new home. If God did not grant her prayer, then she would accept this fact with the peace of knowing that she had done all she could. Hannah's experience, then, witnesses to the centrality of *hope* and *trust* in the life of believers.

Hope is a powerful force. Frederick Buechner attested the power of hopeful wishing when he wrote:

Sometimes wishing is the wings the truth comes true on.
Sometimes the truth is what sets us wishing for it.[1]

Through hope and trust in God, expressed in a place of sanctuary, Hannah found inner peace even before her prayers were answered positively. She learned to entrust to God those things that were beyond her control. The implication of the text is that she would have remained at peace even if her request had not been granted, because she knew that she had done all she could in her relationship with Elkanah and with God.

Hannah's experience speaks to modern believers who may also become despondent about things over which they have no control. Hannah's desire to pray at the temple speaks to the value of a community of faith, a sacred space in which we may draw near to God. Hannah's audacious vow demonstrates how it is possible for one whose stomach has been filled with gall to once again experience hunger for life and joy—even if circumstances do not change.

Hannah hoped for a child, but her trust was in God. Her willingness to make a vow before God demonstrates her belief in Yahweh's power, but even more it reveals her faith in *a God who cares*. Hannah's approach to God was couched in great humility. She carefully referred to herself as the LORD's *maidservant*, but she was a maidservant made bold by her distress and by her conviction that she served a God who cared as much for maidservants as for anyone else.

Hannah is described as a person who was not only trusting, but *trustworthy*. She was willing to make a commitment to God that most people would never consider, and she was the kind of woman who could be trusted to keep her word. This will become even more evident in 1:21-28.

When the circumstances of life bring more misery than joy, believers are faced with several options. They can give up on the future and resign themselves to a life of misery. They can give up on God and decide "to go it alone." Or they can decide to hold on to faith, hold on to hope, and in doing so hold on to God. Hannah's story testifies to one woman's willingness to hold on—whatever the cost—and to God's faithfulness in caring for his own, even for those who are disappointed by life and rejected by society.

Personal Connections

Despite the differences in modern and ancient cultures, women of today face many of the same obstacles Hannah faced. Modern society has allowed women to pursue a greater variety of roles, and contemporary women are appreciated for more than the children they produce. Yet barriers still remain. The "glass ceiling" is firmly in place in many corporations, and certain roles (such as pastoral ministry) remain an almost exclusively male domain. What lesson does Hannah's story suggest for those who can hardly see their goals for the obstacles in between?

Hannah's vow, in effect, was a bargain with God. She made a special request and offered special promises in return. Does Hannah's

Dealing with Reality

One bitterly cold day a rabbi and his disciples were huddled around a fire.

One of the disciples, echoing his master's teachings, said, "On a freezing day like this I know exactly what to do!"

"What?" asked the others.

"Keep warm! And if that isn't possible, I still know what to do."

"What?"

"Freeze."

Anthony de Mello comments: "Present Reality cannot *really* be rejected or accepted. To run away from it is like running away from your feet. To accept it is like kissing your lips. All you need to do is see, understand, and be at rest."

Some aspects of reality can be changed, and should be changed. Other realities, such as the death of a loved one, must be accepted. Living at peace involves both the challenge of action and the call to acceptance, along with the wisdom to know which is appropriate.

Anthony de Mello, *Taking Flight* (New York: Doubleday, 1988), 32.

success imply that all believers should approach God in a similar fashion? Notice that the practice of vow-making in the Old Testament leaves God free to respond either positively or negatively—the believer is obligated only if God grants the petition.

Many persons, both male and female, live under difficult circumstances or with unfulfilled goals. With sufficient determination or ingenuity, many obstacles can be overcome, while other difficulties may be life-long companions. How does one tell the difference and live at peace? [Dealing with Reality]

NOTE

1 Frederick Buechner, *Wishful Thinking: A Theological ABC* (New York: Harper & Row, 1973), 96.

SAMUEL'S DEDICATION
AND HANNAH'S SONG

1:21–2:11

Hannah's remarkable story does not end with the birth of Samuel, for she has promised to give the miracle child back to God. To fulfill her promise, Hannah must take Samuel to the Shiloh temple and devote him to Yahweh's service for life. The reader may wonder if she really will follow through with such a difficult pledge, but the text does not sustain the suspense very long. Indeed, the story is clear in affirming the unflinching devotion of both Hannah and her husband Elkanah. As God had been faithful in responding to Hannah's prayer, so will she be loyal in fulfilling her promise.

This section consists of a narrative description of Samuel's dedication at the Shiloh temple (1:21-28; 2:11), into which has been inserted the "Song of Hannah" (2:1-10); this ancient psalm functions in two ways, drawing attention both to Hannah, who sings, and to Yahweh, who is worthy of great praise.

COMMENTARY

Hannah's Gift to God, 1:21-28; 2:11

The narrator leads us to believe that Hannah became pregnant almost immediately after her return from the previous year's sacrifice. This means Samuel would have been less than three months old when festival time came around again, when "the man Elkanah and all his household went up to offer to the LORD the yearly sacrifice, and to pay his vow" (v. 21). [Going Up] Elkanah's personal piety is evident: not only was he faithful in observing the annual festival rites,

---

Going Up

AΩ Shiloh was located in the central hill country, but that is not why Elkanah and his family "went up" to the temple. It was a customary figure of speech in biblical language that one always "went up" to worship. This probably derived from the fact that early altars were typically located on high places. The idiom is most commonly seen in references to Jerusalem (e. g., 1 Kgs 12:28; Ezra 1:3,5; John 7:14; Acts 15:2; 21:2; Gal 1:17) but was also used in reference to other sanctuaries, such as Bethel (Gen 35:31) or Shiloh (1 Sam 1:7; 2:19).

Elkanah's Vow

The mention of Elkanah's vow serves to reinforce his life of personal devotion, but its presence has troubled some critics, who think it is out of place. Henry Preserved Smith regarded it as a scribal addition, since there was no mention of a previous vow, while H. W. Hertzberg thought Elkanah might be taking on the responsibility of Hannah's vow in accordance with the regulations of Num 30:14 (MT v. 15). This could hardly be the case: even if one could argue that the regulations underlying Num 30 were current in this early period, Elkanah in no way fulfills the requirements of Hannah's vow.

Lyle Eslinger seems to think that it makes no sense for Elkanah to make a vow, and proceeds to emend the text on the grounds that "in the case of a nonsensical text, the way lies open for a judicious emendation." The text is not nonsensical, however, nor is Eslinger's proposed emendation especially judicious. Eslinger would read "and his vow" with the next verse, translating "but with a vow Hannah did not go up." This proposition is invalid for several reasons, the most notable being that it reflects a misunderstanding of biblical vows and confusion with the modern word for "vow." Old Testament vows were always conditional promises. Had she wished, Hannah might have *sworn an oath* not to go up, but would never have made a *vow* not to attend the festival.

Henry Preserved Smith, *A Critical and Exegetical Commentary on the Books of Samuel* (ICC 8; Edinburgh: T. & T. Clark, 1977), 12.

H. W. Hertzberg, *1 and 2 Samuel* (Philadelphia: Westminster Press, 1964), 28.

Lyle M. Eslinger, *Kingship of God in Crisis: A Close Reading of 1 Samuel 1–12* (Sheffield: Almond Press, 1982), 86.

---

but also he had made additional vows of his own and was prepared to pay them.

Most vow accounts in the Old Testament describe vows that arose from some situation of great distress, but there is also evidence that pious worshipers such as Elkanah made vows to Yahweh as a matter of course. [Elkanah's Vow] For example, at the annual harvest festival, Elkanah may have prayed for the seasonal rains to come and for his flocks to be fertile, promising to offer certain sacrifices if the request was fulfilled. If the rains failed or the cattle reproduction rate declined, he would be under no obligation, but if the agricultural year was profitable, he would offer the promised gifts in addition to the standard sacrifices. Such a practice is reflected in the priestly regulations found in Leviticus 27:17-23.

Elkanah went up to worship "with all his household"—except for Hannah. "Hannah did not go up, for she said to her husband, 'As soon as the child is weaned, I will bring him, that he may appear in the presence of the LORD, and remain there forever; I will offer him as a nazirite for all time' " (v. 22; see [Only Child]). The image of Hannah's remaining at home while the others travel to Shiloh immediately draws our attention to the emotional and practical significance of Hannah's plight. Some writers, such as L. Eslinger, argue that Hannah's absence from the feast is intended to add a contrasting negative aspect to her character, creating doubt as to whether she would really fulfill her vow. Indeed, the passage does build limited suspense by retarding the action, but there is no real doubt that she intends to keep her promise.

Hannah's hesitation does draw the reader's attention, however. Samuel may have been a very young infant, but the text gives no indication that Hannah's rival Peninnah had ever stayed home from the festival when *her* several children were small—how else could she have provoked Hannah *every year*? Apparently, Hannah does not intend to take Samuel to the temple until he can stay there, and so she insists on remaining at home until he is weaned. This means that Hannah may have avoided more festivals than this one. In the ancient world, where there was no easily obtainable baby food, children were often breast-fed until they were two or even three years old (e.g., see 2 Macc 7:27).

In practical terms, Hannah could have found a wet nurse for Samuel in Shiloh, but she can hardly be blamed for wanting to nurse her own child. Perhaps the author intends for the reader to remember a similar motif in the story of Jochebed, the mother of Moses (Exod 2:1-10). She and her husband refused to obey the pharaoh's command that all Hebrew male infants be killed, so they hid their son in a watertight basket among the bushes bordering the Nile. Pharaoh's daughter discovered the child and wanted to adopt him, but she needed a wet nurse. In a delightful twist of irony, Moses' sister Miriam offered to find a suitable woman, and Moses' own mother was hired for the task. Thus, while Moses was destined for a life in the Egyptian palace, his mother was able to nurse him through infancy. Likewise, Samuel's future was in the Shiloh temple, but his mother nursed him for the first few years of his life.

There is a textual problem with the part of the verse concerning Hannah's elaboration on her promise. The MT says only "I will bring him, and he will appear before the face of Yahweh, and he will dwell there forever," a reading also reflected in the LXX. However, one of the Dead Sea Scrolls (4QSam^a) preserves a longer reading that adds the clause "and I will give him as a nazirite for life." Kyle McCarter argues for the longer reading, contending that the phrase dropped out of the MT during copying.[1] Since the words "forever" (*'ad 'olām*) appear twice, the scribal copyist's eye may have strayed from one to the other, leaving out the intervening words in the text later adopted by the Masoretes. [Masoretic Text]

Most English translations choose the MT reading, including KJV, NASB, NIV, NEB, JB, and JPS. The RSV likewise followed the MT, but the NRSV translators chose to accept the addition of "and I will give him as a nazirite for life" from 4QSam^a. Thus, for readers of the NRSV, Hannah's promise that Samuel will live in the temple is expanded by a pledge that he will live as a nazirite. The inclusion of the nazirite clause is in accord with Hannah's promise

Masoretic Text

The best-known Hebrew text of the Old
Testament is called the "Masoretic Text" because
it was preserved for many years by a group of specialized
scholars called the "Masoretes." Surprisingly, the Old
Testament text was not codified in any standard way until
the 1st and 2d centuries AD, when Rabbi Akiba (who lived
c. AD 50–132) zealously sought to establish a touchstone
text and have it preserved. This manuscript was then
scrupulously followed by copyists. From about AD 500 until
around AD 1500, different families of scholarly Masoretes,
such as the descendants of Ben Asher and Ben Naphthali,
devoted themselves to preserving the Hebrew text. The
Masoretes first divided the words, added vowel points, and
punctuated the text with accent marks to facilitate public
reading (older versions were written in long run-on lines
with consonants only). These scholars also made notations
of difficult readings, textual questions, and points of
theological interest. The influence of the Masoretes was so
great that the preserved Hebrew text families are much
more uniform than the more numerous Greek New
Testament manuscript families.

Since the Masoretes were concerned only with copying
the *accepted* text, however, older scrolls with divergent
readings were reverently buried or burned so that little evidence remains of other versions. Except for the variants
preserved in the LXX, the Targums, and some other ancient
versions, scholars possessed almost no evidence of variant
Hebrew texts predating the 9th century AD until 1947, when
the "Dead Sea Scrolls" were found, along with other materials from Qumran and Wadi Murraba'at. As expected, these
scrolls and fragments revealed a much less uniform text.
They preserved many variants, some favoring the LXX,
some the MT, and others that were unique.

Today's "standard" Hebrew text is based on a codex preserved in Leningrad designated by scholars as B19A and
includes many editorial notes in what is called a "textual
apparatus." The most common critical edition is usually
called BHS (for *Biblia Hebraica Stuttgartensia*).

For an excellent article on biblical texts and versions, see
Roger Bullard, "Texts/Manuscripts/Versions," *MDB*, eds.
Roger A. Bullard, Joel F. Drinkard Jr., Walter Harrelson, and
Edgar V. McKnight (Macon GA: Mercer University Press,
1990), 890-96.

of 1 Samuel 1:11 that no razor would ever touch Samuel's head,
and serves to emphasize his life of devotion to Yahweh.

The reader notes that Elkanah does not argue with his wife about
the matter. Elkanah's ready acceptance of Hannah's reasoning may
reflect his love for Hannah, his prior knowledge of Hannah's vow,
and his own spirit of devotion. There is, however, some ambiguity
in Elkanah's response: "Do what seems best to you, wait until you
have weaned him; only—*may the LORD establish his word*" (v. 23).
To this point, there has been no word of Yahweh that needs confirmation, so the reader is left to wonder. The LXX and 4QSam^a may
preserve a better reading: "May Yahweh confirm what *you* have
said!" (lit., "May Yahweh confirm [what comes out of] your
mouth").

The slight suspense raised by vv. 21-23a does not last long, for
the narrator quickly passes over Samuel's earliest years (one? two?
three?) with a succinct summary statement: "So the woman
remained and nursed her son, until she weaned him" (v. 23b). The
account of Samuel's dedication at the temple then follows immediately (vv. 24-28), tied to the preceding narrative by the connecting
phrase "when she had weaned him." The text implies that Hannah
took Samuel to the temple as soon as he was weaned, not even
waiting until the next festival journey. Elkanah apparently joined
his wife in this special occasion, but the emphasis is clearly on

Hannah. All of the pronouns refer to Hannah, except for v. 24, where "they" slaughtered the bull and brought the child to Eli.

The MT says that Hannah brought *three* bulls to be sacrificed, along with an ephah of bread flour (roughly half a bushel) and a skin of wine. The better reading, however, is "a *three-year-old* bull," as found in the LXX and the versions. The law required that sacrificial lambs be at least one year old, but said little about age requirements for bulls (see Exod 12:5; Num 7:15, 27). A three-year-old bull would have been fully grown, a large and valuable animal (cf. Gen 15:9, where Yahweh instructed Abraham to bring a three-year-old heifer). There may have been some relation between the age of the bull and the age of the boy Samuel, but the text simply reminds us that "the child was young"—literally, "the lad was a lad."

After the bull was slaughtered, it was Hannah who spoke up and explained their actions to Eli, who may have been bewildered by this unusual presentation. With patronizing words reinforced by an oath sworn on the old priest's life ("*as you live*"), she reminded Eli of the day when she had made her fateful vow: "Oh, my lord! As you live, my lord, I am the woman who was standing here in your presence, praying to the LORD. For this child I prayed; and the LORD has granted me the petition that I made to him. Therefore I have lent him to the LORD; as long as he lives, he is given to the LORD" (vv. 26-28a). If Eli offered any response or showed any gratitude, it has not been preserved.

Scholars have long noted that various forms of the Hebrew root *šʾl*, "to ask," are scattered throughout this chapter (1:17, 20, 27 [twice], 28 [twice]). Hannah points out that she *asked* the LORD for Samuel and has now permanently *lent* the requested child to Yahweh, in accordance with her promise. Many scholars accept a theory that these traditions are borrowed from an ancient birth story originally belonging to Saul, whose name is based on the same root. Indeed, when Hannah says "He is *lent* to the LORD," the word "lent" (or "dedicated") is *identical* to Saul's name: *šāʾûl* (pronounced *Sha-ool*). Evidence for this view is not convincing, however. The narrator's frequent use of *šʾl* may be nothing more than an intentional foreshadowing of the role Samuel will play in Saul's life.

For all of its highly emotional content, the narrative describes the actual leave-taking quite matter-of-factly, with Hannah returning home while Samuel immediately assumes his role of temple servant. The reader would expect young Samuel to be overcome with fear and grief at his parents' departure, but the MT portrays him as

Does Hannah's Song Belong?

Scholars using the tools of historical criticism have long suggested that this majestic poem seems to have derived from a different context. In the first place, the song hardly matches Hannah's particular situation in life. While the mention of enemies in v. 1 and v. 3 could be cryptic references to Hannah's rival Peninnah, they seem better suited to a more nationalistic context, and the military imagery of v. 4 suggests multiple male enemies. The repeated "reversal of fortunes" theme does include a barren woman who gave birth to *seven* children (v. 5b), but Hannah had *six* (Samuel, plus the five mentioned in 2:21). The poem anachronistically concludes with a prayer for God's anointed king. Israel had no king until many years later when Samuel himself, grown old and respected, anointed Saul.

While more conservative scholars may simply assume that Hannah's reference to a king was *prophetic*, the considerable incongruities of the psalm lead historical critics to assume that it was inserted by a later hand to serve a particular purpose in that editor's theological agenda. Indeed, the psalm functions well as an unmistakable claim that

Yahweh is sovereign and active in Israel's affairs. Just as the LORD was responsible for Samuel's conception, the LORD also would be involved in the birth of the monarchy. Just as Samuel proved faithful to his calling, so the kings of Israel would be challenged to faithful service as God's representative leaders.

This source-critical debate is immaterial to modern literary critics, who have virtually abandoned historical criticism for an approach that insists on studying the text as it is, without reference to its underlying sources or history of development. Since it is only the final product that matters, these scholars would not regard the song as an ungainly appendage tacked on by an overzealous editor, but as an integral part of the story, indeed, as a key to its overall interpretation. Thus, Hannah's reversal of fortune appropriately foreshadows the victory that unfortunate Israel will ultimately gain over their Philistine oppressors. Likewise, the concluding prayer for Israel's king lays the groundwork for the remainder of the book, which is largely concerned with the birth of the monarchy and the establishment of a king after God's own heart.

a stalwart child who has absorbed the same pervasive piety of his parents. As soon as Hannah completes her presentation speech ("So now I give him to the LORD"), we find the trenchant comment: "And he worshiped the LORD there." Some commentators ascribe this act of worship to Eli (or even Hannah), but Samuel is the more likely referent. A similar summary statement follows Hannah's song: "Elkanah went home to Ramah, and the boy ministered before the LORD under Eli the priest" (2:11). The reader may ask, "How much ministering can a three-year-old boy do?", but that is not the appropriate question. The point is that Samuel did not run crying after his parents, but stayed on at Shiloh, where he did what he was told (first by Eli and later by God). Hannah's devotion is reflected in her apparently precocious son, who willingly devotes himself to a lifetime of service before Yahweh.

Hannah's Song of Praise, 2:1-10

Emotions may be well hidden in the narrative account of Samuel's presentation, but there is no lack of feeling in the exuberant "Song of Hannah." Certain aspects of Hannah's song fit awkwardly into the context, leading to a considerable amount of scholarly discussion. [Does Hannah's Song Belong?]

We will approach Hannah's song with an awareness that it may not be original to the "real" Hannah, but with an appreciation for the role it plays in the text as presented to us. In the story as we have it, Hannah sings, and she sings powerfully. [Singing Women] As the mother of a child who one day would become prophet and priest to Israel, she sings prophetically and proclaims the awesome power of God. As parent of Israel's future judge and king-maker, Hannah sings of military conflict and the ascendancy of God's anointed king. As one who knew the personal touch of God's power, Samuel's mother sings of Yahweh's central role in guiding Israel's affairs and gaining victory over all enemies, so long as the people were obedient. Samuel would later preach that same message again and again.

Like other psalms in the Hebrew Bible, Hannah's song is a *prayer* (v. 1), couched in the form of *poetry*. [Hebrew Poetry] In form, the song is very similar to those psalms that are called "Hymns of Praise." *Thematically*, it can be divided into three strophes: vv. 1-3 (speak rightly before God, who knows everything), vv. 4-8 (God, the Creator, is able to reverse the fortunes of the oppressed), and vv. 9-10 (God protects his own, and empowers his anointed king). *Poetically*, the structure is more complex. [Poetic Structure]

The first strophe begins with parallel couplets spoken as first-person exclamations: Hannah "exults in the LORD" and rejoices over her enemies because God has granted victory. In the immediate context, this could be seen as an allusion to Hannah's antagonist, Peninnah. In the larger context, it could refer to any of Israel's enemies, such as the Philistines.

The song then turns to direct address through a threefold affirmation of Yahweh's uniqueness: "There is no Holy One like the LORD, no one besides you; there is no Rock like our God" (v. 2, cf. 2 Sam 22:2-3, 32, 47). After addressing God, the poet instructs Hannah's (or Israel's) opponent(s) to give up all arrogant speech in deference to Yahweh's omniscience (v. 3).

Singing Women

Although most biblical psalms are attributed to men, there was also a tradition of significant women who sang praises to God. The Song of Miriam in Exod 15:21 is probably a precursor to the Song of Moses, which precedes it in the text (Exod 15:1-18), and has been regarded as perhaps the oldest bit of poetry preserved in Scripture. The lengthy "Song of Deborah" (Judg 5) celebrates the victory of Deborah, a remarkable woman who led Israel to victory over the Canaanite general Sisera. It is different in style from the Song of Hannah (1 Sam 2:1-10), but similar in theme. In the New Testament, the Song of Mary (Luke 1:46-55) echoes the same primary motif found in the songs of Miriam, Deborah, and Hannah: God is able to reverse the fortunes of the poor and oppressed, leading them to experience unexpected blessings.

Hebrew Poetry

Hebrew poetry differs from typical English poetry (other than free verse) in that it has a rhythm of *sense* rather than *rhyme*, and there is rarely any real meter as English readers know it (though some scholars find meter everywhere). Hebrew poetry most commonly consists of a series of couplets in which the second line repeats, expands, or reverses the thought of the first line. Occasionally, as in 1 Sam 2:2, the same pattern is found in a triplet, or sequence of three lines. This repetition of thought is called *parallelism*, and the relationship of the second line to the first determines whether it is called *synonymous* (repeats the same thought), *antithetic* (reverses the thought), or *synthetic* (expands the thought) parallelism. Like the repetitive chorus of a modern hymn, the constant reiteration of thought adds emphasis to the poet's point of view.

Poetic Structure

The song employs a variety of structural elements, as diagramed here:

Strophe One (vv. 1-3): Exultation over enemies

Two synonymous couplets addressed to all (v. 1)

One synonymous triplet phrased as a direct address to God (v. 2)

Two synonymous couplets addressed to enemies (v. 3)

Strophe Two (vv. 4-8): Yahweh's power to reverse fortunes

Three antithetic couplets addressed to all (vv. 4-5)

Five synonymous couplets addressed to all (vv. 6-8)

Strophe Three (vv. 9-10): Yahweh's blessing of the faithful

One triplet combining an antithetic couplet followed by a comment to all (v. 9)

One synonymous couplet addressed to all (v. 10a)

A concluding synonymous triplet addressed to all (v. 10b)

The second strophe consists of three couplets, which highlight the "reversal of fortune" theme through antithetic couplets that portray various situations in which a divinely wrought inversion of fortune occurs: (1) the weapons of the mighty are broken, while the feeble grow strong; (2) those who were full go begging for bread, while the hungry grow fat with spoil (presumably gained from the previously full!); and (3) the once-barren woman bears seven children, while the mother of many is bereaved. [Eating and Drinking] It is the last reversal, of course, that most closely matches Hannah's situation. "Seven" was often used to indicate perfection or completion, so it should not trouble the reader that Hannah had only six children; the point is that the once-barren mother was blessed with children by virtue of divine assistance.

Eating and Drinking

The theme of eating and drinking appears frequently in 1 Samuel. In 1:8, Hannah did not eat because of her grief, though others around her ate and drank. After making her vow, however, Hannah regained her composure and ate again (1:18). In Hannah's song, the formerly full begged for food, while the poor hungered no more (2:5). In the first prophecy against Eli's house, the wandering "man of God" insisted that Eli's descendants would beg the new and faithful priest for a crust of bread (1 Sam 2:36). During a daring raid on the Philistines, Saul's son Jonathan grew hungry and ate a bit of wild honey so that "his eyes brightened." However, Jonathan unwittingly came under his father's curse upon any who ate that day (1 Sam 14:24-30). Later, Saul visited the witch of Endor (violating his own ban) to seek an audience with the shade of Samuel, who predicted that the kingdom would be ripped from his hands.

Afterward, Saul was weak from hunger, having not eaten all day, and had to eat before gaining strength enough to move on (28:21-25). In a later story, David was searching for his family and others who had been kidnaped in an Amalekite raid on his city of Ziklag. He found an Egyptian in a field who was weak because he had not eaten or drunk for three days. After food and water were provided, "his spirit revived," and he was able to assist David in recovering his family and others who had been taken (30:11-20). In a theological sense, then, eating and drinking represent the gaining of strength, often in conjunction with the aid of Yahweh. Without food and drink, one grows weak, but strength comes with proper sustenance. Perhaps the author intends for the reader to observe that the spiritual starvation of those who reject Yahweh leads to weakness and defeat, while the acceptance of God's way leads to spiritual nourishment and renewed strength.

The "reversal of fortune" theme continues in vv. 6-8. Death and life, poverty and wealth, abasement and exaltation are all within the power of Yahweh. God's power to cause death and give life is most impressive. If Yahweh truly can bring the dead back from Sheol, then surely he is also capable of feeding the hungry and exalting the down-trodden. [Sheol] The LORD is able to do this because "the pillars of the earth are Yahweh's, and on them he has set the world" (v. 8b). The noun underlying the translation "pillars" appears only here and in 1 Samuel 14:5. It could mean "something poured out" (such as a molten pillar) or "something constrained" (like a narrow river). Kyle McCarter translates the word as "straits," arguing that the reference is to the swift-moving rivers of the underworld, where judgment was carried out.[2] Either translation stresses God's power over all the earth.

Sheol

The Hebrews held to a cosmology similar to that of their neighbors in the ancient world, a three-story universe in which the "world of the dead" was located in a great cavern deep in the surface of the earth, between the pillars that supported the earth's surface. In Hebrew thought, Sheol was not necessarily a place of punishment, but simply the natural destination of the dead (e.g., Gen 37:35; 42:38; Job 7:9; 17:13; Ps 6:5; Prov 9:18; Eccl 9:10; Ezek 31:16-17).

The final strophe underscores a primary theme of the Samuel corpus and the entire Deuteronomistic History: God protects the faithful, but punishes the wicked. It is not human might that wins in the end, but the power of God, whose heavenly power shatters all adversaries and rules over the earth. This strophe also contains the most glaring anachronism of the poem: it speaks of divine favor being shown to the *king*, though there was no king in Hannah's time.

The closing couplet of the song could be translated as an assertion (so NRSV) or as an appeal: "May he give strength to his king, and exalt the power of his anointed" (v. 10b). [The Vower's Vow] Even if the couplet is to be read as a prayer, the firm confidence of the preceding verses leaves little doubt that Yahweh is both able and willing to strengthen his chosen king. The later narrative, however, will make it clear that Yahweh's willingness to bless is predicated on the king's willingness to obey.

The Vower's Vow

An interesting variant is found in the LXX and 4QSamᵃ, both of which include an additional couplet in v. 9: "He gives to the vower his vow, and blesses the years of the just." As in most cases, it is impossible to tell if this reflects a harmonizing addition to the vorlage (underlying text) behind the LXX and 4QSamᵃ or if the couplet has simply dropped out of the MT. On text-critical principles, the former seems more likely.

CONNECTIONS

The willingness of Hannah and Elkanah to follow through on their commitments to God stands as a sterling example for all believers who come after them. Elkanah is portrayed as a man of rock-steady, if unexciting, faith, while Hannah is more emotional, experiencing sharper peaks and valleys in her spiritual pilgrimage. Despite their differences, however, Samuel's parents were united in their faithfulness to Yahweh. [Faithful Families]

Faithful Familes

📖 Elkanah and Hannah could serve well as examples of a couple who served God together. Both Hannah and Elkanah had their own spiritual pilgrimages to follow. They each made their own vows and kept their own promises to God. Yet they also supported each other in their spiritual journeys and commitments so that their worship and service to God were shared experiences.

Many believers find it rather easy to make promises to God but much more difficult to remain faithful to those promises. Modern persons may even unconsciously verbalize their promises in the form of an Old Testament vow: "Oh Lord, if you will only get me out of this predicament (or give me this blessing), I will never let you down again"—or "I will attend church every Sunday." Yet those same promises made in moments of crisis are easily forgotten when calm returns. In this sense, the Old Testament vow functions as a means of holding the believer accountable for her promises. In contemporary churches, believers may seek greater accountability through public declarations of their specific commitments to God, either in corporate worship or in small groups.

This story offers an impressive challenge to any persons who make promises to God yet fail to fulfill them. What pledge could be more difficult to keep than giving up a child—especially a long-awaited and *only* child? [Only Child] Yet Hannah kept her word, and

Only Child

📖 Hannah was neither the first nor the last parent who was challenged to surrender her only child. Abraham was called to sacrifice Isaac, his only child by the matriarch Sarah (Gen 22). Jacob, in his declining years, was faced with the difficult decision of allowing his family to starve if he did not send Benjamin to Egypt (Gen 43). Benjamin was the youngest of twelve sons, but the only living child (so Jacob believed) of his beloved wife Rachel. In 2 Sam 12:13-23, King David grieves over his sin and pleads with God when it appears that the child of his illicit union with Bathsheba will die.

In each of these cases, the willingness to give up one's "only" son leads to unexpected, divine blessings. Isaac was spared from death, and he became the second link in the chain of patriarchs, leading to the fulfillment of God's promise to Abraham that his descendants would become as numerous as the sand of the sea. In Jacob's experience, not only did Benjamin survive, but Jacob discovered that his much-lamented son Joseph (also by Rachel) was alive and well in Egypt. David's story is different: his infant child was born in circumstances far outside of God's covenant promise, so when the infant died, his death was regarded as divine punishment. Because of David's attitude of repentance and his acceptance of God's will, however, he was soon blessed with another son by Bathsheba, who had since become his "lawful" wife. This next son born to Bathsheba was Solomon, who would become king after David.

The emotional intensity of these stories prepares the Christian reader for the most significant "only son" story of all: "For God so loved the world that he gave his only begotten son, that whosoever believeth in him should not perish, but have everlasting life" (John 3:16, KJV).

Elkanah supported her. Believers through the ages are called to be faithful, too, and to encourage one another.

Hannah's song functions as a broad reminder of Yahweh's universal rule. The LORD is presented as a living paradox: a God who creates the world and establishes its foundations, yet also knows (and cares) about barren women, feeble soldiers, and hungry peasants. He reverses the fortunes of the downtrodden, lifting up the righteous while toppling the wicked from their lofty perch. Such a song offers hope to the oppressed and abused of every generation, asserting that God has a special concern for the poor, the homeless, and the hungry. New Testament scholars often note that Jesus demonstrated precisely these concerns in his own life and ministry. The Gospel of Luke, for example, emphasizes Jesus' special care for women (Luke 5:38-39; 8:2-3, 43-48), the poor (Luke 6:20-21), and the oppressed (Luke 5:12-14, 17-26; 8:26-39). Likewise, Matthew preserves a tradition that Jesus taught his disciples to extend appropriate compassion to the hungry, the sick, and the imprisoned (Matt 25). In recent years, Marcus Borg has popularized an emphatic view that the historical Jesus understood his ministry in terms of compassion.[3]

In the books of Samuel, God's care for the downtrodden could occur directly (as with Hannah) or through the medium of others (Samuel, Saul, and David) who labored to deliver Israel from the Philistine oppression. In the same manner, Jesus often touched people directly, but he also commissioned his followers to serve the "least of these" in his name, so fulfilling the law of love.

NOTES

[1] P. Kyle McCarter, *I Samuel* (AB 8; Garden City: Doubleday, 1980), 56.

[2] Ibid., 73.

[3] Marcus J. Borg, *Jesus: A New Vision* (San Francisco: HarperSanFrancisco, 1987) and *Meeting Jesus Again for the First Time* (San Francisco: HarperSanFrancisco, 1994).

ELI'S FAILURE
AND SAMUEL'S FAVOR

2:12-26

COMMENTARY

With the departure of Hannah and Elkanah (2:11), Samuel begins a new chapter in his life as an apprentice priest in the Shiloh temple. The narrator quickly sets the stage for Samuel's rapid rise to a position of leadership, not only in the temple, but in all of Israel.

The narrator's method is an effective (if not artful) interlacing of vignettes featuring Samuel and the sons of Eli. Young Samuel is described in glowing, positive terms in 2:11, 18-21, 26, but the sons of Eli are corrupt and intractable (2:12-17, 22-25). The reader soon has no doubt that it will be Samuel, not Eli's unruly heirs, who will succeed the aged priest.

Eli's Worthless Sons, 2:12-17, 22-25

The Bible's pages are filled with villains: Violent Cain, who killed his brother Abel; presumptuous Korah, who led a rebellion against Moses; Queen Jezebel, who promoted the worship of Baal; Judas. There is no shortage of unsavory characters.

Two of the most notable miscreants in Scripture are the sons of Eli, Hophni and Phinehas. Ancient readers, of course, would not have expected much from men with such names. "Hophni" may be from the Egyptian word for "toad." In Hebrew, it is similar to a term describing the empty hollow of a hand. "Phinehas" means "brass lips"—an uninspiring name for one who is called to speak for God.

The reader already knows from 1:3 that Eli is very old and has "emeritus" status of a sort, while Hophni and Phinehas serve as the active priests. Eli is described as being ninety-eight years old when he died (4:15), so his sons would have been at least middle-aged, despite one reference to them as "young men" (2:17). If they are youthful, it is in comparison to their father Eli. Thus, the narrator is not describing rambunctious young priests who lack maturity, but experienced charlatans who have grown fat from their priestly privilege.

"Now the sons of Eli were scoundrels," the text says (v. 12a). "Scoundrels" translates the literal expression "sons of Belial." "Belial" means "worthlessness" or "wickedness," and it was such a strong word that centuries later the Qumran community used it as their primary term for the devil. The narrator uses the term in ironic fashion, for when old Eli had earlier accused Samuel's mother of being drunk, Hannah cried out, "Don't take me for a wicked woman!" Literally, "Don't take me for a daughter of Belial!" (1:16). It was not Hannah who was a descendant of Belial, but Eli's own sons. Hannah's son would represent the future of Israel, but Eli's sons had no future at all.

The most incriminating accusation against Hophni and Phinehas is that "they had no regard for the LORD" (v. 12b). Literally, "They did not know the LORD." The Hebrew word "to know" (*yādaʿ*) is a strong term indicating far more than intellectual knowledge. The word also suggests an intimate relationship. "Now the man *knew* his wife Eve, and she conceived" (Gen 3:1a). To know someone is to live in close communion with them. The narrative picture of

Cooking Pots and Piercing Forks

 The MT describes four separate kinds of cooking vessels: "pan," "kettle," "caldron," or "pot." The LXX mentions three types, while 4QSamᵃ includes only two. The words could indicate either ceramic or metal containers, but the precise distinctions are no longer clear. Ceramic pots were much more common, but metal vessels were often preferred for sacred uses. The fork in question was a large, three-tined utensil (called a "flesh-hook" in KJV) used for spearing, holding, or manipulating meat.

Typical Iron I Cookware (Right)
This storage jare and wide basin date from the monarchic period, 1,000–700 BC.

Haaretz Museum. Tel Aviv, Israel.
(Credit: Erich Lessing/Art Resource, NY)

Hophni and Phinehas acting as personal representatives of a god they did not know is ludicrous.

The priests' lack of regard for God is demonstrated in their failure to conduct properly the duties of the priests to the people (v. 13). Their behavior, in fact, was reprehensible. Priests were entitled to a portion of every sacrifice, but Eli's sons demanded more than their rightful share. The Levitical code established that the priests were to receive the breast and the right thigh of each animal sacrificed (Lev 7:28-36), while the book of Deuteronomy allots them the shoulder, jowls, and stomach (18:3). The temple at Shiloh seems to have practiced an alternate system based on "pot luck."

The custom at Shiloh, according to vv. 13-14, was for worshipers to boil the meat of their sacrifices instead of roasting it. Presumably, this was to avoid giving offense to God by cooking their meat in the same way the sacrifice was burned. In order to receive their portion, the priests (or their representatives) would come to each cooking pot, thrust in a large, three-pronged fork, and take whatever came out on it. [Cooking Pots and Piercing Forks] [Typical Iron I Cookware] Thus, divine providence played a role in the amount of meat the priests received, and they were required to accept it. An expansion in the 4QSam[a] manuscript adds "whether it be bad or good."

Instead of this normative practice, however, Hophni and Phinehas appropriated their portion while the animal was being slaughtered, demanding raw meat with fat left in the trim (vv. 15-16). In the typical sacrificial procedure, the animal's blood would be dashed against the altar, and the fat would be burned (lit., "caused to make smoke") as an offering to God. According to the Levitical code, neither fat nor blood was to be eaten by humans: "All fat is the LORD's. It shall be a perpetual statute throughout your generations, in all your settlements; you must not eat any fat or any blood" (Lev 3:16b-17; cf. Lev 7:23b-25).

Levitical codes may not have been in force at Shiloh, but it is unlikely that the prohibition against eating the blood and fat of sacrificial animals was unknown. [An Alternate View] Certainly Eli's sons would have understood the sacrilege of taking their share before God's portion was offered on the altar. By using strong-arm tactics to seize raw meat in mid-sacrifice, the purloining priests not only showed their personal disregard for the LORD, but interfered with the

An Alternate View

While some scholars argue for the same position taken in this commentary (Ralph Klein, Kyle McCarter), others presume that the Levitical customs were in place at Shiloh, meaning that both vv. 13-14 and vv. 15-17 portray abuses of the sacrificial system (Henry Smith, Gnanna Robinson). Thus the priests, having already received their due portion, would have been guilty of extorting additional meat from the sacrificial stewpots as well as demanding raw meat from the butchering floor. If this view is correct, the dual nature of the offense would intensify the statement that their sin "was very great."

worship of the same people they were responsible for assisting. It is no wonder that the narrator concludes, "Thus the sin of the young men was very great in the sight of the LORD; for they treated the offerings of the LORD with contempt" (v. 17).

The account of the sons' disreputable behavior is interrupted by a contrasting episode from Samuel's young life, demonstrating his innocence and obedience (vv. 18-21). The main account quickly resumes, however, with additional charges. The MT includes an allegation that Hophni and Phinehas were also guilty of sleeping with the women who served at the entrance to the tent of meeting (v. 22), but the clause is missing from 4QSamª and from some versions of the LXX. The wording mirrors the technical priestly language of Exodus 38:8 and may reflect an injection of conditions that prevailed at a later time.

Whether guilty of rampant adultery or not, the two sons were setting an atrocious example and running roughshod over the worshiping community. Their aged father Eli continually heard about his sons' malfeasance—no doubt many people complained (vv. 23-24)—but he was powerless to stop it. Eli argued that his sons were treading dangerous ground: "If one person sins against another, someone can intercede for the sinner with the LORD; but if someone sins against the LORD, who can make intercession?" (v. 25).

Eli's argument that no one could intercede with Yahweh on his sons' behalf fell on deaf ears, for "they would not listen to the voice of their father" (2:26a). The reader is not surprised that the two wicked sons give no credence to Eli's warning of divine retribution, for the text has already insisted that they "did not know the LORD" (v. 12). How could they fear a God they did not acknowledge?

The reader, however, may *not* be prepared for the narrator's additional assertion that the sons continued in their disobedience because "it was the will of the LORD to kill them" (2:26b). Such a statement seems harsh and cruel to modern ears, but the ancient historians of the Old Testament attributed all causality to God. The writer knows that Hophni and Phinehas will soon die (4:11) and believes that their death represents God's judgment on the house of Eli. Thus, just as God "hardened Pharaoh's heart" in order to intensify the lessons of the exodus, so the narrator asserts that Yahweh intentionally fostered the disobedience of Eli's sons for his own purposes. [Can God Do Evil?]

Can God Do Evil?

Many modern readers find it inconsistent to think that God could either carry out or sanction any kind of negative behavior. This view was less of a problem for the ancient Hebrews, for they attributed to God everything that happened. The Deuteronomist could assert that God sent an evil spirit to torment Saul (1 Sam 16:14), brought tragedy upon Israel (2 Sam 24), and enticed Ahab to enter a battle he was doomed to lose (1 Kgs 22:19-23). The theory seems to be, "It wouldn't happen unless God wanted it to happen."

This same view is held by modern persons who respond to every tragedy by asserting that it is the will of God. For example, bereaved persons are sometimes told that God needed their loved one more than they did. Shaken survivors of terrible accidents are often heard to comment, "They say everything happens for a reason."

It is just as possible that some things happen for no good reason at all. If God truly grants to humans the freedom of choice, then humans must be free to act in ways that oppose God's will as well as in ways that follow it. Yet we also hold that God is sovereign over all.

Some theologians deal with the dilemma by distinguishing between God's *permissive* will, which may allow bad things to happen that are not a part of God's *intentional* will. This does not mean, however, that God cannot bring judgment upon the disobedient in the form of physical harm. The Scriptures clearly teach that God can and does bring judgment upon those who choose evil; that is largely the point of the Deuteronomistic History, which challenges Israel to greater obedience.

The Scriptures teach that God is not the author of evil and takes no delight in it (Job 34:10; Ps 5:4; Jas 1:13), but various passages also imply that God may strengthen the resolve of one who has chosen evil, perhaps as a means of making the need for judgment more evident (Exod 7:3; 9:12; 10:20; 1 Sam 2:25; Rom 1:18-32).

Hannah's Worthy Son, 2:18-21, 26

The narrator purposefully punctures the account of Eli's worthless sons with periodic glimpses at Hannah's more worthy child. While Hophni and Phinehas were appropriating Israel's sacrifices for their own gain, "Samuel was ministering before the LORD, a boy wearing a linen ephod" (v. 18). The verb translated "to minister" (*šārat*) was a technical term used to describe priestly service, indicating that Samuel had begun to function as an apprentice to Eli. The linen ephod Samuel wore also suggests his special status. [Linen Ephod]

The writer's added detail that Samuel's mother used to bring him a "little" handmade robe every year gives added emphasis to the boy's youth (v. 19), and Eli's annual blessing upon Hannah and Elkanah underscores what a blessing Samuel had become to the aged priest (v. 20). Eli wished for them the gift of additional children, and over the course of time Hannah gave birth to three more sons and two daughters (v. 21a). This editorial note may seem superfluous, but it serves to provide additional ironic contrast between the families of Samuel and Eli. While Samuel's parents grew more prolific, Eli's descendants were dying out.

This interlude closes with a summary statement to offer yet another contrast between Samuel and the sons of Eli. While

Linen Ephod

The ephod was an integral part of priestly attire. The high priest wore an elaborate vest-like ephod for ceremonial occasions (Exod 28; 39), but ordinary priests wore simpler garments of white linen (1 Sam 22:18) as symbols of their office, as some modern ministers wear a clerical collar. The ephod seems to have been a sort of short shift or apron over which other clothes could be worn; David's wife Michal criticized him for exposing himself while dancing before the ark clad only in a linen ephod (2 Sam 6:14, 20).

(Illustration Credit: Barclay Burns)

Hophni and Phinehas "did not know the LORD" (2:12) and their sin "was very great" (2:17), "the boy Samuel grew up in the presence of the LORD" (v. 21b). We presume that Hophni and Phinehas also had grown up in the temple, but being in the temple and experiencing the presence of the LORD are not the same thing.

The narrative returns a critical eye to Hophni and Phinehas (2:22-25), concluding with their ultimate rejection of Eli's rebuke and the observation that God was planning their death. This is immediately followed by a rather disjunctive but obviously intentional statement about Samuel. Eli's sons are destined to die, but "the boy Samuel continued to grow both in stature and in favor with the LORD and with the people" (v.26). [Samuel's Rise] Samuel's physical vitality contrasts the coming doom facing Hophni and Phinehas, even as his increasing good repute with Yahweh and Israel represents the opposite of their fall from favor. [Great and Greater]

Great and Greater

AΩ The narrator uses a clever rhetorical device to draw the contrast between Samuel and the Elides even more sharply. In v. 17 he describes the sin of the two priests as "very great" (*gᵉdôlâh meᵓōd*). In v. 21 he asserts that Samuel was "growing up" (lit., "becoming great," *yigdal*), and in v. 26 he again pictures Samuel as growing up (*gādēl*). The flexibility of the root *gdl* allows the narrator to contrast the greatness of the sons' evil with the greatness seen in Samuel's growth in physical and spiritual maturity.

CONNECTIONS

The writer's tendentious intent in this text is so obvious as to appear almost overdone. Hophni and Phinehas appear as total renegades with no redeeming qualities, while little Samuel is so pure and sweet that the reader is tempted to regard him as a precious little goody two-shoes. Yet the literary exaggerations serve to make the picture as clear as possible. Those who reject God's way inevitably will hurt other people and ultimately will hurt themselves. In contrast, those who live in obedience and purity of spirit are the ones who find God's approval and accomplish God's work.

This story about two bad boys and one good boy suggests several ways in which modern believers are called to show *reverence* to the things of God and to include a reverent concern for God's leadership in the making of daily decisions. The account also insists that there is a connection between present reverence and ultimate rewards (for good or bad).

Hophni and Phinehas failed to show reverence for the temple of God, while Samuel served there faithfully. There is no temple in Shiloh anymore, nor in Jerusalem. But the Apostle Paul described the human body as the sacred temple of God's Spirit (1 Cor 3:16; 6:19; 2 Cor 6:16). Christian worshipers do not offer animal sacrifices at a physical place, but are called to recognize the sacred character of their own *bodies*, and to offer themselves as living sacrifices to God (Rom 12:1). [Sacred Space] In Judaism, the temple served as a bridge of communication or contact between God and the world. An important way modern believers can communicate their faith is through treating their bodies with the respect they deserve.

Hophni and Phinehas also showed disrespect for the *offerings* brought by God's people. This reminds modern churchgoers to make careful and responsible use of the tithes and offerings contributed for the work of the church. How much should the ministers receive as an appropriate wage? How much should be spent for the church's own local expenses? What is an honorable allotment for missions?

Of course, the most common way modern believers "despise" the offerings of God is by not bringing them at all. Yet the Scriptures teach plainly that all gifts and resources are from God. We show respect for God by returning a portion of our material blessings to him. Hannah and Elkanah were faithful in making an annual pilgrimage to Shiloh to deliver their tithes and offerings. Faithful giving expresses trust *in* God and thanks *to* God. Those who respect what belongs to God, like Samuel and his parents, will enhance their spiritual growth.

Worshipers of God are also called to show reverence in *relationships*. Eli's sons, as priests of God, held a special position as mediators of God's grace to the people, but they violated that relationship and brought harm to others. God's people are to base relationships on love. For example, the bond we have with our spouse is a sacred bond. The connection we have with friends is a holy thing. Even the relationships we cultivate in our work and play have a sanctified character about them because God lives in us.

Sacred Space

Modern Christian parents often warn their children to respect their church buildings as "God's house." The New Testament speaks of our very bodies as temples of God. Thus, we are challenged to respect the sacred character of our bodies. When Christians poison their bodies with alcohol or other drugs, when Christians abuse their bodies through poor diet or lack of exercise, when Christians involve their bodies in unwholesome conduct, they show the same kind of disrespect that Hophni and Phinehas demonstrated toward God's temple. This text challenges believers to make responsible decisions about their health and conduct.

Do we honor the people who trust us? Are we dependable to those who depend on us? Do we remember that people are always to be loved and never used? Basing our relationships on love, trust, and mutual respect is one important way to demonstrate our love and reverence for God.

The skillful narrator has drawn a clearly focused picture. Two bad boys are on one side, thumbing their nose at God and heaping abuse upon God's people. One good boy is on the other side, living in innocence and obedience. In the middle are the worshiping people of God. The text challenges each reader to find himself or herself in the picture. [A Sermon or Devotional Outline]

A Sermon or Devotional Outline

I. Tell the story—two bad boys and one good boy
   A. Eli's worthless sons
   B. Hannah's worthy son
II. Explore the connections—the relevance and reverence
   A. Showing reverence through your physical body
   B. Showing reverence through your giving to God
   C. Showing reverence through your relationships

ELI'S FALL AND SAMUEL'S CALL

2:27–4:1a

COMMENTARY

The writers of Israel's history firmly believed that one's personal behavior brought natural consequences for good or evil. So it is not surprising that the narrator follows his sharp contrast between Eli's sinful sons and Hannah's righteous son (2:12-26) with a prediction that the house of Eli will soon give way before Samuel's ascendant star. The author skillfully combines two distinct accounts to predict this shift in power: the first involves an obscure "man of God" who utters a bleak prophecy in Eli's hearing (2:27-36), while the second describes Samuel's call to the prophetic ministry—and his first devastating oracle (3:1–4:1a).

The careful reader, however, will observe that the author (probably writing during or after the time of Josiah) has something more in mind than Eli and Samuel. His primary concern, barely hidden beneath the surface, is not the long-defunct temple in Shiloh, but the contemporary temple in Jerusalem. While Samuel and Eli act out the stories, the ultimate protagonists are Zadok and Abiathar, David's dual high priests.

The Man of God, 2:27-36

"Man of God" (*'îš 'ĕlōhîm*) is a generic term for a holy man who acts as a prophet. Despite the note in 3:1 that "the word of the LORD was rare in those days," it was not unknown, for an otherwise anonymous prophet appeared in Shiloh to pronounce an oracle of doom upon Eli and his descendants. Utilizing a typical "messenger formula," he begins with "Thus says the LORD" and then speaks in the first person, as if he were quoting God's message verbatim. That message begins with a reminder of Eli's privileged priestly heritage.

The precise origins of the priesthood are mired in an ancient swamp of traditions, filled with tangled roots. Eli may have traced his lineage to Moses, or Aaron, or to the tribe of Levi in general, to

A Stepped Altar
These steps lead to a raised, round platform probably used as a Canaanite altar in Megiddo. Evidence suggests it was still in use during the reign of King Solomon.
(Credit: Erich Lessing/Art Resource)

which both belonged. The text does not say, though it presumes that the Elides belonged to the larger Levitical priesthood whose commission derived from the exodus period: "I revealed myself to the family of your ancestor in Egypt when they were slaves to the house of Pharaoh. I chose him out of all the tribes of Israel to be my priest, to go up to my altar, to offer incense, to wear an ephod before me; and I gave to the family of your ancestor all my offerings by fire from the people of Israel" (vv. 27-28).

The phrase "go up to my altar" suggests that this was written in a time when the altar stood on a raised platform (despite Exod 20:26; see also 1 Kgs 12:33; 2 Kgs 16:12; Ezek 43:13-17). [A Stepped Altar] The words translated "to offer incense" (*lĕhaqṭîr qĕṭeret*) mean something like "to make an offering go up in smoke" and could denote all offerings that were burned, not simply fragrant incense. "To wear an ephod" may allude to the common priestly dress (see [Linen Ephod])or to the elaborate vest-like garment worn by the high priest for purposes of public ceremony and oracle-seeking.

The priests were allowed to keep certain offerings brought to the temple to provide for their daily sustenance. "Offerings by fire" is better translated as "gifts" or "oblations"; the word *'iššeh* has

---

Irreverent Kicks or Greedy Eyes?

AΩ While some translations suggest that Eli and his sons looked upon God's sacrifices "with greedy eyes" (NRSV, JB), other versions suggest that they "kicked at" the offerings made by God's people (KJV, NASB). The discrepancy is due to a very problematic and possibly corrupt Hebrew text. The MT has a word uncertainly translated as "kick at," which makes little sense except in the sense of "show disrespect for." The LXX has a reading that translates "look with greedy eye." Since this seems to fit the context better, some translations follow the ancient Greek version over the preserved Hebrew text. Others choose a more dynamic translation of *intent*: "Why do you scorn my sacrifice?" (NIV). The point seems clear in either case: It is a dangerous thing to show irreverence for the holy things of God.

---

traditionally been related to the word for fire (*'iššeh*), but Ugaritic evidence points to a cognate word (*iṯt*) that more properly means "gift" or "votive offering."[1] The LXX includes the words "for food," making it clear that this was the issue: Yahweh generously provided food for Eli and his family through accepted priestly perquisites, but they were not satisfied with Yahweh's provision. The narrator's earlier accounts laid the blame on Hophni and Phinehas alone, but the man of God includes Eli along with his sons in accusing the family of looking greedily upon the sacrifices and extorting the choicest portions for themselves. [Irreverent Kicks or Greedy Eyes?] If Eli did not *encourage* the practice, he *allowed* it, and apparently profited from his sons' behavior.

As a result of the Shilonites' rampant disrespect for the holy things of God, a remarkable and frightening thing was about to happen. God would abrogate a promise made for eternity. "Therefore the LORD the God of Israel declares: 'I promised that your family and the family of your ancestor should go in and out before me forever'; but now the LORD declares: 'Far be it from me; for those who honor me I will honor, and those who despise me shall be treated with contempt' " (v. 30). The promise of an eternal priesthood (Exod 29:9; Num 25:13) turned out to be stringently conditional. Yahweh's past promise had fallen victim to present circumstances as the sons of Eli proved morally incapable of functioning as priests.

Because of the flagrant sin practiced by Eli's house, the man of God predicted that his family would soon die out (vv. 31-32), with the exception of one man who would spend his days grieving for the family's demise (v. 33a). [Eli's Descendants] All others would die by the sword (v. 33b). Two later events

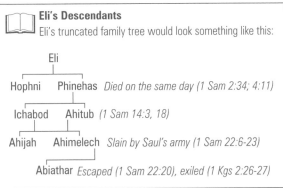

Eli's Descendants
Eli's truncated family tree would look something like this:

Eli
Hophni   Phinehas   *Died on the same day (1 Sam 2:34; 4:11)*
Ichabod   Ahitub   *(1 Sam 14:3, 18)*
Ahijah   Ahimelech   *Slain by Saul's army (1 Sam 22:6-23)*
Abiathar   *Escaped (1 Sam 22:20), exiled (1 Kgs 2:26-27)*

appear in the Deuteronomistic History as evidence that the prophecy was fulfilled. First Samuel 22:6-23 recounts how the priests of Nob first gave assistance to David and then were slaughtered by an angry Saul. Eli's descendants, presumably, were among them. Only Abiathar escaped, surviving to serve as David's personal priest. The favor David showed to Abiathar was not exclusive, however. In a shrewd political move after his capture of Jerusalem, David divided high-priestly duties between Abiathar and a local favorite named Zadok. After David's death, however, Solomon won the throne and sent Abiathar into exile for supporting his rival brother, Adonijah (1 Kgs 1:7-8). This is expressly described (1 Kgs 2:26-27) as the fulfillment of 1 Samuel 2:33.

While these events would require the passing of many years, the man of God predicted a more immediate sign that his words were true: Both Hophni and Phinehas would die on the same day (v. 34). This prediction was fulfilled in 1 Samuel 4:11 when the sons of Eli carried the ark of God into battle with the Philistines and were killed as the ark was captured. Upon hearing the news, Eli also died (1 Sam 4:17-18), though with more apparent concern for the lost ark than for his lost sons.

God would not be left without a witness, however. Despite the Elides' fall, he promised to raise up a "faithful priest who shall do according to what is in my heart and in my mind" and to transfer the perpetual priesthood to him (v. 35). The reader assumes that this new priest would be Samuel, who did in fact succeed Eli and serve God faithfully. But Samuel proves to be an aberration in the priestly lineage. His sons turn out no better than Eli's and fall quickly from the picture.

In the mind of the narrator, then, the faithful priest who fulfills the prophecy is not Samuel, but Zadok. During the struggle for succession prior to David's death, Zadok supported Solomon and was rewarded for his loyalty. Solomon sent priestly rival Abiathar into exile and appointed Zadok to serve as the sole high priest, relegating the Levitical priests to menial roles as temple functionaries (a prospect suggested by v. 36). The narrator seems to have regarded Zadok's ascendancy as a sign of God's favor.

Visions of God

A number of biblical characters were reported to have encountered God through a vision, and prophets were among them. Balaam, though not a Yahwistic prophet, described his words as a vision from Yahweh (Num 24:4, 16). Isaiah reported on a vision of the heavenly temple (Isa 6:1) associated with his call to prophesy.

The term for visionary seeing is used in describing the prophecies of Isaiah (2:1), Amos (1:1), and Micah (1:1) as words that the prophets "saw." At other times, the "visions" of certain prophets are derided as false (Ezek 12:24, 27; 13:6).

The Boy of God, 3:1–4:1a

As if the man of God's scathing prophecy was not devastating enough, the narrator moves immediately to another story in which Eli gets the same message from another prophet, but this time the messenger is a "boy of God"—his own young associate, Samuel. In order to accomplish this, however, the author must first describe how it came about that a message from Yahweh should be entrusted to the young apprentice.

The writer sets the stage with a reminder that the boy Samuel was serving Yahweh under Eli's direction (v. 1a), but Samuel had experienced no personal encounter with Yahweh (v. 7). Indeed, hardly anyone had contact with the God who was worshiped at Shiloh: "The word of the LORD was rare in those days; visions were not widespread" (v. 1b). The word translated as "vision" (*hāzôn*) frequently referred to a visionary encounter with the Deity. [Visions of God] The author says this, despite the fact that the story follows immediately on another account in which an itinerant prophet has proclaimed the word of God. The reader, apparently, is to assume that some time has passed.

The narrator makes no overt claim that the widespread lack of communication from Yahweh is due to Eli's uninspired leadership, but the implication is apparent. Eli's failing eyesight that renders him so dependent on Samuel may be a subtle literary comment on the old priest's lack of spiritual vision. Likewise, while Samuel sleeps in the temple before the ark of God, Eli may be found lying down "in his room," presumably a cell attached to the temple and within easy earshot of Samuel. Through their physical locations, the author suggests that young Samuel, for all his naïveté, is really closer to God.

The temple in Shiloh was probably a small affair, more like a heavy tent than a permanent shrine. Archaeologists have found no clear remains of a temple from the Iron I period in Shiloh (modern Khirbet Seilun), though houses are frequent and pottery abounds.

Sacred lamps were filled with oil and replenished during the day but allowed to go out at night. [Ancient Lamps] On one particular night, the narrator tells us, sometime before the lamp sputtered out, the LORD first spoke to Samuel. In a story grown familiar by many retellings, we learn that Samuel

Ancient Lamps

Pottery lamps of the period were usually simple shallow bowls with lips pinched together to provide a channel for a wick of twisted flax. The wick soaked up oil from the bowl (usually olive oil) and provided a steady source of light.

Oil Lamp from Jerusalem, 1200 BC. Baked clay. (Credit: Erich Lessing/Art Resource, NY)

1 Samuel 3:10—Sir Reynolds, a distiguished portraitist, was the first president of the Royal Academy in London during the period in which he painted this image of the young Samuel. He gave a series of lectures entitled, *Discourses on Art,* to the students and members of the Academy that remain amongst the most important body of art criticism by a British author. Samuel is seen as an innocent, young boy who kneels and clasps his hands in prayer. This Romantic painting evokes emotion and concern for what is happpening to this young child yet there is a calm tone to the composition, perhaps a tone of acceptance.

Sir Joshua Reynolds (1723–92). *The Infant Samuel.* c. 1776. Oil on canvas, 36 x 28". Tate Gallery, London. (Credit: Tate Gallery, London/Art Resource, NY)

twice mistook the voice of God for Eli, assuming that the aged priest was in need of assistance (vv. 4-6). The author's reminder that Samuel "did not yet know the LORD" marks the transition to Yahweh's third call, which Samuel again misinterpreted. There is delightful irony in that Eli, who was blind, finally saw what was happening and discerned that God was calling the boy (v. 8). Eli coached Samuel in the proper etiquette of responding to God's call: "Speak, LORD, for your servant is listening" (v. 9).

God did speak, though not as the reader expects. One might anticipate some small word of praise for Eli, who gave kind guidance to Samuel despite the bitter knowledge that God was speaking to the boy and not to him. Or one might look for some word of introduction or some specific commission for Samuel. Instead, when the LORD spoke again and Samuel responded, the divine message was a nightmare. What Samuel heard was a bone-chilling, ear-tingling prediction of his mentor's doom. Yahweh pledged to fulfill the sentence he had already pronounced against Eli's house (vv.11-12), presumably by the man of God. He described the crime of the Elides as blasphemy, which Eli had done nothing to stop (v. 13). Finally, in bitter words that seems "unGodlike" to modern ears, Yahweh insisted that the time for forgiveness was past; there could be no expiation for their sin—forever (v. 14).

Samuel's sleepless night and reluctance to tell Eli are understandable (v. 15), but Eli pressed for details with a threatening oath, and Samuel revealed all (vv. 16-18a). The old priest's response was one of hopeless resignation in the face of overwhelming calamity: "It is the LORD; let him do what seems good to him" (v. 18b).

The narrator closes the account with a reminder that, while this was the first time God spoke to Samuel, it certainly was not the last. Indeed, Yahweh remained present with Samuel "and let none of his words fall to the ground," an expression that means none of his words were wasted. Samuel spoke truthfully and effectively (v. 19). In v. 20, the narrator first describes Samuel as a prophet. Indeed, he is not a mere prophet, but a *trustworthy* prophet whose reputation extends all the way from Dan (in the far north, beyond the Sea of Galilee) to Beer-Sheba (on the southern border, near the Negeb Desert). The comment in v. 21 that Yahweh continued to appear at Shiloh can refer only to the earliest phase of Samuel's active ministry, for the Philistines probably destroyed Shiloh shortly after they captured the ark (1 Sam 4:10-11). Samuel later made his home in Ramah and traveled a circuit between Bethel, Gilgal, and Mizpah (1 Sam 7:15-17).

CONNECTIONS

1. *A Lesson from the Man of God.* These two stories reflect the prevailing Deuteronomistic theology that centers on one important lesson: Behavior has consequences. The righteous prosper; the wicked fall. The presence of evil appears first as a lack of respect for God. Eli's sons behaved in blasphemous ways, despite their position as priests, and they would suffer for it. [Parents and Children] The traditions are mixed with regard to Eli's role. Whether he personally benefited from his sons' behavior, quietly condoned it, or simply failed to control it, Eli also was affected by it. Sin has consequences that go far beyond the sinner.

No believer can read the story of the man of God (2:27-36) and feel secure in sin again. The wandering prophet declares an amazing thing: an eternal promise of God was not so eternal after all. Yahweh had promised that the descendants of Aaron would lead Israel as God's priestly representatives *forever* (*'ôlām*). Old Testament Hebrew has no special word for "promise." The text literally reads, "I *said* that your house and your father's house would walk before me forever." Words of speaking (like *'āmar* here, and *dābar* in other places) can be translated as

Parents and Children

A mother and father mourn for their only son, who lives in prison because he committed a terrible crime. And they mourn for the victims of their son's irresponsible behavior. They did not teach their son to be selfish, but they allowed him to be so. They did not teach their son how to get into trouble, but they always came to his rescue. They did not teach their son to live with no respect for others, but they brought him up without appropriate consequences for his negative behavior. They did not teach their son to do evil, but neither did they teach him to do good. Now, they share in their son's shame. They share his sleepless nights. They know in their hearts that they are guilty, too.

An Oath, or Not?

Biblical writers sometimes describe divine promises as *oaths*, even when they are not presented as such. For example, when Yahweh promised to establish David's line upon the throne (1 Sam 7), the words used were simple declarative statements. Yet, later writers insisted that Yahweh had "sworn" this to David as a binding oath (Pss 89:3 [MT v. 4]; 132:11; Acts 2:30). While one might credit later writers with embellishing the narrative for literary effect, it is more likely that the ancients regarded any word of Yahweh as the equivalent of an oath. Humans swore *by* the deity, but Yahweh had no reason to call on a higher power; he could swear by himself (Isa 45:23; Jer 49:13; 51:14), by his holiness (Ps 89:35 [MT v. 36]), by his right hand (Isa 62:8), or by his great name (Jer 44:26). Since God's word was backed by his own authority, every divine promise was an implicit oath.

"promise" in certain contexts, and this certainly seems to reflect Yahweh's intent. Of course, the Hebrews regarded any word of Yahweh to be as certain as the strongest human oath. However, God will not be entrapped by his own words. [An Oath, or Not?]

Yahweh's promise to Aaron's descendants was based, apparently, on the condition that they would remain true to their calling. When the Shilonite priests chose personal gain over humble service to God and God's people, they forfeited their right to represent the LORD, and there was no way to regain it. The sons of Eli were so confidently secure in their position that they forgot it was a privilege—and they lost everything.

This text offers a special challenge to libertines of every age who are so certain of God's grace that they overlook God's judgment. We cannot accept God without also accepting God's way of life, because God changes things. Those who live with smug assurance that personal behavior has no consequences are in for a rude awakening.

2. *Lessons from the Boy of God.* While the story of Samuel's call is told for the larger purpose of predicting the fall of the Elides, the nature of the story suggests important truth regarding any individual's personal relationship with God. The story begins with a note that "the word of God was rare in those days" (3:1). The priests did not communicate with God, and only the rare, wandering prophet could bring close the word of God. When Samuel does not immediately recognize the LORD's voice, the narrator takes pains to inform us that Samuel did not yet *know* the LORD—the word of Yahweh had not been revealed to him (3:7).

Surely Samuel would have known *about* the LORD. Neither Hannah nor Eli would have been so remiss as to leave him ignorant of the important stories that revealed the character of God to Israel. However, *knowing about* God and *knowing* God are two different things. In Old Testament Hebrew, the word "to know" (*yādaʿ*) suggested intimate knowledge that grows from a personal relationship (see comments at 1 Sam 2:12). This is what Samuel gained in his nighttime conversation with God.

Parents and teachers of children should avoid communicating the notion that knowing Bible stories and reciting memorized Scripture are equivalent to knowing God. It is much easier to teach abstract knowledge. To teach someone else about relationships requires risk. We must tap into our soul, become transparent, and invite others to view our own relationship with God. If we fail in this task, the word of God will become rare in our days, too.

Yahweh's midnight visit to Samuel suggests that God calls each of us personally, not generically. And God will speak in a way that we can understand. To Samuel, the voice of God sounded like the voice of Eli as he heard his name called again and again. It was a familiar and comforting voice. God may speak to us in the words of a parent or close friend. Of course, ears are not required. God may whisper to our hearts and minds as we drive our cars, or sit by a shady lakeside, or lie awake in the still of the night.

God's call to each of us may not be as specific as it was for Samuel, and the common notion that God has planned our lives to the last detail is almost certainly overstated. Yet God has given special gifts to each of us, and God calls us to use those abilities in service to him and to our world. The first three times Samuel heard God calling his name, he responded in a most appropriate fashion, even though he thought it was Eli calling. Samuel said, "Here I am! You called?" The Hebrew *hinnĕnî* literally means "Behold, me!" Those who follow God best are those who know themselves and who make themselves available in God's service. [Inside and Out]

Inside and Out

How does one determine the shape of God's personal call to service? Sensitive listeners will look *inside* to discover their personal gifts of grace. They know then to look *outside*, discovering places of need. There are many people, places, and situations where the giving of ourselves can make a significant difference. God's call works on many levels. There is not only one way for us to respond to God's call, but many ways. Indeed, the goal is to follow God's call in all of our living, so that all we do brings glory and honor to him.

As we seek to match our own gifts with the needs we see, there are two things that will always be true. God's will for us will be something we *can* do (though we may be unsure), and it will be something that will bring us *joy* even when we don't expect it. We see a need, we know we can meet that need, and we say, "Here I am!" Sometimes God's call can be just that simple.

God may call us when we least expect it, or at the most inopportune time, or in the most unlikely situations. God may have to call more than once to get our attention. God's call is rarely as clear as we like, and the world is filled with distractions that make it hard for us to distinguish God's voice. Nevertheless, we may be sure that God has a word for each of us. Likewise, we may learn from young Samuel that no one is too small or too unimportant or too inexperienced to be used by God for difficult and important work. In fact, God seems to take particular delight in calling "little people" to do big things.

The story of Samuel's call is a perpetual favorite for many reasons, not the least of which is the belief that it can be *our* story, too. It is the story of every one of us who, in our own bumbling and stumbling way, have said, "Speak, LORD, for your servant is listening!"

NOTE

[1] See P. Kyle McCarter, *I Samuel* (AB 8; Garden City: Doubleday, 1980), 90; and detailed articles by J. Hoftijzer, "Das sogannte Feueropfer," *Hebraische Wortforschung* (Leiden: E. J. Brill, 1967), 114-34; and G. R. Driver, "Ugaritic and Hebrew Words," *Ugaritica* 6 (1969): 181-86.

PHILISTINE VICTORIES
AND THE LOSS OF THE ARK

4:1b-22

The Ark of God, 4:1b–7:1

The discerning reader may identify several subsources woven into the larger fabric of the books of Samuel (see "Literary History" in the Introduction). One of the more obvious sources is the "ark narrative," first delineated by Leonhard Rost in 1926.[1] [The Ark Narrative] Rost identified this material as 1 Samuel 4:1b–7:1 plus 2 Samuel 6, noting that the narrative in these sections focuses on the ark of Yahweh rather than on human characters. [The Ark of Yahweh] [The Magnificent Ark]

The ancients commonly thought their gods went into battle with them and could face victory or defeat. Or the gods could choose to desert to the other side as a means of demonstrating discontent with their own people. [Movable Gods] Understanding this cultural background may shed light on our own understanding of this Hebrew account of how Yahweh allowed Israel's defeat, despite the presence of his cultic symbol, to express divine displeasure with Israel.

The Ark Narrative

Rost described the pair 1 Sam 4:1b–7:1 and 2 Sam 6 as a once independent literary unit that focused on the ark of the covenant, rather than on human individuals. He proposed a time of composition sometime after the ark was brought to Jerusalem as a means of explaining why an old Shilonite cult symbol had such significance in the Jerusalem shrine.

The exodus traditions trace the history of the ark to Moses and the time of the wilderness wandering. The ark was such an important cult symbol for Israel that it is only natural that someone should put its history into writing as an ancient "Adventures of the Lost Ark." The narrative is mainly concerned with the theological crisis caused by the loss of the ark (1 Sam 4) and the resulting "war" between Yahweh and Dagon, which led to the ark's return (1 Sam 5–6).

Patrick Miller and J.J.M. Roberts have pointed out the similarity of this narrative to other ancient Near Eastern

accounts concerning the capture and return of an enemy's gods. Israel's contemporaries believed that a nation's gods could be captured by enemies and that the gods might defect willingly to the other side as a means of teaching their own people a lesson. They argue that the ark narrative of 1 Sam 4:1b–7:1 was written soon after the event — before David's victories over the Philistines — as a means of helping Israel come to terms with the theological problem of how Yahweh could have "deserted" his people. Since this would imply the presence of some rationale for Yahweh's displeasure, Miller and Roberts include the earlier account concerning the wickedness of Eli's sons (2:12-17, 22-25) as an integral part of the ark narrative. By the same reasoning, 2 Sam 6 is excluded since it describes events long after the crisis was solved and David had brought the Philistines into check.

Patrick D. Miller and J. J. M. Roberts, *The Hand of the Lord: A Reassessment of the "Ark Narrative" of 1 Samuel* (JHNES ;Baltimore: Johns Hopkins, 1977).

The Ark of Yahweh

AΩ The ark of Yahweh is described in different ways in the various strands of biblical tradition. The elaborate description of the ark in the priestly account of Exod 25:10-22 portrays the ark (*ʾărôn*) as a rectangular box of acacia wood, about four feet long and just over two feet square. The removable top of the box (*kappōret*; called the "Mercy Seat," or better, "Place of Atonement") was adorned with two golden cherubim, arranged so that their wings stretched across the top of the ark.

The two tablets containing the Ten Commandments were to be kept in the ark; thus, it was often called the "ark of the testimony" (Exod 25:22) or the "ark of the covenant" (Josh 3:6). These titles focus on the nature of the ark as a receptacle for holy relics.

Other titles emphasize the gilded cover where Yahweh was thought to abide "between the cherubim" (Exod 25:22). Titles that emphasize God's presence include the "ark of Yahweh" and the "ark of Yahweh of hosts, who is enthroned on the cherubim" (1 Sam 4:4).

The ark was thought of as the throne of Yahweh (Jer 3:16-17) or, more likely, as his footstool, the invisible throne being flanked by the two cherubim (1 Chr 28:2; Pss 99:5; 132:7; Lam 2:1). The cherubim were probably winged sphinxes with both human and animal features. In Canaanite iconography, cherubim often flanked the divine throne.

The Israelites believed that God's presence and power hovered above the ark, where Yahweh appeared in a cloud (Lev 16:2) and spoke to Moses (Exod 25:22; Num 7:89). At God's command, they had carried the ark at the head of their procession through the wilderness (Num 10:35-36), across the Jordan (Josh 3–4), and into battle in the promised land (Josh 6–7).

Traditions suggest that the ark rested at various shrines, including Mount Ebal (Josh 8:30-35) and Bethel (Judg 20:26-27), before coming to reside at Shiloh.

The Magnificent Ark

This unfinished painting was begun by Tissot very late in his career. These later works reflect the deepened spirituality of the artist. Tissot chose subjects from the life of Christ and the Old Testament for his final paintings and engravings.

James [Jacques Joseph] Tissot (1836–1902). *The Ark Passes over the Jordan.* c. 1890. The Jewish Museum. New York, NY. (Credit: The Jewish Museum/Art Resource, NY)

Movable Gods

Ancient enemies sought to humiliate their opponents by capturing the images of the enemies' gods and displaying them in their own temples. Miller and Roberts illustrate with a Babylonian account concerning the capture of Marduk's image in a battle with the Elamites. The account is preserved on two fragmentary tablets. The first fragment claims that evil had become so prominent that "Marduk grew angry and commanded the gods to desert Babylon," with the result that "the wicked Elamites took advantage of the ensuing helplessness of the country to carry off the divine images and ruin the shrines." The second fragment suggests that Marduk devastated the Elamites and returned to Babylon in response to the Babylonian king's constant prayer. "The people of the land stared in joyous admiration of his lofty stature as the jubilant procession led to Marduk's lofty cella, where sacrifices were then offered in great abundance." (The first fragment was published by W. G. Lambert in "Enmeduranki and Related Matters," *JCS* 21 [1967]: 126-38. For the second fragment, see Miller and Roberts, 79-81.)

The author/editor of 1 Samuel has spliced the ark narrative into the larger story of Samuel with considerable skill and a minimum of retouching. As it presently stands, the ark narrative serves to proclaim the supreme power of Yahweh and to reinforce the person and position of Samuel as Yahweh's chosen, prophetic leader.

COMMENTARY

The ark narrative begins with a woeful tale recounting how Israel was defeated in two battles with the Philistines, losing the sacred ark of the covenant in the process. The loss of the ark served as a very painful and tangible reminder that God does not live in a box and cannot be manipulated or taken for granted.

Losing the Battle, 4:1b-11

There is a sharp transition between the summary description of Samuel's growth as a trustworthy prophet (3:19–4:1a) and a sudden situation of grave danger for Israel: the drums of war were beating. The statement "In those days the Philistines mustered for war against Israel" has been lost from the MT but can be restored from the LXX and is certainly necessary for the text to make sense.

No reason for the impending battle is given; border skirmishes between the Hebrews and the Philistines were the natural result of the two nations' desire for the same territory. The Philistines were part of a larger group who invaded Palestine sometime near the beginning of the twelfth century BC. [The Philistines] Known as the "Sea Peoples" by the Egyptians, this advanced society had been

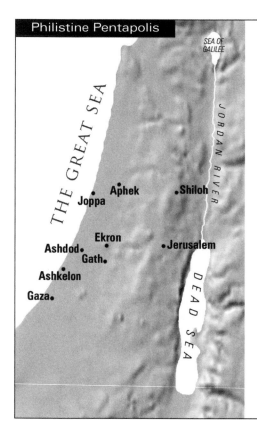

Philistine Pentapolis

SEA OF GALILEE

THE GREAT SEA

JORDAN RIVER

Joppa • Aphek

• Shiloh

Ekron •
Ashdod •
Gath •
Ashkelon •
Gaza •

• Jerusalem

DEAD SEA

The Philistines

The Philistine population was concentrated around the cities of Ashdod, Gath, Ekron, Ashkelon, and Gaza, though their reach extended much deeper inland. This strong pentapolis of city-states provided security and protection for their inhabitants.

The Sea Peoples brought with them new innovations that provided technological advantages in war. The Bronze Age was drawing to a close, and the Philistines were on the cutting edge of the new Iron Age technology. Their skill in the manipulation of iron enabled them to make harder and sharper swords, axes, and arrows than the softer bronze of their opponents. With their large cities guarding a rather small area, the Philistines were able to muster and train reinforcements for their standing army quickly. Their well-trained army, their superior weaponry, and their reputation as a warrior race made the Philistines a fearsome adversary.

The Philistines were not a long-term power in Canaan, but their influence was so great that the entire area now bears their name. "Palestine" derives from the Latin form of "Philistia" (*Palestina*). It came to be used by the Romans in the 2d century AD as a name for their administrative province encompassing the area that included ancient Israel's borders.

pushed from their home country in the Aegean by invading tribes of northern barbarians. After a less-than-successful series of battles with the Egyptians, the Philistines settled along the fertile coastal plain in southwestern Canaan. [Egyptians and Philistines]

As the Philistines were getting settled on the western coast of Canaan, the Israelites were crossing the Jordan and invading the same land from the east. Sooner or later, they were bound to come into conflict over rights to the land. The first recorded clashes between these two neighboring peoples occurred during the period of the judges, not long before Eli came on the scene.

Israel's army is likely to have been a rag-tag affair of farmers and shepherds pressed into duty in defense of their land. The organizing strength of Israel's ancient tribal league is uncertain, and there is little to suggest that all the tribes of Israel were involved. Most likely, those Israelites who lived in the area would have constituted the bulk of the troops. The Philistines, apparently, were much better equipped for battle.

The Philistine army mustered near the city of Aphek, near their northern border. Aphek, just to the east of modern Tel Aviv, guarded an important road leading from the coastal plain into the Ephraimite highlands. The Israelites drew their battle line at

Ebenezer, a site that cannot be identified with certainty. Presumably, it was close to the eastern side of Aphek.

The battle resulted in a clear victory for the Philistines, who killed a large number of Israelites in pitched battle. [Counting Soldiers] When the elders of Israel gathered to assess the situation, their deliberations were dominated by a single question: "Why has Yahweh put us to rout today before the Philistines?" (v. 3) The narrator does not perceive a military crisis so much as a theological one. During the "conquest" of Canaan and the period of the judges, every lost battle was attributed to divine displeasure, and every victory was credited to God's blessing. Yahweh was thought of as a warrior-god who fought on behalf of his people. Why did he not fight for them at Aphek-Ebenezer?

Egyptians and Philistines

This relief depicts Ramses III (1193–1162 BC), who defented Egypt from incursions by the sea peoples, later known as the Philistines. Ramses wears the headress historically associated with the Upper Egyptian kings. His importance is also reflected in his size.

Ramses III Smiting Enemies. Relief from the main temple of Ramses III. Medinet Habu. Thebes, Egypt. (Credit: Erich Lessing/Art Resource)

As the author tells it, the elders did not search for the true cause of Yahweh's displeasure (the corruption of the cult at Shiloh), but assumed that God's absence was related to their failure to actively involve Yahweh in the battle. So they decided to send for the ancient talisman of Yahweh's presence among his people: the ark of the covenant, which was housed at the temple of Shiloh.

The ark served as a battle palladium, a rallying point for beleaguered soldiers. Only priests and Levites were allowed to touch the ark, so Hophni and Phinehas escorted the holy relic into battle. At this point, the text says nothing negative about Hophni and

---

Counting Soldiers

ΑΩ The MT claims that Israel lost 4,000 men in the first battle (4:2) and that 30,000 foot soldiers were slaughtered in the second battle. These numbers seem inordinately high. The ancients possessed no weapons of mass destruction, and wars consisted of hand-to-hand combat, with spears, slings, and arrows the only "long distance" weapons. Armies probably consisted of no more than a few thousand men at most.

Scholars have long wondered if the Hebrew word translated as "thousand" (*'elep*) might actually denote a military unit or squadron of undetermined size. George Mendenhall argued that these units varied in size from five to fourteen men. If these numbers are applied to the battle of Aphek-Ebenezer, the Israelites would have lost from 150 to 420 infantry in the first battle, and from 1,650 to 4,620 soldiers in the second. These numbers would still constitute a serious loss of life.

George Mendenhall, "The Census Lists of Numbers 1 and 26," JBL 77 (1958): 52-66.

1 Samuel 4:12-18—Eli was unfazed by the news that his sons had been killed, but swooned when he learned of the ark's capture.

Julius Schnoor von Carolsfeld. *Eli's Death*. 19th century. Woodcut. *Das Buch der Bucher in Bilden*. (Credit: Dover Pictorial Archive Series)

Phinehas, nor does it indicate whether the priests went willingly. Still, one who has read the earlier account of the rogue priests (2:12-17, 22-25) knows that the sacred "ark of Yahweh who is enthroned above the cherubim" was escorted into battle by the very source of Yahweh's anger against Israel. One could hardly expect victory.

The soldiers of Israel, however, did not know this. They only knew that the mighty ark of God had come into the camp. As the sun shone upon the gilded cherubim, perhaps the infantrymen could imagine the presence of Yahweh as a glowing halo surrounding the ark. They responded with a great cultic shout (*těrûʿâh*), intended to celebrate Yahweh's presence and to frighten the Philistines.

The narrator, who adopts an omniscient view, presumes to speak with the voice of the Philistines, who quailed in fear when they learned of the ark's arrival. Assuming that the Israelites were also polytheistic, they judged that "gods" had come into the camp—mighty gods such as they had never seen—and they cried out in alarm (vv. 5-8).

The story then relates an amazing thing. The *Philistines* remembered how Yahweh had struck the Egyptians on behalf of the Hebrews. By this literary device, the narrator plants a seed in the reader's mind, for the coming saga of the ark will have many similarities with the story of Israel's deliverance from Egypt.

If the Israelites intended to strike fear into the Philistines' hearts, they succeeded; but if they thought the ark's presence would take the fight out of them, they were mistaken. In fact, the terrible challenge of the ark inspired the Philistines to "act like men" and fight bravely for fear that they would be enslaved by the Hebrews (v. 9; cf. 2 Sam 13:28 and 1 Kgs 2:2, where the translation "Be courageous" literally means "Be a man!" [*hayîtah lěʾîš*]).

The Philistines fought, and Israel fought, but Yahweh did not enter the battle. The inspired Philistines overran the dispirited Israelites (had they expected Yahweh to do all the fighting?), who fled—not to a new position, but to their own tents (cf. 2 Sam 20:1 and 1 Kgs 12:16, where returning to one's tent means abandoning the army). Thus, more than seven times the number who died in the first battle were killed, and the remainder deserted.

Two footnotes complete the battlefield report: "The ark of God was captured; and the two sons of Eli, Hophni and Phinehas, died." By their deaths the prophecy of 2:34 was fulfilled, and thus did Yahweh express his displeasure not only with the pandering priests, but with the nation that had spawned and supported them.

Losing the "Glory," 4:12-22

The aftermath of the battle—as it relates to Israel—is told in the form of two connected stories in vv. 12-22. The first of these describes Eli's reaction when he heard the dreaded news (vv. 12-18), and the second recounts how the newly widowed wife of Phinehas responded (vv. 19-22).

For the storyteller, the loss of thousands of Hebrew soldiers is not nearly so important as the loss of one ark, for it was Israel's most sacred symbol of Yahweh's presence. The bearer of bad news was a man from the tribe of Benjamin who ran the twenty miles from Ebenezer to Shiloh with his clothes torn and with dirt on his head to symbolize Israel's loss. It is significant that the messenger was a Benjaminite, since Israel's first king (appointed for the purpose of dealing with the Philistines) was from the tribe of Benjamin. The reader knows that the Benjaminites were personally acquainted with the conflict.

Eli was waiting for news, sitting by the city gates—or, as Kyle McCarter describes (following the LXX), actually *on top of* the broad gate towers.[2] The MT has "on the hand of the gate," a common Hebrew idiom for "beside the gate." Eli was waiting because his heart had trembled for the ark from the moment it was carried from Shiloh.

Despite Eli's advantageous position, he failed to see the messenger come through the gate (a parenthesis in v. 15 points out that Eli was blind). The messenger's torn clothes and dirt-sprinkled head conveyed bad news without speaking, but he also ran crying through the streets, leaving the entire town in an uproar of weeping and wailing. Husbands and fathers and sons were dead, and the Philistines were victorious.

While the city residents mourned their loss and wondered if the survivors would be dragged from their homes to become slaves, the narrator is more concerned with the theological crisis caused by the

---

Messenger Reports

📖 Compare the striking structural similarity of this report with another battlefield messenger's appearance before David in 2 Sam 1:3-4. Both messengers appear in mourning, with clothes torn and dirt on their heads.

1 Samuel 4:16-17	**2 Samuel 1:3-4**
The man said to Eli, "I have just come from the battle; I fled from the battle today."	He [the messenger] said to him [David], "I have escaped from the camp of Israel."
He said, "How did it go, my son?"	David said to him, "How did things go? Tell me!"
The messenger replied,	He answered,
"Israel has fled before the Philistines, and there has also been a great slaughter among the troops; your two sons also, Hophni and Phinehas, are dead, and the ark of God has been captured.	"The army fled from the battle, but also many of the army fell and died; and Saul and his son Jonathan also died."

---

ark's capture. Had Yahweh deserted Israel, or had he really been defeated by the Philistine god Dagon? (See [Dagon]).

The author skillfully raises suspense by having Eli, who is most concerned about the ark, be the last to know. And when the messenger finally reported to Eli, he saved the worst news until last: "I have just come from the battle; I fled from the battle today. . . . Israel has fled before the Philistines, and there has also been a great slaughter among the troops; your two sons also, Hophni and Phinehas, are dead, *and the ark of God has been captured*" (v. 17). [Messenger Reports]

Eli appears unmoved by the news that Israel had fled in battle and that his evil sons, Hophni and Phinehas, had died. He seems to have expected no less. But "*when he mentioned the ark of God,* Eli fell over backward from his seat by the side of the gate, and his neck was broken and he died, for he was an old man, and heavy" (v. 18). McCarter posits that Eli actually fell from the top of the gate and into the street below,[3] but if this had been the case, the explanation that Eli was old and heavy would hardly be necessary to explain his broken neck. A single editorial line adds the final period to Eli's life: "He had judged Israel for forty years." [Was Eli a Judge?]

The second story concerns the late Eli's very pregnant daughter-in-law, the wife of Phinehas

Was Eli a Judge?

📖 First Sam 4:18b is the first and only time Eli is called a judge, and the title is somewhat problematic. There is no record that Eli ever "delivered" Israel as did other judges (compare Gideon, Deborah, Jephthah, and Samson) or that he held any leadership responsibilities beyond the cult at Shiloh. Eli is not included in the lists in the book of Judges, and the claimed forty-year period overlaps with other named judges. Eli's successor, Samuel, was considered the last of the judges (see 1 Sam 7:15).

(vv. 19-22). News of the shocking tragedy sent her into premature labor, and she crouched down to give birth. [Birthing Positions] The labor was difficult and led to her death, but her attendants tried to comfort her with the good news that she had given birth to a son. [A Woman's Worth] In her delirious state, the woman did not respond to their succor but bitterly gave her son the name Ichabod, saying, "The glory has departed from Israel, for the ark of God has been captured" (v. 22). [Glory] Notice again that the deaths of Hophni and Phinehas seem entirely secondary to the loss of the ark.

The glory of Israel was the presence of God, but with the loss of the ark, Israel's most tangible and sacred symbol of God's presence was gone. For the narrator, this was the crucial issue, recognized not only by Eli, but by his daughter-in-law. No one yet knew the full consequences of Yahweh's apparent desertion of Israel, but everyone knew it was a dark day in Shiloh.

Birthing Positions

The women of ancient Israel, like the women of many less developed cultures today, did not give birth in a bed, but in a sitting or squatting position that facilitated parturition. Note the reference to "birth stools" in the story of the heroic midwives Shiprah and Puah (Exod 1:16).

A Woman's Worth

Compare the story of Rachel in Gen 35:17-18. As Rachel died while giving birth, her attendants tried to cheer her with the news that she had borne a son. Remember also Hannah's great desire to bear a son (1 Sam 1). The women tending to Phinehas' wife lived in a culture that declared that a woman's greatest achievement was to bear a son; thus, they truly expected the dying woman to find comfort in the news that her child was a boy.

CONNECTIONS

What can modern believers learn from Israel's experience? Israel's loss at Aphek-Ebenezer grew from one of the oldest problems in any religious system, and that is the human attempt to gain divine advantage. The elders of Israel seem to have thought they had God in a box where they could use, control, and manipulate God to do their bidding. This concept of God is no more sophisticated than a genie in a bottle. Unfortunately, many modern persons share the same concept.

Glory

AΩ The root meaning of the word *kābôd* is "heaviness" or "weightiness." The divine presence was the true substance of Israel's favored position with God.

Most commentators since Josephus have confidently asserted that the name "Ichabod" (*ʾî- kābôd*) means "no glory," citing Phoenician parallels for interpreting *ʾî* as a negative preformative. McCarter, however, draws attention to the Ugaritic word *ʾîy*, which means "Where is?" or "Alas!"; compare the use of *ʾî* in biblical Hebrew for "alas" in Eccl 10:16. Thus, "Ichabod" may not mean "no glory," but "Where is the glory?" or "Alas (for the) glory!" The precise translation matters little; the glory is gone in either case.

P. Kyle McCarter, *I Samuel* (AB 8; Garden City: Doubleday, 1980), 115-16.

What Israel learned from this episode is that you cannot control God. You cannot manipulate God. You cannot tell God what to do. God will be God. If God is not free to act as God wills, then God is not God. We want to believe that God is big enough to conquer all our enemies and work any miracle and yet small enough to come running when we snap our fingers. It doesn't work that way.

Modern believers can hardly carry the ark into battle, but there remain a number of ways in which we might attempt to manipulate God. The most obvious, as noted by Kenneth Chafin, is that many believers have difficulty distinguishing between the Bible, which is the *written* word of God, and the eternal God, who is the *living* Word.[4] They seem to think they have captured God in the Scriptures, and they try to control God and manipulate people with their particular interpretations of Scripture.

Others attempt to control God through prayer. Many persons seem to think they have guaranteed formulas for answered prayer. Television evangelists with "healing ministries" put their hands on the sick and *command* God to drive out their sicknesses. Proponents of "success theology" claim that material blessings are guaranteed for those who show faithfulness to God by contributing to their organization. Thousands of well-meaning Christians purchase expensive books and sign up for extended studies on developing a more "successful" prayer life.

Humans have always desired to gain power with the gods, whether through the building of temples or through sacrifices or ceremonies or prayers. There are things we can do to help bring us into a right relationship with God, but there is nothing we can do that gives us the right or the ability to control God's power or God's relationship to others.

Every day, people pray with all their hearts for something and do not receive it. Every day, people die when others have prayed for them to live. Every day, people are disappointed that God did not protect them in the way they expected. And every day, people are blessed who don't deserve it, don't ask for it, and don't expect it. We must learn that saying our prayers and wearing angel pins on our shoulders give us no guarantee that God will provide miraculous care and protection.

God will be God, or he is not God. The Scriptures do teach us that God cares for his people, and that he hears our prayers, that he is a God of steadfast love and that he has promised abundant life and eternal life to those who believe. But nowhere do the Scriptures say that God has surrendered control of his power to us. He gives *us* no power either to limit or to channel *his* power. God does not live in a magic box. He is not a genie in a bottle. He is like a wind we cannot capture, a power that we cannot hold, a wildness that we cannot comprehend.

One secret to growing in our faith is the recognition that we cannot use God—but that we find our greatest joy when we allow God to use us. God will never lead us into evil. As we give our lives to him, he will lead us to do good and to be good, to bring love and hope and joy into a world of darkness.

Eventually, all of us will learn what the Israelites learned in battle that day. Having the paraphernalia of God and having God are not the same. Having the title "pastor" or "rabbi" and having God are not the same. Being baptized and having God are not the same. Those who bring the most goodness to the world and the greatest glory to God are the ones who choose not to possess God, but to be possessed by him.

NOTES

[1] Leonhard Rost, *Die Überlieferung von der Thronnachfolge Davids*, BWANT III, 6 (Stuttgart: W. Kohlhammer, 1926), 119-253.

[2] P. Kyle McCarter, *I Samuel* (AB 8; Garden City: Doubleday, 1980), 110-11.

[3] Ibid., 114.

[4] Kenneth Chafin, *1, 2 Samuel* (CC; Dallas: Word Books, 1989), 53.

THE HAND OF GOD AND
THE HANDS OF DAGON

5:1-12

COMMENTARY

The first episode of the ark narrative ended on a dark and somber note for Israel: "The glory has departed from Israel, for the ark of God has been captured" (4:22). The second episode is much shorter, relating the aftermath of the ark's capture from the perspective of the Philistines. This episode declares that while the glory of God may have departed from Israel, it had certainly not departed from the earth, or even from the ark. Despite all rumors to the contrary, Yahweh was alive and well.

The account of the Philistines' experience with the ark is one of the most delightful stories to be found in the Scriptures, unless the reader happens to be a Philistine. The author peppers the account with humor and not-so-subtle sarcasm. The story tells of tragedy for the Philistines and confusion for Israel, but from beginning to end it sings the glory of God.

The Philistine misadventures began when the victorious soldiers brought the captured ark some thirty-five miles south from Ebenezer to the city of Ashdod, where they placed it before the divine image in their temple to Dagon (v. 2). [Dagon] Ashdod was not the closest Philistine city to Ebenezer; Ekron was northernmost. Perhaps Ashdod was chosen to house the ark because it was located roughly in the center of the Philistine pentapolis or because it was considered the leading religious or political center among the five cities.

During this period, Dagon was popularly worshiped in the area north and east of Canaan. He was known as the father of Ba`al Haddu, who became the most famous of all the Canaanite gods. Perhaps the Philistines thought to gain power over the indigenous Canaanites by adopting the "father" of Canaan's patron deity.

Setting the ark of Yahweh before the cultic image of Dagon was a way of declaring to all that the Philistines had conquered Israel because Dagon had conquered Yahweh. According to the narrator,

Dagon

The name "Dagon" is ancient but obscure. The Latin father Jerome and some medieval Jewish scholars (Rashi and the Kimchis) considered Dagon to be a "fish god" on the basis of the North Semitic word for fish (*dagg-* or *digg-*) and the Philistines' origin as a "Sea People." This opinion is sometimes repeated, but generally rejected by modern scholars, who associate the name Dagon with an old Semitic root (*dgn*) that may be associated with clouds and rain, leading to the common Northwest Semitic term for grain (*dāgān*). Dagon, then, would be an appropriate name for a fertility god who brought rain for crops in the coastal plain, where the Philistines lived.

If the Philistines brought with them other gods from the Aegean, they left few traces of them. Perhaps they thought it best to adopt a deity that was native to their new locale. Biblical writers apparently regarded Dagon as the Philistines' national deity (cf. 1 Chr 10:10, which refers to the temples of the Philistine gods but names only Dagon).

Even so, it is a bit surprising to find Dagon as the patron deity of the Philistines, for historically Dagon was a West Semitic god worshiped in ancient city-states such as Mari (along the Euphrates, in western Mesopotamia), Ebla (in northern Syria), and Ugarit (near the Mediterranean coast of northern Syria). Military records inscribed for Sargon of Akkad (2334-2279 BC) describe a military foray into these regions, where he "prostrated himself in prayer before Dagan" (note the different spelling), with the result that "Dagan gave him the Upper Region: Mari, Larmuti and Ebla as far as the Cedar Forest (Lebanon) and the Silver Mountain (the Taurus Mountains north of Lebanon, extending into Asia Minor)."

Georges Roux, Ancient Iraq, 2d ed. (Harmondsworth England: Penguin Books, 1980), 147.

W. Hinz, "Persia, c. 2400–1800 BC," in CAH, 12 vols. (Cambridge: Cambridge University Press 1923) 1:644-80.

Dagon lies headless before the ark in this watercolor by Tissot. This painting is a final work by the artist. Tissot is well known for his religious works, especially 365 gouache illustrations for the *Life of Christ*. Recently, Tissot's depictions of genre scenes and views of 19th century life have gained new acclaim (see [The Magnificent Art]).

James [Jacques Joseph] Tissot (1836–1920). *The Idol Broken Down Before the Ark*. Watercolor. 7³⁄₈x10⁵⁄₁₆". The Jewish Mesuem. New York. (Credit: The Jewish Museum/Art Resource, NY)

however, Yahweh had something of his own to declare. After closing up the temple for the night, the Philistine priests returned the next morning to discover that Dagon had "fallen on his face to the ground before the ark of the LORD" (v. 3a).

Anthropomorphic language abounds in the fleshing out of the story. Dagon is found "on his face" before the ark, evidently paying homage. The narrator leaves the reader to imagine the thoughts and emotions that swept over the Philistines, describing their efforts to restore Dagon's solemn decorum with the simple statement, "They took Dagon and put him back in his place" (v. 3b).

If the Philistines had imagined Dagon's fall to be accidental, their illusion was shattered on the following morning when they again found the cult statue of Dagon on his face before the ark, but this time with the head and the hands "cut off" and lying on the threshold of the temple (v. 4). The position of the broken image suggests that Dagon had been trying to escape through the door or perhaps appealing for the aid of spirits who were believed to reside under the threshold. The fact that the head and hands were "cut off" (*kĕrutôt*), rather than simply broken, implies mortal combat in the night, with Dagon coming out the dismembered loser. The Philistine god was left as an impotent stump, without a head for thinking or hands for acting.[1]

Again, the narrator tells us nothing about the emotional reaction of the Philistines, except that he incorporates an etiology suggesting that the event gave rise to the Philistine custom of not stepping on the threshold of the temple since it had been touched by the holy image of Dagon. [Etiology] There is subtle sarcasm here: Dagon is clearly helpless before Yahweh, but the Philistines still revere his image and all that it touches. They require more convincing, it seems.

This leads to a more obvious use of sarcastic humor: while the head and the hands of Dagon lie broken on the temple doorway, the *hand of Yahweh* becomes "heavy" upon the Philistines (v. 6). Now the narrator reveals to us their terror, explaining how Yahweh's heavy hand struck the citizens of Ashdod and its associated villages with a painful bodily affliction usually translated as "tumors." [Yahweh Smote Them with What?] The LXX adds that there also

Etiology

AΩ An etiology (also spelled aetiology) is a story told for the purpose of explaining the origin of a custom, a place name, an ethnic group, or an institution (the Greek word *aitia* means "cause"). The Bible contains many accounts that were probably first preserved as etiological stories but later were given theological significance when they were incorporated into larger narratives. For example, Gen 11 explains why the world's peoples speak different languages, and Gen 22 explains how the village of Bethel came to have its name.

The custom of "leaping over" the threshold was widespread in the ancient world, as was the belief that powerful spirits dwelt under the threshold. The custom probably grew from the fear that putting pressure on the threshold would annoy the spirits underneath. The superstition was apparently extant in Israel since it was roundly condemned by the prophet Zephaniah (1:9). The etiology of 1 Sam 5:5 offers an explanation for the practice, at least in Ashdod.

Yahweh Smote Them with What?

AΩ There is some debate concerning the precise affliction visited upon the Philistines. The word *ʾōpel* normally means "hill" or "mound" (the "city of David" in Jerusalem was located on the "Hill of Ophel"). The plural form used here seems to point to multiple swellings on the body, such as those caused by the plague. At the time the LXX was translated, the dual form of the word (indicating two mounds) could refer to one's hips, for the Greek translation is, "He smote them on the buttocks" (*eis tas hedras*).

This leads to speculation that Yahweh's smiting brought dysentery, perhaps caused by the plague, or hemorrhoids, a common result of dysentery. This question has resulted in an interesting variation in the MT. The Hebrew Scriptures were written without vowels, but the Jewish scholars who preserved the ancient text (see [Masoretic Text]) added vowels to the consonantal text in a process called "pointing." Sometimes the scribes employed a convention

known as *Kethib/Qere* (Written/Read) in which they would point the consonants for one word with the vowels for another. Their intention was for the reader to follow the *vowels*. For example, the name "Yahweh" is written with the consonants *yhwh*, but since it was considered improper to pronounce God's name, the Masoretes added the vowels for "Adonai," meaning "Lord. Any scribe who read the text would *see* "Yahweh" but *read* "Adonai."

Here in chapter 5, the Masoretes pointed the consonants *ʾplym* with the vowels for the word *tĕhorîm*, which is commonly translated as "hemorrhoids."

Whether the Masoretes' intention was to clarify an obscure word, to avoid offense with a euphemism, or simply to add humor to the story is unclear. In any event, the reader is left with the picture of a people so stricken by dysentery that they all develop hemorrhoids. Not only does Dagon lose his head and his hands, but his people lose their dignity.

was a plague of rodents, though mice are not mentioned in the MT until 6:4.

The maladies striking Ashdod remind the reader of how Yahweh had proven his supremacy over Pharaoh by sending an assortment of plagues against the Egyptians (Exod 7–11). Other ancient traditions also connect plagues with the actions of God (Hab 3:5), even against God's own people (2 Sam 24:10-17).

The inhabitants of Ashdod were not without spiritual insight. They attributed their mounting troubles to the presence of the ark of Yahweh, concluding that "the ark of the God of Israel must not remain with us; for his hand is heavy on us and on our god Dagon" (v. 7).

Gath

The city of Gath was located about ten miles inland from Ashdod. As the closest Philistine city to Judah, it was often a place of contention. The Semitic word *gat* means "wine press," a likely reference to a leading local industry. The people of Gath were called "Gittites."

A conference was called to deal with the crisis, bringing together the "lords of the Philistines"—probably a consortium of the rulers of the five major Philistine cities and perhaps leaders from their dependent villages. The people of Gath volunteered to host the ark but soon regretted their bravado (vv. 8-9). [Gath] The "hand of Yahweh" also turned against the Gittites, striking both young and old with tumors and causing a great panic among the populace.

The ark was quickly sent northward to the city of Ekron, back toward the place of its capture. The ark's dangerous reputation had become known, however, and the inhabitants of Ekron wanted nothing to do with it. Accusing their kinsmen of inflicting intentional harm against them, the Ekronites instigated a second meeting of the Philistine lords to deal with the issue of the ark, which was wreaking havoc in the city. The hand of Yahweh was *very* heavy against the people of Ekron so that many died and all were stricken, "and the cry of the city went up to heaven" (v. 12).

In Exodus 2:23 the Israelites who were enslaved in Egypt had groaned so loudly that "their cry went up to God," with the result that God heard them and responded with compassion (Exod 3:7-9). The narrator seems to be suggesting that the Philistines' cry also went up to the heavens—but there were no gods to hear it or to save them.

CONNECTIONS

The Philistines' experience with the living God of Israel is rich with significance. It challenges us to ask questions such as "Who/what do we worship?" and "What do you do when your gods fall?"

1. *Fallen gods and following God.* Through tumors and plague, through falling idols and broken gods, the God of Israel made one thing very clear: When gods do battle, Yahweh wins, for he is the only true and living God. He is the only God whose hands can be heavy—or gentle—the only God whose hands can shape mountains and paint rainbows, the only God whose hands can do anything at all.

That is the primary point of our story, with emphasis. But that is not, perhaps, the most interesting thing to be learned from the account. When the cultic image of Dagon fell before the ark of Yahweh, the Philistines simply set him back on his pedestal. But what good is a god that must be propped up with a stick or held together with pitch (cf. Isa 44:9-20)? How can a god who cannot support itself offer anything to its followers?

When Dagon's image was so thoroughly humiliated that no Philistine doubted Yahweh's power, one might think they would give up on their false and impotent god and offer their worship to Yahweh. Instead, they propped up their false god and sent the symbol of the true God away in hopes of distancing themselves from Yahweh.

In modern English usage, the word "Philistine" describes an immoral or unmannered person who cares nothing for God or for good. Sadly, many persons who claim to follow God still live as if God does not exist. They prefer to keep the Lord at a distance, reserving religion for times of trouble.

2. *Modern Dagons.* The truth is, those persons who want to live without reference to the true God have, in effect, given themselves to the worship of false gods. Yahweh is jealous for the love of his people and bears no rivals (Exod 20:5).

Many persons fall prey to the worship of *materialism*, to the acquisition of *things* or the accumulation of *wealth.* Some worship *career* gods, while others give themselves to *leisure.* To support opulent lifestyles, we put ourselves under great stress, and to deal with our stress we take longer and more frequent vacations. These, of course, require more money, which puts us under greater stress, which makes us want to get away even more. When our gods fall down, we keep propping them back up.

A Prayer

The same divine hands that can wax heavy against God's enemies can also be tender and warm in comforting his own. "My sheep hear my voice," Jesus said. "I know them, and they follow me. I give them eternal life, and they will never perish. No one will snatch them out of my hand. What my Father has given me is greater than all else, and no one can snatch it out of the Father's hand" (John 10:27-29).

God of the heavy hand,
God of the comforting touch,
give us wisdom to hold our own hands up to you,
and trust to leave them there. Amen.

There are other gods to consider. Any *thing*, *person*, or *cause* we trust to bring meaning and fulfillment to life has become, in effect, our god. Money and things can add a measure of joy to our lives, but they cannot be central. Leisure and travel can enrich our lives, but they also can carry us farther and farther from the real God of all journeys. Other persons cannot be expected to meet our innermost, spiritual needs. Political or social causes, in and of themselves, can lead one far from the teaching of Jesus.

When we give our hearts to idols, we will spend much of our time either propping them up or trying to put distance between ourselves and the living God. The Lord may not choose to swat us with his heavy hand, or to afflict us with tumors, but such punishment is not our only concern.

We want God's strong hand to comfort us when we are in darkness, to guide us as we walk life's journey, and to lift us up to a higher plane when this world's walk is over. [A Prayer] If that is going to happen, we want to live without any other gods between us.

NOTE

[1] Ralph W. Klein, *1 Samuel* (WBC 10; Waco: Word Books, 1983), 50.

THE RETURN OF THE ARK
AND A MIXED RECEPTION

6:1–7:1

COMMENTARY

The final episode of the ark's adventures in Philistia consists of two parts: the account of how the Philistines determined the appropriate method of returning the ark to Israel, and the report of how the Hebrew population of Beth-shemesh responded to the unexpected reappearance of the sacred relic. From beginning to end, this episode is infused with evidence of the power of Yahweh at work through the medium of the ark.

The Philistines Return the Ark, 6:1-12

Although the events of chapter 5 are narrated in whirlwind fashion, we learn from v. 1 that the ark actually remained in Philistine territory for seven months. In Hebrew thought, the number seven indicates completion. [The Perfect Number] Thus, the narrator indicates that Yahweh had brought the Philistines to a complete submission (note that the first plague against Egypt lasted for seven days, Exod 7:25).

Since their hosting of the ark had been a harrowing experience throughout, the Philistines were determined to get rid of it. In v. 2, the first question presupposes the second. Returning the ark is a foregone conclusion. Thus, "What shall we do with the ark of the LORD?" is not concerned with *whether* to return the ark but with "what we should send with it to its place." It is unclear whether "to its place" simply means "to Israel" or if the Philistines thought to return it to a particular cult shrine.

To reduce any chance of further offending the God of Israel, the Philistine lords consulted their religious professionals, the priests and diviners. [Divination] By careful augury, the priests determined that the ark could not be returned without some reparation offering, nor should it be carried by ordinary means. The diviners proposed that a

The Perfect Number

In biblical usage, some numbers had a special, symbolic meaning. The numbers three (and its multiples), seven, and forty seem to have had special significance. The number seven apparently represented the idea of completeness or perfection. For example, the creation of the world was said to have taken seven days, leading to the measuring of time in weeks, each of which culminates on the Sabbath, the seventh day (Gen 1:1–2:4). The Sabbath was to be a day of rest for people and animals alike. According to Lev 25:2-7, even the land was to have its own Sabbath, lying fallow every seventh year. The number also plays a significant role in various narratives. The patriarch Jacob worked seven years for his wife Rachel. When Laban deceived him by giving him Leah instead, Jacob worked an additional seven years to obtain Rachel as well (Gen 29:15-30). In the story of Joseph, the Hebrew hero interpreted Pharaoh's dream, in which seven years of plenty were followed by seven years of famine (Gen 41:1-36). Common wisdom seems to have used the number seven as a measure of completion: the sign of high-quality silver is that it was refined seven times (Ps 12:6).

The number seven has similar significance in the New Testament. When Peter asked Jesus if one should forgive seven times, Jesus instructed him to forgive seventy times seven (Matt 18:21-22). Seven deacons were appointed to serve the Jerusalem church (Acts 6:1-6), and seven churches are mentioned in Revelation 2–3.

Multiples of seven also were important and are represented in legal, narrative, and prophetic literature. The same Levitical laws that proclaimed a Sabbath year for the land declared that a "Jubilee" year should occur every forty-nine years. In the year of the Jubilee, all ancestral land that had been sold reverted to its former owner, and Jews who had sold themselves into servitude were released from their bondage (Lev 25:8-55). The Exodus traditions point to an influential assemblage of seventy elders (Exod 24:1, 9), while Jesus sent out seventy disciples on a short-term mission project (Luke 10:1-17). Both Jeremiah (25:12; 29:10) and Daniel (9:2) describe the exile as a seventy-year period. Daniel's eschatological scheme predicted a period of seventy "weeks of years" prior to the arrival of the messianic kingdom (Dan 9:24). This common use of the number seven and its multiples suggests that the number carried with it the connotation of completeness.

suitable "guilt offering" (*ʾašam*) would bring forgiveness and healing to their land, causing Yahweh to withdraw his heavy hand (v. 3).

The gifts designed to accompany the ark serve a dual role as placatory offerings and as the elements of sympathetic magic. According to the MT, five golden tumors and five golden mice were to be sent, representing the five Philistine lords and their people. [Five—Or More?] By sending the golden tumors and the golden mice with the ark, the diviners hoped that their plagues of tumors and mice would depart as well. Note the difference between v. 3, where the diviners express certainty of healing, and v. 5, which reveals more hope than confidence: "*Perhaps* he will lift his hand from you and your gods and your land" (v. 5b).

First Samuel 6:6 makes apparent what has previously remained subtle: There are significant similarities between the return of Yahweh's ark from Philistia and the return of Yahweh's people from Egypt. As the Egyptians had pressed gifts of gold and silver upon the departing Israelites (Exod 12:35-36), so the Philistines

Five—Or More?

The LXX and 4QSam^a, perhaps reflecting a variant textual tradition, omit the reference to five golden mice. Their reading may be closer to the original since 6:18 says the offering included mice to represent the unwalled villages as well as the five fortified cities. This would suggest a number much greater than five.

Divination

Certain cultic officials of most ancient Near Eastern religions were responsible for determining the will of the gods, and they developed many complicated means for divining the will of the gods. In ancient Babylon, for example, divination procedures and results were analyzed with scientific rigor and preserved on a series of clay tablets. A special class of diviners, called *barû* priests, was trained and equipped to serve as royal and cultic advisers.

Divination procedures could be based on naturally occurring events, such as the movements of the stars (astrology), the direction of storms and wind, or the observed behavior of wild animals. More commonly, omens were impetrated through ritual procedures. Like a modern fortuneteller who reads tea leaves, ancient diviners read the minds of the gods in the patterns formed by oil on water (lecanomancy) or by smoke from a censer (libanomancy). Arrows could be shaken and dropped, providing clues in the patterns formed in their fall. Or lots made of marked stones or pieces of wood could be cast.

Perhaps the most common means of augury was through the careful examination of the entrails of sacrificial animals (extispicy), with special attention given to the liver (hepatoscopy), which was thought to be the seat of life. Ritual animals were kept for the purpose. To obtain an omen, the priests would carefully pray over the appointed animal, asking the gods to give a message through the shape of the animal's liver or through the pattern of spots or blemishes found on the organ's surface. Clay models of livers, complete with instructions and diagrams, were used for reference. Many of these have been preserved.

The Deuteronomistic and prophetic strands of Israelite religion roundly condemned the actions of diviners and "soothsayers," believing that the authentic word of Yahweh came only through the prophets (Deut 18:14-15; cf. also Isa 44:25; Jer 14:14; 27:9-10; Ezek 12:24; 13:9; 22:28; Mic 3:7, 11). However, the priestly strands of tradition record how the casting of sacred lots (probably the *Urim* and the *Thummim*) was practiced in Israel, apparently with Yahweh's approval (Exod 28:30; Lev 16:8; Num 27:21; Ezra 2:63; Neh 7:65; see also 1 Sam 28:6 and [Sacred Lots]).

---

sent the ark away with offerings of gold (v. 4). As the *Destroyer* had appeared to ravage the Egyptians (*hammašḥît*; Exod 12:23), so the plague-bearing mice were *destroyers* of the land (*hammašḥîtim*; 6:5). The Egyptian Pharaoh's hardened heart had led to more numerous plagues (Exod 7:14; 8:15, 19, 32; 9:7, 12, 34-35; 10:20, 27; 11:20), but the Philistines were enjoined not to harden their hearts as did Pharaoh and the Egyptians (v. 6).

The ark and its attendant offerings were not to be borne by the Philistine couriers who had carried the ark from one Philistine city to another, but by a new cart and two previously unyoked milch cows who were to be taken from their young calves. [What Is a Milch Cow?] Evidently, the priests intended for these cows to serve a dual role. First of all, since they had not been yoked previously, they were suitable for sacred use to bear the ark on its homeward journey (cf. Num 19:2; Deut 21:3). [Travels of the Ark]

Secondly, the actions of the cows would serve as a further means of divination to determine if the plagues had in fact been caused by the presence of the ark. No one is designated to

What Is a Milch Cow?

AΩ The NRSV and several other versions use the rather archaic term "milch cow" to translate *pārôt ʿālôt*, "cows giving suck." A milch cow is one that is kept for the purpose of raising calves and giving milk, not as a beast of burden or source of meat.

Assyrian soldiers with ox-cart leading Elamite prisoners of war into exile. Alabaster bas-relief. 7th century BC. Palace of Ashurnazirpal in Niniveh, Mesopotamia. Louvre. Paris, France. (Credit: Erich Lessing/Art Resource, NY)

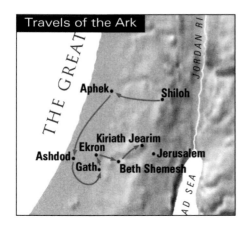

drive the cart or lead the cows; they are left on their own. As untrained animals who had been taken from their young, the new team could hardly be expected to work in unison, much less to bear the cart far into unfamiliar territory. Such a performance would be miraculous, a sign from the gods that the ark was indeed the source of the Philistines' misery, rather than chance (v. 9).

Evidently, the priests set the cart in the direction of Beth-shemesh, a disputed border town whose name ("House of the Sun") suggests the possibility of an earlier shrine to the Semitic sun-god Shemesh (or *šamaš*). [Beth-shemesh]

Having formulated their plan, the Philistines put it into motion, loading onto the cart both the ark and a box (or, as suggested by Kyle McCarter, possibly a pouch) containing the golden offerings.[1] To the Philistines' surprise and amazement, the two cows proceeded directly to Beth-shemesh in the straightest possible line. The phrase "not turning to the right or to the left" is frequently found in Deuteronomistic materials to express faithful obedience (Deut 5:32; 17:11; Josh 1:7). The reader is to understand, apparently, that Yahweh himself is driving the cart, and the untrained cows are perfectly obedient to him. The added detail that the cows were "lowing as they went" contributes a poignant note, reminding the reader that they were leaving their calves behind (vv. 10-11).

The first part of this episode closes with a subtly comical observation. To be sure that the matter was completed, the Philistine rulers followed the cart to the borders of Beth-shemesh. The picture of the great lords jogging along behind the ark—rather than entrusting the task to others—contributes to the overall depiction of Philistine humiliation. The perplexed rulers do not return until

---

Beth-shemesh

There were several pre-Israelite villages named Beth-shemesh. The town to which the ark was directed was alternately called Ir-shemesh (Josh 19:41) and Har Heres ("Mount of the Sun," Judg 1:35). The city (modern Tell er-Rumeileh) was located about 14 miles west of Jerusalem, at the southwestern end of the Valley of Sorek. The word "Sorek" refers to a choice variety of grapevines, suggesting that the area was known for its excellent vineyards. In the Samson stories, the Valley of Sorek was known as the home of Delilah (Judg 16:4).

The fertile area surrounding Beth-shemesh was often contested by the Israelites and the Philistines (2 Chr 28:18). Josh 15:10 assigned Beth-shemesh to the tribe of Judah, but other traditions denote it as a city reserved for the Levites (Josh 21:16; 1 Chr 6:59 [MT 44]). Some authors suggest that Beth-shemesh was still under some measure of Philistine control when the ark was returned, but the text clearly describes it as an Israelite city.

Burnt Offerings

AΩ The *ʿōlâ*, or "holocaust" offering, was so named because the entire animal was burned on the altar. None of the meat was given to the priest or consumed by the worshiper (Lev 1:1-17; 22:17-25), as with other offerings. Burnt offerings were often associated with petitions, public worship, votive offerings, and rites of purification (see [Sacrificial Meals]). In this case, the people of Beth-shemesh were apparently motivated in their worship by a sense of thanksgiving that the ark has returned, and perhaps by fear associated with handling such a sacred object. The cart and cows, having served such a holy purpose, could not be converted to mundane use, so they were appropriately sacrificed to God.

they are confident that the ark has passed safely beyond their borders and has been accepted by the Israelites (vv. 12, 16).

The Israelites Rejoice and Mourn, 6:13–7:1

Harvest time in ancient Israel usually occurred around May or June, the wheat having been planted in time for the seasonal rains of December through February. Because of the harvest, many people were in the fields surrounding the city. There they witnessed the incredible and unexpected sight of the great ark of the covenant, glinting in the sun, rolling through the fields on an unattended cart. The story suggests that no one took charge of the cart until it stopped by itself beside a large rock in the field of a man named Joshua (vv. 13-14a).

The narrator emphasizes the ark's homecoming by beginning the episode with the ark in the field (*śādeh*, here meaning "territory") of the Philistines and ending with the ark coming to rest in the field of Joshua, near Beth-shemesh.

Regarding the ark's return as providential, and wishing to offer thanks, the Israelites offered sacrifices to Yahweh, using wood from the cart as fuel and the two cows as burnt offerings. [Burnt Offerings] Ordinarily, burnt offerings were bulls (Lev 1:3; 22:19), but this does not seem to have troubled the people of Beth-shemesh. With their sacrifice, the two cows have served a third purpose. They have borne the ark, acted as a means of divination for the Philistines, and have been offered as a sacrifice by the Israelites.

As the five Philistine lords return to make their report (v. 16), the narrator summarizes the symbolic significance of their golden offerings, noting that the number of mice represented not only the five major cities but also their dependent villages (v. 17; contrast v. 4). This part of the episode concludes with a remark that the large stone in the field of Joshua remained "to this day" as a testimony to the truthfulness of the story (v. 18). ["To This Day"]

"To This Day"

AΩ   Narrative writers of the Old Testament were quite fond of adding "to this day" as a means of asserting the truthfulness of their words, because readers could check it out for themselves. Often, the phrase is used in the context of etiologies (see [Etiology]). Writers used this expression to remark on the persistence of a particular custom "to this day" (Gen 32:32; 47:26; Deut 10:8; Josh 9:27; 1 Sam 5:5; 2 Kgs 17:34, 41; 2 Chr 35:25) or to point out the continued existence of some physical landmark or object (Gen 35:20; Josh 4:9; 7:26; 8:28; Judg 15:19; 2 Sam 18:18; 1 Kgs 8:8; 2 Kgs 2:22; 10:27; 2 Chr 5:9). "To this day" could be used to indicate the continued presence of a particular people (Deut 2:22; Josh 13:13; 15:63; 16:10; Judg 1:21; 2 Sam 4:3; 1 Kgs 9:21; 2 Kgs 16:6; 17:23) or a special name for a locality (Deut 3:14; Josh 5:9; 2 Sam 6:8; 1 Kgs 9:13; 2 Kgs 14:7; 1 Chr 13:11; 2 Chr 20:26). "To this day," of course, means "to the day" in which the story was written—not necessarily the present.

Serious textual problems make v. 19 difficult to interpret. [A Troublesome Text] Certain persons of the Beth-shemites (probably 70) offended Yahweh and were struck down for their insolence. At issue is the nature of their offense. Was it because some of the people brashly looked inside the ark, or because a particular clan (the otherwise obscure "sons of Jeconiah") refused to celebrate, or because no official priests were present? In any case, the central issue seems to involve a lack of respect for Yahweh's sacred symbol (cf. 2 Sam 6:6-7). The deaths in Beth-shemesh serve as a reminder that even Israel cannot take the ark and the power of God for granted. The awesome holiness of the ark, representative of Yahweh's own holiness, must be respected.

The story lacks details that modern readers would like to have. How quickly did this happen? Did the 70 die a slow death from plague, like the Philistines, or were they all struck at once, as if by a lightning bolt? Patrick Miller and J.J.M. Roberts have suggested that the plague had spread from Philistia, afflicting the people of Beth-shemesh and necessitating an explanation.[2] The narrator does not hesitate to attribute the deaths to the ark, and portrays the people of Beth-shemesh asking themselves, "Who is able to stand before Yahweh, this holy God?" (v. 20). The question may have had cultic significance since the expression "stand before" could be used to describe one who assumed the priestly responsibility of attending the ark (Deut 10:8; Judg 20:27-28). [Attending the Ark]

A Troublesome Text

📖   The MT reads, "But he smote [some of] the men of Beth-shemesh, because they looked into the ark of Yahweh, and he smote among the people 70 men, 50,000 men." The number 50,000 clearly represents some sort of textual corruption, as it would have represented far more than the population of Beth-shemesh. The NRSV, like most translations, follows the LXX: "The descendants of Jeconiah did not rejoice with the people of Beth-shemesh when they greeted the ark of the LORD, and he killed seventy men of them."

Kyle McCarter calls upon an argument offered by Josephus (*Ant.* 6.16), whose text apparently did not mention Levites. Josephus explained God's anger with the argument that none of the people of Beth-shemesh were priests. McCarter supposes that "sons of Jeconiah" (retroverted from the Greek as *bny yknyhw*) may be a corruption for an original *bny hkhnym*, "sons of the priests." Thus, he suggests, Yahweh would have been angry because the people presumed to offer sacrifices with no priests present. A similar issue erupts in 1 Sam 13:8-15, where Saul is punished for offering a sacrifice without waiting for the priest Samuel to arrive.

P. Kyle McCarter, *I Samuel* (AB 8; Garden City: Doubleday 1980), 131.

Assuming they were not qualified (or brave enough) to attend to the ark, the people of Beth-shemesh then asked a further question that sounds surprising in the mouths of Israelites: "To whom shall he go up from among us?" The NRSV adds an interpretive flair that is not in the text: "so that we may be rid of him?" The ark of Yahweh was such an inherently dangerous object that even Yahweh's people feared it. So the people of Beth-shemesh invited the people of Kiriath-jearim to take custody of the holy relic.

> **Attending the Ark**
>
> At times, special priests were given charge of the ark. For example, when the Israelites sought counsel concerning a battle with their kinsmen the Benjaminites, they came to Bethel, where the ark was, "and the Israelites inquired of the LORD (for the ark of the covenant of God was there in those days, and Phinehas son of Eleazar, son of Aaron, ministered before it in those days)" (Judg 20:27-28).

Kiriath-jearim means "City of Forests," though it seems to have been called Kiriath Ba`al before the Israelites took it over (Josh 15:60; 18:14). The city (modern Tell el-Azhar) was about nine miles northwest of Beth-shemesh, located on a high hill near the traditional boundaries of Judah, Benjamin, and Dan. The old name "City of Baal" suggests the presence of a pre-Israelite sanctuary, which may have been appropriated and used for the worship of Yahweh. Whether this is to be identified as the "house of Abinadab on the hill" (7:1) is unclear.

Abinidab is listed as father of the priests Ahio and Uzzah (2 Sam 6:3-4; 1 Chr 13:7-11), as well as Eleazar, who here is consecrated for the special service of attending the ark. No other outbreaks are reported, implying that Yahweh was now satisfied that the ark was being treated with appropriate respect. The ark had proven so troublesome, however, that Israel was satisfied to leave it alone for some time. The following verse (7:2) notes that the ark remained in Kiriath-jearim for 20 years.

CONNECTIONS

Bribing God, 6:1-8

The chapter begins as the Philistines confront a difficult question: How do you get rid of God? The hand of Yahweh had wrought havoc in their cities from the moment they had brought the ark into Ashdod. Yahweh had afflicted them with painful tumors, most likely in the nether regions. Like a spectral pied-piper, God had whistled up a plague of crop-eating, disease-spreading, heart-stopping rodents.

The Philistine lords tried to pass the ark about from place to place, with the only result being that the misery spread. After seven months of undignified distress, all pride was gone, and the only thing that mattered was finding a way to get the hand of Yahweh out of their country.

Trusting in their sacred shamans, the Philistines decided to pay God off through the practice of sympathetic magic, a primitive idea that "like heals like." To seek healing from their tumors, they had five tumors made of precious gold, one for each of the Philistine lords and the people the lord represented. To gain relief from the pestilential rodents, they crafted enough golden mice to represent not only the five major cities, but even the smaller villages that surrounded them (6:18). With this payment and the voluntary return of the ark, they hoped to curry God's favor, but for no other purpose than that he should leave them alone.

The desire to manipulate God's favor through symbolic actions is as old as Adam and as fresh as today. Even if the Philistines did find relief after sending the ark away (the story really does not say), this implies no divine approval of their actions. The Philistines chose to honor Yahweh, but only in a most legalistic, not-more-than-necessary way.

The Philistines ostensibly acknowledged the power of God, yet their greatest desire was not to worship Yahweh, but to be rid of him. Many persons of our own day give lip-service to God and engage in symbolic rituals of the faith; yet, their greatest desire is not to serve the Lord, but to placate him just enough to avert divine anger. Like the Philistines, what they really want is for God to leave them alone.

Testing God, 6:9-12

Even as they sought to soothe the LORD's anger, the Philistines were putting him to the test. One can hardly imagine that two untrained cows, snatched away from their nursing calves and harnessed to a yoke, would obediently and without direction march directly away from their stalls. If such an event should take place, the Philistines reasoned, they could presume that the God of Israel was indeed responsible for their woeful state.

As it happened, the unlikely pair pulled the ark straight into Israelite territory and stopped beside a great stone that would serve as the altar for their ultimate sacrifice. All observers agreed that Yahweh's miraculous power was indeed at work. Even so, the reader must be aware that God acted out of his own freedom, not because he was bound to prove himself to the Philistines. In chapter 4, the Israelites had fully expected Yahweh to bring them victory by bringing the ark into their military camp as a battle palladium. There was good reason, based on Israel's history, to believe that God would not allow his holy ark to be captured or his people to fall. Yet they were surprised. God is always free to act (or not to act) according to divine sovereignty. He is not bound to meet our tests or even answer our prayers in the way we desire.

Still, the story suggests that God does choose—at times—to reveal his power in unmistakable ways. Gideon, in seeking confirmation of God's will, sought an equally improbable sign (Judg 6:36-40) and found divine affirmation. Elijah, desiring to prove the supremacy of Yahweh over Baal, set up a water-drenched altar that a blowtorch would not ignite. But when he called for fire from heaven, Yahweh incinerated the offering and vaporized the water (1 Kgs 18:20-40).

In Jesus Christ, God has revealed himself in an unrivaled way. There is no greater proof of God's concern than the incarnation, no greater proof of his love than the crucifixion, no greater proof of his power than the resurrection of Jesus from the dead. The Christian church owes its existence to the early testimony of God's self-revelation and to the continuing presence of the Spirit in the lives of believers.

The question for persons today is not whether we should test God, but whether we will fare well when God tests us.

Honoring God, 6:13-18

The people of Beth-shemesh appear to have greeted the ark's return with spontaneous acts of celebration and worship (vv. 14-15). The picture presented suggests that all of the people were involved in the worship: chopping the wood, starting the fire, butchering the cows, singing the hymns, answering the questions of children.

This is as it should be. The truest worship comes from the heart, an instinctive outpouring of gratitude to God. Worship happens when the people of God adore the person of God in thought and song and prayer.

Rejecting God, 6:19–7:1

The celebration at Beth-shemesh came to a premature end when some of the people incited God's anger, resulting in the death of at least 70 persons. This troublesome text inspires more questions than answers, and we would be wise to acknowledge its problematic nature and not expect to understand it fully.

Why should God kill 70 of his own people? It is impossible to be dogmatic when dealing with such a difficult text. The narrator seems to imply that it was Yahweh's way of reminding the Israelites that he could not be taken for granted. The power of God is no respecter of persons, and the danger of trifling with holy things applies to the chosen as well as the heathen.

The episode closes as the people of Beth-shemesh confront precisely the same problem the Philistines faced in the beginning of the chapter: how to get rid of a troublesome god. The Hebrews chose the same strategy that twice failed the Philistines and decided to pass the ark along to someone else. The people of Kiriath-jearim had to "come down" to get the ark and "take it up" to its new home because their city was on a hill, considerably higher in elevation than Beth-shemesh. By some unnamed means they transported the ark to the house of Abinadab (possibly a temple; cf. Judg 17:12; 18:2) and consecrated his son Eleazar for the special service of caring for the ark.

In our own day it is discouraging to observe believers who "send the ark away" when times of trial arrive, distancing themselves from God. A marriage dissolves. A child dies. A job evaporates. Believers grow angry. They ask, "Why did God let this happen?" They wonder, "What good is a god who lets his people suffer?" Worship may cease. Prayer becomes a memory. The God who did not meet their expectations is pushed away.

There is nothing comfortable about a god who exercises such raw power and such freedom. Perhaps the narrator wants us to understand that it is not God's job to make us comfortable, but to make us better. The people of God can become better servants of God only when they acknowledge the supremacy of God. The importance of that lesson is not diminished by its painfulness.

NOTES

[1] P. Kyle McCarter, *I Samuel* (AB 8; Garden City: Doubleday, 1980), 135.

[2] Patrick Miller and J. J .M. Roberts, *The Hand of the Lord: A Reassessment of the "Ark Narrative" of 1 Samuel* (JHNES; Baltimore: Johns Hopkins, 1977), 74.

ISRAEL REPENTS AND
THE PHILISTINES FALL

7:2-17

COMMENTARY

This unit of text stands alone and is significant for several reasons. The ark narrative ends with 7:1, and the account of Israel's transition to a monarchy begins with 8:1. Thus, the pericope serves as a transition piece, but its primary purpose is to cast Samuel in the mold of Israel's premonarchic judges. [Israel's Judges] The text portrays Samuel as exceedingly competent in priestly, governmental, and military roles. As such, it supports the later vein of thought that Israel's demand for a king was unnecessary.

The section appears to contain older, traditional materials (vv. 5-12, 15-17) that have been spliced together by Deuteronomistic editorializing (vv. 2-4, 13-14). We recognize the Deuteronomist's hand in the explicit theme of repentance leading to deliverance, in the use of typical expressions such as "return to Yahweh" and "with your whole heart" (v. 3), and in vocabulary choices such as "Amorites" in v. 14.

Israel's Judges

Israel's most notable leaders during the period between the settlement of Canaan and the institution of the monarchy were called "judges," and the accounts portraying their activities follow a fixed pattern in the Deuteronomistic History. The general pattern is described in Judg 2:11-23, and specific examples include the accounts of Othniel (Judg 3:7-11), Ehud (Judg 3:12-30), and Deborah (Judg 4:1-23), among others. With few exceptions, the "judges cycles" contain the following elements:

1. Israel sins against the LORD (usually by worshiping other gods).
2. God punishes Israel by allowing its enemies to defeat and oppress the people.
3. Israel repents and cries out to God for help.
4. God raises up a man or woman to lead Israel to victory over its enemies.
5. The deliverer "judges" Israel for a specified period of time, during which the land experiences "rest" from its oppressors.

The structure of 1 Sam 7:2-17 appears to be designed to fit this pattern and, thus, to depict Samuel as the last legitimate judge of Israel.

Mourning after Yahweh

AΩ The phrase "mourning after Yahweh" is unusual (the verb form appears only here), and scholars have conjectured various explanations. Following LXX[B], for example, Kyle McCarter assumes that *wayyinnāhû* is a textual corruption of *wayyippēnû* and translates "Israel turned after Yahweh." This fits well with 7:3, in which Samuel's words seems to presume a previous expression of repentance.

The meaning of *wayyinnāhû*, however, can be established with some certainty from cognates (cf. Ezek 32:18), and "lamenting" fits the context well. Though the ark had returned to Israel, people had died because of it (6:19). God's favor was no longer assured, and the Philistines were a constant threat.

P. Kyle McCarter, *I Samuel* (AB 8; Garden City: Doubleday, 1980), 141.

Many scholars question the historical accuracy of Israel's dominance over the Philistines during this period, but the astute reader will be interested in the *theological* claims as well as the historical ones. The text invites reflection on Yahweh's ability to protect and guide Israel *without* a royal intermediary, thus leading the reader to understand Samuel's dismay in the following account when the people demand a king.

Samuel Calls Israel to Repent at Mizpah, 7:2-6

The return of the ark to Israel had led to both rejoicing (6:13-16) and sorrow (6:19-20), resulting in the ark's being "quarantined" at Kiriath-jearim (6:21–7:1). The transitional note of v. 2—that the ark remained at Kiriath-jearim for twenty years—does not fit well with the chronological sequence adopted by the Deuteronomists, but the point is that a certain amount of time had passed; time for Israel to fall sway to other gods, time for young Samuel to grow in power and stature within his sphere of influence. We are given no details about this period. Although the Philistines had returned the ark, their oppression of Israel evidently had not ceased. Accounts of the earlier "judges" typically began with a period of sin and oppression. Since the authors are portraying Samuel as a judge, they appropriately include a twenty-year period of Philistine domination, which leads Israel to "lament after the LORD." [Mourning after Yahweh]

Samuel's address in v. 3 presumes that Israel has come to him for assistance in "returning to Yahweh" with a view toward obtaining deliverance from Philistine oppression. Samuel's response betrays some measure of doubt in regard to Israel's sincerity or stability. He lists

"The Whole Heart"

AΩ The Deuteronomists frequently used the phrase "with the whole heart" in the technical sense of complete commitment. (For other examples, see 1 Sam 12:20, 24; 1 Kgs 8:23; 14:8; 2 Kgs 10:31.) In Hebrew thought, the heart was not only the seat of the emotions (Deut 28:47; Isa 65:14; Jer 49:16), but also of the intellect (Prov 19:8; Isa 65:17) and of the will (Josh 22:5; Jer 23:20). In this sense, the heart represents one's inner being where one makes choices and is confronted by God. Pleasing God results from the devotion of one's "whole heart" to following God's way.

Astarte

Astarte was an astral deity whose roots were in Babylonia, where she was worshiped as Ishtar, the "Queen of Heaven," the goddess of love, war, and fertility. Ishtar's popularity extended to the Levant, where her name is spelled in various ways according to language; the later Greek vocalization approximated "Astarte." Astarte is often confused and sometimes identified with Asherah, who sometimes appears to be a different goddess of the same period and sometimes appears to be identical. The Old Testament asserts that these fertility goddesses were enamored of the Israelites, who often worshiped them outright or incorporated Canaanite practices into their worship of Yahweh.

In the Old Testament, Astarte is sometimes called "Ashtoreth," an intentionally insulting name formed by incorporating the vowels of the word *bōšet*, meaning "shame." Late Bronze Age statuettes of fertility goddesses have been found in Palestine, but the Old Testament suggests that they also were depicted by sacred groves or by carved wooden poles, which could be placed near an altar (Judg 6:25-26; 1 Kgs 15:13).

---

several conditions for a true return to God: repentance "with the whole heart" ["The Whole Heart"], removal of all foreign gods and Astartes [Astarte], and a commitment to serving Yahweh alone. Only then, he insisted, could they expect Yahweh to respond to their cries for help. This conditional language is very characteristic of the Deuteronomist.

In v. 4, the "foreign gods" are identified as Baals. [Baal] Baal was the god of weather and hence was responsible for the land's fertility. He was the chief god of the Canaanite and Phoenician pantheons. Asherah (sometimes identified as Astarte) was his astral consort, and together they were worshiped by means of feasts, offerings, and cultic prostitution. It was common for individuals to keep small images of Baal and Astarte in their homes as tokens of their trust that Baal and Astarte would enhance the fertility of individuals, as well as of the land. According to the text, many Israelites had joined their Canaanite neighbors in worshiping the fertility gods, but they demonstrated their contrition by removing all their images of Baal and Astarte and worshiping Yahweh alone.

Satisfied with Israel's show of penitence, Samuel called the people to gather at Mizpah [Mizpah] for a ceremony of prayer, fasting, and ritual repentance. First Samuel 7:6 describes an enigmatic water ritual that involved drawing water and pouring it out before the LORD. This ritual has no exact parallel in the Hebrew Bible. Elijah's water-pouring rite (1 Kgs 18) is sometimes mentioned, but it had a different purpose. David poured out water before the LORD after his heroes had risked their lives in obtaining it (2 Sam 23:13-17), but this also reflects a radically different context. Postbiblical sources describe the ritual drawing and pouring of water during the Feast of Booths,[1] but that later practice offers little insight.

Baal

In Cannan, Baal was worshiped as the weather god, who controlled the storms. This depiction of Baal from ancient Ugarit probably held a lightning bolt in his upraised hand.

God Baal of the Thunderstorm. 2nd–1st mill. BC. Gilded bronze idol with Egyptian crown. Louvre, Paris, France. (Credit: Erich Lessing/Art Resource, NY)

Even though we have no parallels, we may presume that the ritual was intended to demonstrate Israel's repentance in a symbolic way. Perhaps the pouring out of water was to indicate the nation's whole-hearted devotion to Yahweh, poured out in his service. Alternatively, the water could have symbolized Israel's former sin, now poured out completely as the Baals and Astartes were put away. The pouring of clean water may have symbolized cleansing. In any case, the ritual was accompanied by a statement that explains its significance: "We have sinned against the LORD" (v. 6a).

The closing observation that "Samuel judged the people of Israel at Mizpah" is apparently a Deuteronomistic addition, intended to associate Samuel with the earlier judges of Israel. In the book of Judges, God's chosen deliverer usually is not identified until after the people repent. Samuel's case is different since he is already on the scene. The editors, however, do not want their readers to lack appreciation of Samuel's place in history as a judge of Israel like those who preceded him.

Mizpah

The location of Mizpah (which means "outlook") is uncertain. The two most likely candidates are found on suitably high outcroppings for an outlook: Tell en-Nasbeh is eight miles north of Jerusalem, while Nebi Samwil (whose name derives from a tradition that it is Samuel's burial place) is five miles northwest of the city. Mizpah was the site of at least one previous cultic gathering (Judg 20:1, 3; 21:1, 5, 8), and 1 Macc 3:47 identifies it as an old place of prayer for Israel.

Renascent Israel Routs the Philistines, 7:7-14

Israel's repentance is followed immediately by the threat of war. The narrator leads us to assume that Philistine spies had reported the gathering of Israel at Mizpah, prompting the Philistine leaders to attack (v. 7). Did they think that Israel had gathered for cultic rituals leading to holy war? [Holy War] An earlier gathering at Mizpah (Judg 20–21) was indeed for the purpose of preparing for inter-tribal warfare against Benjamin. The Philistines might have presumed that war was in the offing and decided to make a peremptory attack. The Philistines would have had to regard any united activity of Israel as potentially dangerous and deserving of

Holy War

The term "holy war" does not appear in the Old Testament but is used to describe certain battles in which Yahweh was thought to play the central role. God himself was thought to have ordained these sacred battles (Num 31:3; Josh 6:2; 8:1; Judg 7:7) although Israel could also initiate plans for holy war and seek God's approval (Num 21:1-3). To participate in the sacred battle, Israel's warriors were required to be ritually clean (Num 31:19-24; 1 Sam 21:4; 2 Sam 11:11). In a holy war, Yahweh was thought to do the real fighting, delivering a defeated enemy into the hands of Israel (Judg 3:28; 7:15; 1 Sam 7:8). There were strict rules governing the spoils captured in a holy war: All plunder was to be utterly destroyed as an offering to God, in recognition of his aid (Num 21:2; Deut 7:2; 13:15). To gain personal profit from a holy war was considered to be a serious sin, placing Yahweh's future aid in jeopardy (see the story of Achan at Ai, Josh 7–8).

action. In addition, the ritual gathering offered the Philistines a propitious opportunity for a surprise attack while a large number of Israelites was gathered in one place, rather than scattered in their isolated villages.

The reader may presume that Israel's leaders had been expecting a Philistine offensive, and this fear may in fact have prompted the ceremonial return to Yahweh. Samuel had promised deliverance from the Philistines if the people would put away their foreign gods and devote their hearts to Yahweh (7:3). The cry of the people in v. 8, then, is both plea and demand, as they instruct Samuel: "Do not cease to cry out to the LORD our God for us, and pray that he may save us from the hand of the Philistines." "Do not cease to cry out" renders a Hebrew idiom that is difficult to translate. Literally, it means "Do not keep silence (or "be deaf") from us, from crying out to the LORD our God."

Samuel accompanied his sacrifice of a suckling lamb with a cry to the LORD, and "the LORD answered him," apparently with thunder. [Why Sacrifice a Suckling?] To see the connection, the reader must recognize v. 10a as a parenthetical expression within the main flow of the narrative. Yahweh answered Samuel (the Philistines were just about to attack as Samuel burned the offering), and "Yahweh thundered with a mighty voice that day against the Philistines and threw them into confusion" so that they were completely routed before Israel. [Yahweh's Mighty Voice] The verb for "throw into confusion" (*way-hummēm*) is commonly used in holy war contexts (Exod 14:24; 23:27; Josh 10:10; Judg 4:15). Yahweh is always the subject, throwing the enemy into such a state of chaos that the Israelites can easily subdue them.

The movement of the story in 7:2-11 is clear: Israel repents, Samuel cries out to God on Israel's behalf, and Yahweh leads Israel to victory over the enemy. The narration emphasizes that it was Yahweh who fought Israel's war and defeated the enemy (v. 10),

Why Sacrifice a Suckling?

Why Samuel chose to offer a suckling lamb instead of an older animal is unclear. Lev 22:27 requires only that animal sacrifices be at least seven days old, implying that very young animals were acceptable as offerings. The description of the lamb as a "complete whole offering" is as redundant in Hebrew as it is in English. The word ʿôlâ alone describes a holocaust offering, in which the entire animal was burned on the altar, with none of the meat being shared by either priests or people. The addition of the word "complete" (*kālîl*) is apparently for emphasis (see Ps 51:19, where the two terms also appear together).

There is no evidence that the battle at Mizpah was considered to be a holy war, although the text does insist that Yahweh fought the battle in Israel's behalf.

Yahweh's Mighty Voice

In the Old Testament, Yahweh's intervention in human affairs is often mediated by natural elements, especially storms. The tradition that Yahweh spoke in thunder is found throughout the time period covered by the Old Testament: in the ancient hymns (1 Sam 2:10; 2 Sam 22:14 = Ps 18:13; Pss 29; 81:7) and in literature from the exile and onward (Isa 29:6; Job 37:4-5; 40:9). Yahweh was also described as employing lightning (2 Sam 22:15; 1 Kgs 18:38), hail (Josh 10:14), and darkness (Josh 24:7) as weapons against his enemies.

while the Israelite troops participated only in mopping-up operations, pursuing the Philistines back toward their own territory (v. 11). The location of Beth-car is unknown, though we may presume it would have been a few miles to the west of Mizpah, in the direction of the Philistine homeland.

First Samuel 7:12 serves as an etiology (see [Etiology]) to remind modern readers that the place they knew as Ebenezer owed its name to Yahweh's beneficence. Samuel memorialized the victory by raising a standing stone, a common practice in the ancient world (Gen 28:18, 22; Josh 24:26-27; cf. Josh 4:1-9). The Deuteronomistic author, however, is careful to call it a "stone" (*'eben*) rather than a "pillar" (*maṣṣēbâ*) because pillars were often associated with Caananite worship practices. The Deuteronomists strongly opposed such practices, and polemicized against them (Deut 16:22).

The pillar is named "Ebenezer," from the words for "stone" (*'eben*) and "help" (*'ēzer*), thus, "stone of help." Samuel's explanation is a bit ambiguous since "to this point" could have a chronological or geographical meaning; whether he meant "up to now" or "as far as this" is not clear.

The location of the stone-raising ceremony is also uncertain and probably different from the Ebenezer mentioned in 4:1. However, the author clearly intended for his readers to remember the earlier battle of Aphek-Ebenezer. In the first battle, the Israelites were attacked at Ebenezer and routed before the Philistines, despite the presence of the ark, because Israel's sin had prompted Yahweh to absent himself from the battle. In the second battle, Israel comes fresh from a service of national repentance when the Philistines attack again. This time, God is present in the battle, routing the Philistines as far as Ebenezer.

By structuring the account of the battle in this way, the author accomplishes two things. First, he reminds his readers of the central Deuteronomistic theme—that divine favor is conditioned by human obedience. Secondly, he prefaces the account of Israel's demand for a king with a story that maximizes the role of God (and his prophetic spokesperson) in guiding the country. In the author's mind, the battle of Mizpah proved that national security was not dependent on the establishment of a monarchy. [History and Theology]

History and Theology

The author's clear purpose is to pen an interpretation of the battle's consequences in terms that are more theological than historical. He wants his readers to understand that Yahweh's theocratic rule is sufficient to meet Israel's needs. This is seen most clearly in 7:13-14, which summarizes the battle results in exaggerated fashion. Expressions such as "the Philistines were humbled before Israel" and "the hand of the LORD was against them" were common stock in the Deuteronomistic lexicon (cf. Judg 3:30; 8:28; 11:33; 1 Kgs 21:29; 2 Kgs 22:19 for the verb "humbled," and Deut 2:15; Judg 2:15; 1 Sam 12:15 for "the hand of the LORD"). The narrator claims that the Philistines were no longer a threat during Samuel's lifetime (7:13), that the Philistines were pushed back within the borders of their coastal pentapolis (7:14a), and that Israel lived in peace with the Amorites (7:14b). "Amorites" is the Deuteronomists' preferred ethnic term for the indigenous populations of Palestine, many of whom remained after the Israelite "conquest."

Other Scriptures, however, call into question the accuracy of these assertions. It was precisely the continued Philistine threat that led to Israel's cry for a king to lead them like the other nations. When Saul became king (during Samuel's lifetime), he enjoyed only mixed success in battling the Philistines, who were not truly "subdued" until well into David's reign. These historical discrepancies are less troubling when one remembers that the author's primary purpose was theological truth, not historical accuracy.

Samuel's Circuit: The Final Judge, 7:15-17

The section closes with a bit of ancient tradition that identifies Samuel as a judge (v. 15) and describes his activities. Samuel did not remain in Shiloh as Eli had done, perhaps because the Philistines destroyed the city following the battle of Aphek-Ebenezer. Samuel "judged" Israel by traveling a circuit encompassing Bethel, Gilgal, and Mizpah (v. 16) but made his home—and established an altar—in his home-town of Ramah (v. 17).

A quick look at the map of pre-monarchic Israel reveals that Samuel's circuit encompassed only a very small part of Israel's holdings. [Samuel's Circuit] Bethel was about ten miles north of Jerusalem; Mizpah was either five or eight miles north of the city; and Gilgal was probably near Jericho, about fifteen miles northwest of Jerusalem. Ramah was just a few miles south of Mizpah. Samuel's sphere of influence, then, probably did not reach to every geographical part of Israel, but as far as the author is concerned, Samuel's circuit encompassed the heart of Israel. Samuel's activities as a judge would have included some civil or administrative responsibilities, perhaps in deciding difficult cases or in teaching the law to local citizens.

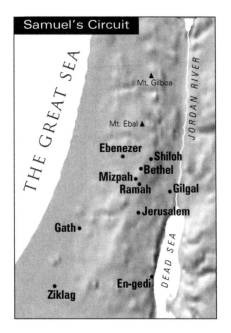

Samuel's Circuit

Samuel judged Israel "for the rest of his days," but he would soon become more than a priest, prophet, and judge; he would become a king-maker and king-breaker. Thus, the narrator transitions us to chapter 8 with a reminder that Samuel's home was in Ramah, for it was there that the elders of Israel first approached him with the request for a king.

For all of its strategic importance within the literary structure of 1 Samuel, this unit also has great homiletical value. [Ideas for Preaching and Teaching] The themes of repentance, trust, and remembering are just as relevant to our own struggling relationships with God as they were in Israel's experience.

Ideas for Preaching and Teaching

One could easily develop a single sermon or devotion from this text, or a series of three separate studies. Here is a suggested outline for a study or sermon on "A Right Relationship with God":

I. The Role of Repentance (7:2-6)
   Real repentance involves:
   A. Sorrow for sin (v. 2)
   B. Turning away from false gods (v. 3)
   C. Whole-hearted devotion to God (v. 3)
   D. Accepting accountability through public commitment (vv. 4-6)

II. The Role of Trust (7:7-11)
   A. In this world we have trouble (v. 7)
   B. We can cry out to God for help (v. 8)
   C. We can trust God to hear our prayers (vv. 9-11)

III. The Role of Remembering (7:12-17)
   A. The importance of symbols (v. 12)
   B. The importance of remembering God's blessings (vv. 13-14)
   C. The importance of remembering where home is (vv. 15-17)

CONNECTIONS

The Role of Repentance, 7:2-6

Like similar stories in the book of Judges, this story reflects a persistent pattern of sin, oppression, repentance, and deliverance for the Israelites. We wonder why Israel never learned that it would be best for them to remain in close fellowship with God, rather than riding the rollercoaster of apostasy and renewal. We wonder why we do not do any better. As a boy once asked, "How can we repent and stay repented?"

Repentance begins with true contrition. Israel "lamented after the LORD" because they recognized their failures and their need for divine assistance. Many persons are not motivated to repent until they are already mourning for some other reason. Perhaps their lifestyle has led to the loss of a job, or a significant relationship, or the respect of a loved one. The important thing, where repentance is concerned, is that our contrition be motivated not only by our troubles (as the Philistines troubled Israel), but by a genuine awareness of personal failure.

Repentance involves change, for remorse is empty without some modification of sinful behavior. Our internal desires and our surrounding culture lead us to extremes of materialism and hedonism that are nothing more than idolatry.

If we repent, we must do away with our idols. Some behaviors must be put away entirely: adultery, abuse, and mind-altering substances are representative of an entire catalog of behaviors that disrupt our relationships with God and others. Other things, such as wealth and recreation, do not need to be forsworn as much as put in their proper place.

Contrition and change lead to an about-face in our relationship with God. The Hebrew word for "repent" (*šûb*) literally means "to turn around." Repentance is not simply a turning *away* from sinful behaviors, but a turning *toward* God. Samuel reminded the Israelites that true repentance must be with the *whole heart*, and he instructed them to *direct their hearts* to the LORD, to serve God only. Ancient Hebrews regarded the heart as the center of volition as well as feeling, and repentance is not only an emotional experience, but an intentional choice.

Samuel understood the importance of public ceremony as a means of internalizing the reality of repentance. He led Israel to gather in worship, to pray, to fast, and to pour out water as an outward symbol of their inward change. In Christian worship, baptism is a particularly appropriate symbol for repentance and renewal. As Paul interprets it (Rom 6:1-4), baptism represents death to the old self and resurrection to a new life in fellowship with God. Every public service of baptism provides an opportunity for believers to relive vicariously their own experience and renew their own commitments. Other services of public worship offer participants an opportunity for intentional repentance and renewal in a setting that encourages accountability. Regular involvement in such worship enhances the probability that we will continue to serve God whole-heartedly, rather than falling back into the sway of our culture's many false gods.

The Role of Trust, 7:7-11

Those who worship God with their hearts can trust him with their lives. The people of Israel put away their false gods and participated in a public ceremony of repentance and covenant renewal. When their faith was tested immediately by an attacking army of Philistines (v. 7), the people turned to Yahweh for help, calling on Samuel to pray on their behalf (v. 8). The narrator tells us that Samuel offered a sacrifice and cried out to God and that *God answered him* (v. 9) in the form of thunder, which comforted Israel but threw the Philistines into a fearful state of confusion, allowing the Israelite troops to rout the invading soldiers (vv. 10-11).

The problem with this story is that it is too simple, too easy. It gives the impression that God always answers with immediate victory. Our personal experience, like other experiences of Israel, often stands in tension with this story. There are times when faithful Christians pray for healing or deliverance that does not come. There are times when God seems utterly, inexplicably silent.

This is not the text to teach us about theodicy. It is enough to recognize that the Deuteronomists' black-and-white picture of "repentance and trust = deliverance" is given added color by other biblical witnesses, such as Job, the author of Ecclesiastes, even Jesus and Paul. Responsible interpretation considers the larger picture, and the larger picture teaches us that suffering is a part of life. God is present with us even in the midst of our suffering and can work with us to bring positive growth even from trials and troubles (Rom 8:28). Even when God does not answer with thunder, we can still hold to the author's central belief: Those who serve God with their hearts can trust him with their lives.

The Role of Remembering, 7:12-17

The closing verses of this text emphasize the importance of memory and encourage the use of aids to remembering. To encourage Israel's continual recall of their divine deliverance at the battle of Mizpah, Samuel erected a stone and named it Ebenezer: "Stone of Help." ["My Ebenezer"?] Like Joshua, who erected a cairn of twelve stones to commemorate God's help when Israel crossed the Jordan upon entering the promised land (Josh 4:1-9), Samuel hoped that the story of the stone would be passed on for generations as a public reminder of God's deliverance.

Such "remembering aids" are still important: a worn Bible that recalls childlike faith, a rounded stone from a stream near a

"My Ebenezer"?

The imagery of this story has made its way into a very familiar hymn that worshipers often fail to appreciate. "Come Thou Fount of Every Blessing" was written by Robert Robinson in 1758. The second verse combines the Old Testament imagery of Samuel's "Ebenezer" with the New Testament deliverance of Christ. As Samuel declared that Yahweh had delivered Israel, so the songwriter sees Jesus as the "stone of help" that brings salvation to Christians.

Here I raise my Ebenezer, hither by thy help I'm come;
And I hope by thy good pleasure, safely to arrive at home:
Jesus sought me when a stranger, wand'ring from the fold of God;
He to rescue me from danger, interposed his precious blood.

---

waterfall where God's closeness was felt, a cross or a woven bracelet designed to recall God's presence.

Verses 15-17 reinforce the importance of remembering in another way. These verses describe Samuel's judicial activity, traveling a circuit between the main cities in the heart of the Holy Land. But the section closes with a reminder that "he would come back to Ramah, for his home was there" (v. 17a). Samuel never forgot that his roots were in Ramah, in the simple piety he had learned from his mother Hannah and his father Elkanah. When the Shiloh sanctuary was abandoned (perhaps destroyed by the Philistines after the loss of the ark), Samuel built an altar as a place of worship in Ramah. When he was not traveling his judicial/administrative circuit, that is where he could be found.

Samuel's return to his physical home symbolizes the importance of having a spiritual home, a place to which we can return on a regular basis for worship, rest, and fellowship with those we love. Many aspects of life clamor for our attention and lead to spiritual distraction. Returning to our spiritual home helps us to re-center our values and commitments. One characteristic of today's baby "boomers" as well as "busters" is a lack of loyalty to institutions, a preference for going it alone rather than being a "joiner." One of the great challenges of today's church is to exhibit such relevance that persons of all ages will realize the vital importance of discovering a spiritual home and returning to it on a regular basis.

NOTE

[1]*Tosefta Sukkah* 3.3; *Sukkah* 5.1-4; 50a; cited by P. Kyle McCarter, *I Samuel* (AB 8; Garden City: Doubleday, 1980), 144.

THE PEOPLE'S REQUEST
AND SAMUEL'S WARNING

8:1-22

The Question of Kingship, 8:1–12:25

Should Israel have a king like other nations, or is there a better way? This is the question underlying 1 Samuel 8–12. [Outline of 8:1–12:25: The Question of Kingship] Answering the question is a complicated affair because the section contains material from at least two different strands of tradition—with completely *different* ideas about kingship! We have already pointed out that chapter 7, which we attributed largely to the Deuteronomist, prepares the reader for the coming question of kingship by demonstrating (to the author's satisfaction) that Yahweh and his prophetic spokesperson together were quite capable of providing all the executive leadership Israel needed.

The elders of Israel, however, wanted more. For reasons that will be discussed below, they demanded a king "like other nations." Samuel's response may strike the reader as inconsistent; at different times he appears both to oppose and to favor a king. Many scholars attribute Samuel's shifting sentiments to the presence of two underlying literary traditions: an older source that favors kingship, and a later contribution that opposes it. The story of Saul's rise to power is favorably related in 9:1–11:15, but even the overlying positive view of kingship cannot disguise variant traditions beneath.

Saul is declared king at least three times in 9:1–11:15, each instance related as if it were the first. In 9:1–10:16, Samuel discovers Saul and privately anoints him as king. In 10:17-27a, Samuel calls for an assembly of Israel, selects Saul by lot, and publicly proclaims

> **Outline of 8:1–12:25: The Question of Kingship**
> I. The People's Request and Samuel's Warning (8:1-22)
>   A. Samuel's sons desire wisdom (v. 1-3)
>   B. Israel's elders want a king (vv. 4-6a)
>   C. Samuel sounds a warning (vv. 6b-18)
>   D. A king like other nations (vv. 19-22)
> II. Saul's Search and a Secret Anointing (9:1–10:16)
>   A. Saul in search of his father's donkeys (9:1-4)
>   B. Saul in search of a seer (9:5-14)
>   C. Samuel's unexpected reception (9:15-24)
>   D. A secret anointing and special signs (9:25–10:8)
>   E. Saul becomes a new man (10:9-16)
> III. A Public Proclamation and Immediate Danger (10:17-27)
>   A. At Mizpah, Samuel proclaims Saul king (vv. 17-26)
>   B. Internal unrest and the Ammonite threat (v. 27)
> IV. Saul's First Victory and the Kingship Confirmed (11:1-15)
>   A. Farmer Saul becomes a warrior and leader (vv. 1-11)
>   B. At Gilgal, Saul's kingship reconfirmed (vv. 12-15)
> V. Samuel's Parting Soliloquy (12:1-25)

him to be the chosen king. Finally, in 10:27b–11:15, Saul is plowing in the fields when he hears of an impending threat from Nahash the Ammonite. He leaves the field to lead Israel to victory, and the people declare him king by popular acclaim. The divergent stories may owe their origin to variant traditions preserved at different sanctuary sites or in other venues.

There are strong hints of displeasure with the concept of kingship even within 9:1–11:15. Before choosing Saul by lot, for example, Samuel insists that Israel's call for a king is tantamount to a national rejection of Yahweh (10:18-19). This may be a Deuteronomistic contribution deftly inserted into an older story. Other sections, however, are more striking in their opposition to the monarchy. In fact, the account of Saul's rise to kingship is carefully bracketed between a strong warning against kingship (8:1-22) and a powerful polemic against trusting an earthly king over a heavenly one (12:1-25). These two chapters also may preserve ancient traditions (especially ch. 12) but are clearly shaped by the Deuteronomist's characteristic hand.

The rise of kingship sets the stage for the demise of the judges, including Samuel. Although Samuel and other prophets continue to play a role, Israel's further history in the Old Testament will be told from the perspective of its kings. Their personalities and proclivities, failures and victories will shape the remainder of the Deuteronomistic saga of Israel's experience.

COMMENTARY

There is no unanimity of opinion regarding the subsources of chapter 8, though most scholars agree that the chapter is a composite work held together by Deuteronomistic glue. If chapter 7 sets the stage for the rise of kingship in Israel, chapter 8 is Act One.

Samuel's Sons Are Wanting, 8:1-3

The observation about Samuel's sons certainly derives from a tradition that is older than the Deuteronomist, and its sudden appearance suggests several things regarding the course of the narrative. Apparently, an indeterminate number of years had passed since the miraculous deliverance at Mizpah. Samuel had

Samuel's Sons

Samuel's personal piety is reflected in the names of his sons. Joel means "Yahweh is God," and Abijah means "My father is Yahweh." Samuel's sons are also named in the Levitical genealogy of the Chronicler (1 Chr 6:28; MT v. 13). The name of Joel is missing from the MT, but is supplied by the versions. Joel is also listed as the father of Heman the singer, one of those "whom David put in charge of the service of song in the house of the LORD, after the ark came to rest there" (1 Chr 6:31-33; MT vv. 16-18). There, Samuel's family is listed as belonging to the clan of Kohathite priests, who had the special responsibility of caring for the ark (see Num 3:29-31; 4:4-15).

---

married and fathered at least two sons, Joel and Abijah, who had grown to adulthood. [Samuel's Sons] Samuel himself had grown old enough to enter semi-retirement, appointing his two sons to serve as judges in Beer-sheba.

The text gives no explanation for the unexpected note that the sons were made judges *in Beer-sheba.* [From Dan to Beer-sheba] Beer-sheba was some fifty miles south of Jerusalem, nearly sixty miles from Samuel's home of Ramah and far from Samuel's accustomed circuit (see [Samuel's Circuit]). Indeed, Beer-sheba was so near the southern extremity of Israel's borders that it was used in conjunction with the northern city of Dan as a figure of speech (technically, a "merism") for all Israel: "from Dan to Beersheba" (Judg 20:1; 1 Sam 3:20; 2 Sam 17:11). [Everything in Between] The mention of Beer-sheba may indicate a southern tradition regarding Samuel, though some regard it as an artificial ploy to attribute to Samuel a larger sphere of influence. Josephus was familiar with an alternate tradition that placed one son in Beer-sheba and another in Bethel (*Ant.* 6.32).

Joel and Abijah were apparently given some judicial responsibilities, but they did not follow in Samuel's ethical footsteps. Like the sons of Eli, they abandoned the way of

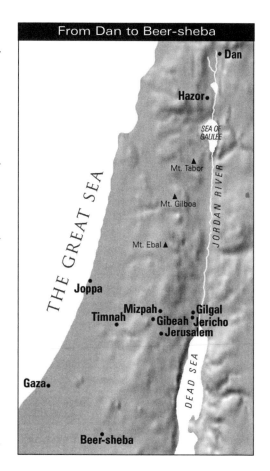

From Dan to Beer-sheba

Everything in Between

"Merism" is a technical term commonly used by literary specialists but still rarely found in dictionaries. A merism is a figure of speech in which a totality is expressed by means of two contrasting parts. In other words, two polar objects, places, or concepts represent the whole of everything in between. For example, some scholars regard the phrase "good and evil" in "the tree of the knowledge of good and evil" (Gen 2:9, 17) as a merism, suggesting that wisdom gained from the tree would not relate to good and evil alone, but to all knowledge. In a similar way, the northern and southern extremities of Israel were used as a merism to describe the country as a whole: "from Dan to Beer-sheba."

the father for the way of the world: "They took bribes and perverted justice" (v. 3b). Some writers have taken note of the similarity between Samuel's sons and the sons of Eli, suggesting that the inclusion of this story is a tendentious attempt to argue against hereditary succession. If that is the case, the theme is a minor one. The story is more concerned with the establishment of the monarchy than with its rules for succession.

Israel's Elders Want a King, 8:4-6a

The elders of Israel approached Samuel at his home in Ramah (see 7:17), acknowledging him as the *de facto* leader of Israel. The failure of Samuel's sons had given them the opportunity they needed to broach the issue of a central governing authority. Their desire for a king "like other nations" had very practical roots. Apparently, the elders saw that the people of Israel were scattered across the land and vulnerable to attack from the surrounding nations. Israel's loose tribal federation often produced more strife and envy than unity, while Israel's neighbors had standing armies and coherent foreign policies, often involving territorial expansion at Israel's expense. The leaders of outlying tribes—those closest to the borders of hostile neighbors—would have been especially enamored with the idea of setting up a central government with the authority to conscript and equip a standing army to provide national defense.

All human reason, then, pointed toward the clear logic of calling out a king. Danger lurked on every side. Samuel was already old and getting older. His sons had proven themselves to be unworthy of leading Israel as Samuel had. The establishment of a central government headed by a king had proven successful in surrounding nations—why not in Israel? Why not accept the fact that Israel's premonarchic tribal federation had grown incapable of dealing with new political realities?

While this line of reasoning makes perfect sense to the modern reader, as it did to the delegation of elders, the text itself reveals no felt need for change. As far as the narrator is concerned, there is no need to challenge the traditional theocratic ideal that Israel should be ruled by Yahweh alone, with the prophets as his spokespersons and a faithful priesthood as the guardian of the law. Yahweh had proven himself quite capable of calling out charismatic judges to lead the people in times of national emergency. Had not Samuel proved to be an effective leader as prophet, priest, and judge? Had not God responded to Samuel's prayer and delivered Israel from the Philistines in the battle of Mizpah (ch. 7)? The author sees the issue through Samuel's eyes, and Samuel seems to have regarded the elders' request as a personal rejection that disregarded the peaceful era of his judgeship.

Kyle McCarter argues effectively that the Deuteronomists present the call for a king as one more episode in humanity's attempt to become more than it should be. The elders want a king so they can be "like the other nations." They are not content with the life Yahweh has granted them, but yearn for change. In McCarter's words, "They are motivated by a perverse and self-destructive urge to rise above themselves. As Adam and Eve in the Yahwistic primeval history desired to become 'like gods' (Gen 3:5), so their descendants desire to become 'like the nations.' . . . They seek a new status that in their impetuosity they regard as more glorious; but in the seeking they repudiate their only true glory."[1] Samuel's response also echoes the story of Eden: he warns the people that life with a king—that is, life outside of God's intended parameters—will be much harder than they think. The institution of kingship will become more of a curse than a blessing.

Samuel Sounds a Warning, 8:6b-18

That Samuel chose to pray about the issue rather than sending the elders away immediately is a tribute to his true reliance on God. His prayer also offers the author a perfect literary vehicle for giving divine authority to his opinions about kingship. Given Samuel's prior statements, it comes as a surprise to the reader when Yahweh responds to Samuel's prayer by instructing him to indulge the elders and grant them a king. In Yahweh's view, according to the narrator, Israel's request for a king is one more rejection in a long string of rebellions, from Egypt onwards (vv. 7-8). God was better prepared to accept rejection than was Samuel, knowing that the people ultimately would do what they wanted in any case. The God who grants human freedom is wise enough and patient enough to know that those same humans often will make inappropriate choices, and is gracious enough not to give up on them.

Thus, Yahweh instructed Samuel to accede to Israel's demand for a king, but only after warning them of the consequences

---

Translating "The Ways of the King"

AΩ The phrase *mišpaṭ hammelek* is subject to varying interpretations because *mišpaṭ* can have multiple meanings. Normally it means "justice," but it can also mean "way," "custom," or "manner." There probably is an intentional wordplay involved: The elders asked for "a king to judge us" (*melek lĕšāpṭēnû*; v. 5), and Samuel responded with a polemic on what "justice of the king" they could expect (*mišpaṭ hamelek*; v. 9).

The varying interpretations may be seen in the variety of modern translations. Most assume that the list describes the practices of a king, whether legitimate or not: "the ways of the king" (NRSV, RSV), "the procedure [custom] of the king" (NASB), "the practices of any king" (NJPS), or "the manner of the king" (KJV). The NIV renders "what the king . . . will do," while the TEV speaks of "what it will be like to have a king." The concept of legitimacy is present in JB's rendering of the term as "the rights of the king" and in McCarter's "the justice of the king" (AB).

Some scholars have argued that the list of royal prerogatives in vv. 10-17 describes the actual practices of King Solomon, while others see a broader spectrum of kings represented. Several, though not all, of the customs Samuel predicted are in fact reflected in the biblical record. A number of scholars believe that "The Rights of the King" may have been an official document representing the accepted powers of Israel's monarch, here attributed to Samuel. At 1 Sam 10:25, the narrative insists that Samuel did this very thing, writing the duties of the king in a book for future reference (see [The Rights and Duties of Kingship]).

---

and advising them what it would mean to live under "the ways of the king" (v. 9). [Translating "The Ways of the King,"] Samuel's stern warning could more aptly be titled "The Problem with Kings," for he paints the rights of monarchy with a decidedly negative palette.

Israel's elders do not respond to Samuel's warning with either shock or dismay; they seem to have weighed the options before coming to him. Since Israel was surrounded by other small nations that already had kings, the general conventions of kingship may have been common knowledge.

The "rights of the king," according to Samuel, are as follows:

1. Power to conscript men for service in the chariot corps, which had both ceremonial and military functions (v. 11; cf. 1 Sam 21:8; 22:17; 2 Sam 15:1; 1 Kgs 1:5; 4:26; 9:22).

2. Power to conscript men to serve as professional officers in the military, to work the royal estates, and to support the military by fashioning weapons and chariots (v. 12). For the military reference, compare the Mosaic tradition of Exodus 18:21; Deuteronomy 1:15; and the practices of later kings, reflected in 1 Samuel 17:18; 18:13; 22:7; 2 Kings 1:9, 11, 13. The Old Testament does not otherwise mention the laborers

who toiled in the fields and equipped the army, but the need for their services is obvious.

3. Power to conscript women to serve the palace as perfumers, cooks, and bakers (v. 13). Some have suggested that "perfumers" is a euphemism for concubines, but this is unlikely. Since Samuel was trying to persuade the elders against having a king, he would not have hesitated to use the more graphic term. Given the enormous task of provisioning a large administration, the number of women conscripted could be considerable (note the incredible size of Solomon's daily provisions, 1 Kgs 4:22-23 [MT 5:2-3]). [Palace Provisions]

4. Power to confiscate choice private land and give it to the "servants of the king" (v. 14). All officials in the palace were called "servants" of the king, but many were really royal courtiers of high standing. The practice of confiscating land for such officials was also known at Ugarit.[2] There must have been some limits to this power, however; witness the incident of Ahab and Naboth's vineyard (1 Kgs 21). [The Wrongs of the King]

5. Power to tax all products of field, vineyard, and flocks at the rate of ten percent (vv. 15, 17a). [A Taxing Tithe] The grain and wine, at least, were for the upkeep and support of the king's court. The word for "officers" (*sārîs*) is an Assyrian loanword meaning "one at the head." Since these Assyrian officers typically were castrated as a condition of their position, the word is more commonly translated as "eunuch," but here the broader definition is appropriate. The reference to "his officers and his servants" implies that the entire court is intended.

Palace Provisions

According to 1 Kgs 4:22-23, the provisions needed to feed Solomon's court with bread and meat alone for *a single day* amounted to 300 bushels of choice flour, 600 bushels of meal, 10 grain-fed oxen, 20 pasture-fed cattle, and 100 sheep, not to mention unnumbered deer, gazelles, roebucks, and grain-fed fowl. One can only imagine the number of farmhands, butchers, cooks, and attendants required to maintain the flocks and fields and to prepare and serve the meals.

The Wrongs of the King

The sordid story of 1 Kgs 21 takes place in the northern kingdom, in the new capital city of Samaria. King Ahab wanted possession of a vineyard near his palace. He attempted to negotiate a land swap or purchase price, but the owner, Naboth, refused to part with his ancestral land. Ahab was so dejected that his Tyrian wife Jezebel plotted Naboth's death by stoning on false charges. After his death, Ahab claimed the land for his own; he apparently had no power to confiscate it while Naboth was alive. Thus, the "rights of the king"—at least in Israel—may not have been as powerful as Samuel suggested.

A Taxing Tithe

AΩ "He will take one-tenth" translates a single verb in Hebrew (*'āśar*), meaning "to tithe." The word is simply a verbal form of the noun that means "ten" (*'eśer*). It is the same word used for the tithes that were given to God for the upkeep of the temple and the priests (Deut 14:22-29; 26:12-15; 2 Chr 31:5-6; Amos 4:4; Mal 3:8). Through Samuel, the author implies the inappropriateness of having a king who takes the same proportion for himself that is also due to God.

Ancient documents reveal that nearby kingdoms, such as Ugarit, also had royal taxes. The Israelite officials who benefited from such taxes are listed for several royal administrations (1 Kgs 22:29; 2 Kgs 8:6; 9:32; 23:11; 24:12, 15; 25:19; 1 Chr 28:1).

6. Power to confiscate the strongest slaves and draft animals for the purpose of "his own work" on the royal estates and on government building projects (v. 16; cf. 1 Kgs 5:13-18; 9:23). Perhaps Samuel wanted the elders to think about what it would be like to serve a king who employed the same kind of forced labor the Hebrews had provided when they were slaves in Egypt.

Servants of the King

AΩ While we have taken this expression as an implication that the Israelites as a whole would live as *de facto* servants or slaves to the king, the word could also bear the sense of "vassal" (Josh 9:8, 11; 1 Sam 4:9; 11:1; 17:9; 2 Sam 10:19; 2 Kgs 16:7; 17:3; 24:1). Thus, some writers contend that 1 Sam 8:10-17 reflects an ancient royal treaty or covenant established between a king and his subjects. Samuel's point would be the same in either case: Whether one lives as a royal servant, vassal, or subject, it is still the king who is in control.

7. Power to conscript any person for royal service, literally, "And you will be to him for servants" (v. 17b). [Servants of the King] Again, Samuel seems to imply that by insisting on a king, the people are returning to bondage, as in Egypt.

The common people's eventual response to such royal domination would add a further parallel to Israel's exodus experience. "And in that day you will cry out because of your king, whom you have chosen for yourselves; but the LORD will not answer you in that day" (v. 18). Israel had cried (*zāʿaq*) for deliverance in Egypt (Exod 3:7) and in the oppression phases of the judges cycles (Judg 3:9, 15; 6:6-7; 10:10), but this time Yahweh would not respond to their cry. In essence, Samuel has given the elders fair warning. "This is how it will be: You will live to regret your choice, and don't expect God to help you out of it!"

A King Like Other Nations, 8:19-22

Samuel's dire warning is cogently argued and might have been convincing—had the elders heard it. The narrator, however, insists that they would not even listen to Samuel's speech. The theme of refusing to hear God's word is common in the Deuteronomistic History (see 2 Kgs 17:14; 13:10). The elders return to their "request" of v. 5, but now it is stronger: "No, but we *will* have a king over us!" (v. 19b).

The elders elaborate on their argument for a king in v. 20. In their minds, a king would: (1) make Israel like the other nations, [The Other Nations] (2) provide a stronger central government, and (3) lead the nation to military success. Each of these

The Other Nations

🔍 While some strands of tradition insist that Israel eliminated the local inhabitants and the threat of other nations during the "conquest" of Canaan (Josh 21:43-45), other traditions insist that the conquest was not complete (Josh 13:1-6; Judg 1:1-36). Indeed, the presence of other nations provided a continual challenge to Israel (Josh 13:12-13; Judg 2:1-3). In response to Israel's repeated unfaithfulness during the period of the judges, the Deuteronomist insists that Yahweh preserved certain nations "in order to test Israel, whether or not they would take care to walk in the way of the LORD as their ancestors did" (Judg 2:22). The writer of 1 Sam 8 would insist that Israel had just failed the test by choosing to follow the ways of the other nations rather than the way of God.

The modern debate concerning the extent of Israel's "conquest" is reflected in a number of books and articles, several of which are cited here for further reading: W. F. Albright, "The Israelite Conquest of Canaan in the Light of Archaeology," *BASOR* 74 (1939): 11-23; Israel Finkelstein and Nadav Na'aman, eds., *From Nomadism to Monarchy: Archaeological and Historical Aspects of Early Israel* (Washington: Biblical Archaeology Society, 1994); Volkmar Fritz, "Conquest or Settlement? The Early Iron Age in Palestine," *BA* 84 (1987): 84-100; Norman K. Gottwald, *The Tribes of Yahweh: A Sociology of the Religion of Liberated Israel, 1250–1050 BCE* (Maryknoll NY: Orbis Books, 1979); George E. Mendenhall, "The Hebrew Conquest of Palestine," *BA* 25 (1962): 66-87; J. M. Miller and J. M. Hayes, *Israelite and Judean History* (London: SCM Press, 1990).

arguments makes logical sense, but each of them also repudiates the theocratic rule of Yahweh over his people.

For the Deuteronomists, the whole point of Israel's being God's chosen people was that they *not* be like the other nations, but be ruled by Yahweh alone (Deut 12:29-31; 18:14). This is especially evident in the elders' desire for a king to "go out before us and fight our battles" (v. 20b). The Deuteronomists believed that *Yahweh* alone was responsible for Israel's military success—witness the story of the battle at Mizpah, just prior to the elders' request (1 Sam 7; see also Deut 20:1-4; Josh 10:14, 42; 23:3, 10; Judg 4:14). Israel's holy wars were called "Yahweh's wars" (1 Sam 18:17; 25:28), but the elders wanted a king to fight *our* battles.

For the narrator, then, Israel's insistence on a king was not so much a rejection of Samuel as it was a rejection of Yahweh, who—surprisingly—instructed Samuel to indulge the people and give them a king (v. 22a; cf. 8:7). We should note that Israel's demand for a king is also a matter of concern in Deuteronomy 17:14-20, which speaks of Israel's adopting a king like the other nations and warns against the potential abuses of a king. [Deuteronomy 17:14-20]

Yahweh's permission for Israel to have a king offers a sort of backhanded sanction to the office. Even so, this qualified consent was not the result of divine desire, but of God's gift of grace to a stubborn people. As God had provided judges in Israel's past, so he would provide kings for Israel's future. Samuel, however, wanted the people to know that kings do not

---

Deuteronomy 17:14-20

📖 Deut 17:14-20: "When you have come into the land that the LORD your God is giving you, and have taken possession of it and settled in it, and you say, 'I will set a king over me, like all the nations that are around me,' you may indeed set over you a king whom the LORD your God will choose. One of your own community you may set as king over you; you are not permitted to put a foreigner over you, who is not of your own community. Even so, he must not acquire many horses for himself, or return the people to Egypt in order to acquire more horses, since the LORD has said to you, 'You must never return that way again.' And he must not acquire many wives for himself, or else his heart will turn away; also silver and gold he must not acquire in great quantity for himself. When he has taken the throne of his kingdom, he shall have a copy of this law written for him in the presence of the Levitical priests. It shall remain with him and he shall read in it all the days of his life, so that he may learn to fear the LORD his God, diligently observing all the words of this law and these statutes, neither exalting himself above other members of the community nor turning aside from the commandment, either to the right or to the left, so that he and his descendants may reign long over his kingdom in Israel."

This text, ostensibly earlier than the rise of the monarchy in 1 Samuel, was probably written at a later point and included in the Deuteronomic code to give Mosaic authority to the rules of kingship. That this law was not extant in Samuel's day is evident from the simple fact that neither Samuel nor the elders appealed to it in the course of their debate, even though it reflects issues addressed by both. The specific abuses the text warns against—such as the taking of many wives or the accumulation of much wealth—clearly reflect the reign of Solomon, whose heart was reportedly turned from Yahweh by the influence of his foreign wives (1 Kgs 11). The insistence that the king have a copy of the law at hand reflects the Deuteronomic themes evident during the Josianic reforms, when just such a book was "discovered" while repairs were being made to the temple (1 Kgs 22:8). Many scholars believe it was during this period that the book of Deuteronomy reached its final form.

---

come with guarantes. The more powerful the office, the more susceptible it is to abuse.

Samuel's dismissal of the elders in v. 22b serves the literary purpose of clearing the stage for the next act in the ongoing drama of Israel's quest for a king. The reader is now prepared for the story of how young Saul went out to look for his father's asses, but found a kingdom instead.

CONNECTIONS

Samuel's sons set the tone for this troublesome chapter. They are not like their father. Like the sons of Samuel's mentor Eli, they do not walk in the path of piety, but use their office for selfish gain. We wonder why. Did Samuel give his children godly names (see [Samuel's Sons]) and then neglect to give them godly upbringing? Was he so busy traveling his administrative circuit from Gilgal to Bethel to Mizpah that he had no time for his children? Those are possible explanations, but the text simply does not provide enough information for anything more than speculation. The story says very little about Samuel's family; it never suggests that Samuel was anything less than a faithful father and a good example to his children. It is entirely possible that Samuel's sons had the best possible upbringing and all the attention they craved yet still chose to follow their own way. They would not have been the first—nor the last.

The narrator uses the story of Samuel's sons as a literary means of introducing the elders' demand for a king, since Samuel's sons had proven to be worthless as leaders. But we can also see in Samuel's sons a metaphor for or commentary on the behavior of Israel. Joel and Abijah had every reason to follow in their father's footsteps, but they surrendered to the temptation of power and gave in to graft. Likewise, Israel had every reason to follow the way of God, who had always been faithful to his people. Yahweh had provided deliverance from Egypt and had brought the Israelites safely to the promised land. The LORD had provided sustenance and guidance in all their times of need and had continued to defend Israel against those who threatened the nation. Yet the elders of Israel came to Samuel and said, "We want a king like the other nations, to go before us and fight our battles."

Samuel could see only the negative side of kingship, but the elders refused to hear anything but the positive aspects. This is the way temptation works. When we are tempted to reject God's way for our way, we focus on all the reasons we *should* do it our way—why we should spend extravagant amounts of money on ourselves, or participate in some questionable behavior, or devote our Sundays to physical fitness and family time that does not involve participation in a family of faith. Somehow we manage to ignore the consequences so that we can adopt lifestyles that are selfish to the core without any awareness that we have rejected God entirely.

The Bible speaks clearly about the dangers of living in ways that promote personal selfishness and have little regard for the needs of others. Amos, perhaps more clearly than any other prophet, emphasized the danger of self-aggrandizement at the expense of the poor and the downtrodden, or the danger of substituting ritual forms for a real relationship with God (e.g., Amos 5). Yet, people through the ages have demonstrated a strong and continuing ability to ignore good advice in the face of strong temptation.

The most amazing thing about this passage is the surprising grace, flexibility, and generosity of God. As the story unfolds, the LORD understands that his people have rejected "Plan A," but instead of writing them off, he agrees to go along with

"Plan B" in hopes that something good will come of it. It certainly is possible that a righteous king could have tremendous influence for good in Israel. Unfortunately, with greater power comes greater temptation and greater potential for harm. Despite the danger inherent in their desire for a king, God chose not to give up on his people. Like a loving parent who works hard to relate to children on their own level, God was willing to meet the people of Israel where they were and to work with them as he could.

Many years later, God would take the ultimate step of meeting his people on the human plane of existence. Through the incarnation of Christ, God came to us, loved us, redeemed us, and taught us what it means to live in the one kingdom that ultimately matters: the kingdom of God.

NOTES

[1] P. Kyle McCarter, *I Samuel* (AB 8; Garden City: Doubleday, 1980), 160-61.

[2] Issac Mendelsohn, "Samuel's Denunciation of Kingship in the Light of the Accadian Documents from Ugarit," *BASOR* 143 (1956): 17-22.

SAUL'S SEARCH AND
A SECRET ANOINTING

9:1–10:16

The account of Saul's secret anointing is the first of three consecutive stories that recounts how Israel's first king was chosen. The preservation of three differing stories is testimony to the importance Israel accorded to the institution of the monarchy. The final text blends all three stories so they appear to be ongoing episodes in a single account of Saul's call to greatness.

COMMENTARY

Saul in Search of His Father's Donkeys, 9:1-4

This story begins, as good stories often do, with the line "There once was a man" (*wayĕhî 'îš*). However, as in 1 Samuel 1:1, the man so prominently introduced is not the hero of the story, but the hero's father. We learn of this man Kish that he was a Benjaminite, and five generations of his family are listed, six if the enigmatic "son of a Benjaminite" (MT has "son of a man of Yamini) that follows Aphiah is intended as the final ancestor rather than a repetitive appelative describing Kish. [Benjamin] [Who Was Kish's Father?] When the focus shifts quickly to Saul, we have the seventh generation, a portentous number.

Kish is said to be a *gibbôr ḥayil*, an impressive appellation that can mean either a "mighty warrior" (cf. Josh 1:14; 8:3; 10:7; Judg 6:12;

Benjamin

AΩ Benjamin (lit., "son of the right hand") was remembered as the youngest son of the eponymous patriarch Jacob, whose descendants received the smallest portion of land when the promised land was divided among the tribes. The Benjaminites had a colorful history. They were vilified following the infamous rape of the Levite's concubine at Gibeah of Benjamin, and so many were massacred by their fellow Israelites that the other tribes had to allow the remaining Benjaminites to "capture" some of their young women so the tribe would not die out altogether (Judg 19–21). Thus, the tribe of Benjamin was remembered as the smallest and least worthy among the tribes, which makes it all the more amazing that Israel's first king would be a Benjaminite. The author intends this, no doubt, as a sign of Yahweh's handiwork, for God delights in taking the small and making them great (1 Sam 2:5, 8).

Who Was Kish's Father?

There is some confusion with Kish's genealogy, both here and in 1 Chronicles. First Sam 9:1 names Kish as the son of *Abiel*. First Chr 8:29-33 and 9:35-39 list *Jeiel* as the father of sons including Kish and Ner, while also insisting that Ner was the father of Kish. This seems to presume that Abiel had both a son and a grandson named Kish. In 1 Sam 14:51, Ner is mentioned as the father of Abner, Saul's general, and as the son of Abiel.

11:1) or a "man of wealth" (Ruth 2:1; 1 Kgs 11:28; 2 Kgs 15:20). Given the context, the latter interpretation is preferable, though Kyle McCarter's rendering of "powerful man" aptly preserves the ambiguity. Saul comes from a small tribe, but from a substantial family.[1]

Saul himself is described as a handsome, or fine (lit., "good"), young man (v. 2). Hebrew heroines and heroes typically are remembered for their striking good looks: Joseph (Gen 39:6), David (1 Sam 16:12), and Esther (Esth 2:7) offer representative examples. Saul is portrayed as a tall man, a fine physical specimen who stood head and shoulders above his contemporaries. Presumably, the reader is to interpret Saul's handsome appearance and impressive size as signs of divine favor. The word for "young man" (*bāḥûr*) is a technical term for one who has reached the age of assuming adult responsibilities such as marrying and going to war. In a battle portrayed as occurring early in his reign, however, Saul already has a son who is old enough to serve in his army (ch. 13).

The story of Saul's anointing is set in the context of a charming story about a search for a cluster of asses gone astray. [The Donkeys of Kish] Saul's diligent search carried him far beyond his immediate neighborhood and the surrounding hills. His journey seems to have encompassed the better part of Benjamin and Ephraim, lasting three days (9:20) and exhausting virtually all of the resources Saul and his servant had brought with them (v. 8). Some of the place names mentioned (Shalishah, Shaalim) are now unidentifiable, and, for our purposes, beside the point. The far-ranging attempts of some scholars to identify these obscure places provide a modern metaphor for Saul's own search: a wandering, frustrating, and ultimately fruitless endeavor.

The Donkeys of Kish

AΩ "The donkeys of Kish" (NRSV) translates an uncommon construction (lit., "the asses [belonging] to Kish") that could be used to designate part of a larger whole. Thus, the text may or may not imply that all of the donkeys had strayed, a potentially significant loss (see P. Kyle McCarter, *I Samuel* [AB 8; Garden City: Doubleday, 1980], 173-74 for an extensive discussion). Kish's command for Saul to search for the donkeys is couched in a string of imperatives: "*Take* one of the servants (lit., "boys") with you, *rise up*, *go*, and *search* for the asses" (9:3b).

Saul in Search of a Seer, 9:5-14

By the time their search had reached Zuph, Saul was ready to stop worrying about the donkeys lest his father start worrying about him (v. 5). [Zuph] The servant who accompanied Saul, however, urged one last try, a visit to the "man of God" who lived "in this town" (for more on the "man of God," see [Prophets and Seers]). [Which

Town?] The reader is left to wonder why the servant, and not Saul, was so well informed about the holy man, whose extensive reputation included the ability to predict the future, so that "whatever he says always comes true" (v. 6).

The unfolding narrative gradually makes it clear that providence is guiding Saul to a date with destiny. His fruitless donkey chase through the hills of Benjamin and Ephraim has brought him within hailing distance of the holy man who will set his life on a different path. He just happened to bring with him a servant who has the knowledge and the persuasive ability to see that Saul meets the man of God. The MT describes this servant as a "lad" or "boy" (*na'ar*), but the term is also used of adult male servants, which seems more likely here. The hand of providence appears again in vv. 7-8; Saul expresses concern that they have no gift to offer the holy man, but the servant unexpectedly discovers that he has a quarter of a shekel of silver. [A Quarter of a Shekel] Under ordinary circumstances, one would expect the man of means, not his servant, to have money. The providential appearance of the silver is stressed by the servant's words: "Here, there is found in my hand" has the sense of "Look what *I* found!" With cash in hand, Saul and his servant seek out the seer. [Seers and Prophets]

The place of Saul's fated meeting remains unnamed, though the women coming from town to draw water seem familiar. The motif of male travelers encountering women at the well is common stock in biblical narratives (compare Abraham's servant's meeting Rebekah, Gen 24:15-20; Jacob's meeting Rachel, Gen 29:2-12; Moses' defending Reuel's daughters, Exod 2:15-19; and Jesus and the woman of Samaria, John 4:3-26). The water-drawers are called "girls" (*nĕ'ārôt*), as Saul's servant is called a "boy" (*na'ar*). These

Zuph

Zuph was a district in the western foothills of Ephraim, presumably named for a man named Zuph whose descendants had settled the area. Samuel's father Elkanah is called a Zuphite (1 Sam 1:1).

Which Town?

AΩ The servant's reference to "this town" is problematic. Saul and the servant had just come to Zuph, which was not a town but a region; the text refers to it as the "land of Zuph." Thus, "this town" is without a referent. When the holy man turns out to be Samuel, we might assume that the town in question is Ramathaim, where Samuel was born (his father Elkanah was called a Zuphite in 1:1), but 1 Sam 7:17 says that Samuel made his home in Ramah. There seems to been some confusion between Ramah and Ramathaim. McCarter contends that a misidentification of Ramathaim of Zuph with Ramah of Benjamin is typical of a prophetic revision of the material.

Fortunately, the specific place name has no real impact on the story. The point is that Saul has stumbled onto the one man who can help him with his problem—the man of God.

P. Kyle McCarter, *I. Samuel* (AB 8; Garden City: Doubleday, 1980), 174.

A Quarter of a Shekel

Coins were not used in Palestine until Hellenistic times. Prior to that, silver and other valuable metals were measured by weight. The standard weight was a shekel, which averaged about two-fifths of an ounce. Thus, the servant's quarter-shekel would have weighed only a tenth of an ounce, quite small enough to have been overlooked until it was needed. A quarter of a shekel would not have been an extravagant gift by any means, but would not have been considered penurious either. It was an appropriate amount to show one's respect for the holy man's time.

Seers and Prophets

AΩ First Sam 9:9 is obviously secondary to the original story and functions as a parenthetical explanation. (Formerly in Israel, anyone who went to inquire of God would say, "Come, let us go to the seer"; for the one who now is called a prophet was formerly called a seer.) The verse seems awkwardly placed, however, since neither of the terms "seer" or "prophet" has yet been used. Since the explanation intends to elucidate the meaning of "seer," the most logical location for the verse would be after v. 11, where the word first appears.

"Seer" (*rōʾeh*) translates a participial form of the verb meaning "to see." It was an old term that emphasized the holy person's divining abilities. The word was not really obsolete when 1 Samuel reached its final form, but the editor apparently feels a need to harmonize the appearance of "seer" in this older story with the previous description of Samuel as a "prophet" (*nābîʾ*). *Nābîʾ* may derive from an old word meaning "to bubble up," describing the ecstatic roots of early prophecy, or it may be a passive form of an archaic verb meaning "to call" (there is an Akkadian cognate). In either case, prophets were considered to be more generalized in function than seers. Prophets could function as seers, but they also spoke in Yahweh's behalf on matters of national and spiritual import, while seers typically were regarded as local fortune tellers. Thus, although Samuel is called a seer in this older story, the editor does not want the reader to forget that Samuel is more than a seer; he is a true prophet of God.

words could be euphemisms to describe adult male and female servants, though the word here may simply mean "girls." In ancient Israel, drawing water was considered to be a woman's work, slave or free.

Saul learned from the women that the seer had just arrived in town and was on his way to assist with a sacrifice (v. 12) on the sacral high place. [High Places] This statement seems to be in tension with the earlier indication that the seer lived in the town (v. 6). The woman's statement suggests that the holy man was an itinerant, though it also could mean simply that he had been outside the city walls for a while, and had just returned. Once we learn that the man of God is Samuel, we remember that he made periodic rounds of the territory in his capacity as judge (7:15-17), and we presume he did the same in exercising his priestly functions.

Verse 13 describes a practice in which the authorized holy man must participate in the consecration of a sacrificial meal before others are allowed to join the feasting. The story implies that the man of God already has made one trip to the high place to preside over the ritual slaughter, division, and preparation of the meat, and is returning for the meal after it has been cooked. So it is that Saul's path propitiously intersects with the man who will turn him to another path altogether.

Samuel's Unexpected Reception, 9:15-24

The various hints at providential leadership find final confirmation in v. 15, where we also learn for the first time that the "man of God" is no less than Samuel himself. On the previous day, Yahweh had revealed his plan to Samuel: "Tomorrow about this time I will

High Places

It was common for an enclosed shrine or simple altar to be built on a high place (*bāmâh*), though the particular place and practice mentioned here is unknown from other sources. Later prophets condemned Israel's worship on the high places because of their association with Canaanite rites, and King Josiah received the historians' accolades for tearing them down (2 Kgs 23:8-10, 19-20). The narrator's quiet acceptance of worship on this Zuphite high place is evidence of the story's antiquity.

This round altar platform, with steps at left, was used as a Canaanite "high place" in Megiddo, which is located on a hill.
(Credit: Mitchell G. Reddish)

send to you a man from the land of Benjamin, and you shall anoint him to be ruler over my people Israel. He shall save my people from the hand of the Philistines; for I have seen the suffering of my people, because their outcry has come to me" (v. 16). [Revelation]

The word for "ruler" (*nāgîd*) is often translated as "prince," for in royal contexts it typically refers to one who has been appointed to reign (1 Sam 10:1; 25:30; 2 Sam 5:2; 6:21; 7:8; 1 Kgs 14:7) or to a "crown prince" chosen to rule after the king (1 Kgs 1:35; 2 Chr 11:22). The use of *nāgîd* also may be part of an intentional wordplay. It is related to the verb *higgîd* (to advise) used in 9:6, 8, 18, 19 and 10:15, 16. Saul asks the seer to inform (*higgîd*) him about the lost asses and is apprised that he will be prince (*nāgîd*).

Revelation

ΑΩ Yahweh's revelation to Samuel is couched in a colorful Hebrew idiom. Literally, the text says that Yahweh had "uncovered Samuel's ear." This implies the revelation of something that was otherwise secret or unknown. The phrase could describe the disclosure of something unknown in human conversation (1 Sam 20:12-13; 22:8, 17), as well as between God and humans (1 Sam 9:15; 2 Sam 7:27).

Yahweh had not only revealed to Samuel that Saul was coming, but had pointed him out when he came through the gate (v. 17). Thus, when Saul approaches Samuel for directions to the seer's house, Samuel already knows who he is. Samuel identifies himself as the seer, and immediately proves it by answering Saul's question about the donkeys—even before Saul has had a chance to request assistance. Verse 19 presents a bit of a conundrum, for Samuel first invites Saul to be his honored guest at the sacrificial feast that evening, then says, "In the morning I will let you go and will tell you all that is on your mind" (v. 19). We know that the donkeys are on Saul's mind, but Samuel does not wait until morning to tell

1 Samuel 9:17—Doré was an illustrator, painter and sculptor who took on the job of illustrating the great works of western civilization. Among those, of course, was the Holy Bible in 1866. His skill at combining symbolism, romanticism and narrative can be found in this scene of Samuel blessing Saul.

Gustave Doré (1832–83). *Samuel Blessing Saul* from the *Illustrated Bible*. 19th century. Engraving. (Credit: Dover Pictorial Archive Series)

Social Structures

Saul's concern about being from the least family of the smallest tribe in Israel is understandable in the context of the social structure of ancient Israel. The word "family" (NRSV) is better rendered as "clan."

In ancient Israel, the word family (*bêt ʾāb*; lit., "house of the father") depicted an extended household including a patriarchal father along with all of his sons. Married sons and their children were still considered a part of the basic family unit, while married daughters became a part of their husband's family.

A larger group of related families, usually living in close proximity, was called a clan (*mišpāḥâ*). Clans exhibited a certain level of independent behavior in matters political and religious.

A tribe (*šēbeṭ*) consisted of a group of clans who claimed a common ancestor and exhibited family loyalty in defending or caring for each other. Saul claimed to be from the smallest tribe (Benjamin) and the smallest clan in all of Israel. This makes his calling stand out as even more unexpected.

The following sources, among others, are helpful for further reading: Roland de Vaux, *Ancient Israel: Its Life and Institutions*, 2 vols, trans. J. McHugh (London: Daughton, Norman, & Todd, 1961); Norman Gottwald, *The Tribes of Yahweh: A Sociology of the Religion of Liberated Israel, 1250–1050 BCE* (Maryknoll NY: Orbis Books, 1979), 237-344; Douglas A. Knight, "Family," *MDB* (Macon GA: Mercer University Press, 1990), 295-96.

---

him that they have been found (v. 20a). He quickly reveals the donkeys' whereabouts, then shifts the focus to Saul: "And on whom is all Israel's desire fixed, if not on you and on all your ancestral house?" (v. 20b).

Saul's response expresses the humility typical of God's chosen leaders (compare Moses, Exod 3:1–4:17; and especially Gideon, Judg 6:11-27). Saul's response that the Benjaminites were the smallest tribe in Israel appears to be accurate (see [Benjamin]), but the claim that his family was "the humblest of all the families of the tribe of Benjamin" seems in tension with the earlier assertion that his father Kish was a powerful man, a *gibbôr ḥayil.* [Social Structures] Perhaps we are to understand that the stress was on Kish's ability as a warrior, rather than on his wealth. The word "family," however, is better translated as "clan." Kish could have stood out as an anomaly in an otherwise unremarkable clan. Saul's question in v. 21b—"Why then have you spoken to me in this way?"—makes it clear that he still will have much on his heart for Samuel to reveal in the morning, even though he knows that the donkeys are no longer an issue.

Samuel's special treatment of Saul at the banquet raises a number of issues since we have no real parallels to a sacrificial banquet on a high place. If the guest list simply comprised the leading men of the town who were accustomed to attending periodic feasts, would the author have called them "invited guests"? The reader is left to infer that this is an atypical banquet, one Samuel has called for the specific purpose of introducing Saul to the invited guests. Note that Saul (along with his servant) is feted at the head of the table (v. 22) and given a choice cut of meat, which Samuel had ordered to be reserved.

The cut of meat itself raises another issue (v. 23). "The thigh and what went with it" is an awkward translation because the underlying Hebrew is obscure and potentially corrupt. [A Troublesome Translation] It seems most reasonable to assume that Samuel gives to Saul a portion, at least, of the thigh that belongs to him as the priest of record. The implication is that Saul's portion was not merely a closely trimmed thigh bone, but a generous cut containing more meat than usual. The fact that Samuel had personally reserved this portion adds to its special quality.

Samuel's gift of meat normally reserved for the priests intensifies the aura of Yahweh's sacred plans for Saul but does not suggest that he is regarded as a priest. The banquet itself bears some similarity to banquets sponsored by Absalom (2 Sam 15:1-12) and by Adonijah (1 Kgs 1:1-10) as a means of announcing their designs on the throne and seeking popular acclaim as king. Both were unsuccessful. Perhaps Saul's participation in a sacral banquet is to be seen as an anticipatory coronation banquet. The significance of having thirty invited guests is unclear. Absalom invited 200 guests. The number thirty brings to mind the count of David's trusted "mighty men" (2 Sam 23:13, 18), but the guests mentioned in 1 Samuel 9 are meeting Saul for the first time.

The banquet, then, incorporates both prophetic and priestly functions, setting Saul apart as a man who is favored by God's representative and worthy of preferential treatment. Saul clearly is destined for greatness he does not yet understand. Through the symbolic act of eating together (v. 24), Samuel has created a special bond with Saul and has given him a taste of what is yet to come.

A Troublesome Translation

AΩ The term translated "what went with it" (*wĕheʿālêhā*) appears to be an ungainly combination of a connective, an article, a preposition, and a pronoun used together as a relative. The resulting term is similar to a word meaning "fatty tail," a portion the Levitical codes reserved as being especially holy to God (Exod 29:22; Lev 3:9; 7:3; 8:25; 9:19). "And the fatty tail" would be *wĕhāʾalyâ*. The fatty tail, however, was always burned on the altar as an offering to God and was forbidden for human consumption (Lev 7:25). According to the same code, the right thigh was given to the priest who conducted the sacrifice (7:32-33). Some versions of the LXX preserve the Hebrew reading, while at least one (LXXᴮ) has only "the thigh." 4QSamᵃ has a slightly different spelling of the word, suggesting perhaps an "upper" portion.

A Secret Anointing and Special Signs, 9:25–10:8

The author adds a bit of dramatic space to the story by describing Saul's descent from the shrine to the town, where a bed was prepared for him "on the roof" (v. 25). We are not told if this roof is a part of Samuel's home or a place in which he, also, is a guest. By

1 Samuel 9:26-27—Samuel anoints Saul as king. Samuel first anointed Saul in a private ceremony outside an unnamed city in the "land of Zuph."

Julius Schnoor von Carolsfeld. *Samuel Anoints Saul as King.* 19th century. Woodcut. *Das Buch der Bucher in Bilden.* (Credit: Dover Pictorial Archive Series)

modern standards, sleeping on the roof does not sound very appealing, but many ancient homes were built with flat roofs that were used as an open-air second story. Rain is infrequent in Palestine, but predictable. Homes of stone or mud brick had few windows, so during the dry seasons it was not unusual for people to sleep in the cooler evening breezes to be found on the roof.

We note that Saul's servant boy, who has been at his side throughout and who was seated with Saul at the head of the banquet table, is not mentioned in vv. 25-26. Perhaps we are to understand that he was sent to sleep with the other servants. The absence of Saul's companion allows us to focus on the future king, who is left alone with an entirely new set of questions.

Samuel, presumably staying in the same house, roused Saul at the crack of dawn (v. 26). Why so early? Was it to speak to him while unmentioned dreams were still fresh in his mind, or while few

Anointing

Persons were anointed, usually on special occasions, by the pouring or smearing of aromatic oils. Israel, like their ancient neighbors, probably used anointing for a variety of secular and religious purposes. In the Bible, however, anointing almost always has a strong cultic significance. Sacred objects of worship, such as the altar, were anointed (Exod 30:22-29; 40:9), as were the priests who handled them (Exod 28:41; 30:30). The high priest's appointment to office was marked by a special anointing (Lev 21:10). Even Elijah the prophet anointed Elisha to follow as his successor (1 Kgs 19:16b).

In the Old Testament, the focus of anointing is often the king. Saul is anointed as the first king (1 Sam 10:1), and David as the second (1 Sam 16:1, 13), setting a precedent that presumably was repeated with each king (for example, see 1 Kgs 19:16a; 2 Kgs 9:1, 3). Anointing, then, was used to set persons aside for some special purpose— as the leaders or saviors of Israel (note 1 Sam 10:1).

Thus, when Israel later toiled under Seleucid and Roman rule, broken only by a brief spell of relative independence under the Hasmoneans (2d and 1st centuries BC), they longed for a divinely inspired leader to deliver them and lead the nation to greatness. They thought of their leader as a "messiah," or "anointed one" (Heb.: *māšîaḥ*). The Greek word for "anointed" is *christos*. Thus, the title *Jesus Christ* means "Jesus, the anointed one." Jesus was anointed with perfume by a friend (Mark 14:8), but more significantly, he was anointed by God with the Holy Spirit (Luke 4:18).

others were up and about? Secrecy seems to be the controlling factor. Once they are outside of town, the servant is again absented from the story. Prompted by Samuel, Saul instructs his companion to go on without him while he remains for a while with the old priest (v. 27a).

The reader is now prepared for the revelation of Samuel's secret. Hints of the message to come began with v. 19, and chapter 9 closes with Samuel's instruction for Saul to "stop here yourself for a while, that I may make known to you the word of God" (v. 27b).

A Recipe for Anointing Oil

Oil was commonly carried in a flask or vial made of pottery (1 Sam 10:1; 2 Kgs 9:1, 3) or in a container made from an animal's horn (1 Sam 16:1, 13). The oil in question was probably an aromatic blend of olive oil and various spices. Exod 30:22-24 provides a formula for sacred anointing oil to be used in consecrating the temple and the priests: "Take the finest spices: of liquid myrrh five hundred shekels, and of sweet-smelling cinnamon half as much, that is, two hundred fifty, and two hundred fifty of aromatic cane, and five hundred of cassia—measured by the sanctuary shekel—and a hin of olive oil; and you shall make of these a sacred anointing oil blended as by the perfumer; it shall be a holy anointing oil" (NRSV). This oil was considered so sacred that it could not be used for any ordinary purpose, and anyone other than the priests was forbidden from using the recipe on penalty of being banished from Israel (Exod 30:31-33).

The word of God is first revealed through a symbolic anointing. When they were alone, Samuel poured a vial of oil over Saul's head and then anointed him with a kiss. Since Saul supposedly was head and shoulders taller than anyone in Israel, the reader can imagine that Samuel had Saul to kneel for the occasion. [Anointing] [A Recipe for Anointing Oil]

Samuel makes it clear that the anointing sets Saul apart by divine designation as Israel's future ruler—and *savior* (10:1). The idea that the anointed one was both ruler and savior played a role in Israel's later hopes for a messiah (lit., "anointed one") to deliver them and be their king. Saul's role as savior is emphasized in the battle stories of chapters 11 and 13–15.

Remembering Saul's incredulity over his favored treatment on the previous day (9:22), Samuel offers to Saul three tangible signs that his word is true. [Signs] The signs reveal Samuel's knowledge of things that only God could have shown him, thus confirming to Saul that a throne was indeed in his future. In the story at hand, the signs also provide the literary structure upon which the remainder of the chapter is built.

The first sign had to do with the object of Saul's original search: Kish's lost asses (10:2). Although Samuel had already revealed their discovery, Saul would hear it again from two men who also would confirm Saul's earlier fear that his father had begun to worry more about him than the donkeys (9:5). He would meet these men by Rachel's tomb, near Zelzeh. Zelzeh is apparently a place name, but is otherwise unknown. Scholars can only speculate as to its location, which was probably near Ramah. [Where Was Rachel's Tomb?]

The second sign is truly enigmatic, but it may have sacral overtones. Beyond Rachel's tomb, as he approached the oak of Tabor, Saul would meet three men carrying sacrificial offerings to Bethel (10:3). [Oak of Tabor] Without prompting, they would offer to Saul two loaves of bread, which he was to accept (10:4). The MT apparently is missing a word since it preserves only "two of bread." The LXX has "two wave offerings of bread," emphasizing the sacral character of the gift. Wave offerings were lifted ceremonially before Yahweh, after which they could be burned on the altar (Exod 29:22-25; Lev 8:25-29) or set aside for the priests (Num 18:11). As Saul had received the choice portion of meat reserved for Samuel (9:23-24), so now he receives bread that had been destined for sacrifice. This appears to give Saul a holy, if not priestly, status.

The third sign would confirm Saul's new position as a holy person of God: At Gibeah-elohim he would fall in with a band of ecstatic prophets. Gibeah-elohim means "the hill of God." This site is also uncertain, though many suggestions appear in the literature. The most likely candidate is Gibeah of Benjamin, Saul's own hometown. Apparently the town contained some sort of outpost manned by the Philistines. Whether the outpost was a garrison of soldiers or an administrative office is unclear, but its presence

Signs

Both the Old and New Testaments make frequent mention of "signs," often coupled with "wonders," as noteworthy events through which divine revelations are mediated. The signs may or may not be miraculous, but are generally unusual. In Saul's case, the signs in themselves are not overly strange; it is Samuel's prediction of the events that sets them apart.

Signs are particularly apparent in the Deuteronomistic works. In Deuteronomy itself, confessional passages such as 26:8 speak of how God has saved Israel from slavery "with a mighty hand and an outstretched arm, with great terror, with signs and wonders" (cf. Jer 32:20; Pss 78:43; 105:27; 135:9; Neh 9:10). The frequent reminder of God's ability to perform such signs and wonders serves not only as an encouragement to Israel, but also as a warning of what God might do if the people turn against him (Deut 28:46).

God makes his presence known to the Egyptian king through a series of devastating signs (Exod 4:8-9) and reveals his involvement with Israel's future king by means of more mundane signs (1 Sam 10:1-8). Isaiah gave prophetic names to his children as signs of God's unhappiness with Israel (Isa 8:18) and predicted the birth of a baby as a sign to King Ahaz that he should avoid entangling military alliances (Isa 7:10-17).

Where Was Rachel's Tomb?

Rachel was the favorite wife of Jacob, mother of Joseph and Benjamin. Her burial is described in Gen 35:19-20 and 48:7, taking place as Jacob's family journeyed from Bethel toward Ephrath. When Rachel was buried, Jacob had a large stone raised to mark the place and testify to his grief. The location of Ephrath was already lost by the time Genesis was put into its final form, as both 35:19-20 and 48:7 include an explanatory gloss concerning Ephrath, "which is Bethlehem." Bethlehem was sometimes associated with the name "Ephrathah" (Ruth 4:1; Mic 5:2). However, Ephrath or Ephrathah almost certainly refers to a territory or region in which the Ephrathite clan was dominant, so that it encompassed an area larger than Bethlehem alone. Ephrathah is listed in the genealogies of 1 Chron (2:19, 24, 50; 4:4) as the mother of the men who founded Bethlehem. Though it is unclear whether more than one ancestress was named Ephrathah, the tradition clearly holds an association between Ephrathah and Bethlehem. First Sam 17:12 and Ruth 1:2 both refer to David as an Ephrathite from Judah.

According to 1 Sam 10:2, however, Rachel's tomb was in the territory of Benjamin, near Zelzeh. It is likely that the Ephrathite clan extended across the often fluid border between Benjamin and Judah, leading to later confusion.

The traditional site of Rachel's tomb, like many similar sacred sites in Israel, is probably not authentic.

(Credit: Tony W. Cartledge)

Gen 35:19-20 and 48:7 say that Jacob had left Bethel for Ephrathah but had not yet arrived there, so we may presume that they were not far from Bethel when Rachel died. The town of Ramah was only a few miles south of Bethel and is associated with Rachel in Jer 31:15.

Modern visitors to Israel can visit a structure near Bethlehem that is called "Rachel's Tomb," but it was built by the Crusaders, long after the biblical period. The original location was probably near Ramah, not far south of Bethel.

underscores Saul's calling to deliver Israel from its enemies, most notably the Philistines.

Samuel predicted that when Saul met the prophets, he himself would be possessed by the spirit of God, and turned into a different person—literally, "another man" (*lĕʾîš ʾaḥēr;* vv. 5-6). Thus, Saul's endorsement as a person of God seems to involve both priestly and prophetic elements, along with his royal designation as the LORD's anointed one.

There is an interesting interplay between v. 7, which is probably original, and v. 8, which seems to contradict it. In v. 7, Samuel offers to Saul a word of true empowerment, authorizing him (as an individual filled with the spirit of God) to use his own judgment in taking the steps necessary to rally the people under his leadership: "Now when these signs meet you, do whatever you see fit to do, for God is with you." However, later editors knew that Samuel would soon criticize Saul for exercising the priestly function of offering a sacrifice at Gilgal when Samuel did not arrive after the prescribed seven-day period (13:8-14). Even though the text implies that Saul's sacrifice occurred some time later (11:1 indicates that more than a month had passed), later editors apparently inserted 10:8 to provide a basis for the command that Saul violated in 13:8-9. Thus, we have v. 7, in which Saul is given freedom to "do whatever you see fit to do," immediately followed by v. 8, in which Samuel instructs Saul to "wait until I come to you and show you what you shall do."

Saul Becomes a New Man, 10:9-16

Despite the narrative's emphasis on *three* signs, we read only about the last one. The author declares that all three signs were indeed fulfilled that very day, but he prefaces the statement with a cryptic comment that, as Saul turned to leave, "God gave him another heart" (v. 9). The Hebrew is unusual. Literally, it reads "and God turned another heart to him," matching the terminology of v. 6, in which Samuel had promised that Saul would be "turned into another person" when he met the prophets and was filled with the spirit. The narrator's insistence that Saul was given "another heart" from the moment he left Samuel may be an intentional effort to fill a

Oak of Tabor

The Oak of Tabor is otherwise unknown, but distinctive trees were commonly identified with certain persons or events and used as landmarks. Some have sought to identify this site with the oak under which Rebekah's nurse Deborah was buried (Gen 35:8), or with the "Palm of Deborah" mentioned in Judg 4:5. There is not enough evidence to make this identification, however. The Hebrew word *ʾēlôn* usually refers to a large tree connected with a shrine, not necessarily an oak. Mamre, where Abraham built an altar (Gen 13:18), was known for its great trees, often called the "oaks" or "terebinths" of Mamre (Gen 13:18; 18:1).

Ecstatic Prophets

The earliest prophets in Israel were quite different from the staid figures of the classical prophets such as Isaiah or Jeremiah. Although the literary prophets were sometimes given to aberrant behavior (witness Ezek 4) and apparently saw visions, they were not portrayed as ecstatics. Israel shared with its neighbors—and with most major cultures and religions of world history—a tradition of roving or temple-based "prophets" who came into contact with the spirit (or spirits) through dervish-like behavior, using chants, musical instruments, or even self-flagellation to induce an ecstatic trance. The prophets of Baal who opposed Elijah used chants, dances, and self-mutilation to induce their frenzy (1 Kgs 18:26-28), but the prophetic troop Saul encountered seemed to rely on musical instruments to achieve their euphoric state. Another account in 1 Sam 19:18-24 connects both Samuel and Saul with a band of ecstatics. In that story, Saul stripped off all of his clothes and lay at Samuel's feet for a full day and a night.

Analogous shamans of primitive cultures (up to and including the modern era) are known to use various naturally occurring drugs from mushrooms, tree bark, or hemp for the same purpose. It is worthy of note that modern rock bands who promote drug usage serve in a similar role as idolized shamans to a vast number of people who are supposedly more enlightened.

There is a sense in which modern charismatic churches that promote glossolalia, "holy laughter," and "being slain in the Spirit" have preserved many of these ancient prophetic traditions. Such churches often rely on powerful music or the chant-like sermons of the preacher to induce the contagious "movement of the Spirit," which may lead even skeptical participants to speak in other tongues, fall senseless to the floor, or laugh uncontrollably. Whether it is the Spirit of God that moves in such ways—or whether these phenomena are self-induced—is beside the point for those who find the experience to be cathartic.

For further reading, see Arthur C. Lehmann, and James E. Myers, *Magic, Witchcraft, and Religion: An Anthropological Study of the Supernatural* (Palo Alto CA: Mayfield Publishing Company, 1985); J. Lindblom, *Prophecy in Ancient Israel* (Philadelphia: Fortress Press, 1962); Robert R. Wilson, *Prophecy and Society in Ancient Israel* (Philadelphia: Fortress Press, 1980).

perceived gap in the fulfillment of Samuel's prophecy. Verses 10-12 describe Saul's infilling with the spirit and his unexpected behavior as he fell in with the ecstatic prophets, but they never use the terminology of Saul's becoming another person. For the narrator, the change in Saul actually preceded his experience with the prophets, for God's gift of a new heart certainly would have made him a new man.

Saul's encounter with the band of prophets is told with an economy of style (v. 10), then followed by a longer account of how others reacted to Saul's uncharacteristic behavior (vv. 11-12). [Ecstatic Prophets] The prophetic troop, just returning from the shrine, used musical instruments—and probably a whirling dervish-like dance—to induce a trance, which they believed put them in contact with the spirit of God. [Musical Instruments] The prophetic band's frenzied behavior was so contagious that Saul lost his inhibitions and joined the band in their ecstatic invocation of the spirit.

The author attributes Saul's behavior to divine initiative: "The spirit of God possessed him" (v. 10). This presence or absence of the spirit becomes a recurring theme for Saul, for the spirit later comes upon him in power (11:6), but also leaves him (16:14a; 18:12) and is replaced by an evil spirit (16:14b-16; 18:10; 19:9).

The account of Saul's encounter with the prophets—like the similar story in 1 Samuel 19:18-24—is used in part as an etiology to explain an enigmatic proverb whose meaning is no longer clear (vv. 11-12). Since the narrator's contemporaries understood the proverb, the narrator did not bother to explain it. The intensive particle *gam* ("even" or "also") may be the key to the conundrum and leads to a reasonable presumption that the proverb later functioned to emphasize any individual's uncharacteristic behavior. Evidently, no one ever would have expected Saul, son of the respected Kish, to writhe on the ground and cry out in ecstatic frenzy. It would have become the subject of much talk and speculation. With Saul's rising notoriety, his atypical ecstasy became emblematic of unexpected behavior. Thus, if a timid recluse suddenly found courage and emerged as a leader, or if a shy young person developed into a paramour, others might observe their change in behavior by saying, "Is Saul also among the prophets?" Other possible meanings are explored by Ralph Klein.[2]

The puzzling question of v. 12 is even more baffling. A man asked, "And who is their father?" A likely assumption is that "father" in this case is a metaphor for "leader." Since prophetic bands were often called "sons of the prophets" (2 Kgs 2:12; 6:21; 13:14), it is reasonable to think that their leader might be called

Musical Instruments

The instruments specified in v. 5 are the harp, tambourine, flute, and lyre. The harp and lyre were popular stringed instruments, while the tambourine was a small, two-sided hand drum. The word translated "flute" by NRSV was really more of a primitive clarinet, a split-reed instrument fashioned from dried cane. Travelers to Israel will see similar instruments sold in the streets of Jerusalem to this day.

Blind Harpist (detail). 19th Dynasty. New Kingdom (c. 1250 BC). Rijksmusum van Oudheden. Leiden, The Netherlands. (Credit: Erich Lessing/Art Resource, NY)

"father" (cf. Gen 45:8 and Judg 17:10). Since Saul's father Kish was mentioned in v. 11, the question in v. 12 may posit that Saul has deserted Kish and adopted Samuel, who "stood in charge" of the ecstatic troop in 1 Samuel 19:20.

Once his prophetic frenzy had faded, Saul returned home. The narrative leads us to believe that he may have been embarrassed, or simply confused. His first conversation was not with his father Kish, but with an uncle (1 Chr 8:29-33 and 9:35-39 suggest that Saul had an uncle named Ner, though the lists do not pretend to be comprehensive). The uncle asked Saul several probing questions, as the narrator tells it (vv. 14-16). Since Saul's encounter with the prophets had occurred not far from home, perhaps the family had heard about it. In any case, Saul holds his peace and limits his conversation to the matter of the donkeys, his original quest: "About the matter of the kingship, of which Samuel had spoken, he did not tell him anything." Like Samson (Judg 14:4, 6), Saul hides his divine encounter, even from his family. This withholding of information serves the narrator well, as it sets the stage for the following accounts in which Saul's previous anointing is unknown (10:17-27; 11:1-15).

CONNECTIONS

A New Goal, 9:1-26

The story of Saul's search for his father's donkeys has a nice, folksy feel to it, but the reader soon learns that it is one of the most important stories in Israel's history. The shape of the story itself serves as a metaphor for the content: a folk story with royal implications, a quest for an ass that culminates with a crown, a farm boy who becomes king of his people. The author delights in telling us that God works in mysterious ways.

Fences are still rare in Israel and were probably nonexistent in Saul's day. Animals could easily wander away, but usually someone was assigned to watch over them. If Kish's donkeys managed to get completely out of sight, someone was not doing their job. Could it have been Saul, or was he called upon to fix someone else's failure? In either case, Saul showed remarkable determination. How many people would spend *three days* searching for donkeys in the rugged countryside of Israel's central hill country? Saul's perseverance in pursuing the lost asses is a testament to his character.

When Saul and his servant finally gave up and decided to consult the seer, they had no way of knowing that God had already revealed his will to Samuel, or that the LORD had sent them out on a "wild ass chase" for the express purpose of bringing them to Samuel. Saul's story prompts us to reflect on our own lives and the hidden ways in which God has been at work. A chance meeting introduces a man to his future mate. A stranger's words lead

Unexpected Developments

Sometime around 1812, in the French town of Coupvray, a three-year-old boy was at play in his father's workshop. Knives for cutting leather and awls for embossing decorations were common tools. As he played, something sharp pierced his eye. An infection set in and moved to the other eye. Soon, the young boy was completely blind. At the age of 10, he was sent to a special school in Paris, where he learned to read by tracing raised Roman letters. He was also exposed to a system of dots and dashes embossed on thin cardboard. At the age of 15, Louis Braille adapted what he had learned to create a simple six-dot code that eventually became the standard method of reading and writing for the blind.

Legend has it that Braille created his code with the same awl that had pierced his eye. An unexpected accident led to the invention of a code that has brought light and hope to countless blind persons since that time. We would overstate the case to claim that God caused Louis Braille's blindness—but it is not unreasonable to see how God led him through the darkness to become more than he ever thought he would be. Braille expressed his thanks to God by working as a dedicated teacher and serving as a talented church organist. His name will be remembered as long as the blind read Braille, because he kept his inner eyes open to new and unexpected possibilities.

---

someone to examine and change her life. An unexpected illness allows the time for serious study. The loss of a job leads one to discover the career she really wanted.

Do we believe that God is at work in our lives, leading us to discover new truths or accomplish new things even in the face of obstacles? Do we believe that God can work through the circumstances of our lives to bring us closer to God? The message of 1 Samuel 9:1-26 is unequivocal. Every day and every action is fraught with divine significance for those who have ears to hear and eyes to see. [Unexpected Developments]

When Samuel began to predict great things for Saul, the young man was incredulous. Although he had personal potential (the author tells us that he was tall and handsome), Saul knew he came from a tribe that was not only the smallest in Israel, but also the most despised (see [Benjamin]). Indeed, Saul's hometown of Gibeah was the very town that had sparked Benjamin's downfall by victimizing a Levite's concubine (Judg 19). If Israel was to have a king, Gibeah is the *last* place to look. Yet God chose Saul.

It is easy for us to belittle ourselves and allow false humility to impede our spiritual development and service to God. We think that we are too small, or too shy, or too poor to accomplish great things. We think we are not smart enough to teach, not wise enough to care for children, not bold enough to share our faith. Saul's call is an ever-present reminder that God can use even the least of us to do great things. God is always waiting to bless us in more ways than we know. [A Taste of Things to Come]

A Taste of Things to Come

Samuel's unexpectedly generous hospitality toward Saul (v. 24) is a token of Saul's future greatness; the ample portion of meat is a taste of things to come. The New Testament speaks of the believer's present experience with the Holy Spirit as a taste of things to come through all eternity. Paul speaks of the Spirit as a present pledge or guarantee of our future inheritance (2 Cor 1:22; 5:5; Eph 1:14), while 1 Peter encourages new believers to grow in their faith, having tasted what the Lord is like (2:2-3). The greatest tragedy, according to the author of Hebrews, is for one who has tasted God's heavenly gift to turn away from the gospel (Heb 5:5-6).

A New Heart, 9:27–10:9

Saul's encounter with Samuel led to an encounter with God in which God made him a different person (v. 6) by giving to him a new heart (v. 9). Saul was changed; he was no longer the same. By the power of God, he became a new man. By the leadership of God, he opened his heart to new experiences, including a spiritual encounter with God. Under ordinary circumstances, Saul would never have joined the troop of prophets outside Gibeah. He would never have given up his inhibitions. He would never have released his control and given God such sway in his life. But that is what it means to have a new heart, to become a new person. In the Christian sense, it means to surrender control of one's life to Christ and, as it were, to be reborn as a new person.

Ezekiel the prophet described such a transformation as he spoke God's word: "A new heart I will give you, and a new spirit I will put within you; and I will remove from your body the heart of stone and give you a heart of flesh" (Ezek 36:26). Paul described the significance of baptism by pointing out that new believers are "buried with him [Christ] into death, so that, just as Christ was raised from the dead by the glory of the Father, so we too might walk in newness of life" (Rom 6:4). As Christians, we no longer conform to the ways of the world, but are transformed into persons who know and do the will of God (Rom 12:2).

God still has the power to change our lives, even as God made Saul into a new person. Our anointing through baptism, like Saul's anointing with oil, sets us apart as God's chosen people. If we are willing to open our hearts, God will give us a new heart, a new hope, a new life.

A New Experience, 10:10-16

Saul's encounter with the prophets added another level of confirmation to his sense of calling. They accepted him and shared with him, while Saul relaxed his own inhibitions to accept the band of prophets and their unusual ways. Through the prophets' fervent devotion to God, Saul experienced something he had not previously known. He allowed the spirit of God to overwhelm him, body and soul. For Saul, his time with the prophets was a high moment of worship, an encounter with God, an experience of true ecstacy. He did not stay long on that mighty cloud of joy, but even after he came down, he was left with the certain knowledge that he had met God.

Saul's experience underscores the importance of worship in our lives. Worship does not always entail a charismatic experience, but true worship always involves a personal surrender of self to God. Through singing God's praise, hearing God's word, sharing God's gifts, or seeking God's forgiveness, we reset our priorities and exalt God to God's proper place in our lives. The support we receive from other worshipers and the fellowship we experience as God's family are ongoing confirmations of God's presence *in* us and God's calling *to* us. The glorious feelings of heartfelt worship may not last through the week, but the memory does. We know that we have been with God and God's people, and in that knowledge we find strength for each day.

NOTES

[1] P. Kyle McCarter, *I Samuel* (AB 8; Garden City: Doubleday, 1980), 173.

[2] Ralph W. Klein, *1 Samuel* (WBC 10; Waco: Word Books, 1983), 92-93.

A PUBLIC PROCLAMATION
AND IMMEDIATE DANGER

10:17-27a

COMMENTARY

The story of Saul's election by lot is the second account of his ascent to the throne, but it does not really follow the first account. The preceding story of Saul's search for the lost asses of Kish and his subsequent anointing by Samuel (9:1–10:16) is told almost as a parenthesis, or as something that takes place offstage. Its wholly positive approach to kingship identifies it as older material.

Saul's selection in the "kingship lottery" (10:17-27) more aptly follows the account of Israel's demand for a king and Samuel's antimonarchical speech (8:1-22). That story ended with Yahweh's acceding to Israel's plea and instructing Samuel to give the people what they wanted. With 10:17-27, we come to the continuation of that narration: Samuel has summoned the people to Mizpah, an important city that sometimes served as a cultic gathering place for all Israel. [Mizpah] The last time Israel had gathered at Mizpah (see 7:2-6), they were there to repent of idolatry and seek deliverance from the Philistines. The text pointedly says that Samuel judged them there. Now Israel gathers at Mizpah to seek a king, and Samuel opens the assembly with words of deliverance and judgment.

Mizpah

The Levant was home to several cities named "Mizpah" (sometimes spelled "Mizpeh"), including representatives in Gilead, Moab, Judah, and Benjamin. There was even a "land of Mizpah" located north of Palestine (Josh 11:3). The most important of these is the location described in 1 Sam 7 and 10: Mizpah of Benjamin.

The name "Mizpah" derives from the root ṣāpâh, meaning "to watch" or "to spy out." Thus, miṣpâ means "outlook" or "watchtower"; we would expect to find Mizpah on high ground. The precise location of this particular Mizpah is uncertain; archaeologists are divided between Nebi Samwil, an impressive high point some five miles north of Jerusalem, and Tell en-Nasbeh, about three miles further north, on a large hill beside the main road to Samaria. The evidence slightly favors the latter.

Mizpah was remembered as a place of cultic significance (Judg 20–21; 1 Sam 7; 10:17-27) as well as a military and political center (1 Kgs 15:22 = 2 Chr 16:6; 2 Kgs 25:23, 25). After the first fall of Jerusalem in 597 BC, Mizpah became the capital of the Babylonian province. In later Jewish history, it was remembered as a great center for prayer and worship (1 Macc 3:44-46).

Sacred Lots

The use of lots as a means of determining the divine will was common in the ancient Near East. In Israel, lots were used in various ways: to determine guilt (Josh 7:14; 1 Sam 14:42; Jonah 1:7), to apportion land (Num 26:55; Josh 14:2), or to select which animals should be sacrificed (Lev 16:7-10). Various ranks of temple personnel were chosen by lot (1 Chr 24:5; 25:8; 26:13), as were assignments for temple provisions in time of need (Neh 10:34 [MT v. 35]; 11:1). The lot could be used to decide contentious disputes in the lack of other evidence (Prov 18:18). And Israel resorted to the lot in order to choose its first king (1 Sam 10:20-21).

The texts cited above cover the greater part of Israel's history, from the entry into Canaan to the postexilic period. The use of lots also appears in the New Testament. Roman soldiers cast lots to determine who should get Jesus' clothing (Mark 15:24 and parallels). More positively, the disciples cast lots in choosing Matthias to replace Judas (Acts 1:26), believing that the choice would be the Lord's.

Israel's law opposed all forms of divination and witchcraft (see [Divination]), but the sacred lot was considered to be something different, for when it is cast, "the decision is the LORD's alone" (Prov 16:33).

We know few particulars concerning the appearance of the objects in question, or about the preferred methods for casting lots. Scholars have surmised that the "Urim and Thummim" associated with the high priest's breastplate (Exod 28:30; Lev 8:8) were a type of sacred lots, since they were used to divine God's will (Num 27:21; Deut 33:8). In 1 Sam 14:41-42, Saul ordered that the Urim and Thummim be used to determine guilt: "If this guilt is in me or in my son Jonathan, O LORD God of Israel, give Urim; but if this guilt is in your people Israel, give Thummim."

Existing evidence, then, suggests that two lots were commonly used, though we know nothing of their appearance. Lots simply may have been drawn from a pouch to determine a "yes or no" answer, or cast toward a given point, with the lot landing closest being the chosen one. Prov 16:33 speaks of lots being thrown into the lap, which would seem to require that upward-facing markings on the lot were used to determine the divine will.

Despite Yahweh's instruction to give the people a king, Samuel cannot resist reminding the gathered tribes that they have rejected the better path of obedience to Yahweh. Although Yahweh had delivered the people from Egypt and rescued them from the grip of other oppressive kingdoms (v. 18)—thus proving the efficacy of the traditional theocracy—the people had rejected Yahweh's salvific leadership in favor of an earthly monarch (v. 19a). Samuel's speech takes the form of a prophetic oracle, and the final part of the oracle—the judgment—consists of instructions for the royal lottery (v. 19b). [Sacred Lots] The implication is that God will judge Israel by giving them what they want; the vagaries of kingship will be punishment enough.

The word for "lot" is not used in this passage, but the technical language of "presenting" the options and "taking" the chosen is evident. If we assume that something like the "Urim and the Thummim" was employed, then only two lots were available, offering two options on each cast. On this basis, the tribes would be presented two by two, with one being chosen of each pair. The "winners" would then be paired again, and the process repeated until only one tribe remained. According to the text, the tribe of Benjamin was chosen (lit., "taken by lot," v. 20). The process was then repeated until the lots indicated a single man: the Benjaminite Saul, son of Kish. [A Postulated Procedure]

Saul was chosen, the narrative says, but he could not be found. Thus, those present ask the obvious question, "Did the man come here?" The unexpected twist is that they ask the question of *Yahweh*, rather than of Saul's family, and it is Yahweh who reveals that Saul can be found hidden among the baggage and gear brought by the family caravan. There is a wordplay at work here: the people asked (*wayyîšʾălû*, from *šāʾal*) for the location of Saul (*šāʾûl*), whose name means "requested one." The only surprising thing is that the wordplay is not more pointed still. The narrator could have inserted Saul's name instead of "the man" in the question "Did the man come here?"

A Postulated Procedure

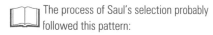 The process of Saul's selection probably followed this pattern:

1. The tribes were paired and ultimately reduced to one: Benjamin.
2. The clans or extended families of Benjamin were reduced to the clan of Matri (NRSV, "the family of the Matrites").
3. The families of the clan of Matri were paired and reduced to the family of Kish.
4. The men of Kish's family were brought forward until only Saul remained.

The actual procedure seems a bit confusing because the text says the candidates were presented "man by man," and Saul was chosen, but the narrative also says that Saul was not present. This suggests that family leaders might have represented others by proxy, offering each individual's name at the appropriate time. We are probably not to assume that every person in Israel had left their homes unguarded and traveled to Mizpah. Indeed, the question asked in v. 22 ("Did the man come here?") presumes that not all men had come to Mizpah.

Did Saul have regal characteristics or abilities to qualify him for kingship? The only thing we learn is that he was "head and shoulders taller" than all the rest—a veritable giant among men (v. 23). Saul's height, like his good looks mentioned in 9:2, would have been considered as signs of divine favor. Samuel himself seemed impressed. The negative tone of vv. 18-19 vaporizes as Samuel presents Yahweh's chosen king to his gathered subjects: "Do you see the one whom the LORD has chosen? There is no one like him among all the people!" (v. 24a). The people's response, literally, "May the king live," is the Hebrew equivalent of "Long live the king!"

Though Saul now stands as king, Samuel is not yet willing to relinquish control of the proceedings or of the nation's future. As he previously warned the elders about the potential abuses of kingship, so now he outlines the proper rights and duties of a king (see the discussion of 1 Sam 8:9, including [Translating The Ways of the King]). [The Rights and Duties of Kingship] Saul is not given *carte blanche* to do whatever he desires. Rather, Samuel "reads him his rights" before all Israel so that all know what to expect of their king (v. 25a).

The Rights and Duties of Kingship

AΩ In 8:11-18, the phrase *mišpaṭ hammelek* was translated as "justice of the king" (see [Translating "The Ways of the King"]). Here (10:25), the term *mišpaṭ hammĕlûkâ* is rendered as "the rights and duties of kingship." The two phrases seem to suggest the same idea, though the different contexts suggest almost opposing connotations. The "abuses" mentioned in 8:11-18 were all considered to be rights within the king's purview; Samuel had simply given them the darkest possible slant in a fruitless attempt to dissuade the people from seeking a king. The negativity has receded in 10:25, where the term has a more positive meaning.

To ensure further that the king's limits would be manifest, Samuel put them into writing and entrusted the official document to the priests' care (lit., he "laid it up before the LORD," v. 25a). This copy of the royal prerogatives would serve as an independent testimony in the event of future abuses (cf. Deut 17:18).

The story concludes with a comment on the people's reaction to Saul's election. After Samuel dismisses the assembly, an indeterminate number of men "whose hearts God had touched" go with him (v. 26). These men are described with the term *haḥyil*, which could mean "valor" or "substance" (compare Saul's father, who was called a *gibbôr ḥayil*, "a powerful man"). Many translations, including the NRSV, call them "warriors" because they become Saul's honor guard. Although the phrase is ambiguous in its specific intent, the overall impression is wholly positive. These are men who will be good and loyal supporters of Saul and of the kingdom.

Saul's loyal supporters are set in contrast with certain "worthless fellows" (*bĕnê bĕliyyaʿal*) who "despised Saul" and refused to support him (v. 27). Similar terms are used to describe Eli's worthless sons (1 Sam 2:21) and other rebellious scofflaws (2 Sam 20:1). With this brief comment, the author has set the stage for the dissension and strife that will yet rip the nation apart. The people of wealth and power support Saul, knowing that the added stability of kingship will strengthen and protect their personal interests. On the other hand, the less powerful and more marginalized societal strata seem less enthused about having another layer added to Israel's power structure.

The seeds of dissension found in v. 27 come to fruition when David later rises to power, for his primary support (outside of Jonathan) is initially found among the lower classes and the "outlaws" of Israelite society. Indeed, David himself lives as an outlaw for a time, though he remains loyal to "the king's anointed."

CONNECTIONS

Getting What You Asked For, 10:17-19

Samuel spoke to Israel an oracle of judgment: "Thus says the LORD, the God of Israel." [Judgment Oracles] He spoke of God's past graciousness (v. 18) and wondered why Israel would reject the sovereignty of Yahweh in favor of an earthly king (v. 19).

As he came to the part of the oracle normally reserved for the pronouncement of judgment, Samuel called the people to come forward and choose their new king. By shaping the story in this way, the author suggests that God's judgment was to give the people precisely what they asked for, allowing them to experience the natural consequences of their choice.

Samuel had predicted the dark side of kingship in 8:11-18, but to no avail. In the author's eyes, the people had rejected the King of Heaven for a king on earth. As punishment for this rebellion, God would simply give them what they asked for.

Modern believers rarely think in terms of seeking a king, but we all have inner conflicts concerning who will rule our lives. When we reject God's leadership and follow selfish desires, we often get what we ask for, and sometimes more than we bargained for.

Judgment Oracles

Later prophets routinely criticized Israel and declared the coming of judgment by means of oracles (e.g., 2 Sam 12:7-15; Amos 2:6-16; Jer 26:1-6). Typical judgment oracles included all or most of the following elements:

1. Introductory formula ("Thus says the LORD")
2. Reminder of Yahweh's faithfulness
3. Description of Israel's (or another nation's or individual's) sin
4. Declaration of judgment
5. Concluding formula (often, "Says Yahweh!")

Items one and five can vary in form, and one of the two may be missing, but rarely both. Items two and three are sometimes reversed or interspersed, and the reminder of Yahweh's faithfulness does not always appear, but the description of Israel's sin and the consequent declaration of judgment are ubiquitous.

Where Was Saul?, 10:20-24

Why was Saul not present when his name was called? If the account in 9:1–10:16 can be presumed as a prior event, then Saul would have had foreknowledge that he was God's chosen. In that case, he might have been hiding, in case his anointing had been a false hope, so that others would not see his disappointment. Or he might have been waiting in the wings, shrewdly building suspense before his grand entrance when they called for him to appear and accept the charge.

The story itself suggests that Saul had to be persuaded to accept the new role assigned to him. Yet he did accept it. That Israel's first ruler was an ultimate failure as a king seems to be more of a commentary on kingship than on Saul himself. When God called, Saul hesitated—but he answered.

This story challenges modern believers to reflect on how many times we have remained hidden amid the baggage of our lives even though God was calling us to positive service and opportunities for leadership. We have many excuses for hiding: Perhaps we are shy or have low self-esteem. Perhaps our personal baggage is so heavy that we think we'll never get away from it. Many great leaders of the Old Testament period were hesitant when God called (e.g., Moses, Amos, Isaiah, and Jeremiah), but they overcame their inner fears and self-doubts to become strong and able leaders. Those who read their stories are moved to consider: how will *we* respond when God calls?

The Rights and Duties of the King, 10:25

Samuel's careful composition of a document outlining the "rights and duties of the king" provides a reminder that great privilege is accompanied by great responsibility.

Jesus expressed the same truth in the parable of the faithful and the unfaithful servants. "From everyone to whom much as been given, much will be required; and from the one to whom much has been entrusted, even more will be demanded" (Luke 12:48).

Believers sometimes want the privilege of constant forgiveness without the responsibility of changing sinful behaviors. Paul pointed out the incompatibility of dying to sin and living in it at the same time (Rom 6:1-4).

There Is Always Trouble, 10:26-27

The last two verses of this story make it clear that kingship did not solve Israel's problems. Instead, internal strife increased as the "valiant fellows" whose heart God had touched rallied around Saul and "worthless fellows" rejected him by refusing to bring gifts to help finance the nascent monarchy.

Samuel did not like the idea of kingship and said as much, but at Yahweh's bidding he pledged his support to the king; others, for their own reasons, refused. Saul responded to the conflict by "holding his peace."

There are times when "holding our peace" is a proper strategy for dealing with cantankerous persons, but also there are times when keeping quiet is nothing more than the psychological defense of denial or avoidance.

Conflict is inevitable so long as we live in relationship with other persons. Learning to confront and manage conflict is a crucial skill, though often avoided. Saul's later escapist behavior (listening to David's music) and his manic depressive personality both suggest that he internalized his troubles, rather than dealing with them in an open manner. The insistence of Jesus that conflict be handled openly and fairly (Matt 18:15-20) reinforces the truth that interpersonal conflict is to be expected, while suggesting appropriate strategies for dealing with it. Mature believers learn to live in peace, not simply to hold their peace.

SAUL'S FIRST VICTORY AND THE KINGSHIP CONFIRMED

10:27b–11:15

COMMENTARY

This passage provides the third account of Saul's ascent to the throne. In the first two accounts, Samuel played a pivotal role in seeking out Saul, first for a private anointing (9:1–10:16), then for a public proclamation (10:17–27) as king. In this third story, Saul's rise is attributed to the exercise of his personal leadership qualities, greatly enhanced by the inrushing upon him of Yahweh's spirit. Samuel's role is limited to a "kingship renewal" ceremony tagged on as the end of the main story.

The story itself bears many similarities to the old narratives describing the "major judges" who typically rose to power in response to crises, and delivered Israel by dint of their charismatic leadership empowered by Yahweh's spirit (Judg 3:7-16:31). [Stories of the Judges] The primary difference is that those judges did not go on to become kings, but remained local heroes. Indeed, the one earlier attempt at establishing a monarchy—by Abimelech, who was not a judge—was roundly condemned and ended in failure (Judg 9).

Stories of the Judges

The hero stories describing the judges were shaped as theological lessons for Israel, following a typical form that began with Israel's sin and consequent "judgment" through the oppression of some enemy. When the suffering people cried out for deliverance, Yahweh's spirit would endow some person to become the agent of Israel's salvation.

Shrewd trickery often played a role in these victories. Left-handed Ehud inserted himself into the enemy king's palace through an intrepid artifice that led to a liberating assassination (Judg 3:12-30). The woman Jael lured the enemy general Sisera into her tent, where a bowl of warm milk and a well-placed tent peg did him in after Deborah and Barak had routed the Canaanite army (Judg 4:17-22). Other judges, such as Gideon (Judg 6:7-25), succeeded by means of superior military strategy. The present account of Saul's most successful military exploits likewise reflects a measure of trickery combined with a careful strategy of troop placement.

The Need for Deliverance, 10:27b–11:4

The present account reveals that the Philistines were not the only enemy to threaten Israel's well-being, for even as the Philistines sought to expand their coastal holdings into the central highlands, the people of Ammon fought to take (or retake?) the land east of the Jordan, an area often called Gilead. [Ammon] Details of the Ammonite oppression that led to Saul's regal response are missing from both the MT and the LXX. It is possible that an ancient scribe inexplicably skipped an entire paragraph. Fortunately, the manuscript tradition preserved at Qumran did not have the lacuna. 4QSam^a preserves (or provides) the missing paragraph, which also was present in the ancient Greek version used by Josephus. Virtually all English translations of the Bible also lack the passage, but the NRSV inserts it at the end of chapter 10, with no new verse designation. We shall refer to it as 10:27b. [The Missing Paragraph]

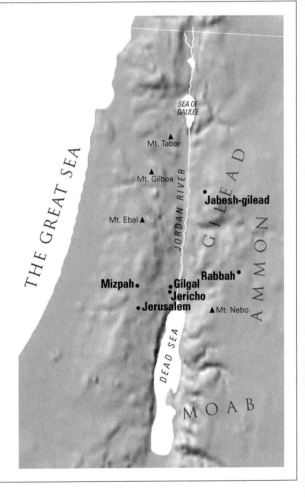

Ammon

The Ammonites, like the Moabites, were linked to Israel by traditional kinship stories tracing their origin to the eponymous ancestors Ben-Ammi and Moab, the sons born to Abraham's nephew Lot as the result of an incestuous encounter with his daughters following the destruction of Sodom and Gomorrah (Gen 19:30-38). Thus, for Israel, the Ammonites were blood relatives (however distant) and occasional allies, but their relationship was usually adversarial because the two nations claimed much of the same territory.

Ancient Ammon was centered in a mountainous area east of the Jordan, just north of Moab's borders along the Dead Sea, and generally south and east of the important River Jabbok. The heart of Ammon was its great city Rabbah (meaning "great"), usually called Rabbath-ammon to distinguish it from other cities named Rabbah. The strength and persistence of this city (now Amman, Jordan) testifies to its fortuitous location and good water supply.

The Ammonites spoke a Semitic language that was very similar to Hebrew, and shared many similarities with Hebrew culture. The chief god of the Ammonite pantheon was called Milkom.

For further reading, see Gerald Mattingly, "Ammon/Ammonites," *MDB* (Macon GA: Mercer University Press, 1990), 23-24; and Stephen J. Andrews, "Molech," *MDB*, 580-81.

The tribes of Reuben and Gad claimed terri- tory in the Transjordan area between the Sea of Galilee to the north and the Dead Sea to the south. Unfortunately, the Ammonites main- tained their own claim to much of the same territory. The king of Ammon had begun a sys- tematic program of terrorizing the Gadites and Reubenites and rendering them malleable to his own designs by gouging out the right eye of each Israelite man. This cruelty left the men not only disfigured, but seriously handicapped in the event of war. Most men, being right-handed, could not aim a bow or a spear effectively without benefit of their right eye.

The text tells us two facts that appear contradictory: "*No one was left* of the Israelites across the Jordan whose right eye Nahash, king of the Ammonites had not gouged out," and "*There were seven thousand men* who had escaped from the Ammonites and had entered Jabesh-gilead." [Jabesh-gilead] The first statement expresses the dire need of the Transjordanian settlers. The second points to a glimmer of hope. But the last remaining holdouts also came under siege, as Nahash and his army encamped around Jabesh-gilead. The phrase "about a month later" (included in the NRSV as part of 11:1) is prob- ably an editorial attempt to connect this story with Saul's public acclamation at Mizpah.

Most descriptions of biblical battles do not include the threats and negotiations that typi- cally preceded the fighting (Judg 11:12-28, also involving Ammon, is a notable exception). The siege at Jabesh-gilead allowed ample time for parleying, however, and the reader is privy to a sample of the treaty talks. The people of Jabesh-gilead seemed willing to become a vassal city to Ammon, but Nahash insisted on gouging out "everyone's right eye" as a condition for lifting the siege and exer- cising suzerainty. For obvious reasons, the elders of Jabesh-gilead found this unacceptable. The Israelite negotiators asked for—and, surprisingly, received—a seven-day respite and permission to send messengers seeking military aid from the other tribes. Their request to seek a "deliverer" (*môšîaʿ*, 11:3), combined with the later use of "deliver" or "rescue" (*tĕšûʿâh*, 11:9, 13), serves as a verbal link to the old stories of the judges, who acted as deliverers.

Nahash, apparently, was supremely confident that no help would be found. The Israel he knew was disjointed and scattered,

The Missing Paragraph

"Now Nahash, king of the Ammonites, had been grievously oppressing the Gadites and the Reubenites. He would gouge out the right eye of each of them and would not grant Israel a deliverer. No one was left of the Israelites across the Jordan whose right eye Nahash, king of the Ammonites, had not gouged out. But there were seven thousand men who had escaped from the Ammonites and had entered Jabesh-gilead. About a month later . . . ." (NRSV).

Jabesh-gilead

The area called "Gilead" was roughly equivalent to the land between the Sea of Galilee and the Dead Sea, on the *east* side of the Jordan River (see map at [Ammon]). The city of Jabesh-gilead usually is associated with Tell Abū Kharaz, about twenty miles south of the Sea of Galilee, where the Wadi Yabis flows into the Jordan. Another possible site is Tell el-Maqlub, located further to the east on the same river.

incapable of any unified response. Nahash, however, had not counted on Saul—or, more precisely, the spirit-enhanced Saul who was galvanized into action by the abhorrent news from Jabesh-gilead.

Farmer Saul Becomes a Warrior and Leader, 11:5-11

Saul's hometown of Gibeah was just over forty miles to the south and west of Jabesh-gilead, on the opposite side of the Jordan. Though geographically separated, Gibeah and Jabesh-gilead were bound together historically as "sister cities" because of an earlier request for aid—one that went unheeded. This story is told in Judges 19–21, a long and involved tale of intertribal warfare, which reputedly began when a Levite from the remote hills of Ephraim went to Bethlehem to retrieve his runaway concubine. As the two traveled back toward the north, they found overnight shelter with an old man in Gibeah of Benjamin. During the night, a rowdy gang of men sought to have forceful relations with the Levite, who voluntarily surrendered his concubine instead. The perverse pack then horribly abused and raped the unfortunate woman, who consequently died. The Levite was so livid that he cut the concubine's corpse into twelve pieces, sending them among all the tribes as a call to action against the Benjaminites for harboring such men.

The other tribes responded in force, attacking the Benjaminites with such ferocity that only six hundred men survived. When they realized, however, how close the ravaged tribe was to extinction, Israel's elders took concerted action to find wives for the remaining Benjaminites. All who participated in the pogrom had sworn not to allow their daughters to marry a man of Benjamin, however, and could not violate their oaths. According to the story, the elders found a partial solution to the problem when they realized that the city of Jabesh-gilead had not responded to the tribal call to arms. As punishment, Israel's leaders sent a contingent of twelve thousand soldiers to Jabesh-gilead with instructions to slaughter every person except the young virgins of marriageable age. Four hundred of these were captured and given to the surviving men of Benjamin. Thus, both Gibeah and Jabesh-gilead shared a reputation as shamed cities; they also came to share a blood relationship, as the surviving men of Gibeah took wives from the captured maidens of Jabesh-gilead.

This bit of background helps to explain why Saul of Gibeah is moved with such anger when he hears of the Ammonite threat against Jabesh-gilead. Saul appears as an active farmer when the

> **Threats, Curses, and Covenants**
>
> AΩ Saul's threat takes the form of an oath, which is unusual in that the curse is directed toward others. In ancient Israel, an oath consisted of a promise to do something, strengthened by a self-imprecation in the event of failure to carry out the promise: "Thus and more may God do to me, if I do not do so and so." The oath and its curse usually were directed toward the speaker (2 Kgs 6:31), but could be aimed at another (1 Sam 3:17).
>
> Saul's oath in 1 Sam 11:7 seems to presume a covenant of kinship in which the tribes have sworn to come to each other's aid. Animals sometimes were dismembered as part of the covenant-making ceremony, implying that covenant-breakers would suffer the same fate. Thus, the Hebrew idiom for covenant-making is "to *cut* a covenant" (see, for example, Yahweh's covenant with Abraham in Gen 15).

narrative begins, suggesting that the story originated separately from the preceding accounts of his anointing. Saul is moved powerfully by the spirit of God (v. 6) to deliver Israel, just as the judges of earlier generations had been moved (e.g., Samson, Judg 14:6, 19; 15:14). Drawing on the Levite's model, perhaps, Saul took two oxen—probably the very ones with which he had been plowing— and cut them into twelve pieces. He sent these out among the tribes as a call to arms, threatening a similar fate for the oxen (at least) of any who failed to muster (v. 7a) in support of Saul and Samuel. [Threats, Curses, and Covenants] [And Samuel?]

> **And Samuel?**
>
> AΩ The words "and Samuel" (in "whoever does not come out after Saul and Samuel," v. 7) may be parenthetical. Many scholars believe that these words, like "to Samuel" in v. 12, were added by later editors, perhaps along with 11:14-15, to incorporate this story into the larger narrative and bring it under the umbrella of Samuel's blessing.

The expression "dread of Yahweh" (v. 7b) is used in a surprising way. In 2 Chronicles 17:10, the expression *paḥad Yahweh* describes a paralyzing fear that falls upon Israel's *enemies* (cf. Deut 2:25). In this text, however (as in 2 Chr 14:14 [MT v. 13]), it is the Israelites who are overcome by the "dread of Yahweh," and the fear of divine reprisal stirs them to immediate action.

Saul mustered his new army at Bezek, about ten miles from Jabesh-gilead, on the opposite side of the Jordan. The number of soldiers seems staggering: 300,000 from Israel and 70,000 from Judah. As mentioned previously (see comments on 4:10), many scholars believe the word *'elep*, when used in a military sense, denoted a contingent of unspecified size, perhaps a "platoon" of from five to fourteen men.[1] Based on these figures, Saul's army would have included a more reasonable two to five thousand fighters.

Like Ehud (Judg 3:12-30) and Gideon (Judg 7) before him, Saul employed a cunning strategy in gaining an advantage over the enemy. He sent word to the inhabitants of Jabesh-gilead that he would attack early in the morning ("by the time the sun is hot, you shall have deliverance," v. 9). With this information in hand, city officials informed the besieging army that they would open the gates on the following day and submit to Ammonite rule (v. 10). This rendered the Ammonites overconfident, perhaps causing them to relax their guard a bit. Thus, when Saul divided his army into companies and attacked at dawn, striking the Ammonite camp from every side but the one facing Jabesh-gilead, he had the strategic advantage and won a resounding victory (v. 11).

At Gilgal, Saul's Kingship Reconfirmed, 11:12-15

Saul's powerful and inspired leadership led to public demand for him to rule actively as king. The text has the people address this demand to Samuel. [Is Samuel In or Out?] Saul's earlier anointing by Samuel had provided no evidence of his ability to deliver Israel from its enemies (see 10:27), but his leadership in the liberation of Jabesh-gilead offered indisputable confirmation of his aptitude for kingship. Thus, Saul's earlier anointing at Mizpah is reenacted publicly at Gilgal, an ancient sanctuary site near Jericho where Israel had reenacted their covenant ceremony upon entering Canaan. [Gilgal]

Is Samuel In or Out?

Some scholars regard v. 12 as an intrusive attempt to get Samuel back into the picture, since it refers to the prior story of Samuel's leadership in the "kingship lottery" leading to Saul's anointing. The verse may be a later addition used to bind the originally disparate stories together, but its function is to get Samuel back *into*, not *out of*, the picture. The people ask *Samuel* to identify those who had earlier rejected Saul's kingship, but it is *Saul* who insists on sparing them (11:13; the LXX, however, has Samuel in both places).

The narrator pays scant attention to Samuel, casting him in a peripheral role, though we assume he led in the ceremony of anointing and in the offering of sacrifices (vv. 14-15). Although Saul now takes center stage, Samuel refuses to leave the picture or to surrender his own leadership role. The next time he

Gilgal

According to Josh 4:19-24, Israel first encamped at Gilgal after crossing the Jordan River and entering the promised land. There, they erected a memorial of twelve large stones and renewed their covenant with Yahweh, circumcising all who had joined forces with Israel en route from Egypt (Josh 5:1-9). This, according to Josh 5:9, led to the name Gilgal, which derives from the verb meaning "to roll": God had "rolled away" the disgrace of Egypt.

Since the word "Gilgal" is also related to the idea of a circle, some scholars posit an alternate view that the 12 covenant stones were arranged in a circle, inspiring the name.

The precise location of Gilgal is unknown despite much speculation. The two leading candidates are Khirbet en-Nitleh, about three miles southeast of Jericho, and Khirbet Mefjer, a little more than a mile north of Jericho (see map at [Ammon]).

and Saul come to Gilgal, Samuel will withdraw his endorsement and repudiate Saul's kingship (13:7b–15a).

CONNECTIONS

1. *A surprising savior.* The story that precedes chapter 11—the account of Saul's anointing at Mizpah—ends when a group of worthless men ask the question "How can this man save us?" (10:27). The story of Saul's leadership in the victory over the Ammonites answers the question in no uncertain fashion: This man can save us when he allows the spirit of God to lead him.

The addition to 10:27 found in the LXX (see [The Missing Paragraph]) suggests that King Nahash already had begun a systematic program of repression targeted against the Transjordanian Israelites. Thus, the people of Jabesh-gilead were not the first to experience his cruelty, but the last holdouts against it. The king's indulgent permission to allow Jabesh-gilead seven days to seek a deliverer was not based on grace or honor, but on the certainty that no help would be found. The king of Ammon, like the worthless men of v. 27, was convinced that there was no deliverer in Israel. Allowing time for an ultimately fruitless search would have served as an effective demoralizing agent in the psychological aspect of his warfare against Israel.

The text does not tell us how the plea for aid was received in other cities of Israel—or even if the messengers of Jabesh-gilead went to other towns. The narrator is concerned only with Saul's response—and God's, for the two go together. When Saul came down the pathway from the fields and found the people of Gibeah already weeping over the news, his life was changed forever.

2. *Unexpected emotions.* Saul's personal response of grief and anger prepared his heart for an inrushing of the spirit of God, which empowered him. This was not the first time Saul had tasted God's spirit (see 10:10), but there was something different about this experience. This time, the spirit did not lead him into a frenzy of physical convulsions and ecstatic speaking, but into a frenzy of fierce anger and decisive action. Saul's anger is described by means of a common Hebrew idiom: literally, "His nose swelled greatly." Saul's nostrils flared with rage when he heard of Ammon's oppression, and he was moved to respond.

We cannot deliver every person from the varied "Ammonites" who oppress them, but a greater concern for justice might spark the inspiration to save some. One mother who became justifiably angry about the irresponsible actions of drunk drivers was moved to action. The end result was an organization called "Mothers Against Drunk Driving" (MADD), whose educational and lobbying efforts have saved many lives. Caring teachers who see obvious signs of child abuse can take action to intervene, and may save a child's life in the process. Concerned citizens who are touched by the oppressive conditions found in migrant camps or sweatshops can find positive ways to bring some measure of deliverance to those who suffer.

What angers us? Are we more prone to anger when our personal boundaries are crossed or when someone else is abused? The Bible has much to say about anger, both positively and negatively. Anger is a powerful emotion that can be extremely destructive to self and to others (Job 5:2; Prov 15:18; 22:24-25; 29:22). The wise avoid anger when possible (Jas 1:19); when it arises, they seek a quick and appropriate resolution (Eph 4:26).

There are times when anger is honorable, especially in the face of physical abuse, social oppression, or cultic corruption. The "dread of Yahweh" can move us to effective action. Like a caustic acid, however, anger is far too destructive to adopt as an everyday lifestyle.

The Saving Power of Anger

Saul was moved to anger by the cruelties Nahash was inflicting upon his kindred. His anger became a door through which the spirit of God found entrance to Saul's heart, filling him and empowering him for needed action. Thus inspired, Saul led the untrained agriculturalists of Israel to a resounding victory over the professionally equipped army of the Ammonites. Thus, like the judges who had come before him, he "delivered" Israel.

Jesus modeled appropriate anger when the self-righteous of his day thought it more important to keep rules than to heal the sick (Mark 3:5) and when he saw how the temple system extorted money from the poor while commandeering the space that should have been set aside for Gentiles to worship (John 2:13-17). There are times when appropriate anger can fuel the flame of needed action. There are times, indeed, when anger is inspired by the spirit of God.

Believers can profit from learning to identify their emotions. When we feel anger, it is good to name it, for this allows us to examine it more closely. Is our anger justified? Has our God-given sense of justice inspired our anger? If so, then what should we *do* about it? Anger does not exist for its own sake; it is a gift of God to empower us to oppose actively those who oppress or abuse the powerless. [The Saving Power of Anger]

3. *Credit where credit is due.* Following Saul's great victory over the Ammonites, some remembered the divisive spirit of those who had questioned Saul's leadership abilities and called for them to be

executed as traitors (v. 12). But the same spirit who had moved Saul to anger and war also moved him to express understanding and grace. Flush with the confidence of victory, and not yet subject to the paranoia that would later afflict him. Saul gave all the credit to God and insisted that it was a day for celebrating life, not inflicting further death (v. 13).

This impressive gesture of grace showed evidence of Saul's growing maturity. Together with his inspired mustering of the army and his charismatic leadership in battle, Saul was proving himself to be a fitting king. Seizing the moment, Samuel proposed a renewed coronation ceremony that would unite all Israel—Saul's supporters and detractors alike—in a covenant of loyalty under Saul and under God (vv. 14-15). Thus, a story that began with cruel suffering and impassioned anger concluded with joy, celebration, and peace. Such a story offers hope that we, too, may find deliverance from our own distress and experience a renewal of joy.

NOTE

[1] See George Mendenhall, "The Census Lists of Numbers 1 and 26," *JBL* 77 (1958): 52-66.

SAMUEL'S SOLILOQUY

12:1-25

COMMENTARY

This carefully constructed chapter is presented as Samuel's final attempt to warn Israel of the dangers inherent in choosing a political monarchy over a theocratic model for leadership. Commentators tend to give it labels such as "Samuel's Farewell Address," but Samuel pointedly *does not* say farewell. Indeed, at the people's urging, he promises to continue praying for them and instructing them, and he later appears in chapters 13, 15, 16, and 19. Though Samuel's death is recorded in chapter 25, his character refuses to go away, as he returns from Sheol to advise Saul in chapter 28. Nevertheless, an important transition does take place with this chapter; from this point on, Samuel is no longer the main character of the book. Reluctantly, Samuel gives over primary leadership to Saul; Israel's last judge hands over the reins to the first king.

This composition, like chapter 8, is concerned with exploring the whole concept of kingship as it relates to Israel. Can Israel have a king and still remain faithful to Yahweh? Are monarchy and theocracy mutually exclusive terms, or can they coexist? How is the king's role to be defined in relation to God?

Samuel's Faithful Leadership, 12:1-5

Chapter 12 seems to contain some ancient source materials, amply embellished by the Deuteronomistic editor(s) and strategically located at the beginning of Saul's active reign. The phrase "Samuel said to all Israel" leads the reader to assume that Samuel made this speech at Gilgal immediately following Saul's public coronation. The content, however, is more in keeping with Samuel's earlier speech to the elders who had brought their demand for a king to the old priest's home in Ramah (8:10-22).

Samuel's soliloquy begins with a concession that the torch has been passed. Samuel has listened to the people's call for a king and has

Literal Leadership

AΩ In v. 2, the concept of leadership is conveyed by a Hebrew idiom, literally, "to walk before your faces." This has been true of Samuel ("I have led you from my youth to this day") and is now true of Saul ("See, it is the king who leads you now"). Effective leadership for the Hebrews was not a matter of forcing others to follow, but of setting such a good example that others would be inspired to follow. Samuel had "walked before" the people as leader for many years. Now it is Saul who has seized the initiative. His bold example in opposing Nahash (ch. 11) inspired an entire nation to follow him.

endorsed Saul, so that "it is the king who leads you now," even though "I have led you from my youth until this day." [Literal Leadership] As he surrenders his role of primary leadership, Samuel pleads for a public vindication of himself and his office. He wants it understood that the institution of kingship in Israel should not reflect any failure on the part of either Yahweh or Yahweh's prior mode of leadership. Indeed, Samuel still understands the call for a king as an act of rebellion against Yahweh's preferred method of leadership through the priests, who served as arbiters of the mundane, and through charismatic judges, who arose to deliver Israel from periodic military threats.

The reference to Samuel's sons (v. 2) is in some tension with 8:1-6. Both texts acknowledge that Samuel has grown old and has passed on some leadership responsibilities to his sons (8:1, 5; 12:2). However, 8:3-5 insists that Samuel's sons, like Eli's, did not follow their father's example. "They turned aside after gain; they took bribes and perverted justice" (8:3). In chapter 8, Samuel does not dispute the failure of his sons, but in chapter 12, he implies that they are fit to rule, though rejected in favor of a king: "I am old and gray, but my sons are with you" (v. 2a).

Indeed, Samuel calls Israel to witness that *he* has not committed the very crimes of which his sons were accused. His defense takes the form of five rhetorical questions (v. 3), all of which would be answered negatively. [Making a Point] "Whose ox have I taken? Or whose donkey have I taken? Or whom have I defrauded? Whom have I oppressed? Or from whose hand have I taken a bribe to blind my eyes with it?" (v. 3). The key word in these questions is "take." Samuel has not used his authority to expropriate a single ox or donkey for his own use. He has not taken bribes, has not defrauded or oppressed anyone. This is in contrast to "the way of the king," who takes whatever he wants and visits hardship upon his people (8:11-18).

Samuel's public challenge has the desired effect; all Israel agrees that he has acted circumspectly, conceding that their desire for a king cannot be associated with any failure on Samuel's part (v. 4). Moreover, Samuel's challenge specifically includes the new king as a primary witness. Samuel does not mention Saul by name, but he calls both Yahweh and *his anointed* to witness his own exoneration by the people. The image of God's anointed being present as a wit-

---

Making a Point

The use of a string of rhetorical questions—all of which have the same answer—was also popular with the prophets. For example, when Amos wanted to stress his own authority to speak in God's behalf, he launched into a litany of seven rhetorical questions, all having an obviously negative answer:

Do two people walk together unless they have met?
Does a lion roar in the forest, when it has no prey?
Does a young lion cry out from its den, if it has caught nothing?
Does a bird swoop down into a snare on the ground, if there is no bait?
Does a snare spring up from the ground for no reason?
Can a warning trumpet blow in a city without causing the people fear?
Does disaster come to a city unless the LORD is behind it?
Surely the Lord GOD does nothing without revealing his secrets to his servants the prophets!
(Amos 3:3-7, adaptation of NRSV)

Having established his point, Amos personalized it with two further questions:

The lion has roared; who will not fear?
The Lord GOD has spoken: who can but prophesy? (Amos 3:8)

The power of such repetitive rhetoric is that it overwhelms the hearer (or reader) with an avalanche of questions that have the same answer, leading to the compelling inference that the issue at hand (has Samuel failed you?) will have the same answer: "No!"

For further reading on rhetorical questions, see Meir Sternberg, *The Poetics of Biblical Narrative: Ideological Literature and the Drama of Reading* (Bloomington: Indiana University Press, 1985).

---

ness is consistent with the idea that Samuel's speech followed the kingship renewal ceremony at Gilgal. Saul was still on stage in a place of honor—but he was forced to sit through Samuel's sermon before he could begin the practical business of setting up the varied institutions of a political monarchy.

Israel's Faithless Record, 12:6-15

Samuel's historical review in 12:6-15 is reminiscent of speeches made by Joshua (Josh 23–24) and Solomon (1 Kgs 8:12-61). These carefully crafted monologues are designed to reprise Israel's history and to reiterate the Deuteronomistic ideals first attributed to Moses. [Deuteronomistic Terminology] They appear at crucial periods in Israel's history, so that the reader (at least) can see that the nation's persistent troubles were predictable, but avoidable.

Deuteronomistic Terminology

AΩ Kyle McCarter provides a helpful list of phrases common to the Deuteronomistic school that appears in vv. 6-15. These include:

"cry out to Yahweh" (Judg 3:9, 15; 6:6, 7; 10:10)
"forget Yahweh" (Judg 3:7)
"sell [the Israelites] to [an enemy]" (Judg 2:14; 3:8; 4:2; 10:7; cf. Deut 32:30)
"abandon Yahweh" (Judg 2:12-13; 10:6, 10, 13; 1 Sam 8:8)
"serve the Baals [and Astartes]" (Judg 2:11, 13; 3:7; 10:6, 10; 1 Sam 7:4)
"fear Yahweh" (throughout Deut; see also Josh 4:24; 1 Kgs 8:40, 43)
"serve Yahweh" (common in Deut; see also Josh 22:5; 24:14)

P. Kyle McCarter, *I Samuel* (AB 8; Garden City: Doubleday, 1980), 214.

Which Heroes? Which Enemies?

The names of the enemies mentioned in v. 9 are fairly clear, but the judges named in v. 11 are quite uncertain. Jerubaal is an alternate name for Gideon (Judg 6–9; see especially 7:1), who fought the Midianites, an enemy that is not mentioned in v. 9.

The name Barak results from the NRSV's choice of the LXX reading, for the MT has "Bedan," who is otherwise unknown. Barak, along with Deborah, opposed the Canaanite king of Hazor, whose general was Sisera (12:9; Judg 4).

The MT's "Bedan" has stimulated much discussion. Some speculate that the name would mean "from Dan," perhaps serving as a nickname for the Danite hero Samson, who fought the Philistines (Judg 14–16). Others suggest that it is part of a dual name for Jephthah.

The presence of Jepthah the Gileadite in v. 11 is uncontested. He delivered Israel from the Ammonites (Judg 11), the same people whose atrocities had inspired Saul to call out his army against the current king Nahash. The Ammonites, however, were not mentioned in v. 9.

The king of Moab (Eglon?) is listed as an enemy in v. 9, but his nemesis Ehud (Judg 3:12-30) does not appear in v. 11.

The last hero listed in the NRSV is Samson, but the name Samson does not appear in the MT or in some versions of the LXX (it is present in the Syriac version and in the LXX^L). The better reading is *Samuel* (MT, LXX^{AB})! For Samuel to name himself among the heroic judges is not inappropriate in the light of his role in leading Israel to victory over the Philistines (1 Sam 7:2-17), an event that would still be fixed in his hearers' memory. Samuel clearly saw himself as the last judge of Israel, a final bridge to the period of the monarchy.

Verse 6 is problematic for two reasons. In content, it nearly duplicates v. 8, though with less fleshing out of God's motive for calling out Moses and Aaron. There is also a grammatical peculiarity: The word translated as "appointed" is the very common word for "do" or "make" (*ʿāśâh*). The word is sometimes used in conjunction with another verb indicating what the person is made to do ("made to fight," 1 Kgs 12:21; "made to pass through the fire," 2 Kgs 21:6). Here, however, it stands alone, suggesting only that God made Moses and Aaron what they were as the pioneers of Israel's faith.

Samuel uses lawsuit terminology in v. 7, as if he is hauling Israel into court to stand before God, who is not only witness (v. 6), but also judge and deliverer. His purpose is to remind the people of Israel's past penchant for rebellion and God's unblemished record of faithfulness (even as Samuel has been faithful). Samuel's historical review begins with the deliverance from Egypt (12:8) and moves to the period of the judges (vv. 9-11) before arriving at the transition to the monarchy (vv. 12-15).

Samuel's précis of the judges period varies considerably from the accounts found in the book of Judges itself, suggesting the presence of an older or variant tradition. The order in which the enemies appear (Sisera of Hazor, Philistines, the king of Moab; v. 9) does not tally with the Judges account, nor does the list of Hebrew heroes (Jerubaal, Barak, Jephthah, Samson; v. 11) match up with the enemies they fought. [Which Heroes? Which Enemies?]

The point of the speech, however, does not require uniformity with the records found in Judges. Samuel (or, at least, the author of his speech) wanted the people to remember Israel's historical proclivity to rebellion. He reminded the people of how God invariably had allowed them to fall into bondage as punishment for apostasy, but had always been sympathetic to their resulting plight, raising up powerful judges in response to Israel's repentant cry for deliverance (v. 10). Samuel's reference to the Baals and Astartes (see [Astarte] and [Baal]) who had tempted Israel in the past may imply that there is something idolatrous about their present devotion to a king.

In essence, Samuel is pointing to the folly of change for the sake of change. God had proven to be faithful in past trials, so why should the people now insist on a king when they faced similar circumstances? Samuel speaks as if the Ammonite crisis sparked by Nahash (v. 12; cf. 10:27b–11:2) had instigated Israel's demand for a king, even though chapter 8 assigns the initiative to a group of elders who previously had brought their demands to Samuel in Ramah. We cannot be dogmatic about this apparent discrepancy, however. Nothing happens in a vacuum, and the elders who badgered Samuel in Ramah could have been motivated by news of Nahash's earlier depredations.

The tone of Samuel's speech in vv. 12-13 makes it clear that he prefers the tried and true method of governance established by the judges, based upon God's covenant with Israel, which grew out of the exodus experience. He does not favor the transition to monarchy. Nevertheless, Samuel points to the possibility that kingship can be acceptable to God—so long as the king and his people continue to accept God's covenant demands.

The covenant reference is clear from the emphasis on the verb for hearing (*šmᶜ*), which also carries the sense of "obey," and is prominent in the Sinaitic covenant introduced by Exodus 19:5-6, as well as in the traditions preserved in Deuteronomy. To "hear" God's word truly is to heed God's voice and obey. ["I Hear and Obey"]

Samuel's concession to kingship remains provisional and is couched in the form of two conditional sentences that emphasize the precarious nature of the new relationship. Verse 14 is expressed in primarily positive terminology: "*If* you fear the LORD and serve him and heed his voice and do not rebel against the commandment of the LORD, and *if* both you and the king who reigns over you will follow the LORD your God, all will be well." The following verse repeats the same theme from a more negative

"I Hear and Obey"

"To hear" implies "to heed." Sometimes a parent may tell a child to do something several times with no response, even though the child is well within hearing distance. In exasperation, the parent may bluster, "Did you *hear* me?" The implication is, "If you hear me, you will obey me." The biblical use of the word is no different; hearing implies obedience. In some cases, as in Exod 19:5, two forms of the same verb may be combined for added emphasis: "If you hearingly hear" leaves no doubt that the listener is expected to obey, leading to the common translation "If you *obey* me."

perspective: "But *if* you will *not* heed the voice of the LORD, but rebel against the commandment of the LORD, then the hand of the LORD will be against you and your king."

Both verses carefully emphasize the importance of hearing, and both verses include the king within the sphere of the covenant. In his call to obedience before God, *the king is no different than any other Israelite*. With his speech, Samuel has granted Israel a king, but has skillfully taken the magic out of the monarchy by insisting that king and people alike are still subject to the same covenant expectations that have governed Israel from the time of the exodus.

Samuel's Final Warning—and Promise, 12:16-25

Samuel's desire to deflate Israel's concept of an all-powerful kingship continues with the performance of a miraculous sign designed to show Israel where the true power lies: with Yahweh, *who listens to his prophet*, not with the king. Pointing out that the fields were ready for harvest—a time of the year when rain is rare—Samuel called upon Yahweh to send thunder and rain upon the land. [Weather Patterns in Palestine] According to the text, the LORD answered with a great storm.

Grain that is ripe for harvest is subject to great damage from the high wind and heavy rain of a thunderstorm, so we presume that Samuel's sign not only was a means of demonstrating his continuing position of influence with Yahweh, but also was to be understood as a pointed punishment for Israel's rebellious demand for a king. The people were suitably impressed, for they "greatly feared the LORD and Samuel" (v. 18b).

Fearing further afflictions, the people finally confessed their sin to Samuel's satisfaction (v. 19), eliciting a comforting response and a final challenge (vv. 20-25). The old prophet/priest/judge repeated his warnings against turning away from Yahweh's way, exhorting the people to serve Yahweh with all their hearts (cf. Deut 11:13) and to turn away from useless endeavors (by implication, from the demand for a king, v. 21).

What little comfort Samuel gives is found in an assurance that Yahweh will not forget his people, since he has called them out to be his own (v. 22), and in the promise that Samuel himself would not turn his back on the Israelites simply because they had turned their faces toward a king (v. 23). Samuel inserts a barb even into

Weather Patterns in Palestine

Rain is seasonal in Palestine, most of it falling in the winter months (early December to early March). In good years, showers in October (the "early rain") soften the ground to facilitate plowing and the germination of seed crops. When rain falls as late as April or May (the "latter rain"), the planting of a second crop becomes possible. Thus, the growing season extends from October to April or May. The Old Testament often links the coming of early and late rains as a special sign of divine beneficence (Deut 11:14; Ps 84:6; Jer 5:24; Joel 2:23).

these words of encouragement: He will not sin against God (as the people are doing) by failing to pray for them or to teach them "in the good and right way" (which evidently they do not yet understand).

Samuel's soliloquy concludes with a final exhortation for Israel to fear God and serve him well, remembering his great acts of salvation (v. 24)—or else. Further rebellion would lead to a certain result: Both Israel and their new king would be swept away by the hand of divine destruction (v. 25). This warning was important especially to the Deuteronomists, for it serves as a theological basis for their conviction that the exile was Israel's punishment for an extended period of rebellion (see discussion of the Deuteronomist in the Introduction). Israel's choice of a king was one of many steps on the road to exile.

CONNECTIONS

Samuel's sermon speaks to a people who lived in changing times, but the issues involved are timeless. The old prophet's complete exoneration in vv. 1-5 points to the importance of personal integrity. Samuel's historical review in vv. 6-15 counsels persons to preserve and to profit from the lessons of history, especially as they relate to divine activity. Prior experience exerts its own call to listen for the voice of God above the din of other entreating temptations and to obey only God. The final section (vv. 16-25) offers both comfort and discomfort. The assurance that God will not forget God's people may bring joy to the faithful (v. 22), but not to the wicked (v. 25).

The Rarity of Integrity, 12:1-5

Samuel's appeal for vindication is a testimony to his integrity as one who had "walked before the faces" of his people during his entire life. Samuel understood the importance of setting a good example for others. He had seen the crimes perpetrated by Hophni and Phinehas, the sons of Eli. He had observed the weakness of Eli's withdrawn leadership style. He was determined to live with integrity and to build his leadership on the foundation of personal piety and probity. Even as a youth, Samuel's devout life and careful words convinced all Israel that he was a trustworthy prophet (3:19-21). Israel's elders might question Samuel's wisdom, but no one could question his character.

How many of us would have the courage to challenge our families, our friends, or even our enemies to find fault with our lifestyles, confident that nothing untoward would be found? We live in an inquisitive society that delights in finding skeletons in closets, or in shining spotlights into the dark corners of others' lives. Those who seek political office must do so with the knowledge that their finances, their morals, and even their language will become subject to public scrutiny. Few emerge unscathed from the rigors of public investigation.

Most of us, of course, do not hold positions of political power, but all of us have influence far beyond our awareness. Others look to us for leadership and follow our example. Samuel challenges us to live with integrity, to be honest in our dealings and truthful in our speaking. All of us "walk before the faces" of our family, our friends, co-workers, and neighbors. Do we want them to walk as we walk?

The Persistence of the Past, 12:6-11

All of us have pasts. We have the memories of our individual lives, which shape our present much more than we generally comprehend. And we share the history of our community, our nation, our culture. Samuel urges us to make the most of our lives by learning from the past. To grow old without benefiting from our years of experience is a terrible waste of living.

Samuel reminds Israel of its long history as God's special people. Although Genesis traces the growth of Israel to the patriarch Abraham, Samuel picks up the story with the exodus from Egypt, when Israel had a distinctly corporate personality. He rehearses the nation's persistent sin and failure, matched by God's great saving acts (*ṣidqôt*, v. 7) of redemption. God delivered Israel from Egypt under the leadership of Moses and Aaron. God delivered Israel from Canaanites, Moabites, Philistines, and other enemies through the inspired leadership of judges such as Gideon, Samson, Jephthah, and Samuel himself.

The lesson to remember is that rebellion inevitably led to bondage, while deliverance resulted from a heartfelt cry of need and repentance. If God's people would live in obedience, they could avoid falling prey to rapacious enemies. If God's people would repent and seek the LORD's favor, they could look forward to faithful deliverance.

Here is the truth for our lives: We all know what it is to fail, to fall away from God, to come under the sway of bondage to unhealthy habits, behaviors, attitudes, or lifestyles. We may have cried out in repentance and found the cleansing freedom of forgiveness, only to fall again into the same snares. Samuel would have us learn where pitfalls may be expected and take caution to avoid them.

God is gracious and forgiving; God does not give up on us, even though we may cycle in and out of personal bondage as if stuck in a revolving door. But our lives are diminished by such repetitive patterns of behavior. Those who are wise will learn from past mistakes so they may avoid them in the future. They will enrich their living by hearing and obeying God's voice, trusting more in God's sustaining power, and relying less on God's willingness to rescue the perishing.

The Steadfastness of God, 12:16-25

Samuel was not content without demonstrating to the people that ultimate power rested with God, not the king. A charismatic king might do wonders on the battlefield, but only God could open the windows of heaven and bring heavy rain out of season. Samuel's speech is a great leveler, for he reminds Israel that the king is no different than other persons in that he also stands under God's judgment.

Samuel's intention probably was not to subvert Saul's kingship or to delegitimatize the monarchy, but to put it into perspective. What Israel's leader is called (judge, king, prophet, or priest) is not so important as whether Israel's leader calls upon the LORD for guidance and so leads the nation rightly. When modern believers vote for a pastor or a president, they should be concerned with the same issue: "Will this person lead us rightly? Will this person promote the kind of justice that God would approve?"

Of course, Samuel was not concerned with the leader's behavior alone. "If *both you and the king* who reigns over you will follow the LORD your God, it will be well" (v. 14), but "if you still do wickedly, you shall be swept away, *both you and your king*" (v. 25). It is not only the leader's justice and behavior we should be concerned about, but our own. God has called us and made us to be a people for himself (v. 22; cf. Exod 19:5-6; 1 Pet 2:9). Samuel would have us to know that our behavior is not immaterial. How we live *matters*.

CROSSED BOUNDARIES
AND A CROSS PRIEST

13:1-22

Part Two: Saul—The Tragic Hero and Warrior King, 13:1–31:13

Saul rarely holds centerstage in the extended drama of kingship's rise in Israel. He owes his position to the call of God, the machinations of Samuel, and one inspired victory in battle over the Ammonites. Although the narrative of chapter 11 ends in triumph and a grand coronation for Saul, it is followed immediately by Samuel's soliloquy of 12:1-25, in which the aged priest acknowledges Saul as king but questions kingship and pointedly refuses to leave the stage.

The narrator's packaging of Saul's story suggests that the new king was doomed from the start. [Was Saul Set Up for a Fall?] We hear little of Saul's accomplishments. Rather, he quickly falls from favor with Samuel by presuming to offer a sacrifice on his own (13:1-22). Saul's popular acclaim also fades, as his son Jonathan wins public sympathy

---

Was Saul Set Up for a Fall?

Kenneth Cohen argues that King Saul was not a tragic hero, but a divine dupe who was flawed from the outset. Cohen notes that the narrator takes the point of view expressed by Samuel that Israel's desire for a king was tantamount to rebellion against Yahweh. Thus, when God instructed Samuel to "make *for them* a king" (1 Sam 8:22), Samuel chose the kind of inept leader that recalcitrant Israel deserved. Thus, "the biblical author portrays Saul as a leader who was thrust into the kingship as God's revenge for the people's rejection of God in their demand for monarchy" (36).

As evidence, Cohen points to Saul's unlikely background. As a Benjaminite from Gibeah, he came from a tribe and a town with the worst reputations in Israel. Saul's choice by lottery at Mizpah seems to reflect Israel's only other such use of a lottery—and that was to identify the criminal Achan in Judg 20:1. Like Achan, Saul later violates the divine ban. Like Achan, Saul is rejected by God for his actions and ultimately dies, along with his entire family. Saul is seen most clearly as a buffoon when he opts to play David's armor-bearer in the battle with Goliath (1 Sam 17:38-39).

Though he is described as the tallest man in Israel, Saul does not make use of his "vertical virtue" in battling the giant as one would expect. Rather, he allows little David to fight the giant, and David prevails by using a sling — a weapon that reportedly was second nature to Benjaminites like Saul (Judg 20:16).

Cohen concludes that the biblical author does not regard Saul as a tragic hero, but "as a hapless fool thrust into the kingship as God punishes his people for demanding a monarchy" (56). When Israel demanded a king, God ordered Samuel to select Saul as a king *for them* (1 Sam 8:19-20). David, however, is portrayed as a different kind of king altogether, for in David, God tells Samuel, "I have provided a king *for myself*" (1 Sam 16:1).

Compare Cohen's argument with the "tragic hero" view effectively argued by Jan P. Fokkelman in "Saul and David: Crossed Fates," *Bible Review* 5 (June 1989): 20-32; or, in a book-length argument, *The Crossing Fates* (Assen: van Gorcum, 1986).

Kenneth I. Cohen, "King Saul: A Bungler from the Beginning," *BRev 10* (October 1994).

after unintentionally violating his father's rash oath (13:23–14:23). The king then infuriates Samuel again by parading King Agag (of the Amalekites) and the best of his flocks as war trophies, when Samuel had decreed their total destruction (15:1-35).

Thus, while Saul's reign remains in its infancy, Samuel already is looking for another king. Young David's rise to prominence is described by means of three separate accounts of his discovery and anointing (16:1–18:5). The remainder of Saul's career is played out in a dangerous tango with David as the troubled king tries first to kill David (18:6–20:42) and then to catch him (21:1–26:25). Even Saul's last days are haunted by the specter of Samuel, and he dies an ignoble death as David positions himself to rule in Israel (27:1–31:13).

So it is that Saul shares the stage with Samuel and David throughout his abbreviated career. It is, however, Saul's show, even if he is upstaged. Thus, the second major section of our commentary is organized around Saul, Israel's most tragic king.

Saul's Fall from Grace, 13:1–15:35

Even casual readers must be confused by chapter 13 because Saul's movements do not always seem logical, and certain elements of the story seem to be misplaced. The first verse even contains blanks, apparently to be filled in later! Commentators often have suggested that the chapter is a patchwork of at least three sources: the Deuteronomistic introduction in v. 1, an old narrative recounting the opening stages of the battle of Michmash pass (13:2-7a; 16-22), and an antikingship episode inserted to discredit Saul's leadership (13:7b-15).

The episode in vv. 7b-15 seems out of place because it appears to be connected to the earlier narrative of Saul's initial anointing in chapters 9–10, the first of three accounts describing Saul's rise to kingship. There, Saul is a young man, still living in his father's house, who has been sent out in search of some lost donkeys. Samuel meets Saul, anoints him as future king, and tells him the whereabouts of the donkeys. Then Samuel instructs Saul to meet him in Gilgal seven days later and *to wait for him there* so that he might offer sacrifices in Saul's behalf (10:8).

Much has happened prior to 13:7. Saul has been chosen as king by public lot (with Samuel's involvement, ch. 11) and has led Israel to victory over the Ammonites in a flashing display of charismatic leadership, after which Samuel again proclaims him king (ch. 12). By the time chapter 13 begins, Saul appears to have been king for some time, has established a standing army, and has a son old enough to command one third of the army. Yet the episode in 13:7b-15 seems to assume Samuel's earlier instruction to meet him at Gilgal in seven days, unless we project that Samuel had set another appointed time for meeting that is not recorded elsewhere (13:8). The ill fit suggests that the account of Saul's presumptuous sacrifice may have been inserted here to add further evidence that Saul was not a fit king for Israel, using Samuel's unresolved instruction of 10:8 as a convenient connective device.

Nevertheless, the story comes to us as it is, and we must seek to understand its canonical form. With an awareness of the various possible subsources, we will now examine the narrative as a unit.

COMMENTARY

Saul Musters Israel and Offers a Sacrifice, 13:1-9

Something is missing from v. 1. The MT begins with the impossible reading "Saul was a year old when he began to reign," leading to the targumic interpretation that he was "like a one-year-old who had no sins." Some versions of the LXX record Saul's age as thirty (perhaps influenced by David's age at accession, 2 Sam 5:4).

The assertion that Saul reigned for only two years also appears too short, though the number is repeated in the LXX and most versions. [Saul's Activities] In the New Testament, the Apostle Paul (who once was a rabbi named Saul) recited a tradition that King Saul ruled for forty years (Acts 13:21), and Josephus attributed to Saul a reign of both twenty and forty years (*Ant.* 10.143; 6.378).

The original text was probably an attempt by the Deuteronomists to fit Saul's reign into their chronological framework, and in this it succeeds (cf. 2 Sam 2:10; 5:4; 1 Kgs 14:21; 22:42; 2 Kgs 8:26; among others). The overall construction of Saul's story in 1 Samuel suggests that his leadership is so inept and fraught with cultic transgressions that we would not expect it to last very long. Even so, two years is a very short

Saul's Activities

In considering the length of Saul's reign, it is helpful to review the major events of his life, as recorded in 1 Samuel:

1. Saul seeks lost donkeys and finds a kingdom (9:1–10:16).
2. Saul is chosen by lottery at Mizpah (10:17-27).
3. Saul rouses Israel, defeats the Ammonites, and is confirmed as king (11:1-15).
4. Saul and Jonathan lead Israel against the Philistines (13:1–14:52).
5. Saul defeats the Amalekites, but angers Samuel (15:1-35).
6. Saul suffers from an evil spirit and is comforted by David's music (16:14-23).
7. Saul faces the Philistines, but David fights Goliath (17:1-58).
8. Saul grows jealous of David and tries to kill him (18–20).
9. Saul hunts David: several encounters (21–26).
10. Saul seeks advice from Samuel's ghost before battling the Philistines (28).
11. Saul and three of his sons die in battle with the Philistines (31).

period in which to pack all of the events described in 1 Samuel 9–31.

Saul had mustered an army of three hundred and thirty "thousands," or military units, for the battle with Ammon, but most of his recruits returned home afterward, leaving Saul with a standing army of only three "thousands," or three units. Two of these remained with Saul at a place called Michmash, in the rugged hill country near Bethel, while the other unit served with Jonathan at Saul's traditional home, Gibeah of Benjamin. [Geba, Gibeah, and Gibeon]

First Samuel 13 describes a period in which Israel lived in an uneasy arrangement with the Philistines, who were clearly the dominant and more powerful party. The Philistines kept the Israelites subservient through maintaining a monopoly on the manufacture and maintenance of iron weaponry and by staffing

---

Geba, Gibeah, and Gibeon

There seems to be some confusion in the text regarding these place names, and no real scholarly consensus for solving it. The problem stems from the fact that all of the names derive from the Hebrew appellative meaning "hill." There are many notable hills in Palestine, and there were certainly several towns or villages named after their physical surroundings.

First Sam 13 refers to a place called Geba, which was apparently located about eight miles north-northeast of Jerusalem, near the edge of the deep and rugged Wadi Sunweinit, across from Michmash. This seems to have been the site of a Philistine outpost that was conquered by Jonathan and later used as an Israelite base of operations (1 Sam 13:3, 16).

The most prominent Gibeah was located about six miles north-northwest of Jerusalem, in the heart of the tribal territory assigned to Benjamin (modern-day Jeba). This Gibeah was named in the tribal allotment lists (Josh 18:28) and was the site of the infamous rape of the Levite's concubine that led to intertribal warfare (Judg 19–21; see comments on 1 Sam 10:5-11).

Gibeah was King Saul's home town (1 Sam 11:4) and eventually became his capital (1 Sam 22:6; 23:19). In 1 Sam 13–14, Gibeah (along with Geba) figured into Saul's initial conflict with the Philistines. Some scholars regard Gibeah and Geba as identical towns with different spellings preserved by variant traditions underlying the final history. Others prefer to think of two places near each other, while others confess the inability to tell when the text means "Gibeah" and when it means "the hill."

Another Gibeah, located west of Jerusalem near Kiriath-jearim, hosted the ark for a period of time (1 Sam 7:1-3; 2 Sam 6:1-3). The city of Gibeon lay northwest of Jerusalem. It also figured prominently in the stories of Israel's early monarchical years (2 Sam 2:12-19; 22:1-2; 1 Kgs 3:8-15).

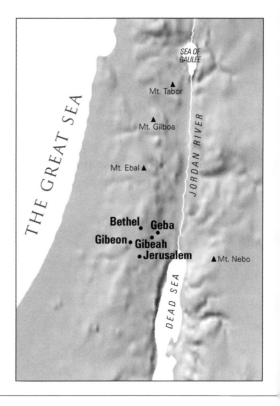

strategic outposts in Israelite territory to keep their less technologically advanced neighbors at bay. One of these garrisons apparently
was located at "Geba," probably on a hill overlooking the deep
Wadi Suweinit, only a few miles northwest of Saul's capital in
Gibeah of Benjamin.

Jonathan engineered some sort of attack on the Philistine outpost
at Geba (v. 3), though it is not clear whether he personally assassinated the local prefect alone (so NJPS, NEB, Kyle McCarter) or
led his troops to overrun the entire Philistine
garrison (NRSV, RSV, NASB, NIV). The word
nĕṣîb could be translated several ways, as "prefect," "garrison," or even "pillar" (see JB).
Jonathan's actions, in any case, were a clear sign
of rebellion against the Philistine hegemony,
made more obvious by Saul's call to arms with
trumpet and word.

The use of the term "Hebrews" is unusual
here, for normally only outsiders referred to
Israel as "the Hebrews." Some writers postulate a textual corruption, assuming an original announcement by the Philistines that
"the Hebrews have revolted!"1 In either case, both parties prepared
for war. Saul summoned Israel's fighters to Gilgal (v. 4), while the
Philistines gathered their troops and encamped at Michmash, three
or four miles south of the ancient sanctuary city of Bethel, on the
north bank of the Wadi Suweinit. [Bethel or Beth-aven?]

The Philistine army was quite impressive: the thirty companies of
chariots and six companies of horsemen were more effective on the
plain than in the rugged hills where the troops were camped, but
there were also foot soldiers "like the sand of the seashore in multitude" (v. 6). As the Philistines were encamped opposite Jonathan's
troops across a deep but narrow defile, reports of the
Philistine armory's intimidating size became widely
known. [Philistine Chariot] Israel's conscripted "soldiers," most
of whom were armed only with farm implements (see
13:19-22), looked for places to hide (v. 6) or deserted
Saul altogether (v. 7a).

At this point the focus of the story shifts from the
Philistine conflict to an equally sharp confrontation
between Saul and Samuel. Nothing in the story itself prepares us
for Saul's being required to wait at Gilgal for seven days so that
Samuel might offer sacrifices and pronounce a divine sanction for
war. The only possible antecedent in the text is in 1 Samuel 10:8,
which seems to be far more removed than seven days. The later

Bethel or Beth-aven?

AΩ First Sam 13:5 and 14:23 speak of a place called "Beth-aven," which is probably to be identified as Bethel, the ancient sanctuary city (see map in [Geba, Gibeah, and Gibeon]). "Beth-el" means "house of God," while "Beth-aven" means "house of sin." Later writers expressed their distaste for Israel's corrupt worship of idols at Bethel by refusing to call it "house of God," giving it instead the pejorative name "house of evil" (see Hos 4:15; 5:8; 10:5).

Philistine Chariot
(Illustration Credit: Barclay Burns)

writers, however, apparently picked up on this unresolved appointment and used it as a bridge to the unhappy encounter in 13:11-15a.

The author appears to have some sympathy for Saul, even though the end result of the story is a break between Saul and Samuel. Saul waited for seven days, despite the fact that his army was deserting him in droves (v. 8). Samuel delayed his coming, even though the distances involved were not great. It seems as though Samuel was testing Saul intentionally, waiting in the shadows, as it were, until Saul despaired of losing his entire army and resorted to offering the ritual sacrifices himself (v. 9). [Petitionary Sacrifices]

Samuel Confronts Saul and Predicts His Doom, 13:10-15

According to the text, Saul had just completed the burnt offering when Samuel appeared. The truly cynical might note that Samuel made his appearance *before* the communion offerings, from which the priest received a share. The communion offerings, however, are not mentioned again. Saul's presumption in the case of the burnt offerings is quite enough to engender Samuel's ire.

Saul's explanation of his actions (vv. 11-12) is perfectly logical and leads the reader to sympathize with his plight. The army was deserting, the enemy was pressing, Samuel was absent, and there seemed no other choice. Still, what Saul saw as creative leadership, Samuel saw as flagrant impertinence and blatant disobedience (v. 13). As a result, Samuel declared that Saul's kingdom would not be established—that is, his descendants would not succeed him on the throne (v. 14a). Rather, God would appoint another who was better suited to rule (v. 14b). [A Pointed "Appointment"]

The obvious reference to God's choice of David as "a man after his own heart" is often misunderstood. A surface reading may suggest that David's heart is patterned after God's heart, that David is superior to Saul because his heart and motivations are in tune with

---

Petitionary Sacrifices

AΩ Saul's proposed sacrifice (1 Sam 13:9) mentions two types of sacrifices: a burnt offering (ʿōlâh) and a "peace offering," or "offering of well-being" (šĕlāmîm). The burnt offering, also called a "holocaust," was so named because it involved the immolation of the entire carcass, after it had been ritually slaughtered, skinned, quartered, and washed. Burnt offerings appear as elements of formal petitions (as here), in the course of ordinary public worship (Num 28–29), as the object of votive or voluntary offerings (Lev 22:18), or as part of a purification ritual (Lev 12:6, 8; 16:24). Sacrifices offered in preparation for war probably involved both petitionary and purification elements.

The "peace offering" might better be called a "communion offering." The purpose of the šĕlāmîm offering was to establish or maintain good relations with God. Unlike the ʿōlâh, which was burned *in toto*, the communion offering was shared between the deity, the priest, and the supplicant. God alone received the blood, the visceral fat, and the fat tail of sheep, because blood and fat were considered to be life-giving (Lev 3:16-17; 7:22-26; 17:11, 14). The priest was given the right forequarter as his portion (Lev 7:28-34; 10:14-15), and the worshiper was allowed to keep the rest. The sharing of this communal meal promoted the sense of unity between God, priest, and person.

the divine will. This claim is hardly borne out in David's actions, however. David schemes constantly; he kills without just cause; he commits adultery; he sanctions the murder of the innocent; he takes many wives; he refuses to be reconciled with his troublesome son. These actions are hardly modeled "after God's heart." While it is true that the author was indeed a great fan of David, his initial intention may not have been to claim that David's heart was the image of God's. Rather, the expression "after his own heart" might also be read as an idiom that means "of his own choosing" (cf. 1 Sam 14:7; Ps 20:4 [MT 20:5]). The fact that David would build a dynasty, rather than Saul, is a matter of divine choice. Later biblical traditions, however, interpreted the phrase primarily as a descriptive portrayal of David's character (see Acts 13:22).

"If anyone is in the wrong here," Hertzberg points out, "it is Samuel, and not Saul." Yet the author clearly imputes the sin to Saul, reaching a theological verdict that "is put before the period of Saul's reign like a clef on a music stave."[2] Samuel symbolically parted company with Saul, going his own angry way from Gilgal, while the belittled Saul was forced to gather his depleted army and proceed toward Gibeah and the battle that awaited (v. 15a).

> **A Pointed "Appointment"**
>
> AΩ Samuel's condemnation of Saul is built upon a careful wordplay between the verb *ṣāwâh* ("to command," "to appoint") and the related noun *miṣwâh* ("appointment"). Since Saul was not careful of the *appointment* that God had *appointed* to him (13:13), God would *appoint* another of his own choosing (13:14). See P. Kyle McCarter, *I Samuel* (AB 8; Garden City: Doubleday, 1980), 228.

Saul's Poor Army and the Philistines' Advantage, 13:16-22

As the preceding section portrayed Saul's poor standing with Samuel, the last verses of chapter 13 are designed to illustrate the pitiful inadequacy of Israel's army. According to the text, frequent desertions caused by a craven fear of the enemy—and exacerbated by Samuel's delay—left Saul with only six hundred soldiers to join with Jonathan's troops and oppose the fearsome Philistine juggernaut.

The "Geba of Benjamin" in v. 16 may be the same "Gibeah of Benjamin" where Jonathan was posted in v. 2, or it may suggest a separate but nearby place closer to the rugged wadi that separated the opposing military camps. The Philistines showed supreme confidence in their

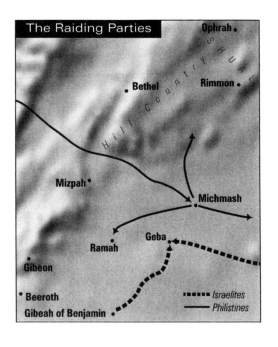

The Raiding Parties

Literary Repetition

The author skillfully uses the technique of repetition to portray the general population's fear and inadequacy before the Philistines. In v. 6, as the Philistine army looms large on the horizon, the troops' fear grows even larger. Thus, according to the narrator, they began to hide out "in caves, in thickets, in cliffs, in cellars, and in pits." The listing of such ignominious hiding places underscores Israel's fear.

Later, the writer uses the same convention to highlight the inadequacy of Israel's armaments in comparison to the Philistines. Since Israel does not possess the technology to make implements of iron, the Philistines hold a monopoly. They do not allow Israelites to own weapons of iron, but only garden tools. The listing of "plowshares, mattocks, axes, and sickles" is reminiscent of the previous string of hiding places, picturing the Israelite army as a cowering collection of conscripted farmers who could hardly expect to have any success against the well-equipped professional fighting force of the Philistines.

fighting force, sending out raiding parties in three entirely separate directions. [The Raiding Parties] The way toward Ophrah was due north, while the road to Beth Horon led west-south-west, and the road "toward the mountain [MT has 'border'] that looks down on the Valley of Zeboim [Hyenas]" went southeastward from Michmash, toward the wilderness beyond the Jordan (vv. 17-18). The parties' intention was probably to punish Israel for Jonathan's rebellion by terrorizing small villages, plundering the people, and confiscating any weapons of iron that could be used against them.

Israel's woeful plight becomes more apparent in vv. 19-22. The Iron Age was just beginning in Palestine, and while the Philistines had mastered the technology, the Israelites had not. Thus, "there was no smith to be found throughout the land of Israel" (v. 19), and the Philistines guarded their advantage as a state secret, allowing the Hebrews to purchase only farming tools. Israel's ineptitude is underscored in that they were not even capable of sharpening their plowshares, mattocks, axes, sickles, and goads, but periodically returned them to the Philistine forges for sharpening or resetting—at a price (vv. 20-21). [Literary Repetition]

The end result of the Philistine policy and the three-pronged raids was that, according to the author, none of the Israelite soldiers save Saul and Jonathan possessed so much as a sword or spear. While we presume that weapons of flint or bronze may have been available, the superior implements of iron were not in Israel's arsenal.

CONNECTIONS

This chapter serves primarily as a "setup" for later events. The military accounts of vv. 1-7a and 15b-22 set the stage for the battle of Michmash Pass, which will unfold in chapter 14. The confrontation between Saul and Samuel (vv. 7b-15a) prepares the reader for the final break in chapter 15 and for Saul's troubled career as a king who is doomed to failure. What lessons can modern readers gain from such an unhappy text?

1. *We are always outnumbered.* The opening and closing verses of chapter 13 emphasize a hard truth: on this earth, God's people seem always to be in a minority. Saul's small and untrained army was overwhelmed in size by the Philistine forces (vv. 2-5, 15b). Their makeshift weapons could not compare with the Philistine armaments, which included not only weapons of iron (vv. 19-22), but large numbers of chariots, the "tanks" of the ancient world (v. 5).

The theme of being outnumbered appears often in Scripture. Without any army at all, Israel escaped from Egypt. Against clearly superior forces, Israel settled large parts of Palestine. Saul led his vastly outnumbered soldiers to victory over the Ammonites. Little David was overmatched by Goliath, but overcame the giant. Elijah stood alone against four hundred prophets of Baal. Daniel and his three friends persevered, though held in an alien land. The returning exiles were surrounded by enemies, yet succeeded in rebuilding Jerusalem.

The common lesson is that God's power overcomes all odds. When our smallness is most apparent, our faith is most likely to grow, because we understand our need for God's help. When we gain a victory (or even survive) against overwhelming odds, we are more likely to acknowledge divine aid. Can a tiny nucleus of Christian believers establish a strong and vital congregation with adequate facilities without God's help? Can a Christian person remain faithful in a sinful world without God's help? Can a believer survive tragedy and grow even stronger without God's help?

Once we reach the point of thinking that we are in a majority position or that we have achieved a secure standing, faith tends to fade into the background. If we have enough money or enough people to handle things on our own, what need do we have of God? For most of our history, neither Jews nor Christians have had the luxury of being in the majority or in control. In those rare cases when it has happened, such as in Europe during the Middle Ages, it has proved disastrous: the Spanish Inquisition was one symptom of an intolerant and all-powerful church. Our world, for the most part, has become largely pluralistic, but echoes of the Inquisition still reverberate when religious parties feel secure enough to impose their beliefs and value systems on others. Whether the parties in question are Muslim fundamentalists in Iran, Orthodox Jews in Israel, or Christian conservatives in America, the same issue applies: True faith cannot be forced, and cultural faith cannot be as meaningful as chosen faith.

2. *Courage makes a difference.* In the face of long odds, courage makes a difference. Jonathan is not presented as an especially pious person in this text, though he may have been, but he stands as a beacon of courage and leadership. His victory over the Philistine garrison disrupted the status quo and encouraged the Israelites to believe that they could overcome their oppressive overlords. Jonathan quickly fades from the picture in the remainder of this chapter, but he will return in chapter 14 to spark yet another victory by dint of his contagious valor. [Jonathan the Brave]

Modern believers rarely find the need to express courageous faith in hand-to-hand combat, but there are many opportunities to express our faith, and they all require courage. Do we dare to stand against the status quo when social issues demand it? Do we dare to go into dangerous neighborhoods to carry the love and the light of hope that God offers? Do we dare to stand up to others in our workplace if their profanity or abusive behavior threatens those who are vulnerable? Do we dare to speak of God in a secular world?

Jonathan the Brave

(Illustration Credit: Barclay Burns)

3. *Obedience is essential.* The story reveals an unexpected (and uncomfortable) aspect of God's character. To the extent that Samuel's condemnation of Saul truly reflects divine displeasure, the LORD appears capricious at worst, impatient at best. Despite the reader's natural sympathy for Saul, however, the narrator interprets the warrior king's actions as a lack of faith in and obedience to God.

The reader, with Saul, is left to struggle with the meaning of obeying a command that seems to fly in the face of rational judgment. Perhaps God intended for Saul's army to dwindle to nearly nothing to inspire greater reliance on divine assistance (cf. Gideon in Judg 7:1-8, who at Yahweh's behest intentionally whittled his army from 32,000 to 300 men—precisely half of Saul's depleted fighting force). Saul could claim any number of human excuses for giving up on Samuel and pressing ahead before losing the last of his soldiers. According to the author, however, he had every divine reason *not to* depart from Samuel's instructions.

Kingship may have become a political expediency in Israel, but Israel's kings were always to be subservient to God's will, *as revealed through his prophets.* In the present setting, the prophet of record is Samuel, and Samuel had instructed Saul to wait for him to offer the sacrifice. No excuses are acceptable for Saul's disobedience;

what a secular person might see as a courageous action under difficult circumstances still fails to pass prophetic muster.

The human brain is highly developed and capable of myriad rationalizations for any circumstance. If we want to do something badly enough, we can find a way to convince ourselves that our actions are logical and just. If we are called to account for our actions, we can offer multiple arguments to justify ourselves. When the base of our logic is entirely internal, we can rationalize anything from apathy to adultery, from materialism to murder.

Saul's encounter with Samuel is a firm reminder that God has established guidelines of behavior for his people and expects them to be followed. We may think we can justify aberrations from the Ten Commandments of the Old Testament (Exod 20) or the one commandment of the New Testament (John 15:12), but our excuses inevitably come up short. The narrative leads us to believe that Saul could have accomplished great things had he been more obedient to God. The beginning of Saul's downfall is marked by the beginning of his disobedience.

NOTES

[1] See P. Kyle McCarter, *I Samuel* (AB 8; Garden City: Doubleday, 1980), 225, n 3.

[2] H. W. Hertzberg, *I and II Samuel* (CC; Dallas: Word Books, 1989), 106.

A COURAGEOUS SON
AND HIS RASH FATHER

13:23–14:52

COMMENTARY

Jonathan's Risky Initiative and a Victory to Remember, 13:23–14:23

The story detailing Israel's victory in the "Battle of Michmash Pass" is very old and shows little sign of later editing. It was preserved in Israel's memory for two primary reasons. First, it was the battle that consolidated Saul's power and strength in the heartland of Gibeah; and secondly, it was the necessary prelude to the emerging conflict between Saul and his son Jonathan.

The scene unfolds with the Philistines encamped just outside of Michmash, on the north bank of a deep and narrow ravine. The Israelites occupy the south bank, just a few miles north of Gibeah, at a place called Geba. Thus, the two camps are quite visible to each other and within shouting distance. Their positions are marked by two rocky outcroppings (lit., "teeth") so noticeable that they have names: Bozez and Seneh, "The Shining One" and "The Thorny One."

Jonathan apparently is in charge of the Hebrew outpost at the overlook, while Saul remains with the main force (still only 600 men; cf. 13:15) at Gibeah. Saul's position "at Migron" (14:2) may be a misreading for "on the threshing floor." Other ancient traditions speak of kings holding court on the communal threshing floor outside the gate of their city.

We learn with great interest that Saul has a court chaplain, Ahijah, the great grandson of Eli, whose family apparently has carried on priestly traditions apart from Samuel (see [Eli's Descendants]). Ahijah's brother Ahimelech maintained a sanctuary at Nob, which figures significantly in the later conflict between Saul and David. Ahimelech was the father of Abiathar, who became David's court chaplain (1 Sam 22:6-23; 1 Kgs 2:26-27). Our first thought is to wonder why

Saul did not call upon Ahijah to offer the sacrifice that got him into so much trouble with Samuel in chapter 13. Did Saul not recruit Ahijah until after that unseemly debacle? Or did Ahijah's presence simply not fit into the storyteller's purpose? That is not, of course, a question we can answer.

Acting on his own initiative, Jonathan persuaded his armor-bearer to join him in an apparently suicidal attack on the entrenched Philistine garrison, climbing up the steep ravine in plain view of the enemy and shouting to gain their attention. Jonathan acted, apparently, by the inspiration of God: "Come, let us go over to the garrison of these uncircumcised; it may be that the LORD will act for us; for nothing can hinder the LORD from saving by many or by few" (v. 6). [By Many or By Few]

By Many or By Few

Jonathan's statement of faith was remembered and possibly reflected in another great hero of Judaism, Judas Maccabaeus. Known as "the Hammer," Judas led Israel to regain its independence from the Seleucids during the early 2d century BC. Prior to his first great victory at "the ascent of Beth Horon"—not very far from the battle site of 1 Sam 14—Judas' army was also vastly outnumbered, but he encouraged his troops with these words: "It is easy for many to be hemmed in by few, for in the sight of Heaven there is no difference between saving by many or by few. It is not on the size of the army that victory in battle depends, but strength comes from Heaven" (1 Macc 3:18-19). Judas' brother, also named Jonathan, later judged Israel from his home in Michmash.

Jonathan proposed a plan that involved requesting a sign from God. He and his companion would descend to the floor of the ravine and attract the attention of the Philistine watchmen. If the enemy guards challenged them to come up and fight, they would take it as a divine omen that God would be fighting with them (vv. 8-10). All went according to plan. After clambering down to the valley floor, Jonathan and his bodyguard were spotted and laughingly challenged to climb up and offer sport to the bored watchmen: "Come up to us, and we will show you something." The Philistine challenge reminds the reader of the cowardice shown by other Israelites: "Look, Hebrews are coming out of the holes where they have hidden themselves" (see 13:6-7). In contrast, Jonathan's courage and confidence shone defiantly as he invited his attendant to "come up after me; for the LORD has given them into the hand of Israel" (v. 12b).

The disdainful Philistine troops had judged Jonathan to be an overconfident cub, but he scaled the cliff like a cat and then fought like an enraged tiger, felling Philistines left and right while his armor-bearer came behind to finish them off (vv. 13-14). Some have postulated that the fighting took place in a narrow pass between rocky outcroppings where the soldiers were forced to go in single file, allowing Jonathan to face one at the time. The narrator, however, does not wish to detract from the miraculous nature of the battle's outcome. Jonathan was successful because Yahweh was fighting with him. The unexpected slaughter led to a panic in the camp, as the Philistines realized that a power greater than Jonathan was working against them. The panic spread from the guard outpost to the field soldiers to the main garrison, fueled by a sudden earthquake that confirmed the activity of Israel's deity in the battle (v. 15). This is underscored in the text by the phrase translated as "a great panic." Literally, it means "a shuddering of God," clear evidence of divine doings in Israel's behalf.

Saul's response to his lookouts' report of the enemy panic seems curious. Instead of striking immediately to take advantage of the confusion, he first sought to discover who was absent, finding that Jonathan and his armor-bearer were the only ones missing. Saul then called for a sacred totem: either the ark or the priestly ephod. The MT has the word "ark" (reflected in NRSV), but most critics prefer the LXX reading of "ephod"; Saul seems to be preparing to have the priest divine the will of God by using the Urim and Thummim, sacred lots that were kept in a pocket or compartment of the priestly breastplate (see vv. 40-42 below).

The text does not record the command to begin the divination, but it does reflect Saul's sudden abortion of the procedure. As the Philistines' dismay became more evident, he commanded the priest to "withdraw your hand," evidently from the pocket containing the lots (v. 19). Capitalizing on the adversaries' disorientation, Saul sent his troops around to an easier crossing of the wadi, where they joined in the battle.

The conflict swung quickly in Israel's favor, aided by a rapid and unexpected increase in the size of Saul's available force, which was strengthened by the return of both defectors and deserters. Evidently, the Philistine camp contained some Israelites who had sided pragmatically with the obviously superior Philistine forces. In the ensuing panic, however, the turncoats reversed course on their new allies, joining the other Hebrews in routing the Philistine army (v. 21). [Hebrews] In addition, earlier deserters from the Israelite force gained confidence, emerged from their hiding places (13:6-7), and attached themselves to the chase (v. 22). The author, however, reminds the reader that these waffling hangers-on were in no way responsible for the rout: "*the LORD* gave Israel the victory that day" (14: 23).

Hebrews

AΩ The etymology of the term *ʿibrî* has caused scholars much consternation. Many have proposed some connection with the people called by the Semitic word *ʿapiru* in second-millennium texts from Egypt, Mesopotamia, and Syria-Palestine. The *ʿapiru* were an ill-defined group of ancient peoples who lived on the fringes of society and generally were regarded as a threat to civilization.

The ancient Hebrews may well have belonged to the ethnic strata known as the *ʿapiru*, but the word *ʿibrî* is not as closely related to *ʿapiru* as it appears. It is more likely that *ʿibrî* is related to the word *ʿēber*, meaning "the region beyond." Some suggest it is a self-given name reflecting the Israelites' historical memory of their origin in Mesopotamia, "from beyond [the river]." Others postulate that the name derives from *eber nari*, the Akkadian term for the western side of the Jordan, the "other side" from the Mesopotamian perspective.

Saul's Rash Oath and a Confrontation to Forget, 14:24-46

As the Philistines retreated westward toward their uncontested territory, the battle was no longer confined to a small area, but spread out across the hill country west of Bethel (or Beth-aven; see [Bethel or Beth-aven?]). Saul's army swelled to ten thousand men (according to the LXX reading of 14:23b), but the Israelites' momentum was slowed by an ill-fated command on Saul's part. The LXX preserves a reading that says "Saul committed a very rash act on that day" (NRSV), or "Saul made a great blunder that day."[1]

Without giving any rationale for Saul's actions, the narrator turns from the battle at large and describes Saul's decision to impose an oath upon his soldiers, declaring that all should fast until sundown, when the battle concluded. Perhaps Saul thought this would increase his level of control over the soldiers as the fighting spread into scattered engagements. Or perhaps he wanted to assure himself that no Israelite soldiers were relaxing over a meal when there were Philistines yet to be killed.

In any event, the soldiers became famished. After a long day of hand-to-hand combat over rugged terrain, the Hebrew troops grew weak and weary. The soldiers respected Saul's authority, however, and obeyed his command, even though the Philistines left behind much spoil. As a single illustration of the larger dilemma, the narrator focuses on one group of soldiers who happened upon a tempting flow of honey from an abandoned beehive. [All the Troops?] Jonathan, who accompanied the group, was unaware of his father's imposition of the oath, so he did not hesitate to indulge in a sweet snack, using the end of his staff as a spoon (vv. 25-27).

All the Troops?

AΩ Although the text insists that *all* the troops came upon the honeycomb, it is hardly likely that 10,000 soldiers (or even 10 "platoons") would have stood around contemplating a single tempting honey tree. Elsewhere, the narrator has taken pains to tell us that the battle had spread out across the hills of Ephraim. Thus, the story cannot refer to "all the troops," but only to the group surrounding Jonathan. It is not uncommon for ancient storytellers to take a relatively small event and extrapolate it to a much larger context.

When the other troops informed Jonathan of the proscription against eating, the young hero spoke openly against his father's command, insisting that the army could have fought more effectively if all had eaten as he had. The refreshment and renewed strength Jonathan enjoyed from the honey is conveyed by means of an idiom: "His eyes brightened" (vv. 27-30).

The narration then jumps to the end of the day and the soldiers' obvious triumph. [From Michmash to Aijalon] Freed of Saul's oath by the setting sun—and possibly encouraged by Jonathan's speech—the victorious troops fell upon the Philistines' provisions like the starving men that they were, slaughtering and eating captured cattle wherever they found it. Unfortunately, this violated a long-standing Hebrew taboo

From Michmash to Aijalon

This expression describes the rout (and the route) of the Philistines as they retreated from Michmash toward more hospitable territory. The Philistine strongholds were in the west, gathered around their pentapolis of five city-states: Gath, Ashdod, Ekron, Ashkelon, and Gaza. Aijalon was over twelve miles west of Michmash, hard by the borders of Philistine territory. The place names involved tell us something about the nature of the battle. Israel won a great victory, but not a complete one. The Philistines retreated all the way to Aijalon, but not completely within their own borders. Israel's failure to win a more resounding victory was attributed to the consequences of Saul's misguided oath.

---

insisting that all meat must carefully be bled upon an altar so the blood would not be inadvertently eaten. The blood of an animal represented its life force and, consequently, belonged to God (see Deut 12:23-27; Lev 19:26). [The Life Is in the Blood]

When the unchecked slaughter was brought to Saul's attention, he immediately recognized Israel's peril, and commanded that a stone altar be constructed so the animals could be butchered properly (vv. 33-35). The narrator notes that this was the first altar Saul built for the LORD—but it was not his first troublesome collision with proper ritual (see ch. 13), nor his last (see ch. 15).

Saul was more skilled at war than at religion, so he immediately proposed a night attack to finish off the enemy, but his priest encouraged him to seek Yahweh's permission, which was not forthcoming (vv. 36-37). Thus, a more complete victory over the Philistines was thwarted by two unexpected results of Saul's unfortunate oath: the troops grew weak and could not fight as efficiently (v. 30), and Yahweh refused to bless a midnight sortie to break the enemy's back (v. 37).

Again, the author skillfully draws the reader into a story within the story. Saul's frustration leads to a search for the man whose sin has brought a halt to Yahweh's battle blessings. Once before, in Israel's memory, the sin of a single man had thwarted an apparent victory, and it had happened in the same general area, near Bethel. Under Joshua, the emerging Israelites had anticipated little opposition from the city of Ai, but were routed unexpectedly. Joshua assumed that someone had violated the ban on taking plunder, thus averting Yahweh's blessing. With the assistance of the priests, Joshua identified the culprit Achan by a progressive casting of lots (Josh 7).

The Life Is in the Blood

The Hebrews regarded both blood and fat as the primary sources of animal and human life (see Gen 9:4; Lev 3:16-17; 7:22-26; 17:11, 14; Deut 12:23). Thus, only God, the giver of life, was considered worthy to partake of them. Animals were to be slaughtered in a prescribed fashion and laid out upon a stone surface so the blood could drain away. Many sacrificial offerings were eaten by both priests and people, but the blood was first sprinkled around the altar and allowed to soak into the ground, while visceral fat and the "fat tail" of sheep were burned on the altar, ascending in redolent smoke offered as a pleasing aroma to God.

Aided by this historical memory, Saul did precisely the same thing, although the exercise did not turn out as he anticipated (cf. 10:20, where the lots unexpectedly chose Saul to be king). The narrator consistently describes Saul as a bumbler who speaks before he thinks; this instance is no exception. Thinking, perhaps, to show that Israel's leaders were no less accountable than all others, Saul insisted that the lot first be cast between the royal house and the common people (vv. 38-39). When the first lot indicated the royalty, Saul was forced to take the process one step further. The next lot pointed to Jonathan, who defiantly admitted eating the honey—though not to knowing it was forbidden—and declared his readiness to die if need be.

Saul, whose own impulsive words had trapped him, refused to back down from his oath. He swore his intention of carrying through on the threat of execution, even though the "sinner" was his son, but the armies of Israel refused to allow it, responding with an oath of their own (vv. 44-45). [Three Oaths and a Ransom] The army's rescue of Jonathan is communicated in the MT by a word that usually means "ransom," but the LXX says they "interceded" for Jonathan. We need not speculate that some innocent soldier was put forward to die in Jonathan's behalf. Rather, the army's oath of solidarity was sufficient to force Saul into another solution. Perhaps an animal sacrifice was offered instead.

The army's internal conflict, the loss of momentum, and the Philistines' retreat into their strongholds brought a temporary lull in the conflict with Philistia, leaving Saul free to pursue other enemies and fight new battles. Despite the victory, however, Saul found himself diminished. The reader knows that this is Jonathan's victory, not Saul's. The king had been under a cloud since his earlier confrontation with Samuel, who predicted that his dynasty

---

Three Oaths and a Ransom

In Hebrew, oaths were characteristically expressed in the form "May God do thus and so to me, if I do not do so and so." Thus, oaths consisted of two parts: a curse (may God do thus and so) and a promise (if I do not do so and so). The use of either part could imply the other. The swearing of oaths was used to give added emphasis to one's veracity or certainty of action. First Sam 14 is punctuated by no less than three oaths, which serve to add drama and structure to the story. First, Saul's order that his troops should fast until sunset is cast in the form of an oath imposed on the soldiers and expressed as a curse on anyone who violates Saul's promise that none should eat (14:24). In the second oath, Saul swears that the offender shall be put to death, even if it is Jonathan (14:39). The last oath is sworn by Saul's troops, who aver that Jonathan will not die, despite the king's word (14:45). Both Saul and the troops call upon the LORD as witness and executor of the implied punishment: "As the LORD lives" means "as the LORD lives who is able to do thus and so to me if I do not."

Both oaths could not be kept since their objects (the condemnation/rescue of Jonathan) were opposite. Saul backed down and did not fulfill his oath, rendering him culpable for divine punishment—and the remainder of 1 Samuel details the ways in which Yahweh engineers Saul's downfall. Saul's rash oath was not the only way in which he crossed purposes with God, but it is one that should not be ignored.

would not endure (ch. 13). The emergence of Jonathan as a true hero, pure and strong, leads the reader to think there is still hope that Saul's dynasty may be redeemed through Jonathan. Saul himself made this unlikely, however, by rashly leading his son to an unwitting cultic violation, then condemning him before Israel. Thus, Jonathan's star also was dimmed and his future rendered uncertain. The story ends with the king's wearing a frustrated scowl, as Jonathan stands no longer in the spotlight of heroism, but in the shadows of paternal disfavor.

A Short Salute to Saul's Rule, 14:47-52

The last few verses of chapter 14 offer what seems to be a summary statement of Saul's reign, even though he remains king to the end of 1 Samuel. The narrator seems to be telling us that Saul's tenure on the throne was as good as over. Thus, he provides a précis of Saul's accomplishments, accenting as many positives as he can, since all that is yet to come will portray Saul in a wholly negative light. The summary includes a list of enemies that Saul fought with both valor and success (Moab, Ammon, Edom, Zobah, Philistia, and Amalek; vv. 47-48). Likewise, it introduces the members of Saul's family and their various connections (vv. 49-51). [Saul's Family]

The final note serves as a bridge to the coming stories of David, who would become attached to Saul's court in a natural way, for "when Saul saw any strong or valiant warrior, he took him into his service" (v. 52).

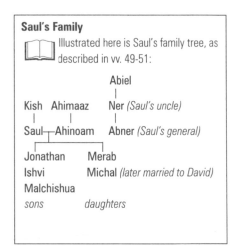

Saul's Family

Illustrated here is Saul's family tree, as described in vv. 49-51:

```
                    Abiel
                      |
   Kish   Ahimaaz    Ner (Saul's uncle)
     |       |         |
   Saul—Ahinoam      Abner (Saul's general)
     |
Jonathan      Merab
Ishvi         Michal (later married to David)
Malchishua
sons          daughters
```

CONNECTIONS

1. *In the presence of my enemies.* The setting for the conflict between the Israelites and Philistines is painted in some detail, enabling the reader to imagine a clear-cut demarcation between the people of God and the enemies who stand against them. The steep sides of the separating wadi, with their prominent outcroppings used as lookout posts, give the impression of a straightforward division between Israel (the "good guys") and Philistia (the "bad guys").

Contemporary worshipers of Yahweh also know that they face many enemies in this world, but they rarely are so clearly marked.

Hatred lurks unseen; even obvious evils, such as racism, are often cloaked by a facade of cultural acceptance. Many persons chronically abuse their families or subordinates, but may successfully hide their machinations from the world under a guise of respectability. Perhaps the most widespread evil is a simple lack of regard for others whom God has created, resulting in the neglect and suffering of individuals or even entire groups—such as the Jews themselves during World War II. Jonathan had no problem recognizing the enemy. Those who would serve God's ends as faithfully as did he must learn to do the same.

2. *Salvation by many or by few.* Jonathan's comment in v. 6 is a clear reminder that any victory is God's victory, not our own. Many people give lip service to God for divine blessings, while quietly congratulating themselves for their personal achievements and their bright future. The greatest victories are won by those who recognize that only God can defeat the greatest enemies. Jonathan is unquestionably worthy of praise for his valiant kamikaze attack upon the Philistines, but the narrator goes to great pains to emphasize that Jonathan's fighting is blessed by God, and that the subsequent panic resulted from a "shuddering of God" that shook the earth and melted the hearts of Israel's enemies.

3. *Fair-weather friends.* As quickly as the tide of battle turned in Israel's direction, a multitude of Hebrews who had either "converted" or deserted suddenly appeared from the woodwork. Some Israelites of flexible or pragmatic allegiance had thrown in their lot with the Philistines when it appeared that the technologically advanced invaders would be victorious. Once the enemy experienced the fear of Yahweh, however, the pseudo-Philistines betrayed their new friends and rejoined the resurgent Hebrews. Likewise, those who had deserted the army and secreted themselves in various hideouts now emerged to play like soldiers and claim an equal share of the spoil with those who truly had earned it.

The negative example of Israel's fair-weather soldiers provides a positive challenge for believers to demonstrate integrity of mind and heart, remaining faithful in times both bad and good.

4. *A brave son and a foolish father.* The story of Saul's impetuous curse upon his son Jonathan brings to mind the many children who fail to gain parental blessing. Sometimes parents have a hard time expressing their love for and pride in their children. Parents sometimes seem afraid that if they affirm a child's artwork or

schoolwork without correcting it, the child will not be motivated to work harder. The truth is that children have an inborn desire to grow and to learn. We can praise them every day for where they are and what they are doing. What *does* happen when we reserve our praise and refuse to express our approval is that we cause them to think something is wrong with them. We may turn our children into paranoid perfectionists who think that greater striving one day will lead to parental approval. Or we may turn them into people who give up and think so little of themselves that others can easily abuse them.

There is nothing better we can do for our children's emotional and spiritual health than to give them our unconditional love and acceptance, to be proud of them and to tell them so. This statement remains true whether the children are five years old, twenty-five, or fifty.

Theological educators know that everything we learn or believe about God is colored by our relationships with our parents. Those who feel rejection from earthly parents will find it difficult to believe that the celestial Parent of all is compassionate, loving, and trustworthy. They will find it difficult to accept God's forgiveness and love.

Something wonderful happens in this story. When Jonathan's father turns on him and threatens his future, the people of Israel will not hear of it. They "ransomed Jonathan" and save him from death, giving to him a blessing his father refused to give. It was not the father's blessing, but it was a needed blessing. One does not have to be a child's biological parent to love them, to be proud of them, and to tell them how special they are.

Those who work with children in tutoring programs, Christian education settings, or mentoring relationships know that opportunities for making children feel special and loved are abundant, but volunteers are few—especially among the children who are most in need. Many children seem condemned or cursed by their place in society, by their neighborhood, by the poor parental examples they are given. Yet those lives can be redeemed if others are willing to step in and demonstrate the acceptance and love that found its origin in the Creator of all things and all people.

NOTE

[1] P. Kyle McCarter, *I Samuel* (AB 8; Garden City: Doubleday, 1980), 243.

SAUL'S REBELLION
AND SAMUEL'S REGRET

15:1-35

COMMENTARY

Samuel's Order and Saul's Response, 15:1-9

In his attempt to explain Saul's fall from grace, the author has spliced together elements of the Saul tradition that highlight his greatest cultic transgressions. We learn little about Saul's administrative achievements as he set about the difficult task of establishing a new kingdom, but in rapid order the author tells us that Saul offered a sacrifice without waiting for Samuel (13:8-15) and that he endangered his own son—the most promising young leader in Israel—by imposing a foolish oath upon the troops (14:24-46). The narrator then compresses Saul's positive military exploits and family records into a few brief comments (14:47-52) before launching into another lengthy recital of an instance in which Saul failed to live up to Samuel's expectations.

Samuel is portrayed as the most influential and the most frustrated man in Israel. He was powerful and influential because God had appointed him as a prophet, with the authority both to anoint Israel's first king and to command him by delivering messages from God. Unfortunately, the first appointed king proved unwilling to follow the divine directives that Samuel brought.

The present episode begins with Samuel's informing Saul that God was ready to settle an old grudge with a recurrent enemy, the Amalekites. [The Amalekites: A Heritage of Hatred] This suggests a time in which Saul was well established as king in Israel and in a position of some regional power. The campaign would have entailed great risk because the Amalekite homeland was south and east of Israel, even beyond the Philistines' coastal pentapolis. Leading his main force so far from Saul's stronghold in central Judea would have left Israel vulnerable to attack from another quarter. Yet neither Samuel nor Saul shows any hesitation in advancing against Amalek. Their confidence

---

The Amalekites: A Heritage of Hatred

Israel had many enemies, but none more despised than the Amalekites, who were purported descendants of Esau through Amalek (Gen 36:12). The Amalekites inhabited the rugged steppes of the Negeb and appear most frequently in the role of an enemy to Israel.

The heritage of hatred went back to the exodus period, when the Israelites were making their way from Egypt to Palestine; they were ambushed by a band of Amalekites who used harassing tactics of cutting off those who were weak and straggling. After a long and bitter battle, Israel prevailed, and Moses declared what he believed to be a word from God: "I will utterly blot out the remembrance of Amalek from under heaven" (Exod 17:14; consult vv. 8-16).

Later, when Moses was giving his farewell speech, he reminded the Israelites never to forget this charge: "Therefore when the LORD your God has given you rest from all your enemies on every hand, in the land that the LORD your God is giving you as an inheritance to possess, you shall blot out the remembrance of Amalek from under heaven; do not forget!" (Deut 25:19).

Amalek's downfall was also predicted by the pagan prophet Balaam, as recorded in Num 24:20. As a perpetual enemy, Amalek was included in several lists of peoples who stood in the way of Israel's possession of the promised land (Num 13:29; 14:25; Judg 3:13; 6:3, 33).

Samuel instructed Saul to exterminate the Amalekites (1 Sam 15:2-9); but he was not successful. Although the text suggests that all were killed save Agag (1 Sam 15:8), the Amalekites appeared again and again. Ironically, it was an Amalekite who mercifully ended Saul's life (according to 2 Sam 1:8-10; but cf. 1 Sam 31:1-6).

David also fought the Amalekites, initiating raids against them, then leading a retaliatory strike after they burned his city and captured his wives (1 Sam 27:8-11; 30:1-20). As David and Solomon consolidated their control over the southern reaches of the kingdom, the Amalekites were forced to pay tribute (2 Sam 8:11-12). By the time of Hezekiah, only a few Amalekites remained, and these supposedly were eradicated by a group of Simeonites (1 Chr 4:42-43).

The Amalekites also figure into the delightful story of Esther, for the hated henchman Haman is described as an Agagite—presumably a descendant of the Amalekite king Agag, spared by Saul but slain by Samuel (1 Sam 15:7-9). Haman is portrayed as one who despised the Jews and wanted to annihilate them all. Haman's heritage helps to explain his enmity for Israel. Nevertheless, Haman failed just as surely as those who came before him (Esth 3–4; 8:2).

---

apparently derives from the belief that Yahweh has ordained the battle and will fight for them.

The battle is portrayed as the direct consequence of an ancient action; it is Yahweh's punishment of the Amalekites for their attacks on Israel during the exodus period (v. 3). Samuel's instructions to Saul thus are spoken prophetically, insisting that both people and property be utterly destroyed in a holy war. [Holy War] The command to "kill both man and woman, child and infant, ox and sheep, camel and donkey" (v. 4) seems highly problematic to modern believers, but it was common enough in the ancient world. [The Problem of War] In a holy war, the entire enemy nation is perceived as the personification of evil, and in 1 Samuel 15, that personified population is named Amalek.

Saul set out to follow Samuel's mandate; he gathered an army of overwhelming size and set an ambush for the Amalekites. After sending a quiet message offering amnesty to any Kenites who lived in Amalek, he and his army set upon the Amalekites across the entire southern frontier of Judah. [Kenites] According to the text, gaining the victory was uneventful, as the Israelites swept through

Holy War

AΩ The ancient concept of holy war assumes that some human battles are merely surface manifestations of a divine conflict between the gods. Many of Israel's battles were believed to be ordained by Yahweh as a means of eliminating the danger of enemies who threatened Israel's physical and spiritual safety. The term "holy war" does not appear in the Bible, but "wars of the LORD" does occur (Num 31:14; 1 Sam 18:17; 25:28).

There were specific rules for establishing and fighting a holy war. Since the people believed they were fighting at God's behest (Num 31:3; Josh 6:2; Judg 7:7), soldiers were required to be ritually clean (Num 31:19-24; 1 Sam 21:4; 2 Sam 11:11). Once the battle was engaged, troops were denied the opportunity to profit from the conflict by looting the enemy. Instead, both people and plunder were to be utterly destroyed. This is expressed by the phrase "to put under the ban" (*ḥerem*; Num 21:2; Deut 2:34; 3:6; 7:2; 13:15; among others).

The purpose of the ban was to demonstrate that it was *Yahweh's* war, not Israel's, and to destroy all evidence or persons that might tempt Israel to worship the enemy's gods. Failure to honor the ban could have disastrous consequences, as Israel discovered in the Ai/Achan episode (Josh 7), and as Saul learned the hard way in 1 Sam 15.

For further reading relative to holy war and the problem of war in general, see [**The Problem of War**]), and Rudolf Smend, *Yahweh War & Tribal Confederation*, trans. Max G. Rogers (Nashville: Abington, 1970); L. E. Toombs, "War, Ideas of," (*IDB*, 4 vols.; New York: Abingdon, 1962), 4:796-801; Gerhard von Rad, *Holy War in Ancient Israel*, trans. Marva Dawn (Grand Rapids: Eerdmans, 1991); and Johnny Wilson, "Holy War," *MDB* (Macon GA: Mercer University Press, 1990), 385-86.

Amalekite lands "from Havilah to Shur." The place name Havilah is in much dispute and may reflect a corruption of "the wadi" where Saul had lain in wait. The land bridge south of the Mediterranean Sea just east of Egypt was sometimes called the "Wilderness of Shur."

Despite Saul's easy victory, the army's treatment of the vanquished violated Samuel's plainly worded dictum to put the entire land under the ban. Since the battle itself was seen as a cultic act of devotion, every thing captured (living or not) was to be destroyed as an offering to God. However, Saul and his army kept alive not only Agag the king, but also "the best of the sheep and of the cattle and of the fatlings, and the lambs, and all that was valuable, and would not utterly destroy them; all that was despised and worthless they utterly destroyed" (v. 9).

Saul's Explanation and Samuel's Sermon, 15:10-23

Saul's transgression was so egregious that Yahweh declared divine regret over choosing Saul, while Samuel expressed his own anger and confusion by spending the night in earnest prayer (vv. 10-11).While Samuel was grieving, however, Saul was celebrating his victory, having erected a monument to himself at Carmel (v. 12)

The Problem of War

The concept of killing innocents, even in the context of an apparently justified war, seems wildly opposed to the ethic of Jesus and out of character for the God who is described in the New Testament. Problems such as this led Marcion (a proponent of the Gnostic heresy in the early church) to argue that the God of the Old Testament was a bumbling lower-level species of divinity who had been superseded by Christ.

If there is any key to understanding the dilemma, it must be found in the differing perceptions of God based on culture and history, and in seeking to hear the word of God even through a text that is steeped in violence. The history of the ancient Near East is a legacy of war in which each people group sought supremacy over the other and tried to ensure success by eradicating the enemy completely. Each nation assumed that its patron gods gave both blessing and victory, and in this regard, Israel was a product of its culture.

In the New Testament, the issue of war is toned down, but not absent. Jesus seems to have taught a simple ethic of nonviolence toward others (Matt 5:38-48), but was not averse to using military metaphors to describe the conflict his teaching could bring: "Do not think that I have come to bring peace to the earth; I have not come to bring peace, but a sword" (Matt 10:34). Paul used military language as well, but in a spiritualized context: God's faithful do battle against the forces of evil as part of the eschatological struggle to actualize Christ's self-sacrificial victory over Satan, the personified enemy of all that is good (Eph 6:10-20; 1 Tim 1:18-19).

For King Saul's contemporaries in the 10th century BC, evil was not a pervasive spiritual force, but a population of particular enemies who threatened their way of life under God and deserved annihilation. Modern adherents of holy war (*Jihad*) continue to think in the ancient way, seeing their victims not as individuals, but as the corporate personification of evil.

The texts do not endorse any modern sort of racial genocide or ethnic cleansing. The point of the story is that evil exists, it must be confronted, and it can be overcome. The realities of each given situation and the whole of the biblical witness must be considered as believers seek God's will in determining the best response to individual or national conflicts.

Kenites

The Kenites were a nomadic group of pastoralists who also were known for their metal-working skills. They lived on the fringes of society, operating from the semi-arid lands east of the Dead Sea and south of Arad. Through the years, the Kenites maintained a tenuous but positive relationship with Israel.

Moses' father-in-law, Jethro (also called Hobab), is described both as a Midianite (Exod 18:1; Num 10:29) and as a *Kenite* (Judg 1:16; 4:11). Jethro/Hobab was not a Hebrew, but surprisingly, he worshiped Yahweh. Since the name "Kenite" bears philological similarities to the name "Cain" (*qēnî; qayin*), some scholars have postulated an old tradition that the Kenites were descendants of Cain, still wandering on the fringes of society and worshiping Yahweh.

In addition to the Jethro/Hobab connection, Kenites are said to have joined the tribe of Judah in conquering southern Canaan (Judg 1:16). Another familiar story from the conquest/settlement period relates how the Kenite woman Jael gave apparent shelter to the Canaanite general Sisera, then calmly dispatched him with a tent peg through the head (Judg 4:17). This was celebrated in the exultant "Song of Deborah" (5:24-27).

Although the Kenites generally remained politically neutral in later conflicts, friendly relations between the Israelites and Kenites continued. Thus, Saul sent a secret word to the Kenites, who lived among the Amalekites, allowing them to escape before the mass slaughter of the coming war (1 Sam 15:6).

before moving on to the ancient cultic altar at Gilgal. [Carmel] The author portrays Saul as being so dense that he did not even realize he was in trouble when the angry Samuel came into view the next morning. Instead, Saul offered a pious blessing on Samuel, announcing his fulfillment of Yahweh's command (v. 13). Samuel's response dripped with sarcasm. "What then is this bleating of sheep in my ears, and the lowing of cattle that I hear?" (v. 14).

Incredibly, Saul still showed no awareness of his sin: "They have brought them from the Amalekites," he replied, "for the people spared the best of the sheep and the cattle, to sacrifice to the LORD your God; but the rest we have utterly destroyed" (v. 15). Thus, Saul blames the offense on his army, but he excuses the troops by insisting that the animals were destined for public sacrifice at a later time, perhaps in celebration of the victory. Saul's assertion that he did this for "*your* God" does not suggest that he did not acknowledge Yahweh as his own God, too, but probably reflects a futile effort to buy favor with Samuel by implying that Saul had fought the battle for his sake.

Samuel's reply was heated and direct. He charged that Saul once had been a humble man ("small in his own eyes") but that his humility had given way to hubris; his obedience has been watered down by temporizing. God's command had been clear: "Kill both man and woman, child and infant, ox and sheep, camel and donkey" (15:3). Instead, Saul had chosen to "swoop down" upon the spoil like a ravenous predator rather than as an obedient conqueror (vv. 17-19).

The narrator insists that Saul *still* failed to understand his transgression, claiming full obedience to God's command, despite having reinterpreted it to suit himself. Saul divided any potential blame between the troops and Yahweh, to whom the animals were to be offered (vv. 20-21). Samuel did not accept Saul's rationalization, however, but indicted him with a prophetic poem that puts the entire issue clearly into focus:

> Has the LORD as great delight in burnt offerings and sacrifices,
>   as in obeying the voice of the LORD?
> Surely, to obey is better than sacrifice,

Carmel

Carmel was a small town in southern Judah, about seven miles south of Hebron. It would have been one of the first Israelite towns Saul passed through on his return from battle, an appropriate site for a monument commemorating his cleansing of the southern frontier. Carmel appears again in 1 Sam 25 as the locale of David's encounter with his future wife Abigail and her "worthless" husband, Nabal.

1 Samuel 15:22-31—This woodcut by Carolsfeld depicts a repentant Saul clinging to an enraged Samuel, unintentionally tearing the old priest's robe. Samuel prophesied that the kingdom would by torn away from Saul.

Julius Schnoor von Carolsfeld. *Saul Is Rejected as King.* 19th century. Woodcut. *Das Buch der Bucher in Bilden.* (Credit: Dover Pictorial Archive Series)

and to heed than the fat of rams.
For rebellion is no less a sin than divination,
    and stubbornness is like iniquity and idolatry.
Because you have rejected the word of the LORD,
    he has also rejected you from being king. (vv. 22-23)

Samuel's energetic invective is highly reminiscent of similar charges from the later "writing" prophets, such as Isaiah (1:10-17), Hosea (6:6; cited by Jesus in Matt 9:13; 12:7), and Amos (5:21-24). Public sacrifices are impressive, but obedience is better. Saul's presumptuous variation on God's command cost him his kingdom.

Saul Repents, but Loses His Kingdom, 15:24-35

When Saul finally acknowledged his error, he still accepted no responsibility for it. He had been afraid to rein in the troops, he said.

Did Saul's fear of the troops have something to do with the earlier incident in which Saul had ordered Jonathan's execution, but had been overruled by the people (14:43-45)? Saul could not perceive why his actions should preclude Samuel from attending the official celebration of victory to offer the captured sacrifices (15:24-25).

Thus, Samuel's grief was compounded by Saul's spiritual obtuseness. He refused to go and worship with Saul, repeating his charge that Saul's rejection of the LORD had led the LORD to reject Saul in return (v. 26). Only when Samuel turned to walk away did Saul absorb the seriousness of his situation and what it meant to lose Yahweh's blessing. He reached for the aged priest and pulled at his robe so violently that it ripped, providing Samuel with a potent prophetic metaphor: "The LORD has torn the kingdom of Israel from you this very day, and has given it to a neighbor of yours, who is better than you" (v. 28).

Only then did Saul acknowledge his sin, begging Samuel to help him save face before Israel by accompanying him to the sacrifice. Samuel finally agreed (vv. 30-31), but when he arrived at Gilgal, he insisted on doing what Saul was unwilling to do. When Agag was brought before Samuel, he came not as a brave and defiant hero, but as a man who knew he was about to die and who was afraid. Even so, Samuel showed no sympathy to Israel's old enemy, but personally hacked him into pieces (vv. 32-33).

The closing verses of the story are drenched with sorrow. Though Saul remained king for several more years, he no longer enjoyed the blessing of Yahweh or of Samuel. Samuel's departure for Ramah and Saul's return to Gibeah reflect a deeper parting of the ways. Both Samuel and Yahweh grieved for Saul, but the king never knew how deeply, for the divine spokesman Samuel—Saul's former patron—never came near him again (vv. 34-35).

CONNECTIONS

Persons who appreciate violent action films would probably enjoy a movie based on 1 Samuel 15. This text is one of the ugliest and most brutal stories to be found in Scripture. It is dark and foreboding. It points to a side of God—or, at least, to an ancient people's understanding of God—that gives many people great discomfort because it seems so much at odds with God as we know him from the New Testament.

1 Samuel 15:33—Samuel had no interest in keeping King Agag alive as a war trophy, as did Saul. Doré's skill as a printmaker can be found in his dramatic use of shading and contrast. The primary action is centered and concentrated on the main protagonists in the narrative.

Gustave Doré (1832–83). *Death of Agag* from the *Illustrated Bible.* 19th century. Engraving. (Credit: Dover Pictorial Archive Series)

And yet, beneath the troublesome parts, there is a very important lesson for those who call themselves the people of God. So parts of this story are rated "R" for "Revolting." Other parts are rated "PG" for "Pretty Good." A couple of verses are rated "X" for "Xtremely Important," but the overall rating is "G" for "God's word." Like it or not, God speaks to us in this text. It is in our Bible. Our task is to understand it and interpret it responsibly.

For many Christians, the idea of a holy war sounds barbaric at best. It appears to be antithetical to the ethics taught by Jesus, who told us to love our enemies, not to slaughter them. Two things help us in interpreting this passage.

The *first* is to remember its historical context. Samuel and Saul lived in an ancient and impassioned culture in which all-out war was seen as a means of survival. We can understand why Samuel advocated holy war, but we cannot use this text automatically to promote war over peace, or to declare that our battleships and jet fighters are the instruments of God. Some groups, such as Muslim fundamentalists of Iran and Iraq, still preserve remnants of that same ancient culture. They may declare war in the name of God as a holy *Jihad,* but New Testament believers can find nothing of this in the teaching of Christ.

To understand Scripture properly—and this is the *second* thing—
we must use the highest point of revelation as the point from which
all other scriptures are interpreted, and for Christians this means
that every scripture must be subject to the light of Jesus Christ.

Jesus' coming did not bring an end to violence and death, but
effected a deeper change. Jesus did not set out to slaughter sinners,
but to deal with sin. And somehow, in the mystery of God, the way
he chose to do that was by allowing the brutality of this world to
rise up and kill *him*. Jesus died in a holy war. He died a violent,
bloody death—for the sake of those who killed him. As Jesus suffered upon the cross and took human sin upon himself, he made it
clear that power and violence as this world knows them ultimately
must fall subject to the law of love.

Fortunately, none of the inherent problems prevent us from
understanding the central point of this story, which is straightforward: To obey is better than to sacrifice. The inner reality of an
authentic faith is more important than any external rituals. "We
forget that God has always been more interested in our character
than our liturgy and more impressed by our compassion than our
doctrine."[1] Here is the heart of the matter. No Sunday ceremony
will impress the Lord if we have ignored God's will every other day
of the week.

We cannot read this story without the voice of Samuel persistently shouting in our ears, reminding us of God's call to
obedience, putting the name to our smug temporizing, and calling
us to repentance and renewal.

We cannot read this story without learning from Saul that sometimes repentance comes too late. As long as we live, forgiveness is
possible, but even forgiveness is accompanied by loss. God did not
stop loving Saul, but the errant king had proven himself unworthy
of his position. Likewise, God will never stop loving us, but there
may come a time when we realize that we have passed by our best
opportunities for serving Christ and accomplishing his work
because we chose to follow our human rationalizations rather than
God's clear word. Though our hearts may be redeemed, opportunities for service may irretrievably be lost.

NOTE

[1] Kenneth Chafin, *1, 2 Samuel* (CC; Dallas: Word Books, 1989), 129.

YOUNG DAVID,
THE ANOINTED

16:1-13

David's Rise to Prominence, 16:1–17:58

With chapter 16, we come to a new piece of literature within the traditional collections that make up the books of Samuel. The section encompassing 1 Samuel 16:1 to 2 Samuel 5:2 is often called "The History of David's Rise." David was such a powerful character in history that many stories grew up around him and were remembered with great reverence. Sometimes these accounts seem to contradict each other, but the editors were so respectful of David's heritage that they included several divergent traditions with little attempt to harmonize them.

There is much debate concerning the historicity of David. So-called "maximalists" and "minimalists" accept more or less of the Davidic traditions as being historical. This issue is discussed at some length in the introduction to this commentary. While historical issues may surface from time to time, the following discussion of David's rise assumes the historical reality of a Hebrew leader named David whose activities and impact were such that he is remembered with profit many centuries later.

The narrative is careful to show that David's ascent to power was authorized and effected by God, who rejected Saul (ch. 15) and chose David to become king of Israel. Like Saul, David is introduced by no less than three separate stories, all as if for the first time. Since the various stories show little cognizance of each other, they seem to have been combined from various independent sources. David is anointed by Samuel in 16:1-13, then joins Saul's court as a favorite musician in 16:14-23. When Israel experienced a renewed threat from the Philistines, David again is introduced to Saul as an unknown but daring young warrior (17:1-58). The common threads are that, in each story, David is described as a shepherd, and in each story, God is working behind the scenes to maneuver David into position as the future king of Israel.

Other records show a similar multiplicity of sources. According to 1 Samuel 16, David was anointed by Samuel in Yahweh's behalf, while 2 Samuel 2:4 describes an anointing by the men of Judah, and

2 Samuel 5:3 insists that David's anointing came at the hands of
Israel's elders.

COMMENTARY

The use of divergent sources, however interesting, distracts only
little from the smooth narrative flow of the final editor. Having
elucidated Saul's unsuitability for kingship and Samuel's declaration that Yahweh would choose another to replace him (ch. 15),
the author turns immediately to the anointing of young David as
the newly selected successor. Surprisingly, Samuel seems less than
enthused. He had been filled with righteous indignation over Saul's
cultic transgressions in the war with Amalek. He had railed at Saul
and insisted that God would give the kingdom to "a neighbor of
yours who is better than you" (15:28). Samuel might be expected
to rush out in search of Saul's replacement. Instead, we find him
sitting at home in Ramah, grieving over Saul's disappointing performance. [Samuel's Grief over Saul]

It is Yahweh who jars Samuel from his glum reverie, reminding
him that Saul's opportunity is past, but the future awaits (v. 1). It is
not mourning that is called for, but action. Indeed, Samuel
learns that Yahweh already has discovered (lit., "seen")
a new king, to be found among the sons of Jesse,
in Bethlehem. Samuel's calling was clear: Fill
your horn with oil, find the new man, and
anoint him. For once, however, Samuel
sought to avoid his duty. He had been
highly outspoken in his criticism of the
king, and he presumed that the suspicious Saul would have spies on his trail.
To anoint a new king was to invite personal disaster.

Yahweh dismissed Samuel's objections by suggesting a reasonable
solution bound up in a small artifice.
Samuel was to take with him a heifer
and tell any potential informant that he
had need to offer a sacrifice in
Bethlehem (v. 2). As Israel's leading priest, the guise of sacrifice
could mask his real motives effectively.

Suppressing his fears, Samuel obeyed (v. 4), only to find that the
elders of Bethlehem were no more happy about his appearance

Samuel's Grief over Saul

Samuel had opposed the idea of kingship, and only
reluctantly gave his blessing to Saul. Yet he had high
hopes for the young king. Now Saul had let him down—not for
the political and social sins that Samuel had outlined in 8:10-18,
but for repeated violations of Israel's cultic ritual.

(Illustration Credit: Barclay Burns)

Elders

In the Old Testament period, each family, clan, or town was led by a group of elders. Originally, elders would have been the oldest and wisest men of the group, but in time the term was applied to other authority figures as well. Moses appointed elders to assist him in governing the wandering Israelites (Num 11:16-30). During the judges period, the officials and elders of one city (Succoth) were said to encompass seventy-seven persons (Judg 8:13-15). Elders appeared during the monarchic period (1 Sam 15:30; 1 Kgs 8:3; Jer 26:17-19), and they seemed to take even stronger leadership roles after the exile (Jer 29:1; Ezra 5:9; 10:14).

Elders commonly met at the city gate, where they adjudged disputes, enforced the law, and witnessed business dealings (Deut 19:12; 22:5-21; Ruth 4:4). It was the elders of Israel who demanded that Samuel appoint for them a king (1 Sam 8:4-5), and elders later gave unheeded advice to King Rehoboam (1 Kgs 12:6).

It is ironic that the same persons who once had pressed Samuel for a king would now interfere with his recruitment of the man who would be Israel's greatest ruler.

---

than he was. [Elders] Saul's traditional power base was among the northern tribes, but Bethlehem belonged to the southern tribe of Judah, which doubtless retained some wariness toward the new king. If Samuel were still Saul's man, he could be scouting the area for future "contributions" to Saul's army or treasury. On the other hand, if Samuel were no longer in favor with Saul, the Bethlehemites could be in even greater danger for giving him refuge. Thus, their query about Samuel's intentions is understandable (v. 4).

Although Samuel invited the village elders to participate in the sacrificial feast, they immediately disappeared from the picture. Only Jesse (presumably an elder) and his sons remain. Curiously, Samuel instructed the village elders to go and sanctify themselves, but Samuel himself supervised the ritual sanctification of Jesse and his sons. [Sanctification]

After preparations were made, but presumably before the sacrificial meal was eaten, Samuel reviewed the sons of Jesse. The author is careful to emphasize Samuel's initial captivation with Eliab, Jesse's oldest son (v. 6). He does this to set the stage for sage words from Yahweh that would be repeated throughout Israel's history: "Do not look on his appearance or on the height of his stature . . . for the LORD does not see as mortals see; they look on the outward appearance, but the LORD looks on the heart" (v. 7). The astute reader will immediately recall 1 Samuel 13:14, where Samuel insisted that Yahweh would seek out a man "after his own heart."

Sanctification

Israel's cultic regulations required that worshipers be "sanctified" or "consecrated" before approaching Yahweh through sacrifice or temple worship. Literally, the word means "to make holy" or "to set apart" for divine service. When Moses met God through the burning bush, the LORD instructed him to take off his sandals to acknowledge the holiness of the place (Exod 3:5). When Israel met God at Sinai, the people were required to consecrate themselves in particular ways (Exod 19:10-15). The "Holiness Code" of Lev 17–26 includes specific instructions for maintaining ritual holiness.

The Sons of Jesse

According to 1 Chr 2:13-15, Jesse's sons were named Eliab, Abinadab, Shimea, Nethanel, Raddai, Ozem, and David—a total of seven. However, 1 Sam 16:10 and 17:12 insist that there are seven brothers in addition to David. First Chr 27:18 mentions another brother of David, named Elihu, though some scholars consider Elihu to be a textual corruption of Eliab (note also the variant spelling of Shammah/Shimea in 1 Sam 16:9 and 1 Chr 27:18). Evidently, there are mixed traditions regarding David's family. The number of brothers is not without significance, however. David's choice as one who is outside of the first seven brothers suggests that he is someone special, above and beyond even the "perfect" number seven.

Eliab was not chosen, despite his firstborn status and his impressive appearance. Saul also had been tall and handsome, but those qualities had not aided his performance. As Samuel had renounced Saul, he also had rejected Eliab. Likewise, Abinadab and Shammah were bypassed, along with four other sons of Jesse (vv. 8-10). [The Sons of Jesse] This might have surprised the ancient reader, who knew that the number seven represented completeness. How could seven sons pass by and none be chosen? Samuel did not comment on the anomaly, however, demanding only to know if all of Jesse's sons were present. Learning that a single younger brother remained, Samuel insisted that he be brought (v. 11).

The narrator masterfully builds suspense by reporting that Samuel would not allow anyone to sit down until the missing son arrived. David could have been far away as he watched over the flocks, but Samuel insists that everyone stand and wait. Samuel waits. Jesse waits. The brothers wait. And the reader waits—all await the arrival of David, the son who was not invited.

This literary tension leads the reader to suspect that the long-awaited David must be the chosen one, though (in the light of v. 7) he probably will be unimpressive in appearance. When David arrives, however, the storyteller unexpectedly reverses field. After making it clear that God looks on the heart and cares not for out-ward appearances, the narrator ebulliently reports that David had fair skin , beautiful eyes, and was altogether handsome! [David's Complexion] Apparently, the author was such an admirer of David—or the David traditions were so rich with praise—that he could not help but admire David's (unimportant) appearance. Even so, the reader learns that David's heart must also be in tune with Yahweh's purpose, for he was clearly God's choice (16:12).

David's Complexion

AΩ The word describing David's complexion usually is translated as "ruddy," for it derives from the same root as the name "Adam," a reference to the reddish dust of the earth. Today, the word "ruddy" describes a pink complexion that often appears flushed. The Hebrews, however, like indigenous inhabitants of the Middle East today, were probably a dark-complected people. A person described as "ruddy" would likely have fairer skin than usual so that the color of the cheeks was more apparent. Presumably, this was considered to be an attractive quality.

The actual anointing (see [Anointing] and [A Recipe for Anointing Oil]) may have been no more than a curiosity to his brothers, but the narrator describes it as a defining moment in David's life. As the sacred oil brought a shine to David's face and hair, the spirit of God gleamed in his heart. "The spirit of the LORD came mightily upon David," the story tells us, "from that day forward" (v. 13). The word translated as "came mightily" (NRSV, NASB) can also mean "rushed" (AB) or even "gripped" (NJPS). It is as if God cannot wait to inspire David with divine power and presence.

1 Samuel 16—Carolsfeld has captured Jesse's surprise at learning that God had chosen David, rather than one of his older sons, to be king.

Julius Schnoor von Carolsfeld. *David Is Anointed King.* 19th century. Woodcut. *Das Buch der Bucher in Bilden.* (Credit: Dover Pictorial Archive Series)

The reader recalls that the spirit of the LORD had come upon Saul, too (1 Sam 10:6; 11:6), but without such compelling force or permanence. Indeed, the narrator underscores the contrast between the two royals by conjoining the account of David's spiritual blessing with the immediate report that "the spirit of the LORD departed from Saul" (v. 14). Though the ruling king was unaware, the torch had been passed.

The final note of this account is both poignant and significant, despite its simplicity: "Samuel returned home to Ramah." The anointing of David was Samuel's last great act. He did not become David's advisor, because David did not need him. As the LORD had come upon Samuel in his youth, so the LORD's spirit now had come upon the youngest of Jesse's children, and David would never be the same again.

CONNECTIONS

Samuel's search for David calls to mind a beauty pageant in which the carefully coifed contestants are shocked to discover that final judging will be based on their ability to define and compare quantum physics and the theory of relativity. Even Samuel—the judge—is surprised, for he began the royal search with an eye for physical size and attractiveness, only to learn that "the LORD looks on the heart."

The story of David's selection compels the reader to ask if God might also be calling us to divine service. We all know others who are better looking, more talented, more mature, more wealthy, or more physically fit than we are. Perhaps we have discounted our abilities or our attractiveness to God as potential servants. We have assumed that God will use others, but not us. We'll just stay in the fields with the sheep.

David was not the oldest, the biggest, the strongest, or the most impressive of his brothers. He was such an unlikely candidate that his father didn't even invite him to the sacrifice! "But the LORD does not see as mortals see; they look on the outward appearance, but the LORD looks on the heart." [The Power of the Heart]

What do you suppose was so special about David's heart that Scripture would portray him as a man after God's own heart? Different interpreters suggest different ideas, but consider the significance of David's openness—his spirit of adventure, his delight in trying new things, his willingness to let God work through him. David's heart was not closed because his mind was not made up and he made no claim to having everything figured out. The impression we get is that David's heart was open to the future, open to new possibilities, open to mystery, and therefore open to the spirit of God. As David remained open to the spirit's presence and leadership in his life, God's spirit remained with him *from that day forward.* As a result, God accomplished great things through David. Most of us are familiar enough with our own frailties and failures to know that if great things come through us, it will be God's doing, and not ours.

The surprising truth about the spirit of God is that we do not *do* something to *get* it. We do not have to become more attractive or even more worthy. Our openness is enough. Our not knowing is enough. Our willingness is enough. The Bible makes it clear that God *delights* in surprising the world by doing great things through small people.

We may never be anointed with royal oil, as was David, but we can be anointed by the spirit of God. We can look forward to a future that is filled with unknown opportunities for life and service and joy. We can become the persons God wants us to be; there is no greater goal in this life.

The Power of the Heart

No moment of the 1996 Olympic Games in Atlanta is more memorable than Keri Strug's final vault in the team competition of women's gymnastics. The American team was poised to win the gold medal if either of the last two competitors succeeded in completing a clean vault. The vault did not have to be spectacular, but neither could the team afford any major deductions. The penultimate competitor attempted two vaults, but fell on both of them, leaving it to Strug to clinch the gold medal. Strug was not the best gymnast on the team, nor the flashiest, nor the most decorated. Before the Olympics, she was hardly known outside of gymnastic circles. When the tiny competitor raced down the floor to attempt her first vault, she slipped on the landing and injured her ankle. With one last chance remaining, she limped gingerly back to the starting line, testing her leg, fighting back pain and tears. With the encouragement of her coach and her teammates, she sprinted down the runway again, launched herself into a series of aerial gyrations, and executed a solid landing before reflexively lifting her injured foot, then collapsing in pain. With victory assured, the tiny but courageous gymnast was carried off the floor by her coach, placed on a stretcher, and wheeled to the medical center.

One could say that Keri Strug made that final landing not with her feet, but with her heart. It wasn't the outward appearance or reputation that mattered, but the stuff she was made of.

SWEET DAVID,
THE MUSICIAN

16:14-23

COMMENTARY

David is introduced for the second time in an entirely separate story that is linked to the first by the activity of God's spirit. The text reports that David's initial anointing at the hands of Samuel was accompanied by a powerful inrush of the spirit of the LORD (16:13). The very next verse introduces the ensuing account with the pointed observation that "the spirit of the LORD departed from Saul, and an evil spirit from the LORD tormented him" (v. 14). [An Evil Spirit from the Lord?] The spirit of the LORD had come upon Saul first shortly after he was anointed by Samuel (10:9-11), leading him into an ecstatic frenzy. Later, Saul experienced the motivating and empowering touch of the spirit before doing battle with the Ammonites (11:6).

The text suggests that David's encounter with the spirit of God was on an entirely different level. Saul's infusion with the spirit was more reminiscent of the judges, who each experienced a temporary rush of

---

An Evil Spirit from the Lord?

It seems oxymoronic to speak of God as the source of an evil spirit, but there is no getting around the text. Kyle McCarter suggests an ancient belief that a person who had been touched by the divine spirit could never be free entirely again. When Yahweh's empowering spirit came upon David, it was as if an evil spirit rushed upon Saul to fill the vacuum (compare Jesus' comment about the seven evil spirits in Matt 12:43-45). However, the evil spirit seems to come and go (16:23; 18:10), rather than being a permanent affliction. Indeed, Saul experienced a more positive influx of the spirit on at least one other occasion (19:23-24; though some scholars consider this to be a doublet of 10:9-13).

Modern psychologists can easily spot signs of manic depression or paranoia and other indications of mental illness in Saul's behavior. These concepts, however, were unknown to the ancients. Hertzberg correctly noted that Saul's suffering was clearly described in *theological* terms, not psychological terms. The Old Testament writers were so opposed to dualism or polytheism that they had little choice but to assign both evil and temptation to God, who was the source of all things (e.g., Deut 13:2-4; Amos 3:6; 2 Sam 24:1; 1 Chr 21:1). An evil spirit between Abimelech and the men of Shechem was attributed to God (Judg 9:23), as was the lying spirit that came over the false prophets who opposed Micaiah (1 Kgs 22:19-22).

The concept of Satan as the source of evil and chief of demons developed rather late in the Old Testament period, probably based on ideas picked up from the Persians, following the exile. Prior to the development of this more dualistic view, and apart from an understanding of evil as an abstract quality inherent in humankind, evil, like everything else, was thought to come from God.

P. Kyle McCarter, *I Samuel* (AB 8; Garden City: Doubleday, 1980), 280.

Hans Wilhelm Hertzberg, *I & II Samuel*, (Philadelphia: Westminster Press, 1964), 141.

power enabling them to accomplish some great act of deliverance (Judg 3:10; 6:34; 11:29; 14:6, 19; 15:14). The narrator insists, however, that David's experience was ongoing: "The spirit of the LORD came mightily upon David *from that day forward*" (16:13).

The bounty of David's blessing was matched by the depth of Saul's misery. Not only did the empowering "spirit of the LORD" desert the king, but "an evil spirit from the LORD tormented him." In ancient Israel, there were no secondary causes; all things were traced back to God. If Saul were afflicted by the inner torments of manic mood swings, there was no attempt to explain his malady as a mental illness or demonic possession—even evil spirits owed their existence to God. In the narrator's scheme, Saul's emotional affliction sets the stage for David's physical arrival. The remainder of the story identifies young David—newly endowed with God's spirit— as the only medium of relief for Saul's manic attacks.

When one of Saul's officials suggested that the king seek someone skilled with the lyre to soothe his raw nerves, the king urged them to go forward (vv. 15-16). The author employs a touch of artistry by having Saul use an imperative form of the word "to see," as in "spy out for me" an appropriate musician (v. 17; some prefer the dynamic translation "provide," but the literal meaning is "see"). As Yahweh had revealed to Samuel that he had "seen" (or "provided") a new king among Jesse's sons (16:1), so now one of Saul's aides responds: "I have *seen* a son of Jesse the Bethlehemite who is skillful in playing the lyre" (v. 18). [Lyre] Why should this courtier of Saul's northern-based kingdom be so familiar with a young man from the obscure southern village of Bethlehem? The narrator's silence suggests a tacit assumption that the earlier contact was providential.

Lyre

David's lyre, the *kinnôr*, was the most common stringed instrument of the day. It was built on a rectangular or trapezoidal sound box with strings attached to wooden uprights extending from either end. Archaeological evidence suggests that ancient lyres had from three to twelve strings, which could be plucked with the fingers or a type of pick called a plectrum. The pleasant music of the lyre, it was hoped, might offer a calming distraction during Saul's manic moods, when "the evil spirit from God" was upon him.

This ancient lyre was found in a Sumerian tomb in Ur. The lines and proportion reflect not only its functionality but its beauty.

Lyre. Early Dynastic, Ur. 2450 BC. Iraq Museum. Baghdad, Iraq.
(Credit: Scala/Art Resource, NY)

David's Résumé

AΩ David's initial qualification was his skill with the lyre, literally, "He knows harp-playing." Two unexpected epithets follow: "Man of valor" translates *gibbôr ḥayil*, an appellative that can emphasize physical prowess, financial power, or family stature (see commentary at 9:1). "Warrior" means, literally, "a man of war." Both of these titles seem overblown when describing a shepherd boy! David's intelligence and poise are conveyed by the phrase "prudent in speech," for the word rendered "prudent" means "insightful," "discerning," or "intelligent."

David not only was intelligent and skilled, but also he was handsome and fit, described as "a man of good presence." The word "presence" literally means "form" or "outline." David was physically fit and attractive.

David's final attribute is his best one: "Yahweh is with him." What Saul did not realize is that it was the spirit of Yahweh in David that would give him comfort, not simply his music.

King David Playing the Lute. Relief from Pueto de las platerias. Romanesque. 12th century. Santiago de Compostela, Spain. (Credit: Giraudon/Art Resource)

(Right) Michelangelo (1475-1564). *David.* 1502-04. Marble. 14'1". Museo di Accademia del Disegno, Florence, Italy. (Credit: Planet Art)

(Above) Andrea del Verocchio (1435–88). *David.* c. 1470. Bronze. 49⅝" Museo Nazionale del Bargello. Florence, Italy. (Credit: Scala/Art Resource)

These three sculptures indicate very different approaches to visualizing the biblical hero. The 12th century artist is directed to depict King David in a traditional Romanesque pose of crossed ankles and striated drapery. This figure was to fit within the architectural space desginated for it. As a relief, it is fully attached to the architecture. Verrocchio, a 15th century Florentine, reveals an adolescent and confident David seen after the defeat of Goliath. This figure is free-standing in the Greek tradition and was commissioned by Lorenzo de'Medici for the Medici Palace in Florence. Michelangelo also chooses the David and Goliath story but his colossal, fully developed figure concentrates on the activity about to begin. David had for several centuries been a symbol of the city of Florence. Florence considered themselves an underdog continually able to conquer a formidable foe. One can only imagine the size of Michelangelo's Goliath as his David (standing at over 14') mentally prepares for him. Michelangelo's David was originally commissioned to be placed on the buttress of the Florentine Cathedral. After the civic committee saw Michelangelo's work, however, it was located prominently as a symbol of the city in the main governmental square, the Piazza della Signoria.

David's skill with the lyre, however, is only the beginning of his emerging talents, though perhaps it is David's later glory that is reflected in the glowing résumé of v. 18. [David's Résumé] Saul was looking for a good musician, but his aide's enthusiastic

David the Musician

Renaissance and modern literature have reflected David's stature as an archetypal poet and musician. Sir Philip Sidney's *Defence of Poetry* (1579–80) cited David to bolster his argument for the antiquity and value of poetry, while, according to Christopher Smart's *A Song for David* (1763), David's "muse, bright angel of his verse, / Gives balm for all the thorns that pierce, / For all the pangs that rage." Lord Byron paid homage to David's verse in "The Harp the Monarch Minstrel Swept" in his *Hebrew Melodies* (1815).

Michael Drayton's *David and Goliah* infuses David's music with epic qualities; with it David not only calms Saul, but also tames fierce animals and inspires docile sheep to resistance:

What wondrous things by Musick he had done,
How he fierce Tigars to his hand had wonne,
Had layd the Lion, and the Beare to sleepe,
And put such spirit into his silly sheepe,
By his high straines, as that they durst oppose
The Woolfe and Fox, their most inveterate foes. (ll. 243-48)

Robert Browning's poem *Saul*, published in 1855, also focuses on David's music, his "soul-wine." Influenced by the Romantic movement, the poem extols David's ability to play "the tune, for which quails on the cornland will each leave his mate / To fly after the player" (ll. 42-43).

---

recommendation went far beyond David's musical ability. Saul's advisor characterized the young Bethlehemite as a "man of valor, a warrior, prudent in speech, a man of good presence, and the LORD is with him." This paean of praise seems unsuited for a mere shepherd boy, however gifted. Perhaps the author, once again, cannot pass up the opportunity to sing David's praises. Or perhaps he is purposefully enhancing David's image so the reader will react more strongly when Saul turns against him, understanding why God rejected Saul and chose David. Noting how David demonstrates these specific traits in the succeeding chapters, J. T. Willis has labeled this section as an "anticipatory redactional joint."[1]

David's reputed musical abilities become quickly apparent (16:23). [David the Musician] The title "man of valor" could refer to David's descent from a respected family (as with Saul, 9:1), but the "warrior" title suggests individual accomplishment. David's courageous victory over the giant Goliath (17:41-51)—while the rest of the army cringed in fear—soon demonstrates the aptness of the epithet. Likewise, David's "prudence in speech" and his charismatic "good presence" are confirmed quickly in the way he confidently handles himself before Saul, persuading the dubious king to sanction his challenge of the Philistine champion (17:31-37). The reader also knows the all-important fact that "Yahweh is with him" because of the previous reference in which the spirit of the LORD came upon David (16:13). While Yahweh's presence with David is related as a promise in 17:37 and 20:13, it is a reality in 18:12, 14, 28, and 2 Samuel 5:10. Though Yahweh works behind the scenes with David, the narrator is convinced that only God's presence could explain the young man's meteoric rise and successful reign.

The flattering report of v. 18 does not include David's name, which is invoked first by Saul (v. 19) as he sends messengers to Jesse requesting his son's services. Saul's comment that David was "with the sheep" provides a second link with the previous story: David was a shepherd, but also more than a shepherd. Though Saul is mysteriously privy to David's name and occupation, there is much about David that he has yet to learn.

Saul's message to Jesse was couched as more of a command than a request ("Send me your son David!"), though his later missive regarding David's permanent appointment was more diplomatic (v. 22). Nevertheless, Jesse acquiesced without argument, sending his son to Saul along with a donkey load of bread, a skin of wine, and a kid from the flock. Some writers have sought special significance in the content of Jesse's gift (cf. 1 Sam 10:3), but it seems no more than a simple sign of respect for the king, composed of elements that would have been readily at the Bethlehemite's disposal. It may have been nothing more than an offer to provide for David's board. Jesse's most significant gift, however, was not what the donkey bore, but the young man who walked beside it.

David wasted no time in making a favorable impression within the royal court. Although the MT is ambiguous—it simply says "He loved him"—there is not doubt that Saul is the one who became enamored with the irresistible David. As he had taken valiant men into his service before (14:52), so Saul engages David as a permanent member of his entourage, not only as his musical therapist, but also as his armorbearer (v. 21). A king's armor-bearer was usually a man of valor, a talented warrior who acted as the king's personal servant and guardian. According to the narrative, David served well in both capacities (v. 23). Blessed by Yahweh's beneficent spirit, David's music overcame the effects of Saul's "evil spirit." [The Original "Spiritual"]

> **The Original "Spiritual"**
> AΩ English readers rarely see the narrator's special artistry in v. 23. In describing how the evil spirit came upon Saul, who found relief only when David played, the writer employs a clever wordplay; the term for "spirit" and the word for "relieved" have the same three consonants (*rwh*). Though usually translated as "made wide" (thus, "given relief"), the verbal form could mean something like "inspirited." As David (who was blessed by the spirit of Yahweh) played for Saul (who was afflicted by an evil spirit), Saul was refreshed or "inspirited" by his contact with David, and the evil spirit departed.

By neatly juxtaposing the two stories found in chapter 16, the narrator continues to show how God, in his sovereignty, has blessed

David with the spirit and maneuvered him into position to become not only the sweet singer of Israel, but the future leader of God's chosen people.

CONNECTIONS

This charming story of Saul and David compels the believing reader to ask some basic questions. "What kind of spirit rules my life? What kind of reputation do I have? What kind of willingness do I have to share my gifts with others?"

What Kind of Spirit?, 16:14-17, 23

Saul's life, once blessed by the positive and powerful spirit of the LORD, had changed. As Saul chose time and again to follow his own wisdom rather than the divine leadership mediated through Samuel, he hardened his heart to the touch of the spirit. Ultimately, he was bereft of the comforting spirit of God and overwhelmed by an evil spirit the narrator also traced to deific activity. As if a spiritual vacuum existed within Saul, the departure of God's beneficent spirit created a powerful attraction for some other spirit to fill the void. Jesus hinted at the same sort of image in Matthew 12:43-45/Luke 11:24-26. There, he spoke of an evil spirit that had been exorcized from a person who presumably made no effort to fill his life with anything better. When the evil spirit saw that its former abode was still available and in good order, it returned, bringing with it seven companions.

Saul's experience, like Jesus' lesson, points to our spiritual nature and our spiritual needs. Every person, knowingly or not, seeks to fill the spiritual void within. Some attempt to furnish their spiritual house with material possessions, or to combat the emptiness with a parade of relationships. Some seek joy through the spirits that come in a bottle or through other mind-altering drugs. These false friends are like evil spirits that can take over people's lives and prevent them from experiencing the beneficent Spirit of the Creator, who has stamped human life with God's own image.

The Scriptures are clear in teaching that God desires to bless all people with the Spirit of life, but we are always free to choose other spirits, evil spirits that lead to alienation and death. This is the way life is. We are created as spiritual persons with spiritual needs. The free gift of God's good Spirit is available to all whose hearts are open to God's leadership and love. Those who do not seek divine inspiration will, by default, find lesser spirits dominating their lives.

What Kind of Reputation?, 16:18

David's glowing résumé may be a bit overdone, but it still points to the importance of one's reputation in the community. Our public standing, of course, grows from what we do as well as who we are. David's skill with the lyre would not have been known had he not been willing to share his talent with others. The title "man of valor" would not have been applied to David for his family status alone. Honor cannot be inherited, but must be earned. So it is with believers. Public respect as people of God is not a legacy to be received from those who die, but a standing to be earned by those who live. Special talents are not meant to be hidden, but to be shared with the community.

Scholars question whether David's reputation as a warrior was earned before or after his first appearance in the court; but in either case, David showed a willingness to fight for what was right. When the Philistine giant Goliath shouted insults at Israel, it was David who took offense and had the courage to stand against him. As David sought to convince Saul of his battle-worthiness, the young man insisted that he had subdued singlehandedly both lions and bears that had threatened his father's sheep. Thus, he proved himself to be a man of principle, willing to take the risks and make the efforts necessary to defend the right. The defense of what is right and good is rarely a military matter, however. More often, standing for justice involves courageous social action, intelligent voting, and a willingness to be involved in the community.

David's reputation as one who was prudent in speech did not derive from genetics, but from wisdom, and wisdom is never gained without effort, attentiveness, and a willingness to learn. The mark of wisdom in speaking is not in the volume or the length of one's conversation, but in its content. The Apostle Paul later would encourage his Christian readers to "let your conversation be always full of grace, seasoned with salt, so that you may know how to answer everyone" (Col 4:6).

David's evident courage, his stalwart honor, and his unexpected maturity combined to produce in him a "man of good presence" (NRSV), although the phrase can (and probably should) be translated "a man of good form"—that is, "a handsome man." Many of us may never be labeled as "good-looking," but we *can* be known as people of good presence. If we sense that others prefer *not* to be around us, it is worth asking ourselves why.

The most admirable quality of David, of course, was the last one mentioned: "Yahweh is with him." David was blessed with a special measure of "the spirit of the LORD," but he did not have a permanent monopoly on God's spirit, which continues to bless God's people. Followers of Jesus take comfort in his promise always to be present with them through the Holy Spirit (John 14:15-27). It is impossible to be infused with the spirit of God and not live a life that is noticeably marked by the presence of God. In this, the young David stands as a perpetual role model.

What Kind of Willingness?, 16:19-22

David's willingness to serve in Saul's court goes without saying in the text. He seems to relish the challenge and to thrive on adventure. The narration as a whole suggests that David was happy to leave Bethlehem and venture out to do great things. The person who shows the most heartfelt willingness to serve, then, is not David, but his father Jesse. How could one give up such a son as David? Given the unfeeling nature of Saul's initial "request," we might expect Jesse to resist, to delay, or to send David into hiding. Instead, he proudly sends young David to the king, and even includes a gift of food, perhaps to help defray his son's living expenses and thus be less of a burden to Saul. David did not inherit his exemplary character from his father, but our text suggests that he had a worthy teacher.

NOTE

[1] J. T. Willis, "Function of Comprehensive Anticipatory Redactional Joints in 1 Samuel 16–18," *ZAW* 85 (1973): 294-314.

SHEPHERD BOY DAVID, THE GIANT'S KILLER

17:1-58

COMMENTARY

The remarkable story of David and Goliath is the third consecutive account in which David is introduced as if for the first time. In the first two stories, David was anointed by Samuel as Israel's future king (16:1-13) and appointed by Saul to be the king's personal musician and armor bearer (16:14-23). Yet, in chapter 17, Saul has never heard of David. The culprit for such confusion is the variety of tradition histories that make up the composite work of the Deuteronomistic historians. The story of David and Goliath derived from one or more separate traditions about Israel's hero, and seems to have had a complex history of its own. [One Story or Two?] The Deuteronomistic authors preserved it *in toto*, with little or no effort to harmonize it with surrounding material. Despite the differences, the stories all agree on the one point that really matters: David's growing success was due to the LORD's favor and guidance.

One Story or Two?

The story of David and Goliath includes several rough spots and seeming inconsistencies, even in the English version. For example, Saul meets David and has a lengthy conversation with him in vv. 31-39, but in vv. 55-58, Saul has no idea who David is. There seem to have been two separate traditions about David's defeat of a Philistine champion that later were combined; this suggestion is reinforced by the fact that the LXX[B], probably the oldest exemplar of the Greek translation, is lacking a substantial portion of the story as found in the MT. In all, vv. 12-31, 41, 48b, 50, and 55-58—along with 18:1-5, 10-11, 17-19, and 29b-30—are missing from the Old Greek. When read together, these verses make up a relatively complete story in themselves, emphasizing David as a youthful, unknown shepherd who defeated the giant by his cunning and courage. Without these verses, the account also makes sense, though it seems to build on ch. 16, portraying David as a member of Saul's entourage who ventured forth to challenge the Philistine hero. Thus, two ancient versions of the same story seem to have been combined to form the story as found in the MT.

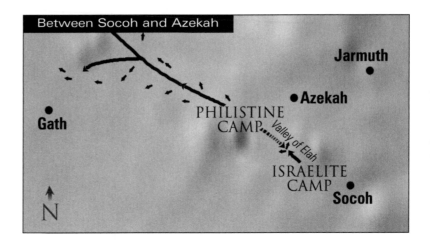

Goliath's Challenge, 17:1-11

It was the Philistine threat that had led Israel to press for a king, and though Saul had enjoyed some success as a military leader, he had not been able to vanquish the Philistines. The author prepares the reader to see that David will do what Saul could not do, underscoring David's status as the more legitimate king.

As the story begins, battle lines were drawn on either side of the Valley of Elah in western Judah (vv. 1-3), also called the "Valley of the Terebinth." [Between Socoh and Azekah] This area was disputed often between Israel and Philistia (see also 2 Chr 11:7; 28:18). In this particular confrontation, the Philistine troops apparently had overrun the western village of Azekah and set their sights on Socoh,

Battle of the Champions

Other incidents of one-on-one combat are found in the Bible, including 2 Sam 21:15-22 and 2 Sam 23:20. In a similar scheme, twelve of David's soldiers battled twelve representatives from Ishbosheth's camp (2 Sam 2:12-17). In ancient Babylon's epic literature, Marduk was remembered for doing battle with Tiamat, creating the earth from her body (from the *Enuma Elish*). Such battles were also recorded in Hellenistic epics such as the *Iliad*, in which Paris and Menelaos do battle, as well as Hector and Achilles. For further reading, see Roland de Vaux, "Single Combat in the Old Testament," *The Bible and the Ancient Near East* (Garden City NY: Doubleday, 1971), 122-35.

only fourteen miles west of Bethlehem. Before they reached Socoh, Saul's army intercepted them near a place called Ephes-dammim, leading to a standoff. Ephes-dammim may be identified with modern Damun, about four miles northeast of ancient Socoh.[1]

If the Philistine army had been vastly superior, they surely would have pressed the battle. Instead, the two armies had reached a stalemate. The Philistines advanced their aims by means of psychological warfare; relying on their strongest resource, they outwardly adopted the stratagem of a battle by proxy, sending out a champion to challenge any single fighter that Israel could muster. Roland de Vaux has collected many examples of similar battles between representatives in the ancient Near East, but in most cases (as here), a battle between the armies followed the battle by proxy. [Battle of the Champions] Armies who promise to lay down their arms and submit if their champion loses can hardly be expected to follow through when the hero falls and swords are drawn. Saul and his generals responded as the Philistines had hoped, quailing in fear before their giant champion's taunts.

The warrior's name is mentioned only in vv. 4 and 23, where he is called Goliath (*golyāt*), from Gath. Elsewhere in the story, he is called "the Philistine." This peculiarity has led some scholars to speculate that the Philistine champion was anonymous in the original, surmising that the name Goliath was imported from 2 Samuel 21:19, which credits Elhanan, son of Jaareoregim—one of David's "mighty men"—with killing "Goliath the Gittite, the shaft of whose spear was like a weaver's beam." With this we must compare 1 Chronicles 20:5, which says that "Elhanan son of Jair killed Lahmi the brother of Goliath the Gittite, the shaft of whose spear was like a weaver's beam." Some writers have suggested that Elhanan was an alternate name for David, but Elhanan is clearly identified as the son of Jair/Jaareoregim, not Jesse, and as one of David's personal entourage of heroic warriors (2 Sam 23:24). It is more likely that some details of the stories were confused in the telling and retelling.

The narrator takes special pains in vv. 4-7 to describe Goliath's large girth and the gigantic size of his various armaments. The Hebrew text depicts the Philistine champion as being nearly ten feet tall (six cubits and a span), but the Greek version and some other ancient sources ascribe a height closer to 6 feet 9 inches (*four* cubits and a span), still far above average in ancient times. A "cubit" was the distance from a man's elbow to the tip of his fingers, about 18 inches. A span measured the distance from the tip of the thumb to the tip of the little finger of a man's outstretched hand, about 9 inches.

Ancient Armor
Illustration of Myceanean warrior wearing bronze armor based on an early twelfth century Warrior Vase motif.
(Illustration Credit: Barclay Burns)

Despite Goliath's advantage in size, he took few chances. He was armored heavily from head to toe, and he kept his armor bearer standing before him with a large shield. [Ancient Armor] The author spends more time describing Goliath's armaments than he does in relating the battle itself. [Goliath's Armaments] There is a purpose in this; while providing such a detailed description of the giant, the narrator builds suspense and paints a more fearsome image of Goliath. At the same time, however, the storyteller leaves a clue to the warrior's vulnerability: he was virtually immobile, and everything was armored but his face.

Goliath's Armaments

Goliath was equipped with a diverse collection of offensive and defensive armaments, both domestic and imported. Pictorial representations from Egypt suggest that Philistine soldiers normally wore a feathered headdress, but Goliath wore a more substantial helmet. The giant's entire torso was protected by heavy scale armor, weighing in at 5,000 bronze shekels, or nearly 126 pounds. Neither the helmet nor the cuirass was typical of Semitic armaments. "Greaves" of bronze protected the warrior's lower legs like giant shin guards, though they may have encircled the entire calf and probably had a leather lining.

The weapon slung between the giant's shoulders is called a bronze javelin in NRSV, but Molin has argued convincingly that the word *kîdôn* describes an Oriental curved scimitar, sharpened on the outer edge. The Philistine's spear was massive, the iron point alone weighing fifteen pounds. The description of the spear's shaft (2 Sam 21:19; 1 Chr 20:5) may be designed to emphasize its weight ("like a weaver's beam" [NRSV]) or that it was equipped with a throwing loop like a typical Aegean javelin ("like a weaver's heddle rod"). Working from the heddle rod comparison, Kurt Galling suggested that it was wound with cords to cause a rifling motion when thrown. In any case, Goliath's spear seems to have been both large and exotic, adding to its fear-provoking appearance. Like a modern tank, Goliath was bristling with armaments. Like the poorly equipped conscript army they were, the Israelites were shaking with fear. Only David saw the gaping hole in Goliath's armor.

P. Kyle McCarter, *I. Samuel* (AB 8; Garden City: Doubleday, 1980), 293, building on Yadin, "Goliath's Javelin and the *měnôr 'origîm*," PEQ 86 (1955): 58-69.

Kurt Galling, "Goliath und seine Rüstung," *Volume du Congrès: Genève*, VTSup 15 (Leiden: E. J. Brill, 1966): 150-69.

The giant antagonist's harassments were a daily reminder of his unanswered challenge, and they had the desired demoralizing effect on Israel's army of conscripted farmers and townsmen: "They were dismayed and greatly afraid" (vv. 8-11). So Israel's army was shamed, and that shame was reflected on its leader, King Saul.

David's Appearance, 17:12-30

The stage was set for a hero to appear. As if for the first time (though it is actually the third), David is introduced: "Now David was the son of an Ephrathite of Bethlehem in Judah, named Jesse, who had eight sons" (v. 12a). This reminds us that we are reading a story that was preserved separately from the others and integrated later with little attempt at harmonizing. The account in chapter 16 credits Jesse with seven sons, not eight.

Jesse was old, we are told, and his three eldest sons had followed Saul into battle. Though Saul retained a small corps of professional soldiers, Israel had no standing army of consequence. Regional farmers and others were mustered to battle

Battle Rations

David (or his donkey) carried an ephah— a little more than half a bushel—of roasted grain, along with ten loaves of bread. Parched grain and bread was a common meal for Israel's agrarian people (1 Sam 25:18; 2 Sam 17:28; Lev 23:14; Ruth 2:14), easily prepared and substantial. The ten cheeses (or possibly "slices of cheese") for the commanding officer were more of a luxury.

whenever there was a serious threat to their area. These erstwhile soldiers had to provide their own supplies. Thus, David served as a go-between, delivering food to his older brothers when he was not in the fields near Bethlehem, watching the sheep (vv. 12b-15). [Battle Rations] This was no mean job in itself: the battle site was some fourteen miles west of Bethlehem, in disputed territory. The fact that Jesse was so old and that he assigned David such dangerous undertakings suggests that David was no mere lad, but a fully grown man, albeit the youngest. Even so, the Bethlehemites' simple fare and their contribution to the officers underscores David's lack of prestige, contributing to the story's image of the small overcoming the great.

A Royal Reward

Saul's offered reward (17:25) consisted of three prizes: an unnamed but large bequest of riches, permission to marry one of Saul's daughters (thus becoming a member of the royal family), and freedom for his family. Just what it means for the victor's family to be "free in Israel" is a matter of some dispute, though it probably meant only that the family would be free from taxes and exempt from military and labor corvées.

The military posturing had gone on for forty days when Jesse sent David with fresh supplies and in search of news from his brothers (vv. 17-18). David first left the sheep with a keeper (v. 20) and, when he arrived, left the food with a supply officer (v. 22) before walking calmly into the battle line to greet his brothers. When David heard the Philistine champion's challenge, he was appalled that no one had dared to answer. The soldiers about him spoke of Saul's promise to reward richly anyone who defeated Goliath, and how not even Saul's mightiest men had ventured forth to fight the giant warrior (vv. 23-25). [A Royal Reward]

David was not disinterested in the promised reward for one who defeated Goliath, but showed greater concern that Israel's army was being shamed: "What shall be done for the man who kills this Philistine, and takes away the reproach from Israel? *For who is this uncircumcised Philistine that he should defy the armies of the living God?*" (v. 26). The sharp retort of his oldest brother Eliab suggests that David was prone to doing outrageous things (and also explains why God had rejected Eliab, 16:6-7). The reader may note a subtle use of irony in the narrator's portrayal of the conversation: Eliab charges that David has an "evil heart" (v. 28), but the reader knows that David is a man after God's heart (13:14). David deflected his brother's criticism and moved among the people, continuing to express his outrage at Israel's reproach (vv. 28-30).

David and Saul, 17:31-40

When David's dauntless words brought him to the attention of Saul, the young man volunteered before the king to enter mortal combat with Goliath (vv. 31-32). Saul responded reasonably: "You are not able to go against this Philistine to fight with him; for you are just a boy, and he has been a warrior from his youth!" (v. 33). David's response—that he had routinely killed ferocious lions and bears that had threatened his sheep—is couched in a series of verbs suggesting continuous action. [Biblical Beasts] David reasoned that if *the living God* had granted him courage and skill to defeat such dangerous wild animals in one-on-one conflict, he also should be able to defeat a lowly Philistine, however large (vv. 34-38).

Saul seemed impressed with David's *chutzpah*, if nothing else, and finally agreed to sponsor David in the battle. A comic moment is effected as Saul offers David the protection of his own armor; David could hardly walk in the unfamiliar outfit. The separate pieces of Saul's armor were similar to those of Goliath (helmet and plated mail), but not as impressive. David, however, would be different. Discarding the awkward armor, he chose to confront the giant with nothing more than his shepherd's staff, his slingshot,

---

Biblical Beasts

In ancient times, the range of the African lion and the Persian lion overlapped in the Middle East, though neither is native to the area now. The Syrian bear may still be found in the mountainous areas of Lebanon. As the two largest and most dangerous of wild carnivores, lions and bears are often mentioned together in the Bible (1 Sam 17:34, 36-37; Prov 28:15; Isa 11:7; Lam 3:10; Hos 13:8; Amos 5:19; Rev 13:2).

Frieze of lions from the palace of Darius I of Persia at Susa. Glazed Ceramic Tiles. c. 500 BC. Louvre, Paris. (Credit: Mitchell G. Reddish)

1 Samuel 17:45-51—David was no child when he slew Goliath, as indicated by this illustration.

Julius Schnoor von Carolsfeld. *David Slays Goliath.* 19th century. Woodcut. *Das Buch der Bucher in Bilden.* (Credit: Dover Pictorial Archive Series)

and five carefully chosen stones for ammunition (vv. 38-40). The contrast is obvious and intentional. On the one side is Goliath, a giant of a man, trained in military techniques and armored in the best protection the world could offer. On the other side is David, who is young, untrained, unprotected, and virtually weaponless. David, however, carries his armor on the inside. He is steeled within by faith in God, emboldened and empowered by a force that is greater than himself.

David and Goliath, 17:41-51a

Modern athletes often attempt to gain a psychological advantage through "talking trash" to their opponents. Apparently, this is not an innovative strategy. The narrator uses seven verses to describe how Goliath and David traded insults and threats (vv. 41-47), while only two short verses are required for the battle itself (vv. 48-49). The Philistine took offense that Israel would send such a young opponent, handsome though he was (cf. 16:12), and he cursed David by his own gods (probably Dagon). The reader, however, already knows that Dagon is a dead god and no match for Yahweh (ch. 5), in whose name David fights. Goliath also expressed outrage that Israel would send out such a measly opponent, not only young and inexperienced, but apparently armed with nothing more than a *stick.* While Goliath focused on David's

Desert Scavengers

Vultures were a common sight in the ancient Near East. These were carved into a column in the Temple of Ramses III in Thebes, about 200 years before the emergence of David.

Two Vultures. Detail. Temple of Ramses III. 20th dynasty. Medinet, Habu. West Thebes. Egyptian Museum. Cairo, Egypt. (Credit: Scala/Art Resource, NY)

shepherd's staff, however, he seemingly failed to notice the thin leather straps of the young man's sling.

When Goliath threatened to kill David and leave his body exposed for scavenging birds and animals to eat, David predicted that *he* would turn the entire Philistine army into bird food. For people familiar with the sight and habits of vultures and hyenas, this offers a particularly gruesome image. [Desert Scavengers]

David's speech is filled both with bravado and faith. It is precisely the sort of speech that pious storytellers would embellish to add a theological element to the drama, for David's challenge encompasses the central point of the story: "You come to me with sword and spear and javelin; but I come to you in the name of the LORD of hosts, the God of the armies of Israel . . . the LORD will deliver you into my hand, and I will strike you down and cut off your head . . . so that all the earth may know that there is a God in Israel, and that all this assembly may know that the LORD does not save by sword and spear, for the battle is the LORD's and he will give you into our hand" (vv. 45-47). [God of the Armies]

The contrast between the Philistine's powerful weaponry and David's reliance on the LORD reflects a technological imbalance between the two armies. The Iron Age was still young, and the Philistines were proficient in the new technology. Israel had not mastered iron-working, however, and the Philistines were careful to keep their knowledge proprietary (see 13:19-22). The point David made was that it did not matter. The power that would prevail in this battle was not the might of advanced weapons and trained armies, but the power of Yahweh, Israel's God, the only true god.

God of the Armies

AΩ David's reference to "the LORD of hosts, the God of the armies of Israel" is composed of a title and an explanation. In the Old Testament, "Yahweh Sabaoth" was a favorite title for God, especially among prophets such as Elijah (1 Kgs 19:10, 14), Amos (3:13; 6:14; 9:5), Hosea (12:6), Jeremiah (5:14; 15:18; 35:17; 38:17; 44:7), and Isaiah (47:4; 48:2; 51:15; 54:5), among others. The term actually may have originated during the war-torn time of David and probably means "Yahweh of hosts," with "hosts" meaning "armies." In fact, the narrator makes a point of having David explain the name by paraphrasing it in 1 Sam 17:45: "Yahweh Sabaoth, the God of the armies of Israel."

The battle itself was over almost as quickly as the opponents' taunts faded. When the giant approached, David ran quickly (to make a more difficult target?) toward Goliath, probably dropping his staff so he would have both hands free to load his sling. After all of the lengthy and suspenseful buildup, here is the entire account of the battle: "David put his hand in his bag, took out a stone, slung it, and struck the Philistine on his forehead; the stone sank into his forehead, and he fell face down on the ground" (v. 49). The young shepherd was smart enough to discover the giant's weakness, clever enough to distract his attention from the sling, and skillful enough to deliver a mortal blow on the first shot. The reader, however, has no doubt that God is at work in David; he did not accomplish this alone.

The fact that David was no mere lad is apparent from the battle's denouement: David drew out Goliath's giant-sized sword and used it to cut off his head, removing all doubt that the giant was defeated (v. 51). [A Popular Image] A sword (*ḥereb*) was not included in the inventory of the Philistine's weapons in 17:4-7, but in v. 45 David spoke of Goliath's coming at him "with sword (*ḥereb*) and spear and javelin" (*kîdôn*, which may mean "scimitar"; see comments on 17:6 above).

A Popular Image

The image of David triumphantly holding Goliath's head has been a popular subject for artists. Caravaggio's realistic painting of David holding the head of Goliath clearly reveals the artist's love of the grotesque and the dramatic. Considered one of the founders of the Italian Baroque, Caravaggio's tenebrist light, deep colors and emotionality set the bar for artists to come.

Michelangelo Merisi called Caravaggio (1571–1610). *David with the Head of Goliath.* 1609–10. Oil on canvas, 3'4"x4'1". Borghese Gallery, Rome. (Credit: Planet Art)

Reprise, David and Saul, 17:51b-58

Understandably, the Philistines had no intention of honoring Goliath's pledge that they would become Israel's servants if he lost the battle (17:9). However, Goliath's demoralizing defeat led to a rout, as the combined troops of Israel and Judah chased the Philistines all the way back to their strongholds in Gath and Ekron, the easternmost cities of the Philistine pentapolis (vv. 51-53). The narrator's note that their dead bodies were found all along the road to Shaarim is a reminder that David's prediction of v. 46 had come to pass.

An obvious and interesting anachronism appears in v. 54, which insists that "David took the head of the Philistine and brought it to Jerusalem; but he put his armor in his tent." The city of Jerusalem did not come into Israelite hands until years later, when David led his personal army to conquer the Jebusite stronghold in the early days of his own reign as king. Perhaps David kept Goliath's head as a souvenir and later displayed it in Jerusalem, leading to the tradition. The same verse also claims that David kept Goliath's armor for himself, putting it in his tent. However, the story line is that David had just arrived to bring supplies to his brothers, leaving the goods with the quartermaster so he could rush to the battle line. There is no mention of David's having a tent of his own. Goliath's sword later shows up in the temple at Nob (1 Sam 21:10). Some scholars have suggested a textual emendation to read "in the tent of Yahweh," rather than "in his tent."

Even though Saul had met David already and sought to clothe him in his own armor (17:31-39), he suddenly appeared to have no knowledge of David's identity (vv. 55-58). This probably is due to the separate traditions underlying the Goliath story (see [One Story or Two?]). The story ends as Abner, Saul's commander, seeks out David, then makes the formal introductions. Despite its awkward nature, this interlude functions to shine a literary spotlight on David, who now has been introduced for the fourth time (twice in this story). He is Israel's future king, the man upon whom the dynasty and the glory of Israel as a nation will be built—but the reader cannot forget that David's strength is found within, for he is a man after God's own heart (1 Sam 13:14; Acts 13:22).

CONNECTIONS

1. *In the Face of Giants.* Homileticians through the ages have used the story of David and Goliath as a springboard for challenging believers to be courageous in the face of the "giant" obstacles that come their way. No doubt, the narrative's early popularity had something to do with Israel's recurrent status as a small nation going up against the world's great powers from Egypt and Mesopotamia.

In the modern era, Goliath has been metaphorically morphed into the shape of illness and rejection, the fear of failure and the threat of persecution. Athletic teams (particularly poor ones) have taken courage from David's amazing victory against all odds. Hopeful small business owners have adopted David's "can do" attitude in going up against giant competitors in the hope of carving out a niche for themselves. Some of those who visualize themselves in David's sandals have succeeded. Others have failed. But is this what the story is all about?

Using David's unlikely victory as an inspirational lesson may be helpful, but that is not the intended purpose of the story, which insists that it was not David who defeated the giant opponent, but Yahweh. David may have been both courageous and skillful, but he succeeded because he was *faithful.* He was a man after God's own heart, empowered by God's own spirit.

The author finds several opportunities to contrast David's behavior with Saul's action—and non-action. Readers may remember that Saul once had resisted God's call to leadership by hiding in the baggage (10:22), but David was so anxious to leap into the arena that he left his brothers' provisions (his primary mission) with the unit's baggage so he could rush to the front lines (17:22).

While Saul and his army were paralyzed by inaction before the Philistine threat, David never wavered. Why? Not just because he was fearless, but because he was so devoted to Yahweh that he could not bear to hear the giant's taunts against Israel and its God. He could not endure seeing God's people shamed or God's honor besmirched.

Saul's attempt to clothe David in his own armor suggests that the king, like other men, put his trust in armaments and numbers and physical ability. In contrast, David put his trust in God alone. Yahweh had given David the ability to defeat fearsome lions and dangerous bears—why should it be any different with a heathen soldier?

Perhaps it is significant that David was the only person to mention Yahweh's name until Saul finally picked up on David's faith and sent him into battle with the blessing "May the LORD be with you" (17:37). What is more significant is that David seems to be the only person who regarded Yahweh as a *living* God (17:26, 36). Israel's army, stymied and scared, seems to have regarded their god as irrelevant. There is no suggestion that Saul had called for a priest to offer sacrifice or pray for the people, no indication that Yahweh's favor or aid had been invoked. Goliath proclaimed *his* god's power, but Israel did not answer. Perhaps David's greatest accomplishment is that he reintroduced the presence, the power, and the *life* of Yahweh to the equation.

When modern believers fall prey to the discouraging obstacles of life, they often do so with little hope that there really is a living God who loves them and cares for them. The difference between growing people of faith and non-practicing religionists may come down to the issue of whether they think of God as a cultural icon or a living presence. If Yahweh had no more life than Dagon, then Israel's army was surely in trouble. But if Yahweh was *living* and active and willing to fight for his people, a whole new script was in order. When modern readers come to 1 Samuel 17 in search of inspiration or guidance, their central challenge is not to take courage in their own smallness, but to find hope in their God's reality and relevance. Faith communities cannot stand firm amidst the gods of modern culture unless they are willing to trust the same faithful God who empowered David's victory over the giant.

2. *In the Face of Discouragement.* The story suggests that David had more difficulty in overcoming discouraging allies than in defeating his opponent. Like Joseph's brothers in Genesis 39, David's older brothers consider him to be a presumptuous glory-grabber. They fail to see God at work in David. Eliab was the oldest brother—a man so handsome and impressive that Samuel had once thought he should be king (16:6). Yet Eliab saw David's brash challenge as nothing more than the impetuous irresponsibility of an immature dreamer (17:28). David responded by deflecting Eliab's criticism ("It was only a question!") and turning to someone else for information. David could have been discouraged by Eliab's verbal barrage, but he simply chose not to be dissuaded.

When David's stirring bravado brought him to Saul's attention, the king offered no more encouragement than Eliab. "You are not able to go against this Philistine to fight with him; for you are just a boy, and he has been a warrior from his youth" (17:33). Again,

David ignored the opportunity to be discouraged. Again, he deflected the implicit criticism of his abilities, because he saw personal ability as irrelevant. Yahweh had empowered him to defeat lions and bears, and Yahweh could work through him to defeat the imposing Philistine (17:34-37).

Thus, David overcame the opposition of both enemy and friends in the same way—by trusting in the living presence and potential power of God. The emphasis on David's youth, more than anything, underscores the purity of his child-like faith in Yahweh's living reality and God's concern for his people.

3. *In the Face of Doubt.* Even when David had convinced Saul of his willingness and competence to confront the enemy, the king could not imagine sending him into battle without a full set of armor. So, in a remarkable display of kindness (or perhaps cowardice), Saul offered his own armor to David: a heavy helmet made of bronze, an awkward coat of chain mail tailored to Saul's tall physique, and a hefty battle sword suitable for a large man (17:38-39). David, however, was unaccustomed to wearing armor—especially armor that didn't fit. He could hardly walk!

David cast off King Saul's armor and chose to go in shepherd's array, but he was not unarmed. Like the faithful believers whom Paul later described in Ephesians 6:11-17, David was clothed with "the whole armor of God." David's fresh naiveté suggests Paul's reference to the belt of truth and the breastplate of righteousness. David's professed trust in Yahweh's victory reflects Paul's reference to shoes that would make one ready to proclaim the gospel. David's absolute confidence in the presence and power of God could have inspired Paul's advice that Christians equip themselves with the shield of faith, the helmet of salvation, and the sword of the Spirit.

To the natural eye, David may have appeared defenseless, but one gifted with the eyes of faith could see that he was armed to the teeth. When David went into battle, he did not go alone. God offers no guarantee that believers will win every battle of life. Sickness comes and tragedies befall us. Marriages may fail and jobs may disappear. The obstacles and discouragements of life sometimes may seem overwhelming, but those who still believe in a living God know that, come what may, they are never left to go it alone.

NOTE

[1] P. Kyle McCarter, *I Samuel* (AB 8; Garden City: Doubleday, 1980), 290.

DAVID IN DANGER —IN SAUL'S COURT

18:1–20:42

A Struggle for Survival, 18:1–31:13

The remaining chapters of 1 Samuel are devoted to a variety of similar stories surrounding a central theme: David's struggle to survive despite Saul's attempts to eliminate him as a court rival. [David's Struggle to Survive: 18:1–31:13] By this point in the book, David has established himself as a charismatic warrior with far more leadership potential than Saul. Not only Saul's son Jonathan (18:1-6), but the entire nation falls in love with David (18:6-19). Saul, overcome by his manic anger, tries unsuccessfully to kill his young nemesis (18:20–19:24), who escapes with the aid of Saul's own children (19:11-17; 20:1-24).

David finds shelter with Samuel at Ramah (19:18-24) and later among the priests of Nob (21:1-15), escaping just ahead of Saul's forces, who slaughter the "traitorous" priests (22:1-23). Saul then goes in direct pursuit of David through the hinterlands of Judea, but it is David who has the best opportunity to eliminate his rival, though he refuses (23:1–25:1). As he roams the countryside, David acquires a new wife (25:2-44) and continues to frustrate Saul (26:1-25).

Finally, Saul presses the issue to the point that David finds greater safety among the Philistines than in his own country. In an apparent defection and coup for the Philistines, David accepts the

> **David's Struggle to Survive: 18:1–31:13**
>
> Here is a general outline of this tumultuous period:
>
> I. David in Danger—In Saul's Court (18:1–20:42)
>   A. David's fame and Saul's jealousy (18:1-19)
>   B. A failed trap and greater fear (18:20-30)
>   C. Attempted murder and a daring escape (19:1-24)
>   D. Jonathan's love and David's departure (20:1-42)
>
> II. David in Danger—On the Run (21:1–26:25)
>   A. The priests of Nob help, and David "plays the fool" (21:1-15)
>   B. David travels, and the priests of Nob pay for it (22:1-23)
>   C. Saul hunts David, and the tables are turned (23:1–25:1)
>   D. Nabal's demise is David's gain. (25:2-44)
>   E. Saul keeps hunting, and David keeps winning (26:1-25)
>
> III. David in Danger—Among the Philistines (27:1–31:13)
>   A. Achish's protection and David's deception (27:1–28:2)
>   B. Saul's distress and Samuel's ghost (28:3-25)
>   C. Philistine aid and Amalekite trouble (29:1–30:31)
>   D. Saul's last battle and an honorable death (31:1-13)

protection of Achish and is given the city of Ziklag to defend (27:1–28:2). A desperate Saul breaks his own laws against necromancy by invoking the shade of Samuel to assist him, but hears a depressing prophecy (28:3-25). Faced with enemy encroachments from both Philistia and Amalek, Saul leaves his pursuit of David to fight his last battle (in which David is not allowed to participate). Saul's story ends with an ugly scene in which both he and his son Jonathan are killed, paving the way for David's accession to the throne (29:1–31:13).

COMMENTARY

David's Fame and Saul's Jealousy, 18:1-19

It is likely that several traditions have been intertwined in this complex chapter, and scholars have struggled to untangle the various sources and develop a more cogent chronology. For example, 18:1-5 may not have been in the original story, since it is absent from the Greek version of the Old Testament, and seems to summarize in advance what takes place more gradually over the following verses. Likewise, the story about Saul's daughter Merab (18:17-19) is not in the LXX, and it duplicates some elements of the similar story that follows (18:20-29). For the sake of simplicity, we will take a "canonical" approach to the text; thematically, at least, the chapter holds together quite well.

The previous chapter ended as David, fresh from defeating Goliath, introduced himself to Saul, and chapter 18 picks up on that conversation to push the story forward: "When David had finished speaking to Saul, the soul of Jonathan was bound to the soul of David, and Jonathan loved him as his own soul" (v. 1). The word "soul" translates *nepeš*, a Hebrew word that refers to one's innermost being, one's true life-essence. [A Holistic View] From the beginning, Jonathan loved David from the depths of his being.

David did not immediately obtain Saul's daughter in marriage, as promised (17:25), but he did get the love of Saul's son.[1] This implies a strong "male bonding," but does not insinuate a homosexual attraction, as some suggest. More significantly, such a close friendship between a king's son and his chief rival would have unavoidable political implications. Peter Ackroyd points to the ambiguity of the verb *qāšar*, which could mean not only "bound," but "joined in conspiracy."[2] No obvious or intentional conspiracy

A Holistic View

AΩ While modern persons often adopt the Greek view, which draws clear lines of distinction between body and soul, the Hebrew concept of personhood was much more holistic. The term *nepeš* is often translated "soul," but it refers to a person's whole being, from the inside out.

As a noun, *nepeš* occurs 755 times in the Old Testament. Verbal cognates in Hebrew and other ancient Near Eastern languages suggest that its original meaning may have been "breath," which was expanded to include the one who breathes, who has life and desires. According to Gen 2:7, when God created Adam, "the man became a living being [*nepeš*]"—but the word is also used to describe the living *creatures* of Gen 1:20, 21, and 24. *Nepeš* is often translated by the word "soul," as in Ps 42:1—"As the deer longs for the flowing streams, so my soul longs for you, O God" (also v. 2). The *nepeš* yearns for or craves the presence of God (Isa 26:8-9; Ps 119:20) and the closeness

of other persons (Cant 3:1-4), even as it desires material things (Deut 12:20; 14:26; 1 Sam 2:16).

The theological significance of *nepeš* is found in verses like the commandment in Deut 6:5: "You shall love the LORD your God with all your heart, and with all your soul, and with all your might." The word for heart (*lēbūb*) emphasizes one's will or intention, while *nepeš* (here translated as "soul") implies the whole self, and "might" translates a word (*mĕʾōd*) that signifies "muchness."

In other texts, *nepeš* is best translated with words like "life": the life of a person (1 Sam 26:21; 2 Kgs 1:13), or life in the abstract (Lev 17:11). In the priestly, legal texts, *nepeš* can even be used to describe the dead (Lev 19:28; 21:1, 11; Num 5:2; 6:6, 11; and others). The wide variety of possible translations for *nepeš* illustrates the word's basic meaning—a reference to one's full personhood as a living, thinking, spiritual being.

---

between David and Jonathan was evident, but Saul would soon imagine one.

Saul apparently loved David, too—as long as David was useful to him: "Saul took him that day and would not let him return to his father's house" (v. 2). But while Saul's love was utilitarian, Jonathan's love is described as entirely unselfish. Like two men becoming "blood brothers," Jonathan and David made a covenant bond. Significantly, Jonathan marked the event by giving to David his own robe, his armor, and even his weapons (vv. 3-4). This covenant gift of his royal regalia seems to be an obvious symbol of Jonathan's willingness to hand over to David even his own right to the throne.

The conditional nature of Saul's love is again contrasted in v. 5. When David proved successful at every mission Saul assigned him, the king showed his favor with military promotions, appointing David to higher positions of responsibility (though perhaps not over the entire army, as the story implies). Jonathan and Saul were not the only ones who loved David, however. "All the people, even the servants of Saul," admired the young man and approved of his ascendancy.

The author underscores David's growing fame—and Saul's growing paranoia—with songs from the mouths of Israel's common people. As the army marched through various villages on its return to Jerusalem, the local populace would come out to cheer. The narrator paints a charming picture of local women who sang, danced, and played musical instruments in the traditional way of honoring the returning warriors (cf. Exod 15:20; Judg

11:34). A refrain that proved troublesome to Saul was growing in popularity as quickly as its subject: The women sang, "Saul has killed his thousands, and David his ten thousands" (v. 7). The attribution of greater numbers to David may have been nothing more than a poetic convention, for the movement from "thousands" to "ten thousands" was a standard way of expressing large numbers. [Thousands upon Thousands] Nevertheless, the chants fed Saul's insecurity and sealed his conviction that David was in pursuit of the throne (v. 8) and would have to be eliminated. So "Saul eyed David from that day on" (v. 9). As in English, the Hebrew turns the noun "eye" into a verb, suggesting that Saul kept a close and suspicious watch on every activity of his new and unsuspecting rival.

Walter Brueggemann points to the keen irony of the situation. The reader knows that though David is destined for the throne, his anointing remains a secret. Saul remains ignorant of Yahweh's resolve that David should be king, but looking through the prism of his own deep suspicions, Saul sees David's future. "Saul has it right, but for all the wrong reasons. Saul knows more than he understands, for he sees David only as ambitious, not as destined."[3]

Thousands upon Thousands

The women's song is a poetic couplet in what appears to be synonymous parallelism, a typical form in which the second line repeats or amplifies the first. The word pair translated "thousands" and "ten thousands" (*ǎlāpîm* and *rĕbābôt*) seems to be a standard pair used to express large—but not necessarily different—numbers. For example, Ps 144:13b offers the prayer:

May our sheep increase by thousands,
   by tens of thousands in our fields.

Likewise, Ps 91:7 assures protection from the plague to one who would see others fall:

A thousand may fall at your side,
   Ten thousand at your right hand,
   But it will not come near you.

The same pair occurs in Ugaritic with the same force. McCarter cites a text, labeled *CTCA* 4 (= 51), that describes the impressive work of Kothar-wa-Hassis, who was the god of craftspersons:

He casts silver by the thousands,
Gold he casts by the ten thousands. (Tablet 1, lines 27-29)

Even if the couplet is not intended to suggest that David's heroic deeds were greater, the fact that he is mentioned as Saul's equal is reason enough to arouse Saul's suspicion and fuel a natural jealousy. The couplet may not be as innocuous as it seems, however. It is very unusual that the "thousands" and "ten thousands" are attributed to different subjects. The record shows that David's heroism in battling the Philistine champion far exceeded that of Saul, who appears to have remained on the sidelines.

P. Kyle McCarter, *I Samuel* (AB 8; Garden City: Doubleday, 1980), 311-12.

Saul's paranoid fear of David erupted in periods of madness not unlike his earlier "prophetic" ravings, but with a decidedly negative bent. The earliest persons to be called prophets in Israel were ecstatics who "bubbled over" with the spirit, and Saul had experienced such ecstacy shortly after he was anointed (10:10, 13). The same word is used here, but is translated "raving" instead of "prophesying." The author suggests that when one's heart is turned away from God, even the visitation of God's spirit can be turned into something negative.

The narrator paints David as innocent of any ambition for the throne, seeking only to be of service to the king. He returned to his role as a musician, playing his lyre in an attempt to calm Saul's troubling spirit (cf. 16:14-23), but David's sweet singing did nothing to allay Saul's perception that David was more of a threat than a comfort. The text implies that Saul kept a constant hand on his spear, further emphasizing his paranoia, though some writers suggest that he held the spear like a scepter, as a symbol of his office. In any event, the narrator declares that Saul twice attempted to nail David to the wall with his spear, without success (vv. 10-11).

Saul became more and more convinced that Yahweh had deserted him in favor of David, but his every attempt to reverse the process backfired. Transferring David from his post as court musician, and perhaps hoping that David might be killed in battle, Saul appointed him as "commander of a thousand" (cf. v. 5, which says that Saul had already set David over the army). David, however, was not killed in action, but led his battalion in a series of victorious forays. The terminology used—that David "marched out and came in"—underscores David's success: When his soldiers went to battle, they survived to return and fight again (v. 13). Apparently, this state of affairs existed for some time.

The reader knows that David's success is due to the LORD's blessing as well as the young soldier's cunning, but the narrator underscores God's aid in v. 14: "Yahweh was with him." The effect of David's success set Saul in opposition to his own people as well as his rival. Saul "stood in awe" of his young general, but "all Israel and Judah loved David" (vv. 15-16). The expression "stood in awe" also could be rendered "lived in fear." Likewise, the people's "love" for David probably implies political loyalty as well as personal affection. The king and his people had vastly different feelings about David. It was especially troublesome for Saul that "all Israel and Judah" loved David.

Saul's small kingdom was centered in the northern part of Canaan, among the tribes who one day would form a separate kingdom called "Israel." David was a native of the southern area dominated by the tribe of Judah. David later would become the first leader to bring real unity to the northern and southern tribes as a single kingdom. That successful venture began here, as the people of both Israel and Judah grew in their admiration of David. Saul, unfortunately, could see it coming.

Saul's growing break with David—and his attempt to remove him from the picture—is illustrated by a broken promise (vv. 17-19). The king supposedly had promised his daughter in marriage to anyone who defeated the Philistine Goliath (17:25). David had accomplished that feat, but the promise remained unfulfilled. Saul manipulated this promise in his efforts to rid himself of David by offering his daughter Merab in marriage, on one condition: "Only be valiant for me and fight the LORD's battles" (v. 16b). Again, the narrator tells us, Saul was hoping that David would die in battle (v. 17).

Marriage to the king's oldest daughter would have been a great coup for David, putting him in a potential position to succeed Saul to the throne. David expressed great humility that Saul should make such an offer ("Who am I . . . that I should be son-in-law to the king?", v. 18), and the implication is that he continued to fight valiantly. Some commentators suggest that David's humble reply was a polite refusal of marriage to Merab, but v. 19 clearly indicates that Saul reneged on his promise, betrothing Merab to another man (v. 19) and depriving David of his promised membership in the royal family. [Adriel the Meholathite]

Adriel the Meholathite

This person probably came from Abel-meholah, which was east of the Jordan, not far from Jabesh-gilead, a city to which Saul had strong ties (see comments at ch. 11). In 2 Sam 21:8-9, he is called "Adriel son of Barzillai the Meholathite," and we are told that he and Merab had five sons. In a political gesture of conciliation to the Gibeonites, David turned these five sons over to the Gibeonites, along with two of Saul's children by Rizpah. To exact revenge for an earlier slaughter of their people by Saul, the Gibeonites "impaled them on the mountain before the LORD."

A Failed Trap and Greater Fear, 18:20-30

Saul had other daughters, however. When the crafty king heard that his younger daughter Michal loved David, he saw another opportunity to ensnare the man he now saw as an adversary (vv. 20-22; lit., "It was well pleasing in his eyes"). Communicating through palace intermediaries, Saul offered Michal to David, who demurred slightly (as in v. 18), noting that such a marriage was easier proposed than done, considering that he came from a poor family and could hardly pay the expected "bride price" for a king's daughter (v. 23). A typical bride price, or *mohar*, was probably about 50 shekels of silver. The price was usually set through negotiations between the fathers of the bride and groom.

Sensing that his prey was entering the trap, Saul set for David a bride price designed to cost him his life: "The king desires no marriage present except a hundred foreskins of the Philistines, that he may be avenged on the king's enemies" (v. 25). Now, however, it was David who saw a window of opportunity (again, "It was pleasing in his eyes," v. 26) to advance his standing in the court by marrying the king's daughter. Whether David knew of Michal's professed love for him is unstated and apparently beside the point.

Obtaining the bride price entailed a serious risk. Philistine men could hardly be expected to give up their foreskins willingly—not while they lived. Saul expected David to be killed by the enemy warriors, but David expressed full confidence that he would succeed and marry Michal.

Well before the time allotted had expired, David and his men returned after killing at least 100 Philistines. The Hebrew text magnifies David's feat by saying he killed *200* men, as most translations suggest. The NRSV, however, follows the Greek version, which has 100. In a grisly but memorable scene, David publicly counted out each severed and bloody prepuce so all the royal court could see that he had accomplished his goal, thus holding Saul to his promise (v. 27). As Saul saw the evidence that both God and his daughter loved David, his feelings became even darker. He grew even more threatened by David, "so Saul was David's enemy from that time forward" (v. 29).

It is no wonder that Saul became an embittered, frustrated, and isolated man. His every effort to manipulate and control David turned against him so that David only became more powerful and more loved. This theme of love that implies both affection and attachment runs throughout the chapter: Saul's son Jonathan loves David (18:1, 3). Saul's people throughout Israel and Judah love David (18:16). Saul's daughter Michal loves David (18:20). Saul has no choice but to watch as David succeeds in all that he does (18:5, 15, 30), because Yahweh is with him (18:12, 14), a truth that is obvious even to Saul (18:28). David's star rises without any special initiative on his part, and it becomes evident to the reader that God is at work in David's life. He succeeds because it is God's good pleasure for him to follow Saul as king.

Attempted Murder and a Daring Escape, 19:1-24

The saga of David and his tenuous standing with Saul continues in chapter 19 with three separate stories that describe an attempted reconciliation brokered by Saul's son Jonathan (vv. 1-7), a daring escape engineered by Saul's daughter Michal (vv. 8-17), and an attempt to capture David that is thwarted by the spirit of God (vv. 18-24).

David and Jonathan

Rembrandt, a master of the Dutch Baroque, conveys the emotional departure between the two figures through the drama of light and the sense of the momentary. The two figures embrace as a son would hug his beloved father. Rembrandt's focus on the figures is amplified by the hazy and indistinguishable area surrounding the men. There are no details to detract our attention from the scene at hand.

Rembrandt van Rijn (1606-69). *David and Jonathan.* Oil on panel, 29"x24". Hermitage, St. Petersburg, Russia. (Credit: Scala/Art Resource, NY)

Saul made no secret of his antipathy toward David and his desire to eliminate him as a rival. If he expected a sympathetic hearing, however, he did not receive it. While Saul sought to kill David, his son Jonathan "took great delight in David" (v. 1). [David and Jonathan] This surprising contrast emphasizes the underlying work of God. Some find it strange that Jonathan would show more solidarity with David than with his father, but we must not forget that Saul, in a moment of darkness, had once tried to kill his own son, too (ch. 14), and would do so again (20:33). The people of Israel had saved Jonathan from his father's rage. Now Jonathan hoped to save his friend from the same angry man.

Saul Attacks David

1 Samuel 19:9-10—David's music had the power to calm Saul's troubled spirit, but there were times when the king's mania overcame even that small respite.

Julius Schnoor von Carolsfeld. *Saul Tries to Kill David.* 19th century. Woodcut. *Das Buch der Bucher in Bilden.* (Credit: Dover Pictorial Archive Series)

Jonathan offered to speak to his father on David's behalf, attempting to defuse the volatile situation and prevent David's assassination. There is a strange contradiction in Jonathan's offer. He tells David to hide, then promises to sound out his father about David "in the field where you are" (v. 3). This implies that David is to overhear the conversation, but Jonathan also promises to report to David on the outcome of his meeting.

Jonathan's diplomacy evidently caught Saul in a moment of sanity. As Jonathan recounted David's heroic exploits and faithful service, Saul relented and swore that he no longer would seek David's death (vv. 5-6). This was an oath, however, that Saul soon would forget—or ignore. The narrator continues to portray Saul as a man who possesses the capacity to appreciate David, but who cannot suppress an inner urge to eliminate him. For a time, however, the commitment held. Jonathan apprised David of his father's promise, and brought him back to the court, where David resumed his duties, presumably as court musician and army commander. The text simply says that "he was in his presence as before" (v. 7). David and Saul lived with an uneasy truce.

The next story (vv. 8-17) begins with David leading an army into battle, and ends with him fleeing for his life, covered only by his wife. Conflict with the Philistines escalated to the point of renewed war (inspired, perhaps, by David's foreskin foray?). David, leading at least a part of the army, had great success in driving back the Philistines. The account of the war, however, is compressed into one verse (v. 8)—just enough to renew Saul's jealousy toward his triumphant young general and provide a transition from reconciliation to attempted murder. The scene shifts quickly to a domestic encounter: The battle has ended, and David has returned to his post as Saul's personal musician. Afflicted once again by "an evil spirit from the LORD," Saul repeated his efforts to pin David to the wall with his spear (v. 9; cf. 18:10-11), but David eluded him and escaped. [Saul Attacks David]

Two themes are evident in this brief interlude. One is the repeated reminder that the growing shift in power is the work of God. Saul's rapid deterioration is not simply a sign of his own inner weaknesses, but a response to the "evil spirit from the LORD" that afflicts him. Secondly, Saul's persistent attempts to kill David lead only to a mounting sense of frustration and public humiliation. David's popularity grows as Saul's reputation declines in a death spiral that continues through the remainder of 1 Samuel.

A Favorite Escape Route

David's escape through a window—presumably by means of a rope—echoes Josh 2:15; Joshua and the other spies make a similar escape with the aid of the harlot Rahab. Perhaps we are to understand that David's house, like Rahab's, was built into the city wall. A similar story is found in the New Testament, where the newly converted Saul is forced to flee for his life and escapes by being let down through a window in a basket (Acts 9:23-25; 2 Cor 11:32-33).

Gustave Doré (1832–83). *The Escape of David Through the Window* from the *Illustrated Bible*. 19th century. Engraving. (Credit: Dover Pictorial Archive Series)

David soon found that there was no more security in his own house than in Saul's, for the king had set a watch for him there to kill him (v. 11); Kyle McCarter suggests that this account originally followed 18:27, assuming that Saul planned for David's wedding night to be his last.[4] Once again, however, Saul was frustrated by one of his own children. As Jonathan had interceded for David, so Michal arose to intervene and thwart the attempted assassination. Given David's popularity, it is not surprising that someone in the palace guard would warn Michal of the impending danger. Alerting David, Michal assisted his furtive escape through an unguarded window, then covered his tracks with an elaborate ruse to make it appear that David was still in bed. [A Favorite Escape Route]

Michal's artifice offers an interesting insight into tenth century religious practices, as she disguised David's absence by filling his place in bed with an idol (v. 13). [Idols in Israel] The word translates the Hebrew term *ṭĕrāpîm*, often transliterated as "teraphim." The word form is plural, but it may be used to describe a single idol, or multiple ones. In Genesis 31, Rachel escaped with the teraphim belonging to her father Laban (v. 19), who described them as his gods (v. 30). There, however, the teraphim were small enough to fit into Rachel's camel saddle and be hidden by her robe (19:34-35). In the present story, the teraphim belonging to David and Michal was evidently the same size and shape as an adult human. With the addition of a matted goat's hair wig and some of David's clothes, Michal hoped to give any visitors the impression that David was sick in bed. When Saul discovered the ruse and confronted his daughter, Michal skillfully eluded personal guilt by veiling the truth in an implication that David had threatened to kill her if she did not aid in his escape.

David's escape from Gibeah marks the last time he would ever live in Saul's court. From this point on, so long as Saul lived, David would be a man on the run. Instead of ascending to fame as a leader of Saul's army, David would gain new fame as an outlaw chieftain who lived by wits and bravado, always managing to stay at least one step ahead of pursuing King Saul.

David's first step in evading Saul was to seek out the old prophet/priest Samuel, who lived a few miles to the north in the rustic village of Ramah. There, David found himself protected, not by Samuel and the "prophets" who attached themselves to him, but

> **Idols in Israel**
>
> Despite the monotheistic teachings of Yahwism, it apparently was not unusual for ancient Israelites to possess household idols. Ezek 21:21 (MT v. 26) suggests that teraphim could be used in divination, though Zech 10:2 declares that the results would be nonsense. In Judg 17:5, the traveling priest Micah had a shrine containing teraphim that obviously served religious purposes. In many cases, teraphim were probably old family heirlooms representing traditional clan deities or popular Semitic patrons such as Baal or Astarte. When King Josiah instituted his religious reforms, he insisted that the teraphim be destroyed.

Saul Among the Prophets

This painting by Battista Zelotti portrays Saul, in a manic state, being restrained by his family. Battista Zelotti (1526–78). *Saul Restrained by His Family.* Museo Civico, Padua, Italy. (Credit: Cameraphoto/Art Resource, NY)

by the very spirit of Yahweh. The narrator's inclusion of this story adds another link to the chain of events that leads David to the throne as the chosen one of God, for Samuel's protection of David reads as an endorsement.

After hearing David's story, Samuel agreed to shelter him, and together they "went and settled at Naioth" (v. 18). Since Naioth was "in Ramah" (v. 19), it could not have been a very large place. Though the MT treats it as a place name, McCarter argues that it should be translated as "camps," since the word is very similar to the plural form of *nāweh*, meaning "shepherd's camp."[5]

In either case, Saul learned of David's whereabouts and sent messengers to retrieve him. The messengers, however, were ambushed by the spirit of God (v. 20). Samuel is portrayed as the leader of a group of ecstatic prophets (see commentary at 1 Sam 10:5-16). Prompted by activities such as prayer or frenzied dance, and presumably under the influence of the spirit, such prophets typically would fall to the ground in rapt ecstasy thought to result from a personal encounter with divinity. Saul's emissaries came in search of David, but when they approached Samuel's band of prophets, they also came under the spell of the spirit and joined in the group's writhing frenzy. Such behavior would never be expected of the king's servants—some of whom were presumably soldiers—but the spirit of God overwhelms ordinary expectations.

So infectious was the spirit that a second group of messengers encountered the same fate, and a third search party fell victim to delirium as well (v. 21). Finally, Saul himself came to Ramah, where he stood alone by "the well of a threshing floor on a bare height" (LXX; the MT has an enigmatic phrase, "the great well that is in Secu"). Inquiring after David and Samuel (v. 22), the king came to Naioth, where he fell under the influence of the same spirit that had taken his messengers. "The spirit of God came upon him," we learn (v. 23), "as he was going"—even before he came to Naioth, where the others were gathered. Saul's ecstasy was so deep that he stripped off his clothes and fell into a quaking frenzy that lasted for a day and a night (v. 24).

For the second time, we are reminded of the proverbial question: "Is Saul also among the prophets?" (cf. 10:11-12). [Saul Among the Prophets] Some scholars regard this as a doublet, a retelling of the same story. This story is different, however. In 10:11-12, Saul came to the prophets as a young and welcome novice; in 19:23-24, he comes as a powerful intruder seeking to harm. In 10:11-12, Saul is the beneficiary of God's spirit; in 19:23-24, he is its victim. Saul is no stranger to the spirit of God—his initial ecstasy had given way to a series of experiences in which his rapture was perceived as evil rather than good (16:14; 18:10; 19:9). Saul's encounter with the spirit in 19:23-24 seems almost bittersweet—a reminder of what his relationship with God could have been. Even this apparently "positive" encounter is another reminder that Saul is utterly power-less—and openly foolish—before the choices of Yahweh.

Jonathan's Love and David's Departure, 20:1-42

The book of Proverbs says "There is a friend who sticks closer than a brother" (Prov 18:24). David and Jonathan not only were brothers-in-law, but also had the kind of friendship that goes even deeper than family loyalty. Sadly, the friendship was fated to exist under extreme tension, for Jonathan's father Saul had sworn enmity against David and sought to kill him.

First Samuel 20 is a fascinating story describing the effect of this strain on Jonathan and David. Though it is David's story, it is Jonathan who wins our sympathies, for his heart was torn. He loved his father and was loyal almost to a fault. Despite Saul's sev-eral attempts on David's life, Jonathan remained unconvinced of his father's evil intent (vv. 1-2). Yet he was also bound to David by a love as deep as his own soul (18:1-5). When his father (whom he loved) was trying to murder his best friend (whom he also loved), what was he to do? Jonathan's fre-quent use of the phrase "my father" adds special poignancy to the narrative.

David convinced Jonathan that his father might be withholding information about future assassination attempts precisely because he knew of Jonathan's love for David. David elicited his friend's aid by using the strong language of an oath: "But truly, as the LORD lives and as you yourself live, there is but a step between me and death" (vv. 3-4). [A Step or an Oath?]

The following verses seem awkwardly placed, for they assume it would be normal for David to appear at Saul's table for the New Moon festival. David had already fled from Saul, and even though he easily could have returned to Gibeah for a clandestine meeting with Jonathan, he hardly could be expected to show up for dinner as if nothing had happened. There may be some confusion in the chronology of the stories, but that is beside the point. In *this* story, David anticipated that Saul would expect him to attend the next Feast of the New Moon, and he feared that Saul would try to kill

---

A Step or an Oath?

AΩ The reading is difficult in this verse. The MT can be read as "[it is] only a step between me and death." The LXX has "because, as I said, he is sated." Kyle McCarter prefers to presume a different Hebrew word underlying the Greek for "sated" (*nšbʿ* instead of *nśbʿ*), resulting in "he [Saul] has sworn a pact between me and death." There is not enough evidence to choose a certain reading, but all point to the same truth: Saul's rage left David in danger of death.

Feast of the New Moon

AΩ "New moon" refers to the first sliver of the crescent moon, beginning the lunar cycle. A new moon occurs every 29½ days. Since the Hebrews observed a lunar calendar, the word for "new moon" (ḥōdeš)also meant "month." Some ancient cultures worshiped the moon as a god and saw the new moon as a sign of the god's continual rebirth and power. Thus, in ancient times, the new moon was celebrated with feasting and religious ceremonies.

In Israel, the new moon festivities apparently included feasting that could continue for as much as three days (1 Sam 20). Though it seems to have begun as a family festival (as in the story of Saul and David), it came to be celebrated with rituals and special sacrifices at the temple (Num 10:10; 28:11-15; Ezek 46:6-8). The book of Amos suggests that ordinary work was to be suspended during the New Moon festival (Amos 8:5).

---

him. The new moon celebration involved extra sacrifices to God (Num 28:11-15; Ezra 3:5), and since the worshipers' share of the sacrificial animals had to be eaten within three days, the time of feasting could last several days. [Feast of the New Moon]

David had no intention of sitting at the table with Saul, but with Jonathan's assistance he contrived to employ his absence as a test of Saul's mood. If the king commented on David's empty chair, Jonathan would reply that David had asked permission to attend an annual family festival in Bethlehem. They would discern Saul's plans by his reaction to this news: If he became angry, this would be a sign that he intended harm to David (vv. 5-7). The story seems to give added stress to David's innocence and his loyalty to Saul. David, as a subject of the king, referred to himself as Jonathan's "servant," and he offered to let his friend kill him if he could find any guilt in him (v. 8). On the other hand, the same verse could be read to suggest that David was questioning Jonathan's loyalty, reminding him of the covenant that bound them, and expressing his preference to die at the hands of his friend than to be turned in by him. After Jonathan's astonished assertion of loyalty, the two friends agreed on a covert manner of communication. Since Jonathan's aid to David would make him guilty of treason in his father's eyes, caution was essential (vv. 9-10).

Having moved out into a field for greater privacy, Jonathan swore a strong oath that he would not leave David uninformed (vv. 11-13). In a touching fashion, Jonathan's self-imprecation ("The LORD do so to Jonathan, and more also, if I do not disclose it to you") is followed by a blessing on David ("May the LORD be with you, as he has been with my father"). In this blessing, as in 18:4, Jonathan tacitly acknowledged his assumption that David would succeed Saul as king, and asked God's blessing upon him.

Knowing that nascent kings were prone to assassinating all rival families, Jonathan asked that David continue to show faithful love to him and to his descendants (vv. 14-15). The MT's text suffers from problems in v. 16: The NRSV reading, "Thus Jonathan made a covenant with the house of David," must presume that the word "covenant" is understood, since the text has only "Jonathan cut with the house of David." The expression "to cut a covenant" is a typical Hebrew idiom. [Cutting a Covenant] Although the word for "covenant" (*bĕrît*) typically is present, there are a few instances in which it may be understood (1 Sam 11:2; 20:6; 22:8; 1 Kgs 8:9 = 2 Chr 5:10; 2 Chr 7:18). Some versions of the LXX understood the word "cut" to mean "if Jonathan is cut off from the house of David."[6]

> **Cutting a Covenant**
>
> AΩ The idiom "to cut a covenant" goes back to a formal custom of marking a covenant by dismembering an animal as a sacrifice to be shared by the covenant partners, and as a sign that any covenant-breaker should suffer the same fate. The expression is used more than 80 times in the Old Testament (Gen 21:27, 32; 31:44; 1 Sam 18:3; 1 Kgs 5:26; Hos 10:4; among others).

There is no question that oaths are sworn in v. 17, but some uncertainty exists about the person doing the swearing. The MT uses a causative verb form ("So again Jonathan caused David to swear"), while the LXX translates the verb as a simple active form ("So again Jonathan swore to David"). Whether the oath arose from David's insecurity or Jonathan's, its intent reflects Jonathan's deep affection for David, "for he loved him as he loved his own life" (v. 17).

Finally, the narrator gets to the covert plan for Jonathan to communicate Saul's disposition toward David. They would come again to the same field on the third day of the New Moon festival, and while David hid behind a particular mound, Jonathan would feign target practice with his bow and arrow. A short shot and shouted instructions for the servant boy to fetch the arrows close in would suggest safety. If, however, Jonathan shot the arrow beyond the boy, so that he had to cry something like "It's beyond you! Keep going farther," then David would take this as a sign that he, too, should travel farther away from Saul's sphere of influence (vv. 18-23). With a final reminder of their covenant bond before Yahweh (v. 23), Jonathan returned to his father.

The narrator paints a banquet scene that was filled with tension as the day for the New Moon festival arrived. The storyteller includes a colorful note that Saul sat in his accustomed place, with his back to the wall (so no one could sneak up on him), while Abner (his chief general) sat by Saul's side. Jonathan appeared too nervous to sit at all. On the first day of the feast, Saul took little notice of David's absence, assuming that he did not attend due to some ritual uncleanness. [Ritual Uncleanness]

When David did not appear on the second day, Saul revealed his angry mood by asking why the "son of Jesse" was not in his accustomed seat. Jonathan offered the prearranged excuse, carefully using David's given name, and stressing that David's brothers had insisted on his presence. Saul's rage erupted so violently that he not only threatened David, but turned on his own son. He cursed Jonathan, insisted that he had brought shame on the family, and then attempted to spear him with the same lack of success as in his three previous attempts on David. Speaking with a wisdom that went deeper than his rage, Saul insisted that Jonathan would never be king if David remained alive (vv. 30-31). There was no longer any doubt concerning Saul's hostile intentions. Showing a bit of his father's temper, Jonathan left the table "in fierce anger," outraged by both grief and shame over his father's actions (v. 34).

> **Ritual Uncleanness**
> Any number of things could make a person ritually unclean for one day, precluding them from participating in religious festivals. Examples include such things as experiencing a nocturnal emission or touching some "unclean" thing, such as a corpse (Deut 23:10; Lev 7:20-21; 15:16-18). This excuse, however, would not hold for the second day.

According to their plan, Jonathan waited until the next day, then went out to the field where David was hiding. He gave David the secret signal by shooting an arrow beyond his servant boy, and cleverly devised a way to emphasize the urgency of his message. Not only did he shout "Is the arrow not beyond you?" but also he called out, "Hurry, be quick, do not linger!" (vv. 35-39). With all the secrecy of this enterprise, the reader expects David to slip out of the field and leave quickly.

Yet the story does not end here. In a touching scene that some scholars regard as a later addition, there occurs a moment of high drama as Jonathan and David say their goodbyes. The narrator tells us that Jonathan sent the boy back to town with the bow and arrows, so that he was left alone in the field and David could safely appear (v. 40). When David emerged from hiding, he demonstrated his loyalty to the kingdom and his love for Jonathan by prostrating himself three times before Saul's heir. The two friends embraced, kissed, and wept, and surprisingly, *David wept the more.*

David's loss of composure is unexpected because, until this point, the narrator has only described Jonathan's love, not David's. From the beginning, the reader knows that Jonathan loved David as he loved his own life (18:1-4; 20:17). Now the author reveals that David's love for Jonathan also ran deep: "David wept the more." The Hebrew is uncertain here, but "until David made great" (the literal reading in the MT) makes little sense unless it is connected to his weeping. Some time later, when he learned that Jonathan had died in battle with the Philistines, David lamented their friendship in poignant poetry (2 Sam 1:19-27), insisting that

Jonathan's faithful love meant more to him than the love of a woman.

It is usually David who appears as the strong and composed figure, but here it is Jonathan who has the strength to say goodbye, reminding David once again of their covenant oath before the LORD, a promise of fidelity that extended even to their descendants (v. 42). This was a painful farewell for the two devoted friends, but though divided by danger, their friendship never ceased. Once David was recognized as king, one of his first questions was this: "Is there still anyone left of the house of Saul to whom I may show kindness for Jonathan's sake?" (2 Sam 9:1). When he learned that Jonathan's crippled son Mephibosheth still lived, David was careful to bring him under his patronage (2 Sam 1:3, 7). The memory and the effect of their mutual love lived on.

CONNECTIONS

The contrasting stories of Saul and David are reminiscent of a convention center or department store in which two or more lengthy escalators are located side by side, one going up and the other down. David is riding high and headed higher on the fast track to political power and human adulation. Saul, on the other hand, finds himself in a rapid descent that he cannot stop. With every paragraph, Saul grows closer to the bottom, while David climbs steadily upward. Saul throws obstacles into David's path with increasing desperation, but he is unable to impede David's ascent to power or to dislodge himself from the downward track. It seems that every barrier David overcomes serves only to build his character and increase his strength.

1. *Words about Friendship.* The story of Jonathan and David's friendship is one of the more heart-warming stories in all the world's literature of any age. [David and Jonathan in Literature] That friendship begins here (18:1-4), grows through the next few months or years (compacted into chs. 19–20), and ends only with Jonathan's death (31:2). Even after Jonathan died, David continued to show loyalty to Jonathan's descendants (2 Sam 9).

What elements underlie such a firm and lasting friendship? Close friendships often begin with *chemistry*. David and Jonathan were different in many ways: one a king's eldest son and heir apparent, the other the youngest son of a village shepherd. Yet they shared a common idealism and the kind of heroic courage that made them

David and Jonathan in Literature

Several works from the post-Renaissance period treat the friendship of David and Jonathan. While most of the works are dull paraphrases of the biblical story, one stands out—Abraham Cowley's *Davideis* (1656). Utilizing Thomas Aquinas' discussion of love in the *Summa Theologica*, the classical ideas about friendship found in the philosophies of Plato, Aristotle, Cicero, and Seneca, and the ideas about love set forth by Renaissance Neoplatonists, Cowley portrays the friendship between David and Jonathan in classical Greco-Roman categories: virtuous, trusting, selfless. Their complete trust forged a bond closer even than that between twins or spouses:

No weight of Birth did on one Side prevail,
Two Twins less even lye in Nature's Scale.
They mingled Fates, and both in each did share,
They both were Servants, they both Princes were.
If any Joy to one of them was sent,
It was most his, to whom it least was meant. . . .
Never did Marriage such true Union find, . . .
'Till Nature's self scarce look'd on them as two. (ll. 96-101, 104, 126)

In modern literature the friendship of David and Jonathan takes a new turn, being used for the exploration of homosexual relationships. The most notable work is that of Nobel Prize-winning French writer André Gide, whose *Saul* (1922) suggests a homosexual triangle between David, Saul, and Jonathan. Gide was himself a homosexual. Raised in a strict, even puritanical Protestant environment, he frequently explored in his work the tension between religious authority and individual feelings. In *Saul*, Saul has an ambiguous relationship with David: He wants him as a lover, but he also sees David as a threat to Jonathan's kingship, since Jonathan is a weakling. According to Gide, Saul's unrequited affection turns to jealous hatred when David and Jonathan have a sexual relationship. By projecting homosexuality into the biblical narrative, Gide provides emotional motivations for some of the actions described in 1 Samuel.

immensely popular with the people. When they first met, there seems to have been a certain chemistry that formed an immediate bond, especially from Jonathan's perspective ("The soul of Jonathan was bound to the soul of David," 18:1; cf. 19:1).

Friendships that begin with great chemistry, however, often end with gradual corrosion or explosive reactions. Good friendships require careful *cultivation*. The friendship of Jonathan and David endured and grew like a fruitful vine because the two cultivated it over time. The narrator has compressed the events of chapters 18–20 into a short time period, but it is likely that they encompassed many months or even years. The two friends proved to be true to each other throughout that time so that they grew closer and closer.

Lasting friendships also require *commitment*. Western movies have popularized a custom purportedly practiced by Native Americans, the act of sealing a friendship by becoming blood brothers. Jonathan and David also "cut a covenant together" (18:3; 20:8, 16-17), a covenant not only between themselves, but before the LORD (20:23, 42). Jonathan marked their covenant by giving to David his royal robe and princely armaments (18:4), revealing his willingness to sacrifice his own political ambitions for the sake of his friend. David accepted Jonathan's friendship and his position as heir apparent because God also had revealed this to be his destiny (1 Sam 16:1-13). Yet, even when David became king, he included Jonathan's family in his court (2 Sam 9:1-7).

Lasting friendships require trustful *cooperation*, even in times of apparent conflict. Jonathan was torn by divided loyalties, for his own father (whom he also loved) turned against David. For their friendship to endure—and for David to survive—the two men had to trust each other. The narrator makes no attempt to hide the tension between Jonathan and David over this matter (20:8-9, 13-17). Nevertheless, their trust endured, and their clandestine cooperation effectively saved David's life.

Friendships cannot endure for long without effective *communication*, which seems to have come naturally to David and Jonathan. Such was their love that they contrived to communicate even when it was dangerous for the two of them to be seen together (19:2-7; 18-24; 20:10-12; 35-39). In many relationships, one person tends to be more vocal about their feelings than the other. This is the case with Jonathan, whose love for David appears at times to be one-sided (18:1-3; 19:1; 20:17). David's love is less apparent until the time comes for the friends to part. David prostrated himself before his friend before they embraced for the final time, kissed each other, and wept (20:41). The telling phrase comes at the end of the verse: "David wept the more." Later, when Jonathan is killed, David would express his love for Jonathan in one of the most poignant laments ever written (2 Sam 1:19-27). David and Jonathan were not ashamed to express either their feelings or their concerns to each other.

Close relationships in any context can benefit from these same characteristics. Friendships may begin with chemistry, but they grow only through intentional cultivation and stated commitment. They function best through open communication and trustful cooperation.[7]

2. *Words about Power.* As the theme of friendship runs throughout chapters 18–20, so does the theme of power. Saul has great power as the series of stories begins, but he sees his own power deteriorate even as David's influence grows. The mighty king's decline becomes apparent when the village women sing greater praise for David than for Saul (18:7), after which he descends into a black mood of jealousy from which he is unable to escape (18:10-16, 29; 19:9-10), except for short periods of clarity (19:6). Saul's

debasement reaches a nadir when he loses all self-control and lies naked and helpless before Samuel, writhing in a frenzy (19:22-24). Saul seems to understand that ultimate power is in Yahweh's hand, and the reader suspects Saul knows in his heart that David is fated to succeed him. Even so, Saul will not willingly give over his throne.

As Saul's power dissipates, David achieves greater popularity and acclaim without apparent effort. He did not ask Jonathan to love him so (18:1-3), nor did he organize the cheers that proclaimed him ten times the warrior that Saul was (18:6-7). David gives no clue that he consciously seeks to supplant Saul—his primary energy goes into serving the king and surviving Saul's string of attempted murders.

Jonathan has less power, but he uses his influence skillfully. While Jonathan could have swung his weight behind Saul to eliminate David, his heart would not allow him to do so, for he loved David as he loved himself (18:3; 19:7). Instead, Jonathan used his position to protect David from Saul. He utilized intercession when possible (19:4-7; 20:32) and deception when necessary (20:18-29). Jonathan also seemed to know that David was destined for the throne (20:12-16). Yet he seemed happy to advance David's cause, even to his own detriment.

As the narrator presents the story, then, Saul uses his power in selfish ways, seeking to maintain his own position despite the obvious fact that he has lost favor with God. David uses his power with simple honesty and ambition, serving the king by fighting his battles, surviving the king by artful dodges, and preparing himself for whatever lay ahead. Jonathan, more than any other, uses his power unselfishly. He willingly protects his friend at the risk of his father's wrath, even though he suspects that David ultimately will supplant him.

The story leads modern readers to examine what power they possess (for everyone has a measure of personal power) and how they are using it. Do we, like Saul, cling to our power and use it only to advance our own causes, climbing over others' backs if necessary to achieve our goals and fill our pockets? Are we more like David, driven but honest, taking what comes and growing in influence? Or do we live like Jonathan, using our power for the benefit of others, even when our own power is lessened?

These same power issues were just as evident in the New Testament as in the Old. Both Matthew and Mark preserve a story of how James and John sought to gain ascendancy over the other disciples, creating dissension within the group (Matt 20:20–28;

A Different Path

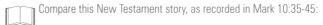 Compare this New Testament story, as recorded in Mark 10:35-45:

James and John, the sons of Zebedee, came forward to him and said to him, "Teacher, we want you to do for us whatever we ask of you." And he said to them, "What is it you want me to do for you?" And they said to him, "Grant us to sit, one at your right hand and one at your left, in your glory." But Jesus said to them, "You do not know what you are asking. Are you able to drink the cup that I drink, or be baptized with the baptism that I am baptized with?" They replied, "We are able." Then Jesus said to them, "The cup that I drink you will drink; and with the baptism with which I am baptized, you will be baptized; but to sit at my right hand or at my left is not mine to grant, but it is for those for whom it has been prepared."

When the ten heard this, they began to be angry with James and John. So Jesus called them and said to them, "You know that among the Gentiles those whom they recognize as their rulers lord it over them, and their great ones are tyrants over them. But it is not so among you; but whoever wishes to become great among you must be your servant, and whoever wishes to be first among you must be slave of all. For the Son of Man came not to be served but to serve, and to give his life a ransom for many."

Mark 10:35-45). Jesus responded by teaching his followers that they were to choose a different path from the standard rules of society. [A Different Path] In God's kingdom, those who serve are counted as greatest: the first will be last, and the last will be first.

3. *Words about Ethics.* First Samuel 18–20 presents the ethicist with a dilemma, for the stories are fraught with deception, sometimes on behalf of God's favored one. Saul is consistently deceptive, clearly in a negative fashion. He offers David a secure position in his court, but then attempts to murder him more than once (18:10-11). Saul promised not to harm David again (19:6), but quickly broke his promise with another violent spear thrust (19:9-10). Surprisingly, these attacks are attributed to "an evil spirit from Yahweh." Later, Saul promises David his daughter Merab's hand, but then reneges on his promise (18:17-19). Saul offers Michal instead—but only if David is willing to risk certain death by obtaining a bride price of 100 Philistine foreskins (18:20-25).

After this, Saul makes no secret of his efforts to eliminate David, but now he becomes the victim of deception at the hands of his own children. Michal helped her husband David escape, covered his absence from bed with a disguised idol, then lied to her father, insisting that David had forced her to do it (19:11-17). Jonathan later developed an elaborate ruse to secure David's safety, lying to his father when Saul complained about David's absence from the Feast of the New Moon, and meeting covertly with his father's sworn enemy (20:18-42). The narrator tells these stories with a wink, suggesting that God would approve their actions. Indeed, there is a sense in which Saul is betrayed by Yahweh. When David flees to Samuel, Saul follows him, only to be overtaken by the spirit of God, which renders him naked, incoherent, and helpless (19:18-24).

Both Jonathan and Michal were torn by divided loyalties, wanting to remain in good standing with their father but also wishing to protect their beloved David from Saul's irrational onslaught. In order to do this, they found it necessary to oppose Saul on his own level with deceptions of their own. The narrator seems to suggest that Saul got what he deserved, that the crafty betrayal of his children was the natural reward for his own deceitful demeanor. The story gives no hint that Yahweh was unhappy with the turn of events.

Is this series of stories a case study for those who promote situational ethics? Hebrew storytellers delighted in portraying heroes who survived and succeeded by means of their wits, even when deception was involved. Perhaps the deceitful behavior in 1 Samuel 18–20 is not intended as a model for emulation, but the willingness to do what has to be done to accomplish God's work certainly is presented in high regard.

[Doing What Has to Be Done]

Doing What Has to Be Done

Here is an ethical question to ponder. Today, many independent and denominationally supported individuals are working as missionaries among peoples that do not welcome missionaries—and, in some places, where mission work is expressly forbidden. In many cases, persons enter the country based on their qualifications to do work that is approved of or needed by the local government or populace, but their real agenda is to spread the gospel in the process. Should practices such as this be condemned or congratulated?

The issues, of course, are complex; there are matters of trust between governments and the possibility that such practices may harm future possibilities for more "legitimate" or officially recognized mission work. In the simpler case of Jonathan and Michal protecting David from Saul, however, the issue is more clear-cut, at least in the light of one biblical writer. The narrator of 1 Samuel seems to take delight in the cleverness and courage that Jonathan and Michal demonstrated in effecting David's deliverance, even though both employed an artifice to accomplish their aim.

NOTES

[1] Ralph W. Klein, *1 Samuel* (WBC 10; Waco: Word Books, 1983), 182.

[2] Peter Ackroyd, "The Verb Love-*Aheb* in the David-Jonathan Stories–A Footnote," *Vetus Testamentum* 25 (1975): 213-14.

[3] Walter Brueggemann, *First and Second Samuel* (IBC; Louisville: John Knox Press, 1990), 137.

[4] P. Kyle McCarter, *I Samuel* (AB 8; Garden City: Doubleday, 1980), 325.

[5] Ibid., 328.

[6] Ibid., 337.

[7] This description of friendship expands on a scheme suggested by Kenneth L. Chafin, *1, 2 Samuel* (CC; Dallas: Word Books, 1989), 151.

DAVID AND
THE PRIESTS OF NOB

21:1-9

David in Danger— On the Run, 21:1–26:25

David's departure from Jonathan marked his exit from Saul's court as well. It did not, however, remove him from the king's "Most Wanted" list. David remained in danger as Saul's paranoia led him to pursue his young rival throughout the hinterlands of Judea. As before, David continued to walk a gilded path of success, while Saul spiraled downward in one embarrassing defeat after another, venting his anger on the innocent while the object of his search remained simply out of reach. This ugly episode in the Saul/David saga is delineated in 1 Samuel 21–26. [A Man on the Run]

A Man on the Run

Here is a brief outline of the deadly cat-and-mouse game Saul and David played:

1. The priests of Nob help, and David plays the fool. (21:1-9)
David fled first to the sanctuary at Nob, where he was supplied with food and allowed to take Goliath's sword. Unfortunately, a spy was present.

2. David travels, and the priests of Nob pay for it. (21:12–22:23)
David sought sanctuary with the Philistine king Achish, but the Philistines turned on him. David escaped by feigning madness. While David hid in the cave of Adullam, his visit to the priests at Nob was reported to Saul by an Edomite mercenary named Doeg. Saul ordered his men to slaughter the helpless priests, but they refused. Saul then called on Doeg the Edomite, who murdered 85 priests, along with their families and cattle. Only Abiathar, son of Ahimelech, escaped.

3. Saul hunts David, and the tables are turned. (23:1–25:1)
When the Philistines ravaged the Judean city of Keilah, David and his men came to the rescue, defeating the Philistines and rescuing the city. Abiathar joined David as his personal priest and effected an oracle indicating that the

residents of Keilah would turn David over to Saul. David and his 600 men escaped from the city. David's army tried to hide in the Wilderness of Ziph, but certain locals reported his whereabouts to Saul, so David moved on to the Wilderness of Maon. As Saul's army approached David's men from the opposite side of the same mountain, the men were called back to fend off a Philistine invasion. After dealing with the Philistines, Saul took 3,000 men in pursuit of David, who had taken refuge at En-gedi. David had an opportunity to kill Saul, but did not. Saul declared a truce and swore that he would call of the chase.

4. Nabal's folly and David's prize (25:2-44)
David sought provisions from a wealthy man named Nabal, who refused to give any aid. Nabal's wife Abigail provided for David's men, however. When Nabal conveniently died shortly after, David and Abigail were married.

5. Saul keeps hunting, and David keeps winning. (26:1-25)
When it was reported that David had returned to Ziph, Saul broke his oath and renewed the pursuit. David secretly entered Saul's camp, but again refrained from killing the king. When Saul learned what David had done (and *not* done), the king again swore love for David and returned home.

COMMENTARY

David and the Priests of Nob, 21:1-9

The account of David's visit to the temple at Nob begins with 21:1-9 (21:2-10 in MT) and is interrupted by three episodes relating to David's flight before finding its conclusion in 22:6-23.

Counting Verses

The numbering system for Hebrew verses differs at many points from the English system. For example, the last line of 1 Sam 20:42 ("He got up and left; and Jonathan went into the city.") appears in the MT as 1 Sam 21:1, pushing the remaining verses in that chapter one number higher than in English.

The familiar system of dividing the Bible into chapters and verses is a rather modern phenomenon—the Old Testament was originally written without either punctuation marks or even vowels, and certainly without chapter and verse divisions. Vowel points and accents (which served as punctuation) were added to the Hebrew text by the Masoretes (for whom the "Masoretic Text" is named) between the 6th and 10th centuries AD. Hebrew scrolls were divided into sections for weekly reading as early as the Talmudic period, but the current system of chapter and verse divisions was not applied to the MT until the 14th century, following an earlier system applied to the Vulgate by Stephen Langton (see Ernst Würthwein, *The Text of the Old Testament* [Grand Rapids: Eerdmans, 1979], 21).

[Counting Verses] The sanctuary at Nob had apparently replaced the Shiloh temple, which was probably destroyed by the Philistines shortly after they defeated Israel's army and captured the ark (1 Sam 4:10-11). [Nob]

Nob was called "the city of the priests" (1 Sam 22:19), suggesting that it served as Israel's primary sacred site during Saul's monarchy. At least 86 priests and their families lived and worked in Nob, a sizable population of religious professionals. [Counting Priests] When David first came to Nob, he sought out Ahimelech, who acted with authority, indicating that he was the leading priest at the Nob sanctuary.

Ahimelech's apprehension over David's arrival (he "came trembling to meet David") was based on the fact that David came alone, rather than with the usual cortege of soldiers who were assigned to him. It is likely that Ahimelech knew of Saul's antipathy for David: His lone arrival gave him the appearance of a fugitive, and Ahimelech could only imagine the penalty for harboring Saul's enemy (compare the fear of the elders of Bethlehem when Samuel arrived unexpectedly, 16:4). Ahimelech was the brother of Ahijah, who served as Saul's own court chaplain (14:3, 18).

David's claim that he had stationed his men elsewhere for a later rendezvous may well have been an artifice, but it was effective in winning Ahimelech's aid. [At Such-and-Such a Place] The narrator depicts David as being alone when he fled from Gibeah (20:42) and alone when he sought refuge with King Achish of Gath (21:10). We cannot assume that the soldiers under David's command would have deserted their posts and followed him into hiding. Also, David requested only five loaves of bread (21:3), more

Counting Priests

First Sam 22:18 asserts that Doeg the Edomite killed 85 priests at Nob, but at least one escaped (Abiathar, v. 20). Abiathar was the son of Ahimelech, who was apparently the chief priest at Nob and the great-great-grandson of Eli, patriarch of the Shiloh temple (see [Eli's Descendants]).

Nob

The location of Nob is uncertain, but it was probably located just north of Jerusalem. In Neh 11:31-32, Nob appears in a list of Benjaminite cities that were near Gibeah. Isaiah predicted a day when the LORD would pass through the city of Anathoth (3 miles north of Jerusalem), then halt at Nob and shake his fist at Jerusalem (Isa 10:28-32). This suggests that Nob was located on a high place between Anathoth and Jerusalem. Archaeological evidence is lacking, but some have proposed Mount Scopus as a possible location, since it is less than a mile from Jerusalem and easily visible. The closest high place north of Jerusalem is the Mount of Olives, which offers a panoramic view of the Hill of Zion.

---

suitable for one man's travel than for provisioning a detachment of soldiers. Even the oversized temple loaves would not have gone far in feeding a band of hungry men. David would later recruit an outlaw army, which numbered 400 at first (22:2) and later swelled to 600 (23:13).

Ahimelech may also have spoken less than the truth when he claimed that no bread was available except for the sacred bread of the Presence that was placed before the LORD each Sabbath, unless the reader presumes a clandestine meeting in which Ahimelech could not leave the temple to obtain more. [Bread of the Presence] Bread that had been removed was reserved for the priests alone, but the exigency of the situation prompted Ahimelech to allow David to take it—provided that his men were ritually pure.

Ahimelech seemed especially concerned about sexual purity— namely, that the men had foregone any recent sexual relations. According to Leviticus 15:16-18, men or women who had engaged in intercourse had to take a ritual bath and were considered unclean until the following evening. It was customary for soldiers

At Such-and-Such a Place

AΩ David expressed his purported plan to meet his troops "at a certain place" by using the alliterative Hebrew term *pĕlōnî ʾalmônî*, which roughly translates to "such-and-such." See also 2 Kgs 6:8 (translated "such-and-such a place") and Ruth 4:1, in which Boaz refers to Naomi's nearer kinsman as "Mr. So-and-So."

Bread of the Presence

According to the priestly regulations (which may not have been codified until after David's time), twelve cakes of pure wheat flour were to be baked every Friday. As part of the Sabbath observance on Friday evening, the warm loaves were placed in two rows (or, perhaps, "two piles"—the word means "arrangement") before the LORD. The bread was to be accompanied by frankincense, all placed upon a rather small table covered with gold plate. On the following Sabbath, fresh bread was offered, and the old bread was removed (1 Sam 21:6) for distribution to the priests. The gift of the bread as provision for the priests is significant because it makes a direct statement that God was not expected to eat the bread (as other religions expected of food placed before their gods). Rather, the bread was symbolic of God's provision for Israel and the mutual covenant between them.

Rules governing the preparation and use of the bread of the Presence (called "shewbread" in the KJV) are found in Exod 25:30 and Lev 24:5-9, which requires that each loaf should contain $1/5$ of an ephah of choice flour. Since an ephah may have been about $7/10$ of a bushel (dry measure equivalents are not certain), this represented about 3 quarts—or about 3 pounds—of flour for each loaf. The resulting loaves would have been huge, rendering their symbolic presence highly visible and providing a significant amount of food for the priests (see G. J. Wenham, *The Book of Leviticus*, [NICOT; Grand Rapids: Eerdmans, 1979], 309-10). In later years, certain kindred of the Kohathites were responsible for preparing this bread (1 Chr 9:32).

to practice ritual purity when preparing for battle, and David assured the priest that every soldier carefully refrained from touching a woman while on active duty (v. 5; cf. Deut 23:9-14; Josh 3:5; 2 Sam 11:11-12). The soldiers' "vessels" (a euphemism for genitals) were surely pure, or "holy." David's emphatic point about the men being particularly careful about purity at that time goes back to his earlier claim that he was on a secret mission for Saul. David's men kept themselves pure even during ordinary ventures. How much more would they take care while on such a special assignment?

The author interrupts David's conversation with Ahimelech to notify the reader that all they say is being overheard by a man named Doeg, a mercenary from Edom who was in the employ of Saul (v. 7). Textual difficulties render Doeg's official position uncertain; speculation ranges from "shepherd" to "mule-keeper" to "runner." The reason for Doeg's detainment at the temple is likewise uncertain, as the word has no parallel in the Old Testament. It was probably from some ceremonial ritual, perhaps of purification. The sinister presence of Doeg casts a dark shadow over David's meeting with Ahimelech, for he will soon become both informant against and executioner of the priests at Nob.

The narrator returns quickly to David and Ahimelech. Emboldened by the priest's willingness to share the sacred bread, David compounds his duplicity by asking for a weapon, claiming that his secret mission caused him to leave in such haste that he had no time to gather his armaments. The reader is left to wonder if Ahimelech was exceedingly gullible, or if he simply was willing to do whatever it took to get David out of the temple. Ahimelech's grant of Goliath's renowned sword adds further force to the winds of change that are sweeping David toward kingship. The narrator paints it as an endorsement of David's rise, however unintended.

The last time Goliath's weapons were mentioned was in 1 Samuel 17:54, where David was said to have stashed them "in his tent." Since David had no tent of his own at the battle site, some commentators have suggested emending the text to read "in the tent of Yahweh." This would explain why the sword of Goliath was now to be found in the temple at Nob. Since David apparently had donated the sword to the temple, Ahimelech could hardly refuse to return it.

The sword apparently had been hidden or stored behind an "ephod." Ordinarily, the word "ephod" describes a priestly garment or robe (1 Sam 2:18; 22:18; 2 Sam 6:14), and here the sword is described as being wrapped in a cloth. However, there are indications that "ephod" could also describe a worked image of metal that could serve as an object of veneration (see Judg 8:27; 17:5; 18:14-20; Hos 3:4) or in the invocation of oracles (Exod 28:15; 1 Sam 14:3; 23:6, 9; 30:7). This particular ephod may have held Goliath's fearsome weapon, which would have served the Israelite community as a forceful reminder of Yahweh's power. In any case, David accepted the sword with delight: "There is none like it!"

CONNECTIONS

1. *Trouble Happens.* David seems to have led a charmed life up to this point. He enjoyed heroic exploits as a young shepherd (17:34-37). He was exalted above all his elder brothers to be anointed by Samuel as the future king of Israel (16:13). He was chosen from obscurity to be King Saul's personal musician and armor-bearer (16:21-23). He surprised Israelites and Philistines alike with his daring defeat of the giant Goliath (17:41-51). He garnered the admiration and love of Israel's peasants (18:7) as well as the king's own son (18:1-4) and daughter (18:20). He was successful in all that Saul gave him to do, for the LORD was with him (18:5, 14). In time, he would become the undisputed king of Judah (2 Sam 2:4) and of all Israel (2 Sam 5:1-5).

Yet, despite David's many accomplishments—and despite the narrator's claim that the LORD was with him—David's upward march was tinged with trouble. Saul became jealous of his prolific retainer and threatened his life, both directly (18:10-11; 19:9-10) and through subterfuge (18:17, 25). In short order, David was forced to flee for his life (19:12), venturing at first only so far as Ramah (19:18), but later realizing that he could no longer remain near Saul's stronghold (20:35-42). With chapter 21, David begins a long and arduous period of life in which he is hunted like an animal with no one to trust but the retinue of soldiers who remained faithful to him.

David's experience illuminates a question many believers ask: Why doesn't God keep those who love him from harm? Why do bad things happen to good people? David was known as a man "after God's own heart" (1 Sam 13:14), and the Scripture tells us time and again that the LORD was with David (1 Sam 18:12, 14, 18; 2 Sam 5:10). Why should David experience such danger and deprivation?

Some would argue that David's troubles were necessary for the building of his character. The biblical author asserts that at least some of Saul's attacks on David were inspired by "an evil spirit from the LORD" (18:10-11; 19:9-10). This was an attempt on the part of the writer to provide a theological explanation for Saul's illness and David's trouble.

Adherents of modern popular religion often assert that everything happens for a reason, that even tragedy comes as the direct result of God's will and plan for one's life. This is nothing more than a modern attempt to do what the Deuteronomist did, to explain life's trouble theologically. [Theological History] The truth, despite the promised blessings of Deuteronomy 28:1-6, is that God's followers have never been guaranteed shelter from every trial. We live in a sinful, troubled world, and adversity is a part of life. God does not buy our love by promising perfect peace. If trusting in God could buy lifelong health and assured safety, then everyone would worship God, and all for the wrong reasons. Few would refuse to follow a God who promised a trouble-free life.

But we do not live in a perfect world, and we cannot expect a perfect life. Troubles will come to all of us, and for all of us, those trials can serve as character-builders or character-breakers. Our response will determine whether adversity makes us bitter people or better people. David faced his trials with courage, cunning, and a determination to succeed. As a result, he emerged a stronger man. Later episodes in 1 and 2 Samuel show that David never fully escaped adversity. David fell into personal sin. His children fought with each other and with him. His heart was broken over the death

---

Theological History

1 and 2 Samuel are part of a larger section of the Bible that critical scholars call the "Deuteronomistic History." This term was first coined by Martin Noth (*The Deuteronomistic History*, trans. J. Doull et al., JSOT Sup 15 [Sheffield: University of Sheffield, 1981]) and is widely used to denote the historical books from Joshua through 2 Kings, with the exception of Ruth. Although these books derive from many different sources, it is likely that they were last edited by a single scholar or group of scholars working during the exile, trying to explain how God's special people could have experienced such utter and bitter defeat. The editors were greatly indebted to those persons responsible for the final version of Deuteronomy, and their work is grounded firmly on the same theological presuppositions, namely, that those who obey God will prosper, while the disobedient will fall under God's curse (see Deut 28).

Thus, the editors are careful at each juncture to emphasize whether significant persons in Israel's history (as well as Israel as a whole) were faithful to God, and to demonstrate the sure result of blessing or cursing. For example, in 1 and 2 Kings, the account of each king's rule is prefaced by a statement as to whether he did good (such as Asa and Josiah, 1 Kgs 15:11; 2 Kgs 22:1-2), evil (Nadab and Ahaz, 1 Kgs 15:25-26; 2 Kgs 16:1-4), or some of each (Jehoshaphat and Amaziah, 1 Kgs 22:41-44; 2 Kgs 14:1-4). Since the larger work is based on the principles found in Deuteronomy, scholars call it the *Deuteronomistic* History, and its purpose is to proclaim the editors' theological understanding of the exile as punishment for Israel's sin.

One interesting thing about the editorial work of the Deuteronomists is that there is so very little of it in the books of Samuel. Most of the ancient stories in Samuel were handed down in large segments, leaving less room for redaction.

of his son. He died as a decrepit old man, no longer able to make his own decisions.

The story of David and Ahimelech contains within it a dark reminder that disaster is always lurking. As the popular refugee and the temple priest talked, a spy was skulking about. Doeg the Edomite hangs like a vulture over the otherwise happy story of David's finding succor from the priests of Nob. The reader suspects, and rightly so, that Doeg will inform Saul that Ahimelech had given aid to David. The result would be utter disaster. Although they were blameless of knowingly aiding an outlaw, the entire temple staff, their families, and even their livestock would soon fall beneath Doeg's bloody sword. Only Abiathar would escape. Abiathar chose to remain a priest and served David well for many years.

Life comes to us with joy and sorrow, pleasure and pain. Those who follow God cannot expect to escape all affliction, but through continued faithfulness, they may hope to emerge as stronger people for the experience.

2. *The Common and the Holy.* There is a delightful interplay between the words "holy"(*qōdeš*) and "common" (*ḥol*) in 21:4-6. Ahimelech assured David that he had no common bread, only sacred bread. Because the bread was holy, it could be eaten only by persons who were also holy. David assured the priest that his men always kept themselves holy (ritually pure) when they were on duty—even when they were on "common" missions. Satisfied with David's explanation, Ahimelech allowed David to take the holy bread normally reserved for the priests.

God's people are called to be holy in all aspects of their lives, even the common ones. Christian believers no longer observe the strict Old Testament laws of ritual purification. For example, intercourse between a husband and wife is no longer considered an "impure" act that would interfere with worship on the following day. Even so, modern believers must not presume that all things are equally acceptable in God's sight or profitable for spiritual growth. We are called to be holy, even in the common days of life.

It is interesting that Jesus recalled this specific story as a means of teaching the first century

Mark 2:23-28

"One sabbath he was going through the grainfields; and as they made their way his disciples began to pluck heads of grain. The Pharisees said to him, 'Look, why are they doing what is not lawful on the sabbath?' And he said to them, 'Have you never read what David did when he and his companions were hungry and in need of food? He entered the house of God, when Abiathar was high priest, and ate the bread of the Presence, which it is not lawful for any but the priests to eat, and he gave some to his companions.' Then he said to them, 'The sabbath was made for humankind, and not humankind for the sabbath; so the Son of Man is lord even of the sabbath.' "

Compare the parallel stories in Matt 12:1-8 and Luke 6:1-5.

Pharisees that human needs take precedence over the ritual law (Mark 2:23-28). [Mark 2:23-28] The religious leaders had criticized Jesus for allowing his disciples to pluck grain from the side of the road and eat it on the Sabbath. Jesus argued that, just as David and his men needed food, so Jesus' men were hungry. Even though "reaping" and "threshing" a handful of grain was technically a violation of the law, Jesus insisted that human necessity took precedence over the sacral law. This dynamic approach to religion was a hallmark of Jesus' ministry—people always came first. Nothing was more holy or demanding than human need.

Apparently satisfied, the priest allowed David to take the sacred bread. Although this was normally a violation of cultic regulations, the human need of the moment superseded the law.

DAVID TRAVELS, AND THE PRIESTS OF NOB PAY FOR IT

21:10–22:23

David's encounter with the priests of Nob is separated from its grisly aftermath by a series of three brief interludes that seem unrelated except for two undergirding themes. First, David is now taking the initiative rather than passively waiting to see what happens. Secondly, in each of these three bits of tradition, David seeks an alliance with others who are the sworn enemies of Saul. David himself never speaks of Saul as an enemy, but the company he keeps cannot endear him to Israel's first monarch.

The first episode involves a puzzling foray to the Philistine city of Gath and a rejected appeal for sanctuary with King Achish (21:10-15). The second describes David's establishment of a stronghold at Adullam, where he recruited an outlaw army of other fugitives and dissidents (22:1-2). The third piece is an enigmatic assertion that David secured a safe haven for his family with the king of Moab (22:3-5).

COMMENTARY

David at Gath, 21:10-15

David's curious and unsuccessful interview with Achish seems to presage his later position as a vassal to the Philistine king (ch. 27). Even so, the two accounts are hard to reconcile. The city of Gath was about 23 miles to the west and south of Nob, though somewhat further by foot. The territory was rugged, but a hard-pressed man could make the journey in the space of a day (v. 11).

Achish, whose name probably reflects Aegean roots, is called the "king" of Gath, which is a bit unusual since leaders of the Philistine cities were typically called "lords" (1 Sam 5:8, 11; 6:4, 12, 17-18). The story may reflect a shift in Philistine politics, or it may simply be the narrator's way of magnifying Achish's importance as a counterpoint to the Gittites' reference to David as "the king of the land"

Triumphal Traditions

It was a tradition in the ancient world that conquering heroes be feted as they passed through villages and towns along their way home, not unlike ticker-tape parades awarded sports heroes in our own culture. The victory songs of the women were a memorable aspect of this tradition, and notable songs were remembered and repeated over a wide area. Thus, when David came to Gath seeking refuge, even the Philistines had heard how the women sang, "Saul has killed his thousands, and David his ten thousands" (2 Sam 21:10-11; cf. 18:7). They also knew that the "thousands" in question were Philistines.

Two Mad Men

It is interesting to compare David's intentionally irrational behavior with Saul's equally bizarre but less deliberate actions. On at least two occasions, Saul was possessed by the spirit of God and fell into an ecstatic trance (10:9-13; 19:23-24). The difference is that Saul was powerless to fend off the frenzy that left him writhing naked on the ground. In contrast, David's "madness" was evidence of his ability to stay in control and keep his wits about him even in times of great danger and stress.

(v. 11). Even if the Gittites' title for David means no more than "local chieftain" (cf. Josh 12:1, 7), it is an impressive appellation for a fugitive.

The Philistines' immediate recognition of David seems less related to his victory over Goliath than to the songs of the women who had praised David as he marched victoriously through their villages. [Triumphal Traditions] The subjects of Achish recite the women's song from 18:7 as if they had heard it, and indeed they may have. There was much interchange between the Philistines and Hebrews during this period.

Any monarch worth his salt has a functioning intelligence network at his disposal, so it is also likely that Achish's spies helped identify David as a Hebrew leader so popular and powerful that they called him "the king of the land." Achish would have known, no doubt, that Saul was still the titular king. Some scholars consider the reference to David as "king of the land" to be a historical anachronism, but it is also possible that the narrator has purposefully postulated a Philistine prophecy, adding to the swelling chorus of voices and events that point to David's future kingship.

If David had hoped to sneak unnoticed into Gath and find a quiet mercenary role in Achish's army, he failed. David's canny reaction to being found out illustrates his quick and cunning mind, which was also evident in the previous story (and may be an intentional link between the two). David quickly denied any hint of royalty or power by feigning madness: The expression literally means he "changed his judgment" or "changed his behavior." This behavior involved some sort of abuse to certain doors. The text is difficult, for the verbal root *tpp* can mean "to beat," in Hebrew, or "to spit," in Aramaic. Whether David beat on the doors or spat on them, and whether it was the doors of the palace or the city gate, is really immaterial. His hyper-erratic behavior and the drool running down his beard clearly marked him as insane. [Two Mad Men]

Achish's public response to David's behavior may be an intentional effort by the narrator to portray the Philistines in an unfavorable light. "Do I lack madmen, that you have brought this fellow to play the madman in my presence?" (v. 15). The king's retort implies that the

Philistine city had more than its share of deranged inhabitants. This unflattering portrayal of the Philistines may suggest another reason why this particular story was preserved, even when it is difficult to reconcile with David's later mercenary service in Achish's army. Would Achish have given one of his cities to a man he thought was mad (27:6)?

David's escape from the Philistines is so uneventful that it is not recorded, though there may be a clue in Psalm 34, whose superscription suggests that it was traditionally associated with this episode. The superscription reads: "Of David, when he feigned madness before Ahimelech, so that he drove him out, and he went away." The scribe who appended this note to the psalm has apparently confused the priest Ahimelech from the previous story with the Philistine Achish, but the comment about David's being "driven away" may suggest a variant tradition that David engineered his escape by baiting Achish's subjects to force him out of town.

David at Adullam, 22:1-2

The narrator has pieced together these bits of tradition like beads on a string, though the modern reader cannot be certain that they preserve an accurate chronological picture. The present order suggests that David, once free from the Philistines, wiped the spittle from his beard and headed straight for the stronghold of Adullam, deep in the Judean desert. [Adullam]

There, David drew to himself two groups of people. The first group was his family (v. 1), who apparently recognized that Saul could not be trusted to hold them guiltless and that their lives

---

Adullam

Adullam was about ten miles east and south of Gath and about sixteen miles southwest of Jerusalem. It was a fortress city, designed to guard the *Shephelah*, a Hebrew term used to describe the fertile lowland area between the coastal plain dominated by the Philistines and the uplands of Judah and Samaria. Originally a Canaanite royal city-state, it was conquered by Joshua and brought under Israelite control (Josh 12:15; 15:35).

Although in a low-lying area, Adullam probably sat on a well-fortified hilltop (modern Tell esh-Sheik Madhkûr is usually suggested), but it is unlikely that David's fortress was in a large cave. The traditional identification of the "cave of Adullam" with the cave of Khareitun just southeast of Bethlehem in the central hill country has been refuted since Adullam was clearly in the Shephelah. The MT uses the word "cave," but many scholars have adopted Wellhausen's proposed emendation from *m'rt* ("cave") to *msdt*, "the stronghold" (see also 2 Sam 23:13 and 1 Chr 11:15), as found in vv. 4-5.

Adullam seems to have served David as a base of operations during his "outlaw" period as a fugitive from Saul and a leader of the discontented.

would be in jeopardy as long as David was on the run. The second group seems to have been drawn by David's personal magnetism and his newfound reputation as an outlaw. He attracted an assortment of marginal people who were either fugitives themselves or unhappy with the current state of affairs in Israel (v. 2).

The text describes David's new allies as being made of "everyone" who was "in distress" (lit., "bitter in spirit"), who was in debt, and who was discontented. This suggests that David gave hope to a band of economically challenged people who wished to oppose the more wealthy and politically powerful populace (cf. Saul's taunt in 22:7). Elsewhere, the phrase "bitter in spirit" is used to describe Hannah's feelings about her childlessness (1 Sam 1:10), the grief of the men of Ziklag over the kidnapping of their families (1 Sam 30:6), and David's own concern over the loss of his city, compared to a mother bear bereft of her cubs (2 Sam 17:8).

Having suffered great loss himself, David becomes the hero and leader of others who have experienced deprivation, disenchantment, and discontent. The text numbers David's followers at 400, though they would quickly swell to include at least 600 fighting men (23:13; 25:13; 27:2; 30:9, 10). For attentive readers, David's position as the leader of an outlaw army may call to mind Jephthah of Gilead, who led his ragtag army to victory over the Ammonites and so became a "judge" in Israel (Judg 11).

David in Moab, 22:3-5

The unusual interlude in 22:3 suggests that David had negotiated some sort of alliance with the king of Moab. On the surface this seems strange, because Israel and Moab were perennial enemies. David's friendlier connection could have grown from an international political agenda: It would be in the Moabite king's desire to foment trouble in Israel by assisting David, who had gained a reputation as a rebel leader. Saul had once defeated Moab in battle (14:47). The king had no way of knowing that David would later do the same thing (2 Sam 8:2; 1 Chr 18:2).

A second suggested scenario is that David appealed to a family connection. According to the genealogy of Ruth 4:18-22, David's great-grandmother was Ruth, a Moabite. Indeed, some Jewish traditions held that Ruth was of royal blood. [Princess Ruth?] Thus, when David sought safe haven for his parents, he could have claimed family relations in high places.

Princess Ruth?

Some traditions hold that Ruth was of royal blood, that she and Orpah were both daughters of King Eglon. One tradition even holds that Orpah remarried and became the ancestress of the Philistine giant Goliath! (Étan Levine, *The Aramaic Version of Ruth* [Rome: Biblical Institute Press, 1973], 55, 486).

The reference to Mizpeh of Moab is somewhat problematic, since it is mentioned only in 1 Samuel 22:3. [Mizpeh of Moab?] The word *mispâh* means "watchtower." It could have referred to a Moabite outpost where David parleyed with royal representatives, or it may have been an otherwise obscure royal city.

The location of the "stronghold" in vv. 4-5 is uncertain. The Syriac version reads "Mizpeh" instead of "stronghold," suggesting that David stayed in Moab for a while, and the words of Gad in v. 5 also imply that the "stronghold" was not in Judah. The sense of the story, however, is that David took his parents to Moab for safe-keeping, then returned to his stronghold at Adullam. In this case, the prophet's warning that David should leave the stronghold and "go into the land of Judah" can only make sense if one presumes that Adullam was within the borders of Philistine influence at the time, and not considered a part of Judah proper.

The "forest of Hereth" is otherwise unknown in Scripture. Kyle McCarter has noted the similarity of the name to the modern village of Kharas, near the ancient city of Keilah, which David later rescued (1 Sam 23:1-13).[1]

The presence of the prophet Gad is surprising so early in David's career, though the seer played a much larger role later on, serving as a court prophet (2 Sam 24:11-19; 1 Chr 21:9-19). Gad is best known for his later prophecy in connection with David's ill-fated census of the populace. The narrator's inclusion of Gad's guidance is a gentle reminder that the hand of God was at work with David, even during his years as an outlaw. Gad's warning put David and his company safely in hiding when Saul's minions descended upon the pitiable priests of Nob (22:6-19).

Mizpeh of Moab?

Several places named Mizpeh (or Mizpah) are mentioned in the Bible, including a region in northern Palestine (Josh 11:3), a town in northern Gilead (Gen 31:49), an important cult site in Benjamin (Judg 20; 21; 1 Sam 7:5-6; 10:17; 1 Kgs 15:22), and even a small town in the Shephelah region of Judah, not far from David's stronghold at Adullam (Josh 15:38). Mizpeh of Moab is mentioned only in 1 Sam 22:3.

The Priests in Danger, 22:6-23

With 22:6, the interrupted tale of the priests of Nob continues (the first part is found in 21:1-9). The traditional episodes inserted between the two parts lead the reader to imagine that, just as David found refuge in the forest of Hereth, the priests back in Nob were left in need of asylum, but unable to find it. Instead, they began to reap the consequences of having abetted David's escape, however unwittingly.

The scene opens with a characteristic image from Northwest Semitic literature: the king sits under a sacred tree, his court

Trees and Kings

Ancient Near Eastern kings were often depicted holding council beneath a tree. For example, this Ugaritic text from the Late Bronze Age (shortly before David's time) describes the great hero Daniel as follows:

Then Daniel, man of Rapi'u,
Ghazir, man of Hrnmy,
Sits erect before the gate
Under the mighty tree which is on the threshing floor.
He judges the cause of the widow,
Decides the case of the orphan.

CTCA 17[=2 Aqht].5.4-8; 19[=1 Aqht].1.19-25, trans. P. Kyle McCarter, *I Samuel* (AB 8; Garden City: Doubleday, 1980), 239.

---

around him. [Trees and Kings] Saul had earlier appeared by the threshing floor (also often associated with kingship), beneath a pomegranate tree (14:2). Threshing floors were typically located on high places. In 22:6, the text places Saul "on a high place" in his stronghold at Gibeah, this time beneath a tamarisk tree. [The Tamarisk Tree] As in previous scenes (18:10; 19:10), Saul holds court with his spear in hand (22:6).

The narrator portrays Saul in an angry mood. The besieged king accuses his officers of knowing about David's illegal activities, berates them for failing to inform him of David's movements, and charges them with conspiring against him in hopes of winning David's favor (vv. 7-8). In response, only the sinister Doeg speaks. The reader is left to wonder if Doeg had also been holding his peace or if he had only now arrived. Since the earlier account spoke of Doeg's being detained at the temple in Nob (21:7), the latter seems more likely.

The Tamarisk Tree

The tamarisk was a desert tree with widespread branches. Its leaves are small and flat, aiding in the retention of moisture. Tamarisk trees appear on two other occasions in the Old Testament. According to Gen 21:33, Abraham planted a tamarisk in Beer-sheba to mark the site where he prayed to "Yahweh, the Everlasting God." And 1 Sam 31:11-13 recounts how the men of Jabesh rescued the defiled bodies of Saul and Jonathan from the walls of Bethshan. After burning their bodies to purify them, they buried the bones under a tamarisk tree in Jabesh.

(Credit: James L. Reveal)

Doeg's recollection of the events he witnessed at Nob provides an intriguing detail about David's visit that was not mentioned earlier. According to Doeg, David not only obtained food and weapons from Ahimelech, but also divine advice: "He inquired of the LORD for him" (v. 10). The resulting oracle's content is not revealed, but it incriminates Ahimelech, who could hardly be ignorant of David's intentions after seeking for him an oracle from Yahweh. The narrator's emphasis on David's interest in oracles portrays David as a man who sought God's will both eagerly and frequently—all the more so given Ahimelech's claim that David had frequently requested his aid in ascertaining divine guidance (v. 14). This bit of information also nicely sets up the two following stories, in which David conspicuously inquires of the LORD before taking action (23:1-5, 6-14).

Saul appears no longer capable of rational judgment or willing to hear a rational argument, and was neither impressed nor swayed by Ahimelech's attestations of innocence (vv. 14-15). When Saul ordered his personal guards to kill the priests, however, they refused. If Saul previously had cause to doubt his army's loyalty, this rejection of his order could only have increased his suspicions. For the narrator, however, something else is at work; another element of the plot is being set in motion. Saul's palace guard refused to lift their hands against the priests of God. Later, David would have two easy chances to kill Saul, but he would also publicly eschew the opportunity, declaring that he could not lift his hand against Yahweh's anointed (24:6, 10; 26:9, 11).

The Edomite Doeg is pictured as having no such scruples, however. At Saul's order, he single-handedly slaughtered eighty-five priests—all of the descendants of Ahitub, "who wore the linen ephod," a sign of priesthood. There is some tension in the story. According to v. 11, Saul had ordered every priest from Nob to present themselves in Gibeah, where they presumably were murdered (v. 18). The account in v. 19 draws a somewhat different picture, in which Doeg went to the city of the priests, where he put to the sword "men and women, children and infants, oxen, donkeys, and sheep." To avoid conflict, one must presume that the "men" in v. 19 were spouses of priestly daughters, or independent, non-priestly males who also lived in "the city of the priests." The more difficult part of the story is to imagine how one man could have tracked down and killed every resident of Nob, unless Saul's army assisted by hemming them in, though they would not actively shed priestly blood.

Despite Doeg's earnest effort to eliminate the priests, one managed to escape. This priest, Abiathar, lived to fulfill Samuel's prophecy that Eli's descendants would be destroyed with the exception of one faithful priest (3:33-36; see [Eli's Descendants]). Abiathar had little choice but to seek refuge with David, who was eager to appoint the fellow fugitive as his own court priest. Later, Abiathar would employ the ephod he had appropriated to inquire of the LORD for David (23:6-14), as his father had done before (vv. 10, 15).

There is an interesting interplay between vv. 7-8 and v. 22. Saul accused his courtiers of knowing about David's activities but refusing to tell (vv. 7-8). None denied it. In v. 22, David spoke words of self-deprecation, insisting that he had known Doeg would incriminate the priests. Yet he had also failed to do anything about it. Perhaps there was nothing he *could* do. In an effort to make amends, David promised Abiathar his personal protection and sponsorship.

As it fits into the larger narrative, this story supports the Deuteronomist's contention that the Jerusalemite priesthood of Zadok was destined to win out over the Shilonite priesthood of Eli. Abiathar was the last of the Elides, the one destined by prophecy to survive Saul's pogroms and then wear out his eyes with weeping (1 Sam 2:27-36). Abiathar would eventually become David's high priest in Jerusalem, sharing power with a Jerusalemite priest named Zadok. This was temporary. When Abiathar supported Adonijah over Solomon as a potential successor to David, Solomon banished him from the temple, leaving Zadok in full control (2 Sam 20:25; 1 Kgs 1:5-8; 2:26-27).

The immediate focus of this story, however, is not on Abiathar, but on David. Saul is pictured as the destroyer of the priesthood, while David, by giving shelter to Abiathar, is its preserver. Through the story, David gains a priest and, hence, access to God. Saul, in contrast, is left without a priest or any legitimate means of seeking God's leadership (for an *illegitimate* attempt, see 1 Sam 28:3-25). In a sense, David is portrayed as the savior not only of the priesthood, but of Yahwism itself. By destroying the priesthood, Saul endangered the future of Yahwism, but David ensured the safety of its one remaining priest.

CONNECTIONS

The three episodes in this section occupy only a small part of the text, but imply a great deal of activity on David's part. David's behavior during this stressful period may offer clues to others who must cope with difficult situations.

1. *Be Proactive.* Modern management gurus encourage business leaders to be proactive in their business relationships and management style, as well as in their personal lives. The battle with Goliath displayed David's penchant for taking initiative, but during his court service, David is portrayed in a more passive role. Once David understood that Saul's desire to kill him had moved from an occasional manic attack to a continual conscious threat, he had no choice but to shift back into a proactive mode.

Society is filled with "professional victims" who passively accept inequity or abuse. They may complain about their fates but spend their days in a perpetual pity party without working for change. Saul's vendetta against David is a reminder that even God's chosen leader can also experience great difficulty and trials. David made a conscious choice that he would *not* live his life as a victim. Rather, he took matters into his own hands, did what was necessary to assure his own safety, and then began aiding other people who were in similar circumstances.

Saul's animosity toward David was undeserved, and his violent attacks were certainly unfair. David could have allowed such abuse to make him bitter, but chose instead to let it make him better. David's years as an unlikely outlaw do not sound like an ideal proving ground for leadership, but David chose a determined path calculated to result in victory, not victimhood.

2. *Know When to Retreat.* There is a difference between running from problems and retreating to find the safety and strength needed to confront those problems. When David left the priests of Nob and made his way toward a place of temporary safety, he was taking initiative for his own well-being, though God continued to work in his life. The fact that King Achish rejected David's request for political asylum and declared him fit for an insane asylum is immaterial. David was making the effort to regain control of his life—even if he had to feign being out of control in order to do it! Furthermore, even David's apparent failure at Gath may have helped pave the way for his later success in forging a temporary alliance with the Philistine king (ch. 27).

When life seems overwhelming, it is wise to retreat to a place of safety where we can find relief and release. Sometimes the best thing we can do is let go of our public persona and allow ourselves to act in ways that seem crazy or uncharacteristic for us. There is a great catharsis to be found in a good vacation for the workaholic, or in a structured retreat for the "control freak." Sometimes the best way to regain control of our minds is to step outside of our normal thinking processes and see life from a different perspective. Surely David did not journey to Gath with that intention—his "retreat" did not turn out as planned—but he was cunning enough to shift into survival mode, and he learned from the process.

3. *Rely on Friends and Family.* Once David had escaped from the Gittites and found refuge at Adullam, his first order of business was to seek the support of his family, and to broaden his network of friends. This became a mutual support system, for David's family and newfound friends needed him as much as he needed them. David's parents and brothers would not have been safe from Saul's predations as long as David remained unaccounted for. There may have been lingering tension between David and his brothers over the fact that Samuel had anointed him rather than one of the older brothers (16:6-13). The prelude to the story of Goliath implies a continued rivalry between the brothers (17:28-29). The brothers may have resented David even more for incurring Saul's wrath and thus bringing them into jeopardy, but none of this is evident in 22:1, where all of David's family comes to him, or in 22:3, where David requests a safe haven for his parents with the king of Moab.

Perhaps there is no greater source of hurt—or of healing—than our families. None of us grows up without some reason to complain of unfair treatment. Unfortunately, many persons carry teenage grudges into later life and miss out on the great strength that can be found in loving family relationships. Others learn to put past offenses behind them and build better families for the future. Some families are so dysfunctional that they may never be redeemed, but the potential reward is worth the effort.

David also took the initiative to create a new network of friends, drawing to himself "everyone who was in distress and everyone who was in debt and everyone who was discontented." David was not the only person to experience loss or deprivation. The social changes brought about by the monarchy had brought hardship to many. Together with David, these 400 (and soon more) persons became a veritable support group. [Support Groups] Alone, their bitterness of spirit had accomplished nothing. Together, their mutual

Support Groups

Many persons find tremendous value in joining a small support group of persons who face similar trials in life. Increasingly, local churches are finding it beneficial to sponsor support groups for persons with common needs: divorcees, parents with special-needs children, or persons fighting co-dependency, for example. One does not need to have an identified "problem" to benefit from support groups, however. Small groups of men and women who consciously form a covenant of support with each other are finding enormous strength in community. Churches, on a larger scale, serve this same function. David's actions remind us that life is better in community—not only more enjoyable, but more productive as well.

---

concerns gelled them into a group that had hope and strength and a future. Surely this group tested David's leadership skills, but he, like his new army, became stronger for the experience.

4. *Trust in God.* God is not often mentioned in this series of episodes (21:20–22:23), but God's presence is evident throughout. David had spent sufficient time with Samuel and the ecstatic prophets to know the characteristic behavior of someone in the throes of mad frenzy. A quick adoption of this behavior saved his skin when the Gittites were about to turn on him.

David's trust in God is often unstated, but it emerges in a telling phrase. When David petitioned the king of Moab for asylum for his parents, he asked for such assistance "until I know what God will do for me" (22:3). This suggests that David was always cognizant that God was at work in his life, even through the difficult days. David knew that Samuel had anointed him to be king, but he did not know how or when that promise would be fulfilled. David was apparently content to trust in God's timing and to trust as well in his own judgment as he lived in the present while looking toward the future.

A second reminder of God's hand in David's affairs comes through the prophet Gad, who suddenly appears in David's entourage. Gad may have been among the distressed, indebted, or discontented persons who joined David's movement. Gad urged David to leave his stronghold and go out into the Judean country-side. Since this advice came from one identified as a prophet, the reader presumes that it came as a word from God. David's respect for the word of God given through Gad is evident in three words: "So David left."

God's word to modern believers may come through the words of Scripture, through the words of a sermon, or through the words of a trusted friend. The prophet Gad brought God's word to David, and one may presume that God's ability to communicate has not been lost. David's response to Gad's warning serves as an example for others to be willing and ready to hear God's word—and to obey.

5. *Acknowledge Your Influence.* Saul's pogrom against the priests of Nob (22:6-23) brought home to David a hard reality: his every action would have consequences upon others. David accepted responsibility for drawing the Nob priesthood into the line of fire (22:22), though he did not repent of it. Still, he sought to make up for the harm he had caused by aiding the one priest who had escaped. In the process, he gained a priest who could assist him in divining the will of Yahweh—and he would keep Abiathar very busy.

David's difficult lesson remains true: our actions will have an impact on others, for good or ill. A thoughtless word can lead to hard feelings. A momentary act in the heat of passion can lead to an unwanted pregnancy and hard questions for the future. A drink too many and a set of car keys can leave innocent persons lying dead in their crumpled cars.

On the other hand, a word of encouragement and support can lift another's self-esteem. A random act of kindness can refresh another's troubled spirits. A conscious effort to care for others can leave behind a host of persons who will rise up to call their benefactor blessed.

No one is so great or so small that they can ignore the reality of their influence upon others, or the consequences their actions may bring into the lives of others. Unfortunately, even David would not always remember this important lesson.

NOTES

[1] P. Kyle McCarter, *I Samuel* (AB 8; Garden City: Doubleday, 1980), 350.

SAUL HUNTS DAVID, AND THE TABLES ARE TURNED

23:1–24:22

COMMENTARY

The Rescue and Betrayal of Keilah, 23:1-14

The narrator's treatment of the Keilah episode seems to include two older bits of tradition (vv. 1-5, 7-14) and an editorial splice (v. 6). [Keilah] The unifying theme of these verses is the storyteller's stress on David's ready access to Yahweh. David defeats the Philistines, delivers the Keilahites, and escapes from Saul—all after consulting with Yahweh and receiving divine guidance or blessing.

The word of Keilah's plight comes to David through an enigmatic "They told David." Perhaps we are to presume that the leaders of Keilah themselves never asked for David's help. This would explain their natural suspicion of David (who had moved his army into their city) and their later willingness to sell him out to Saul.

The terminology suggests that the conflict did not involve a concentrated push by a large Philistine army intent on conquering the town, which was surrounded by fortified walls. Instead, the picture is drawn of a Philistine raiding party that had come to rob the threshing floors of grain, bringing with them herds of their own cattle! The raiders could harry the residents with such impunity

---

Keilah

Though Keilah is little known, it would be classified as an ancient city because it was enclosed by protective walls (23:7). In David's day, the city of Keilah was about three miles south of his stronghold at Adullam. The ancient name is preserved today by the village of Khirbet Qîlā, about eight miles northwest of Hebron.

Keilah is portrayed as an independent sort of city, nominally assigned to Judah (Josh 15:35, 44) but well within the Philistines' sphere of influence, which was expanding into the Shephelah. The conflict portrayed in 23:1 suggests that the enemy army had not mounted a full-scale assault on the walled city, but was simply raiding the more accessible threshing floors and making away with grain for the army's cattle. This affront sparked David's intervention on the city's behalf (23:1-5), but the populace showed little appreciation for his valiantry (23:12).

because Keilah was not far from other Philistine strongholds, where larger armies waited in ready reserve. Threshing floors were located outside of cities, often on open hillsides, where seasonal winds could catch the chaff and separate it from the grain. [Threshing Floors]

David probably saw the political advantage in aiding the beset city, and may have felt a desire to help the people of Keilah. Previously, the narrator has portrayed David as one who acted on the basis of intuition or instincts. In this instance, however, the author takes great pains to show that David did not act without first conferring with Yahweh. There is no explanation here about *how* David did this. Such consultations were normally done through a priestly oracle, but there has been no mention of such a priest in David's retinue. The prophet Gad has appeared in David's company, however, and had previously advised David on his movements. One might surmise, then, that David sought Gad's advice, since the narrator does not bring Abiathar into the picture until after the victory at Keilah. Perhaps the reader is to understand that David was comfortable with prophets and priests alike.

Threshing Floors

Threshing floors appear frequently in Old Testament narratives because they were outdoor places where people often congregated, and their locations were usually well known. The temple in Jerusalem was built atop what was once the threshing floor of Araunah the Jebusite, purchased by David for that purpose (2 Sam 24:18-25; 1 Chr 21:18-28).

Threshing floors were typically located on a high, open point outside of a village or city. The floor itself was of necessity flat and smooth, with a surface of natural rock or tightly fitted stone. Grains such as wheat and barley would be piled upon the hard surface and then threshed in various ways. Oxen might be driven back and forth, doing the work with their hooves, or they might pull wooden sledges with stones or metal teeth set into the underside to break the grain apart. The sledges were weighted with stones or children. Large stone or iron rollers might also be pulled across the grain. Smaller, softer grains such as dill and cummin were beaten out with sticks.

This huge storage pit at Megiddo may have been used for storing grain. Note the circular stairway leading into the silo. (Credit: Mitchell G. Reddish)

Once the grain was thoroughly threshed, it was winnowed —thrown high into the air with pitchforks so the prevailing westerly breezes could separate the chaff from beaten grain, which was then stored in large clay jars or in silos dug into the earth.

In any case, David's query found an immediate and positive response (v. 2), though it did not satisfy his fighting men, who argued that they were frightened enough while hiding in the woods and desired no open conflict (v. 3). To assuage their doubts, David once again sought Yahweh's will, perhaps in a more public forum, and received the answer (v. 4).

Emboldened by the clear sanction of Yahweh, David and his men dealt the Philistines "a heavy defeat." The NRSV says that they "brought away their livestock"—that is, livestock that the Philistines had brought with them to feast on Keilah's grain. The word usually means "drive away," though it could suggest that David's men drove the cattle back with them as plunder.

The summary statement, "Thus David rescued the inhabitants of Keilah," closes the pericope neatly, strengthening the supposition that it was originally an independent unit. The following verse describing the arrival of Abiathar appears to be an editorial insertion explaining why David's future inquiries of Yahweh would be directed through his new "court priest." Prior to escaping the slaughter at Nob, Abiathar had apparently appropriated the ephod containing the Urim and Thummin, commonly used for divining God's will (see [Sacred Lots]), along with the discussion at 10:20 and 14:40-42).

The following account describes how David once again eluded Saul's clutches, with the obvious point being that David escaped because he had a secret weapon far more powerful than anything Saul possessed: David had the ear of Yahweh. Both David and Saul had a network of informers, so that Saul quickly learned of David's new residence in Keilah, and David soon heard about Saul's plan to besiege the town and effect David's capture (vv. 7-9a). The difference between Saul and David is reflected in their responses to the respective news. Saul summoned his army to war, while David summoned Abiathar and his oracle-producing ephod.

A further contrast between David and Saul is seen in their vocabulary choices. Upon learning that David was bottled up in the city of Keilah, Saul remarked that "*God* has given him into my hand." Saul's choice of the more impersonal name "God" (*ʾĕlōhîm*) hints at his growing isolation from the Deity, while David's habitual use of the personal name "Yahweh" augments the portrait of a man who is so close to God that they talk on a regular basis.

David asked two questions of Yahweh, both of which could be answered with a "yes" or "no," a required format when seeking divine guidance through casting the sacred lots. He learned not only that Saul was indeed planning to attack, but also that the elders of Keilah would turn him over to Saul rather than jeopardize their city by defending him (vv. 9b-12).

The narrator's comment that David and his band left Keilah and "wandered wherever they could go" really implies that they went wherever they chose. Literally, the phrase means "they went about where they went about" (v. 13), though v. 14 relates that they remained in various wilderness strongholds in the "wilderness of Ziph." [The Wilderness of Ziph]

The Wilderness of Ziph

Ziph was a city in Judah, listed in Josh 15:55. Today Tell Ziph lies about thirteen miles southeast of Keilah and about five miles southeast of Hebron. Presumably, the "wilderness of Ziph" describes the rugged hills and valleys surrounding the city, which were wooded in ancient times but became barren. During the 20th century, massive reforestation projects have returned trees to many such places in Israel.

The heart of vv. 1-14 is found in the final verse. Though Saul gave up the expedition against Keilah, he continued to seek David "every day," but without success, because "the LORD did not give him into his hand." By giving this theological interpretation to David's continued escapes, the narrator leads the reader to expect more of the same. Saul has no hope of capturing David unless Yahweh gives him up. Saul expects the LORD to deliver David to him (note the vocabulary of v. 7), but unlike the elders of Keilah, that is not something Yahweh intends to do.

From Ziph to Maon and a Close Call, 23:15-28

After escaping Saul's trap at Keilah, David took his men deeper into the desert, where ancient Ziph sat high on a ridge overlooking the bleak wilderness some twelve miles southeast of Keilah, about five miles south of Hebron. David's flight from Saul was interrupted by a visit from Saul's son, who seemed to have no trouble locating and approaching the fugitive camp. The narrator uses Jonathan's visit as another pointer to David's future enthronement. Jonathan seeks not to harm David (as does his father), but to bless him. In a summary description of Jonathan's positive effect on David, the writer tells us that "he strengthened his hand through the LORD" (v. 16b). [Give Him a Hand!] This common idiom could be used to convey the idea of encouraging words or actual support (Judg 9:24; Isa 35:3; Jer 23:14; Ezek 13:22; Neh 6:9).

Jonathan's speech sounds like an "oracle of salvation" that typically would be pronounced by a priest, beginning with "Be not afraid" and moving to specific reasons why David had no cause to fear. Jonathan was confident that Saul would not find David. He spoke with confidence of David's future enthronement, framing his support for David in the offer to serve as David's second in command, even though he would normally be first in line for the

Give Him a Hand!

AΩ In Hebrew, the word "hand" (*yād*) could be used in a variety of metaphorical expressions. The author(s) of the Deuteronomistic History made frequent use of the term, but it is especially evident in chs. 23–24, where it functions as a unifying leitmotif. In 23:4, David learned from an oracle that Yahweh would deliver the Philistines near Keilah into his *hand*, just before the reader learns that the priest Abiathar had arrived to join David, with an oracle-producing ephod in his *hand* (23:6). Saul mistakenly thought God had delivered David into his *hand* at Keilah (23:7), and David inquired of God twice to ascertain whether the elders of Keilah would deliver him into Saul's *hand* (23:7, 11). After failing to capture David at Keilah, Saul continued to seek David, but the narrator pointedly reveals that Yahweh did not deliver him into Saul's *hand* (23:14).

Jonathan's arrival served to "strengthen his [David's] *hand* in the LORD"—that is, to encourage David (23:16), as Jonathan assured his friend that the *hand* of Saul would not find David (23:17). In contrast, the Ziphites offered to deliver David into the king's *hand* (23:20), but were unable to fulfill their promise.

The scene shifts in ch. 24, where David has a perfect opportunity to dispatch his tormentor. David's men insist that Yahweh has delivered Saul into David's *hand* (24:4), but David refuses to "stretch out his *hand*" against the LORD's anointed (24:6), choosing only to cut off a corner of Saul's robe. This prediction is played out in 24:10-11, where Yahweh delivered Saul into David's *hand*, but David refused to stretch out his *hand* against Saul, and declared this to Saul by pointing to the severed fabric from the royal robe that was in his *hand*. Twice, David declares that he is no threat to Saul, that "my *hand* will not be against you" (24:12-13). David prays that Yahweh will continue to deliver him from Saul's *hand* (24:15).

Finally, Saul himself acknowledges that Yahweh had indeed delivered him into David's *hand* (24:18) and that the kingdom would ultimately be established in David's *hand* (24:20). Through this long-running play on words, skillfully interlaced throughout the account of the conflict between David and Saul, the writer makes it certain that the hand of Yahweh is *with* David and *against* Saul, clearly leaving David with the *upper hand* in the conflict.

throne (cf. Jonathan's plea in 20:14-17; the expression for "second" can also be found in Esth 10:3 and 2 Chr 28:7). The surprising news—soon to be confirmed in 24:16-22—is Jonathan's contention that Saul also knows the truth of David's destiny.

For the third time, Jonathan and David entered into a covenant together (v. 18; cf. 18:3 and 20:8). In each case the initiative appeared to lie with Jonathan, but David freely and gladly embraced the bond offered by his friend. With Jonathan's departure, leaving David in Horesh, the narrator effectively resumes the main course of the story.

David would eventually build a strong base of support in Judah, but it did not come easily. The residents of Keilah had been ready to turn David over to Saul, despite the fact that he had delivered them from Philistine domination. Likewise, certain Ziphites found it expedient to report David's whereabouts to the king, even though they had to travel all the way to Gibeah to do it. Perhaps the Ziphites were afraid that Saul would punish them for appearing to shelter David if they did not report him. Word of the massacre at Nob had probably spread throughout Judah, making it clear that even those who innocently abetted David's effort could be subject to the severest of penalties.

An Ironic Blessing

There is some irony in Saul's blessing of the Ziphites for "showing him compassion" by offering to assist him. As residents of Judah, the Ziphites were not of Saul's tribe, yet they supported him. In the previous chapter, Saul had criticized his own people of Benjamin for failing to feel sorry for him—or, if we accept a commonly proposed textual emendation, showing a lack of compassion for him.

Keeping in mind that David's army was made up of outlaws, it is also possible that the residents of Ziph were simply uncomfortable with the presence of such a rough gang in their territory. An army of 600 men would need constant provisions, and the scattered villages of southern Judah would be tempting targets for extortion or plunder. It is no wonder, then, that the Ziphites offered to lead Saul to his prey.

The locations of "the hill of Hachilah" and "Jeshimon" are unknown, though their apparent proximity to Maon (v. 24) suggests that they were simply further south and east of Hebron. Maon can probably be identified with Tell Ma'in, which occupied a strong position atop a tall hill about eight miles southeast of Hebron. Since Hachilah and Jeshimon are also mentioned in the introduction to a very similar story beginning in 26:1, several scholars have suggested that 23:21b is interpolated from the later story as an expanded duplicate.[1]

The verbal interchange in vv. 20-23 is illuminating. Saul had been embarrassed when David slipped from his grasp when he thought the renegade was bottled up at Keilah. Now that David was in the open country, Saul was even more concerned that his intelligence be accurate. So he accepted the Ziphites' offer with a bit of skepticism, though he blessed them for offering to surrender his enemy (v. 22). [An Ironic Blessing]

Saul's command to find out where David is and "who has seen him there" (NRSV) is emended by some scholars to read "where his fleet foot is" (the Hebrew for "who saw him" is very similar to the word for "swift"). Saul wanted to know precisely where David was hiding (v. 23), lest he be embarrassed again. The narrator's focus on Saul's self-concern seems to be intentional, as it sets him up for even greater humiliation when David again escapes.

Saul's decision to follow the Ziphites despite his doubts is evident in that they went "ahead of Saul" (v. 24). Technically, "the Arabah" describes the depression of the Jordan Rift Valley, from the southern tip of the Sea of Galilee all the way through the region of the Dead Sea and down to the Gulf of Aqaba. [The Arabah] David's position near Maon, in the Arabah, positions him to the east of the city, on the craggy slope leading down to the Dead Sea near En-gedi. It was (and is) a rugged, desolate area.

The narrative focuses on a certain unnamed crag ("rock," v. 25) to which David had retreated, with Saul in hot pursuit. As David and his men hurried down the far side of the craggy mountain,

Saul reached the near side and sent his soldiers to circle the mountain and cut off David's retreat with a strategic pincers movement. It seemed that Saul's larger and better-equipped army would finally be successful in apprehending David, and the narrator suggests that Saul would indeed have caught his enemy—if not for an urgent message that forced Saul to call off the chase. The Philistines were raiding the land, and Saul, who had not forgotten his duty as king, turned his army about and led it into battle with the Philistines.

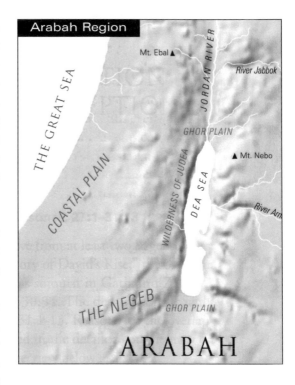

David had escaped once again, but the fact that Saul was forced to turn away from the chase reveals just how much effort the king was expending on his fruitless quest to capture his nemesis. Apparently, Saul was using most of his army to hunt down David, leaving insufficient troops to man the outposts and defend the territories from Israel's real enemies. For David, the seemingly providential message that led to his close escape affirmed once again that the hand of Yahweh was upon him and that Yahweh had no intention of handing him over to Saul. Saul might come close, but with God's protecting hand upon him, David would always manage to slip away. [Slippery Rock]

The MT brings the chapter to a close with 23:28, suggesting that 23:29 (MT 24:1) was thought to begin a new textual unit. The note that David traveled on to En-gedi and hid out there serves as a fitting close to the previous pericope, however, and is presupposed by the following story of how David turned the tables on Saul but chose to spare his life.

Slippery Rock

AΩ The etiology of v. 28 has given rise to much discussion. *Selaʿ hammaḥlēqôt* can be interpreted in two ways, for the root verb *ḥālaq* can mean either "to divide" or "to be slippery." Thus, it may be rendered "Crag of Division," suggesting the place where Saul departed from David, or it could be translated as "Crag of Slipperiness" (or even "Slippery Rock"), indicating the way David slipped from Saul's clutches.

A Confrontation at En-gedi, 24:1-22

The encounter between David and Saul at En-gedi (24:1-22) is so similar to the later confrontation in the Wilderness of Ziph (26:1-25) that many critics assume they are two versions of the same

1 Samuel 24:2-7—This Carolsfeld woodcut imagines that Saul was asleep when David crept up on him in the cave. The euphemism "to cover his feet" probably means that Saul had chosen the cave as a private toilet.

Julius Schnoor von Carolsfeld. *David Spares Saul's Life.* 19th century. Woodcut. *Das Buch der Bucher in Bilden.* (Credit: Dover Pictorial Archive Series)

story. For the most part, older source critics (plus some modern scholars, such as Kyle McCarter) imagine 24:1-22 to be a later version of 26:1-25, with revisions intended to make the story more clearly tendentious—David's piety and innocence are much more noticeable in 24:1-22. More recent writers tend to think of two alternate accounts of the same event, preserved in differing streams of tradition.

There are in fact many parallels between the two stories, but also significant differences. [Two Similar Stories] In both stories, Saul was pursuing David in the wilderness when the tables were turned and David had an opportunity to take the measure of Saul. David's companions insisted that Yahweh had delivered Saul into David's hand, but David refused to harm the LORD's anointed. Even so, David appropriated a bit of evidence to prove that he could have killed Saul, leading the king to recognize David's innocence and supremacy.

Yet the first story takes place in a cave, while the second occurs in an open encampment. In the first story, Saul ignominiously falls into David's hands by chance, while in the second, David makes a daring foray into Saul's camp. In the first account, only David and

Two Similar Stories

The following table illustrates some of the more obvious similarities and differences between the two accounts (with acknowledgement to Ralph Klein's helpful comparison, *1 Samuel* [WBC 10; Waco: Word Books, 1983], 236-237, which served as the starting point for this expanded table). Italics are used to indicate differences of detail in places where the story structure is very similar:

1 Samuel 24:1-22	1 Samuel 26:1-25
Unnamed informers reported David's position to Saul. (v. 1)	Certain *Ziphites* reported David's position to Saul. (v. 1; cf. 23:14-19)
Saul's pursuit team included 3,000 select men from all Israel. (v. 2)	Saul's pursuit team included 3,000 select men of Israel. (v. 2)
Saul *came to the sheepfolds* beside the road. (v. 3; also v. 7)	Saul *camped* beside the road. (v. 3)
David and company were sitting in the *cave*. (v. 3)	David and company were sitting in the *desert*. (v. 3)
David's men insisted that *Yahweh* was providing an opportunity to kill Saul. (v. 4)	*Abishai* argued that *God* was providing an opportunity to kill Saul. (v. 8)
David cut off a corner of Saul's cloak. (v. 4)	David took Saul's spear and water jar. (v. 12)
David swore, "The LORD forbid that I should *do this thing to my lord, the LORD's anointed, to* raise my hand against *him, for he is* the LORD's anointed." (v. 6)	David swore, "The LORD forbid that I should raise my hand against the LORD's anointed." (v. 11; cf. v. 23)
David called Saul "my lord." (vv. 6, 8, 10)	David called Saul "my lord." (vv. 17, 18, 19)
David called Saul "the LORD's anointed" (vv. 6 [twice], 10)	David called Saul "the LORD's anointed" (vv. 9, 11, 16, 23)
After taking evidence to prove he could have killed the king, David called out to *Saul*. (v. 8)	After taking evidence to prove he could have killed the king, David called out to *Abner*. (v. 14)
David *asked why* Saul listens to *men* who turn him against David. (v. 9)	David *suggested* that *mortals* have stirred Saul up against him. (v. 19)
David claimed that "the LORD gave you into my hand." (v. 10; cf. v. 4)	David claimed that "the LORD gave you into my hand." (v. 23)
David insisted on his innocence "today." (vv. 10, 18, 19)	David insisted on his innocence "today." (vv. 8, 19, 21, 23, 24)
David demonstrated his innocence by showing Saul *a piece of his robe*. (v. 11)	David demonstrated his innocence by showing Saul *his spear and water jar*. (v. 16)
David *protested*, "There is no *wrong or treason* in my hands." (v. 11)	David *asked*, "What *guilt* is on my hands?" (v. 18)
David insisted that *he did not sin*. (v. 11)	*Saul* admitted that *he did sin*. (v. 21)
David claimed that Saul, the king of Israel (v. 15), was hunting him *to take his life*. (v. 11)	David said the king of Israel had come out to hunt him *like a single flea, like one who hunts a partridge in the mountains*. (v. 20)
David asked, "*Whom* do you pursue?" (v. 14)	David asked, "*Why* does my lord pursue *his servant*?" (v. 18)
Saul asked, "Is this your voice, my son David?" (v. 16)	Saul asked, "Is this your voice, my son David?" (v. 17; cf. vv. 21, 25)
Saul said, "You are more righteous than I" (v. 17), and "May the LORD reward you with good." (v. 19)	*Saul* said, "I have done wrong. . . . I have been a fool, and have made a great mistake" (v. 21). *David* said, "The LORD rewards everyone for his righteousness and his faithfulness" (v. 23).
Saul confessed, "You shall surely *be king*." (v. 20)	Saul confessed, "You will *do many things and will succeed in them*." (v. 25)
David and Saul go their different ways. (v. 22)	David and Saul go their different ways. (v. 25)

Cliffs and Caves
The desolate cliffs lining the western edge of the Dead Sea contain many caves, including these near Qumran.
(Credit: Tony W. Cartledge)

Saul are mentioned by name, and David confronts Saul directly. The second account speaks of Ahimelech the Hittite and Abishai the brother of Joab as David's companions, while Abner, son of Ner, is identified as the commander of Saul's army. When David acquires evidence to prove his mastery in chapter 26, he first confronts Abner, not Saul, and taunts the Israelite general (who has failed to protect his king) before speaking to Saul.

Whether one chooses to regard these two stories as separate events or as differing versions of the same encounter, their placement in the text functions with the surrounding material to magnify the role of David as God's true anointed while discrediting the inept Saul, to whom David ironically and frequently defers as the LORD's anointed.

The western shore of the Dead Sea was home to several spring-fed oases, of which En-gedi was the most important. Lying just below the steep limestone cliffs leading into the Judean wilderness, En-gedi was roughly eighteen miles east and slightly south of Hebron, about the same distance from and slightly north of Maon. As an oasis, it provided a refuge for humans and animals alike, including the ibexes, who lent their name to a nearby area called "The Wild Goat Rocks."

The rugged cliffs above En-gedi, like those further north near Qumran, were pock-marked with caves, some of which must have been massive. [Cliffs and Caves] It was in one of these caves that David and his 600 men were hiding when Saul came in pursuit with 3,000 men (or three contingents of men; see [Counting Soldiers]). According to the text, it just so happened that Saul felt the call of nature as he was passing a sheepfold that lay beneath (and possibly connected to) David's hideaway. Seeking privacy, Saul made his way into the cave to relieve himself by defecating (expressed in Hebrew by the euphemistic idiom "to cover his feet").

With Saul in this ignoble stance, David was given the perfect chance to eliminate his persecutor. Certain aspects of the story seem to stretch credulity, however. Could David and his men carry on even a whispered conversation in the echoing cavern without Saul's hearing them? Could David *really* sneak up and slice off a piece of Saul's robe without rousing the king's awareness? Yet this is the way the story is told. Perhaps we are to imagine that Saul cast aside his heavy outer robe before assuming the position, facilitating David's clandestine cutting of a corner from the cloak.

The focus of the story, however, is not on the action so much as the dialogue. David's men argued that Saul's defenseless presence was the fulfillment of a divine promise, though we know nothing more about the purported "day of which the LORD said to you, 'I will give your enemy into your hand' " (v. 4). David chose to cut only Saul's robe, not his throat, and was conscience-stricken even at that (v. 5). The apparent piety of David's insistence that he could not lift a hand against the LORD's anointed (v. 6) should be weighed against the knowledge that David also was anointed of Yahweh (16:1-13), and he did not wish to establish a precedent. Later, David would take strong measures against those who harmed the LORD's anointed (2 Sam 1:14, 16).

The forceful way in which David verbally brought his men into line is apparent, though the translation is uncertain. The word preserved in the MT means "tore to pieces," which would be severe even for a metaphor, leading scholars to propose various emendations, all of them unsatisfactory. Whether David "scolded his men severely" or "restrained his men with words,"[2] he succeeded in preventing them from doing harm to the king. The effort required to bridle David's men reminds the reader that they were also no friends of the king and his imperial policies (22:2).

David's emergence from the cave to confront Saul publicly was a moment of high and risky drama, unless there was a back way out of the cave through which his men could escape. The narrator suggests that David knew his enemy well enough to know that Saul would be shamed into withdrawing, at least temporarily. David demonstrated his fealty by carefully referring to Saul as "my lord the king" and by bowing down before him (v. 8). To this point, the narrator has portrayed Saul's dogged determination to capture David as an entirely personal vendetta, but David offered a way for the king to withdraw with honor by suggesting that Saul had been misled by his advisors (v. 9).

David's presentation of the clear evidence that he could have taken the king's life strikes Saul like a thunderbolt. As the narrator tells it, David used the tension-filled event to prove his loyalty to Saul: "that you may know for certain that there is no wrong or treason in my hands. I have not sinned against you, though you are hunting me to take my life" (vv. 11b-12). Plaintively, David calls Saul "my father," perhaps suggesting the former closeness of their relationship when David had served as personal musician and assistant to the king (16:21).

David's speech is carefully calculated. He calls on the wisdom of the ages by citing a traditional proverb, "Out of the wicked comes forth wickedness," using it to demonstrate that he is *not* wicked, for he did not harm Saul even though he had the chance. David insists that he is not only blameless, but undeserving of such an expenditure of the king's energy and resources. In a surprising self-deprecation, David insists that he is as insignificant as a single flea on a dead dog (v. 14). [Dead Dogs and Fleas] For the king to devote such energy to his destruction is shameful. Twice, David appeals to Yahweh for vindication before Saul (vv. 12, 15), reminding the king that there are spiritual dimensions to their conflict, not only political ones.

In his disconcerted response, Saul—for the moment, at least—exonerates David completely and accepts full responsibility for misjudging him. He calls David "my son" and weeps as if he has found a long lost child (v. 16). Picking up on David's righteous/wicked terminology (vv. 11, 13), Saul acknowledges David's superior righteousness, for David could have repaid the king evil for evil but chose to respond with good by withholding his hand (vv. 17-18). Saul is so impressed by David's gracious and

Dead Dogs and Fleas

In ancient Israel, dogs carried a decidedly negative connotation. There is little evidence that dogs were kept as pets by the Israelites, though ritual burials of dogs have been documented among the Philistines. Perhaps the Israelites' antipathy for dogs arose from their experience in Egypt, where Anubis was worshiped in the form of a jackal-headed god. Wild dogs were much like modern hyenas, dangerous scavengers who inspired little affection.

Comparison of oneself to a dead dog was a common form of self-abasement. For example, when David later showed kindness to Jonathan's crippled son Mephibosheth, the grateful man responded, "What is your servant, that you should look upon a dead dog such as I?" (2 Sam 9:8; cf. 2 Kgs 8:13).

Israel's neighbors shared the same expression, for the use of "dead dog" as a disparaging term also occurs in various Akkadian letters and other inscriptions from ancient literature (for samples, see [Dead Dogs in Literature] at the commentary on 2 Sam 9:8).

---

unexpected act (v. 19) that he declares David to be truly royal material, destined to become king (v. 20).

As the narrator tells it, Saul is so humbled before the ascendant David that he is reduced to pleading for mercy for his descendants when David inevitably takes the throne (v. 21), much as Jonathan had done previously (20:14-16). As he had done for Jonathan (20:17), David swore to protect Saul's descendants (v. 22).

The reader has some cause to expect the conflict to be over, as Saul and David departed in peace. Saul returned to Gibeah, and David took his men "up to the stronghold," presumably Adullam. Yet the chase will resume, for the account in 26:1-25, however similar, is presented as yet another chapter in the Saul/David conflict. Earlier accounts have already demonstrated Saul's mental instability, for the king could love David one moment and try to skewer him in the next (18:10-11; 19:9-10). Thus, the reader is not surprised when Saul later returns to his deadly pursuit.

CONNECTIONS

Lessons from Keilah, 23:1-14

David's experience at Keilah asserts *the importance of trusting in God*, rather than in persons—even those who have every reason to show us kindness! The narrator takes great pains to focus on David's habit of consulting Yahweh before making important decisions. When word was brought to him that the Philistines were harassing the people of Keilah, David was motivated to take action, but in some unnamed manner he sought divine guidance—not once, but twice (vv. 2, 4)—before venturing out.

After ridding Keilah of the Philistine threat, David and his men sought succor from the city but soon learned that Saul had hopes of entrapping them there. Again, David sought divine guidance, this time by consulting with Abiathar, who had custody of the oracle-producing ephod (vv. 9-12). Upon learning that the Keilahites would gladly surrender him to Saul, and with the news of what happened at Nob still fresh in his mind, David departed from Keilah and saved its residents the unpleasant task of betraying him.

David had reason to expect that the people of Keilah would defend him as their deliverer, but their fear of Saul was greater than their gratitude to David. The people of our own world are no different from the residents of Keilah. Some people are so selfish that they seem entirely unacquainted with gratitude. Even when we wish to be loyal and trustworthy, we are often weak, afraid, or simply limited in our ability to help. As David learned, when all is said and done, our only dependable source of strength and guidance is found in God. Those who are wise will place their trust accordingly. [In God We Trust]

David's experience at Keilah also underscores *the importance of listening to God* when God speaks. Divine revelation has a purpose,

---

In God We Trust

The prophet Jeremiah, like David, demonstrated an intense trust in God. This remarkable poem (similar to Ps 1) expresses an awareness that the wise learn to put their trust in God rather than in other persons—even when that person is oneself:

Thus says the LORD:
Cursed are those who trust in mere mortals
    and make mere flesh their strength,
    whose hearts turn away from the LORD.
They shall be like a shrub in the desert,
    and shall not see when relief comes.
They shall live in the parched places of the wilderness,
    in an uninhabited salt land.

Blessed are those who trust in the LORD,
    whose trust is the LORD.
They shall be like a tree planted by water,
    sending out its roots by the stream.
It shall not fear when heat comes,
    and its leaves shall stay green;
in the year of drought it is not anxious,
    and it does not cease to bear fruit. (Jer 17:5-8)

whether it is made known through the casting of the priestly lots, the inner quickening of the heart, or the living words of the Scriptures. It was not enough for David to seek divine guidance— it was equally important that he act in accordance with God's revelation. Suppose David had heard the LORD's call to go out against the Philistines, but refused? Such behavior would certainly be reprehensible. Today's faith community would do well to look at the many ways in which the Philistines continue to badger the innocent. In modern English, the word "Philistine" conventionally describes a reprobate person. Drug-pushers steal the lives of men, women, and children every day. The beer and liquor industries bombard us through the media with a pounding message that drinking alcohol is the key to happiness and acceptance. The purveyors of pornography profit daily from the shameless exploitation of men and women. The gambling industry fattens itself on the broken hearts and dreams of men and women who become addicted to gambling, whose children pay dearly. Such realities announce that the Philistines continue to attack. Is there not enough revelation already available to make it clear that God's people are called to oppose those who bring such harm to others? Should this impact believers' behavior?

Another important truth underlies the narrator's treatment of David's experience at Keilah: No matter what we may think, *God is ultimately in control.* Furthermore, we must be careful what purposes and motivations we ascribe to God. Saul presumed that God had delivered David into his hand at Keilah (23:7), but "the LORD did not give him into his hand" (23:14). Perhaps the narrator intends to show the growing distance between Saul and the LORD, for he has Saul use the generic attribution "God" (*'ĕlōhîm*), while David consistently employs the personal name "Yahweh." It is not at all unusual for people to stridently proclaim competing versions of what they perceive to be God's will, reminding us of the danger of daring to speak for God. We are called to be perceptive in our search for divine guidance and always humbly aware that we may be wrong. The mind of God is not easily penetrable, and it is God, after all, who is in control.

Lessons from Maon, 23:15-28

The account of David's flight from the Wilderness of Ziph to the Wilderness of Maon is punctuated by a dramatic and unexpected visit from Saul's son Jonathan, who could get through to David when his father could not. Jonathan came for a single purpose: to *encourage* his friend by expressing his confidence that Saul would fail in his quest to capture David and that David would indeed become king. The summary statement describing Jonathan's visit is couched in language that emphasizes the faith in God shared by David and Jonathan alike: Jonathan "strengthened [David's] hand through the LORD" (v. 16). David is often portrayed as a man larger than life, a man who rises above others, but he was never a man who did not need others. David needed Jonathan's friendship to encourage and strengthen him in a time of great stress and potential disillusionment. [Two Are Better Than One] As a perceptive friend, Jonathan provided the support David needed.

This element of David's flight, culminating in his near-capture at "Slippery Rock," revealed a serious flaw in Saul's management of both his personal life and the country. Saul had committed so much of his time and so many of his soldiers to chasing David that he had left the borders untended and his people unprotected. When the Philistines attacked, he was forced to turn from the chase and confront the Philistines with soldiers who were already fatigued and frustrated by long and fruitless travel. While the reader presumes that Saul successfully repelled the Philistine incursion, the text says nothing about it. This is significant because of the strong way in which *David's* victory over the Philistines at Keilah had been presented: He "dealt them a heavy defeat" (23:5).

Thus, the narrator subtly stresses David's superiority over Saul by the way in which the two men managed their resources. David habitually sought divine leadership and made decisions accordingly, spending his army's energy only when necessary. In contrast, Saul mismanaged his much larger army by sending them scurrying through the wilderness in search of David, rather than stationing them strategically to protect the populace.

Every person has a limited budget of time, energy, and resources. How do we spend it? Do we waste precious hours on vapid, mind-numbing "entertainment" before the television set? Do we spend

---

Two Are Better Than One

The importance of supporting others (and being supported) is also illustrated by two well-known proverbs. "Iron sharpens iron, and one person sharpens the wits of another," says Prov 27:17. "Wits" is used by the NRSV to translate the Hebrew word "face," but it leaves something to be desired. The mutual interaction of two caring persons sharpens more than their wits—it hones all the edges of life.

A proverb found in Ecclesiastes contributes a similar thought. Expressing a traditional truth at least as old as the Babylonian *Epic of Gilgamesh*, "Two are better than one because they have a good reward for their toil. For if they fall, one will lift up the other; but woe to one who is alone and falls and does not have another to help. Again, if two lie together, they keep warm; but how can one keep warm alone? And though one might prevail against another, two will withstand one" (Eccl 4:9-12a).

S. N. Kramer, JCS 1 (1947): 17, ll. 106-108; see also Jeffrey Tigay's discussion in *The Evolution of the Gilgamesh Epic* (Philadelphia: University of Pennsylvania Press, 1982), 165-67

limited resources on unneeded luxuries or harmful habits? Do we neglect our families and our neighbors because we have expended so much time and energy on selfish pursuits? Saul's failure revealed inner flaws in his character and commitment. Those who are wise will seek constantly to grow in their skills for managing time, talents, and treasure.

Lessons from En-gedi, 24:1-22

The encounter between David and Saul in the caves of En-gedi offers several lessons for life. The first has to do with *recognizing opportunity.* Every day is filled with many opportunities to do good or evil. When Saul unwittingly fell into David's hands, he was totally vulnerable. David's friends saw this as the perfect opportunity to dispatch their nemesis and make a bid for the throne. David may have been tempted to agree, but he was more concerned with doing what was right than with achieving power by ill-gotten means. David used the opportunity to do something good by proving his innocence to Saul, leading the abashed king himself to proclaim the certainty of David's future rule. The kingdom would indeed be "established in David's hand" (v. 20), but at the proper time and in the proper way.

Jesus would face similar issues in his own ministry. His disciples urged him to take advantage of various opportunities to rally support from the populace, defeat the Romans, and lead Israel to establish a new and powerful kingdom. Jesus fully intended to establish a kingdom, but the realm he envisioned would be something far greater than any earthly empire. It would be established in the proper way, at the proper time. Jesus' disciples could not understand how Jesus could establish an eternal kingdom through his own suffering and death, nor could they understand why he would not reveal to them the time of its final manifestation. Jesus called his followers to trust him and have faith. His call to contemporary disciples has not changed.

Another lesson grows from the contrasting *choices of good or evil.* David's deliberate decision to repay Saul's evil with good was something so unusual that Saul declared, "For who has ever found an enemy, and sent the enemy safely away?" (v. 19). Saul recognized that he had repaid David's good and faithful service with evil, while David had continued to respond with goodness, despite Saul's harmful treatment (v. 17). The narrator thus upholds good as superior to evil and a person who pursues good as more noble than one who goes after what is evil, even when there seems to be just cause.

David's legacy of repaying evil with good is one reason why it was appropriate that Jesus be known as a descendant of David. Yet David did not always remain true to his convictions. There were times when he even repaid the goodness of others with evil of his own (for example, Uriah the Hittite in the Bathsheba incident, 2 Sam 11–12). In contrast, Jesus demonstrated goodness beyond any previous human measure. He withstood evil, not with evil of his own, but with goodness—even when it led to his suffering and death. Jesus taught his followers to do the same (Matt 5:43-48). Loving our enemies is no easier now than it was in the ancient world, but our calling remains constant. [Love Your Enemies] It is not our place to take vengeance on those who harm us. Rather, both vindication and vengeance belong in the hands of God (vv. 12, 15).

The culmination of the En-gedi encounter leaves the impression that all is calm, but the reader soon learns that the apparent peace will not last. Despite his public deference to David, Saul would soon be on the trail again. We can learn, like David, *never to rest on our laurels* or on the seemingly serene appearance of things. Trouble always lurks beneath the surface of life like an alligator waiting to strike its unwitting prey. We never know when a friend may turn away, when a quiet enemy may attack, when someone's feelings may unexpectedly be hurt, when tragedy may rear its ugly head

---

Love Your Enemies

Within the culture that spawned the Hebrew Bible, vengeance was not only accepted, but applauded. As criminal action disrupted the social order, retribution was necessary to restore moral balance and set things right. Actions that called for vengeance could be as minor as a personal insult (1 Sam 25:39), or as serious as murder (Gen 4:15) or defeat at the hands of one's enemies (Ezek 25:14). When a death was involved, the closest male relative was obliged to become an "avenger of blood" and to take vengeance by pursuing and killing the one who had caused the death. This custom was so common that ancient Israel established several cities of refuge in which persons could find asylum from the kinsman's vendetta while appealing their innocence (Num 35:9-28; Deut 19:4-13; Josh 20:1-9; 2 Sam 14:11). Blood vengeance was so common that the psalmists routinely prayed for God to take vengeance upon their enemies (Pss 58:10; 94:1; 149:7).

Since vengeance was so ingrained in the ancient mindset, Jesus' contemporaries were shocked and amazed at his radical contention that one should return good for evil by loving one's enemies:

You have heard that it was said, "You shall love your neighbor and hate your enemy." But I say to you, Love your enemies and pray for those who persecute you, so that you may be children of your Father in heaven; for he makes his sun rise on the evil and on the good, and sends rain on the righteous and on the unrighteous. For if you love those who love you, what reward do you have? Do not even the tax collectors do the same? And if you greet only your brothers and sister, what more are you doing than others? Do not even the Gentiles do the same? Be perfect, therefore, as your heavenly Father is perfect (Matt 5:43-48).

In Jesus' teaching, vengeance was not the responsibility of blood kin, but of God. As Jesus demonstrated love and forgiveness to all persons, so his followers were to show kindness and love toward others, even those who had wronged them. Only in this way could they truly demonstrate love that was unselfishly motivated.

For further reading, see Bruce Dahlberg, "Vengeance/Avenger," MDB (Macon GA: Mercer University Press, 1990), 947-48; Moshe Greenberg, "Avenger of Blood," (*IDB*, 4 vols.; New York: Abingdon, 1962), 4:321.

with no warning or explanation. This is not to say that we should be mistrustful of others or pessimistic about life—but it does suggest that we have appropriate expectations. When we learn to expect trouble, we are less likely to be surprised and better equipped to deal with the consequences. This is a part of what it means to practice humility in living. According to an ancient proverb, "Pride goes before destruction, and a haughty spirit before a fall" (Prov 16:18). Those who are humble also learn to be nimble.

NOTES

[1] P. Kyle McCarter, *I Samuel* (AB 8; Garden City: Doubleday, 1980), 379.

[2] Ibid.

NABAL'S FOLLY
AND DAVID'S PRIZE

25:1-44

COMMENTARY

Samuel's Death, 25:1

The Saul/David conflict is interrupted in 25:1 with a surprisingly simple note that Samuel had died. Samuel was one of the great figures of Israelite history, acting as priest, prophet, and judge in Israel. He was a maker and a breaker of kings, an extremely powerful personage. Yet the account of his death is limited to this: "Now Samuel died; and all Israel assembled and mourned for him. They buried him at his home in Ramah."

Despite its unpretentious austerity, the text does speak of the near-universal respect Israel had for Samuel. "*All Israel* assembled and mourned for him." The mourning could have lasted for some time, involving many ceremonies. They are beside the point for the narrator, however, who simply wants the reader to know that Samuel is dead in order to set the stage for Saul's later appeal to Samuel's shade (28:3-25). The notice is repeated in 28:3 but presented as something that happened in the past. The interlude serves one other function, however: it illustrates the momentary peace that existed between Saul and David. Saul undoubtedly would have presided over some aspects of the national mourning for Samuel. If David also attended the ceremonies, as the text implies, there is no hint of trouble. Outward animosity was suspended out of respect for the deceased leader.

David's activity *after* the funeral is a bit unclear. The MT says he went down to the "wilderness of Paran," which describes the southern extremity of the Arabah, a location that seems much too far south. One of the better versions of the Septuagint (LXXB) has "Maon" and another (LXXL) has "Yeshimon," as does the Syriac version. In any case, David's further activities in chapter 25 do not take place in Paran, but in the area surrounding Maon.

David's New Wife, 25:2-42

The story of David's encounter with Nabal and Abigail is sandwiched between the two parallel accounts in which the future king has the opportunity to kill Saul, but chooses to render him good rather than evil. In the Nabal episode, David also comes close to shedding blood, though in this instance he is restrained not by his inner aversion to harming the king's anointed, but by the persuasive words of Nabal's charming wife. Thus, the three episodes share a common theme illustrating how the future king must be saved from himself in order to become the wise and just man who is fit to rule.

Nabal's story begins much as 1 Samuel began: "There was a certain man" (v. 2; cf. 1:1). [The Foolish Fool] This style of narration introduces the character before revealing his name, which in this case is necessary to present a properly impressive picture of the powerful Nabal before revealing what a fool he is. The man lived in Maon, a city in the wilderness area of southern Judah that has already figured into David's story (23:24-25). The bulk of Nabal's property was in the vicinity of Carmel, a smaller village about one mile north of Maon. [Carmel]

The narrator reveals that the man was *very rich*, a fact that will become of strategic importance later. His wealth was measured by the size of his flocks: 3,000 sheep and 1,000 goats (compare the description of Job's wealth in Job 1:3). The story also relates that the man was occupied with the difficult but festive occasion of shearing his sheep before finally stating his name, almost as a parenthesis: "Now the name of the man was Nabal, and the name of his wife Abigail." The Hebrew reader would quickly discern the nature of these two characters, for *nābāl* means "fool" or "foolish," especially in a moral or religious sense, while *ʾăbîgayil* means "my father rejoices." Some scholars speculate that no one would really name their child "Fool," so they assume that the man's real name has been shuffled to the background, or else they postulate other, more noble meanings for "Nabal."

The Foolish Fool

📖 In a sense, Nabal serves as a counterpart to Saul: a gruff man who does foolish things and who shows no kindness to David. As J. D. Levinson has shown, however, Nabal and Abigail also appear as the prototypical "foolish man" and "wise woman" of Israel's wisdom tradition. The text portrays Abigail as both "clever and beautiful," while Nabal was "surly and mean" (v. 3). The narrator even has Abigail describe her own husband by saying, "As his name is, so is he; Nabal [Fool] is his name, and folly is with him" (25:25; cf. Isa 32:6).

"1 Samuel 25 as Literature and as History," CBQ 40 (1978): 11-28; "1 Samuel 25 as Literature and History," *Literary Interpretations of Biblical Narratives*, vol. 2, ed. K. R. R. Gros Louis (Nashville: Abingdon, 1982), 220-42; and B. Halpern, "The Political Import of David's Marriages," JBL 99 (1980): 507-18.

Carmel

🏛 For most Bible students, the name Carmel calls to mind the famous mountain by the Mediterranean Sea that stands at the entrance to the Valley of Jezreel, leading into the heartland of Israel. This site, however, is an entirely different location, far to the north of Maon. The Carmel of 1 Sam 25:2 was a small village in southern Judah, about one mile north of Maon and seven miles south of Hebron. First mentioned in Josh 15:55, Carmel was also where Saul had erected a monument to celebrate his victory over the Amalekites (1 Sam 15:12). Modern Khirbet el Kirmil preserves the name of this ancient village.

Calebites

The Calebites claimed as their ancestor one of the heroes of the wilderness and conquest traditions, a man named Caleb (Num 13, 14). There is some evidence that Caleb was of non-Israelite origin (Num 32:12 calls him a Kenizzite; also Josh 14:6, 14), but his family was accepted as members of the tribe of Judah (Josh 15:13). Of the twelve scouts sent to spy out the promised land, only Caleb and Joshua returned with confidence that Israel should proceed. As a reward for his heroism, Joshua gave to Caleb Hebron and its surrounding territory "because he wholeheartedly followed the LORD, the God of Israel" (Josh 14:13-14). While Caleb's progeny inherited his territory and continued to live in the regions surrounding Hebron, Nabal demonstrates that not all of his descendants inherited Caleb's piety or his prudence.

Just in case any reader missed the point of the names, however, the narrator spelled out the differences in this unlikely couple: "The woman was clever and beautiful, but the man was surly and mean; he was a Calebite." The significance of the last note is not to cast aspersions on Calebites, but to identify the politically powerful clan to which Nabal belonged. [Calebites] Despite his contemptuous nature, he was a rich and powerful man.

The reader senses that any dealing between Nabal and David will lead to conflict between the two strong-willed men, and there is no disappointment on that score. David's men had inhabited the southern reaches for some time, and apparently had taken it upon themselves to offer protection to shepherds and others who shared their open-air quarters. Thinking that a properly grateful businessman would gladly reward such services, David waited until sheep-shearing time, when the flock was fleeced and Nabal would be flush with profit from his wool operations. Then, David sent a contingent of ten representatives to explain their past service to Nabal, and politely to request some benison from him.

Acting on David's instructions, the men approached Nabal with great caution and decorum, saluting him with a magnanimous threefold blessing: "Peace be to you, and peace be to your house, and peace be to all that you have" (v. 6). After reciting the way in which they had offered protection to Nabal's shepherds—while asking or taking nothing in return—David's message noted the joyous nature of the festive day, and he humbly requested a gift of "whatever you have at hand" (v. 8).

Nabal's response was an explosion of anger, as he apparently interpreted David's request as a poorly disguised attempt at extortion by soliciting "protection money." "Who is David?" he asks. "Who is the son of Jesse?" Implying that David was no better than the outlaws, debtors, and escaped slaves who made up his fighting force, Nabal refused to offer anything to David and his hungry men (vv. 9-11).

When the embassy returned with Nabal's reply, David responded with uncharacteristic anger of his own, ordering his men to prepare for a bloody raid against Nabal's household ("Every man strap on his sword!"). As 400 of his men readied themselves to take vengeance on Nabal, David seemed in danger of sullying his positive reputation and sidetracking his march to the throne. This is the first glimpse the narrator reveals of David's dark side, which ultimately would take its toll on him in the Bathsheba/Uriah affair (2 Sam 11–12).

Fortunately, however, David was saved from himself by none other than the beautiful and prudent wife of the callous Nabal. One of Nabal's young workers, far wiser than his employer, brought word of the situation to Abigail, insisting that Nabal was leading the household into certain danger, but no one could penetrate his stubbornness to talk to him about it (vv. 14-17). Upon learning of Nabal's offensive behavior, Abigail quickly gathered up a healthy stock of provisions for delivery to David, whose men had indeed been "a wall of protection" to Nabal's shepherds. [Feeding an Army]

As wily Jacob had done when seeking to placate his brother Esau (Gen 33), Abigail sent the provisions ahead in the care of her servants, hoping to mollify David before meeting him herself. Without her husband's knowing, Abigail mounted her donkey and rode out to meet David, who was leading his armed band to wreak vengeance against Nabal, who had repaid his good with evil (vv. 19b-21; note the similarity of the good/evil theme to 24:17). Indeed, the text insists that as she met the raiding party, David had just sworn a powerful oath of vengeance: "God do so to David and more also, if by morning I leave so much as one male of all who belong to him" (25:22). [Euphemisms] Since David withheld his hand and did not keep his oath—but did not face the consequences that Yahweh was thought sure to exact—a later editor emended the MT to read "May God do so to *the enemies of* David," and this is followed in some versions of the LXX. This robs the oath of its very intention, however, which is to motivate action by threatening oneself.

Feeding an Army

The provisions Abigail gathered would not feed an army for very long, but they would have provided at least one good meal for David's men. Her gift (literally, "blessing") included 200 loaves of bread, 2 skins of wine, five dressed sheep, five measures of parched grain (about a bushel), 100 clusters of raisins (the LXX has "one omer"), and 200 fig cakes (25:18).

Euphemisms

AΩ The NRSV translation "one male of all who belong to him" renders a Hebrew idiom that literally means "he who urinates against a wall," a pithy phrase that appeared in the KJV as "he who pisseth against the wall," before "pisseth" took on a vulgar connotation. In a literary sense, the vulgarity is not out of place on David's lips, however, for it illustrates his angry, near out-of-control mood. The euphemism appears again in 25:34 and in 1 Kgs 14:10; 16:11; 21:21 and 2 Kgs 9:8. In every instance, the earthy expression is used with reference to the extermination of all males in a particular household.

Abigail, then, arrived in the nick of time. Hurrying (a key motif in this account; see vv. 18, 23, 42), she climbed from her donkey and prostrated herself before David. Just as David's messengers had spoken to Nabal with carefully calculated words, so Abigail shrewdly curried David's favor through an overt show of humility, calling David "my lord" and speaking of herself as "your hand-maid." Her opening statement, "Upon me alone, my lord, be the guilt," was intended to draw David's anger away from Nabal and defuse it (vv. 23-24), for he could hardly harbor ill will toward the charming woman who showed such deference to him.

Abigail urged David to dismiss Nabal's behavior and pleaded for-giveness for having delayed the presentation of provisions, since she had just heard of David's need. In a sense, Abigail presents herself as the intellectual power behind her crude but wealthy husband, assuring David that things will be better now that she understands his situation (vv. 24-25).

Abigail then entreated David with a curse upon David's enemies: "As the LORD lives, and as you yourself live, since the LORD has restrained you from bloodguilt and from taking vengeance with your own hand, now let your enemies and those who seek to do evil to my lord be like Nabal" (v. 26). Since this statement seems to presume that David has already called off his attack and that God has already punished Nabal, some commentators assume that it is misplaced, and move it to a later location in the chapter. It is more likely, however, that the chronological inaccuracies are due to sloppy work by a later redactor who sought to expand upon the theme of David's narrow escape. As he had escaped from Saul's clutches, so David evaded his own inner demons, avoiding the guilt that would have accompanied his ill-advised plan to massacre every male in Nabal's household. David was a better man than that, and Abigail is presented as one who brings out the best in David.

The redactional quality of Abigail's speech becomes increasingly apparent in vv. 28-31, in which the narrator has Abigail predict that Yahweh will establish for David a sure house (v. 28) as a prince over Israel (v. 30). She speaks of David as the one who fights Yahweh's battles (v. 28), one whose life will be preserved in the "bundle of the living," and one who will certainly be king by virtue of Yahweh's work (v. 31). [A Sure House] [The Book of Life] The twin dangers

A Sure House

AΩ The expression "sure/secure house" translates *bayit neʾĕmān*. The word *neʾĕmān* derives from the same root as "Amen," and can mean something like "firmly established." The terminology is reminiscent of Nathan's dynastic prophecy in 2 Sam 7:11, 16, 25, 26, 27 and in 1 Kgs 2:24; 11:38. The prophecy in 2 Sam 7 is the key to understanding the Josianic version of Israel's history, as expressed in the earliest redaction of the Deuteronomistic History. Kyle McCarter points to parallels such as this to suggest that 25:28-31 was written in Jerusalem by none other than the Josianic historian himself (*I Samuel* [AB 8; Garden City: Doubleday, 1980], 402).

The Book of Life

AΩ Abigail's wish that David's life be bound up in the "bundle of the living" is a
metaphorical wish for him to remain alive. The expression itself parallels the "book
of the living" in Ps 69:28 (MT 69:29; cf. Isa 4:3), which includes all who live on the earth. In
Exod 32:32-33, Moses interceded for rebellious Israel, praying that if they must come under
judgment, he would also be blotted out of God's book. In the eschatological writings of later
Jewish thought, and in the New Testament, the concept of the "Book of Life" came to be
associated with the list of those who would enjoy the afterlife (Dan 12:1; Rev 3:5; 13:8;
17:8; 20:12; 21:27).

---

of acting out his hostility toward Nabal were that David would kill
unnecessarily and that he would be guilty of taking his future into
his own hands, rather than trusting in Yahweh's guidance. Saul had
failed by trusting his own wisdom, rather than Yahweh's instruction
(e.g., chs. 13 and 15), but David has the potential to avoid that
fatal error and remain dependent on Yahweh.

David's response to Abigail was one of joyous confession. He
would indeed have acquired bloodguilt, he said, if Abigail had not
prevented him; he surely would have taken mat-
ters into his own hands and diverged from
trusting in Yahweh alone (vv. 32-34). Thus,
David blessed Yahweh, blessed Abigail's good
sense, and blessed Abigail herself for coming to
his rescue (v. 33; cf. to the threefold blessing of
peace upon Nabal's house in v. 6). David gladly
accepted Abigail's gift, and granted her petition
seeking mercy for her family—a petition that Jonathan (20:14-17)
and Saul (24:21) had also made. [Another Idiom]

Another Idiom

AΩ David's acceptance of Abigail's petition
was expressed by means of a Hebrew
idiom, literally, "I have lifted your face." The use of
this idiom to denote the granting of a request is
also found in Gen 19:21, where God granted the
fleeing Lot's petition that Zoar not be destroyed
so that he might find refuge there.

Abigail's clandestine rendezvous with David could not go unnoticed for long, but she chose not to inform Nabal of her activities at
the feast, where he was filled with wine and thus incapable of
rational thought and possibly prone to unpredictable behavior. The
narrator emphasizes Nabal's personal culpability by describing the
wealthy man's sumptuous feast as one fit for a king (v. 37a). There
was no lack in Nabal's house. He could have assisted David and his
men at no detriment to himself, but he had chosen to refuse them.
That would cost him far more than the gift David requested.

The next morning, "when the wine had drained out of him,"
Abigail explained her activities to Nabal. The reader expects the
uncouth Calebite to rise up and attack her, but instead, "his heart
died within him; he became like a stone" (v. 37b). This seems to
describe some sudden physical impairment, such as a massive
stroke or heart attack. Nabal lived ten days more before dying a
death that the narrator attributes directly to Yahweh (v. 38). Thus,

it seems, David is rewarded for withdrawing his own plans for vengeance and putting his trust in Yahweh. David's enemy was neatly dispatched, but David acquired no guilt in the process. He would soon acquire something else, however.

Once David learned of Nabal's death, he wasted no time in setting his sights on obtaining Abigail as his wife. He sent messengers to her with a message that would be considered both presumptive and sexist in most modern cultures: "David has sent us to you to take you to him as his wife" (v. 40). Abigail took no offense, however, but responded with obvious, almost overdone humility. Many commentators have noted that in v. 41 Abigail seems to be speaking to David, even though David is not present. Perhaps the reader is to understand that she was dictating a message to be carried to David before her arrival. Or, since she declares herself willing to wash the feet of David's servants, perhaps she would have spoken to David's representative with the same deference she would have shown to David himself.

Surprisingly—to modern readers—Abigail seemed delighted at David's proposal, which leaves the impression that the two had already felt a mutual appeal. Abigail hurriedly mounted her donkey and followed the messengers back to David, accompanied by five personal maids. [An Unusual Picture] This is the fourth time that Abigail is pictured as hurrying in her response to David (vv. 18, 23, 34, 42).

David's marriage to Abigail gained him several things. Not only did he obtain a wealthy wife who presumably could help finance his army, but he gained a position of real political power in Judah by marrying into the powerful Calebite clan, who controlled the important city of Hebron. The narrator's way of emphasizing this political connection is to describe Abigail consistently as Nabal's widow (1 Sam 27:3; 30:5; 2 Sam 2:2; 3:3). The Hebron connection apparently became the base of David's political power in the south. After Saul's death, David would be crowned as king of Judah, several years before he was also acclaimed king of the northern tribes. That first coronation took place in Hebron (2 Sam 2:1-4).

An Unusual Picture

The text of the MT, as preserved, offers a poor example of Hebrew grammar and syntax. Literally, the text says that Abigail mounted her donkey along with the five maidservants who followed her. The image of six women on a single donkey is surely incorrect. It is more likely that the maidservants followed on foot.

Wedding Notices, 25:43-44

To the story of David's marriage to Abigail, the narrator has attached two additional redactional notes to update the reader regarding David's marital status. David had also married Ahinoam of Jezreel (v. 43). This is almost certainly not the same Ahinoam who was Saul's wife (14:50), though some have suggested it. Nor is it likely that Ahinoam's home is the same Jezreel found far to the north of David's operating theater in southern Judah. There was probably a town named Jezreel somewhere in the hilly country around Maon, Ziph, or Hebron. While the beautiful and clever Abigail would give birth to an unremarkable son named Chileab (2 Sam 3:3)—or Daniel (1 Chr 3:1)—Ahinoam would become the mother of Amnon, who later would rape his half-sister Tamar, sparking Absalom's rebellion when David refuses to address Amnon's crime (2 Sam 13–15).

The significance of David's marriages to Abigail and Ahinoam becomes even more apparent when the narrator reveals that Saul had annulled David's previous marriage to his daughter Michal, wedding her instead to an otherwise unknown man named Palti, the son of Laish, from Gallim (v. 44). According to Isaiah 10:30, there was a town by that name just north of Jerusalem. Saul had apparently sought to reduce any claim of legitimacy that David might have to the throne by erasing any family ties between them. All the while, however, David was forging new bonds with substantial southern clans who offered power of their own.

CONNECTIONS

The story of Nabal and Abigail is, among other things, a story about names. Nabal brings great shame upon himself because he lives up to his name, which means "fool." In v. 3, we are told that Nabal was surly and mean. In vv. 9-11, he acts toward David's men with what seems to be coldly calculated contempt and scornful derision. When Nabal's own servants reported his behavior to Abigail, they spoke of him being so ill-natured that no one could talk to him (25:17). Finally, when Abigail sought to pacify David, she described her uncouth husband by saying, "As his name is, so is he; Nabal [Fool] is his name, and folly is with him" (25:25). Later, Nabal compounded his foolish behavior by getting "very drunk" at his own feast (25:36). He is the prototypical "rich fool" (Luke 12:13-21) who lets his selfishness and wealth blind him to the needs of others, and whose untimely death underscores the peril of riches—especially for the rich who do not share their wealth (Matt 19:23; compare Luke 12:16-21; 16:19-31).

David and Abigail

Guido Reni was a master of the 17th century Baroque style in Bologna. This "academic" style was in strong contrast to the southern Italian Caravaggesque style. (see [A Popular Image]). Reni's compositions draw from Greco-Roman paintings and works by Raphael. This "classicizing" element is found in his religious and genre scenes. His figures may be dramatic and have a theatricality to their poses but they maintain a consistent elegance and grace. This can be seen in both David and Abigail.

Guido Reni (1575–1642). *David and Abigail.* Museum of Fine Arts (Szepmuveszeit Muzeum). Budapest, Hungary. (Credit: Alinari/Art Resource, NY)

The only similarity between Nabal and Abigail is the significance of their names. [David and Abigail] "Abigail" means "My [divine?] father rejoices," or "Joy of my father." And she was indeed a delight in every way, both beautiful and intelligent (25:3), perceptive (25:14-17) and quick-witted (25:18-19). Abigail's relationship skills were so strong that she knew how to handle both David's anger (25:23-31) and Nabal's hangover (25:36-37) with equal aplomb. The wise woman of Proverbs 31 had nothing on Abigail.

As the story is told, both Nabal and Abigail lived up (or down) to their reputations and got what they deserved. Nabal died like a heavy stone, sinking in the middle of all his wealth (25:37-38), but he could not take his riches with him. Abigail was released from her burdensome husband to marry the future king (25:39-42) and offer him all of Nabal's wealth.

What is generally overlooked in this story is that David's name also has significance: *dawid* means "beloved," and the reader knows that he also bears the title "anointed of Yahweh." David is God's beloved, chosen one. In the beginning of the story, David does not live up to his name, for his dark side prompts him to declare a pogrom against every male in Nabal's sizable household (25:13, 21-22). Through Abigail's timely intervention (25:23-31), David was able to gain control of his emotions and avoid incurring the blood-guilt of Nabal's death, thus remaining worthy of his status as God's beloved, chosen one.

Persons who follow the teachings of Jesus Christ bear the name "Christian." This passage challenges those who claim Christ's name to live up to their calling as the beloved children of God, rather than choosing to live in hypocrisy and bring shame upon the name. As Nabal's servants could see his true nature, so our friends and neighbors can recognize what is truly within us by virtue of our words and deeds. Let it be said of us, "As her name is, so is she: Christian is her name, and Christlikeness is in her."

David's personal struggle in the conflict with Nabal points time and again to the importance of leaving vengeance with God and trusting divine direction rather than heatedly taking matters into our own hands. David's anger led him to the brink of slaughtering many innocent men because of the crudeness of a single foe (25:13, 22). Abigail warned him of the dangers of acquiring such blood-guilt (25:26, 31), which would be unworthy of a king, as David was destined to be (25:28-30). Afterward, David acknowledged how Abigail had saved him from an egregious sin (25:33), and praised Yahweh for giving to Nabal his due (25:39). David had been in danger of usurping Yahweh's prerogative and of taking his fate into his own hands. Modern believers can learn the importance of trusting God to deal with those who hurt us and to provide direction for life. We may achieve impressive things by our own efforts, but if they are not the things God wants for us, they will be as empty as Nabal's wealth.

SAUL KEEPS HUNTING,
AND DAVID KEEPS WINNING

26:1-25

COMMENTARY

The commentary on chapter 24 contains an extensive comparison of the many similarities between 24:1-22 and 26:1-25, and should be consulted in conjunction with the present text. In both stories, the pursuing Saul falls into David's power, but David refuses to harm "the LORD's anointed." David chooses instead to declare the innocence of his intentions by taking a token from Saul, but not Saul's life. In both stories, Saul responds with repentance and acknowledges that David is in the right.

As noted above, the reference in 26:1 to Ziphites approaching Saul in Gibeah to report David's movements near Hachilah and Jeshimon is very similar to 23:19. Many critical scholars believe 26:1 is more original, with the reference in 23:19 having been borrowed for an expanded or alternate version of the same story.

The reader who wishes to approach chapters 24 and 26 as originally separate events must come to terms not only with the similarities between them, but also with why Saul would go out in search of David when he had just confessed his error in pursuing his rival, agreeing that David was in the right and acknowledging that David was certain to follow him as king (24:17-20). Two possible scenarios come to mind. One is that, though the stories appear in close proximity in 1 Samuel, the text does not indicate how long a period might have passed between the two. The stories may reflect two accounts separated by several months, or possibly years. The more likely explanation, if indeed there is one, is found in Saul's manic-depressive behavior and his growing paranoia, which could easily give rise to both penitent and vengeful moods within a short period of time, and with no necessary relation between them.

Again, Saul chose 3,000 select soldiers to join him in pursuing David (26:2; cf. 24:2). This time, however, Saul's camp is set "on the hill of Hachilah, which is opposite Jeshimon beside the road" (26:3).

General Abner

Abner the son of Ner is first mentioned in 1 Sam 14:50, which identifies him not only as Saul's commander-in-chief, but also as Saul's uncle. After Saul's death, Abner was powerful enough to assume control in Israel, placing Saul's weak son Ishbosheth on the throne and virtually ruling Israel as the power behind the throne (2 Sam 2:8-10). Abner continued the war with David and his archrival Joab, who was David's commander (2 Sam 2:12-31). Abner came into conflict with Ishbosheth when he presumed too much and took one of Saul's concubines for himself. The resulting breach led Abner to desert to David's side (2 Sam 3:6-21). Though David welcomed Abner, Joab exercised a blood vendetta against Abner and killed him, for Abner had killed Joab's brother Asahel in a previous battle. Abner's death prompted the politically shrewd David to mourn his loss in the public forum (2 Sam 3:22-34), gaining sympathy with the northern tribes, who also admired Abner.

These geographical features cannot be located with certainty, but their relation to Maon suggests a distance of about eight miles south of Hebron and at least ten miles west of the "Wild Goat Rocks" above En-gedi, where chapter 24 is set.

Perhaps the most notable difference between the two accounts is found in the method by which Saul came into David's power. In the En-gedi encounter, Saul fell into David's hands by (providential) accident, as he unwittingly chose David's hideout for a private toilet (24:3). In 26:4-7, however, David took a strong initiative to approach Saul, who was sleeping out of doors in his armed camp. David first *sent spies* to learn Saul's position, then *traveled* to a spot overlooking Saul's position, where he could see the king's sleeping arrangements for himself. David then *recruited* Abishai to accompany him into the heart of Saul's camp on a daring and dangerous raid.

As with chapter 24, certain elements of the story seem far-fetched. Would a soldier of Saul's caliber leave his camp unguarded, or would his personal sentries be so incompetent as to allow two enemy raiders to infiltrate the camp? Could David and Abishai really have carried on an extensive conversation beside the sleeping forms of Saul and his general Abner without their waking? [General Abner] The unlikelihood of these events accentuates the miraculous aura that seems to surround David, reminding the reader that he is blessed by the presence and the power of Yahweh. There was no explanation in chapter 24, but here the narrator tells us that David and Abishai were able to operate freely among Saul's immobile soldiers "because a deep sleep from the LORD had fallen upon them" (26:12). [The Sleep of Yahweh]

The Sleep of Yahweh

AΩ The *tardēmat Yahweh*, or "sleep of Yahweh," suggests a deep trance-like sleep. The same term is used in Gen 2:21 to described the divine anaesthesia used when Yahweh removed a rib from Adam, and in Gen 15:12 to portray the torpor induced on Abraham before Yahweh symbolized their covenant by passing between the dismembered remains of several animals.

As in chapter 24, David's companion argues that Yahweh has put Saul in David's power so David could kill him, the differences being that in this story the companion is identified, and David's friend Abishai offers to kill Saul, rather than urging David to do it. Abishai's confidence was such that he was certain of killing Saul with one silent thrust of his spear, but again David would not allow it. Even if one of his men killed Saul, David knew that he would incur the guilt of having endorsed violence against the LORD's anointed, and this he would not do (26:8-9). In the earlier story, David simply called for Yahweh to judge between him and Saul (24:12, 15). In 26:10-11, however, David gives voice to his expectation that Yahweh will do his own striking of Saul through illness or through the vagaries of battle. Since this seems to anticipate chapter 31, some scholars regard it as secondary (compare also David's words in 2 Sam 1:14-16).

David dared to cut a corner from Saul's robe in the cave above En-gedi, but here he chooses to take Saul's personal spear and water jar, both of which stood at Saul's head. Earlier narratives often showed Saul with his spear in hand as a symbol of his power (1 Sam 18:10; 19:9; 22:6). More than once, Saul had hurled his spear at David (1 Sam 18:11; 19:10). Undoubtedly, David would have found some special satisfaction in taking from Saul his status symbol. The water jug was a personal item that David also took as an obvious symbol that Saul had been in David's power. Anyone who could pull the sword from the ground at Saul's head also could have plunged it through his neck. Anyone who could have taken Saul's water jar also could have smashed it over his head. David would later return the spear, but not the water jar. Perhaps he kept it as a personal trophy, a reminder of Yahweh's blessing, and a token of greater victories yet to come.

David's public challenge to Saul (26:13-16) is also comparable to 24:8-15. In both cases, David shouts from a safe distance (here, from a neighboring ridge) and holds aloft the evidence of his innocence. The greatest difference is that in chapter 26, David addressed his first words not to Saul, but to Abner. In chapter 24, David taunted Saul for chasing him like an insignificant flea on a dead dog. In chapter 26, David's taunts are reserved for Abner, who had failed to protect the king. With merciless sarcasm, David first asked, "Are you not a man?"—implying that a *real* man, as Abner claimed to be, would not have left his king defenseless (26:15). Such dereliction of duty was a capital offense, so David added, "You are a dead man!" (lit., "a son of death"), which gives rise to the NRSV's translation, "You deserve to die!" (26:16).

The narrator offers no answer from Abner's quarter beyond his initial query to know who was calling. [Wordplay] Whether he was too ashamed to speak, or whether Saul simply cut him off, Abner is left in his humiliation for having failed the king. Saul, in turn, replied to David's challenge. He had undoubtedly missed his spear when he rose after David began shouting. If the story does preserve a separate event from chapter 24, one might suggest that Saul knew what to expect: If his spear was missing, David was the most likely suspect.

Saul's first words are precisely as in 24:16, "Is this your voice, my son David?" This time David answers the question: "It is my voice, my lord, O King" (26:17). Note that both David and Saul continue to use proper pleasantries and honorific terms throughout the discussion. As before, David queried Saul concerning his intentions (26:18), but in this account, he skips any further sarcasm and focuses on the participant in the drama that Saul seemed to have forgotten: Yahweh.

On the one hand, David imagines the unlikely possibility that it is Yahweh who has stirred Saul against him. If Yahweh had done so, David argued, divine anger could be appeased with a burnt offering (literally, "Let him smell an offering"). [A Sweet-Smelling Savor] If, however, human persons had stirred Saul's anger against David, they deserved to be put under a curse, for they were forcing a subject of Yahweh to live outside of Yahweh's land. "The inheritance of the LORD" was a reference to Israel, thought to be Yahweh's special possession. David, like all Israelites, had a share in that land, but Saul's army was forcing him to leave, to live among people who served other gods (26:19). Significantly, once David and Saul parted company after this confrontation, David left the borders of Judah to enlist in the service of King Achish, who ruled the Philistine territory surrounding the city of Gath, and he did not return to live in the land of promise until after Saul's death.

Wordplay

AΩ Abner's request to know who was calling from such a distance gave rise to a delightful wordplay in the narrator's version of the event. Literally, he asked, "Who are you who calls to the king?" The words "who calls" translate *haqqōrēʾ*, a participle meaning "the caller" or "one who calls." That same word meant "partridge," the "calling bird." Thus, when David complains that the king hunts him like a single flea, "like one who hunts a partridge [*haqqōrēʾ*] in the mountains," he is throwing Abner's words back at him. "Who is the caller?" "The calling bird that you pursue through the mountains!"

A Sweet-Smelling Savor

The ancients believed that burnt offerings were a special way of communicating with God by means of smell. Though the Hebrews could not see God, they thought of the Deity as inhabiting the heavens, and believed that their smoky offerings, fueled by the prized fat portions of sacrificial animals, would provide an aroma as pleasing to God as steak on the grill (Gen 8:21; Exod 29:18, 25, 41; Lev 1:9, 13, 17; 2:2, 9, 12; plus many others). Various compounds of incense served the same end inside the temple (a recipe for sacred incense may be found in Exod 30:34-38). The image of a sacrifice as a sweet-smelling aroma before God was abstracted in the New Testament as a metaphorical means of describing one's service to God or God's people (Eph 5:2; Phil 4:18).

David's concern was not only that he must live apart from Yahweh's land, but that he might die apart from the LORD: "Now, therefore, do not let my blood fall to the ground, away from the presence of the LORD" (26:20a). The irony of David's expressed fear is that he would die as an old man in his own bed in his own city in the heart of the promised land (1 Kgs 2:10-11). Saul, on the other hand, would die an ignominious death far from home, and his body would be defiled and hung on the walls of Beth-shan, an ancient Canaanite city that had long been controlled by Egypt, but which apparently had fallen under Philistine jurisdiction. The same Saul who lost touch with Yahweh in life would be displayed in death on the walls of a pagan city that was within the promised land, but not in Israelite hands. In this, Saul's death became a metaphor for his life and relationship with Yahweh: so near, and yet so far away.

Saul's response to David's plea for peace (26:21-25) is just as repentant as in 24:17-21, though not as specific. Saul's confession of the error of his ways ("I have been a fool, and have made a great mistake!") is not, as might appear, a pointed play on the previous story about Nabal, the man whose name meant "fool." Instead, Saul employs the causative form of a different verb (*sākal*) that means "to be foolish," hence, "to play the fool."

David's response, as the narrator relates it, reminds the reader that the heart of Saul's foolishness was not in chasing David, but in deserting Yahweh. David declares his own faithfulness to Yahweh and his expectation of divine reward for his display of "righteousness and faithfulness" in withholding his hand (and his man Abishai) from harming the king (26:23). David's piety seems a bit overdone, as he curses those who would drive him away from Yahweh (26:19) but blesses himself: "As your life was precious today in my sight, so may my life be precious in the sight of the LORD, and may he rescue me from all tribulation."

The hero's self-blessing makes evident what the reader already suspects, namely, that David has a hidden agenda. The future king does not withhold his hand from Saul simply because he loves him, but because, as another anointed by Yahweh, he wants to cultivate the same respect from others. By building a powerful taboo around the idea of harming Yahweh's anointed, David protects not only Saul, but himself. David's words echo the typical Deuteronomistic theology: Those who are faithful (in this case, by respecting Yahweh's anointed) may expect blessings, while those who ignore God's commands may anticipate only curses. Two men have been anointed: Saul and David. Saul rebelled and was rejected. In contrast, David remained "faithful and righteous" (two of the Deuteronomist's favorite words). Thus, the theological legitimation of David's future kingship is fully realized.

Saul ultimately added his own blessing to David, but it is not nearly so specific as the prediction found in 24:19-20, where Saul confessed his conviction that David would succeed him as king. In 26:25, he offers a much more ambiguous forecast: that David would "do many things" and "succeed in them." The more general nature of this prophecy suggests that the engagement on the hill of Hachilah preserves an older tradition than that found in the En-gedi encounter.

The reader may note that three times in this chapter, Saul calls David "my son" (26:17, 21, 25) and even invites David to return to his court (26:21). David, however, does not call Saul "my father," as he did in 24:11, though he does use the properly deferential "my lord" (vv. 17, 18, 19). The reader senses a greater level of tension in chapter 26, especially on David's part. Here, David takes the initiative to penetrate Saul's camp and accuses Saul of forcing him to live outside of Yahweh's land. When the story ends with David and Saul going their separate ways, the reader suspects correctly that they will not see each other again.

CONNECTIONS

Our exploration of modern connections from 26:1-25 will be limited to those elements of the story that stand as distinctive from 24:1-22, which is discussed above (see "Lessons from En-gedi").

One notable distinctive is the introduction of additional characters. David is accompanied on his daring mission into Saul's camp by Abishai, the son of Zeruiah, while Saul is personally (though ineffectively) guarded by Abner, the son of Ner. [The Sons of Zeruiah] Abishai was David's first cousin, as Abner was the son of Saul's uncle. Both were regarded as fearless and sometimes bloodthirsty warriors.

The Sons of Zeruiah

Abishai was David's first cousin, the eldest son of his sister Zeruiah. He and his brothers Joab and Asahel were David's closest companions, strongest supporters, and most fearless warriors (see 2 Sam 16:9-11; 21:17; 1 Chr 18:12). When the fleet Asahel pursued Abner from the battle at the Pool of Gibeon, Abner killed him (2 Sam 2:12-23). Joab and Abishai continued to chase Abner, but finally called a retreat (2 Sam 2:24-32). They did not forget who had killed their brother, however. As quickly as Abner defected to David's side, Joab murdered Abner by treacherous means in order to gain blood vengeance for Asahel's death (2 Sam 3:22-30), leading David to disavow his relationship with the two remaining brothers and call for divine retribution upon "the one who does wickedly" (2 Sam 3:38-39).

When the LORD granted David and Abishai safe passage by blanketing Saul's camp with a deep sleep, Abishai argued that David should have killed Saul on the spot, and even offered to do it for him. David held Abishai back, not for the last time. The zealotry of the sons of Zeruiah would eventually lead to bad ends for all of them.

One of Jesus' disciples was named "Simon the Zealot," and several of the disciples probably shared sympathies with armed bands of Jewish patriots who harried the Roman occupation troops. They urged Jesus to proclaim himself king, declare war, and use his mighty powers to grasp political control. Some scholars suggest that Judas Iscariot shared such sympathies and turned Jesus in when it became evident that Jesus would not support the Zealots' cause.

Political or military zealotry is often ugly and usually harmful. David knew that it was better to trust the LORD to save him from Saul without taking Saul's life into his own hands, even though it might lead to more long years of exile and dangerous trials. Jesus knew that the kingdom as God envisioned it could not come through a military rebellion, but through the life and death of a trusting, suffering servant.

As some Jewish leaders sought to stamp out the early church as a danger to orthodoxy, Rabbi Gamaliel pointed to several zealots who had risen like stars and then burned themselves out. He concluded that the wise should beware of presuming all knowledge lest they find themselves to be fighting God. If something is of God, he argued, it will ultimately succeed no matter what we do (Acts 5:33-39; Luke's accounts of Judas and Theudas are in reverse order from Josephus' version).[1]

Modern zealots could learn from David the importance of trusting in God for one's personal guidance and refraining from the temptation to impose their own values upon others by hurtful or oppressive means.

Abishai's action stands in stark contrast to Abner's *in*action. Though he had the good excuse of having been entranced by the "sleep of Yahweh," Abner failed to protect the king whose life was entrusted to his care. Few others can avail themselves of such an excuse, for we have little evidence that God prompts followers to spiritual slumber. Apathy and inactivity are no better than zealotry. Abner failed to protect his king.

Modern believers are called to do their part in supporting and building up the kingdom Jesus introduced, calling others to faith and discipleship (Matt 28:19-20). This cannot be done through the apathy that holds too many churches in its thrall. Those who would learn from Scripture know the value of being alert for every opportunity to do what is good (as David did, in returning good for Saul's evil), while avoiding the temptation to compound one evil with another, as Abishai sought to do. Saul's life was precious in David's sight. Even so, we are to regard others as precious in our sight and to seek their welfare through our work and witness.

NOTES

[1] Josephus, *Antiquities* XX.5.1

ACHISH'S PROTECTION AND DAVID'S DECEPTION

27:1–28:2

David in Danger—Among the Philistines, 27:1–31:13

The final chapters of 1 Samuel derive from at least two larger sources: one, the final chapters of the "History of David's Rise," the other, an account of Saul's last days. David's sojourn in Gath and Ziklag is recorded in 27:1–28:2 and 29:1–30:31. The description of Saul's final fall is found in 28:3-26 and 31:1-13. Reasons for the overlapping of the sources will be discussed in the detailed commentary on each section, following the brief overview below.

Despite David's remarkable success in eluding Saul's pursuit, a time came when he decided to choose a different course. Instead of continuing to hide out in the Judean backlands, David did something that only a remarkable personage such as himself could do—he defied every reasonable expectation and cast his lot with Israel's perennial nemesis, the Philistines. [Regions of the Negeb] Or so it appeared. The reader soon learns that David was playing a risky game of subterfuge as a double agent, feigning fealty to the Philistines while raiding other ancient enemies of Israel and sharing the spoils with the grateful residents of southern Judah (27:1–28:2; 30:26-31).

David's ruse did in fact win him respite from Saul, who won no peace from any front. Rather, Saul appears as a mere shell of his former self as he breaks his own rules to seek out

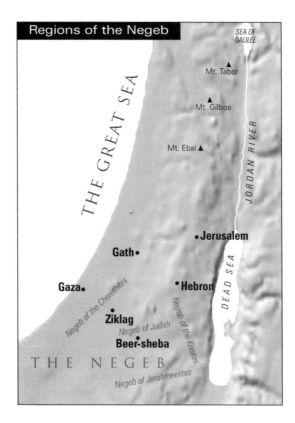

Regions of the Negeb

comfort from the shade of Samuel, who was as displeased with Saul in death as he was in life. Samuel's ghost offered only the nightmarish prediction of an early death and the confirmation of what Saul already knew—that Yahweh would hand the kingdom to David (28:3-25).

David, meanwhile, had troubles of his own. The first was fortuitous: Achish had planned an attack on Israel, with David's troops as his own honor guard (28:1-2), putting David in an extremely untenable position. Other Philistine leaders recalled David's earlier victories against them, however, and called for his dismissal. Achish relieved David of duty for the attack on Israel, sending him and his troops back home to Ziklag. There, David discovered that his city had been ravaged by the Amalekites, who had also kidnaped their wives and children. David and his men effected their rescue, however, and gained vengeance (29:1–30:31).

The camera returns to Saul just long enough to record his final battle, at Mount Gilboa. There, the overmatched Israelites fell in short order. The hapless king fought valiantly, but without success. Not only Saul, but three of his sons died, including the favored Jonathan. The Philistines defiled the royal family's remains and displayed them on the walls of Beth-shan, but the men of Jabesh-gilead heroically rescued their bodies in order to give them an honorable burial (31:1-13).

COMMENTARY

David's Defection, 27:1-4

David's separation from Saul in 26:25 was apparently a peaceful parting, but long experience had proven that there would never be lasting amity between the two of them. The reader presumes that David grew weary of running and hiding from Saul, choosing instead to escape Saul's clutches by ensconcing himself among the Philistines, where Saul certainly would not follow (v. 1). This remarkable story of David's defection to the enemy would have been quite embarrassing to Israel's later storytellers, who no doubt would have preferred to omit it altogether had it not been so firmly entrenched among the Davidic traditions. Thus, its very presence vouches for at least some measure of authenticity.

To ameliorate the disconcerting nature of David's Philistine foray, the editors have carefully shaped the narrative to portray David not as a deserter, but as a double-agent. Though he appeared to have

Philistine Fools

Scholars have long debated the relationship (if there is any) between David's reported earlier—and unsuccessful—attempt to find safe haven as a vassal of Achish (21:10-16). The following table compares the two stories' portrayals of David's interaction with Achish:

1 Samuel 21:10-16	*1 Samuel 27:1–28:2; 29:1-11*
David goes to Achish in Gath to escape from Saul. (21:10)	David goes to Achish in Gath to escape from Saul. (27:1)
David arrives in Gath alone. (21:10)	David arrives in Gath with two wives and 600 fighting men, plus their families. (27:2)
	David is accepted as a resident of Gath (27:3), then is granted the city of Ziklag as a military fief. (27:5-7)
The people of Gath urge Achish to reject David, recalling his heroism against the Philistines, as reflected in the popular dance song: "Saul has slain his thousands, and David his ten thousands." (21:11)	When Achish assigns David's men to serve as his personal bodyguard in battle with Israel, other Philistine generals urge Achish to reject David, recalling his heroism against the Philistines, as reflected in the popular dance song: "Saul has slain his thousands, and David his ten thousands." (28:1-2; 29:1-5)
In order to escape from Gath, David feigns madness, playing Achish for a fool by convincing him that he is deranged. (21:12-15)	Bowing to pressure from other generals, Achish sends David home to Ziklag, praising David for his honesty, never knowing that David has been playing him for a fool. (27:8-12; 29:6-11)

Both accounts seem scandalous on the surface, but the narrator has used them effectively to build David's reputation as an ingenious, quick-thinking man who is able to turn every situation to his advantage. Despite the apparent embarrassment of Israel's future king serving as a Philistine vassal, the narrator demonstrates that the cunning David had in fact made fools of the Philistines not once, but twice.

gone over to the Philistines, he was really practicing an elaborate artifice by which he might simultaneously punish Israel's ancient enemies, enrich his Judean neighbors, and make fools of the Philistines. [Philistine Fools]

Having determined that the only way to escape Saul's predations was to leave the country, David gathered up his considerable retinue of 600 men and their families and "went over" to King Achish of Gath (v. 2). Achish is assigned a patronymic for the first time, the "son of Maoch." This name differs only slightly from "Maacah," who appears in 1 Kings 2:39 as the father of Achish, king of Gath. The accounts are separated by about forty years, but it is possible that they refer to the same king.

The reader must presume that David had negotiated some sort of arrangement in advance, for Achish would certainly not allow an army of 600 men to simply walk into his city and take up residence, as the text implies (v. 3). David's outlaw status in Israel would have been well known, however, so Achish had reason to believe the renegade captain was indeed ready to defect from Israel and bring his mercenary band under the Philistine umbrella.

To all appearances, David's daring plan was working. Along with his two wives and his 600 men, he had found refuge among the Philistines. In addition, the defection had the desired effect upon Saul, who "sought him no longer" (v. 4).

David's Deception, 27:5-12

As quickly as David achieved asylum with Achish, he began setting other plans in motion to further his ends. Noting the considerable size of his entourage, and the unseemliness of continuing to rely on imperial largesse in the royal city, he requested a military fief in one of the outlying towns. [Lords and Vassals] There, his army could assist in protecting and perhaps extending the Philistine region of influence. By raiding Philistia's enemies, David's band could provide for its own needs and perhaps even turn a profit for the king. Achish honored David's request by giving to him the frontier city of Ziklag. [Ziklag] David's hold on Ziklag was so firm that the city continued to be thought of as his personal property even after he became king and beyond, prompting the narrator's editorial note that Ziklag remained a royal city for the kings of Judah "to this day" (v. 6).

David's sojourn among the Philistines is generally understood (and usually translated) as lasting for a year and four months, a number that is meant to include both the time in Gath and in Ziklag. The MT actually says "days [*yāmîm*] and four months," while the LXX has only "four months." The plural of "days" could sometimes be used idiomatically for "a year," as in Judges 17:10 and 2 Samuel 14:26.

The amount of time David spent in Philistia is not so important as the activities in which he engaged while there. Using the isolated southern city as a base of operations, David and his men made periodic raids against several of Israel's ancient enemies, including the Geshurites and the Amalekites (v. 8). The MT adds "the Girzites," with a note that it should be read "the Gezerites," but

Lords and Vassals

During the Bronze Age, and in some places during the Iron Age, the ancient Near East was dominated by the political model of powerful city-states, each ruled by a "lord," who held power over a limited area of farm and pasture lands needed for support. Neighboring city-states sometimes cooperated with each other to expand their spheres of influence. The Philistine pentapolis of Gath, Ekron, Ashdod, Gaza, and Ashkelon offers a textbook example of the practice.

Villages and towns in the outlying areas were beholden to provide food and other goods to the central city, which in turn offered the protection of its fortified walls in the event of enemy attack. Within this feudal economy, it was common for favored servants of the king to be granted landed properties to rule as their own fiefs under the aegis of the king.

Ziklag

The location of Ziklag is uncertain. The proposal currently enjoying greatest favor is Tell esh-Sheri'ah, about fifteen miles southeast of Gaza. This would put Ziklag nearly forty miles to the southwest of Gath, well out of daily commerce with the Philistine king.

According to Josh 19:5 and 1 Chr 4:30, Ziklag was formally assigned to the tribe of Simeon following Israel's establishment of power in the promised land. However, it also appears in a list of cities in the Negeb that belonged to Judah (Josh 15:31). Some scholars suggest that Josh 15:20-63 may reflect a 9th century revision of the rolls, reflecting a situation in which some Simeonite cities had been captured by the Philistines and later recovered by Judah, which retained control.

Gezer was too far north to have come into play; the extra word may have crept in due to a conflation of variant sources. The Geshurites mentioned here are not the inhabitants of Geshur, which lay east of the Jordan (Deut 3:14; Josh 12:5), but an obscure tribe that is otherwise known only from Deuteronomy 2:23 and Joshua 13:2-3 as a people who lived near Gaza and were associated with the Philistines and the Aviim.

The Amalekites are well attested as entrenched enemies of Israel, as discussed above in relation to Saul's ill-fated victory over them in 15:1-9. Samuel had instructed Saul to wage against Amalek a holy war, thus taking no loot and leaving no survivors. Saul, however, returned with the Amalekite king Agag in tow, along with herds of the best cattle and sheep. Samuel's outrage over Saul's disobedience led to his declaration that the kingdom would be taken away from Saul and given to another (15:10-35).

That other person was David, of course, and the narrator makes a point of saying that when *David* raided his enemies, he took no prisoners (v. 9). David's reasons were different; he was not involved in a holy war, but simply wanted to leave no survivors who could report his duplicity to Achish (v. 11). Even so, the narrator's care in pointing to this practice is a subtle jab at Saul, whose failure lay in precisely the same area.

David did, however, take captured property and animals as plunder, using at least some of it to ingratiate himself to Achish. Later, the narrator will reveal that he also shared spoils with the people of Judah, earning friendship and support that would serve him well in years to come (30:26-31).

The reader can almost hear the narrator's laughter bubbling through the scene between David and Achish as the king's vassal arrived with yet another gratuity from the spoils he had taken. When Achish would ask from whom the spoils had been seized, the duplicitous David would answer vaguely, "against the Negeb of Judah," or "against the Negeb of the Jerahmeelites," or "against the

The Negeb(s)

Ordinarily, "the Negeb" refers to the southern region of Palestine, roughly defined by the triangular area between Gaza on the west, the Dead Sea on the east, and the Gulf of Aqaba to the south. The term could also refer to areas inhabited by particular population groups. Thus, "the Negeb of Judah" was the area surrounding Beer-sheba, where Judahites lived (2 Sam 24:7; 2 Chr 28:18). Jerahmeel was an independent tribe traditionally related to Israel through their eponymous ancestor, listed in the genealogies as the brother of Ram, David's forefather (1 Chr 2:9, 25-33). Likewise, the Kenizzites (listed in the LXX) were thought to be descendants of Kenaz, the grandson of Caleb, another of Ram's brothers (1 Chr 2:42; 4:15). The precise location of the Jerahmeelite and the Kenizzite tribes is a matter of speculation, but the implication is that they were either near or within Judahite territory. The MT has "Kenites" rather than Kenizzites. The Kenites were long-time allies of Israel, though they lived among the Amalekites (cf. 15:6, where Saul warned the Kenites to withdraw before he attacked the Amalekites; and 30:29, where David distributed some of his plunder to various Kenite cities).

Negeb of the Kenites" (vv. 9-11). [The Negeb(s)] The population of these areas was all either Israelites or traditional kinsmen/allies of Israel. By convincing Achish that he had burned all bridges by attacking his own people, David solidified his position among the Philistines and increased Achish's level of trust in his allegiance (v. 12).

David's Dilemma, 28:1-2

David's plan proceeded perfectly until Achish did the one thing David could not afford for him to do: he laid plans to attack Israel, incorporating David's band into the Philistine forces. It appears that David's show of allegiance to Achish had been *too* convincing. The conversation between the two reveals that David was still thinking on his feet, though now in danger of a major gaffe. When Achish said "You know, of course, that you and your men are to go out with me in the army" (v. 1), David's reply was eager. Ever the actor (at least with Achish), David disguised his inner anxiety and

A Servant Forever?

Achish's appointment of David's band as his personal bodyguard was not unusual on the surface, since ancient kings traditionally kept around themselves a small number of particularly faithful or skillfull men. What stands out to the reader is Achish's declaration that David should serve as his permanent bodyguard. David's duplicity was so complete that Achish was convinced of his fealty to the Philistines, considering David to be a permanent vassal (27:12; lit., "a servant forever"). Now, he designates David and his men as "guards of the king *forever*" (this time, "all of the days"). The narrator has intentionally underscored the apparently immutable nature of David's alliance with the Philistines. David is about to enter a battle against Israel, casting an irretrievable die. This creates tension-filled curiosity even for the reader, who knows that everything will turn out alright. How would David escape?

replied, "Very well, then you shall know what your servant can do" (v. 2). David's braggadocio won him a place where Achish could indeed see what David could do, for the Philistine king appointed David and his men to serve as his personal—and permanent—bodyguard. [A Servant Forever?]

This turn of events spelled nothing but bad news for David. As the force closest to Achish, there was no way he could aid Israel without being detected. Having boasted so much of his abilities (which were already legendary), he would either have to betray Achish or else fight against his own people with vehemence and valor. All the years of preparation, all the years of waiting, all of David's hopes and dreams now rested on the fulcrum of this crucial battle. The king had called David's bluff, and there seemed to be no escape from the risky path of deception David had chosen. The author has skillfully built the narrative tension to a heart-pounding peak. Then, as a most effective storyteller, he leaves the reader hanging and turns to other matters.

CONNECTIONS

Proposing positive homiletical lessons from David's bloody and deceitful behavior seems as fraught with risk as David's own perilous path. Is there anything morally or ethically good to be said about what happens between Achish and David? David deserts his country to save his own skin. David dupes his host and works to undercut his strength. David ravages the Amalekite and Geshurite villages nearby, pillaging their goods and slaughtering every man, woman, and child so there will be no witnesses to his duplicitous piracy. David agrees to join Achish in battle against his own people, promising to demonstrate his military prowess on behalf of the Philistines. Where is the sermon in that? Where is the lesson for life?

One might say: "This is a negative example. Even good people sometimes do wrong. Learn from David's mistakes." The text, however, offers no such judgment. Rather, the narrator submits a wholly positive assessment of David's activities. In the author's view, David is inflicting proper punishment upon Israel's enemies, presumably with Yahweh's endorsement, and in a more thorough fashion than Saul.

For example, even though David was motivated by a fear of being found out, rather than by the dictates of holy war, the author carefully tells us that David took no prisoners, as had Saul (27:9, cf.

15:8-9). Even though 15:8 declares that Saul killed everyone except Agag, the presence of Amalekite cities for David to raid proves that many others had survived. The imposing prophet/priest Samuel had criticized Saul severely for his restraint before he took an axe in his own hands and "hewed Agag in pieces before the LORD" (15:33), to the narrator's implied cheers. It was this failure, the author says, that cost Saul his kingdom (15:17-29), which would be given to "a neighbor" who was more worthy. That neighbor, of course, was David, who would prove his worthiness by succeeding where Saul had fallen short. Apparently, the storyteller considered Yahweh's declared war on Amalek to be still in effect. Thus, David's "take-no-prisoners" approach to his marauding operations is not seen as reprehensible, but as responsible: David is only doing what Saul failed to do. For the narrator, then, David's ability to punish one enemy while hoodwinking the other is an indicator of genius rather than culpability. Thus, David's bloodthirsty behavior does not reflect a flaw in his character, but a level of obedience to God that Saul could not match.

Can modern readers learn anything positive about God through this bloody story and other "holy war" (see [Holy War]) texts of the Old Testament? We must acknowledge that such texts teach us something about God, without pretending to paint a complete picture of God. The image of God as a warrior who leads his people in holy war suggests that God is *involved* in human history. And God's involvement is toward the end of both judgment and redemption. This does not mean that God is the author of war or that God endorses war as a moral enterprise. What it suggests is that God's providence allows humans the freedom to act as they will. War is a decidedly human evil, but if God is to allow human freedom *and* to act in human history, he may choose to act through the human institution of war—through the world as it is—in order to accomplish his purposes. It is the conviction that God participates in our human world that holds within it the hope of ultimate redemption.[1] The cross on which Jesus died was a particularly cruel, *human* creation, but God's work in human history made even that abominable invention an agent of redemptive grace.

Even so, Jesus called his followers to be not military warriors, but spiritual ones. When dealing with abstract evils that tempt the soul and harm the world, it is appropriate to attack them whole-heartedly and take no prisoners. Let there be no mercy shown to bigotry, injustice, and selfish aims that harm others. When confronting *persons*, however, even though they may embody great wickedness, our response is to be one of compassion, opposing the sin but loving the sinner. Other faiths may declare a holy jihad against their enemies and may terrorize the innocent, but the god who endorses such behavior is not the one who was made known through Jesus Christ.

NOTES

[1] Peter C. Craigie, *The Problem of War in the Old Testament* (Grand Rapids: Eerdmans, 1978), 95-97.

SAUL'S DISTRESS
AND SAMUEL'S GHOST

28:3-25

COMMENTARY

With David on the dramatic verge of permanently severing his ties with Israel by joining the Philistines in battle, the author leaves the reader hanging and shifts his narrative camera to the Israelite encampment. There, he focuses upon the fearsome-turned-fearful commander Saul, who has crept away from his camp in search of succor from one whose memory still haunts him. This remarkable story, which originally formed a unit with chapter 31, has been detached from the larger corpus and inserted here. The critic, of course, wants to know why. Perhaps it is simply a matter of skillful literary artistry, the shifting of focus at a moment of high drama in order to build and preserve narrative tension. On the other hand, the author may be trying to preserve some chronological symmetry, interweaving the two stories so that one does not get ahead of the other. Unfortunately, splicing the text leads to a geographic anomaly regarding the Philistines' movements. [Where Were the Philistines?]

The story begins with two background statements that help set the scene. The first is a virtual repetition of 25:1, which recorded the death of Saul's former ally but frequent adversary, Samuel. One should understand that Samuel has been dead for some time. Secondly, the reader needs to know that Saul "had expelled the mediums and the wizards from the land," no doubt at Samuel's

---

Where Were the Philistines?

The military notes in 28:4 put the Philistines at Shunem (which would be north of Jezreel) and Saul's troops at Gilboa, though in 28:2 the Philistine army was still mustering for battle, presumably in Philistine territory. In 29:1, the Philistines are still many miles to the south and west, at Aphek. They do not arrive at Jezreel until 29:11. This irregularity can be explained by the reasonable assumption that 28:3-25 was originally attached to ch. 31 but was shifted by the editors to its present position, where it intensifies the narrative tension of David's dilemma while reminding the reader of Saul's impending demise.

Mediums and Wizards

AΩ Exact translation of this phrase is difficult, but the subject matter is rather clear. "Wizards" (NRSV) is an especially unfortunate rendering since it brings to mind the image of powerful men who cast spells, which is not the intent. The first word (ʾôbôt) is similar to the term for "fathers" (ʾābôt) and may have originated as a variant pronunciation or spelling of the same word, used in reference to the spirits of deceased forbears. Thus, it would refer to "spirits of the dead" or "ghosts," perhaps even including images or shrines intended to represent them (ʾôbôt can be made or burned; 2 Kgs 21:6; 23:24; 2 Chr 33:6). The NRSV and similar translations assume that the word's meaning extends to those who communicate with the dead, generally called "mediums" or "necromancers." Saul could hardly banish ghosts from the land, but he could outlaw the accouterments and practice of necromancy.

Another interpretive approach relates the word to a similar (but not identical) nonbiblical word that describes a ritual hole in the ground from which spirits are thought to travel between the world of the dead and the land of the living, assuming it could also refer to the man or woman who controlled such access to the spirit realm. For the first

view, see J. Lust, "On Wizards and Prophets," *Studies in Prophecy*, VTSup 26 (Leiden: E. J. Brill, 1974): 133-42. For the latter, consult H. A. Hoffner, "אֹב ʾôbh," *TDOT* (Grand Rapids: Eerdmans, 1974),I, 130-34.

The second word (yiddĕʿōnîm) derives from the verb "to know" (yādaʿ), thus "knowing ones." It always appears in parallel with ʾôb or ʾôbôt (1 Sam 28:3, 9; 2 Kgs 21:6; Isa 8:19; 19:3) and is often translated as "familiar spirits." The root meaning suggests the belief that spirits of the dead were knowledgeable of the future. Again, some translations (such as the NRSV) assume the meaning incorporates those who communicate with the dead, thus "mediums."

The person Saul consults in v. 7 ("woman who is a medium") is literally "woman/wife/mistress of a ghost (ʾôb)." McCarter suggests that this is an unwieldy conflate, and translates simply as "ghostwife." The NRSV renders the MT without emendation as "woman who is a medium," presumably as opposed to a man who is a medium. "Spirit woman" is a reasonable alternative.

Thus, the overall intent of the words is clear, though individual translations may be suspect. Saul, who had once banished the practice of necromancy, now wants to speak to the dead.

urging, and in accord with the law (Lev 19:31; 20:6; 27; Deut 18:9-11). [Mediums and Wizards] Since Saul is about to consult a medium, it is important for the reader to recognize that Saul is breaking his own laws. As Ralph Klein notes, "No reader can miss the irony that Saul was both lawmaker and lawbreaker."[1]

Saul appears as a hollow man, plagued by insecurity and ravaged by doubts. The Philistines had penetrated far to the north of their southern coastal strongholds and deep into the fertile Valley of Jezreel, which stretches across the width of Israel from Mount Carmel near the Mediterranean and into the city of Beth-shan, hard by the Jordan River. Commanding the Jezreel Valley would not only put the Philistines on Saul's northern flank as well as the western one, but also would cut off the Galilean tribes from those in the south. The massing of Philistine forces for a further offensive thrust was unmistakable, a move fraught with such imminent and obvious danger that Saul "was afraid, and his heart trembled greatly" (v. 5). Recognizing the enormity of the situation, Saul did the proper thing by seeking Yahweh's counsel, but the LORD refused to answer (cf. 14:37) through any of the approved means of divine communication: dreams, sacred lots, or prophetic speech. [A Word from God]

A Word from God

The ancients believed that the gods could communicate with humans in various ways. Traditions from Mesopotamia, in particular, contain many means of communicating with the gods, usually through the divining capabilities of the *barû* priests. These priests might produce impetrated omens by consulting the liver or other internal organs of a sacrificial animal for ominous markings (hepatoscopy, extispicy) or examining the motion of oil on water (lecanomancy) or smoke from a censer (libanomancy). Other more passive omens could be observed from the movements of the stars, the sighting of wild animals, or the behavior of domesticated livestock. Dreams were also important; many portentous dreams are recorded in the Akkadian annals.

In Israel, it was believed that God could initiate communication through immediate confrontation with the divine presence (Gen 15; 17; Exod 3; 20) or through an angelic messenger (Judg 13). God was also thought to speak through dreams, as in the case of the patriarchs Jacob (Gen 28:10-22) and Joseph (Gen 37:5-11). Elihu rebuked Job by reminding him that God may speak through dreams:

> For God speaks in one way,
> and in two, though people do not perceive it.
> In a dream, in a vision of the night,
> when deep sleep falls on mortals,
> while they slumber on their beds,
> then he opens their ears,
> and terrifies them with warnings,
> that he may turn them aside from their deeds,
> and keep them from pride. (Job 33:14-17)

God's refusal to speak to Saul through dreams, as mentioned in 1 Sam 28:6, implies that one could take steps to request a divine communication through dreams, perhaps through prayer or some sacred ritual that would prepare the worshiper to receive a cataleptic communication. Jacob was sleeping at a sacred site (Bethel) when God spoke to him in a dream. Near the beginning of his reign, Solomon went to "the principal high place" of Gibeon to offer sacrifices to God. That night, while still in Gibeon, Solomon slept, and God conversed with him in a dream, offering the new king whatever gift he should ask (1 Kgs 3:3-15). The story implies, though it does not state clearly, that Solomon slept at the sacred site in hopes of receiving a divine communication. Saul evidently tried whatever methods were known, without result.

Other means of divine communication (sacred lots and prophecy) have been discussed in previous boxes (see [Divination and Sacred Lots]).

The reader will recall that Yahweh readily advised David through the use of sacred lots (1 Sam 22:10, 13-15; 23:2, 4; 30:8) and by the prophetic word (1 Sam 22:5; 2 Sam 7:3-17; 12:1-15). The LORD had rejected Saul, however (15:23, 26; 16:1, 7), and having departed from the king (16:14; 18:12), would no longer speak to him (see also 14:37). The Hebrew reader would also note a pun in the text, as the narrator plays on the meaning of Saul's name: "asked." Thus, he says, "Saul *sauled* Yahweh," or put another way, "Mr. Asked *asked* Yahweh." Asking was inherent in Saul's name, but his questions were no longer recognized by the source of all answers.

Poetic Echoes of the Witch of Endor

The witch of Endor is mentioned in Robert Frost's humorous "A Masque of Reason" as a friend of Job's wife. A proto-feminist, Job's wife believes the witch was burned for witchcraft and demands that God explain why "women prophets should be burned as witches / Whereas men prophets are received with honor." On a more somber note, Rudyard Kipling opens his poem "En-Dor" with haunting lines that evoke the desperation of the grief-stricken:

> The road to En-dor is easy to tread
> For Mother or yearning Wife.
> There, it is sure, we shall meet our Dead
> As they were even in life.
> Earth has not dreamed of the blessing in store
> For desolate hearts on the road to En-dor.

When ritually sanctioned methods no longer obtained Saul an audience with God, he ventured to gain knowledge of the future by a more illicit means of communicating with the supernatural. Although he himself had outlawed the practice, Saul demanded that his servants search out a medium who could perform a seance and put him in touch with the dead, who were presumed to be knowledgeable about the future. Underground information soon surfaced a medium—*not*, as some translations suggest, a *witch*—in the tiny village of Endor. [Poetic Echoes of the Witch of Endor]

Saul traveled in disguise, lest the medium recognize him and conclude he was laying a trap to convict her of wrongdoing. Practically, Saul's subterfuge would also have aided in passage as he and two companions made their way north to Endor, for their path skirted the Philistine encampment at Shunem, on the southwestern side of "the Hill of Moreh." Endor was on the opposite side of the hill, only a few miles away. Moreover, by narrative symbol, Saul's disguise bespeaks how far the king had fallen from his former position of confidence and power.

The ghostwife's questioning of Saul's intent (v. 9) is natural, given the royal edict banning the practice of her art. It also functions to enhance narrative tension as the reader, with Saul, awaits the arrival of the dead, the fearsome shade of Samuel. Though no ritual is described, the reader presumes that the necromancer performed some ceremony, after which Samuel appeared. The spirit woman, according to the story, seemed shocked and amazed by what she saw. If a modern reader surmises that the woman had no real power to contact the dead, but made her living through pseudo-seances grounded on the superstitions of people easily deceived, her consternation is understandable. Accustomed to manufacturing answers for her conventional clientele, the necromancer would have been astounded at the sight of a spirit actually rising from the earth. [Sheol] Perhaps this is why she described Samuel's shade as an *elohim*—a "divine being" or "god."

According to the MT, it was the appearance of Samuel's ghost that prompted the woman to recognize Saul. Perhaps she assumed that the dead would not truly appear for anyone less than royalty, or that Samuel, at least, would not appear for anyone short of Saul. Kyle McCarter argues that vv. 11-12a intrude on the story from a later prophetic redactor, suggesting that the shade was originally anonymous and that the woman recognized Saul because of his authoritative tone in swearing that no harm would come to her (v. 10).3 Saul responded to the woman's charge of deception by repeating his promise that she would not be held liable for her crime of necromancy—the hollow king was concerned only with what he might learn from Samuel's shade.

Expected or not, the narrator draws a dark and macabre image of the old priest's ghost arising from the netherworld, still wrapped in his prophetic robe, still cantankerous, and even more intimidating in death than he was in life. Saul's obeisance (v. 14) did nothing to palliate Samuel's querulous mood, for the imposing apparition wondered only "Why have you disturbed me in bringing me up?" (v. 15a). Saul's response, which reprises the information in v. 6, was a confession that he had been abandoned by God, who would no longer speak to him by legitimate means.

Saul's name is once again the focus of a play on words and a source of irony. Saul—"Mr. Ask"—has asked Yahweh for guidance, without result. Samuel's spectral presence was no less identified with Yahweh in death than in life, however, and thus not inclined to offer succor to Saul. His response pointed to the logical fallacy of Saul's thinking: "Why then do you ask me, since the LORD has turned from you and become your enemy?" (v. 16). If God had

Sheol

 The Hebrew Bible offers no comprehensive doctrine regarding the fate of the dead, for Israel's theologians insisted that the knowledge of such secret things belonged to God alone (Deut 29:29). There is, however, a background of Semitic folk beliefs about the dead and their destination, beliefs that were common to Israel's Caananite and Mesopotamian neighbors.

Ancient Semites believed that the dead lived on, in some shadowy sense, in a place called *Sheol*. In the Hebrew Bible, Sheol was variously described as being beneath the earth (Num 16:30) or beneath the roots of the mountains (Jonah 2:6; cf. Job 26:5-7). A later view (Enoch 22:1-5) put it in the west, where the sun goes down; but, by far, most references insist that it is "down," a place into which the dead "descend" (Gen 37:35; 42:38; 44:29, 31; Num 16:30, 33; Deut 32:22; Job 11:8; 21:13; Pss 55:15; 86:13; Prov 15:24; Isa 7:11; 14:11, 15; 57:9; Ezek 31:15-17; Amos 9:2).

Sheol was a place where the dead lived on as spectral shades (*rephaim*) who existed in a state of weariness and weakness (Job 3:17; Ps 88:4 [MT 88:5]), with only tenuous connections to the earth or to God. It is described as a place of both dark chaos (Job 10:20-21) and grim silence (Pss 94:17; 115:17). In general, the path to Sheol was a dead-end road (Job 16:22), but popular lore believed that the dead could still be consulted through necromancy (1 Sam 28:13). Thus, when the spirit woman of Endor conjured Samuel, he came "up out of the ground" and castigated Saul for disturbing him (1 Sam 28:13, 15).

In the New Testament, the word "Hades" is used for Sheol as a term describing the land of the dead. Only in Luke 16:23 is Hades described as a place of punishment for the unrighteous dead. That purported place is more commonly called *Gehenna*, the Hebrew term for the "Valley of Hinnom" southwest of Jerusalem, a place that served as the city dump, where garbage burned perpetually and worms were ubiquitous (Mark 9:48).

1 Samuel 28:11—Saul faints before the shade of Samuel. Like the other Doré prints illustrated in this volume, this piece originates in the artist's enormous project of illustrating the *Holy Bible* in 1866. He chose to illustrate other "great texts" of western civilization such as Dante's *Divine Comedy,* Milton's *Paradise Lost* and Cervantes's *Don Quixote.* Doré's art was especially influential on Vincent van Gogh.

Gustave Doré (1832–83). *Saul and the Witch of Endor* from the *Illustrated Bible.* 19th century. Engraving. (Credit: Dover Pictoral Archive Series)

---

rejected Saul, why should he choose to speak through Samuel more so than any other way?

The ghostly oracle of vv. 17-19 may have been limited to v. 19b in the earliest version of this story: "Tomorrow you and your sons will be with me; the LORD will also give the army of Israel into the hands of the Philistines." Many scholars agree that the hand of the Deuteronomist is evident in vv. 17-19a, which point to the fulfillment of earlier predictions (15:18-28) in the same style as other Deuternomistic remarks such as 1 Kings 15:29 and 16:12. [Prediction and Fulfillment]

Saul's greatest guilt, according to this text, was his failure to enforce the requirements of holy war against the Amalekites, for his actions were seen as willful disobedience to the clear word of God. As Samuel had conveyed that call to holy war, so now he uses the language of holy war to describe Israel's coming defeat, in which Yahweh would wage war *against* his people rather than *for* them. If the scholars who see a deuteronomistic insertion in vv. 17-19a are correct, Samuel's original prediction was that "tomorrow you and your sons will be with me; the LORD will also give the army of Israel into the hands of the Philistines" (v. 19b). The expansion, however, goes further, asserting that "the LORD will give Israel, along with you, into the hands of the Philistines" (v. 19a). That is, not just "the army of Israel," but *Israel.*

The narrator knows, of course, that Israel was not exterminated according to the dictates of holy war, or else he would not be alive to write the story. For a time, however, Israel did fall under the sway of the Philistines, where it remained until David emerged as king and led Israel's armies to repel the Philistines and regain a national independence.

On a personal level for Saul, the scene ends with deep irony. He has disturbed Samuel by calling him up from the grave, only to find Samuel's presence so fearsome and condemning that he must surely wish he had left well enough alone and avoided the cantankerous prophet. Yet the future knowledge Saul had sought contained the worst possible news: Not only would he die on the following day, but he would be in Samuel's company permanently!

The closing section of this anguished story (vv. 20-25) finds the great and tall King Saul reduced to a quivering mass of hollow humanity stretched out full-length on the necromancer's floor. Saul's supine state symbolizes his fall from power. Yahweh has surely torn the kingdom from his hand. The narrator, however, is not content to leave Saul comfortless. The spirit woman, who has

---

Prediction and Fulfillment

A primary trademark of Deuteronomistic redactions is the penchant for saying "I told you so" in regard to the fulfillment of an earlier prediction of serious consequences for transgressing the law. For example, compare the Deuteronomistic notice of 1 Sam 28:17-19a with the earlier predictions of 1 Sam 15. The note is introduced by the obvious "The LORD has done to you just as he spoke by me" (28:17a).

Prophetic prediction	*Notice of fulfillment*
"The LORD has torn the kingdom of Israel from you this very day, and has given it to a neighbor of yours, who is better than you" (15:28).	"The LORD has torn the kingdom out of your hand, and given it to your neighbor, David" (28:17b).
"And the LORD sent you on a mission, and said 'Go, utterly destroy the sinners, the Amalekites, and fight against them until they are consumed.' Why then did you not obey the voice of the LORD?" (15:18-19).	"Because you did not obey the voice of the LORD, and did not carry out his fierce wrath against Amalek, therefore the LORD has done this thing to you today" (28:18).

been a rather marginal character thus far, steps to center stage and assumes responsibility for restoring Saul's composure. She who professes power to command the dead also commands Saul, the nearly dead.

The woman's conversation with Saul revolves around the pointed repetition of the word *šāmaʿ*, "to hear" or "to listen." "Your servant has *listened* to you," she said, pointing out that she had risked her own life by *listening* to Saul and conjuring up Samuel in violation of Saul's own law (v. 21). "Now, therefore, you also *listen* to your servant . . . eat, that you may have strength" (v. 22). At first, Saul refused, but at the urging of the woman and his companions, he *listened* to her words, got up from the ground, and ate (v. 23).

The repeated use of *šāmaʿ* underscores an important theological point. "To listen" is also "to obey." Saul had failed to *listen to* Yahweh and obey his commands, as Samuel often reminded him.

When Saul finally does *listen* to someone, it is to the voice of a divining woman, who acts in direct violation of Yahweh's law, and to the voices of his own servants. This is Saul's legacy: He is one who *asks* (the meaning of his name), but not one who *listens*. Samuel, on the other hand, is one who has listened to God and obeyed. His name, as pointed out in chapter 1, embodies the root *šāmaʿ*, "*heard* of God." The central theme of the Deuteronomist is that Yahweh blesses those who listen and obey and curses those who reject the law. The image of Saul lying crushed on the floor as Samuel's shade stands spectrally above him draws a clear picture of one who is cursed. [Cursed Is the Man . . .]

A final motif within this closing section involves food. Saul had not eaten for a day and a night, the narrator reveals (v. 20b), but with no clue as to whether his fast was prompted by requirements of the seance, by the danger of his slinking journey so near to the enemy camp, or by simple nervous preoccupation. The woman insisted that Saul listen to her and have something to eat. The storyteller confides no more about the motive behind Saul's initial refusal than the reason for his hunger. Perhaps he was afraid of becoming more entangled with the forbidden nature of the woman's profession. Perhaps he was simply lost in self-pity. In either case, Saul's conjurer and his companions managed to cajole him into taking enough sustenance to strengthen him for his final, fateful day.

The generous nature of Saul's final meal—a stall-fed calf and bread cakes for only four people—suggests that the king partook of

The Stall-Fed Calf

The prophet Amos used the image of eating a stall-fed calf as an example of luxurious living practiced by those who ignored the needs of the poor (Amos 6:4). Elsewhere, the image appears as a metaphor for those who are proud and well fed (but destined to destruction, Jer 46:21), or as an image of those who are blessed on the day of the LORD (Mal 4:2 [MT 3:20]). Since most cattle were left to range Palestine's poor pasturage, a stall-fed calf was considered particularly fortunate and healthy—at least until the day it appeared on the table.

Josephus passed on a tradition that the ghostwife of Endor owned nothing other than this calf that she had raised in her own home before offering it to Saul and his companions. Thus, the historian commended her gracious hospitality to the king (*Ant.* 6:339-340).

---

one last royal repast, which served to strengthen Saul for his final hours. [The Stall-Fed Calf] The reader, however, must hold this thought in abeyance, for the narrator has business with David before returning to the sad saga of Saul's demise.

CONNECTIONS

Saul's unhappy position in this chapter is not unlike the state of countless others who have abandoned God but seem surprised to discover that their prayers are unanswered. Saul disobeyed God's clear command on several occasions, most notably in the case of the Amalekites in chapter 15. This led to a predictable result: The LORD rejected Saul as king and withdrew from him God's anointing spirit. "The spirit of the LORD departed from Saul" (1 Sam 16:14a). Sadly, however, the king seemed unaware of his desertion. He had trusted his own judgment before, and was comfortable in continuing to do so.

In chapter 28, however, something happened which, in a sense, is the same thing that happens to most of us at some point in our lives—Saul found himself in trouble so deep that he knew there was no solution outside of divine intervention. So Saul did the natural thing most of us would do in similar situations: he prayed for help. In response, God did the same thing he would be inclined to do for others who live for themselves and pray only from exigency: *nothing*. There is no hint that Saul thought so much as to repent of his past failure or to promise future faithfulness. He simply prayed on the tacit assumption that God would always be there to answer his prayers.

Saul was wrong, and so are we if we make the same presumption. Self-centered living is *not* the key to answered prayer. When God did not answer Saul's prayer, Saul simply tried harder, and by other means. He offered sacrifices and slept in holy places in hopes that God would speak through a dream, but his sleep was uninterrupted. He asked the priest to cast the sacred lots for him, but no answer came. He instructed his court prophets to seek God's aid for him, but no help was forthcoming.

Finally, Saul became so desperate that he consulted an occult spiritualist to conjure the spirit of Samuel in hopes that the dead prophet might intercede for him, but he found himself only closer to death rather than life. As he collapsed upon the ground, the mystic woman insisted that he heed her voice and take some food. Saul's reluctant obedience to the advice of the woman and the encouragement of his companions was a symbol of his basic problem: *he would heed the voice of a diviner, but not of the divine.*

Saul's pattern has been repeated countless times, in various guises, and continues to be a way of life for a staggering portion of the populace. Surveys persistently reveal that the vast majority of people believe in God, though few put much effort into living in an obedient relationship with God. We reject the voice of God and listen instead to our own inner voices, or to the voices of our friends, or to the voices of superstition and pseudo-science. As a result, we find ourselves cut off from God. Sensing the emptiness within, we look for God in all the wrong places. We read our horoscopes, call "psychic hotlines," and give credence to Hollywood clairvoyants who claim to "channel" the wise voices of ancients they have been in previous lives. We buy into the quieter appeal of new age books such as *The Celestine Prophecy,* imagining its nine mystic "Insights" to be divine revelation rather than James Redfield's imagination. We think of ourselves as spiritual, but we wander far from the path outlined in Scripture, and we wonder why God does not answer when we call!

Saul's dark meeting with the medium of Endor served only to symbolize his sure demise, and the narrator uses it to underscore the bleak end awaiting those whose spirituality is so twisted that they search for God, as it were, by looking inward and down rather than outward and up. Those who reject the Lord will be rejected in return, and for them the end of the road will be the end of the road. Such is the legacy of Saul.

NOTES

[1] Ralph W. Klein, *1 Samuel* (WBC 10; Waco: Word Books, 1983), 271.

[2] P. Kyle McCarter, *I Samuel* (AB 8; Garden City: Doubleday, 1980), 421.

PHILISTINE AID AND AMALEKITE TROUBLE

29:1–30:31

COMMENTARY

David Is Saved by the Philistines, 29:1-11

With 29:1, the narrator resumes the interrupted story of David's dangerous defection to the Philistines—one that threatened to put him in the untenable position of waging war against his own people. David had feigned fealty to the king of Gath, and Achish had called his bluff by designating David and his men to serve as his personal honor guard. David played along, professing an eager desire to exhibit his fighting prowess to Achish. The reader knows, however, that doing battle against Israel is one thing even the remarkable David cannot afford to do. The ambiguity of David's enthusiasm for battle keeps open the possibility that David has seen an opportunity to kill not only Achish, but also the other Philistine commanders by attacking from behind. Thus, when the king saw David's skill in battle, it would be from the wrong end of the sword.

In chapter 29, the narrator reveals how David was saved from his predicament by the other Philistine commanders, who were free of David's charm and who suspected treachery. A geographic note in v. 1 places the Philistines in Aphek and the Israelites near Jezreel, a picture that is at odds with the previous chapter (see [Which Were the Philistines?]) but can be explained by understanding that the account of Saul's encounter with the spirit woman of Endor has been inserted into its present position for dramatic effect. David's dilemma would have been played out as the Philistine troops were still mustering and organizing for war ("passing on by hundreds and thousands"), not on the very eve of the conflict.

The Philistines' dismay at seeing David in Achish's company is expressed by the question "What are those Hebrews?" (MT). English translations usually add "doing here" for greater clarity. The Israelites rarely referred to themselves as Hebrews (*ʿibrîm*; cf. Deut 15:12 and

Hebrews

AΩ Many scholars believe the ethnic term "Hebrew" derives from the root *ʿābar*, "to pass over," meaning "those who pass over or through," hence, foreigners. In the Old Testament, the term is most often used by other nations when referring to Israel, rarely as a means of self-identification.

In recent years, there has been much debate about the significance of the term "Hebrew" since it was noticed that the phonologically similar term *habiru* or *apiru* was used in ancient diplomatic correspondence to describe a socially marginal class of people of varied ethnicity who were regarded as deserters or escaped slaves. Egyptian documents found at Tell-el-Amarna describe these *habiru/apiru* as a people of no social status who renounced the authority of Egypt, caused trouble along the borders, and

generally threatened the pharaoh's control over Egypt's vassals. Babylonian letters also use the term in reference to a similar group of socially marginal peoples, identified by the ideograms SA.GAZ.

Some scholars have made a strong case for identifying the *habiru/apiru* with the Hebrews. Yet current thought tends to regard the Israelites as people who were probably separate but who may have been regarded by other nations as being on the same marginal level as the *habiru/apiru*, and thus subject to the same pejorative social slur, which became confused with the ethnic term *ʾibrîm*. David's band of 600 men, the subject of the Philistines' contempt in 1 Sam 29:3, was made up of precisely the sort of renegade and social outcasts described by the disparaging term *habiru/apiru*.

Jer 34:9), but other nations did (1 Sam 4:6; 14:21), usually in a disparaging way. [Hebrews]

Achish seemed to take great pride in David's defection, insisting that he had shown nothing but loyalty to the king (v. 3). [David the Deserter?] The other Philistine leaders, however, did not share his enthusiasm for David. They remembered him only as a Philistine killer, reciting the popular verse "Saul has killed his thousands, and David his ten thousands" (v. 5; cf. 1 Sam 21:11 and [Philistine Fools]). They knew that little song and dance was favored among the Israelites precisely because it commemorated the killing of *Philistines—and* because it closely linked the two popular heroes, David and Saul. Even if David *had* fallen from favor with King Saul, what better way to redeem himself than by wreaking havoc behind the enemy lines and assassinating the Philistine leadership? (v. 4).

David the Deserter?

AΩ The MT expresses this idea by a form of the word *nāpal*, which normally means "to fall" or "to fall away." This word was also used in the sense of "defect" or "desert" in 2 Kgs 7:4 (of the beggars who thought to desert to the Aramaeans) and in 2 Kgs 25:11 = Jer 52:15 (to describe Israelite deserters to Babylon). Jeremiah was accused of deserting to the Chaldeans (Jer 37:13, 14), as had other Hebrews (Jer 38:19; 39:9). See also Jer 21:9 and 1 Chr 12:19, 20 (MT 20, 21).

The length of David's "desertion" to Achish is ambiguous. The MT's "for days and years" is probably a conflate reading of two indefinite expressions; either one could mean "for some time."

Achish's colleagues demanded David's departure, and the lord of Gath had little choice but to acquiesce to them. He did not wish to alienate David, however, who had proven to be a profitable servant. In dismissing David, then, he spoke very tactfully and carefully, affirming his belief in David's honesty and covering over the other Philistine lords' suspicions by asserting that they also considered him a good man (LXX). [Did Achish Swear by Yahweh?] The NRSV follows the MT, which has "In the eyes of the Philistines you are *not* a good man," but the LXX may be the better reading. Achish seems to be concerned only for David's reputation, and sensitive to the precariousness of his new vassal's situation (vv. 6-7).

David's response ("What have I done?") may have been calculated to cover his relief at being dismissed from action, but it may also have expressed true disappointment, for David was indeed losing a golden opportunity to decimate the Philistine leadership.

David professed abiding loyalty to Achish and a great desire to "fight against the enemies of my lord the king" (v. 8), but his words contain enough ambiguity to leave the reader wondering if he has Saul or Achish in mind when he speaks of "my lord the king."

> **Did Achish Swear by Yahweh?**
> The attentive reader will be surprised by v. 6, in which the Philistine Achish swears to David "as Yahweh lives." Was this a calculated effort by Achish to win David's trust by swearing an oath by David's God, rather than his own? Or was it an accidental slip by the Yahwistic narrator? Either is possible, though most critics prefer the latter option.

Achish continued to display consummate diplomacy in assuring David that *he* had found David to be as faithful as an angel (lit., "messenger") of the gods. Nevertheless, the other lords did not yet share his high opinion. Thus, to preserve his standing among the Philistines, it would be best for David to gracefully bow out and return to his city of Ziklag (v. 9). Achish's tact breaks down in v. 10, however, when he encourages David not to take the others' "evil report" to heart, but presses the issue by urging him to depart "early in the morning, as soon as you have light."

Through skillful narration, the author shows how David weathered the dangerous storm and emerged with the best possible outcome: Not only is he saved from the problematic position of fighting against his own people, but Achish is forced to apologize to him in the process, leaving David in a stronger position for future negotiations with the Philistine king. The narrator does not offer an explicit theological explanation for this fortunate turn of events, but the invisible hand of Yahweh is pervasive in the Deuteronomistic narrative. The Philistines marched on to the region of Jezreel for a showdown with Saul, while David returned to Ziklag to discover that his city did not lead such a charmed life as its leader.

David Rescues His People from the Amalekites, 30:1-31

The distance from Aphek to Ziklag was on the order of fifty miles, and David's men traveled on foot, so it was on the third day of their march that they discovered the smoking ruins of Ziklag. The narrator reveals that the city had been sacked by Amalekite raiders, who had also left a swath of destruction through much of the Negeb. The Amalekites seem to have been more concerned with profit than vengeance, taking captives rather than killing. Thus, though every woman and child left in Ziklag was gone, none of them had been killed (vv. 1b-2).

The reader knows this, but David and his men did not; they saw only the charred remains of the city they called their own. Given the absence of bodies or bones, David's troops could deduce that their families had been captured rather than killed immediately (v. 3), but their fate was still uncertain. Who had taken them? Had they been raped or abused? Would they be sold as slaves?

David and his men responded to the tragic scene in three ways. First, they collapsed into an enormous well of grief: "They raised their voices and wept, until there was no more strength to weep"

Was There More Than One Ephod?

Some scholars assume that only one ritual ephod existed in Israel and that when Abiathar brought it to David (23:6), the sacred lots were no longer available to Saul. If this ephod and its accompanying lots are to be associated with the ephod and breastplate of the high priest, only one was called for in the ritual instructions of Exod 28:1-30. There was more than one sanctuary during the period of 1 Samuel, however, and there is some evidence of rival priesthoods, each of which probably possessed priestly vestments. When Abiathar defected to David, the text does not say he brought *the* ephod, but *an* ephod. Afterwards, Saul continued to consult Yahweh through the use of sacred lots (28:6), implying that a priest and the appropriate vestments were at hand. The fact that Yahweh refused to answer Saul may imply, however, that only the vestments in Abiathar's care were considered to be authentic and acceptable. (See artist's representation of the priestly ephod at [Linen Ephod].)

(v. 4). David joined his troops in bewailing the loss of their loved ones, for his two wives, Ahinoam and Abigail, were among the missing (v. 5; cf. 25:42-43; 27:3).

The display of grief was quickly followed by a near mutiny. It had been David's choice to leave the city unguarded when responding to the Philistine muster. The men, who were "bitter in spirit" (cf. 1:10 and 22:2), spoke of stoning David, so that he was literally "in a tight spot" (v. 6a). The MT uses the idiom "*It was very narrow* for David," an expression also used for Jacob (Gen 32:7 [MT 32:8]) and for Israel (Judg 2:15).

The narrator offers an intriguing juxtaposition: Saul had been similarly constricted (1 Sam 28:15), and he had dealt with his distress by turning to illicit means of soliciting supernatural aid. David, in contrast, responded to his narrow straits in a different way: He "strengthened himself in Yahweh" (v. 6b). Specifically, David took courage by consulting Yahweh through the legitimate priestly oracle that was available to him since Abiathar had defected to his side (v. 7). [Was There More Than One Ephod?] Surprisingly, David does not ask if he will succeed in rescuing his people, but whether he should pursue their kidnapers at all. This suggests that David is relying on Yahweh for guidance as well as for strength.

Yahweh's response is couched in the form of two infinitive absolutes, offering emphatic assurance that David *should* pursue the raiders and that he *would* succeed in rescuing the women and children of Ziklag. [Infinitive Absolutes] Yahweh's encouraging answer not only underscores the close relationship between David and Yahweh, but also reminds the reader of how completely Saul is cut off from Yahweh.

Suitably strengthened, David and all 600 of his men began an immediate pursuit of those who had destroyed their city and abducted their families, following the trail as far as the Wadi Besor, probably 12 to 15 miles south of Ziklag. [The Wadi Besor] There, David left behind one-third of his troops, those who were too exhausted to cross the deep wadi. These remained to guard the baggage, freeing the remaining 400 men to travel more quickly.

In vv. 11-15, the narrator introduces one of those characters, like Abiathar and Abigail, who "happens" to come along at just the right time to hasten David's triumph. A scouting party discovers an enervated Egyptian slave who has been left behind by his master, abandoned to die in the wilderness when he could not keep up with the raiding party's retreat. He had not taken food or drink for three full days, the storyteller reveals, suggesting that the pirates had quite a head start.

Revived by ample water and a meal of sweet fig cake and raisins (vv. 11-12; the LXX omits the raisins), the young man was able to identify his former owner and to detail the activities of his companions. For the first time, David and his men learned that the marauders were Amalekites, the very same people who had been the bane of Saul and the fulcrum of his fall. The substantial Amalekite band had taken advantage of the imminent battle between Israel and Philistia, which robbed the countryside of its

Infinitive Absolutes

AΩ In Hebrew grammar, infinitives can take one of two forms, "absolute" or "construct." When the "infinitive absolute" is conjoined with a finite form of the same verb, it adds special emphasis. There are two examples in 1 Sam 30:8. "You shall surely overtake" is literally "Overtaking, you shall overtake" (*haśśēg taśśîg*). Similarly, "Rescuing, you shall rescue" is translated "You shall *surely* rescue" (*haṣṣēl taṣṣîl*). By combining two sequential infinitive absolute formations, the narrator reveals why David found such strength in the LORD—the oracle revealed to him an emphatic promise that he would succeed.

The Wadi Besor

Most scholars agree that ancient Ziklag is to be identified with Tell esh-Sheri'ah. The first large wadi southwest of Tell esh-Sheri'ah is now called the Wadi Ghazzeh. Though only 12–15 miles from Ziklag, the distance would have been sufficient to exhaust many of David's companions, who had been on the march for three days and had taken little rest in Ziklag. The wadis of southern Judah are not just small ditches or gullies; they can be quite large and difficult to cross.

The Wadi Qelt, as it merges into the plain near Jericho, illustrates how large desert wadis can become. (Credit: Mitchell G. Reddish)

Amalekite Targets (28:14)

The rescued Egyptian slave provided inside information for David, indicating four areas targeted by the Amalekite raiders. The "Negeb of the Cherethites" was probably located in the southern desert area controlled by the Philistines, for the Cherethites and Philistines were closely related and may have shared a common Aegean homeland (Ezek 25:16; Zeph 2:5). In v. 16, the narrator speaks of spoil taken from "the land of the Philistines" and "the land of Judah," apparently reckoning the Cherethite Negeb as Philistine territory. David seems to have forged an alliance with the Cherethites during his tenure in Ziklag, for his army later included a Cherethite contingent (2 Sam 8:18; 15:18; 20:7, 23; 1 Kgs 1:38, 44).

Raids had also taken place in territory belonging to Judah and in the "Negeb of Caleb," almost certainly descriptive of the area surrounding Hebron, which was the Calebite capital (see [Calebites]). Even though many local men probably had answered the call to arms for the upcoming battle between Israel and the Philistines, the marauders probably had harried outlying villages during their forays, stealing mostly the lightly protected flocks of sheep and goats that remained outside of city walls. Ziklag was different, however. Finding the city undefended, the Amalekites had taken its remaining inhabitants captive and burned the city to the ground.

---

best fighting men. The voracious raiders had swept through a large area of the Negeb, pillaging Cherethites, Judahites, and Calebites before attacking and burning Ziklag (30:14). [Amalekite Targets] Plied by food, friendly hands, and a pledge of immunity from retribution for his own role in the despoliation, the Egyptian gladly agreed to lead David's troops to the Amalekite encampment, which had probably served as their base of operations during the campaign.

The narrator offers no indication of the time required to reach the raider's camp, but David's lightly laden men were capable of much faster travel than the plunder-heavy Amalekites, who had already gained their bivouac when David and his troops found them "spread out all over the ground, eating and drinking and dancing because of the great amount of spoil they had taken from the land of the Philistines and from the Land of Judah" (v. 16). The word translated as "dancing" ordinarily means "making a pilgrimage," perhaps here with the sense of "as if it were a festal gathering." Inserting this word for a religious pilgrim celebration augments the author's description of the camp as a distasteful, disgraceful scene in which the Amalekites exult in the injustice they have brought upon others. In doing so, they prove themselves worthy of Yahweh's judgment and the severe punishment David and his men are about to inflict. The festal image also pictures the Amalekites as being completely off their guard and thus easy prey for David's angry troops.

Though exhausted from the journey, David's much smaller contingent "attacked them from twilight until evening of the next day" (NRSV), or, perhaps, from daybreak until evening. [When Did the

Battle Begin?] David's attack was so successful that *only* 400 Amalekite warriors escaped, a number that is significant because David's troops also measured 400 men. The apparent fraction of the Amalekites who escaped on camelback were as many as David's entire fighting force— another not-so-subtle sign of Yahweh's hand of blessing upon David.

Having routed the raiders, David "recovered all that the Amalekites had taken . . . nothing was missing, whether small or great, sons or daughters, spoil or anything that had been taken; David brought back everything" (vv. 18-19; cf. v. 8). One might presume that the desert pirates would have eaten, ruined, or lost at least some of the plunder taken during their operation, but the narrator insists that David recovered it all, including the flocks and herds that had been driven in advance of the raiding party. As leader, this part of the loot was ceded to him as "David's spoil" (v. 20).

The reader will note immediately the contrast between David and Saul in their dealings with the Amalekites. Saul was commanded to wage holy war on the Amalekites, which required the total destruction of Amalek, both property and person. Saul won a decisive victory, but chose to keep King Agag alive, along with the best of the cattle (15:9, 21). This act of willful disobedience led directly to his permanent rejection by Yahweh, symbolically declared by Samuel (15:26-29; 28:18). David also attacked the Amalekites, but when he also took spoil, it was celebrated! One could argue that David was not subject to the same restrictions of the *ḥerem* ban that had been imposed upon Saul. On the other hand, it seems that David represented such a new paradigm for kingship in Israel that the old rules no longer applied to him. Taking spoil spoiled Saul's future, but the plunder David took was seen as a sign of blessing.

What David did with the goods is as important to the storyteller as how he obtained it. When the triumphant troops and their reunited families regained the bivouac where the tired 200 waited with the baggage, David insisted that equal shares be given to those who remained with the gear, reasoning that Yahweh had given the victory and Yahweh's blessings should be shared. This ruling—over the stringent objections of the "corrupt and worthless fellows" in David's company—is presented as a noble act of grace and tact, underscoring the royal fitness of Israel's future king (vv. 21-25). Though Moses (Num 31:25-31) and Joshua (Josh 22:8) had made

When Did the Battle Begin?

AΩ The word *hanneŝep* usually means "twilight," but it can also carry the sense of "morning light," as in Job 7:4 and Ps 119:147. If we translate with "twilight," the battle would have lasted for at least 24 hours, going through the night. It seems more reasonable to assume that David's troops would have attacked at dawn (lest their families be injured in the darkness). In this case, the combat would have lasted only for the better part of the daylight hours.

Political Connections

There are some discrepancies between the MT and the LXX regarding which cities received grants from David. The MT has Bethel, Ramoth, Jattir, Aroer, Siphmoth, Eshtemoa, and Racal, in addition to the towns of the Jerahmeelites and Kenites—Hormah, Borashan, Athach, and Hebron. The LXX has Beth-zur for Bethel (which seems too far north), and Ararah for Aroer (which was in the Transjordan). To Siphmoth and Estemoa, the LXXᴮ adds Geth, Keimath, Saphek, and Theimath. Also, the LXX has Carmel in place of Racal, Kenizzites instead of Kenites, Beer-sheba for Borashan, and Ether rather than Athach.

Of these cities, at least one (Siphmoth) is otherwise unknown (contrast 1 Chr 27:27), and many are obscure, though their names appear in ancient lists of cities assigned to various tribes. All the cities and territories mentioned were in the southern part of Judah in the vicinity of Hebron, which was the principal city of the region. David's gifts to the elders of these cities contributed to the growing list of alliances he would need as a power base for his future political aspirations.

similar rulings, the narrator insists that it was David who made this a perpetual rule that remained in effect "to the present day."

David's political astuteness was also revealed in his decision to send parts of the spoil as a *present* (the same word used by Abigail in 25:27) to the leaders of various towns in the southern part of Judah. [Political Connections] David's purpose seems obvious: he was cultivating favor with those leaders who could and would support his kingship when the opportunity arose. The town mentioned last, significantly, is Hebron, where David would be crowned as king of Judah (2 Sam 2:1-4).

CONNECTIONS

The stories of 1 Samuel 29–30 are largely built on the theme of how God works in mysterious ways his wonders to perform—for David. Saul, it appears, cannot win and cannot do anything right. David, on the other hand, cannot lose. His actions sometimes appear to be foolhardy, risky, or misguided, but because Yahweh is with him, he always comes out on top. David's apparent defection to Achish (whatever his inner motives may have been) almost ruined his future by putting him in the position of fighting his own people, but Yahweh delivered him from his narrow straits by using the suspicions of his own enemies to carry David far from the scene of battle and any hint of collusion in the death of Saul.

Likewise, David's return to Ziklag revealed that he had made a grave mistake in leaving the city unguarded—an error in judgment that led to a near mutiny among his men. Yet David's appeal to Yahweh for guidance pulled the troops together, and the propitious discovery of the Amalekites' ailing Egyptian slave provided the intelligence necessary to rescue all persons and property taken by the raiders. As was often the case in David's life, Yahweh was clearly at work, though behind the scenes, quietly assuring David's success.

Modern believers have no guarantee that they will be as successful in business or politics as David happened to be. God's blessings upon David served a divine purpose for Israel's benefit and do not suggest an eternal principle that those who call upon the Lord shall prosper. After all, Saul also sought God's leadership, without result. The difference between Saul and David was a contrast between disobedience and obedience. Rebellious Saul could not hope to receive God's blessing. David, the man after God's own heart, could hardly escape it. Those who serve God faithfully in our own world have no promise that they will prosper in this world as David did, but they do have assurance of an ultimate and eternal victory.

Today's faith community may find it significant that when David found himself in distress, he "strengthened himself in the LORD" by seeking God's guidance. Asking for an oracle by sacred lot may seem strange to modern minds, but in David's world it was understood as a divinely endorsed means of ascertaining God's will. Today, we have other avenues of divine revelation available to us. We have the Scriptures, which include the teachings of Christ as well as the full message of the Old Testament. We have the presence of the Holy Spirit, who has now been promised to all believers, even as the spirit of God brought unique blessing to the lives of a few exceptional persons of the Old Testament period. We have the invitation to pray directly to God in Jesus' name, without need to seek the mediation of a priest or oracle. We have the long history of the Christian church and the insight it has garnered through the years. With these abundant resources, there is little excuse for modern believers to claim ignorance of God's revealed will.

Those who celebrate the generosity of Jesus will also appreciate David's noble act of sharing the bounty of battle with all of his people, with those who guarded the gear as well as those who fought the actual battle. For some readers, this may call to mind Jesus' parable of the laborers in the vineyard who worked different hours but received the same pay (Matt 20:1-16). For others, it may recall Paul's insistence that all believers belong to a single body and deserve equal honor even though they may serve quite different functions (1 Cor 12).

Beneath every lesson of these two chapters lies the basic truth that God is at work—in cooperation with God's people. God's work may not always be evident to those who are spiritually dense (like the "corrupt and worthless fellows" among David's entourage), but for those who have eyes to see and ears to hear, the blessings of life are the blessings of the Lord.

SAUL'S LAST BATTLE AND AN HONORABLE DEATH

31:1-13

COMMENTARY

With 31:1, the narrator returns to the story of Saul's last days, a story that began in 28:3 with a hollow man's pleading before the spirit woman of Endor and ends with a dead man's falling before the Philistines in an ignominious demise that necessitated an act of heroism just to rescue his bones for a decent burial. As mentioned above, the story is sandwiched around the account of David's activities during the same period (chs. 29–30), a strategy that serves not only to raise narrative tension, but also to draw a sharp contrast between the hapless history of Saul and the charmed achievements of David.

Saul's story is as depressing as David's is delightful. Although his death is fully expected, its telling is so understated that the reader feels almost let down, as disappointed with the story as with Saul. The narrator's omnipresent eye returns to the battle scene that was laid out in 28:4—the Philistines were encamped at Shunem, near the southwestern slopes of the Hill of Moreh, while Israel's camp was on the opposite side of the valley, on the northern edge of Mount Gilboa. According to 29:1, Saul's actual encampment was near the spring of Jezreel, a crossroads town near the foot of the mountain.

The all-too-brief account of the battle suggests that the Philistines took the initiative, which was probably necessary. The technologically advanced Philistines, with their iron chariots, would have a distinct advantage on the open valley floor. Saul's only hope was to force the Philistines to engage his lightly armed men on the rugged slopes of Gilboa, where the Israelites' chances for success would be enhanced. The Philistines did indeed attack Saul's army on Mount Gilboa, but their superior numbers enabled them to make quick work of the Israelite soldiers.

In the course of the battle, Saul was quickly deprived of his army, which "fled before the Philistines, and many fell on Mount Gilboa"

The Death of Saul's Sons

The number and names of Saul's sons are presented differently in various texts. The genealogical notes of 1 Sam 14:49 list Jonathan, Ishvi, and Malchishua, while the narrative description of the battle at Gilboa says Saul's three sons were killed and lists them as Jonathan, Abinadab, and Malchishua (1 Sam 31:2=1 Chr 10:2). Other genealogical lists in the Chronicler's work list four sons: Jonathan, Abinadab, Malchishua, and Eshbaal (1 Chr 8:33; 9:39).

The text of 2 Samuel insists that at least one son survived the battle, presumably because he was not present at the site. With the support of Abner, Saul's general, Saul's son Ishbaal (also called Ishvi, Eshbaal, and Ishbosheth) presided over a makeshift government for a short time prior to David's accession to the throne (2 Sam 2:8–4:12).

(v. 1). He was then bereaved of his family: Three of Saul's sons died in battle, as Samuel had predicted. [The Death of Saul's Sons] Saul himself was pinned down by the Philistine archers, who may have wounded him and in any case left him in a hopeless situation. [Was Saul Wounded or Worried?] Saul had no doubt that he would die, for Samuel had told him so (28:19), but he had no desire to suffer humiliation at the hands of the Philistines. Thus, in the last moments of his life, hapless Saul mustered the courage to make a choice, and it was a choice to die on his own terms.

Was Saul Wounded or Worried?

AΩ Most translations assume that Saul was seriously wounded by the Philistine archers, who are said to have "found him." English readers are familiar with the idiom of an archer "finding his mark," but the Hebrew term may not have implied the same thing. The only places in the MT where *māṣāʾ* is translated as "hit" are here, the parallel text in 1 Chr 10:3, and the reference to an axehead flying off and "finding" someone in Deut 19:5. The LXX[B] asserts that Saul was "wounded in the belly," but the MT states only that "he writhed in fear of the archers."

Thus, the reader is uncertain whether Saul had suffered a mortal wound and feared only short-lived torture before his death, or whether he was unwounded but certain of capture, which would undoubtedly lead to public humiliation before the Philistine peoples.

Julius Schnoor von Carolsfeld. *Saul's Death.* 19th century. Woodcut. *Das Buch der Bucher in Bilden.* (Credit: Dover Pictorial Archive Series)

Saul entreated his armor-bearer to run him through, but his lone companion recoiled from the deed, "for he was terrified" (v. 4). The text does not reveal the source of his terror. Was it the fear of harming God's anointed? The natural fear of killing someone so highly regarded as Saul? The fear of being tortured by the Philistines for ruining their sport? The aide's refusal left Saul even more alone, forced by his circumstances to make a fateful choice, but with just enough strength to escape becoming a living laughingstock for the Philistine commanders. Despite his own strained relationship with Yahweh, Saul despised the Philistines as "uncircumcised" to his dying day and would not willingly suffer at their hands.

And so, Saul died on the blade of his own sword, with his closest attaché standing by. Saul expired quietly—too quietly—with no parting instructions, no last words, no final message to his subjects or his family. "He took his own sword and fell on it" (v. 4). In a touching display of solidarity, Saul's armor-bearer followed the king's example and died with him (v. 5).

As the narrator paints the scene, there are no witnesses to tell the tale, for Saul was all alone in the end. This suggests the extent to which the story of Saul's final moments may have been created by the storyteller, rather than simply reported. It was necessary that Saul be pinned down by archers, who would remain at a sufficient distance to prove an ominous threat, yet not close enough to identify Saul or to interfere with his suicide. The dialogue between Saul and his aide would have to come from the narrator's imagination, for there was none other living to tell the tale. It was this lack of witnesses that allowed an ambitious young Amalekite to offer David an uncontested, much different account of Saul's demise (2 Sam 1:1-10).

The narrator provides a stunning summation of the battle in v. 6, one that must be read slowly and darkly for maximum effect: "So Saul—*and* his three sons—*and* his armor-bearer—*and all* his men died together on the same day." When other Israelites in the area saw the outcome, they fled, leaving the plain of Jezreel under the full sway of the Philistine armies. [Far-Sighted Folk] The constant Philistine threat had been one of the main motivating

Far-Sighted Folk

The text claims that the Israelites "on the other side of the valley and those beyond the Jordan saw that the men of Israel had fled and that Saul and his sons were dead," causing them to flee in fear, allowing the Philistines to occupy their towns. "On the other side of the valley" describes those Israelites who lived in towns and villages on the northern edge of the Valley of Jezreel—not to a contingent of reserves who were waiting to ambush the Philistines from the rear. "Those beyond the Jordan" is a reference to Israelites living on the eastern side of the Jordan River. They were, of course, much too far away to *see* Saul's defeat, but they would have heard about it quickly enough.

The narrator uses this verse (31:7) to emphasize the extent of the Philistine conquest, for they now controlled the entire valley and plain of Jezreel, effectively cutting the northern tribes off from the south. In addition, the Philistine hegemony extended to the Jordan River and beyond, leaving Israel only the southern hill country as their uncontested homeland.

factors leading Israel to call for a king. Saul, however, had failed to ameliorate the situation. At his death, the Philistine presence was even more oppressive, for they not only ruled the coastal lands to the south and west of Israel, but also controlled the entire Jezreel Valley, which ran across the heart of the nation, and even part of the Transjordanian lands to the east. Thus, at Saul's death, Israel was more threatened and divided than before. The reader is well prepared to anticipate that David will save the day, but not without the knowledge that Israel's first experiment with kingship was an abject failure.

Saul's dismal fall is balanced in small part by the closing vignette about the valorous men of Jabesh-gilead. The Philistines waited until the following day, the narrator says, to come and strip the dead of their weapons and valuables. As unlikely as it seems from the earlier story, it was only then that the Philistines discovered Saul and his sons among the victims. Tall Saul may have been well known by sight. He and his sons also could have been distinguished by the higher quality of their armor, perhaps, or identified by Israelite prisoners of war.

Saul's fear of humiliation at the hands of the enemy was fulfilled in death. The Philistines cut off his head (as David had done to Goliath) and displayed it as a grisly trophy, perhaps sending it with the messengers who carried the news of victory "to the houses of their idols and to the people" (v. 9). [Houses of Their Idols] Saul's armor was displayed in a temple to the Canaanite goddess Asherah (vocalized as Athtart or Astarte in other ancient languages; the MT has the plural, Ashtaroth). The Philistines' primary god was Dagon, in whose temple they had once placed the ark (1 Sam 5), but they apparently participated in the local Canaanite cults as well.

Houses of Their Idols

The pejorative reference to the "houses of their idols" offers a narrative hint that the Philistine power is transient. When David comes to defeat the Philistines, they will abandon their idols (2 Sam 5:17-25), even as the Israelites had abandoned their dead and their cities.

Saul's body—with or without the head—was carried to the crossroads city of Beth-shan, where the Jezreel and Jordan Valleys meet. There, the Philistines fastened his body to the city wall (or perhaps in the public square, 2 Sam 21:12) as a public display of their superiority. According to v. 13, Saul's three sons were also hung on the wall. The Philistine warrior Goliath had once threatened to feed David to the birds of the air (1 Sam 17:44); now his colleagues carried out that same dreadful deed against the ruling royalty of Israel. The word for "fastened" (NRSV) translates a word that means "to strike with a sharp blow," as in pounding a nail or a tent peg. City walls were generally made of stone, but some sort of wooden

City Walls

AΩ Remains of the ancient city wall surrounding Beth-shan. These crumbling walls, deep in Israelite territory, were used to display the bodies of Saul and his sons. (Credit: Tony W. Cartledge)

---

superstructure could have been fastened to the wall to support the gruesome exhibition. [City Walls]

Saul's life was lost, and much of his dignity with it, but there were some in Israel whose long memories contained a young Saul who had fire in his eyes and valor in his heart. The men of Jabesh-gilead, the city Saul had once heroically rescued from the Ammonites (1 Sam 10:27–11:15), were moved to return the favor by retrieving the royal bodies to save them from further degradation. Their city was about thirteen miles east of Beth-shan. By marching through the night, the valiant men of Jabesh were able to reach the Philistine stronghold, surreptitiously remove the bodies, and regain their city. There, they burned the bodies, perhaps as a means of purifying them from the offensive handling of the unclean Philistines, and gave them a decent burial beneath a tamarisk tree. The reference to burning is highly unusual, for cremation was not ordinarily acceptable in Israel. Perhaps this is why the duplicate account in 1 Chronicles 10:12 does not mention it. David would later have the bones exhumed and reburied in the Benjaminite tomb of Saul's father, Kish (2 Sam 21:12-14).

The daring deed of the Jabeshites allows 1 Samuel to close on a note of small triumph, but even that rings hollow against Saul's monumental demise. The true renascence of Israel is yet to come. The reader is left waiting for David, who is still a nominal vassal of the Philistines, still in Ziklag. How will David react to Saul's death? What will he do? When will he come? The answers to those questions form the largest part of 2 Samuel.

CONNECTIONS

Saul's ignominious end is an Old Testament example of a New Testament truth, that "the wages of sin is death" (Rom 3:23). The narrator makes it clear that Samuel had instructed Saul to obey Yahweh, but Saul chose to follow a path more to his liking. The immediate result was the loss of his kingdom (1 Sam 15:17-29); the ultimate price was the loss of his life (1 Sam 28:18-19). Saul's death by his own hand is a pointed reminder that he had brought himself to that point by his own choices. [A Stark Reminder]

The saddest aspect of Saul's fall is that he brought so many others down with him. Three of Saul's sons died, including the heroic and loyal Jonathan. Many Israelite soldiers lay in their blood on Mount Gilboa. Other Israelites were forced to flee from their homes and land, leaving the Philistines free to run rampant over the Israelite heartland and to separate the northern and southern tribes from one another. The dark end that had its genesis in Saul's disobedience had consequences that affect innocent lives from one end of Israel to the other.

The one glimmer of hope in this story comes from the courageous men of Jabesh-gilead, who proved that even in dark and difficult times, there are still

A Stark Reminder

This forlorn tree was mounted at the edge of the tall Tell of Beth-shan and used as a prop for Judas' suicide in the film version of *Jesus Christ Superstar*. The skeletal form remains long after the filming and is a fitting reminder of Saul's dark demise.

(Credit: Tony W. Cartledge)

choices to be made, and they can be choices for good rather than evil. At the risk of their own lives, the Jabeshites showed unselfish kindness to Saul and in doing so earned for themselves a reputation for loyalty and valor that will remain as long as people read their story. Out of darkness, there is the hope of light.

Little imagination is required to connect Saul's experience with our own. We also have the power to make choices for good or for bad. We can trust in God as the source of all life, or we can choose our own paths—but not without the knowledge that the wages of sin is death. We know that we do not live in a vacuum. There are others who look to us for leadership. If we fall, we may bring them down with us, and thus our guilt is multiplied. All is not lost, however. The men of Jabesh-gilead offer proof that the power to make good and redeeming choices exists as long as we live, if only we have the courage to carry those out.

2 SAMUEL

DAVID MOURNS FOR SAUL AND JONATHAN

1:1-27

Part Three: David—King of All Israel, 1:1–24:25

The book called "2 Samuel" in the Hebrew canon continues the narrative that began in 1 Samuel. Originally, the two were almost certainly preserved as a single book. The Samuel scroll from Qumran suggests that the two books existed on one scroll. The MT preserves a Masoretic note at 1 Samuel 28:24, indicating that it was the halfway point in "the book of Samuel," as well as a note from the end of 2 Samuel, giving the total number of verses in both 1 and 2 Samuel. This would be correct only if the Masoretes had considered Samuel to be one book. The division into two may have been introduced by the Greek translators.

Like 1 Samuel, 2 Samuel is made up of a variety of source materials, drawn together by the ancient editors commonly known as the Deuteronomists. [Sources for Samuel] As such, it belongs to the larger corpus that includes the books of Joshua through 2 Kings, exclusive of Ruth. Some of the materials found in 2 Samuel are continuations or fragments of the same sources found in 1 Samuel. For example, the so-called "History of David's Rise" (HDR), which began with 1 Samuel 16 (some say 15), may continue through 2 Samuel 5 (some

---

Sources for Samuel

With an awareness that the limits of these sources are a matter of great debate, and that not all scholars use the same descriptive terms, here is a list of source materials commonly assigned to 1 and 2 Samuel:

(1) The Biography of Samuel (1 Sam 1–3)
(2) The Ark Narrative (1 Sam 4–6; 2 Sam 6)
(3) The Rise of Kingship (1 Sam 9–11)
(4) Saul's Battles (1 Sam 13–15)
(5) The History of David's Rise (1 Sam 16–2 Sam 5)
(6) The Succession Narrative (2 Sam 9–20; 1 Kgs 1–2)
(7) Appendices (2 Sam 21–24)

Material not included in these sources is generally thought to be the creation of the Deuteronomists, probably incorporating other isolated bits of traditional material.

say 7), and the "Ark Narrative" (AN) found in 1 Samuel 4–6 finds a brief reprise in 2 Samuel 6.

The largest source block in 2 Samuel is a document commonly called "The Succession Narrative" (SN). This narrative, an apparent apology for why David's son Solomon was allowed to succeed him—despite Davidic sins, which appear more serious than Saul's—is found in 2 Samuel 9–20 and 2 Kings 1–2. Some scholars see HDR roughly extending as far as 2 Samuel 8, while others prefer to think of SN beginning as early as 1 Samuel 1. Still others have observed that the two sources may have preserved similar stories so that there is some overlap, in which the Deuteronomists have chosen the materials that best suited their own tendentious interests.

The final four chapters of 2 Samuel are generally referred to as "Appendices," which describe various details of David's rule that were considered important, but not included in the other documents.

David's Rise from Hebron to Jerusalem, 1:1–5:10

The book begins with the portentous phrase "after the death of Saul." The first five chapters of 2 Samuel concern themselves with the awkward transition from Saul's death on Mount Gilboa to David's ascension to the throne in Jerusalem. How could David acquire both the throne and Israel's loyalty without appearing to be self-serving or duplicitous? The task required the skills of a consummate communicator and a polished politician. Fortunately, David possessed prowess and proficiency in precisely these areas. David's time had come, but his part would have to be played with deftness and confidence. There was precious little room for mistakes.

COMMENTARY

Killing the Bearer of Bad News, 1:1-16

The first sixteen verses of 2 Samuel 1 make up a fairly uniform literary unit. The story describes how David learned the news of Saul's death and came into possession of certain royal emblems that had been in Saul's possession. As it marks the most important turning point in David's rise to the throne, it is a fitting beginning

Why an Amalekite?

The Amalekites played an important role—at least in the literary sense—in the lives of Saul and David. According to the Old Testament tradition, the Amalekites were descended from one of Esau's grandsons (Gen 36:12; 1 Chr 1:36). Thus, they were linked with the Edomites and remembered as perpetual enemies of Israel (Exod 17:8-16; Num 14:43-45; Deut 25:17-19). The Amalekites who troubled Saul and David did not live in the neighborhood of Edom (south of the Dead Sea), but to the south and west of Judah. Yahweh sent Saul against the Amalekites in a holy war, but Saul refused to carry out the proscribed bans, leading to his rejection as king (1 Sam 15). David also fought against the Amalekites, always victoriously (1 Sam 27:8; 30:1-20).

The narrator has skillfully sandwiched David's success against the Amalekites around the account of Saul's unhappy consultation with the ghost of Samuel (1 Sam 28), who reminded him that his failure in the Amalekite matter had cost him the throne.

Thus, it is most appropriate that the harbinger (and perhaps the cause) of Saul's death should be a scavenging Amalekite—and that he should be given his comeuppance by David, who has no patience with those who would toy with Yahweh's anointed, no matter what the circumstance.

---

for 2 Samuel. "After the death of Saul" is reminiscent of the introductory verses of Joshua ("After the death of Moses," 1:1) and Judges ("After the death of Joshua," 1:1). If the book of Samuel had to be divided, this is as good a place as any.

The narrator is careful to point out that David learned the news while camped out in the ruins of Ziklag, far removed from the site of Saul's death. Ziklag was a frontier city located in the deep south, while Mount Gilboa, where Saul died, was north of Judah, on the southern flank of the Jezreel Valley.

The author reveals not only that David is in Ziklag, but that he has only been there for two days, following his defeat of the Amalekite raiders who had stormed his city and taken hostage all the women and children (1 Sam 30). Thus, the reader knows that David cannot possibly be guilty of any complicity in Saul's death. The Philistines had ousted him from their army prior to the battle (1 Sam 29), and he had been occupied with pursuing the Amalekite pirates since that time (2 Sam 1:1). Supporters of Saul may have accused David of collusion in the death of Saul, but the author insists that no one could be more innocent than David.

Ironically, the news of Saul's demise is brought to David by a certain Amalekite, perhaps a mercenary soldier, but one who is clearly serving his own purposes when he arrives in Ziklag. [Why an Amalekite?] His claim to have "escaped from the camp of Israel" implies that he had fought on Israel's behalf. His torn clothes and dirt-strewn appearance bear all the marks of ritual grief, as if the fallen king were his own liege (vv. 2-3). [Signs of Mourning]

Signs of Mourning

The tearing of one's clothes and sprinkling of dust on the head were typical tokens of mourning in the ancient world, as illustrated by Jacob's actions when he heard that Joseph was dead (Gen 37:34). Joshua tore his clothes and put dust on his head after the defeat at Ai (Josh 7:6), and David did the same when he learned of Absalom's death (2 Sam 13:31). Another story of a messenger demonstrating grief is found in 1 Sam 4:12, where a Benjaminite reported the death of Eli's sons and the capture of the ark by the Philistines at the battle of Aphek-Ebenezer.

Another common emblem of mourning was the wearing of sackcloth (2 Sam 3:31; Lam 2:10; Joel 1:8; Amos 8:10). Various personal behaviors also depicted grief, including fasting (1 Sam 31:13; 2 Sam 3:35), voicing lamentations (Gen 37:35; 2 Sam 1:12; 18:33), and lying prostrate on the ground (Josh 7:6; 2 Sam 13:31). These behaviors may have at times been spontaneous, but also bore the mark of socially expected observances.

The Amalekite's account of Saul's death (vv. 4-10) differs from the story in 1 Samuel 31 in several ways. For example, The Amalekite mentions the deaths of Saul and Jonathan only, while 1 Samuel 31 records the deaths of three royal sons. The armor bearer who refused to kill Saul in 1 Samuel 31 does not appear in the Amalekite's tale. Also, 1 Samuel 31 suggests that Saul fought from the mountain crags, where only the Philistine archers could reach him. In 2 Samuel 1, however, the herald insisted that the Philistine chariots and horsemen were bearing down on Saul. The chariots, at least, could not traverse the mountain paths where 1 Samuel 31 says Saul had chosen to make his last stand.

The most significant difference, however, relates to the manner of Saul's death. The previous story insists that Saul, pinned down by the enemy, died by his own hand when his man-at-arms refused to slay him and so prevent the Philistines from capturing him alive. In contrast, the Amalekite claims to have happened upon a wounded Saul who was close to death, enduring convulsions (or perhaps dizziness), and in danger of imminent capture. At Saul's plaintive request, the Amalekite claimed, he took pity on the doomed man and killed him. Not wanting Saul's crown and royal amulet to fall into Philistine hands, he had brought them to David.

It is obvious that both accounts cannot be true literally. Many scholars give greater credence to the second, since it draws the least savory picture, and consider it to be a variant account from a different source. More recently, a majority of commentators have agreed that the story is a continuation of the same source found in 1 Samuel and that the discrepancies can be explained by assuming that the messenger was lying. He was, after all, an Amalekite, and thus automatically suspect of treachery. He may have been nothing more than a battlefield scavenger who found Saul already dead by his own hand. He stripped Saul of his royal insignia and calculated that David might grant him a large reward for them. In his mind, he might also have expected to curry greater favor with David by claiming to have killed his rival personally. He was neither the first nor the last to misjudge David.

Fortunately, whether the messenger's story was true or not is immaterial. David had nothing else to go on. He had to take the Amalekite at his word. David's response was immediate, forceful, and, to all appearances, genuine. One of the magic qualities of David's leadership was his uncanny ability to do the right thing at the right time, with convincing integrity.

David tore his clothes and fell into a paroxysm of weeping, wailing, and fasting (vv. 11-12) as he grieved publicly, not only for his friend Jonathan, but also for King Saul. Despite their dissonant relationship, David respected Saul as Yahweh's anointed, and he gave every appearance, at least, of truly grieving over Saul's death. As the narrator notes, David and his followers wept as well for the warriors of Israel who had fallen and for the fate that lay ahead for the remaining Israelites, who were largely defenseless against Philistine predations.

David's second response was directed toward the herald of such bad tidings, who responded to David's query by identifying himself as an Amalekite by birth, but a resident alien of Israel. David's single question carries with it an inevitable verdict: "Were you not afraid to lift your hand to destroy the LORD's anointed?" (v. 14). No quarter was given, no opportunity to explain, no rationalizations. David ordered one of his guards to slay the Amalekite on the spot, as if he represented an evil too vile to be given space to exist any longer.

In a later account, when men with similar motives brought David the head of rival Ishbosheth, David claimed to have killed the Amalekite messenger himself (2 Sam 4:10). For a king, however, the command to kill someone is not so much different from swinging the sword; the responsibility is the same. In David's eyes, there was no room for interpretation or excuse when it came to harming the LORD's anointed: "Your blood be on your own head; for your own mouth has testified against you, saying, 'I have killed the LORD's anointed' " (v. 16).

As described by the author, then, David's handling of the situation was masterful. The Amalekite had brought what many would consider to be marvelous news for one who would be king, for one who had been relentlessly pursued by the same man whose death had been announced. The reader might expect David to exult, at least secretly, over such tidings. Yet David did not receive it as good

news. The loss of Saul and Jonathan may have been politically felic-
itous, but it was still emotionally trying. Legally, it involved the
intentional striking down of the LORD's
anointed, which intensified the sense of tragic
loss.

A Note on the Anointed

AΩ The concept of the king as the "anointed of Yahweh" is virtually unique to the books of Samuel. The phrase appears eleven times in the Old Testament. Except for Lam 4:20, all of these instances are in 1 and 2 Samuel (1 Sam 16:6; 24:6, 10; 26:9, 11, 16, 23; 2 Sam 1:14, 16; 19:21). The author/editors seem to imply that the later kings whose histories they describe were not chosen or anointed by God as were Saul, David, and Solomon.

In every arena, then, David responded in ways
that seemed both genuine *and* effective in winning popular favor. The cynic will note that
David, who was also anointed by Yahweh, had
good reason to build on and preserve the
absolute taboo on harming Yahweh's anointed,
as he had done before (1 Sam 24:6-7; 26:9-11).

[A Note on the Anointed] The reader might suspect that David's primary
concern is with his own future security, but the narrator insists that
David's motives were pure. Saul was dead and the crown was in
David's hand, but Israel (and later readers) must know that David
was wholly innocent.

Lamenting the Loss of a Friend and His Father, 1:17-27

David's elegy for Saul and Jonathan probably derived from another
ancient source and was inserted here to give added poignancy to
the grief already expressed in vv. 11-12. The traditional view is that
the dirge reflects the actual words of David, who was famed as the
author of many psalms, and there is no particular reason to question the attribution. To that extent, it offers the modern reader an
open window into David's mind and heart.

The actual lament is found in vv. 19-27, while vv. 17-18 form an
introduction. The word for "lamentation" in v. 17 is *qînâ*, and it
refers uniquely to a funerary lament or dirge. [The *qînâ* Lament] The
introduction in v. 18 has been the occasion of much comment, as
the MT contains an anomalous word (*qāšet*), which is usually

The *qînâ* Lament

AΩ Songs that fall into this literary type frequently have an unbalanced beat (a 3 + 2 rhythm) that produces an incomplete, haunting effect when chanted. *Qînâ* laments tend to be reflective, looking back at the life and accomplishments of the dead. In contrast, the many "psalms of lament" in the book of Psalms tend to be more forward-looking—they are prayers of the distressed, hoping to gain succor. Of all the laments contained in the psalms, none of them are dirges.

Funerary laments could be pronounced over peoples or cities as well as individuals (Lam 1; 2). On occasion, the prophets used the literary form of a dirge to bewail Israel's loss before the fact (Ezek 26:17-18), assuring their hearers of Israel's future fall.

The questioning grief of funerary laments commonly began with the word translated as "how" (Lam 1:1; 2:1; 4:1; Jer 9:19 [MT 18]), as in David's lament over Saul and Jonathan: "How the mighty have fallen!" (2 Sam 1:19, 25, 27).

Dirges are usually addressed to the deceased, in the second person, and rarely mention God. They are exercises in grief, not religious rituals.

translated by the normal meaning "bow" but seems out of place. Literally, the MT reads, "He said to teach the sons of Judah the bow." David is *not* talking about archery training for the Judahites, however, for the following line—"it is written in the Book of Jashar"—makes it clear that the subject of David's command is the elegy itself.

A few authors simply omit the word on the basis of a few Greek manuscripts in which it is lacking. More recently, some scholars have chosen to interpret the word "bow" as a title or tune for the dirge. Thus, they regard the phrase as a superscription after the order of the similar instructions in the psalms, such as "According to Alamoth" (Ps 46) or "According to Mahalath Leannoth" (Ps 88). Thus, for example, the NRSV translates, "He ordered that the Song of the Bow be taught to the people of Judah."

Of further interest is the Book of Jashar, often interpreted to mean "The Book of Upright." [The Book of Jashar] The book was probably a collection of poetic paeans to heroic figures in Israel's history. Though now lost, the author calls upon it as a source of authority for his recounting of David's elegy over Saul and Jonathan.

David's song consists of two unequal stanzas set apart by the threefold occurrence of the refrain "How the mighty have fallen." The first stanza (vv. 20-24) addresses the loss of Saul and Jonathan together, while the second stanza (vv. 25b-26) mourns for Jonathan alone. The refrain (vv. 19, 25, 27) punctuates the lament with a repeated cry of grief, which might have been voiced by those who heard the elegy as a means of congregational participation. In typical Hebrew style, the poetic parallelism is predominantly synonymous and based on couplets, with occasional irregularities for emphasis. [Hebrew Poetry]

The Book of Jashar

The Book of Jashar is also quoted in Josh 10:12-13, a poetic description of Israel's victory over the Amorites, when Joshua commanded the sun to halt in the sky. These two examplars suggest that the book was a poetic collection of heroic stories from Israel's history. The Deuteronomistic History was probably compiled in the 6th century BC, and the editors speak of the book as if it were commonly known. Like the equally enigmatic "Book of the Wars of Yahweh" (Num 21:14), however, it has now been lost.

The two verses are introduced by similar statements announcing the reason for the lament. "Your glory, O Israel, lies slain upon your high places!" (v. 19a, NRSV) is a typical translation, though it is by no means certain. "Glory" (*haṣṣĕbî*) derives from a word (*ṣb*) for "gazelle" which may carry a secondary meaning of "beauty" or "honor." Several modern scholars prefer to read the initial *h* not as the definite article, as in the MT, but as the particle *hō*, meaning "Alas!" Some also conjecture that the word "gazelle" could have been used as a sobriquet for royalty, thus, "Alas! The prince lies slain." This interpretation preserves a closer symmetry between the

---

Hebrew Poetry

Hebrew poetry is marked not by a rhythm of sound, but of *sense*. Hebrew poetry does not rhyme, as much English poetry does, nor does it always have a discernible meter, as does English poetry (aside from free verse). Rather, Hebrew poetry is distinguished by a repetition of thought that is called *parallelism*, usually occurring in dyads (also called couplets or bicola), though triads are not uncommon.

The most obvious and frequent style of parallelism is called *synonymous*, meaning that the second line restates or augments the sense of the first, but in different words. For example, "Tell it not in Gath / proclaim it not in the streets of Ashkelon" (2 Sam 1:20a) are parallel statements expressing a desire that the news the deaths of Saul and Jonathan not be told to the Philistines. This is made clear in the following couplet: "or the daughters of the Philistines will rejoice / the daughters of the uncircumcised will exult" (2 Sam 1:20b).

Hebrew poets occasionally employed *antithetic* parallelism, in which the second statement expresses the opposite of the first. This is especially popular in Israel's

wisdom literature, including poems such as Ps 37: "The wicked borrow, and do not pay back / but the righteous are generous and keep giving" (v. 21; see also vv. 17, 22, 28b).

The third style of parallelism is called *synthetic* or *formal*, for it advances the thought of the first line in some way, but without repeating the same idea. For example, David's elegy contains the following lines: "Saul and Jonathan, beloved and lovely! / In life and in death they were not divided" (2 Sam 1:23a). Both lines offer praise to Saul and Jonathan, but in different ways. The second line does not reiterate the handsome pair's popularity with the people, but adds a statement about their loyalty to one another.

The use of parallelism serves an important literary purpose in Hebrew poetry. Whether the poet utilizes synonymous, antithetic, or synthetic parallelism, the second (and sometimes third) line almost always serves to intensify or elaborate upon the thought of the first, adding emphasis in creative and delightful ways.

For further reading, consider Robert Alter, *The Art of Biblical Poetry* (New York: Basic Books, 1985), among others.

---

introduction to the refrain in vv. 19 and 24: "The prince lies slain / Jonathan lies slain."

The first stanza expresses deep resentment of the Philistines (v. 20) and of Mount Gilboa (v. 21), while saluting the admirable qualities of Saul and Jonathan (vv. 21-23) and calling upon the women of Israel to weep for those who had enriched their lives (v. 24). The "daughters of the Philistines" in v. 20 are nicely balanced by the "daughters of Israel" in v. 24. This serves as an effective *inclusio*, further marking vv. 20-24 as a unit. [Always Include the Inclusio]

Always Include the Inclusio

Inclusio is a term used by literary critics to describe a word or phrase that appears at the beginning and ending of a given section of the text, setting it apart from its surroundings. Some complex texts contain a series of embedded inclusios, tightly binding the passage into a unity of related ideas. More often, especially in poetry, inclusios are used to delimit one section only.

David's elegy makes it clear that the deaths of Saul and Jonathan were a blow to the entire nation, an event that warranted great mourning. "How the mighty have fallen!" is a cry from the heart, intended to express personal grief and to appeal to the hearts of others.

The insistence that the news not be carried to Ashkelon and Gath, two representative Philistine cities, is moot, for surely Philistine runners would have already reported the victory before David's secretive visitor alerted him to the death of Israel's royalty (see 1 Sam 31:9). [Tell It Not in Gath] Since the ill-fated Amalekite had brought to David Saul's battlefield implements of royalty, perhaps

Tell It Not in Gath

AΩ The phrase "Tell it not in Gath" seems to have achieved proverbial status in Israel. More than two hundred years later, when the prophet Micah bewailed the coming destruction of Judah, he cried, "Tell it not in Gath / weep not at all" (Mic 1:10). Since the Philistines were not a strong threat in Micah's time, there would have been no reason for him to use the phrase except for its popular or proverbial status.

David hoped that Saul would not have been recognized amid the carnage. Surely, however, the quality of his armor would have identified him, as well as his notable height and appearance.

David's concern has to do with the Philistine response to Saul's death—he cannot bear the thought of Philistine women dancing in the streets to celebrate Saul's death. The memory of how Israelite women had sung and danced to celebrate the victories of Saul and David (who "killed thousands / ten thousands" of Philistines) adds irony to the lament.

The site of Saul's death on Mount Gilboa is also a target of David's angry grief, for he pronounces a curse upon the mountain and its surrounding fields, calling for drought to leave them withered and sterile (v. 21a). Saul's army probably carried shields of heavy leather, which were prone to cracking and thus in need of frequent oiling. David lamented the bloody defilement of Saul's personal shield, now spoiled and no longer in need of oiling (v. 21b). The perceptive reader will recognize a double entendre in David's plaint: Saul's shield is no longer anointed with oil because Saul, *the anointed one,* is dead.

With vv. 22-23, David turns from his outrage over the royalties' deaths and pours out his praise for their great valor. Though he had not been present for the battle on Mount Gilboa, David had fought beside Saul and Jonathan in previous battles. He was confident that they would have fought until the bitter end. The image of the heroes' weapons shedding the blood and slicing through the fat of the enemy may appear overly graphic, but it serves to bring the horrors of battle to life, the warriors' heroism in the midst of it. Since blood and fat are often paired in sacrificial terminology, David may have imagined the heroes' valiant feats as an offering to God.

Saul's popularity in Israel was not as evident as Jonathan's, but David could safely speak of the leaders as being beloved by the people. David also praised their beauty; ancient kings were commonly praised for their appearances (1 Sam 9:2; 10:23-24). A quality that set Saul and Jonathan apart was their loyalty to each other. Jonathan loved David and swore his life in covenant to him, but he never defected from his father's camp. Despite the tension between them (see 1 Sam 20:30, 33; 22:8), he remained faithful to his father, even to the point of death.

As modern television writers praised Superman as "faster than a speeding bullet, more powerful than a locomotive," David eulogized Saul and Jonathan as being "swifter than eagles, and stronger than lions." The speed of eagles was proverbial (Deut 28:49; Prov 23:5; Lam 4:19), as was the strength of lions (Judg 14:18; 2 Sam 17:10).

The first section of David's elegy ends by contrasting the daughters of Israel (v. 24) with the daughters of the Philistines (v. 20). David did not want the Philistine women to celebrate Israel's defeat, but he did want the women of Israel to weep for Saul, even as they had sung praises to him in earlier days (1 Sam 18:7). The reference to crimson cloth and ornaments of gold implies that Saul had gained much plunder in his various wars and had shared it with the populace, increasing the material wealth of the country. There is no corroborating evidence for this beneficent activity, so it may be intended as a poetic exaggeration—*or* as a subtle reminder that David himself had enriched the people of Judah by sharing his plunder with them (1 Sam 30:26-31).

The introductory formula to the second section is reversed from its first appearance. In v. 19, the poem bemoans the glory (or prince) of Israel lying slain on the high places, followed by the line "How the mighty have fallen." In contrast, v. 25 begins with "How the mighty have fallen" and then moves to "Jonathan lies slain upon your high places." This serves to add greater emphasis to David's distress over Jonathan, which is deeper and more personal than the sadness motivated by his political loyalty to Saul.

Here, David shifts to the first person, in words more typical of a dirge: "I am distressed for you, my brother Jonathan" (v. 26a). The phrase "greatly beloved were you to me" serves as a synthetic parallel to the opening line and as a transition to the plaintive couplet "Your love to me was wonderful, / passing the love of women" (v. 26b). In 1 Samuel 18:1-5; 19:1; and 20:17, Jonathan's love for David seems primary, but 1 Samuel 20:42 stresses the depth of David's love for Jonathan. Some recent interpreters have suggested that David and Jonathan shared a homosexual relationship, but there is little evidence for such a conclusion. [Does "Love" Mean "Lover"?]

Does "Love" Mean "Lover"?

AΩ Tom Horner has argued that David's love for Jonathan was the equivalent of a homosexual relationship. Poetic language, by its very nature, may imply any number of things, but the idea that David and Jonathan were homosexual lovers is unsupported by the text.

David and Jonathan are portrayed as being linked by close ties of friendship, mutual appreciation, and binding commitments. Though their "male bonding" was clear and strong, any further conclusions are indefensible.

Tom Horner, *Jonathan Loved David: Homosexuality in Biblical Times* (Philadelphia: Westminster Press, 1978).

The elegy concludes in v. 27 with a third repetition of the phrase "How the mighty have fallen." Note the progression: In v. 19, the phrase appears alone, "How the mighty have fallen!" At the point of division between the two parts of the dirge (v. 25), the line is simply augmented, "How the mighty have fallen in the midst of the battle!" Finally, the line is paired with another line in synonymous parallel, intensifying the pathos attendant upon the fallen heroes, "How the mighty have fallen, / and the weapons of war perished!" (v. 27).

Some exegetes argue that "the weapons of war" is a euphemism for Saul and Jonathan, but it is more likely that "weapons" is meant in a literal sense. As David had bemoaned the encrusting of Saul's shield with battle grime, so now he grieves the loss of the beloved heroes' weapons. Like Saul and Jonathan, they will fight no more.

David's lament over Saul and Jonathan bears every sign of genuine emotion and sincerity. It was also a politically astute move, but the narrator insists that David was not making a fraudulent play for Israel's sympathies. Rather, with full integrity, he was expressing his own sympathy for the loss of God's anointed king and David's covenant friend.

CONNECTIONS

1. *The importance of integrity.* The two parts of this chapter portray a contrast between the ways in which two men dealt with the deaths of Saul and Jonathan. The young Amalekite gives every outward appearance of mourning. He has torn his clothes and put dirt on his head. When he falls to the ground, however, it is not to mourn for the lost but to seek his own gain. The narrator implies that the Amalekite had stolen Saul's battle crown and royal armband from the body, then brought them to David in hopes of a reward. As such, his obsequious mourning was hypocritical and unworthy.

In contrast, David's mourning is genuine. This is surprising because it is David who stands to gain the most from Saul's death. Saul had been making David's life miserable, seeking to kill him and, in essence, running him out of the country. David still had a large following in Judah, however, and the death of Saul and his sons cleared the way for him to seek the kingship. One might expect David to have rejoiced in knowing that his bitter rival was dead, but he did not. David ripped his raiment. He mourned. He wept. He wrote poetry and music to honor the dead. And he did so in such convincing fashion that Israel's authors remembered his grief as both genuine and deep.

Whether it is expressed through sorrow or joy, God's people are called to lives of integrity. We are called to seek God's will for our lives, rather than using other persons' sorrow for personal gain. Ultimately, the deaths of Saul and his sons did in fact pave the way for David to become king, but David did not allow the hope of future benefit to cloud the reality of his present grief.

2. *The power of God—and good.* This story is only the beginning, but the fact that something positive did emerge from the national tragedy offers a reminder to believers of all ages that God is never ultimately defeated. Even when bad things happen, those who trust in God and seek God's purposes may yet see good. The psalmist prayed, "Hope in God, for I shall again praise him, my help and my God" (Pss 42:5, 11; 43:5). Jesus' death was nothing if not tragic, yet humankind's future was changed for the better because of it. Paul promised, "We know that all things work together for good for those who love God, who are called according to his purpose" (Rom 8:28).

Difficult things are difficult. There is no way around this truth. Sad things are sad, and bad things are bad. Yet, even from tragedy, God can bring good. The good that comes does not lessen the significance of the calamity, but in time it may add perspective and lessen the pain.

3. *Self-incrimination.* Even though the young Amalekite may have fabricated his story about striking down Saul in an act of mercy, David accepted his testimony at face value. David felt the sanctity of God's anointed so strongly that he immediately pronounced a death penalty on the Amalekite runner. David himself had twice refused to harm Saul (1 Sam 24; 26), even though the king was seeking David's death and David had the king in his power. No matter how convenient, David could not accept any excuse for harming the one whom God had anointed as Israel's king.

When David pronounced the surprising sentence of death for the shocked Amalekite, he intoned, "Your blood be on your head; for your own mouth has testified against you, saying, 'I have killed the LORD's anointed' " (1:16). David's observation is a reminder that we bring our own judgments upon ourselves. We sin. We rebel. We turn away from God. We seek our own profits rather than the good of others.

As the prophets reminded Israel, and as John, Jesus, and Paul reminded persons of the first century and beyond, we are responsible for our actions and choices. We may choose to sin, but we may also choose to repent and seek forgiveness. If we choose to live and die in our sin, then our future lives (or lack of them) are upon our own heads.

4. *A lesson in good grieving.* David's elegy for Saul and Jonathan offers to modern readers an effective example of healthy grief. Many of us are conditioned by our upbringing to "keep a stiff upper lip," to deny our feelings, and to shortchange the essential process of grieving when loss comes into our lives. "Big" boys and girls, we are taught, don't cry.

David demonstrated no such recalcitrance when it came to grief. He expressed his grief in physical ways: tearing his clothes, fasting, mourning, and weeping aloud—and in the company of "all the men who were with him" (1:11). David also expressed his sorrow through poetry, as seen in the plaintive elegy of vv. 19-27.

Through giving vent to his grief, rather than bottling it up inside him, David was able to absorb the shock of the tragedy and move past it, rather than becoming emotionally stuck and incapable of functioning. His expression of sorrow remains a helpful model for others.

A NEW KING WHO
RESPECTS THE OLD

2:1-7

COMMENTARY

With Saul's death now a painful memory, the future for Israel lay open and uncertain. Saul had been the first king, so there was no established procedure for transferring power to his successor, or even for choosing who that successor might be. The narrator's periodic focus on Jonathan suggests that dynastic succession was presumed, but this may be anachronistic. The obvious power vacuum existing in Israel following Saul's death implies that the populace did not automatically turn to Saul's lone surviving son.

The reader knows that David will rise to the occasion and give focus to the chaos that followed Saul's death, but the narrator is careful to show how David moved at a measured pace, never overstepping his bounds or even putting himself forward for kingship. David will be king, but not unless his kingship is seen as legitimate in the eyes of the people and intentional in the plan of God.

David Becomes King in Hebron, 2:1-4a

The narrator is careful to show that David's rapid rise to power was directed by Yahweh rather than by David's personal ambition. David previously has shown a pattern of consulting Yahweh before making crucial decisions (1 Sam 23:9-11; 30:7-8), and will do so again (2 Sam 5:19, 23).

"Shall I go up into any of the cities of Judah?" implies an ascent to power in one of those cities. Many people in Judah had supported Saul, and they were now without leadership. Should David make himself available?

The reader presumes that David inquired of the LORD by means of the sacred lots, cast ritually by the priest Abiathar. If so, the precise wording of the questions would have varied from the text, for inquiring by lot required the imposition of a yes/no or either/or

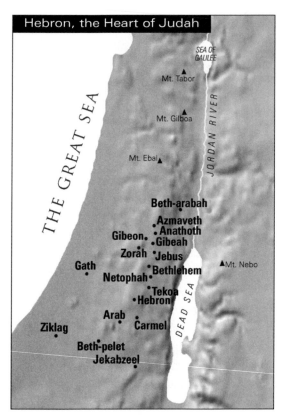

Hebron, the Heart of Judah

question. The text, presumably, summarizes the results without repeating each question verbatim. Other cities could have been posed as possibilities before the affirmative lot fell when the query named Hebron. [Hebron, the Heart of Judah] The text does not give such information.

Nor does the text say how David's plans for achieving power impacted his vassal status to the Philistine hegemony that controlled large portions of Israel and Judah. His previous association with King Achish of Gath plays no obvious role in any of the ensuing events. When David next meets the Philistines, it will be in a battle that his former allies precipitate, but lose (2 Sam 5:17-25). [Did David Rule Judah as a Philistine Vassal?]

If David wished to go in search of Judah's power brokers, Hebron was the natural choice. Geographically, Hebron was located in the heart of Judah, about nineteen miles south-southwest of Jerusalem. At roughly 3,000 feet above sea level, it was higher in elevation than any other city in Palestine.

Politically, Hebron's importance was long-standing in Israel. Abraham and Sarah were buried near the city (Gen 23; 25), which had links with other patriarchs as well (Gen 13:18; 35:27; 37:14). During Israel's drive to settle the promised land, Joshua reportedly led the armies in defeating Hebron (Josh 10:36-37), which was then granted to Caleb and his descendants (Josh 14:6-15).

David already had ties by marriage with the Calebites who controlled Hebron, having married Ahinoam and Abigail, from the nearby villages of Jezreel and Carmel (not to be confused with the Jezreel Valley and Mount Carmel areas far to the north). The future king had also strengthened his ties with Hebron by including that city in the distribution of plunder during his tenure as a token vassal to the Philistines.

The account of David's removal to Hebron is told very quickly and matter-of-factly. With his two wives—who make him a kinsmen of the Calebites who rule the city—David moves to Hebron. With him, he brings his entire retinue of at least 600 men

---

Did David Rule Judah as a Philistine Vassal?

Some scholars (such as A. A. Anderson, *2 Samuel* [WBC 11; Waco: Word Books, 1989]) are confident that David's vassal status remained intact when David assumed power in Hebron. Thus, his actions would have been approved by the Philistines as a means of extending their own influence into Judah. The narrator, however, gives no hint that any obligation to the Philistines followed David to Hebron.

It is more reasonable to postulate that David's move into Judah signaled a permanent break with his former overlords. The bond between David and the Philistines was tenuous to begin with. After the Philistine lords rejected David's service in the battle against Israel at Gilboa, the covenant agreement between David and Achish must have been weakened, despite Achish's efforts to put a good face on it (1 Sam 29:6-10).

David may have been allowed to withdraw gracefully, with the presumption that he would continue as an ally. Or it is equally possible that David simply withdrew without permission and there was little the Philistines could do to stop him. Previously, David had moved about freely, making only occasional reports to Achish. Those reports were routinely fallacious, but Achish believed them (1 Sam 27), suggesting that his intelligence network was limited. David's city of Ziklag (now burned, 1 Sam 30), was so isolated that he could have been absent for weeks before the Philistine king took notice.

David's power in the south seems to have been established quickly. The Philistine forces would have been engaged in subduing and defending their substantial northern intrusion into the Jezreel Valley (1 Sam 30:1-7). As a result, sending an army to whip David into line would have been impractical, putting other, richer gains at risk.

Furthermore, there is no indication that David's takeover in Hebron was anything but peaceful. The narrative suggests that David's fealty to the Philistines was commonly known as a ruse in Judah, where David routinely distributed plunder from his raids against other traditional enemies (1 Sam 27:8; 30:26-31). The "men of Judah" would hardly have anointed David as their king if they thought he was also beholden to the Philistines.

The evidence, then, suggests that David made a clean break with the Philistines after the battle of Gilboa and was acting independently of their influence when he made a play for power in Judah.

(1 Sam 30:9), along with their wives and children, recently rescued from the Amalekites, who had burned their city and left them homeless (1 Sam 30). The total number of people easily could have topped 2,000.

Some writers argue that David moved his personal army to Hebron in a show of force, taking over the city in a bloodless coup. Others presume that the elders of Hebron invited David and his sizable cortege at their own initiative, in hopes of gaining a favored position in the new order following Saul's death.

The narrator presumes, at least, that when the "people of Judah" came to anoint David as king, it was a voluntary and hopeful act. In 2 Samuel 19, the "elders of Judah" (v. 11) and the "men of Judah" (v. 14) seem to indicate the same persons, the leading men of the towns of Judah. These "elders" have authority to make decisions for others as well as to receive diplomatic gifts (1 Sam 30:26-31). Their presence suggests that some sort of cooperative and at least quasi-independent government was already functioning in Judah.

David's anointing by the elders of Judah, no doubt with a scented oil little different from that used for his first anointing, gives a secular endorsement to the spiritual affirmation he had received already from Samuel (1 Sam 16:12-13). David will be anointed yet again when he assumes the throne of Israel and is publicly acclaimed by the elders of Israel (2 Sam 5:3). There is no mention of priest or prophet in either of these civil ceremonies, though both were instrumental in the subsequent anointing of Solomon as David's successor (1 Kgs 1:34).

David Wins New Friends, 2:4b-7

The storyteller's version of David's accession to kingship is so succinct that readers may be disappointed with the author's swift dispatch of the new king's crowning moment. The brevity of the story, however, is a signal that David's enthronement in Hebron is only the beginning. There is much to be done before he rules over all Israel.

But David wastes no time. The Hebrew text was written without the verse notations included in modern versions, but the immediate conjunction of David's installation and his first act as king is unmistakable. In English translations, both take place in v. 4. The men of Judah anointed David as king; then "they told David" about the valiant men of Jabesh-gilead who had risked their lives to give Saul and Jonathan a decent burial.

The antecedent of "they" is unclear. If the story was written as a single piece, one would assume it was the elders of Judah who passed on the news about Saul's burial. Some, however, argue that v. 4b marks the beginning of a new strand in the tradition, so that "they" refers only to some anonymous messengers. The point, in either case, is that David wasted no time in beginning the work of an astute king who knows how to curry favor with possible allies, and to foster dissension among his rivals.

Jabesh-gilead was located far to the north of David's center of power in Hebron, not many miles from the new seat of northern power in the Transjordanian city of Mahanaim. David's efforts to win over the populace of Jabesh-gilead are bold, brilliant, and timely. Jabesh-gilead and Saul's hometown of Gibeah shared an ancient bond as shamed but kindred cities who played unflattering roles in the traditional story of the rape of the Levite's concubine (Judg 19–21; see commentary at 1 Sam 11:5-11).

More recently, Saul had shown loyalty toward his kindred by rescuing Jabesh-gilead from the overwhelming force of Nahash the Ammonite in a brief outburst of truly charismatic leadership (1 Sam 11). For the men of Jabesh-gilead, their daring recovery of the royal bodies from the walls of Beth-shan was in part an expression of gratitude and loyalty for Saul's earlier show of heroism.

If anyone should be loyal to Saul and his house, it is the city of Jabesh-gilead.

Yet David skillfully seeks support even there, sending an official envoy from his seat of power in Hebron to the heart of "Saul country" in Jabesh-gilead. David's message reflects a deft strategy built on religious and political terminology, revolving around the theme of *hesed*. *[Hesed]* Though sometimes translated with compounds like "loving-kindness," in this context *hesed* carries the connotation of covenant loyalty.

First, David blesses the men of Jabesh-gilead, congratulating them for having demonstrated such faithful *hesed* toward Saul and his sons. Their loyalty is truly praiseworthy.

Secondly, David offers the wish "Now may Yahweh show *hesed* to you!" (v. 6a). This outward blessing is a veiled way of reminding them that Saul, being dead, is no longer available to show them loyalty, so it will be up to Yahweh to bless them in the future (cf. Ruth 1:8 and 2 Sam 15:20).

Having set the diplomatic stage, David humbly offers to act as the agent of Yahweh's future *hesed* toward the people of Jabesh-gilead: "And I too will reward you because you have done this thing" (v. 6b). David does not use the word *hesed* of himself, but instead employs the term *hattôbâ* ("goodness") in a phrase that literally translates "and also *I* [emphatic: the pronoun is present though unnecessary] will do with you this goodness," or "*I* will make with you such a friendship."

Thus, David seeks an alliance with those who were most loyal to Saul and therefore most likely to support Saul's successor in Israel. Having blessed their service to Saul and having offered his own service to the city of Jabesh-gilead, David closes the message with an overt invitation for them to show continued valor by entering *his*

Hesed

AΩ *Hesed* is a Hebrew term that defies translation into English. It appears nearly 250 times in the Hebrew Bible. Between human persons, families, or political entities who share a convenantal bond, *hesed* describes the kind of fidelity or loyalty that is befitting of solemn commitments (Ruth 1:8; Gen 21:23; 1 Sam 20:8). The concept of *hesed* implies a reciprocal relationship, in which each party demonstrates loyalty and beneficence to the other (Gen 21:23, 27; Josh 2:12; 14).

When used to describe Yahweh's love for Israel, *hesed* is often translated as "mercy" (KJV, 120 times) or "kindness" (RSV, 177 times). Sometimes the compound "loving-kindness" is used. When the Hebrew Bible tries to describe

God's character, it does so most often in terms of *hesed*, as in Exod 34:6-7, where Yahweh himself described the divine nature to Moses as "abounding in steadfast love [*hesed*] and faithfulness, keeping steadfast love [*hesed*] for the thousandth generation." This description of Yahweh is frequently quoted in the Old Testament (Num 14:18; Neh 9:17; Pss 86:15; 103:8; 145:8; Joel 2:13; Jonah 4:2).

At once, the word *hesed* describes the full range of meaning that surrounds God's eternal love, kindness, and loyalty toward Israel. Humans are called to show such loyalty to God, but often fail. In contrast, the Lord's steadfast love endures forever (see especially the celebratory Ps 136, which repeats the refrain "for his steadfast love endures forever" in all 26 verses).

service, with this pointed reminder: "For Saul your lord is dead, and the house of Judah has anointed me king over them" (v. 7).

David's appeal for support from the people of Jabesh-gilead is remarkable for its careful, calculated approach. David does not coerce or threaten. He presents himself not only as Saul's legitimate successor, but also as their best hope for the future, the most valid vehicle for Yahweh's future blessing upon the city.

CONNECTIONS

1. *Seeking the kingdom.* The author of this brief but significant text insists that David made no strategic decisions without first seeking to know God's will about the matter. The particular decision David struggled with in this text related to the establishment of a kingdom. "*Shall* I go up?", he asks, and "*Where* shall I go up?" The narrator implies that Yahweh guided David in his calculated quest for the kingdom and that David understood that the kingdom was not for his benefit alone.

Later accounts will reveal that when David followed Yahweh faithfully, he and his kingdom were blessed. When he chose to follow his own desires, however, misery and turmoil became his constant companions (2 Sam 11–12), and the nation suffered. Even so, Yahweh promised never to withdraw his steadfast love from David and his descendants (2 Sam 7:15).

Christians are also called to seek a kingdom—the kingdom of God. In the teachings of Jesus, the kingdom of God is not a physical place, but the spiritual reign of God in the individual's heart and life. Thus, seeking God's kingdom leads the believer to follow God's will in every area of daily living, and to experience God's steadfast love in all its fullness. Jesus taught his followers not to become obsessed with material needs, but to "strive first for the kingdom of God and his righteousness, and all these things will be given to you as well" (Matt 6:33).

2. *Loyal love.* In David's missive to the people of Jabesh-gilead, the importance of both accepting and demonstrating loyal covenant love (*ḥesed*) is aptly affirmed. Despite the occasional militaristic overtones, the core concept of divine nature in the Hebrew Bible insists that God is compassionate, gracious, slow to anger, and abounding in steadfast love (Exod 34:6-7; see other references in commentary above). The prophets called Israel to reciprocate by

showing the same kind of love for God (Mic 6:8; Hos 12:6), but were disappointed with the response.

In the New Testament, the word *agapē* carries many of the same connotations. Though originally a rather nondescript Greek term, in Christian writings *agapē* came to mean "Christlike love": love that is unselfish, loyal, and self-sacrificing. Like the Old Testament concept of *hesed,* New Testament *agapē* is reciprocal, motivated by the love so aptly demonstrated in Jesus' life and death. "This is my commandment," Jesus said, "that you love one another as I have loved you. No one has greater love than this, to lay down one's life for one's friends" (John 15:12-13). The ultimate source of loyal love is the heart of God, but those who live after God's heart (as David was said to have done, 1 Sam 13:4) can become agents of blessing to others, even as David sought to show kindness to the people of Jabesh-gilead.

In the modern world, loyalty often seems to be in short supply. Covenant love pledged in marriage is replaced by the cold technical agreements of a divorce decree. Promises made in friendship are broken when loyalty is no longer convenient. Corporations are far less loyal to their employees, with the result that many workers feel little commitment to their employers. The term "denominational loyalty" has become almost oxymoronic. The courageous, risky loyalty shown by the men of Jabesh-gilead and praised by David still stands as a reminder to all persons that there is no greater gift than loyal love.

A RIVAL KING
AND HIS FIERCE GENERAL

2:8-32

COMMENTARY

Abner Makes Ishbaal King over Israel (2:8-11).

The narrator has juxtaposed two accounts of kingship, drawing a sharp contrast between David's popular ascension to the throne in Judah and Ishbaal's military appointment in Israel. David was anointed by the "men of Judah" as a result of his acclaim among the people, but Saul's surviving son Ishbaal had no comparable support in Israel. [Ishvi, Ishbaal, Eshbaal, or Ishbosheth?]

Ishvi, Ishbaal, Eshbaal, or Ishbosheth?

AΩ This son of Saul is given a variety of names. The difficult name "Ishvi" (actually *yišwî*, MT) appears only in 1 Sam 14:49, probably in reference to the same person. The Chronicler used the name "Eshbaal" (1 Chr 8:33; 9:39), but the Deuteronomist, at least in the MT, consistently calls him "Ishbosheth" (2 Sam 2:8, 12). "Ishbosheth" is also reflected in most versions of the LXX (*Iebosthe*) with the exception of one manuscript (LXX^L [e₂]), which has *Eisbaal*. This distinction is lost in modern translations, such as the NRSV, which routinely use "Ishbaal," even when the Hebrew has "Ishbosheth."

The variations in the name of Saul's son are usually attributed to a thoroughgoing attempt by the Deuteronomists to discredit the Israelite pretender to the throne (which rightly belongs to David) and to eliminate the term "baal" as an acceptable component of personal names in Israel. Thus, the argument goes, the name was originally "Ishbaal," but the Deuteronomist preferred to use the euphemism "Ishbosheth," meaning "man of shame."

"Ishbaal" means "man of Baal," or "man of the lord" The name "baal" originally meant "husband," "lord," or "master" in a generic sense. In later periods (as reflected in the 8th century prophets), it was used more specifically as an epithet for the most prominent Canaanite male deity. In

the time of David and Saul (the 10th century BC), it is possible that "baal" could have been used as an eponym for Yahweh. According to 1 Chr 12:6, one of David's "mighty men" was also named Baaliah, a name that probably meant "Yahweh is Lord." David himself seems to have had a son whose name contained the epithet. He is named Baaliada according to 1 Chr 14:7, but is called "Eliada" in 2 Sam 5:16 and 1 Chr 3:8. The LXX^B also preserves the name Baaliada, which is probably the original. It is easy to understand why some writers would substitute "El" (God) for "Baal," but it is difficult to imagine that the opposite would occur.

So Saul could have named his son "Ishbaal" (or possibly "Eshbaal," for "the LORD exists") as an innocent tribute to Yahweh. For all of his faults, there is no indication that Saul ever deserted Yahwism. When these stories were being edited in the 7th or 6th centuries, however, the name "Baal" was clearly and specifically associated with the male deity of the Canaanites. Thus, the Deuteronomists routinely substituted the word *bôšet* ("shame") for *ba'al*, a euphemistic means of identifying the man without using the name Baal. At least one writer has proposed a less pejorative meaning for *bôšet* based on an Akkadian cognate ("protective spirit"), but has won few followers.

The most powerful man in Israel was clearly Abner, Saul's military chief and first cousin (or possibly his uncle, 1 Sam 14:50-51). By some means, which the narrator feels no need to explain, Abner had escaped unharmed from the deadly battle at Gilboa, though his king and three royal sons lay dead in the field. Abner managed to keep intact not only his life and health, but also his command and reputation. As the strongest remaining leader—and as a man who appears hungry for power—he sought to give some direction to the chaotic period following the Philistine victory and occupation of Israel's heartland.

Mahanaim

The precise location of ancient Mahanaim remains a mystery, but it must have been somewhere near the Jabbok River in the forested hills of Gilead, allowing protection from the Philistines but relatively easy access to the surrounding territory still controlled by Israel. Saul's former capital in Gibeah was far too vulnerable, for the Philistine presence extended into the hills of Benjamin after the battle at Mount Gilboa. Some have argued that Mahanaim was a Benjaminite colony to begin with, and thus a natural refuge for Abner, Ishbaal, and their supporters.

Many Israelites had fled their homes and sought refuge in the Transjordan (1 Sam 31:7), and it was there that Abner "had taken Ishbaal" and "made him king" at Mahanaim (vv. 8-9a). [Mahanaim] Although v. 10 says that Ishbaal was forty years old, it is more likely that he was a minor, or at least young and weak enough to be completely under Abner's sway. David's age was given as thirty (2 Sam 5:5), and he was a contemporary of Jonathan, Saul's oldest son. Ishbaal, then, was probably younger. As presented by the narrative, Ishbaal

2 Samuel 2:1-4—David's early reign was marked by a constant seeking of God's will, including whether he should allow the people of Hebron to crown him king.

Julius Schnoor von Carolsfeld. *David Is Made King.* 19th century. Woodcut. *Das Buch der Bucher in Bilden.* (Credit: Dover Pictorial Archive Series)

may have held the regnal title, but Abner was clearly the power behind the throne in Israel, while the "house of Judah" followed David.

The author attributes a rather extensive and probably exaggerated list of holdings to Ishbaal (v. 9). *Gilead* was sometimes used to describe the entire Transjordan between the Sea of Galilee and the Dead Sea, but its proper boundaries were limited to the lands assigned to Gad and Reuben (cf. 1 Sam 10:27). The *Geshurites* lived in the northern Transjordan, east of the Sea of Galilee. ["Geshurites" or "Ashurites?"] The term *Jezreel* may refer to the entire valley separating Samaria from Galilee, or to the small city near Mount Gilboa where Saul and his army had camped before being routed by the Philistines (1 Sam 29:1). To think that Ishbaal's court held sway over the entire Valley of Jezreel is decidedly optimistic. If anything, Abner may have retained some influence in and about the city of Jezreel.

Ishbaal's kingship supposedly extended over *Ephraim,* the northern heartland of Israel, and *Benjamin,* Saul's original homeland in the hills north of Jerusalem. The whole of these five territories is called "all Israel," a much more limited area than what would come to be considered "all Israel" under David and Solomon. [All Israel]

The chronology provided in vv. 10-11 presents a conundrum. David seems to have gained the throne over all Israel shortly after Ishbaal's death (2 Sam 4:1–5:5). Yet David is accorded a reign in Judah of seven and one-half years, while Ishbaal is credited with a reign of only two years. Since v. 10b naturally follows v. 9, it seems likely that the information about Ishbaal's two year reign was inserted by a later hand, in the spirit of the Deuteronomistic

"Geshurites" or "Ashurites"?

AΩ The MT does not have "Geshurites," but "Ashurites," a word that normally refers to the Assyrians. This, of course, is problematic, and the LXX offers no clarification. The Syriac version and the Vulgate have the word "Geshurites," which fits more appropriately into the geographical setting, though Geshur was also known as an independent kingdom, unlikely to have been under Ishbaal's control. David's wife Maacah, the mother of Absalom, was reportedly a Geshurite princess (2 Sam 3:3). There is no clear explanation for the use of the gentilic form ("-ites"), when the other territories are listed by place name only.

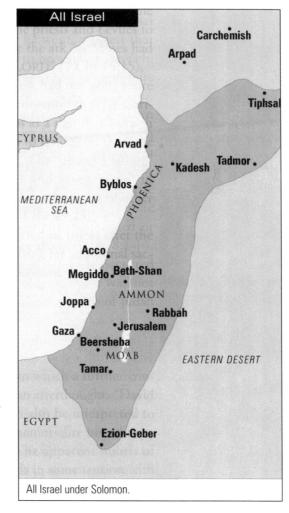

All Israel under Solomon.

tendency to synchronize the reigns of northern and southern kings (e.g., 2 Kgs 3:1; 8:16-17, 25-26).

If the given numbers do reflect an accurate tradition, one must presume an interregnum of a least five years in Israel during which Abner maintained some sort of power base before setting up his rump government with Ishbaal on the throne. This may provide the best explanation.

The Battle at the Pool of Gibeon, 2:12-17

Having described Ishbaal's assumption of the throne in Israel, the narrator promptly ignores him and begins an extended narrative that may seem at first glance to be overly concerned with the interplay between the opposing generals and their families. The editor has intentionally chosen these stories, however, precisely because they are foundational for explaining how it was that David remained perfectly innocent while his most important opponents conveniently died.

The battle outside of Gibeon described in vv. 12-17 marks the beginning of a bloody civil war between Judah and Israel. Yet the inter-family aspect of this feud is well illustrated: The battle's beginning is described as if it were a sporting contest of combat skills, while its denouement focuses on the conflict between the two opposing generals' families.

Neither David nor Ishbaal is involved in this story, though both will feel its effects. Presumably by some pre-arrangement, Abner of Israel and Joab of Judah brought their select troops to the city of Gibeon. There, they gathered on opposing sides of the "pool of Gibeon," which was apparently well known (vv. 12-13). [The Pool of Gibeon] The choice of Gibeon seems a bit strange. Gibeon was located in Benjaminite territory, but was not far from the border with Judah. Though technically in Israel, there was enmity between Gibeon and the house of Saul, who apparently had killed many Gibeonites in a sort of ancient ethnic cleansing (2 Sam 21:1-9). Perhaps the two generals judged that the balance of location and history would make the site relatively neutral.

The most remarkable part of this account is found in the preliminary negotiations between Abner and Joab, who agreed to "let the young men come forward and have a contest before us" (v. 14). It

The Pool of Gibeon

The location of Gibeon is well established as modern el-Jîb, about seven miles north-northwest of Jerusalem. The ancient city contained a huge rock-cut cistern on the northern side, just inside the city wall. The cistern was thirty-seven feet around and eighty-two feet deep, accessible by a circular stairway cut into the pit walls. This was probably not the "pool of Gibeon," however, for water would rarely have reached the top (as is common for a "pool"). Also, the text suggests that the pool was located near an open field, rather than inside the city walls.

quickly becomes evident that there is nothing sporting about the competition, which turns out to be a fight to the death in gladiatorial combat between twelve representatives from each side. Such battles by proxy were known in the ancient world, the most familiar one to Bible students being David's combat with Goliath.

The narrator's innocent language—"let the lads come out and have a contest before us"—leads the reader to imagine a friendly match between rival families. Thus, when the deadly result of the contest is revealed, the reader experiences a greater sense of poignancy. In this way, the storyteller reminds the readers that the bloody civil war to come was from start to finish a battle between brothers.

The twelve hand-picked warriors from either side were apparently evenly matched and identically trained in individual combat, for "each grasped his opponent by the head, and thrust his sword in his opponent's side; so they fell down together" (v. 16a). Some scholars detect a note of betrayal,

2 Samuel 2:15-17—This depiction of the "battle of the champions" imagines the use of more weaponry than was actually mentioned in the passage.

Gustave Doré (1832-83). *Combat between the Champions of Ish-Bosheth and David* from the *Illustrated Bible*. 19th century. Engraving.
(Credit: Dover Pictorial Archive Series)

arguing that the contest began as a wrestling match, but the Benjaminites drew hidden weapons and went for the kill. There is no evidence in the story itself to support this view, however. The men of Judah had swords as well.

An etiological note explains that this battle near Gibeon gave rise to the place name Helkath-hazzurim. [What Does "Helkath-hazzurim" Mean?] Since the contest ended in a draw, the entire armies of either side engaged each other in an attempt to settle the issue. The southern forces prevailed, putting Abner's troops to rout. A later note will report that Joab lost only 20 men, while Abner lost 360 (2:30-31).

Several things stand out in this brief battle account. Man for man, the forces of Judah and Israel are roughly equal, for they are brothers. In a pitched battle, however, David's forces have the advantage, presumably because Yahweh is on their side. This text

What Does "Helkath-hazzurim" Mean?

AΩ Most translations offer no English meaning for Helkath-hazzurim, which is of uncertain interpretation. *Ḥelqat* means "portion of" and, by extension, "territory of," or possibly "field of." *Haṣṣurîm* is more problematic and makes little sense as it is. Various emendations have been made, leading to proposals such as "Flint's Field" (Kyle McCarter, presuming that they used flint daggers, *II Samuel* [AB 9; Garden City: Doubleday, 1980], 93), "Plotter's Field," "Field of Sides" (because they stabbed each other in the side), and "Field of Adversaries."

---

does not mention divine involvement, but other battle accounts make it clear that David was successful because Yahweh was with him (1 Sam 18:14, 28; cf. 1 Sam 16:18; 2 Sam 5:10). As the narrator tells it, a day that began with negotiations suggesting a playful contest ended with a battle that was "very fierce." In this way, the account serves as an appropriate introduction to the tragic civil war that followed. The account suggests that it was not David's intent to do battle against Israel, but it was forced upon him.

Abner Retreats, and Asahel Dies, 2:18-32

The lengthiest part of this initial military encounter focuses not on the twenty-four representatives, but on two men only: Abner and Asahel. Asahel is introduced as one of the three sons of Zeruiah, who was David's sister (1 Chr 2:16), or possibly his half-sister (2 Sam 17:25). Strangely, Zeruiah's husband is never named, though ancient persons were usually identified by patronymics. Perhaps it is the mother's relation to David that is deemed most important.

The three sons of Zeruiah were zealously devoted to David and prone to solving problems by violence (1 Sam 26:6-9; 2 Sam 3:39). [The Sons of Zeruiah] David, being more politically astute, sometimes had to restrain them. Both Abishai and Joab were strong leaders in David's military organization. Asahel, the youngest, was known more for his swift running than his quick thinking.

In the course of the rout, Abner's soldiers fled the field. As Joab's men gave chase, Asahel set his sights on Abner himself. The story is told in breathless fashion, for the two panting soldiers carry on a running conversation even as they sprint across the battlefield. When Abner perceived that the man in hot pursuit was the swift Asahel, he knew that Asahel would catch up with him. He was just as certain, however, that Asahel could not defeat him in combat.

The writer's sympathies are clearly with Abner, who faced a stunning dilemma. Abner was discerning enough to know that killing the brother of David's general, even in battle, would have ramifications beyond the death of a soldier. Thus, Abner entreated Asahel to choose an easier target among the fleeing soldiers—effectively offering to sacrifice one of his own men to satisfy Asahel's bloodlust (vv. 19-21).

Asahel, however, would not be dissuaded by the offer of easy plunder. He turned "neither to the right nor to the left as he followed him." When it became clear that joining arms was inevitable, Abner decided to end it quickly. Apparently, as the relentless Asahel drew near, Abner quickly halted, braced himself, and thrust his spear backwards so that his over-eager pursuer would run on to it. Abner held the spear normally, with the butt end pointed behind him. Perhaps Abner intended to avoid drawing attention to the spear, or maybe he hoped to do no more than knock the breath from the young soldier so he could get away. Asahel came on so fast, however, that the force of the collision caused even the blunt end of the spear to run him through completely (v. 22).

Some scholars argue that the two had stopped the chase and were facing each other during their conversation, suggesting that Abner killed Asahel with the blunt end of his spear as an overt means of demonstrating his supremacy. This goes entirely against the grain of the narrative, however. The writer's emphasis on Asahel's speed and Abner's desire to avoid conflict is calculated to show that hasty Asahel fell victim to his own speed and Abner's cunning. Abner sought to avoid killing Asahel, not to draw attention to his victory over the valiant Judean.

The death of Asahel had a shocking effect on Joab's army: "All those who came to the place where Asahel had fallen stood still" (v. 23). It also had the effect of staining Abner with bloodguilt, at least in the eyes of Joab. [Bloodguilt] Ordinarily, bloodguilt was associated with premeditated murder, not unintentional killing or death in the heat of battle. Joab, however, held Abner personally responsible for Asahel's demise, and his desire for vengeance played a significant role in later events, becoming a heavy political liability for David (see 2 Sam 3:22-39).

The shocking sight of Asahel's body caused the Judean soldiers to pause, but not to stop their pursuit. With Joab and Abishai leading, they returned to the chase and pursued Abner until sunset, as far as

The Sons of Zeruiah

Abishai was the eldest of the brothers (1 Chr 2:16). It was he who joined David in a daring infiltration of Saul's camp (1 Sam 26:6-12), and who wanted to assassinate Saul on the spot. Despite his heroism, his ruthless streak needed restraint on other occasions, as well (2 Sam 16:9-12; 19:21-22).

Joab, the middle brother, served as commander of David's army, though Abishai shared some responsibility for leadership, especially during the early part of David's reign. After the siege of Jerusalem, in which Joab's heroic strategy won the day, Joab's supremacy was unchallenged (1 Chr 11:6).

Asahel was probably the youngest of the three, as his name is usually listed last in sequence (see 1 Chr 2:16). The text assigns him one distinguishing characteristic: He was "as swift of foot as a wild gazelle," the narrator says (v. 18). Josephus added a tradition that Asahel could outrun a horse (*Ant.* 7:14).

Bloodguilt

According to the law, one who intentionally killed another was guilty of murder, and thus subject to capital punishment at the hands of a kinsman who was called the "avenger of blood" (Num 35:16-21). If the death was not premeditated, blood vengeance was not allowed. This ancient "law of the desert" could be quite savage if unchecked, leading to vengeance against those who did not deserve it. The custom of blood vengeance was ameliorated in some ways by biblical law, which designated certain "cities of refuge" to which one who killed without intent might flee for respite until it was determined if bloodguilt should be assigned (Deut 4:41-43; 19:1-13; Josh 20).

"the hill of Ammah, which lies before Giah on the way to the wilderness of Gibeon." Though meaningful to the Deuteronomist's initial audience, the place names Ammah and Giah remain unidentified. "Ammah" can be translated as "water channel," and "Giah" can mean "spring" or "valley," but little more can be ascertained. The conflict seems to have moved well beyond Gibeon proper.

Abner had carried on a conversation with Asahel while on the run, but he rallied his troops on a hill before turning to address Joab, who had fallen back. Abner is looking for an end to the immediate conflict, and apparently Joab is likewise looking for an excuse to call off the chase, which is serving only to exhaust his soldiers. Abner's plaintive plea retains its haunting quality, especially in the ears of those who are prone to seek peace: "Is the sword to keep devouring forever?" Abner reminded Joab that the two armies were kinsmen, lending their conflict a bitterness that went beyond war and death alone (v. 26).

Joab recognized Abner's words as a call for a truce, and his response took the form of an oath ("As God lives!"). Joab swore that his soldiers would have kept up the pursuit through the night if Abner had not spoken (cf. 1 Sam 14:36). Almost gratefully, it seems, he "sounded the trumpet" to signal his troops to cease fighting and reconnoiter for the return journey (vv. 27-28). [Blowing the Horn]

Both commanders seemed anxious to be done with the distasteful conflict and to put as much distance between themselves as possible. Abner led his men to the Jordan, where they followed the Arabah (here meaning the rift valley between the Dead Sea and the Sea of Galilee) before crossing the Jordan and arriving back in Mahanaim at midday (v. 29). Some older translations, such as the KJV, say they traveled "through all Bithron," but most modern scholars understand *bitrôn* as a time designation ("half a day") rather than as a place name.

For its part, Joab's army took time to count the dead, determining that they had lost 20 men (including Asahel), while the Benjaminites had left 360 dead in the field. The text suggests that the Judeans carried Asahel to Bethlehem for burial that same evening, then marched through the night, arriving in Hebron at dawn (vv. 30-32). This would have been a difficult feat, involving a nighttime journey of at least thirty miles through rugged country. Some writers propose that the army tarried in Bethlehem and trekked home to Hebron the following night. If that were the case, however, there would have been no need to travel at night. The journey described by the text would have been rigorous but not impossible, surely within the abilities of soldiers so superior that they took only one casualty for every eighteen inflicted. The narrator is interested in enlarging the reputation of Joab's army as well as stressing the determination of both armies to march through the night to put the bothersome battlefield behind them.

The reader will note that David is notably and intentionally absent from this conflict. It is Joab who leads his soldiers in battle, and Joab who will later assassinate Abner, creating both confusion and consternation for David. Thus, the author carefully draws a clear distinction between David, a "gentle" leader who is worthy of kingship, and the rough actions of his military men (2 Sam 3:39). Though David may benefit from the precipitate and violent actions of his aides, there is no Israelite blood on his hands.

Blowing the Horn

AΩ In Israel, the "trumpet" was not made of brass or silver. The word *šôfar* describes a curved ram's horn, hollowed and pierced to form an ancient bugle. When blown, the *šôfar* emits a high, piercing, almost haunting sound.

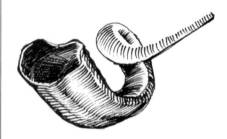

(Illustration Credit: Barclay Burns)

CONNECTIONS

Choosing Leaders, 2:8-11

"Abner . . . had taken Ishbaal son of Saul, and . . . made him king." With these words the narrator tells us that, while Yahweh has endorsed David's kingship, Ishbaal's claim to the throne has no divine sanction. Ishbaal was crowned king over the surviving Israelite tribes for one reason only: The most powerful man in Israel needed a Saulide figurehead to legitimize to his own ambition. [Naming Names] In doing so, Abner only exacerbated the chaotic conditions in Israel, created deeper enmity between the tribes, and postponed the inevitable ascension of David to the throne.

Yet the narrator has sympathy for Abner. Abner thought he was doing the right thing. He had believed in Saul, and wanted to

Naming Names (2:8-11)

The narrator's refusal to call Ishbaal by his given name reflects an awareness of the importance of names. The Deuteronomists' determination to call Ishbaal by the disparaging nickname "Ishbosheth" is a way of underscoring the unhappy consequences of acquiring a bad name.

Despite the pejorative connotations of "baal" in later times, Saul probably intended for his son's name to mean "man of the LORD." Yet he was remembered as a "man of shame." Every person who bears the name "Christian" has been named a "person of Christ." It is worth the asking to wonder whether others would grant us that same name if all they had to go on was our likeness to Jesus.

---

preserve his kingdom. Perhaps he had not recognized the obvious signs that Saul's rule had lost Yahweh's support. Abner had tasted power and rejoiced in Saul's kingship. Now he did not want to see it end, so he tried to revive the Saulide dynasty, with no more success than someone attempting to inflate a balloon full of holes.

Abner's determination to keep Saul's dynasty alive led to a bloody civil war and a divided nation. If Abner had been more in tune with the will of God, one suspects, David would have had a much easier time establishing a true and lasting kingdom in Israel. When the kingdom split again after Solomon's death, the roots of division were at least as deep as Abner's determination to retain a separate northern monarchy.

Tiny churches dot the countryside, many of which have few members and meager resources. Some maintain a meaningful ministry, but others require constant life support. The parishioners of these churches might better be served by closing the doors and joining other, healthier churches, or by banding in common cause to form a single church with adequate resources for ministry. But they continue their hopeless struggle, often because some strong leader or family in the church *wills* it to be so. They refuse to give up the memory of a church that once prospered, though reason suggests it will not prosper again.

Even successful churches sometimes find their calendars clogged with programs that are poorly attended and unsuccessful by any measure. Yet the programs persist because they are grounded in long-standing tradition, or because they continue to be promoted by persuasive denominational agencies. Whether the work of God is being done seems less important than the maintenance of sacred traditions.

When evaluating present and future programs, contemporary believers would do well to consider seriously whether it is best to follow Abner or David.

War Games, 2:12-38

One of the great oxymorons of our time is the term "war games." This is what the conflict at the pool of Gibeon seems to be—a game that became a war. The conflict between Israel and Judah may have begun as a "friendly" rivalry, but it ended in a bloody fight to the death. For the opposing parties, it was easier to fight than to learn to live in peace.

Surprisingly, in this text the call for peace comes from the lips of the same man whose actions had led to the conflict. Perhaps it was the queasy experience of feeling the blunt end of his own spear skewering the body of Asahel that changed his mind. From that point, Abner seems more concerned with avoiding war than with fighting it. From the hilltop called Ammah, he cried, "Is the sword to keep devouring forever? Do you not know that the end will be bitter?" (v. 26). Abner learned how bitter the end of conflict is, but not until he himself had set it into motion. By that time, the conflict had gained such momentum that Abner could not even slow it down, much less bring it to a halt. The Furies were free.

Competition can be an ugly thing, even within the family of faith. Individual churches and larger denominational bodies have found themselves ripped apart by persons who push pet agendas, believing that their way is the only way. The spirit of divisiveness, whether it is clad in the robes of royalty or academia, the clergy or the Ku Klux Klan, always results in conflict and confusion and some kind of death. The carnage covering the field of Helkath-haz-zurim is a continuing reminder that the best hope of accomplishing God's work is not found in competition, but in cooperation.

LIFE AND DEATH

3:1-39

COMMENTARY

David Grows Strong—and Prolific, 3:1-5

The summarizing statement of 3:1 appears to some scholars to be the author's closing comment on the battle of Gibeon (2:12-32), while others see it as an appropriate beginning for the story of Abner's defection and assassination (3:6-39). The verse, in fact, is clearly transitional. It fits awkwardly into exegetical outlines, but it serves well to guide the reader from one story to the next. As the text now stands, however, the intrusive list of sons born to David in Hebron (3:2-5) clearly binds the verse to the following account. There, Ishbaal is portrayed as pitifully weak and impotent, an intentional and blatant contrast to David's political strength and fecund virility.

The civil war between the "houses" of Saul and David was so disagreeable in Israel's memory that the narrator has little to say about it, choosing to summarize the "long war" in a single verse that claimed "David grew stronger and stronger, while the house of Saul became weaker and weaker" (v. 1). Thus, David's rise to power continues, while Saul's house continues to decline. The narrator does not reveal the duration of the "long war," though it must have continued for at least the two years attributed to the reign of Ishbaal (2 Sam 2:10).

The storyteller does inject specific evidence of David's strength and Ishbaal's weakness, however. He includes a list of sons born to David during his sojourn in Hebron. [David's Descendants] This list probably

---

David's Descendants

The list of David's sons born in Hebron (3:2-5) may have been drawn from some sort of state archives, but probably not from the same source as the list of his sons born in Jerusalem (5:13-16). The former list is probably not complete, listing only the firstborn son of each mother and none of the daughters. The first list is also notable for its inclusion of the mothers' names. We have identified the reason for this in the body of the commentary: The author was interested in accentuating the size of David's harem as well as his sexual potency. When the two lists are synthesized in the Chronicler's version (1 Chr 3:1-9), the differences remain.

The Royal Harem and the Politics of Power

The appropriation of another's harem as a symbol of personal power is a surprisingly frequent theme in the Deuteronomists' work. Abner's association with Rizpah may have been intended to remind Ishbaal where the real power lay (3:7), though the story is somewhat ambiguous. There is no uncertainty, however, that Absalom's public cavorting with his father's harem was an intentional show of power intended to underscore his claim to the throne (16:20-22).

Later, in the chaotic period following David's death, both Adonijah (the oldest son) and Solomon (the son of Bathsheba) had designs on the throne. Solomon won out, for David willed it. Adonijah conceded the throne, but requested that he be given Abishag, a concubine David had taken in his old age. Adonijah may have thought his request was innocent, since David had never known Abishag sexually (1 Kgs 1:4). Solomon, however, angrily interpreted Adonijah's request as a bold play for the throne, and ordered him executed (1 Kgs 2:13-25).

One sentence is particularly telling in regard to this custom of identifying political legitimacy with control of the royal harem. When Bathsheba interceded on Adonijah's behalf, Solomon responded: "And why do you ask Abishag the Shunamite for Adonijah? Ask for him the kingdom as well!" (1 Kgs 2:22a). Solomon's fury may have been contrived in part, since Adonijah's request offered the new king a convenient pretext for eliminating his rival. Even so, his reasoning seems to be based solidly on a widely accepted custom: He who controls the harem has the keys to the kingdom.

---

was not part of the traditional stories about the military and political maneuvering that led to David's enthronement over Israel, but instead added by a later hand. The roll call of sons adds narrative shaping of the story, reminding the reader that while David is still in Hebron, he already has sons born to him who will re-enter the picture. In this sense, vv. 2-5 also serves as an introduction to and a rough outline for the later stories of Amnon (v. 2, ch. 13), Absalom (v. 3, chs. 14–9), and Adonijah (v. 4; 1 Kgs 1–2).

The most obvious function of the list, however, is to illustrate David's growing strength by demonstrating his ability to build a sizable harem and sire children by multiple wives. In the ancient world, the size of a king's harem—and the evidence of his sexual prowess as exhibited through regular pregnancies—was an accepted symbol of royal power. [The Royal Harem and the Politics of Power] The sons being born to David in Hebron prove that he is growing "stronger and stronger." In contrast, Ishbaal inherited a harem from his father Saul, but was unable to claim it though it was his by right. When he accuses Abner of sleeping with Rizpah, she is still "my father's concubine," not his own (3:7). Thus, Ishbaal is portrayed as whining and impotent, having no more control over his father's harem than he does over his father's general. "The house of Saul became weaker and weaker."

The list of David's children born during his seven and a half years in Hebron includes the names of six sons who are born to six different wives, only two of whom were previously known. It is entirely possible that some of these sons were born *before* David took up residence in Hebron, for the text assigns him two wives from the time when he roamed the wilderness of the Negeb. It is also likely that other sons or daughters were born during David's rule in Hebron, but the narrator's purposes are fulfilled with the naming of one son for each of David's wives.

Amnon was David's oldest son, born to Ahinoam of Jezreel (v. 2). David's marriage to Ahinoam is mentioned as a sort of footnote in 1 Samuel 25:43, following the account of how David gained the more notable Abigail as a wife. "Amnon" means something like "faithful," but David's eldest did not live up to his name. The account of how he raped his half-sister Tamar—and was murdered by a vengeful Absalom—is found in 2 Samuel 13.

Chileab is given in the MT as the name of David's second son, born to Abigail of Carmel, the widow of Nabal (v. 3a; see 1 Sam 25:2-42). There is some uncertainty about this son's name, for the LXX has the name "Daluiah," while 1 Chronicles 3:1 and Josephus name him "Daniel." Some later Greek versions call him "Abiah." The name "Chileab" could mean "the father prevails" or, perhaps, "all of the father." It is apparently related to the name "Caleb." Abigail probably belonged to the Calebite clan, which had ruled Hebron since the time of Joshua. For all the confusion about his name, Chileab never again figures into the story. Scholars generally presume that he died young.

Absalom is listed third. He was born to Maacah, who is carefully identified as the "daughter of King Talmai of Geshur" (v. 3b). Geshur was far to the north of Judah, where it lay just south and east of the Sea of Galilee. This suggests that David had already begun a policy of extending his political reach through marriage alliances of convenience. Ishbaal claimed sovereignty over the Geshurites (2:9, presuming that "Geshurites" is a better reading than "Ashurites"), but David claimed the daughter of the king. Absalom's name was probably vocalized as "Abishalom," meaning "my [divine] father is peace." When Absalom fell from favor after murdering Amnon, he fled to his mother's people in Geshur for three years (13:37-39). Later, he returned to lead a rebellion against his father, building support in both Hebron and Jerusalem (chs. 14–15).

Adonijah, the son of Haggith, is mentioned fourth. Nothing else is known of Haggith, except that her name could mean "born during a festival." Adonijah is the first son of David to have "Yahweh" (*yah*) as a divine element in his name, unless the LXX reading "Daluiah" for "Chileab" is correct. "Adonijah" means "Yahweh is Lord" or "my Lord is Yahweh." Adonijah was at least fourth in the birth order, but he was probably the oldest surviving son when he sought the throne with the support of Abiathar and Joab (1 Kgs 1:5-10; cf. 1 Kgs 2:22). Solomon, his rival for the throne, brought Adonijah's survival to a quick end.

Shephatiah, son of Abital, is mentioned only here and in the Chronicler's list (1 Chr 3:3). Nothing else is known about how Abital came into David's harem. Shephatiah's name also has a Yahwistic element (*iah*). It means "Yahweh has judged."

Ithream, born of Eglah, is the final son listed from David's reign in Hebron. His name could mean "remnant" or, perhaps, "may the god protect," depending on which root is presumed. Like Shephatiah, his name appears only here and in 1 Chronicles 3:3. Eglah's name means "heifer" and is related to the name "Eglon," who was once king of the Moabites (Judg 3:12-30). Biblical genealogies hold that David had connections with Moab through his grandmother Ruth, and 1 Samuel 22:3-5 claims that David sought for his parents safe haven in Moab while he was on the run from Saul. Eglah is not a uniquely Moabite name, however.

Eglah is specifically called "David's wife," the only woman in the list to be so designated. The significance may be nothing more than that she is mentioned last, and the narrator wants to leave the reader with the thought that Eglah was one of David's many wives.

David Parleys with Abner in Peace, 3:6-21

As the mate to v. 1, v. 6 circumscribes the recitation of David's Hebron scions within a neat inclusio, repeating the thought of v. 1 and moving it forward along the main story line. As the civil war continued, the house of David grew strong in Hebron and the house of Saul grew weak in Mahanaim (3:1), while *Abner grew strong* within the house of Saul (3:6). The form of the compound verb (*hyh* [verb of being] + the causative/reflexive participle of *ḥzq* ["to be strong"]) indicates that Abner was continuing an action he had begun in the past: He was making himself stronger.

Apparently, one means by which Abner flexed his political muscle involved Saul's harem, which Ishbaal apparently had not taken for himself. Some writers suggest that Ishbaal had not assumed control of the harem because he was a minor, but the narrator (who claimed Ishbaal was forty years old [2 Sam 2:10]) is more interested in portraying Ishbaal as inept, incompetent, and perhaps impotent. The king accused Abner of sleeping with

The Custom of Concubinage

Concubines were related to men as mistresses or secondary wives. Their legal status was recognized by law and custom in ancient Israel, but was always inferior to that of a full wife. Concubines could be acquired in various ways: by capture in war, by purchase (Exod 21:7-11 describes how a poor Hebrew father could sell his daughter as a concubine), or through forced slavery (Gen 16; 30:1-13).

In some settings, the rationale for concubinage was the bearing of additional sons to aid in the workforce. Thus, in seminomadic and agricultural societies, concubines should not be perceived as the objects of lust alone.

Kings added concubines to their harems as a means of building political power, which was enhanced by a show of sexual prowess. Thus, taking one or more of the king's concubines was an act of treason, equivalent to usurping the throne (see 2 Sam 3:6-8; 16:20-22; 1 Kgs 2:13-22).

Nevertheless, in other contexts concubines may have been kept primarily for their sexual favors. In Eccl 2:8, the concubine is called "man's delight." In these contexts, at least, "legally and socially, she is not the equivalent of a wife but is virtually a slave, secured by a man for his own purposes."

Concubinage has been practiced in societies worldwide, in the modern as well as the ancient world. Although condemned by law, concubinage was practiced in Western civilization throughout the Middle Ages and into the early modern period. However, sociologists who study family and marriage patterns detect strong trends worldwide toward monogamy and egalitarian status for women, trends that continue to diminish the practice of concubinage.

Phyllis Trible, *Texts of Terror* (Philadelphia: Fortress Press, 1984), 66.

Rizpah, his father's concubine. [The Custom of Concubinage] The MT gives no clue regarding the accuracy of Ishbaal's claim, though the LXX adds "and Abner took her." Some scholars presume that Abner's activity was an intentional foundation for making his own play for the throne, while others suspect he was only flaunting his power over the hapless Ishbaal.

Rizpah, daughter of Aiah, is the only concubine mentioned in relation to Saul. She will return to the narrative in 2 Samuel 21:8-14 when she boldly and openly mourns the loss of her two sons, whom David sacrificed to satisfy a claim of bloodguilt between the house of Saul and the people of Gibeon.

Abner answered Ishbaal's complaint about Rizpah with intense fury, but *without* answering the specific charge. Whether guilty or not, he regarded the offense as inconsequential compared to the favors he had done for Ishbaal. Abner's initial response—"Am I a dog's head?"—has occasioned much discussion among scholars. [Was Abner the Head Dog?] He probably intended the expression as nothing more than a colorful assertion that the ungrateful Ishbaal had no respect for him, despite that fact that he owed his position entirely to Abner's strength. Abner reminded Ishbaal of his continued loyalty (*ḥesed*) to Saul's house, despite the obvious strength and popularity of David. Abner had single-handedly placed Ishbaal on the throne and kept him there. He seems outraged that the young whelp would chide him over his relationship—real or not—with Rizpah (v. 8).

Abner's fiery rhetoric in vv. 9-10 is most remarkable. He claims to have knowledge that Yahweh has sworn to give the kingdom to

---

Was Abner the Head Dog?

AΩ Abner's expression is curious in part because the Hebrew word for dog (*keleb*) contains the same consonants as the personal name Caleb (*kālēb*). Some ancient scribe assumed that Abner was taking offense at the insinuation that he was a Calebite, and added the phrase "which belongs to Judah," which makes no sense if the word is interpreted as "dog." Ancient Hebrew was written without vowels, leading to a variety of interpretations.

Abner's use of the phrase *rōʾš keleb* is anomalous. Literally, it means "head of a dog," and with its received spelling cannot be interpreted as "chief dog," which would otherwise make good sense. Some scholars wonder if the proverbial promiscuity of dogs has something to do with Abner's idiom, while others look for interpretive clues in the "dog-faced baboon," which was known in the ancient Near East and commonly depicted in Egyptian art. The baboon at right is from South Africa. Yet other writers take a cue from 2 Kgs 6:25, which suggests that a donkey's head is the most worthless part of a donkey, presuming that Abner intended to say "Am I a worthless dog?" Scholarly counterparts take another track, assuming that being identified with the dog's rear end would be most demeaning but too coarse for public consumption, so "dog's head" was used as a euphemism for "dog's rear"!

The specific nuance of Abner's expression may be lost to us, but the basic import is obvious. Abner has not only treated Ishbaal like a king, but *made* him king. The thanks he gets is that Ishbaal now treats him like a dog.

David, leading the reader to wonder why he has been opposing Yahweh's choice knowingly. [How Did Abner Know?] Since Saul's house has shown no gratitude for his loyalty, Abner swears a firm oath that he will accomplish Yahweh's desire personally by delivering the kingdom into David's hand.

"So may God do to Abner and so may he add to it" is a typical oath form, though modern translations mask the serious nature of the oath. Ancient oaths were constructed of two parts: a curse and a conditional sentence. "So may God do [terrible things] to Abner and so may he add [even more terrible things] to it"—but only *if* he failed to fulfill the following promise, in this case, to hand the kingdom over to David. Abner's oath makes it clear that he had in mind adding all of Israel to David's realm, so that he would rule "from Dan to Beer-sheba," the traditional extremities of Israelite territory. [From Dan to Beer-sheba]

Ishbaal's reaction to Abner's explosion reveals the true nature of their relationship, hinted at in earlier texts. The puppet king was rendered silent before Abner's anger, "because [Ishbaal] feared him." From this point forward, Ishbaal is completely passive, whether dealing with Abner or with David. It is as if he knows that others are pulling the strings and he has no power to resist.

How Did Abner Know?

The narrator has Abner claim knowledge that "Yahweh has sworn to give the kingdom to David" (v. 9). On what basis could Abner make this assertion? Others, according to the narrator, had predicted David's eventual rise to power. Samuel had twice informed Saul that his kingdom would be given to another who was more qualified (1 Sam 13:13-14; 15:28). Presumably, he would have announced Yahweh's plan before anointing David (1 Sam 16:13). At various times, Jonathan (1 Sam 23:17), Saul (1 Sam 25:58; again in 26:26), and even Abigail (1 Sam 25:28) voiced their personal expectations that David's star would rise.

Nevertheless, the text describes no previous public declaration of Yahweh's intent, and certainly not of a divine oath on David's behalf. Thus, many scholars presume that these words are a secondary interpolation, based perhaps on Nathan's dynastic oracle in 2 Sam 7. It is quite possible, however, that Abner simply recognized which way the wind was blowing. David's growing success and Ishbaal's weakness were equally palpable. The only explanation, for an ancient Yahwist, was that Yahweh's favor had been given to David, making his ultimate supremacy a certainty.

Without regard to how Abner knew, the narrator's insistence on having Abner acknowledge David's divine right to the throne serves his apologetic purpose well. Abner's claim that Yahweh had "sworn" to give David the throne fits nicely with the Israelite strong man's own oath that he would personally deliver the kingdom into David's hand.

Abner's initial parley with David is mediated through official envoys who convey the commander's willingness to swing his support to David and bring all Israel with him. Abner seeks to make a covenant, though particular conditions or expectations are not recorded. The rhetorical question "To whom does the land belong?" is ambiguous. Is Abner implying that the land of Israel truly belongs to him rather than Ishbaal, thus reinforcing his authority to negotiate its future? Or does his question acknowledge that the land already belongs to David, since Yahweh's favor is self-evident? Behind either option lies the reality that the land of promise belongs to Yahweh, who disposes of it at his pleasure.

David's quick acceptance of Abner's offer carried one condition: the return of David's wife Michal, whom he had gained at the cost of risking his life for the bride price of 100 Philistine foreskins

---

From Dan to Beer-sheba

This expression was commonly used to denote Israel's traditional boundaries by naming the northern and southern extremes. The Israelite city of Dan had been known as Laish before the Danites took it from the Canaanites (Judg 18:7, 29). Dan was about twenty-five miles upstream from the north shore of the Sea of Galilee. It sat at the foot of lofty Mount Hermon, straddling the important trade route between the Syrian capital of Damascus and the seacoast city-state of Tyre. When Jeroboam I led the formation of a new northern kingdom after Solomon's death, he established a royal sanctuary at Dan containing a golden calf, hoping to attract northern pilgrims who might normally go to Jerusalem (1 Kgs 12:29).

Beer-sheba was located in the parched lands about twenty-three miles southwest of Hebron. It was located at an oasis amid the hills of southern Judah, along a trade route leading to Egypt. It's name may mean "well of seven," indicating the source of its importance in that arid country. Archaeological excavations of the ancient site (Tell es-Seba) have uncovered several wells, one of which was over twelve feet in diameter and cut through sixteen feet of solid rock. Beersheba was often visited by the patriarchs (Gen 21; 26; 28; 46), and may have hosted an ancient shrine.

Was David's Remarriage against the Law?

Some writers have pointed out that David's remarriage to Michal was in violation of the law, at least as expressed in Deut 24:1-4 (compare Jer 3:1). The laws that are codified in Deuteronomy may not have been in force during David's reign, however. Even if they were, Deut 24:1-4 deals with a different situation: one in which the husband had divorced his wife because she lost favor with him. If she should happen to marry another man and be divorced again, the first husband was not allowed to remarry her. David did not divorce Michal, nor had he desired to give her up. David had been forced to flee for his life; then Michal's father Saul had forcibly given her in marriage to another.

ZaFrira Ben-Barak has discovered intriguing parallels in Mesopotamian case law that apply specifically to a situation in which a man is forced to flee the country and leave his wife behind. After a certain period, she becomes a technical widow and is free to remarry. But if the first husband should return, he may reclaim her as his wife, and she must leave the second husband and return to the first. This established practice may have been known in Israel, as well (see "The Legal Background to the Restoration of Michal to David," VTSup 30 [1979]: 15-29).

(1 Sam 18:20-27) and then lost through Saul's capriciousness (1 Sam 25:44). As the narrator tells it, David's primary objective was to procure a token of Abner's good faith. The phrase "see my face" was idiomatic for "appear in my presence." Only those who had special privilege could "see the face" of the king (2 Kgs 25:19 = Jer 52:25; Esth 1:14).

David's decision to demand the return of Michal as a sign of Abner's good faith suggests deeper designs. David wanted to regain what was rightfully his. Michal was not only his first wife, but also provided him a legitimate claim to being a member of Saul's family. From a political standpoint, reconstituting their marriage would strengthen David's claim on the throne. [Was David's Remarriage against the Law?]

The unexpected content of vv. 14-15 has led some scholars to propose that these verses derive from a different tradition. If David was relying on Abner to return his wife, why should he send a concomitant demand to Ishbaal, and why should Ishbaal honor it? There is some logic to David's actions. He was a man of *public* principle, at least, and proper protocol would require that Ishbaal, as Saul's heir, should approve Michal's return, lest she appear to be a victim of kidnapping. Ishbaal had proven so politically infirm that he knew there was no point in resisting David. Refusing to return Michal might serve David as a pretext for war, and Ishbaal would have wanted to avoid that at all costs. Abner escorted Michal to Hebron, fulfilling David's demand.

The narrator reveals nothing of Michal's feelings about being returned to David, but he draws a pitiful picture of her second husband Paltiel's following behind, whimpering like a whipped puppy (v. 16). [Who Was Michal's Husband?] At Bahurim (just outside of Jerusalem, on the road to Jericho), Abner apparently grew weary of

Paltiel's weeping, and ordered him to return home. Paltiel's whimpering obedience reminds the reader of Ishbaal, a further reminder that the house of Saul had grown weaker and weaker.

Having passed David's test of honor, Abner set about fulfilling his promise. His message to the elders of Israel (the leading men and decision-makers, however official) suggests that there had been prior rumblings from some elders who had lobbied for Israel to switch its allegiance to David (v. 17). Many scholars regard all or part of vv. 17-18 to be secondary, and v. 18b certainly has the signs of it. There is no known referent to the quoted promise of Yahweh outside of 2 Samuel 7, which uses different language. As Abner cites it, the promise is reminiscent of Yahweh's earlier promise to Saul (1 Sam 9:16; 10:1), and it may have been shaped by the same hand as a way of accenting the continuity between the reigns of Saul and David. [Comparing Promises]

It seems that Abner was more certain of success with the elders of Israel in general than with those of Benjamin in particular. Saul was of the tribe of Benjamin. If anyone still supported Ishbaal, it would be the Benjaminites. Thus, while Abner "sent word" to the elders of Israel, he "spoke directly to the Benjaminites," pleading his case on a personal level, and apparently with success. After the consultation, "Abner went to tell David at Hebron all that Israel and the whole house of Benjamin were ready to do" (v. 19b).

The twenty men who accompanied Abner to Hebron (v. 20) are not named. The narrator probably would have mentioned it if the men had been representative elders from Israel, so we may postulate that the twenty men were Abner's personal bodyguard. After all, he was traveling in hostile territory.

David recognized the importance of the occasion and the incredibly significant *coup* that Abner's defection represented. The Israelite general's work as a liaison with the tribal elders was an invaluable

---

Who Was Michal's Husband?

ΑΩ There is some confusion concerning the name of Michal's second husband. In v. 15, he is called "Paltiel the son of Laish," while in 1 Sam 25:44 a shortened form of his name ("Palti") is used, and his hometown is identified as Gallum, a small Benjaminite town located north of Jerusalem. In 2 Sam 21:8, however, Michal's second husband was named Adriel, son of Barzillai. According to 1 Sam 18:19, Adriel was the husband of Michal's sister Merab. Evidence suggests that there has been a textual corruption of 2 Sam 21:8, for at least two Hebrew manuscripts and the LXX have "Merab" in that verse, which is correct.

Comparing Promises

Compare the content of Yahweh's earlier promise to Saul and his purported later promise to David.

Yahweh's Promise to Saul	The Alleged Promise to David
1 Sam 9:16	2 Sam 3:18
"You shall anoint him to be ruler over my people Israel. He shall save my people from the hand of the Philistines."	"Through my servant David I will save my people Israel from the hand of the Philistines, and from all their enemies."
1 Sam 10:1	
"The LORD has anointed you ruler over his people Israel. You shall reign over the people of the LORD and you will save them from the hand of their enemies all around."	

contribution to David's cause. The negotiations, however, were still preliminary. Having reported Israel's readiness to transfer allegiance, Abner begged leave to gather Israelite representatives for an official covenant-making ceremony (v. 20a). David, obviously delighted with the prospects, dismissed Abner to carry out his plan, and the Israelite strongman "went away in peace" (v. 21b). This last phrase is of immense importance, so much so that the narrator will repeat it twice more in the next two verses. Disaster will soon befall Abner, and the reader must know that David had nothing to do with it. *David* sent Abner away *in peace*.

Joab Settles a Grudge, and David Plays Politics, 3:22-39

As Abner departs in peace, Joab returns with the fruits of violence. Two things stand out in v. 22. First, the verse suggests that David was still supporting himself through surgical raids against Judah's traditional enemies (cf. 1 Sam 27:8-12). [An Unusual Raid] The reference to "much spoil" suggests that the raid was designed for profit rather than defense. According to the chronology supplied, this would have taken place at least seven years after David became king in Hebron. Were the people of Judah too poor to support him, or was David's self-sufficiency a key to his popularity? The answer is not provided, apparently because it is beside the point.

The propitious nature of Joab's absence leads the reader to suspect that David anticipated trouble and sent him away intentionally. If that is the case, the raid may have been an exception to David's royal practice, rather than the rule. Thus, one cannot presume that David continued to rely wholly on piracy to support himself.

David's apparent suspicions about Joab were well advised. When the hot-headed commander returned, he was incensed to learn that David not only had entertained Abner, but had sent him away in peace (note again the careful repetition of that thought in vv. 21, 22, 23). The verbal barrage with which Joab accosted David was straightforward. Joab did not trust Abner, and accused him of being nothing more than a top-level spy who had come "to learn your comings and goings and to learn all that you are doing" (v. 25b). [Comings and Goings]

An Unusual Raid

AΩ The word translated as "raid" (*gĕdûd*) has that meaning only in 2 Sam 3:22. Derived from the root *gĕdad*, meaning "to penetrate" or "to go in troops," the noun form usually refers to a marauding band, such as the Amalekites who raided Ziklag (1 Sam 30:8, 15, 23), or to troops in general, as in 1 Chr 7:4 and 2 Chr 26:11. That meaning cannot apply to 2 Sam 3:22, where the mention of spoil makes it clear that *gĕdûd* must refer to the raid itself, carried out by Joab's own band of marauders.

Comings and Goings

AΩ The phrase "going out and coming in" most commonly refers to an army's marching to and from battle (e. g., 1 Sam 18:13, 16; 29:6). Thus, Joab accuses Abner of seeking to gain intelligence about the military maneuvers of David's army so he could use it against them in the civil war.

Gateways
This gateway from
ancient Megiddo may
date from Solomon's era.
(Credit: Tony W. Cartledge)

The narrator records no reply from David, leaving the reader to presume that Joab's ensuing actions resulted from his own initiative. In a bold move that bordered on treason, Joab set out to sabotage David's regnal plans for no greater purpose than to satisfy his own sense of vengeance. As the story is told, Joab's accusations of espionage are entirely secondary to the old rage that still holds Abner personally responsible for his brother Asahal's death (2 Sam 2:18-23).

Joab sent messengers to retrieve Abner, who only recently had departed. Josephus claimed that the "cistern of Sirah" (or *Bor-has-sirah*, v. 26) was twenty stades, or two and a half miles, north of Hebron.[1] The ease with which Joab then assassinated Abner is surprising. Was Abner so naive that he suspected nothing? Were his twenty men totally ineffective in protecting him? The narrative account is short and bitter: "Joab took him aside in the gateway to speak with him privately, and there he stabbed him in the stomach. So he died for shedding the blood of Asahel, Joab's brother" (v. 27). Ancient cities had large and complex gateways that usually included room for merchants, benches from which the city's elders dispensed justice, and side rooms or pockets for the use of the city's guards. [Gateways] It was probably into one of these recesses that Joab invited Abner for his pointed and deadly conversation.

Again, the author takes great pains to underscore David's innocence. When Joab recalled Abner to the city, "David did not know about it" (v. 26a). Once David learned of Joab's deadly deed, he

The Content of David's Curse

David's withering curse upon Joab's house requires little comment, but these notes may be helpful. "To suffer from a discharge" may have referred to some sort of venereal or urinary disease. The biblical term often translated as "leprosy" is generic, describing a number of potential skin diseases, and not limited to what is now called leprosy (Hansen's Disease). The distinguishing characteristics of biblical leprosy were whitish, scaly skin and festering sores. Lev 13–14 gives a lengthy discussion of "leprosy" and the ritual uncleanness that resulting from it.

Some writers interpret one "who holds a spindle" as someone who clings to a crutch. In a Phoenician inscription from Karatepe, the word *plkm* means "crutches" (so Kyle McCarter, *II Samuel* [AB 9; Garden City: Doubleday, 1984], 118). In Hebrew, however, the word routinely refers to a spindle used in the production of yarn or cloth, too small to be used as a crutch. Since this work was done primarily by women, some commentators presume that David's curse pointed to a man who was handicapped in some way, so that he was relegated to doing "woman's work."

The last two parts of the curse—"who dies by the sword, or who lacks food"—are self-evident. The end result of David's curse is that Joab's family should constantly be affected by the wasting effects of disease, famine, and war. When Joab's death is ordered by Solomon, the narrator pointedly ascribes it to David's curse (1 Kgs 2:31-34).

---

issued a statement that not only disavowed any responsibility, but also castigated Joab publicly (vv. 28-29). David pronounced no specific judgment on the legality of Joab's blood vendetta, choosing to render punishment through a curse rather than the courts.

A curse was a serious matter, believed to become effective by the power of the spoken word. David's curse upon Joab is a curse upon his family and descendants. [The Content of David's Curse] David calls for sickness, weakness, war, and famine to be constant companions to Joab's house (v. 29). The inclusion of Joab's family in David's curse may seem surprising, but v. 30 suggests that at least one other family member shared responsibility for Abner's assassination: "So Joab *and his brother Abishai* murdered Abner because he had killed their brother Asahel in the battle at Gibeon." Abner had died to satisfy the honor of Joab's family; now Joab's entire family was cursed to feel the consequences of their actions.

David's curse, though severe, was an ingenious political ploy. David knew that he still needed Joab. He could not afford to court-martial him or to disavow his service. Thus, he issued a blistering curse upon Joab's house—winning him favor with the disconcerted Israelites—but he did not remove Joab from his powerful position.

David had good reason to be angry with Joab, whose precipitate actions doubtlessly postponed his acquisition of power in the north. At the same time, David knew that Joab's strong leadership was indispensable to him. Thus, Joab's punishment was more showy than substantive. The Judean general was forced to dress in mourning clothes and lead the state funeral procession for a man that he himself had killed (v. 31). Joab lost face, but not force. He suffered in reputation, but not rank.

The reader must wonder if David's personal show of mourning was entirely sincere, asking to what extent David simply sought to win public approval. David not only demanded that others mourn, but he wept loudly over Abner's grave, inspiring all others to join him (3:32). David then led an elegy for Abner (3:33-34), much as he had done for Saul and Jonathan (2 Sam 1:19-27).

David's eulogy for Abner is neither as lengthy nor as eloquent as his lament over Saul and Jonathan, though it was probably longer than the excerpts preserved in 2 Samuel 3:33-34. It lacks the *qînâ* meter and the "how" questions often associated with elegies. David's primary lament is that Abner, who was "a prince and a great man," has died the ignoble death of a common criminal. The word for "fool" in "Should Abner die as a fool dies?" is the same term (*nābāl*) that lay behind Nabal's name (1 Sam 25:3). A fool, in this case, is one who acts criminally and is worthy of arrest. Abner was neither a fool nor a convicted criminal ("your hands were not bound / your feet were not fettered"), yet he died ignominiously, denied the dignified demise deserved by one of his standing (v. 34).

David's lead role in the mourning rites is emphasized in two further ways. First, the narrator notes that the king's touching eulogy for Abner again moved all the people to tears (v. 34b). Afterward, David appeared disconsolate, refusing to eat. When encouraged to take nourishment, David swore an oath that he would fast for the remainder of the day (v. 35).

David's skills as a public relations "spin doctor" were so polished that he achieved the desired result: "The people took notice of it, and it pleased them, just as everything the king did pleased all the people" (v. 36). It was imperative that David convince the public—who would naturally be suspicious—that he was completely innocent of complicity in Abner's death (v. 37). If David's public relations gambit had not succeeded, his assumption of the northern throne could have been derailed, rather than simply delayed.

David's closing speech is filled with the vocabulary of power and puzzles. Abner was "a prince and a great man," but he had fallen (v. 38). David was the anointed king, yet he was "gentle" and powerless to prevent Abner's death (v. 39). Thus, both David and Abner had fallen victim to the same violent sons of Zeruiah. David's political skills enabled him to survive, but Abner, despite his martial prowess, could not.

David's closing wish that the LORD give the wicked (that is, Joab) what he deserves may be intended as a final exclamation point, or as a weak excuse for why David did not punish Joab personally. The lack of this phrase in 4QSam*a*, the best-preserved text of Samuel from Qumran, has led some writers to presume that it was a pious platitude contributed by a later scribe.

The end result of the Abner adventure is that David achieved the best of all worlds. David would have understood that Abner and Joab could not co-exist in his government, especially if one was expected to take orders from the other. Something would have had to be done to resolve the inevitable conflict between them. Although his actions created a temporary crisis, Joab's hunger for blood not only resolved the issue for David, but absolved David from later political repercussions. Even when things did not go according to plan, the house of David grew stronger and stronger.

CONNECTIONS

Using People, 3:1-5

The list of David's sons born at Hebron is intended to illustrate the new king's growing power by highlighting his charismatic ability to attract many wives and his connubial success in siring children by them. As acceptable as this practice was in the ancient world, it still amounts to using other people for one's personal gain. Even the charming Abigail, who seemed to have sparked a romantic chord (1 Sam 25:39b), is listed as just one more prize wife suited for the production of children.

Desperately Seeking Something

The desire to mollify one's internal cry by abusing other persons is expressed in practices as private as leering over debasing pictures provided by "adult sites" on the Internet, or as patently serious as child abuse or rape. Sex is not our only outlet for expressing the need for power that grows from our inner need for self-worth, however. People may "gather a harem" of persons or things that meet felt needs for respect or influence in other ways as well.

In modern Western culture, harems such as David possessed exist primarily in the fantasies of men who long to express their need for power by exploiting women. For some men, collections of pornographic magazines take the place of the palace harem, as readers imagine that the women pictured within belong to them alone.

Multiple marriages are no longer allowed in Western society, but many persons practice serial polygamy, constantly in search of the "trophy wife" or the powerful husband who can provide the ego massage they seek so desperately. Others do not bother with marriage, but engage in frequent sexual relationships with a stable of willing partners. [Desperately Seeking Something]

The practice of *using people*, whether ancient or modern, always carries a price. Initially, it hurts the person who is being used.

Children who are born as a result of sexual conquest rather than mutual commitment face added obstacles in growing up. Perhaps it is no coincidence that, so far as we know, *none* of the six sons mentioned in 3:1-5 lived a full life or died a natural death. Their lives were filled with jealousy, suspicion, infighting, and pain. Eventually, the abuser will suffer, too.

People are meant to be loved, not used. *Things* are meant to be used, not loved. Yet many persons continue to love things and use people. David's successful and prolific harem is presented in the text as a positive sign of personal power, but the same narrator will later point to painful lives and cruel fates suffered by the children. Other persons, whether male or female, are not tools to be used, and cannot be exploited without consequences.

Power Plays, 3:6-21

Abner's initial support and later betrayal of Ishbaal is yet another example of one person's using another for personal gain. Abner set up Ishbaal as a puppet king in order to advance his own power. Through Rizpah, Saul's concubine, he sought to enjoy the rewards and exploit the symbols of power. When confronted by Ishbaal, Abner quickly switched his allegiance to David, hoping to gain even greater influence.

Abner is routinely presented as a man who looked out for himself. Though usually considered loyal to Saul, he was conspicuously elsewhere when Saul's position was overrun by Philistines during the battle at Mount Gilboa, resulting in the demise of Saul and three royal sons. Abner escaped the battle intact, emerging as the most powerful man in Israel. Abner had no personal rights to the throne, but he apparently waited five years before lending Ishbaal enough support to assume the title of king, meaning that Abner probably assumed primary leadership during the interregnum.

When pursued by Asahel, Abner continued to look out for himself. He encouraged Asahel to turn and take one of his younger soldiers, who would be easier prey. When Abner finally killed Asahel, it was in self-defense—not to protect his men, whom he would have sacrificed gladly to avoid the personal and political complications involved in dueling and defeating Asahel.

Abner's later use of Rizpah and his willingness to undermine Ishbaal were further efforts to put himself in a position of greater power and influence, no matter what the cost to others. Perhaps the narrator means for the reader to understand that Abner's dishonorable death in the gateway of Hebron was a just reward for his lifetime devotion to attaining power through disreputable means.

Stomach Stabbing, 3:22-30

Joab's untimely assassination of Abner probably grew from mixed motives. No doubt, Joab would have perceived Abner as a threat to his power and position in David's court. He might have resented Abner's presence under the best of circumstances. However, the narrator insists that Joab's main motivation was the desire to gain vengeance on Abner for the death of his brother Asahel. In doing so, Joab allowed his personal agenda to take precedence over everything else—including his king's explicit desire to maintain a relationship of peace with Abner.

No less than three times, the text reminds us that *David* sent Abner away *in peace*. When Joab called Abner back without David's knowledge, however, he met him with lethal violence. There was nothing subtle about Joab. He gained a private audience with Abner through the pretense of a parley, then openly stabbed him in the stomach.

The text may encourage readers to search for ways in which we allow our personal agendas to undermine larger families, organizations, or movements. The cost of internal controversy is painfully high, and often that dissension has its roots in personal agendas held by one or a few persons.

Joab's particular agenda also raises a red flag for readers. Joab was consumed by inner hatred that grew from a desire for revenge. The bereaved brother was so overcome by this personal vendetta that he was willing to jeopardize an entire kingdom to satisfy his hunger for vengeance. Harboring hatred and giving ground to grudges

---

The Cost of Rage

Jesus suggested that harboring anger without forgiveness left one liable to judgment: "But I say to you that if you are angry with a brother or sister, you will be liable to judgment; and if you insult a brother or sister, you will be liable to the council; and if you say, 'You fool,' you will be liable to the hell of fire" (Matt 5:22). This quotation from the Sermon on the Mount expands upon the Old Testament commandment against committing murder. In Jesus' ethic, harboring rage and expressing contempt toward others were only a step removed from murder itself, and equally reprehensible.

Jesus himself experienced anger, but he knew what things to be angry about, as well as how to express anger in appropriate ways. Jesus grew most angry when he saw persons oppressing others who were unable to defend themselves. Jesus expressed indignation to his disciples when they sought to keep children away from him (Mark 10:14), and he created havoc in the temple when he saw the courtyard designed for Gentile worship taken over by Jewish merchants (Mark 11:15-19 and parallels).

The Apostle Paul advised: "Be angry but do not sin; do not let the sun go down on your anger" (Eph 4:26). Paul knew that anger is unavoidable and is sometimes appropriate, but it must always be confronted in one way or another. It is best dealt with quickly and redemptively.

inevitably leads to trouble, whether on a large scale or a small one. [The Cost of Rage] The harm that nursing anger brings to one's own digestive system and internal sense of well-being is bad enough, but others often feel the bite of our gall as well.

When Great Men Fall—and Problems Rise, 3:31-39

Abner's death was a blow to David not only because of his apparent appreciation for the man who had once been David's own commanding officer, but because of the serious complications that Abner's assassination brought to his quest for kingship. A lesser man than David might not have recovered from the blow, but the narrator wants us to understand that David is no ordinary man.

David is both wise and quick-witted. As a result, he engineers a brilliant recovery, turning Abner's death to his own advantage by publicly cursing Joab (without removing his valuable general from office), and by engaging in loud lamentation for Abner as he honored the fallen enemy with a state funeral fit for a king. Trouble reared its ugly head before him, but David found a way to rise above it.

How could David continue his remarkable pattern of facing difficulty and actually gaining strength from it? The narrator does not say, but the implication is clear: It is because Yahweh is with him. David can overcome even the roughest of obstacles, can walk through the valley of the shadow of death, because the LORD is with him.

The Apostle Paul underscored the same reality when he said, "We know that all things work together for good *for those who love God*, who are called according to his purpose" (Rom 8:28). Even bad things can work together for good, but only when we are working together with God.

NOTE

1 Josephus, *Ant.* 7.34.

ISHBAAL DIES,
BUT DAVID IS INNOCENT

4:1-12

COMMENTARY

This chapter completes a sequence of timely deaths (Saul's, Abner's, and Ishbaal's) that worked to David's benefit in ascending to the throne of Israel. Each death was, in its own way, necessary to pave the way for David's accession. Yet the narrator is careful to show that David was unequivocally innocent of complicity in any of the deaths.

Walter Brueggemann has pointed to an interesting corollary: The death of each potential threat to David is balanced by the death of another.[1] In a sense, these connected fatalities atone for the deaths of David's opponents, balancing the books and leaving David free to pursue the kingship. [Three Timely Deaths]

When Abner was killed, Ishbaal was left as good as dead. The king was sired by Saul, but his kingship rested solely on Abner's strong shoulders. When Abner was cut down, Ishbaal knew he was bound to

---

Three Timely Deaths
Consider this comparison:

The Extinguished Opponent	The Balancing Death	David's Response
Saul (and Jonathan) (1 Sam 31)	the Amalekite who claims to have put Saul out of his misery (2 Sam1:1-10)	David orders the Amalekite's death (1:13-16) and publicly laments Saul and Jonathan. (1:11-12, 17-27)
Abner (2 Sam 3:22-27)	Asahel, whom Abner had killed in battle, causing his brother Joab to seek revenge (2:18-23; 3:27, 30)	David publicly curses Joab (3:28-29) and laments Abner (3:31-38), "so all the people and all Israel understood that day that the king had no part in the killing of Abner."
Ishbaal/Ishbosheth (2 Sam 4:5-8)	Rechab and Baanah, who assassinated Ishbaal (4:1-3, 5-8)	David orders the assassins killed and mutilated to show his abhorrence of their crime, and he ceremonially buries Ishbaal's head. (4:9-12)

fall. "His courage failed" translates an idiom that literally means "His hands hung loose" (cf. 2 Chr 15:7; Neh 6:9; Zeph 3:16). An equivalent English idiom would be "He lost his grip." Firm and steady hands suggest confidence and power, while loose and unsteady hands betray fear. The narrator insists that Ishbaal was not alone in growing fearful: "All Israel was dismayed." In this case, "all Israel" refers to the areas over which Ishbaal claimed sovereignty (see 2:9), and does not include Judah.

The name "Ishbaal" (or "Ishbosheth") does not appear in v. 1 or v. 2 of the MT, but is supplied in the LXX. Some ancient versions (including the one reflected at Qumran) had "Mephibosheth," which is obviously incorrect. Some writers suggest that the MT reading intends to cast aspersion on Ishbaal by calling him merely "the son of Saul," but the deletion of any personal name may reflect nothing more than a simple way to correct a corrupt text.

The narrator quickly introduces the villains who will conspire to assassinate Ishbaal, fully expecting David to reward them for doing his dirty work. They are Baanah and Rechab, sons of a man named Rimmon, who is pointedly identified as a Benjaminite, despite his residence in Beeroth. [Why Is This Strange?] The parenthesis in v. 3 (which may be the work of a later hand) makes it clear that the two men are native Benjaminites, and thus not motivated by ethnic rivalry. They were legitimate captains of Ishbaal's raiding bands, who had undoubtedly served to enrich the king by plundering his enemies (compare. 2 Sam 3:22 and the accompanying note). In assassinating Ishbaal, they seek to enrich only themselves.

Surprisingly, the narration is interrupted once again for a different reason. The writer finds it important to point out that Jonathan had a surviving son, one who had been lame since the age of five, when his nurse (who was terrified when she heard that Saul

---

Why Is This Strange?

The text interrupts a crucial story to add an internal footnote explaining how it is that a Benjaminite family hailed from Beeroth. Beeroth (which means "wells," and is identical in form to modern "Beirut") was one of four Gibeonite cities that had made a covenant of peace with Joshua to avoid being overrun by the Israelites (Josh 9:17). Along with the people of Gibeon, Chephirah, and Kiriath-jearim, the Beerothites lived as resident aliens in the midst of the land allotted to Benjamin (see also Josh 18:25-27). The cities of the tetrapolis were all located within a few miles of Gibeon, which was about six miles northwest of Jerusalem.

The parenthesis in v. 3 explains that, at some point, the indigenous Beerothites had fled their city and settled in Gittaim. The location of Gittaim (which means "dual winepress") is unknown, though it must have been relatively near Jerusalem. It is listed in Neh 11:33 as one of the cities repopulated after the exile.

The text does not say why the people of Beeroth had left their homes. Most scholars assume it had something to do with an earlier attempt by Saul to exterminate the Gibeonites "in his zeal for the people of Israel and Judah" (2 Sam 21:1-2). Presumably, the surviving Gibeonites fled, and people from the tribe of Benjamin took up residence in their cities. Thus, it was possible for Rimmon and his family to be residents of Beeroth and Benjaminites simultaneously.

Why Is This a Problem?

AΩ The MT calls this son of Jonathan "Mephibosheth," and is followed by the LXX, except for LXXL, which has "Memphibaal." However, in 1 Chr 8:34; 9:40 the same son is named "Meribaal" (in 9:40 the name appears twice, with variant spellings [Meribaal/Meribbaal]). Saul also had a son named Mephibosheth by his concubine Rizpah. Along with his brother Armoni, he was given by David to the Gibeonites, who executed them to satisfy an old score against Saul (2 Sam 21:7-9).

It is likely that "Meribaal" was the original name, at least of Jonathan's son. How it became "Mephibosheth" is a matter of debate. The traditional view is that "bosheth" ("shame") was substituted for "baal" ("Lord," but in later times more commonly used as the personal name of the Canaanite male deity; see [Ishvi, Ishbaal, Eshbaal, or Ishbosheth?] on Ishbaal/Ishbosheth). However, this altered name could have meant "shame is my master" (if *mĕrî* is related to the Aramaic term *mar*, meaning "master, lord"), which is also undesirable. Thus, "meri" might have been changed to "mephi," producing a combination that could mean "one who disperses shame," or "out of the mouth of shame."

Kyle McCarter proposes a less convoluted solution, presuming that Saul's son was originally named Mippibaal ("out of the mouth of Baal" or "from the mouth of the Lord"), and that later scribes changed it to the euphemistic "Mephibosheth." McCarter conjectures that the same name was then foisted upon Jonathan's son in 4:4, leading to the confusion. The conundrum defies a clear solution. Fortunately, it has little effect on the story, whose characters are sufficiently identifiable.

P. Kyle McCarter, *II Samuel* (AB 9; Garden City: Doubleday, 1984), 125

and Jonathan had been killed) accidentally dropped him. The boy's name was Mephibosheth. [Why Is This a Problem?] The narrator probably wanted to remind the reader that, although Ishbaal would soon die, the Saulides were not dead. David would still have to deal with Saul's descendants, who could have potential claims on the throne. The young and physically challenged Mephibosheth, however, was hardly a threat.

With these asides introduced like so much stage furniture, the narrator returns to the account of Ishbaal's assassination. Rechab and Baanah came to the house of Ishbaal at a time when Ishbaal was known to escape the heat by means of an afternoon siesta (v. 5). Precisely what happened next has fallen victim to a corrupt and possibly conflated text (vv. 6-7). The MT preserves two accounts of the murder. In v. 6 the two soldiers enter the house on the pretext of fetching some wheat, stab the sleeping Ishbaal in the stomach, and quickly escape. Verse 7 could then be read as a more elaborate reprise, adding the detail that they also decapitated Ishbaal and took his head with them before gaining the Arabah road for a night-long journey to Hebron. Some scholars suggest that the two verses preserve separate traditions of how Ishbaal met his demise: through a stab in the stomach or by losing his head.

The LXX combines the two into a single account and adds a female doorkeeper to the list of characters. According to the Greek, the doorkeeper was tired from cleaning wheat and dozed, allowing Baanah and Rechab to "slip in" (a difficult translation to defend for the word "escape"). They then went about the bloody business of removing Ishbaal's head.

The account of Ishbaal's death adds insight to the precarious nature of Ishbaal's rump kingship. He lives in a house with no more protection than a sleepy woman sitting at the door. He naps through the afternoon. The reader is inclined to have little admiration or even sympathy for him. His treacherous subordinates, however, earn even less respect. When the brutal brothers arrive in Hebron and present their gruesome trophy to David, they brazenly profess to have been doing God's work, claiming that "the LORD has avenged my lord the king this day on Saul and on his offspring" (v. 8b).

The brothers allege that they killed Ishbaal because he was the son of Saul, who had wrongly sought David's life (v. 8a). The deadly duo clearly expected David to be overwhelmed with gratitude that they had effected vengeance in his behalf, but they seriously misread the king of Judah. They would not like the reward he offered.

For obvious reasons, David could not rejoice in the death of Ishbaal, even if he wanted to. He did not wish to have his road to kingship littered with corpses for which he was responsible. David was innocent of Saul's death, and Jonathan's, and Abner's. He must also make it clear that he is not complicit in the death of Ishbaal.

David's response to Rechab and Baanah began in typical oath formula ("As the LORD lives"), adding weight and certainty to the succeeding condemnation. The words immediately following the oath formula are significant: "As the LORD lives, *who has redeemed my life out of every adversity*" (4:9b). David had found Yahweh to be an adequate and trustworthy redeemer—he did not need the help of Baanah and Rechab any more than he had needed the help of the Philistines, the Amalekite, or Joab. David professed a belief that more appropriate solutions could have been reached, and refused to let the blood of his rivals touch his hands.

The Amalekite mercenary who had brought Saul's crown and armband to David received death for his reward, even though Saul had asked for a mercy killing (v. 10). If that man deserved to die, was there any question that cold-blooded killers who murdered the innocent deserved even worse? [Was Ishbaal a Righteous Man?] Acting on the basis of their self-condemnation, David passed an immediate sentence, announcing that the two opportunists would die for their crimes. Assuming, perhaps, that no closer relative had the power to

Was Ishbaal a Righteous Man?

AΩ In the NRSV, David accuses Baanah and Rechab of "killing a righteous man on his bed in his own house" (4:11). The rendering (also found in the KJV) is a bit unfortunate. David was not making a moral judgment about Ishbaal's *righteousness*, but simply stressing his *innocence*. Ishbaal had done nothing to deserve the fate he found at the hands of the cruel Benjaminite soldiers. The word used is *ṣadîq*, which normally means "righteous" but can also carry the connotation of "innocent" (NIV, NEB), "blameless" (NJPS), or even "honest" (JB).

seek blood vengeance, David issues orders for their execution (vv. 11-12).

David had implied that Rechab and Baanah deserved worse than death, so he ordered that their bodies be mutilated and displayed as a lesson to all—and as a testimony of David's innocence. [Is This a Problem?] The reader may note an interesting wordplay. David sought to "require his blood at your hand" (v. 11), then ordered that the *hands* and feet of the unwanted assassins should be chopped off as a sign of disgrace (cf. Judg 1:6-7).

The object of "hanged" is not stated, but it is more likely that the bodies were hung up for public view, rather than the hands and feet. The pool of Hebron was likely the most frequented spot in the city, making it an ideal choice for public exhibitions. Just as David made the dishonorable death of the two assassins a public matter, he also made a point of honoring Ishbaal by having his head interred in Abner's tomb. There is no indication of royal ceremony or lamentation, as with Abner. In this case, the public impact resulting from David's treatment of Ishbaal's killers speaks more loudly than any lamentation.

With the close of this chapter, David is left without rivals. King Saul and his popular son Jonathan are dead. Abner, the northern strongman, is dead. Ishbaal, Saul's ineffective heir, is dead. Only Jonathan's son Mephibosheth remains, and he is both young and crippled. The doorway to kingship over all Israel lies open before David. In chapter 5, he will close it behind him.

Is This a Problem?

David ordered the bodies of Rechab and Baanah to be publicly exposed as a means of public education and maximum humiliation. The Deuteronomistic law prohibited the exposure of bodies overnight (Deut 21:22-23), but that law may not have been practiced in David's time—it does not seem to have been followed in 2 Sam 21:9-10, either. The text does not say that the bodies were left out overnight, however. If the men had first appeared before David after an overnight march down the Arabah road, and if they were dispatched as quickly as the text implies, they may have been garrotted for the day only, which would have been sufficient to make David's point.

CONNECTIONS

In one sense, this story highlights the way in which God is able to work out his purpose through persons who are both good and bad. Rechab and Baanah are two of the most repugnant characters in all of the Bible. They committed a horrible crime. Yet God's purpose superceded even their despicable deed as David demonstrated that his kingdom would be of a different sort.

On a more intimate level, the cruel wrong wreaked by Rechab and Baanah speaks to the reader about the importance of judging opportunity correctly and responding appropriately. The two brothers from Beeroth came from an opportunistic family. When

Saul's zealous purge forced the Gibeonites to flee from their ethnic tetrapolis, the family of Rimmon moved into the vacated city of Beeroth. Rechab and Baanah were also professional opportunists. As captains of raiding parties, it was their job to look for situations in which a bold, quick strike could reap great rewards.

So it is not surprising that the two brothers saw Abner's death and David's rise as a golden opportunity to make themselves rich by engineering Ishbaal's assassination. There is no evidence of political intrigue in this story, no suggestion that Rechab and Baanah were acting in behalf of any nationalistic or ethnic group. They, like Saul and his descendants, were Benjaminites, but kinship was no obstacle to their greed. The narration suggests that their cold-blooded murder of Ishbaal was carried out with precision, and without hesitation. For these opportunists, it was all in a day's work.

Rechab and Baanah were so deadly, in fact, that the insertion about Jonathan's son Mephibosheth may be intended for no other purpose than to explain why the lethal duo did not kill him, too. The insertion carefully points out that he was a minor who suffered physical handicaps, and thus could hardly be considered a rival to David.

The brothers were so immersed in their rapacity and so certain of success that they were not prepared for David's response. Ishbaal may not have deserved to be king, but he deserved better than he got from Rechab and Baanah. The narrator stresses his innocence by calling him a "man of righteousness." Ishbaal may or may not have been anointed as Saul was, but David could not condone the cold-hearted murder of an innocent man (though he would later commit the same crime against Uriah the Hittite, 2 Sam 11). For the sake of public appearance, at least, David had to condemn their actions and distance himself from any responsibility. David insisted that the blame and retribution belonged to the opportunistic brothers and no one else. The same hands that had shed the blood of Ishbaal on the previous day were soon covered with their own blood, cut from their executed bodies and displayed as a lesson to Israel.

The crass siblings had come to David expecting a reward, and they received one. Their just recompense, however, was not political favor, military appointments, or a sack full of money. Their just reward was a humiliating death and an uneasy grave. [An Uneasy Grave]

Our own world abounds with opportunities for both good and evil, and all of them carry consequences. Our culture offers

An Uneasy Grave

The ancient Semites believed that the dead, though in Sheol, retained some tenuous contact with their bodies. For this reason, one's manner of burial was extremely important. Bodies were placed in tombs, and when they had decomposed, the bones were carefully collected and stored in a shallow depression, or under the burial shelf, along with the bodies of earlier generations. This is what it means to be "gathered to one's fathers" (Gen 49:29; Judg 2:10; 2 Kgs 22:20).

If the corpse of the deceased was exposed to the elements, dismembered, or otherwise mistreated, it was believed that the dead would experience greater suffering, even in Sheol. Thus, ancient tombs were often protected by curses engraved on or beside the entrance. These curses threatened ruin upon anyone who dared to disturb the bones of the dead.

For example, an inscription in Hebrew from the 8th century BC was discovered in the village of Silwan (Siloam), and is attributed to a man who identifies himself as a royal steward (lit., one who was "over the house"). Though broken, it appears to read: "This is [the tomb of Sheban]iah the royal steward. There is no silver or gold here, only [his bones] and the bones of his maidservant with him. Cursed be the man who opens this" (author translation).

Inscription from J. C. L. Gibson, *Textbook of Syrian Semitic Inscriptions*, vol. 1 (Oxford: Clarendon Press, 1971–82), 24.

---

competing messages about what those rewards will be. Should we seek the golden trophy of material gain, even if we must take advantage of the weak to achieve it? Should we seek the proceeds of personal pleasure and sexual conquest, even though others must be exploited along the way? Should we seek the prize of power, even though we must climb over other persons to attain it? Is the reward worth the cost?

The Old Testament answer was clear: The righteous are those who follow the law, which gives special protection to the innocent and the weak. The righteous were promised God's blessing, and David himself had testified that effect, claiming that the LORD had "redeemed his life" out of every adversity (4:9b). In contrast, the wicked were destined to be cursed.

Jesus took a different approach. He also urged his followers to show love for other persons and special care for the weak and downtrodden. He did not, however, promise earthly rewards for doing so. To those who entrusted their lives to his way, Jesus promised an abundant inner life on earth and an eternal life beyond this earth.

Jesus also taught that, when the rewards were awarded, many would be surprised. The story of the "sheep and goats" judgment (Matt 25:31-46) suggests that many who consider themselves righteous will be shocked to find themselves numbered among the goats, while others will be pleasantly surprised to find themselves with the sheep. The criterion for judgment, Jesus taught, is the way in which we treat other people. Those who use other people for personal gain will not be pleased with their reward. Those who, inspired by Jesus, give of themselves in love for others will find themselves embraced by the gracious love of God.

The road of life has many branches, each of which is an opportunity to choose good or evil. The Scriptures are very clear in teaching that each road leads to a certain destination (e.g., Matt 7:13-14). No one should be surprised when they get there.

NOTE

[1] Walter Brueggemann, *First and Second Samuel* (IBC; Louisville: John Knox Press, 1990), 232-33.

DAVID: KING OF ALL ISRAEL

5:1-16

Second Samuel 5:1-16 has been woven together of disparate parts and traditions for the singular purpose of elucidating David's long-awaited arrival as the king of all Israel, established in his own city and accepted by his peers. The tapestry includes the account of David's enlistment by the elders of Israel (5:1-5; derived from at least two sources) and a brief report on David's capture of Jerusalem as his personal base of power (5:6-9; an old account with several expansions). The theological interpretation attached to this significant victory (5:10) may have marked the original end of the document that began with 1 Samuel 16, the "History of David's Rise." Two further bits of tradition complete the transition from aspiring monarch to ruling king: a chronologically misplaced note about Hiram of Tyre building David's palace (5:11-12) and a court record listing sons of David born in Jerusalem (5:13-16).

COMMENTARY

Anointed by the Elders, 5:1-5

The description of David's ascension to the throne in Israel is decidedly understated. After all of David's years of living in tension with Saul (1 Sam 18-31), and after the detailed accounting of his careful manipulation of events surrounding the elimination of all rivals (2 Sam 1–4), David's "crowning moment" is depicted via a brief notice in which he is virtually passive. The narrator has constructed the text in this way to underscore the underlying theme that David did not seek the throne on his own, but was brought to it by Yahweh.

Scholars have long noted that vv. 1-2 and v. 3 appear to be duplicate versions of the same event. The oldest part of the account is probably v. 3, which has been expanded by the Deuteronomistic addition of vv. 1-2 and chronological note in vv. 4-5.

No clue is provided regarding the amount of time that passed between Ishbaal's death and the arrival of Israel's elders in Hebron. [Tribes, Elders, or Staff-Bearers?] The lack of contrary evidence leads the reader to assume that it happened rather quickly. Abner had already set the process in motion, preparing the elders to approach David even while Ishbaal lived. With both Abner and Ishbaal dead, the elders had scant choice but to turn to David for leadership.

Tribes, Elders, or Staff-Bearers?

AΩ The word used to describe Israel's representatives is *šibṭê*, from a root that could mean "tribe" or "staff." It is unlikely that all the tribes of Israel made a pilgrimage to Hebron. McCarter revocalizes the word as *šōbĕṭê*, meaning "staff-bearer," or one who exercised authority over a tribe. Others, such as Anderson, note that *šbṭ* can also mean "ruler" or "judge" and translate as "chiefs." The intent seems to be clear: Representative leaders from Israel came to parley with David and invite him to become king over Israel as well as Judah.

P. Kyle McCarter, *II Samuel* (AB 9; Garden City: Doubleday, 1984), 74-75, 131-32.

Without Abner's organizing strength, the northern leaders had little with which to bargain. It is as if they appeal to David, trying to convince him that he should accept the position. As arguments, they point to the biological kinship between David (as a representative of Judah) and the tribes of Israel: "We are your bones and flesh." This metaphor, like the modern expression "flesh and blood," was commonly used to denote kinship (Gen 29:14; 2 Sam 19:12, 13 [MT 13, 14]). Some writers regard the expression as anachronistic, but the traditions giving to Israel's tribes a common ancestry could certainly be as old as David.

David's kinship with Israel had been expressed already in his service to Saul and his marriage to Saul's daughter; the leaders acknowledge that even when Saul was king, it was David whose military valor bore the marks of true royalty. The terminology of "leading out and bringing in" is from the vocabulary of ancient war, in which the king led his soldiers out to battle and brought them safely home.

Finally, the elders employ a more spiritual argument. They appeal to David's piety by reminding him of how God had called him many years previously, and had commissioned him to become king of Israel. The divine promise they quote is not found elsewhere, but must refer to David's encounter with Samuel in 1 Samuel 16. How could David refuse such an eloquent plea?

The obvious reference to Samuel's initial call to David allows the author to reprise the important motif of David as shepherd. God had called David away from watching the sheep of his father Jesse (1 Sam 16:11), but not from being a shepherd. Now he is to "shepherd" Israel (2 Sam 5:2), offering protection and guidance to the beleaguered nation. This motif also appeared in 1 Samuel 17:34-36 and will surface again. It is no accident that Nathan used the illustration of a poor shepherd and an abused sheep to spotlight David's sin against Bathsheba and Uriah (2 Sam 12:1-4). Psalm 23, attributed by ancient tradition to David, accentuates Yahweh's role as shepherd to his people.

The metaphor of the king as shepherd was fairly common in the ancient Near East. [The King as Shepherd] In v. 3, it clearly stands as a parallel to the word *nagîd*, translated as "ruler" by the NRSV but also used to mean "crown prince" or "designate to the throne." Though their intention is clear, the elders of Israel seem to be dancing around the use of the word "king." Perhaps they intend by this verbal bandying to limit what David is being asked to do; he is not being given a blank check to run roughshod over Israel, as Samuel had predicted the new kings would do (1 Sam 8:11-19).

> **The King as Shepherd**
>
> AΩ As early as the 3rd millennium BC, the Sumerian king Lugal-zagesi was described as a shepherd-king appointed by the deity. In both Babylonian and Assyrian, the nominal and verbal forms of the word for "shepherd" could be used in the sense of "ruler" or "to rule." The same metaphor was common in Egypt, especially favored during the Middle Kingdom period (21st–18th centuries BC). For specific references, see J. Jeremias, "ποιμήν, κτλ," *TDNT*, 6:485-502.

The older tradition in v. 3 has no qualms about using the word "king" (*melek*) in reference to David. Indeed, the word is emphatic, appearing three times: "So all the elders of Israel came to the *king* at Hebron; and *King* David made a covenant with them at Hebron before the LORD, and they anointed David *king* over Israel." The conditions of David's covenant are not revealed, but his obligations would have been minimal. It was the tribes of Israel who sought to become David's vassals, not vice versa.

The anointing of David to be king over Israel may not have differed much from his earlier anointing by Samuel. Though the covenant ceremony was made "before the LORD," the text does not reveal whether a priest officiated at the anointing, making it a sacral event, or whether the elders themselves anointed David in a secular ceremony. The same type of scented oil would have been used in either case. The primary difference is in the level of publicity and ceremony. No longer a secret future king, David is now exalted to become the popular and powerful ruler of all the tribes, the first king of a truly united Israel.

The chronological notes in vv. 4-5 (cf. 2:10a, 11) are probably in round numbers, though most scholars accept the general accuracy of a forty-year reign for David. There is a minor disparity between v. 4 (forty years total) and v. 5 (forty years and six months total), perhaps due to their derivation from different sources. This discrepancy would not have troubled ancient readers, who would recognize symbolic, rounded numbers when they saw them. Whether this notice is a part of the Deuteronomistic chronology or the work of a later hand is a matter of scholarly dispute.

Ensconced in His Capital, 5:6-16

David's City, 5:6-10

David's acceptance by the tribes of Israel was an important step in his ascension to power, but not the final one. To achieve the superstar status that would make David legendary, he had yet one conquest to make. David's supporters in Hebron obviously would not approve if David chose to move his capital into the larger northern territories. At the same time, Hebron was too far removed to serve as a tenable seat of government for a nation that included the far-flung northern tribes.

David's conquest of Jerusalem has long been recognized as a stroke of political genius. [Jerusalem] The city was not aligned with either the north or the south, being one of the last remaining Canaanite enclaves that the emergent Israelites had failed to dislodge (Josh 15:63; Judg 1:21). The city was also conveniently located near the border between Judah and the northern tribe of Benjamin. When David led his private army to conquer Jerusalem, the city became his own personal property, an autonomous seat of government not beholden or belonging to either Israel or Judah. [The King and His Men] This allowed the ascendant king a greater measure of freedom to exercise his influence over all the tribes while resting securely in his own fortress-like city.

The text of vv. 6-9 is among the most problematic in the Old Testament. It has been the object of many detailed studies, none of which is entirely satisfactory. The main issues surround the meaning of the word *ṣinnôr* in v. 8 and the significance of the lame and the blind, who appear in the short text no less than three times (5:6, 8).

Jerusalem

AΩ Jerusalem was an ancient city, attested by documentary evidence as old as the Ebla archives (c. 2500 BC), the Egyptian execration texts (19th century BC), and the letters from Tell Amarna (14th century BC).

The name "Jerusalem" probably meant something like "foundation of [the god] Shalem." This deity Shalem was mentioned in texts from Ugarit. In later periods, however, the element *šlm* was naturally associated with the Hebrew word *šalôm*, whose meanings range from "peace" to "wholeness."

The King and His Men

David conquered Jerusalem with the aid of his private army, which had begun to gather about him during his wilderness period (1 Sam 22:1-2) and had continued to grow (1 Sam 30:9). David's mercenary army included close relatives such as Joab and his brothers, but consisted mostly of men who were social outcasts before finding a place of acceptance among David's personal troops. Thus, David's men were fiercely loyal to him. The king's decision to attack Jerusalem using his own soldiers, rather than a royal levy of men from Judah or Israel, worked to his advantage. Jerusalem was unquestionably the "city of David," to which both Judah and Israel must look for leadership.

The most common interpretation goes back to rabbinic times. It assumes that the text describes a city so strong that its rulers taunted David, claiming that even the lame and the blind could defend it (so NRSV, RSV, NASB, NIV, NJPS, JB). A few interpreters understand the taunt to mean that David must first kill or lead away the blind and the lame (KJV, NEB), perhaps imagining that the handicapped would have been lined up as a shield of defenseless persons. Some interpreters imagine that their presence was symbolic of a magical incantation, a public warning that all invaders would be made blind and lame. Kyle McCarter proposes an emendation to the verb, arguing that it was the blind and the lame who incited the city rulers to speak so strongly to David.[1]

> **Jebusites**
>
> There is no extrabiblical evidence that Jerusalem was ever called "Jebus" or that the mountain was called "Mount Jebus," despite Judg 19:10-11 and 1 Chr 11:4-5. The pre-Israelite inhabitants of Jerusalem seem to derive their name from a tribal or ethnic appellation. The Jebusites were most closely related to the Amorites (Josh 10:5; compare Num 13:29), one of several ethnic groups generally referred to as Canaanites (Gen 10:16).

Either interpretation gives David little chance of penetrating Jerusalem's reputedly impregnable walls. One thing the text is very clear about is that David surprised everyone by conquering the city in what appears to be a quick and convincing manner (v. 7).

Most interpreters read v. 8 as a mark of David's strategic genius: the recognition that Jerusalem's Achilles' heel was a hidden water shaft leading from the inner city to the Spring of Gihon, which was located outside of the walls. Some years later, a gently sloping tunnel would be built by Hezekiah, but the Jebusite water shaft was virtually vertical. It could only have been climbed with great difficulty, adding to the miraculous nature of David's victory.

The Chronicler's version of the story (1 Chr 11:4-9) attributes to David an additional promise that the first man to strike one of the Jebusites who inhabited the city would become his chief general. [Jebusites] The honor was won by Joab, who appears to have been leading the army already.

While some authors interpret the word *ṣinnôr* as

> **The Water Shaft**
>
> Ancient cities, including Jerusalem and Megiddo, used tunnels as a strategic means of obtaining water from outside of their walls, even during times of siege. The tunnel pictured here may have provided water for Jerusalem, but recent studies suggest it could not be the feature described in 2 Sam 5:8.
>
> Hershel Shanks, "I Climbed Warren's Shaft (But Joab Never Did)," *BAR* (Nov–Dec 1999): 30-35.

Gibeon Springs. (Credit: Scott Nash)

"grappling iron" (NEB), most interpreters prefer "water shaft," based on its meaning in rabbinic Hebrew. [The Water Shaft] This makes for a reasonable explanation, except that it leaves the reader puzzled about why it is said that David hates the lame and the blind. McCarter offers a unique solution. He proposes that *ṣinnôr* does not mean "water shaft" at all, but should be interpreted as "windpipe." In McCarter's interpretation, David insists that his men strike to kill (at the windpipe), rather than leaving maimed soldiers lying around to become a future financial liability. This analysis has some advantages, but leaves the reader with no explanation for how David and his limited army managed to penetrate the formidable city that had withstood all previous assaults.[2]

The motive for David's alleged antipathy toward the lame and the blind—whether based on religious scruples, fiscal callousness, or personal animosity—must remain an object of speculation. Most authors agree, however, that the last sentence of v. 8 is surely a later addition, a brief etiology identifying David's hatred of the lame and the blind as the motivation for a rule prohibiting them from entering "the house," apparently a proleptic (before-the-fact) reference to the Jerusalem temple (cf. Acts 3:1-10). David was later regarded as the founder of many cultic practices (1 Chr 22–28), but the account in 1 Chronicles 11:4-9 mentions neither the lame and blind nor the establishment of any cultic rules.

After occupying Jerusalem, David renamed the city in honor of himself, leaving no doubt as to who was in charge. [The City of David] He then proceeded to build up the city, limited at that time to the Hill of Ophel, by expanding its borders as far as the steep-sided hill allowed. At some point in time, part of the hillside was terraced with balks and filled in, creating a more gradual slope that allowed for additional building projects. This earthwork was called the "Millo," from the Hebrew verb meaning "to fill" (*ml'*). In 1 Kings, Solomon is credited with the construction of the Millo (1 Kgs 9:15, 23; 11:27), but it is possible that Solomon repaired an existing structure. One would expect David's building program to proceed *outward* from

The City of David

David's decision to rename the city for himself was not without precedent in the ancient world. For example, the Assyrian king Tukulti-Ninurta (c. 1244–1208 BC) built a new capital and named it "Tikulti-Ninurta City." Likewise, when Sargon II (721–705 BC) founded the Neo-Assyrian Empire, he established his capital at Khorsabad and called it *dūr šarru-kīn*, which meant something like "Sargonton."

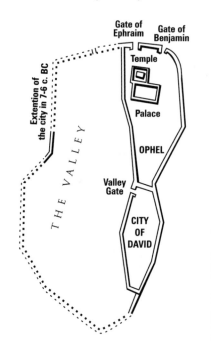

the inner fortress, but the text says that "David built the city all around from the Millo *inward.*" Archaeological evidence regarding the age of the ancient terraces is subject to variant interpretations.

Many scholars consider v. 10 to be the triumphal close of the History of David's Rise. It is unmistakably an editorial comment, added for the specific purpose of spelling out the theological underpinning that buttresses the growing edifice of David's achievements. In 2 Samuel 3:1, the narrator had commented that David was growing stronger, while the house of Saul grew steadily weaker. Now he remarks that David continued on the path to increasing greatness, precisely because "Yahweh, the God of hosts, was with him." The Hebrew text itself is less pointed than most English renderings. To the assertion that David was growing in greatness, it adds the quiet comment, "And Yahweh was with him." Subtly and effectively, the narrator leads the reader to make the causal connection. David's ascendancy is not due to the young king's innate excellence alone, but to the favor of Yahweh's presence.

David's Ally, 5:11-16

A comparative chronology of Semitic rulers suggests that King Hiram of Tyre did not begin to reign until the final decade of David's lengthy regime. [Hiram's Gift] Thus, the notice that Hiram sent his own carpenters, masons, and materials to build David's palace seems chronologically out of place by many years. This suggests that the author has telescoped several later events into a brief synopsis to give the reader a brief glimpse at the kinds of things David did while he ruled in Jerusalem. The list of David's sons in vv. 13-16 reinforces this assumption.

However, the narrator carefully marks Hiram's royal gift as a sign to David that he had truly arrived as an established peer among the kings of neighboring nations (v. 12a)—something that would be more appropriate near the beginning of David's reign. This suggests that the narrator may have moved the event forward arbitrarily to suit his purposes, that he was simply mistaken about the date of Hiram's gift, or that he had confused Hiram with his lesser-known father, Abibaal. Hiram's famed assistance in building the temple (1 Kgs 5:1-12 [MT 5:15-26])—

Hiram's Gift

Tyre was an ancient seaport located on the Mediterranean coast to the immediate north of Israel. During the Iron Age, Tyre was the capital of the Phoenicians, who preferred to call themselves "Sidonians" (cf. 1 Kgs 5:6 [MT 20]; Homer's *Iliad* [23.743]; and the Ugaritic *Keret* epic [14:202]).

The cedar trees that grew tall and straight in the forests of Lebanon were known throughout the ancient world and were exported (either willingly or forcibly) to both Mesopotamia and Egypt as early as the 3rd and 4th millennia BC. Cedar logs were used to make durable and strong pillars, and fragrant cedar paneling lined the houses of the well-to-do and ancient royalty (cf. 2 Sam 7:2; Hag 1:4). Because of the great demand, Lebanon was largely deforested by the end of the second millennium, making Hiram's gift even more remarkable.

and Abibaal's less-than-acceptable name ("my father is Baal")—may have led to a situation in which the son completely eclipsed the father in popular memory.

It should be noted that the present mention of David's cedar house also prepares the way for 2 Samuel 7:2, in which David set his mind to building a house for Yahweh because he recognizes the inequity of living in a cedar house while Yahweh's ark remains in a tent. This may be a supporting reason for the author's insertion of the notice in chapter 5. The overriding point, however, is clear: The Tyrian monarch's ready acceptance of David added political legitimacy to the theological validation of David's reign found in v. 10.

The vocabulary of v. 12 is decidedly dynastic: Yahweh "established him [David] as king" and "exalted his kingdom for the sake of his people Israel." Such language rightly begins with Nathan's dynastic oracle in chapter 7, and so seems out of place here. However, the author already knows the end of the story, and does not hesitate to use language derived from events that are yet to be.

The author brings his account of David's capture and occupation of Jerusalem to a close by inserting a list of sons who were born to David while he was in Jerusalem. As with the enumeration in 3:2-5 (see [David's Descendants]), the purpose of this notice is not just to put David's children on the record, but to emphasize David's increasing power by pointing to his growing harem of concubines and wives, as well as to his obvious virility as illustrated by a regular issue of progeny. [Concubines and Wives]

The NRSV stresses that David took these additional partners *in* Jerusalem, after he came from Hebron. The MT actually says that he took these wives and concubines *from* Jerusalem. The MT may be the original reading, but even so, the primary point is that David's harem continued to grow after he reached Jerusalem. Some wives (such as Bathsheba) he found in Jerusalem. Others undoubtedly came from neighboring nations, as royal marriages were common means of sealing political alliances. Although the text states that daughters were born to David in Jerusalem, none are mentioned by name.

The same list appears separately in 1 Chronicles 14:3-4, and in combination with 2 Samuel 3:2-5 in 1 Chronicles 3:1-9. The list in 1 Chronicles 3:1-9 asserts that all sons listed were born of David's wives, in addition to unnamed sons that were born to concubines. The Chronicler also mentions the name of one daughter, Tamar,

Concubines and Wives

The MT word order ("concubines and wives") was so troublesome that some versions of the LXX reversed it, and the Chronicler's version drops the word "concubine" altogether (1 Chr 14:3). Unlike 3:2-5, the male progeny are listed without reference to their mothers. The parentage of some is known (Solomon, for example, was Bathsheba's son), but for most of the sons listed, their pedigree remains as much of an enigma as their respective careers.

who is better known than most of the sons. The Chronicler's account does not include the story of Tamar's rape by Amnon, known from the tradition behind 2 Samuel 13. The mention of Tamar by name only may represent an acknowledgment of Tamar's fame, without repeating a story that would cast an ill light on David's house.

> **Nathan, Son of David**
>
> David's son Nathan should not be confused with his court prophet of the same name. Christian readers should note that Luke's genealogy traces Jesus' descent from David through Nathan (Luke 3:31), rather than through Solomon, as Matthew's version has it (Matt 1:6).

According to 1 Chronicles 3:5, the first four sons in the list were born to Bathsheba, who is there called "Bathshua, the daughter of Ammiel." Shammua probably means "Yahweh has heard," though only the vowel remains from the suffix "*yah.*" Shobab is of uncertain derivation, possibly meaning "substitute." Nathan means "gift," and may be a hypocorism for "Netanyahu" (gift of Yahweh) or "Nethaniel" (gift of God). [Nathan, Son of David] The name Solomon is probably derived from the word *šalôm*, meaning "peace" or "wholeness." Since Solomon is widely regarded as the first son born to David and Bathsheba after the ill-fated child of their adultery, some scholars presume that his name suggests he is a replacement ("one who makes whole") for the deceased child.

The female progenitors of the other sons are not given, and the later careers of the seven remaining sons are obscure. Ibhar may reflect a wish: "May he [God] choose." The name of Elishua, at least, is fairly obvious, though he is called Elishama by the Chronicler. It means "my God is salvation" and is similar in form to the name Joshua, which means "Yahweh is salvation."

First Chronicles 3:5-8 and 14:5-7 add two additional names at this point: Eliphelet (Elpelet in 14:5; the name Eliphelet also appears at the end of both lists) and Nogah, who is otherwise unknown. It is likely that these two "sons" reflect a textual corruption, not additional children. The duplication of Eliphelet suggests a possible haplography, and Nogah may be a variant of Nepheg.[3]

The meaning of Nepheg is baffling, but Japhia probably means "may he [God] shine." Elishama clearly means "my God has heard," while Eliada means "my God knows." First Chronicles 14:7 preserves this name as Beeliada, or "Baal knows," adding to the evidence from the naming of Saul's son Ishbaal (see [Ishvi, Ishbaal, Eshbaal, or Ishbosheth?]) that "baal" was used in Davidic times to mean "Lord," with reference to Yahweh rather than the Canaanite deity Baal alone. The last son mentioned is Eliphelet, whose name means "my God is deliverance." Eliphelet should not be confused with the military hero of the same name (2 Sam 23:34).

CONNECTIONS

This chapter contains a mélange of events and commentary that combine to assert a single truth: David has arrived. He is accepted by his own people as well as neighboring allies, and his growing success is evident in his occupation of Jerusalem and his stream of sons. All of this, we are told, is due to the beneficence of Yahweh, who is "with him."

1. *The advantages of cooperation.* The account of David's coronation over Israel illustrates the importance of recognizing God's wisdom and of working together. David had been alienated from the people of Israel for many years, but the tribal elders were able to look past their differences with David and cast a vote for unity (5:1-5). They appealed to David on the basis of three things they had in common. First of all, they were family (our bones and our flesh). Not only was David's tribe of Judah descended from the same ancestor as theirs, but David had married into the Israelite tribe of Benjamin through his union with Michal, daughter of Saul.

Secondly, David had already proven himself to be a superlative leader, able to win the loyalty of others and to guide them wisely. Israel was in need of such leadership. Thirdly, the elders believed that it was God's will for David to become king over Israel as well as Judah. With no indication of how they knew, the elders cited a prophecy that David would become king over all Israel.

David's opinions in these matters are left unspoken because the narrator wants to portray him as the passive beneficiary of Israel's trust, rather than an avaricious glutton for personal power. The reader presumes, however, that David concurs with the elders. Together, they agree to put their differences behind them and build a new life based on the common ties that bind them. This agreement is celebrated through a sacred covenant, which strengthens those same ties and makes them inviolable. At last, the people and their king became a truly united kingdom.

Modern believers would benefit from similar wisdom. The kingdom of God, as represented by the community of faith, is far from united. We make far more of our differences—even within individual denominations and churches—than we do of our common ties. Our differences may be theological, methodological, ecclesiastical, or cultural. Though we are bound by a common faith in Christ and by a common call to share Christ's love, our tendency is to allow our differences to overshadow common cause. Instead of celebrating diversity and allowing it to empower growth, we often fail to fellowship or work together with those whose gender, creed,

Unity in Diversity

Paul insisted that in Christ "there is no longer Jew or Greek, there is no longer slave or free, there is no longer male and female; for all of you are one in Christ Jesus" (Gal 3:28). Paul did not mean that ethnic, economic, and gender differences would disappear, but that they would become meaningless in the light of a unity that was far greater, the common bond of Jesus Christ (cf. Rom 12:4-8 and 1 Cor 12:4-31).

---

culture, or worship style fall outside the lines we have drawn. [Unity in Diversity]

This text also points to the importance of sacred symbols, such as the covenant ceremony that bound David to Israel. The memory of this covenant would add accountability to their stated desire to work together. There is great power in symbols, especially those that are public. For Christians, baptism is such a symbol. For the clergy, it is ordination. For husbands and wives, it is the marriage ceremony. Such covenants are made with the understanding that both parties express mutual obligations to the other, and commit themselves to fulfilling those commitments. Also, these covenants are made, like the one between David and Israel, "before the Lord." God is witness to the promises we make through sacred symbols, and God is a source of strength in helping us keep our promises.

Kenneth Chafin has pointed to the elder's quotation of an earlier prophecy as a reminder that "there is often a great distance between the beginning of a dream and its fulfillment."[4] David's patient dependence on God—even when he fled to the wilderness and seemed farther than ever from the promise—is a reminder that we, too, can trust in God even when our dreams seem far from fulfillment. Our natural temptation is to expect things to happen *now* and to devote our efforts to gaining the objects of our desire, but our best qualities are those that grow patiently through adversity (cf. Rom 5:3; 2 Cor 6:4; Col 1:11; Jas 1:3).

2. *The signs of God's favor.* Having elucidated David's invitation to reign, the narrator injected several bits of tradition, each of which serves as a clear sign of God's favor upon David. Jerusalem had a reputation of being impregnable. The steep cliffs and strong walls surrounding the city were so advantageous that even the blind and lame were said to be capable of defending it. Yet David and his men conquered the city, and David took it to be his own city and seat of power (5:6-9). Immediately afterward, the narrator notes that David's power grew because "Yahweh was with him" (5:10).

Yahweh helped David not only militarily, but politically. The author includes a snippet of tradition about the king of Tyre's being so impressed with David that he offered to build a cedar palace for him (5:11-12). This notice does not appear for the purpose of explaining how David found a place to live, but as an illustration of how neighboring kings were used by Yahweh to legitimate and enrich David's reign.

Finally, the list of David's new wives and the sons born in Jerusalem (5:13-16) is added as a further sign of divine favor. In underdeveloped societies that depend on manual labor to tend the crops or care for the sheep, the munificence of God is measured by the number of children one produces. In that category, David was clearly blessed.

By bringing together these signs of divine favor, the narrator "counts David's blessings." Modern believers would do well to count their blessings from time to time. [Today I Am Thankful For...] While counting our blessings, however, believers must remain leery of measuring God's presence by political power or material prosperity. Athletes and race car drivers often attribute their success to God "being on their side," as if God cares who wins a ballgame or a race. The measure of God's presence with the believer is not gauged by physical health or financial success, but by the spiritual power that grows in the heart of those who trust in God and find him faithful through all the circumstances of life. [The Significance of the Zion Traditions for the Old Testament and Beyond]

Today I Am Thankful For . . .

In 1996, Sarah Ban Breathnach published a book called *The Simple Abundance Journal of Gratitude* (New York: Time Warner, 1996). The book contains a short introduction, followed by a yearly calendar in which each day is represented by five blank lines. Readers are encouraged to spend time each day thanking God for the simple things that add abundance to our lives, and are asked to record five of those things. Many readers testify that this simple exercise has made a large difference in their attitudes toward life.

NOTES

[1] P. Kyle McCarter, *II Samuel* (AB 9; Garden City: Doubleday, 1984), 135-38.

[2] Ibid.

[3] Ibid., 148.

[4] Kenneth L. Chafin, *1, 2 Samuel* (CC; Dallas: Word Books, 1989), 267.

The Significance of the Zion
Traditions for the Old Testament and Beyond

The word "Zion" appears in the books of Samuel only at 2 Sam 5:7, but the traditions surrounding Israel's "Zion theology" have their roots in David's conquest of Jerusalem. "Zion" originally referred to a Jebusite fortress in Jerusalem, located on a ridge (also called the "Hill of Ophel") in the southeastern part of the city, lying between the Wadi Kidron and the Tyropoeon Valley. The name Zion later became associated with the temple mount as well, hence "Mount Zion." In time, the term Zion referred to the entire city.

David's capture of Jerusalem and his subsequent transformation of it into his political and religious capital gave Zion/Jerusalem particular theological significance. Jerusalem, along with Sinai, became one of the two major geographical foci in the Hebrew Bible. Sinai remained significant for its ties to the ongoing law, but Jerusalem had more of a future focus, becoming the centerpiece of Old Testament eschatology. The Zion traditions are particularly prominent in the books of Psalms and Isaiah.

Jerusalem became known as the place of God's presence, the city that "the LORD has chosen . . . for his habitation" (Ps 132:13; see also 78:68; 1 Kgs 8:44, 48; 11:13, 32, 36; 14:21; 2 Chr 6:6, 34, 38; 7:12; 12:13; 33:7; Zech 3:2). As the place of Yahweh's presence, Jerusalem was sometimes identified with Mount Zaphon, the traditional place of Baal's abode in Canaanite thought, a cosmic mountain located at the center of the earth (Pss 48:3; 78:68-69; Isa 14:13-14).

The presence of Yahweh in Zion meant protection from both historical enemies and mythological powers of chaos. Thus, Jerusalem was thought to be a place of peace and safety (Pss 2; 46; 48; 76; Isa 10:24-34; 31:1-5; 33:20-22). This belief was abused by some Israelites who presumed upon God's protection regardless of their own faithlessness (Mic 3:9-12; Jer 7:1-15).

The destruction of Jerusalem in 587 BC did not put an end to Zion theology, but sparked an eschatological hope that the city would be restored (Isa 49:14-26; 52:1-10). Since God would again be present in Jerusalem (Zeph 3:14-15; Ezek 43:7, 9; 48:35; Zech 8:1-3), it would become a place of peace and security (Isa 33:17-24). The Gentile nations, drawn to God, would make pilgrimages to it (Isa 2:1-4; 25:6-10; Mic 4:1-4; Zech 8:20-23).

Early Christian theologians, building upon an implication of Heb 12:22-23, identified Jerusalem with the church. The power of Jerusalem as a religious symbol continues to be seen today in millennialist strands of Christianity, in nationalistic Zionism, and in the conclusion of the Passover Seder: "Next year in Jerusalem."

DAVID DEFEATS
THE PHILISTINES

5:17-25

The Consolidation of the Kingdom, 5:17–10:19

Having brought David to the throne of Israel—which the new king chose to locate in Jerusalem—the narrator delineates the various things David did to consolidate his personal power over all Israel and to position Israel as a secure and expanding nation. As the text presents it, David first moved to eliminate further Philistine encroachment into Israelite territory (5:17-25), then focused on domestic matters.

David sought to integrate the state and the faith by establishing Jerusalem as the official residence of the ark of the covenant (6:1-23), and made plans to construct an impressive temple as a symbol of his piety and power (7:1-3). Yahweh rejected David's building proposal, but promised instead to forge a dynastic house from David's descendants (7:4-29).

The author suggests that David continued attending to both external and internal affairs as needed. Flexing newfound military muscle, David engaged in a period of empire-building by conquering neighboring kingdoms on every side, until he had "won a name for himself" (8:1-14).

Refocusing on domestic issues, David delegated authority to a number of governmental officials (8:15-18) and cemented relationships within Israel by showing ostentatious kindness to Mephibosheth, the son of Jonathan and last remnant of Saul's line (9:1-13).

Not everyone loved David. When a new king arose over Ammon and led a brief rebellion, David was ruthless in putting it down, overwhelming both the Ammonite forces and the mercenary Aramaeans they had hired to assist them (10:1-19). With these victories, David's personal power reached its zenith. Yet, for the remainder of the book, David enters a period of decline, leaving active leadership of the kingdom to others. The most significant question shifts to the issue of which son would succeed him.

COMMENTARY

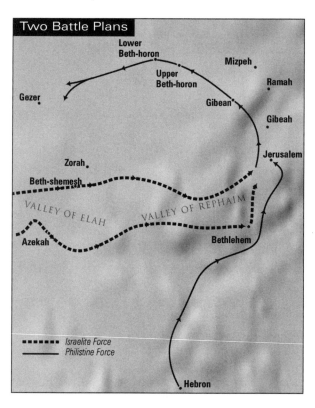

Two Battle Plans

Lower Beth-horon · Mizpeh · Upper Beth-horon · Ramah · Gezer · Gibean · Gibeah · Jerusalem · Zorah · Beth-shemesh · VALLEY OF ELAH · VALLEY OF REPHAIM · Azekah · Bethlehem · Hebron

▪▪▪▪▪▪ Israelite Force
———— Philistine Force

The two battles described in 5:17-25 offer a thorny dilemma to the exegete, for they appear to be out of place chronologically. [Two Battle Plans] In its received form, the text has already recorded David's coronation (vv. 1-5), his conquest of Jerusalem (vv. 6-8), his construction projects within Jerusalem (vv. 9-10), Hiram's gift of a cedar house (vv. 11-12), and the taking of additional wives, along with the birth of several children (vv. 13-16). This implies a period of many years.

We have suggested in the previous chapter that the narrator seems to have telescoped several important events in vv. 6-16 as a means of underscoring David's firm hold on the kingdom. Thus, the Philistine conflicts that now appear may have been passed over because the narrator wanted to give quicker attention to these other milestones.

The most obvious reason for presuming that these battles took place prior to David's occupation of Jerusalem is that the text associates the first battle with David's anointing as king over Israel (v. 17). The reader must remember David's prior tenure as a Philistine vassal. The beginning of David's servitude is described in 1 Samuel 27, but no official dissolution of the relationship is recorded. One might perceive David's seven-year kingship over Judah as a clear break with the Philistines. Surprisingly, however, no conflict is reported between David and his former overlords. The Philistine leaders may have continued to regard David as a vassal even after he moved his base of operations from Ziklag (which had been burned) to Hebron.

David's anointing and appointment to the throne of a united Israel, however, could not have been acceptable to the Philistines, who had expanded deep into Israelite territory (1 Sam 30). A united monarchy would present a more formidable foe than the Philistines could manage. Thus, when they heard of this new development, David's former allies had no choice but to deal forcefully with Israel's new ruler, presumably to depose him. Strangely, they did not seem to know where David was: "All the Philistines went up in search of David" (v. 17a). The reader is reminded of Saul's persistent and unsuccessful attempt to locate David in the rugged, far-flung wilderness of southern Judah. If David had already occupied Jerusalem as his capital, discerning his whereabouts should not have been a problem.

A second clue is that when David learned that the Philistines were after him, he "went down to the stronghold" (v. 17b). The word "stronghold" (*hammĕṣûdâ*) is also used of Jerusalem in 5:7 (where it is called *mĕṣudat ṣiyyôn*, the "stronghold of Zion") and in 5:9. However, it is unlikely that the narrator would have said that David "went down" to the stronghold of Jerusalem. In biblical thought, one *always* "went up" to Jerusalem, never down.

The stronghold in question, then, is probably at Adullam, some sixteen miles southwest of Jerusalem, in the hills of the Shephelah. David had established a strong presence at Adullam early in his career (1 Sam 22:1, 4; 24:23), and another conflict involving the Philistines and the Valley of Rephaim also found David at Adullam (2 Sam 23:13-14). It is possible, but less likely, that David was already ensconced in Jerusalem, and chose to leave the city and oppose the Philistine encroachment from a base of operations at Adullam.

The precise location of the Valley of Rephaim is uncertain, but it probably describes a low-lying area southwest of Jerusalem, bordered on the north by the deep Valley of Hinnom and now known as *el Baqʿa* (see Josh 15:8; 18:16). [Rephaim] The word "spread out" (v. 18) is unusual in a military context, suggesting that the Philistines had dispersed to search for David, rather than encamping in strength to prepare for battle (cf. Judg 15:9).

Another possibility is that the troops dispersed to set up various outposts to block the border between Judah and Israel, forcibly occupying the borderlands to prevent David from uniting the two kingdoms. This would follow from the claim that the incursion was inspired initially by David's anointing as king of Israel (v. 17). The Philistines could not afford to have this new alliance go forward and tip the balance of power against them.

Rephaim

AΩ The Hebrew word "rephaim" (*rĕpāʾîm*) usually refers to the shades or ghosts of the dead (Job 26:5; Prov 2:18; 9:18; 21:16; Ps 88:11; Isa 14:9), though the word is also used to describe a legendary race of ancient giants (Gen 15:20; Josh 17:15; 1 Chr 20:4).

The lowland plain or "valley" of Rephaim is mentioned in Josh 15:8; 18:16; 2 Samuel 5:18, 22; 23:13; 1 Chr 11:15; 14:9; and Isa 17:5. Its location is uncertain, but it is probably to be identified with what is now called the *Beqʿa* Valley, just southwest of Jerusalem.

The name of the Valley of Rephaim is not explained in Scripture. It may have been a traditional abode of the giants, or perhaps was thought to be haunted by shades emerging from the nearby Valley of Hinnom, a deep and fearsome cleft that served Jerusalem as a garbage dump and was frequently smoldering.

The narrative insists that, at this stage of David's career, his power and piety are still closely connected. Even though the Philistines have advanced nearly to Jerusalem and clearly mean him harm, David does not "go up against them" without Yahweh's express permission. As in earlier battles, he "inquired of the LORD" (cf. 1 Sam 23:9-12; 30:7-9; 2 Sam 2:1), probably by means of the sacred lots associated with the priestly ephod (1 Sam 14:41-42). Previously, the priest Abiathar had facilitated David's request for an oracle.

Seeking oracles by lot required one to ask a series of "yes/no" questions that become more specific as needed. Thus, David first asked, "Shall I go up against the Philistines?", before proceeding to the more critical, "Will you give them into my hands?" (v. 19a). The narrator has combined the answers into a single response from the priest, who spoke for the LORD: "Go up; for I will certainly give the Philistines into your hand."

According to the text, David's army met the Philistines at a place called Baal-perazim, probably in the southern reaches of the Valley of Rephaim, and dealt them a stinging defeat.

Baal-perazim

AΩ The name of the place could mean "Baal of Perazim" or "Lord of Perazim," or it may have meant "The Lord of Bursting Forth" or the like. If the battle etiology is secondary, perhaps the name originally referred to a strong spring gushing from somewhere nearby. The addition of "Baal" suggests that there may have been a sanctuary to Baal in the area, or possibly even a shrine to Yahweh, for "baal" seems to have been used in early periods as an epithet for Yahweh (witness the presence of "baal" in the theophoric name of Saul's son Ishbaal [2 Sam 2:10]).

In Isa 28:21, Yahweh's outburst is reported to have occurred at "Mount" Perazim. Despite the helpful etiology, the precise location remains undiscovered—or unidentified.

[Baal-perazim] A brief etiology explains the place name as deriving from this conflict, when Yahweh empowered David's army to "burst out like an outburst" and overwhelm the enemy. The word-play derives from the verb *pāraṣ* ("to burst upon") and the noun *pereṣ* ("outburst").

The Philistine retreat was so tumultuous that the enemy troops "abandoned their idols there," leaving them to be captured by David's men. The word "idols" reflects a Hebrew word meaning "shaped image," used pejoratively to mean "idol." Just as the Philistines had once captured the ark of the covenant, used as a battle palladium to rally the troops (1 Sam 4:1-11), so now the Hebrews capture the Philistine images that had been brought on site to bolster their war effort.

It was customary in the ancient world for victorious armies to carry away the "gods" of the defeated as a sign of their own deity's supremacy. The present text asserts that "David and his men carried them away," but the parallel passage in 1 Chronicles 14:12 insists that David commanded that the images be burned on the spot. The latter text, composed at a later date, is fashioned to protect David from charges that he may have violated the laws described in Deuteronomy 7:5, 25; 12:3.

The battle, like the capture of Jerusalem, is won by David and his men alone, without assistance from the Israelite levy (cf. 1 Sam 23:5, 24, 26; 24:3, 4, 23; 25:20; 27:8; 29:2, 11; 30:1, 3; among others). This is a significant statement about David's military ability and the blessing of Yahweh upon his efforts.

The second battle account occurs in the same general location, but there are no clues as to how much time had passed since the previous battle or what prompted the Philistines to return to the location of an earlier defeat. Some writers have proposed that the second account is a duplicate of the first preserved in a different tradition. The two accounts share common elements: The Philistines are "spread out" in the Valley of Rephaim, the protagonists are the same, and David seeks an oracle from Yahweh. The stories differ in that there is no mention of David's location, the oracle is much more elaborate, and David's army is not identified as his private militia.

We have argued above that the two battle accounts are chronologically out of place, probably occurring prior to David's acquisition of Jerusalem. Most of the evidence relates to the first story, however. This second account could have taken place after David's occupation of Jerusalem, though not necessarily. It may have been lumped with the previous account because of the common battlefield. Since David seems to have preferred to operate from Adullam when fighting in the lowlands of Rephaim (cf. 5:17-21; 23:13-17), we presume that is the case in this story as well.

The Philistines' occupation of the low plain of Rephaim is again described by the word meaning "to spread out," as if their intention is simply to possess the land, rather than to fight for it. And, once again, David seeks Yahweh's endorsement before pursuing military conflict. In this case, however, he gets a much more extensive answer, leading the reader to presume that he sought some other means of divination than the usual sacred lots or that the presiding priest had considerable prophetic latitude in interpreting the lots. It is possible that the detailed instructions could have come as the result of a long series of "yes/no" questions, but this is not likely.

In 2 Samuel 2:1 David also had sought Yahweh's guidance and was given specific instructions to go to Hebron. In 5:23 he is told not to confront the Philistines directly, but to circle around and attack from the rear at Yahweh's signal. This much about the battle strategy is clear. Interpreting the specifics obtains less certainty. If we conjecture that David's troops were advancing from Adullam and that the Philistines had entered the plain through the Valley of Soreq, then David would have circled around to the north side of the Philistine encampments.

The rejoinder to "come upon them opposite the balsam trees" (NRSV) is subject to varying translations. A literal rendering is, "Come upon them from in front of *běkā'îm*." The uncertainty is with the interpretation of *běkā'îm*, most frequently understood to refer to some type of trees. Balsam trees (based on an Arabic cognate) and pear trees (based on a similar word in rabbinic Hebrew) are commonly suggested, along with mulberry trees and mastic trees, or the untranslated alternative, "*bākā'* bushes."

The lack of the definite article implies that the word was also used as a place name, and it must have been well known for David to understand the directions. The article does appear in v. 24, however, where David is instructed to wait until he hears "the sound of marching in the tops of the balsam trees" (*habběkā'îm*, NRSV's translation). [Treetops or Asherahs?] This can be explained if we imagine a place that is named for a large and uniform grove of trees, perhaps one that is well known because it is a sacred grove.

Treetops or Asherahs?

AΩ While the MT has a compound word meaning "in the tops of" (*běrā'šē*), some versions of the LXX have "in the asherahs," reflecting the consonantal text *b'šry*. McCarter presumes that this is original and that the Hebrew text has become corrupt by a transposition of the two consonants (*b'šry* → *bš'ry*). The term "Asherah" refers to a wooden pole or tree used to represent the presence of a female deity in the Canaanite pantheon. A cluster of these would form a "sacred grove," which McCarter presumes is the intent of the narrator's vocabulary.

P. Kyle McCarter, *II Samuel* (AB 9; Garden City: Doubleday, 1984), 152

"The sound of marching in the treetops" suggests a strong storm wind, which is frequently associated with the appearance of Yahweh (Job 38:1; 40:6; Pss 18:7-15; 50:3; Ezek 1:4; Nah 1:3b). The storm wind is sometimes associated particularly with Yahweh's rushing against his enemies (Jer 23:19; 30:23; Zech 9:14). The sound of the wind is the sign to David that Yahweh has already gone before him to strike down the enemy, which is characteristic of a divinely ordained "holy war." There is a nice interplay of images: As the wind is heard "marching in the treetops," Yahweh has marched out to war.

Presumably by means of the storm wind, Yahweh apparently struck the Philistines and weakened the enemy troops so that David's forces were able to rout them, pursuing the Philistine army "from Geba all the way to Gezer" (v. 25). [From Geba to Gezer] With this victory, David effectively pushed the Philistines back into the territory they had occupied prior to the offensive that led to Saul's death (1 Sam 30).

The Deuteronomist attributes special significance to David's success over the Philistines. Some time earlier, when the Israelite

From Geba to Gezer

First Chr 14:16 and the LXX have "Gibeon," rather than "Geba." Gibeon was about six miles north-northwest of Jerusalem, while Geba probably lay about eight miles north-northeast of the city. Some writers identify Geba as Saul's stronghold of Gibeah, but others think "Geba" was used for "Gibeon" in certain early documents.

Gibeon was closer to the scene of the battle, and is preferable in this context. Gezer was about twenty miles west and slightly north of Jerusalem. It lay at the northern edge of the gently rolling Shephelah, near the western slopes of Palestine's central ridge. Gezer was about five miles northwest of Ekron, the easternmost city of the famed Philistine pentapolis. Thus, David's rout of the enemy pushed the Philistines back within their traditional territory, along the southern coast.

---

general Abner defected to David, he had prophesied that David would deliver Israel from the Philistines (2 Sam 3:18, probably a Deuteronomistic expansion). The same had been said of Saul (1 Sam 9:16; 10:1), but Saul had not lived up to expectations. Once again, the reader is reminded of how David's abilities and accomplishments have eclipsed those of Saul. Both here (5:17-25) and in 8:1-14, the narrator underscores David's perfect mastery of the Philistine threat. David triumphs, however, not only because of his personal charisma and brilliance, but because Yahweh fights on his side.

CONNECTIONS

These twin stories of bloody battles may seem far distant from the real world of most modern readers. Are there lessons here that might benefit believers? Both stories emphasize how much David depended on God for leadership and how willing he was to follow. In both stories, David was presented with a crisis that was not of his own making. It was obvious that action needed to be taken, but David carefully sought Yahweh's endorsement before proceeding.

The first story illustrates the principle. The second account is more embellished, emphasizing the importance of being continually alert for the guidance of Yahweh. David, who had been instructed to watch and wait, recognized Yahweh's active presence when he heard the sound of the wind in the treetops.

The book of Acts records how Jesus' disciples were also instructed to wait for the Holy Spirit, and to watch (Acts 1:4-5). The gathered disciples perceived the Spirit's arrival when "from heaven there came a sound like the rush of a violent wind, and it filled the entire house where they were sitting . . . all of them were filled with the Holy Spirit" (Acts 2:2, 4a).

The wind of the Spirit may take different forms. God may not come to us in a violent whirlwind, as he came to Job (Job 38:1), though anyone who has experienced a hurricane or raging thunderstorm must appreciate the elemental power behind the forces of nature. God may not speak through a blinding light, such as was required to gain the Apostle Paul's attention (Acts 9), or through a fearsome angel, as with Zechariah (Luke 1:11-20), Joseph (Matt 1:20-23), and Mary (Luke 1:26-38). Rather, God may speak in a still, small voice, as he did to Elijah (1 Kgs 18:13), through the words of a trusted friend, or in a simple certainty of heart.

The means by which God deigns to speak is less important than our willingness to hear God's voice and to obey it, responding as David did in faith and trust. That is when victories are won. Even when the battlefield is no larger than the human heart, every triumph is a miracle of God's grace and a testament to God's glory.

Christians are called to be people who actively seek peace rather than conflict (Matt 5:9) and who go so far as to love their enemies (Matt 5:43-45), rather than wishing them harm. The reader must first appreciate the narrator's assertion that the victories in question were won not only by the *will* of God, but by the *activity* of God. Acknowledging the realpolitik of the Old Testament world is not equivalent to endorsing it in our own. Indeed, Jesus taught, "You have heard it said. . . . But I say" (Matt 5:27-28; 31-32; 33-34; 38-39; 43-44). The teaching of the new rabbi Jesus brought radical changes to many old ways of thinking.

The teaching of Jesus suggests that if God speaks to us about dealing with our enemies, the strategy will involve winning them over with love, defeating evil with kindness. God led David to adopt novel battle strategies that proved successful. Combating evil with good may seem entirely backwards to the world in which we live; adopting that strategy is an act of faith and obedience. David's example suggests that wise believers will follow God's leadership, even when it does not match conventional wisdom.

THE CITY OF DAVID
AND THE CITY OF GOD

6:1-23

The materials in chapter 6 are generally considered to be part of an ancient traditional corpus known as the "Ark Narrative." Leonhard Rost first proposed that 1 Samuel 4:1b–7:1 and 2 Samuel 6 originated as a single compositional unit that later editors pieced into the longer Deuteronomistic History. Some recent writers have disagreed, pointing to several discrepancies. For example, Eleazar was appointed priest of the ark in 1 Samuel 7:1 but does not appear in 2 Samuel 6, unless he is to be identified as Uzzah. [A Strange Change?] Also, the place of the ark's residence is called Kiriath-jearim in 1 Samuel 7:1, but Baal-judah (or perhaps Baalah) in 2 Samuel 6:2.

These variants could be explained by assuming that the Ark Narrative itself was made up of earlier traditions in which different terminology was already embedded. The arguments for including 2 Samuel 6 appear stronger than the evidence for exclusion. One's position on this matter has little bearing on the interpretation of the passage, however; more significant is the Deuteronomist's placement of the piece, from whatever source it springs.

The exegete will also note that the passage, whatever its origin, is rife with textual difficulties. The Greek version is quite different throughout, and the synoptic passages in 1 Chronicles 13:1-14; 15:1–16:6 have been rewritten with a heavy hand.

> **A Strange Change?**
>
> AΩ There seems to be little in common between the names "Uzzah" and "Eleazar," but other names show a similar shift in pronunciation from 'z to 'zr. For example, 1 Chr 25:4 mentions a priestly musician named Uzziel, who seems to be the same man who is called Azarel in 1 Chr 25:18. More notably, Israel's most successful king of the 8th century BC is sometimes called Uzziah (2 Kgs 15:13, 32; among others) and at other times named Azariah (2 Kgs 14:21; 15:6).

COMMENTARY

The narrator's arrangement of the various David traditions has brought the heroic leader to the kingship of all Israel (5:1-5), to a new capital city (5:6-10), to a place of acceptance by neighboring heads of state (5:11-12), and to a new demonstration of power and virility (5:13-16). In two pitched (and apparently quick) battles, David successfully repelled the Philistines from Israelite territory, bringing their occupation to an end and pushing them back "from Geba [or Gibeon] to Gezer" (5:17-25).

David had brought a new concept of kingship to Israel. It was a kingship that included a mercenary army, a huge harem, a truly royal city, and an imperialistic attitude—all the accouterments of a typical Near Eastern kingdom. David's imposing vision of kingship far eclipsed the modest ambitions of Saul, and could not be sustained without extensive support from his subjects (as predicted by Samuel in 1 Sam 8:11-18). There would be natural resistance to David's active governance, especially among the tribes of Israel. Thus, David sought creative ways to bring together the old and the new, solidifying his position and legitimizing his rule.

The new king recognized the essential importance of claiming Yahweh's support. Later readers may question the purity of David's piety, but the Deuteronomist insists that David was influenced as much by sincerity as by strategy when he sought to make Jerusalem the tangible heart that would pump life into Israel's religious as well as political institutions. David knew that if he could orchestrate a working marriage of cult and state, he would be unassailable.

An Aborted Attempt to Return the Ark, 6:1-11

How does one go about transforming a Canaanite city into the nerve center of Israelite worship? The loyalties of the priests and the locations of sanctuaries were rather flexible in David's day. David needed something more stable. So he cast about for some strong symbol of Yahweh's presence that could make Jerusalem not only David's city, but Yahweh's city. He found it in the ancient cultic emblem that embodied for Israel the very presence and power of Yahweh: the hallowed ark of the covenant. In the absence of anyone strong enough to forbid him, David determined to transport the ark to Jerusalem and thus transport Jerusalem to a new position in Israel.

According to the MT, David gathered "all the chosen men of Israel" to serve as an escort for the ark. The thirty thousand troops suggested by the NRSV is an enormous number. If taken literally, the size of the force would witness to the seriousness of the endeavor. As mentioned in [Counting Soldiers] at 1 Samuel 4:10, however, the word *'elep* seems to denote something other than "thousand" when used to describe military contingents. Available

Where Was the Ark?

First Sam 7:1 placed the ark in Kiriath-jearim, but the MT of 2 Sam 6:2 says that David and his entourage took the ark from *mibba'ălê yĕhûdâ*, which is rendered in the NRSV as "from Baale-judah" but which can also be read as "from the lords [elders?] of Judah." The parallel text in 1 Chr 13:6 expands the problematic text to bring it into line with 1 Sam 7:1: There, they came "to Baalah, that is, to Kiriath-jearim, which belongs to Judah." The Dead Sea Scroll text called 4QSamᵃ has a reading almost identical to that of the Chronicler.

Most versions of the LXX have only "to Baalah," which may be more original. There is other evidence that Baalah and Kiriath-jearim were either alternate names for the same town or individual neighboring towns that grew together. It is called Baalah in the description of Judah's northern border (Josh 15:9, 10), which contains a parenthesis noting the alternate name Kiriath-jearim (see also 1 Chr 13:5). The same city is called Kiriath-Baal (the City of Baal) in Josh 15:60; 18:14, and Kiriath-jearim (the City of Forests) in 1 Sam 6:21; 7:1-2.

Kiriath-jearim was one of the four cities of the Gibeonites (Josh 9:17). It is probably to be identified with modern Tell el-'Azhar, about fourteen miles northwest of Jerusalem.

---

evidence suggests units of five to fourteen men per *'elep*, similar to a modern platoon. By this reasoning, the ark's honor guard would have numbered between 150 and 420 men.

The stated location of the ark illustrates the kind of textual difficulties found in this chapter. [Where Was the Ark?] The ark's resting place is called Baale-judah in the NRSV, an alternate name for Kiriath-jearim. There it had resided for the previous twenty years. The ark had been taken from Israel by the Philistines after the sons of Eli had presumptuously brought it into battle, expecting Yahweh's help (1 Sam 4). Afterward, the ark was taken on a tour of Philistine cities, wreaking havoc in each of them (1 Sam 5). Finally, the Philistines returned the ark to Israel, mounting it on a cart drawn by two milk cows who took it to Beth-shemesh. There, the ark broke out against the descendants of Jeconiah when they showed it no respect, killing seventy men (1 Sam 6). The ark evoked such alarm that only the people of Kiriath-jearim would take custody of it, entrusting it to the care of a man named Abinadab and anointing his son Eleazar to serve as priest before it (1 Sam 6:21–7:2).

No record exists that Saul ever dared to approach the ark, or to incorporate it into Israel's life. But David dared to do what others only feared. Nevertheless, he dared carefully. David recognized that the ark was no simple sacred box. It was "the ark of God, which is called by the name of the LORD of hosts who is enthroned on the cherubim." "Ark of God" and "ark of Yahweh" are used interchangeably in the account. Israelite tradition held that Yahweh sat invisibly enthroned above the outstretched wings of the cherubim

Musical Instruments

Musical instruments in Israel utilized either wind, strings, or percussion. A variety of these appear in 2 Sam 6:5, including lyres, harps, tambourines, castanets, and cymbals. David himself was known as a skilled player of the lyre. Lyres and harps were the most common stringed instruments.

Tambourines, castanets, and cymbals are all percussion instruments. The tambourine was a small double-sided skin drum that was carried in one hand and beaten with the other. Cymbals were made of metal and struck together.

There is some uncertainty about the translation "castanets" for the third percussion instrument, as it appears only here in the Bible. A similar word in rabbinic Hebrew means "to shake," and the Vulgate renders it as *sistra* (some modern translations use the word "sistrums").

Wind instruments are not mentioned until the ark finally came into the city, where it was accompanied by the blowing of "trumpets" made of rams' horns. The shofar was commonly blown as a signal, not as an accompaniment to music; anyone who has heard the particularly piercing ululations of a shofar will readily understand why.

---

that covered the ark. The name of God and the presence of God went hand in hand. Both were intimately associated with the ark.

Recognizing the power of the holy, David took with him a substantial honor guard. He prepared a new cart in which the ark would ride, to be guided by the sons of Abinadab. He "and all the house of Israel" demonstrated their respect for the ark and their celebration of its presence by dancing before it with all their might and playing an assortment of musical instruments. [Musical Instruments]

Despite David's careful preparations, tragedy struck quickly and violently, reminding all present that handling the ark of God was no trifling matter. It was more than an ancient talisman. It was the visible symbol of the invisible God, and it could take care of itself. The ark was accompanied in the procession by the sons of Abinadab. Uzzah (perhaps = Eleazar; see [A Strange Change?]) walked beside the ark, while Ahio went ahead, presumably guiding the oxen. The LXX translates the word *'aḥyô* as "his brothers," rather than as a proper name. Either interpretation is plausible.

As the cortege approached a certain threshing floor, the cart apparently became unstable, and the ark seemed in danger of overturning or sliding off. [Whose Threshing Floor?] Threshing floors were located by custom on the side of a hill, to better catch the prevailing winds as an aid in winnowing grain. Perhaps the ground was uneven and the oxen lost their footing. The MT reads, "The oxen shook it." In any event, all traditions agree that Uzzah reflexively reached out his hand to steady the ark, and died on the spot. The text asserts that "the anger of Yahweh was kindled against Uzzah, so that he struck him." [The Anger of Yahweh]

Whose Threshing Floor?

AΩ The MT says it was the threshing floor of Nachon (*nākôn*). Most interpreters read the word as a proper name (so KJV, RSV, NRSV, NIV, NJPS, JB), though some translate it as the passive participle of a verb meaning "to be firm." Thus, the NEB has "a *certain* threshing floor." The parallel text in 1 Chr 13:9 has "Chidon," as does Josephus (*Ant* 7.81), while the LXX has "Nodab." The Dead Sea Scroll text of 4QSam³ has "Nodan," which may be original since the others can most easily be explained as corruptions of it.

he Anger of Yahweh

The idea of an unpredictable god who lashes out against his people with little or no warning is not ncommon in the ancient Near East, or in the Greek and oman pantheons. In general, the God of the Hebrew Bible remarkable by his restraint; when Yahweh's anger does are, it is typically in response to specific unfaithfulness and omes after prolonged patience with a rebellious people.

In a few instances, however, Yahweh's anger is nexpected and inexplicable. The strange story of Yahweh's ported attempt to kill Moses on the way to Egypt is one xample (Exod 4:24-26). The night visitor who wrestled with acob and left the crippled patriarch convinced that he had ught with God is another (Gen 32:22-32).

Our present text—Yahweh's outburst against Uzzah—is third exemplar of this curious phenomenon. Many attempts have been made to explain Yahweh's fatal wrath against a well-meaning man. They vary from the idea that the ark's inherent holiness, like spiritual radioactivity (Rudolph Otto called it *mysterium tremendum*), rendered it hazardous, to the notion that Uzzah's act was presumptuous because he dared to assume that the ark could not take care of itself.

The psalmists were sometimes puzzled by Yahweh's anger in other contexts, for trouble was often considered to be the result of divine wrath. Witness Ps 77:9: "Has God forgotten to be gracious? Has he in anger shut up his compassion?" Likewise, Ps 85:5 asks, "Will you be angry with us forever? Will you prolong your anger to all generations?" There is some comfort in knowing that modern readers are not the first to be bewildered by the expression of divine wrath.

Uzzah's misfortune is as troublesome to modern readers as it was to ancient hearers. Why should Yahweh break out in wrath against someone who was only trying to help? The common assumption is also a presumption—that Uzzah's helping hand showed entirely too much familiarity in dealing with the holy ark. Another part of the picture, but one rarely noted, is that Uzzah's actions, though well intended, violated the freedom of the ark to choose its own course.

By Yahweh's power, the ark had proven perfectly capable of looking after itself before. It had ravaged the gloating Philistines (1 Sam 5), guided itself safely back to Israel (1 Sam 6:1-18), and taught the sons of Jeconiah a lesson that Israel would never forget (1 Sam 6:19-20). Presumably, the ark could have kept itself on the cart without Uzzah's assistance. More to the point, even if the ark had fallen from the cart or rolled down the embankment, such misfortune would have been an obvious sign of divine displeasure with the move to Jerusalem. Uzzah's helpful gesture, however benign its design, presumed too much.

Ancient exegetes sought to rationalize Uzzah's death in other ways, generally based on a violation of Levitical rules. The Chronicler attributed Uzzah's death to David's failure to include Levites in the sacred procession (1 Chr 15:13). Josephus presumed that Uzzah was not a priest, and blamed him for daring to touch the ark despite his lay status.[1]

David's anger over Uzzah's demise is self-explanatory. Not only had Yahweh fatally struck down an apparently innocent man, but the same blow impacted David's highly publicized plans to bring the ark to Jerusalem. David's frustration was remembered in an etiology for the place name "Perez-uzzah," meaning "Uzzah's breach" (v. 8). The location of Perez-uzzah is unknown, except that it must

have been somewhere on the road from Kiriath-jearim to
Jerusalem. Some students presume that it must have been close to
Jerusalem (since the final leg of the journey seems to have involved
a burnt offering after every six paces), but Kyle McCarter's idea that
it names the particular breach by which it entered through
Jerusalem's wall would probably leave the ark too close for David's
comfort.[2]

Yahweh's "breaking out" against Uzzah caused a breach in Uzzah's
family tree by eliminating Uzzah from the picture. The divine outburst also caused a breach in David's plans, leaving him afraid and
unsure of himself (v. 9). Something had to be done with the ark,
however, so it was deposited in the house of Obed-edom the
Gittite (v. 10). Some interpreters are certain that Obed-edom was
from the Philistine city of Gath, one of many whose loyalty to
David went back to his days as a vassal of Achish, the king of Gath.
Second Samuel 15:18-23 says that 600 men from Gath, under the
leadership of Ittai, had followed David and sworn allegiance to
him.

It seems logical that David would have entrusted the ark to a par-
tisan supporter, though others argue that David had to leave it with
a Philistine because the Israelites were too afraid of it. The
Philistine city-state was not the only place named Gath, however.
There were at least two in Israel, so it is not a given that Obed-
edom was a Philistine.

Later tradents, such as the Chronicler, were uncomfortable with
the idea that the ark could have rested with a non-Israelite. So they
delineated a priestly identity for Obed-edom, complete with a
Levitical genealogy that identified him as a musician and gatekeeper in the temple, a man who was blessed by Yahweh with no
less than eight sons (1 Chr 15:18, 21, 24; 16:5; 26:48). The
obvious difficulty with accepting this identification, of course, is
the name: Obed-edom means "servant of [the deity] Edom," an
unlikely name for a Yahwistic Levite.

Whatever his past may have been, Obed-edom's future was surprisingly blessed. For the three months that the ark remained with
him, "the LORD blessed Obed-edom and all his household" (v. 11).
With this brief statement the narrator underscores the bipolar
nature of Yahweh's power, incarnate in the ark. It is, in short, the
tangible embodiment of the Deuteronomistic theology. Yahweh has
the power to bless or to curse, and does not hesitate to exercise
either option. The determining factor is human conformity to
divine directives.

A Successful Return and an Angry Wife, 6:12-23

David's initial effort to install the ark in Jerusalem fell short of demonstrating appropriate respect for the venerable talisman of Yahweh's presence with Israel. The good fortune showered upon Obed-edom's household convinced David that Yahweh's good pleasure still rested upon the ark, and he determined again to ensconce the holy relic in Jerusalem.

The narrator emphasizes the extra care David took in assuring that no offense came to the ark. Since the use of an oxcart had proven disastrous, the ark—which was equipped with two golden poles designed for carrying—was now borne into the city on the shoulders of men who undoubtedly were chosen specially and consecrated for the task. The corresponding text in 1 Chronicles 15:11-15 embodies later traditions and is designed to demonstrate how carefully David followed the law. In that text, which is much expanded, David connects the previous tragedy to the failure of the Levites to carry the ark. Thus, he ordered the priests and Levites to consecrate themselves, and the Levites bore the ark "as Moses had commanded according to the word of the LORD" (1 Chr 15:15).

As an additional gesture of respect, the ark had not gone more than six paces before David stopped the procession to offer sacrifices. Perhaps he saw the successful six steps as a sign that Yahweh had given permission for the ark to proceed to Jerusalem; thus, the sacrifices expressed both relief and gratitude. The "ox and a fatling" of 2 Samuel 6:13 becomes "seven bulls and seven rams" in 1 Chronicles 15:26 and 4QSamᵃ (compare the examples of other sevenfold sacrifices in Num 23:1; Job 42:8; Ezek 45:23).

Some interpreters assume that David offered sacrifices after the first six paces only, while others see him halting for additional sacrifices with every six paces of the sacred procession. [The King as Priest]

The King as Priest

Biblical evidence insists that the kings of Israel sometimes assumed the office of priest, at least for the purpose of offering sacrifices. David offered sacrifices as the ark made its way to Jerusalem, and later at the threshing floor of Araunah (2 Sam 24:25). Solomon made sacrifices and offered intercessory prayer for his people at the dedication of the temple (1 Kgs 8; cf. 3:3). A psalm used during royal coronations in Israel contains this declaration from Yahweh: "You are a priest forever after the order of Melchizedek" (Ps 110:4; this psalm applied to the coronation of kings long before it was given an eschatological interpretation).

Some interpreters believe that certain psalms allude to the king's entering the temple as head of a cultic procession (Pss 40:9; 42:4; 66:13-15; 118:19, 27; 132 [perhaps a cultic re-enactment of David's installation of the ark in Jerusalem]).

The legitimation for an Israelite king's functioning as priest derives from the unique relationship he enjoyed with Yahweh: He is Yahweh's "son" (2 Sam 7:14), adopted and installed in office by Yahweh (Ps 2), symbolically sitting at Yahweh's right hand (Ps 110:1). For an era knowing no distinction between "church and state," it made sense that a political leader invested with such authority should also be a cultic leader. These concepts of the king's priestly role were held throughout the ancient Near East.

For those who object that repeated sacrifices would involve an unbelievable number of animals, several comments are apropos. First, since the distance from Obed-edom's house to Jerusalem is unknown, the quantity of sacrifices cannot be calculated with any accuracy, so arguments are largely moot. There is also some extrabiblical evidence of periodic sacrifices during the transport of national gods to their temples. [The Return of Marduk]

A comparison to Solomon's installation of the ark in the new temple also suggests that enormous quantities would have been deemed appropriate: There, he reportedly offered "so many sheep and oxen that they could not be counted or numbered" (1 Kgs 8:5). A later note in the same account puts the tally at 22,000 oxen and 120,000 sheep. The Hebrew text of 2 Samuel 6:13 could be interpreted either way, as a one-time event or as a series of sacrifices on a trail of sacrificial altars. The initial sacrifice alone is the most natural reading, however. Additional burnt offerings and peace offerings were made after the ark reached its designated resting place, in sufficient quantities to share portions with the worshipers (2 Sam 6:17-19).

According to 6:5, David's first attempt to transfer the ark to Jerusalem had been accompanied by frenzied dancing, accompanied by music. There, "David and all the house of Israel were dancing before the LORD with all their might." In the second attempt, David is the only one reported to have danced, though still "with all his might." Perhaps as a sign of humility designed to abet safe passage of the ark, David was clothed "with a linen ephod" alone. [Israelite Underwear]

The Return of Marduk

Patrick Miller and J. J. M. Roberts have collected a number of comparative examples from ancient Near Eastern literature. For example, annals of the Assyrian king Assurbanipal describe the return of Marduk, chief god of Babylon, after eleven years of exile in Assur. The deity's journey to his temple in Babylon was marked by much music and rejoicing along with sacrifices every "double mile" (text from Streck 1916: vol II: 265-69).

Patrick D. Miller and J. J. M. Roberts, *The Hand of the Lord: A Reassessment of the "Ark Narrative" of 1 Samuel* (Baltimore/London: Johns Hopkins Press, 1977).

Israelite Underwear

The term "ephod" had multiple meanings in the Hebrew Bible. One of the items described by the term was a short loincloth reaching from the hips to the thighs. It seems to have been the accepted attire for priests who ministered in the sanctuary, and originally may have been the only garment worn during temple duty. Its shortness is implied by the ancient law of Exod 20:26 (cf. Exod 28:42), which prohibits that the altar be built so high that steps were necessary to reach it, "so that your nakedness may not be exposed on it." Later laws required the priests to dress more circumspectly, wearing linen trousers or breeches (Exod 28:42; Lev 6:10 [MT 6:3]; Ezek 44:18).

In normal, moderate activity, this loincloth provided adequate cover to safeguard the wearer from public exposure. It was insufficient, however, to keep David covered during his ecstatic dance.

The second attempt is also distinguished by a change in the musical accompaniment to David's dance. Whereas the first stage of the journey had involved widespread singing and a whole cacophony of instruments, the procession from Obed-edom's house into the city was marked "with shouting, and with the sound of the trumpet." [The Sound of the Trumpet] The failure to mention other musical instruments does not preclude their use, but it seems that the narrator is carefully pointing to differences between the two stages of the ark's journey. Perhaps the ritual aspects of blowing the *shofar* and responding with cultic shouting seemed more appropriate (or more subject to control) than the apparently riotous atmosphere surrounding the ark's departure from Kiriath-jearim.

> **The Sound of the Trumpet**
>
> The trumpet, or *shofar*, was a hollowed ram's horn that served many purposes in Israel. It was used for signaling troops in battle (2 Sam 2:28; 18:16; Neh 4:20; Job 39:24-25; Jer 4:19, 21), or for warning the populace that war or other troubles were imminent (Jer 6:1, 17; Ezek 33:3-6; Hos 8:1; Joel 2:1). It could be used as a signal, calling for some action (Judg 7:18; 2 Sam 15:10), or to herald some announcement, such as the advent of a new king (1 Sam 13:3; 1 Kgs 1:34, 39, 41; 2 Kgs 9:13; Isa 58:1). The trumpet was also used for ritual purposes, calling the people to special assemblies (Exod 19:13, 16, 19; Judg 3:27; 6:34; Joel 2:15) or announcing religious observances (Lev 23:24; 25:9). The *shofar* was used less frequently for its musical qualities, though. Ps 150:3 seems to provide the exception.

There is still wild dancing going on in the second attempt, but it is David who leaps and dances on behalf of the people. David's scanty clothing is made more sedate in the Chronicler's version, where the linen ephod becomes a fine linen robe (1 Chr 15:27). In both versions, however, the combination of David's dress and David's dance causes great offense to David's wife (2 Sam 6:16; 1 Chr 15:29).

Scholars often compare the account of Michal's parade posture to the literary motif of the "woman at the window" that appears occasionally in ancient Near Eastern literature. To suggest on this basis that she represents a hierodule or goddess, however, is far-fetched. The narrator implies that Michal watched from the window because she refused to attend the celebration in person. Michal is the daughter of Saul, whose house makes one last attempt to spoil David's successful rise. Michal's act of "despising David in her heart" cannot be separated from what David is doing, however. To despise David's joyous dance is to cast disdain on the reason for his euphoria. The consequences incumbent on Michal's attitude await the denouement of the story in vv. 20-23.

The high intensity of the narrative associated with the ark's travels renders the actual installation story something of an anticlimax. They brought it in, set it down in the tent David had prepared for it, and offered sacrifices to God. The most remarkable thing about the story is the narrator's insistence that *King David* assumed the high-priestly role of offering the sacrifices and blessing the people. David could do this because Israel's king was ideally

Yahweh's representative (God's adopted son, according to Ps 2:7), so sacerdotal functions naturally followed (see discussion in [The King as Priest]). Also, as far as the Deuteronomistic story goes, no high priest has yet been appointed. Abiathar continues to accompany David, though Zadok has not been introduced (as he has in Chronicles; see 1 Chr 15:11).

David's supervision of the sacrifices is also a natural extension of his desire to assure that the ceremony is successful. As David took on the role of representative liturgical dancer for the worshipers (cf. 6:5, 14), he also presided over the sacrifices, leaving as little to chance as possible.

Two kinds of sacrifices were mentioned: "burnt offerings" and "offerings of well-being." With the burnt offering (ʿ*ôlâ*), sometimes translated as "holocaust offering," the entire animal was consumed on the altar. [How to Perform a Burnt Offering] Burnt offerings most commonly played a role in petitions (1 Sam 13:12), public worship (Num 28–29), votive or voluntary offerings (Lev 22:18), and rites of purification (Lev 12:6, 8; 16:24). Any or all of those motivations would have been appropriate for the rites of dedicating the ark's new resting place and asking Yahweh's blessing upon the endeavor.

The offering of well-being (*šĕlāmîm*), frequently called a "peace offering" or "communion offering," functioned to establish or maintain good relations with God. [How to Perform a *šĕlāmîm* Offering] The root *šlm* suggests wholeness or completion, well-being or peace. Unlike the burnt offering, *šĕlāmîm* offerings were largely consumed by the priests and worshipers rather than the fire. Thus, David would have distributed portions of the *šĕlāmîm* offerings to the people, along with the cakes of bread and raisins that rounded out the celebratory meal.

How to Perform a Burnt Offering

The latest strand of Levitical tradition insisted that a burnt offering be an unblemished male calf, sheep, or goat (cf. Lev 22:17-25). In the case of the poor, two pigeons or turtledoves could be substituted. After laying hands on the animal in an act of identification, the worshiper would personally cut the animal's throat, and the high priest then would ritually dispose of the blood around the large outdoor altar. After the carcass was skinned, quartered, and washed, everything but the hide was immolated in the fire upon the altar.

How to Perform a *šĕlāmîm* Offering

With minor exceptions, the ritual for the *šĕlāmîm* offering followed that of the ʿ*ôlâ* sacrifice (see Lev 3), with the major exception being that the meat was shared by all parties involved. God alone received the blood, the visceral fat, and the fat tail of sheep, because both blood and fat were regarded as life-giving (Lev 3:16-17; 7:22-26; 17:11, 14). The priest was given the breast and the right leg as his rightful portion (Lev 7:28-34; 10:14-15), and the worshiper was allowed to keep the rest. This practice was once the primary means of slaughter in Israel (thus the common use of *zebaḥ*, "slaughter," as a synonym for

sacrifice), but the killing of animals for meat was later desacralized (Deut 12:15-16).

The purpose of *šĕlāmîm* offerings was to establish or maintain close relations with God; thus, both parties participated in the disposal of the animal. The parts reserved for Yahweh went up in smoke, while the remaining parts were consumed by the human participants. This does not suggest, however, the same sort of mystic union supposedly gained by sharing a meal with the gods, as in other ancient cultures. The practices may share common roots, but Yahweh, unlike the Mesopotamian gods, did not need to be fed (Ps 50:12-13).

The word that seems to designate the portions of distributed meat (*'ešpār*) has no biblical parallel except the synoptic text in 1 Chronicles 16:3. The rabbis related it to a choice cut of meat on the basis of the root *špr*, which means beautiful or pleasing. The LXX translates the word as some kind of cake, but the more logical preference is for "a cut of meat," since the distribution of meat regularly accompanied the *šĕlāmîm* offering, and it is not mentioned elsewhere.

The blessing David offered at the conclusion of the sacrifices would later become the purview of the Levitical priests (Deut 10:8, cf. Num 6:22-27). [The Priestly Blessing] To bless someone "in the name of Yahweh of hosts" was to wish Yahweh's blessings upon them. The theme of blessing carries into the conclusion of the story: David's confrontation with Michal when he went home to "bless his household" (6:20).

As the other worshipers departed for home (6:19), David returned to his own house with a cheerful heart and a desire to pronounce blessings upon one and all. David's joy was quickly eclipsed by Michal's rage, however. The story implies that David had not begun his blessing before Michal pounced upon him with a string of sarcastic, verbal barbs. Michal's accusation that David had disgraced himself before the common maids suggests that the king's loincloth had failed to remain in place during David's daring dance. Some suggest that Michal took offense at David's dancing because her values were more conservative than David's, but her haughty tone suggests that the issue was not moral scruples but royal pride.

Michal's implication is that her father Saul would not have acted in such vulgar fashion. David's reply was to remind Michal that Yahweh had rejected her father and chosen him instead. David's animated display had not been intended to please Saul or Saul's daughter, but to honor Yahweh, even if it required self-abasement. Though David's leaping dance inspired Michal's scorn, the young maidens she was so concerned about held him in higher regard for his exuberant exhibition. David was no haughty recluse, but a king who was willing to share himself with his people—in more ways than one. His show of humility was a *show* of humility.

Michal's criticism of Yahweh's man showed disregard for Yahweh as well, and the narrator's judgment of the royal wife is succinct but certain. The penalty for her pride is expressed through a simple historical note: "And Michal the daughter of Saul had no child to the

The Priestly Blessing

As related in Num 6:22-27, the descendants of Aaron were to bless the Israelites as follows:

The LORD bless you and keep you;
the LORD make his face to shine upon you,
  and be gracious to you;
the LORD lift up his countenance upon you,
  and give you peace.

day of her death" (6:23). The author does not disclose whether Michal's childlessness resulted from divine intervention, or the natural consequence of presumably being excluded from David's bed. Two significant results emerge in either case. The point most pertinent to the immediate story is that Michal would have been shamed, for the failure of a married woman to produce children was considered a curse in ancient Israel (see comments relative to Hannah's barrenness at 1 Sam 1).

There is an issue of deeper significance, however. Earlier passages emphasized David's virility and fertility, pointing out that "the house of David grew stronger and stronger, while the house of Saul grew weaker and weaker" (3:1-5; cf. 5:13-16). Saul's house was dying out (in 2 Sam 9, only one grandson was left, and he was crippled). Michal's union with David had promised the possibility of keeping the Saulide line alive, but her failure to produce children removed the last brick supporting the house of Saul.

CONNECTIONS

No object in Israel was more precious than the ark of the covenant. It was a treasure of singular sacredness. The power of God was in it. The presence of God was upon it. The promises of God went with it.

Inside the ark was the proof of God's care for his people: the two tablets of stone on which the Ten Commandments had been engraved by God's own finger as a reminder of God's just law, a jar of manna saved from wilderness days as a sign of God's loving providence, and Aaron's rod that had budded as a sign of God's prophetic future with his people.

Nothing in Israel was more holy. Nothing in Israel was more sacred. Nothing in Israel was closer to God himself than the ark of the covenant, also known as the *Ark of Yahweh*, the *Ark of Testimony*, and the *Ark of Yahweh of Hosts Who Is Enthroned Above the Cherubim.*

That last title explains the inherent power associated with the ark of the covenant: The power of the ark was the power of God, who was believed to rest upon the wings of the cherubim as if it were his earthly easy chair, or at least his footstool.

The holy relic was about four feet long, according to the instructions for its construction. The main body of the ark was about two and a half feet square, constructed of acacia wood and covered with pure gold, both inside and out.

The Concept of the "Mercy Seat" in New Testament Thought

AΩ The author of Hebrews spoke of the "mercy seat" in a literal way, comparing earthly and heavenly sanctuaries (Heb 9:5). Paul expanded and developed the concept of the mercy seat to describe the atoning work of Christ, "whom God put forward as a sacrifice of atonement by his blood, effective through faith. He did this to show his righteousness, because in his divine forbearance he had passed over the sins previously committed" (Rom 3:25, NRSV).

The phrase "sacrifice of atonement" (NRSV, NIV) is also translated as "propitiation" (KJV, NASB). Both are efforts to translated the Greek word *hilastērion*, which means "a place of propitiation." Since the LXX used *hilastērion* to translate *kipporet*, the Hebrew term for "mercy seat," Paul seems to be adopting the Old Testament concept of Yahweh's forgiveness emanating from the mercy seat on the Day of Atonement. On that day, the holy of holies was ceremonially filled with clouds of incense before the high priest entered to daub blood from a special sacrifice upon the mercy seat as a means of gaining atonement for his own sins and for the sins of the people (Lev 16:1-28). Paul saw the sacrificial death of Christ as a final re-enactment of that ritual, an eternal atonement. Thus, the cross became a "place of propitiation" by which believers might experience the atoning grace of God, and the curtain demarcating the holy place was torn apart.

On top of the ark was a special cover; this was the source of its striking visual power. The cover was called the *kipporet*, translated as "mercy seat" or "seat of atonement." [The Concept of the "Mercy Seat" in New Testament Thought] The top was also made of acacia wood and covered with gold. On top of this were two golden cherubim, arranged on either end with their wings outstretched so that they touched in the middle.

The ark sat upon four feet, one at each corner, and to each foot was attached a golden ring. Through the rings were inserted strong poles made of acacia wood, covered with gold. The poles could not be removed; by them alone could the ark be moved, for once it was constructed, it was considered far too holy for any human person to touch. Yahweh's very presence was thought to dwell between the cherubim, atop the ark.

The traditions recorded in the Pentateuch say that Yahweh instructed Moses to have the ark constructed while Israel was still in the wilderness. Whenever the people were encamped for a period, the ark was to be enclosed in a special room far in the back of the portable tabernacle, a room called the "holy of holies." Whenever the people journeyed, the ark went first, carried by the Levitical priests who led the way.

The ark had a rich and colorful history in ancient Israel. It played significant roles in Israel's crossing of the Jordan as the people entered the promised land (Josh 3), and in the battle of Jericho, their first major obstacle west of the Jordan (Josh 6). The ark is crucial to the narrative in the Books of Samuel. It was lost through presumption at the battle of Aphek-ebenezer (1 Sam 4); it caused great loss to the conquering Philistines (1 Sam 5); and it found its own way back to Israel, wreaking havoc at Beth-shemesh before coming to rest at Kiriath-jearim (1 Sam 6).

The sacred symbol surfaces again in the story of David's grand plan to remove the ark to Jerusalem after its twenty-year hiatus from Israel's life and worship. The story is one of tragedy and triumph. Uzzah died when he touched the ark while attempting to save it from a fall. The power of the ark flared against him with immediate and deadly force. When the ark was parked in the house of Obed-edom, however, Yahweh's blessing became apparent, inspiring David to make a second—and successful—attempt to ensconce the ark in Jerusalem. David's joy over the ark was so great that he danced wildly while clad only in his underwear, leading to an estrangement from his wife Michal. [A Psalm about the Ark]

What can modern readers make of stories like this one? Can we really believe old tales of a golden ark that had supernatural powers? Can we learn anything today from Israel's experience? Should we, like Indiana Jones, go out in search of the lost ark?

The answers are "yes," "yes," and "no." Yes, we can believe that there is truth behind these ancient stories. God works in mysterious ways, and we never become so enlightened that we can claim to understand them all. These things may not have happened in exactly the same way we have them today. Stories are never told exactly the same way twice, and some of the details may have changed with the telling. But *something* happened. The traditions are too strong. God wanted Israel to understand the power of the holy, and he used the ark to teach them, and we can also learn from those stories.

The answer to the last question is "no" because there is no point in attempting to find the ark. If God had wanted us to have it, he would have preserved it for us. God knows that if we had it, we would turn it into an object of worship, like some believers do with the Bible. The ark, for all of its mystery and power, was a teaching tool. Its purpose has passed. The ark was probably captured when Jerusalem fell to the Babylonians in 587 BC,

---

A Psalm about the Ark

Scholars have long noticed that Ps 132:1-10 seems to be a liturgical remembrance of David's desire to bring the ark to Jerusalem:

O LORD, remember in David's favor
all the hardships he endured;
how he swore to the LORD
and vowed to the Mighty One of Jacob,
"I will not enter my house
or get into my bed;
I will not give sleep to my eyes
or slumber to my eyelids,
until I find a place for the LORD,
a dwelling place for the Mighty One of Jacob."

We heard of it in Ephrathah;
we found it in the fields of Jaar.
"Let us go to his dwelling place;
let us worship at his footstool."

Rise up, O LORD, and go to your resting place,
you and the ark of your might.
Let your priests be clothed with righteousness,
and let your faithful shout for joy.
For your servant David's sake
do not turn away the face of your anointed one.

though there is an old theory that Jeremiah saved it from the Babylonians by taking it to Egypt with him. Wherever it is, the ark is lost to us, and we do not need it.

But that does not mean we cannot learn something from Israel's experience. That is why the answer to the second question is "yes." What we learn from this story of the ark is that the power of the divine is very real. It can bless, but it can also be dangerous. One cannot toy with it and expect to remain unscathed. There are things in this world that are so closely associated with God that they are truly sacred. They are *holy*, and one cannot treat them lightly without suffering consequences.

Consider, for example, our bodies. The Scriptures speak of our bodies as holy and sacred to God. Jeremiah promised a day when we would no longer find the law of God written on tablets of stone, like those within the ark, for God's law would be written on our hearts (Jer 33:31-34). That promise was fulfilled in the work of Jesus, who called for a paradigm shift in our understanding of the law and taught us simply to love one another. To the Corinthians Paul wrote, "Do you not know that your body is a temple of the Holy Spirit within you, which you have from God, and that you are not your own?" (1 Cor 6:19).

How do we see these dangers manifested? For one thing, you cannot mistreat your body without suffering consequences. If you misuse it through abusing alcohol or other drugs, through smoking or unhealthy eating, there are consequences.

One aspect of our bodies relates to sexuality. Just as our bodies are holy to God, so also are relationships sacred, especially marriage. If we misuse our bodies by engaging in sexual activity outside of marriage, there will be consequences. This does not suggest that God will strike dead every person who commits adultery or has premarital sex, but neither does it imply that there are no consequences to immoral behavior. Unwanted pregnancies. Abortion. Guilt. Sexually transmitted diseases. The loss of innocence. A sense of shame that won't go away. Broken marriages. Broken homes. Sometimes, broken bones. Innocent children suffering for their parents' mistakes. And all because we fail to recognize the danger of profaning the sacred.

There are many ways in which we are tempted to treat the things of God lightly, for which we suffer consequences. But it is important to see the positive side, too. The power of the holy becomes dangerous only when it is misused. As the ark brought victories to Israel and blessings to Obed-edom, God desires to bring goodness and joy into our lives through the celebration of the sacred.

When gathered for worship, people of faith feel the power of the divine in their midst. When we sing, when we pray, when we join our hearts in common cause, we sense the presence and the power of God at work in our hearts, giving strength not only for today, but for tomorrow as well.

That is one of the reasons why worship is so important, and worthy of effort to make it meaningful. To use an inadequate but obvious analogy, our spiritual "batteries" need frequent recharging. A good personal prayer life is important for that, but alone it is not enough. God made us to be relational people. Congregational worship is not the only way in which we come into contact with the power of the divine, but it is perhaps the most common and certainly the most accessible. Jesus promised that where even two or three were gathered in his name, he would be with them (Matt 18:20).

We do not gather now to stand in awe before a sacred talisman, a gilded ark or throne on which God is thought to dwell. Rather, we gather as a community of individual believers, knowing that God dwells in us—not in the ark, but in our hearts. Together, as we worship, the power of God's holiness becomes very real to us. Together, as we join in confession and hearing and open our hearts to God's word, the corrosion of sin is wiped clean from our spiritual cables, and we can feel the power of our holy God surging through our hearts and lives. That is why we keep coming back— because we know that we are prone to internal corrosion, to power failures, to occasional internal meltdowns. We come back because we know the power of the divine, and we know how greatly we need it, and we know that we can find it here whenever we join our hearts in worship.

The image of the ark of God is a powerful and sacred symbol. We would profit from the effort to burn it firmly into our minds and never forget the power of the divine—not to *fear* the holiness of God, but to *embrace* it.

NOTES

[1] Josephus, *Ant* 7.81.

[2] P. Kyle McCarter, *II Samuel* (AB 9; Garden City: Doubleday, 1984), 170.

A HOUSE FOR GOD
AND A HOUSE FOR DAVID

7:1-29

This chapter is the ideological and theological climax of the books of Samuel, as well as of the entire Deuteronomistic History. All that follows is an extended denouement. Second Samuel 7 declares Yahweh's intent to establish David's line upon the throne of Israel in an everlasting dynasty. This puts it at the heart of Israel's theological and political self-understanding from that time forward. The story has shown remarkable flexibility and an ability to be reinterpreted with changing times, even during its development. It has been and continues to be a central source of hope and comfort for Judaism as well as for the Christian church.

The chapter readily falls into two parts: the narrative surrounding Nathan's dynastic oracle (7:1-17), and David's consequent prayer of gratitude (7:18-29).

COMMENTARY

David's Desire and God's Desire, 7:1-17

This story about David's house and God's house is so significant that it has been the subject of many learned treatments from a variety of perspectives. [David's House and God's House] Virtually all scholars agree that there is a multi-stage literary history behind the pericope, but most will also concur that the final product possesses an impressive unity. It is beyond the purview of this work to compare and contrast these often conflicting studies. We will, however, sketch an outline of the text's present form and suggest some general ideas that may have played a role in its development.

One plausible suggestion of the story's history is that the earliest core (probably including most of vv. 1-3, 11b-12, and 13b-15a) relates Yahweh's

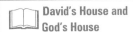 **David's House and God's House**

As it stands, vv. 1-17 may be outlined as follows:

I. David's desire to build Yahweh a house (7:1-3)
II. Yahweh's opposition to David's plan to build a house (7:4-7)
III. Yahweh's desire to build David a house (7:8-17)

positive promise in response to David's pious desire to build a temple in Jerusalem. During the exile, when the temple lay in ruins, the idea arose in prophetic circles that Yahweh had never approved of an earthly house to begin with. At that time, vv. 4-9a and 15b might have been added to express Yahweh's antipathy toward the temple, emphasizing that David's success was due to Yahweh's gracious favor alone. The final editing, at the hands of the Deuteronomists, transformed the negative attitude toward the temple into a positive one by insisting that Yahweh's opposition was not to the temple itself, but to the *timing* of its construction. The addition of vv. 13a and 16 would accomplish that goal.

The final form of the narrative now includes an interweaving of attitudes with an overriding theme of divine blessing upon David and the eternal establishment of David's house upon the throne of

---

Semantic Variations of the Word *Bayit*

AΩ Second Sam 7 utilizes a play on the word "house" (*bayit*), which, in addition to its basic meaning as a simple dwelling (for example, Judg 11:31), may also refer to a palace (2 Sam 5:11; Jer 39:8) or a temple (1 Sam 5:2 [of Dagon]; 1 Kgs 6:5 [of Yahweh]). In a familial sense, the same word may refer to a household (Gen 7:1; 2 Sam 6:20), a tribal group (2 Sam 2:10-11), a nation (2 Sam 6:5), or a royal dynasty (1 Kgs 12:26).

Readers easily recognize the shift of meaning that occurs in 2 Sam 7: David desires to build Yahweh a house (that is, a temple), but Yahweh disapproves and promises to build David a house (that is, a dynasty). Less apparent are the subtle shades of meaning that go beyond the simple play on words.

First, in the ancient Near Eastern cultural milieu, god, king, and temple were closely associated. The king hoped that building a temple would obligate the deity to endorse the royal dynasty. For example, King Nabopolassar of Babylon (626–605 BC) described his wish on this inscription dedicating his temple to Marduk, the Etemenanki:

At that time Marduk, the lord, ordered me firmly to found the base of Etemenanki. . . . O Marduk, my lord, look joyously at my pious work! By your noble command, that will never be changed, may the work, the work of my hand, last forever! As the bricks of Etemenanki are firm forever, establish the foundation of my throne for all time to come!

In addition, a temple served a propagandistic purpose for an illiterate audience, as a visual symbol connecting the sovereignty of the king who built it with the sovereignty of the deity (see Carol Meyers).

Thus, David's desire to build a temple for Yahweh may imply his desire to control God by forcing God's sanction of his reign. Yahweh refuses, however, to be obligated in this way, and replaces David's manipulative request with a divine promise: "I will build your dynasty." What David wants—security for his reign—will not be found in a temple, but only in his faith in Yahweh's promise. It is ironic that after the temple was built, the people of Judah came to see it as a guarantee of security, a notion against which Micah (3:9-12) and Jeremiah (7:1-15) railed.

Second, it is noteworthy that house-building is a common motif in Samuel–Kings (note 1 Sam 2:35 [particularly important for its similarity to 2 Sam 7]; 25:28; 2 Sam 5:11; 7:5, 7, 13, 27, 29; 1 Kgs 2:24; 3:2; 5:17-18; 6:2; 7:40; 8:13, 17-20, 44, 48; 11:38). Several of these houses are said (through declaration or petition) to be "forever." Nevertheless, at the end of the Deuteronomistic History, "forever" has come to an end: The temple is destroyed, the dynasty is no more, and even the houses of the people have been obliterated (2 Kgs 25:9). By juxtaposing "forever" with the undeniable dissolution of both houses, dynasty and temple, the historian has invited reflection on the mysterious complexity of promise and faith.

Inscription text from Tomoo Ishida, *The Royal Dynasties in Ancient Israel: A Study on the Formation and Development of Royal-Dynastic Ideology*, BZAW 142 (New York: Walter de Gruyter, 1977).

Carol Meyers, "David as Temple Builder," *Ancient Israelite Religion: Essays in Honor of Frank Moore Cross*, ed. Patrick D. Miller Jr., Paul D. Hanson, and S. Dean McBride (Philadelphia: Fortress Press, 1987), 364.

Israel. The key motif is built upon the dual use of the word "house" (*bayit*), and is introduced immediately: "Now when the king was settled *in his house.*" [Semantic Variations of the Word *Bayit*]

Readers often note that the claim of v. 1b ("the LORD had given him rest from all his enemies around him") seems out of place, since the following chapter launches into a series of highly unrestful battle accounts. The idea of a divinely granted rest was a typical way of expressing safety and security. The final editors seem to have treated chronology lightly in other places, and it is not at all unlikely that the wars of chapter 8 actually preceded the events of chapter 7. The account of Yahweh's dynastic promise has been placed after chapter 6 because of the natural connection with David's introduction of the ark to Jerusalem.

In the received text, Nathan first appears in 2 Samuel 7:2. Some writers have proposed that Nathan was originally a Jebusite prophet whom David astutely appointed to his own court after the capture of Jerusalem, as he did with Zadok the priest. There is no other evidence nor any real need to support this idea. It is unlikely that a formerly pagan prophet could have achieved such respect in the eyes of the community.

Nathan is often depicted as a court prophet, and may well have been a voice from the tribes of Israel who was brought on board to complement the Judean prophet Gad (cf. 1 Sam 22:5). When David experienced an inner tension over the dichotomy of living arrangements in Jerusalem, he brought the problem to Nathan. David already occupied a palatial house of cedar (cf. 5:11), but the ark of God remained in a tent—literally, "in a curtain." [In a Curtain?]

> **In a Curtain?**
>
> AΩ The normal term for "tent" is *'ōhel*, but the word used here is *yĕrî'â*, the singular form of the word meaning "curtain." Presumably, it is used in a collective sense. First Chr 17:1 uses the plural form. According to Exod 26:1; 36:8, the wilderness tabernacle was made from ten curtains made of goatskin.

David's desire to build a permanent structure for Yahweh is not stated outright; it is implied by the raising of the issue, but seems clear from the context. Nathan's initial response was positive (though also imprecise): "Go, do all that you have in mind; for the LORD is with you" (v. 3). The motif of Yahweh's presence with David is an open secret in the Davidic stories (cf. 1 Sam 18:12, 14, 28; 2 Sam 5:10), reminding the reader of the source of David's good fortune.

The pro-temple stance of vv. 1-3 is immediately counterbalanced by vv. 4-7. The reader is led to believe that Nathan first responded to David out of his own heart, without consulting Yahweh, who rectified the matter by appearing to Nathan that very night, presumably in a dream. "The word of the LORD came to" (v. 4) is a typical prophetic formula, as is the connected formula, "thus says

Yahweh" (v. 5). ["Thus Says Yahweh"] Both appear frequently in the Hebrew Bible. The appearance of these standard prophetic phrases underscores Nathan's status as a true prophet, to whom Yahweh speaks, as does the double commissioning phrase "Go, say" (cf. Isa 6:9; 38:5; Jer 1:7; 2:2; 3:12).

"Thus Says Yahweh"

In the ancient world, formal messengers typically were expected to repeat their communiqué verbatim, as if the sender were speaking. Thus, we have the typical messenger formula—"Thus says _____"—to be followed by a direct quotation of the sender. Since prophets considered themselves to be messengers of God, they simply adapted the messenger formula to incorporate the name of Yahweh: "Thus says Yahweh." The following speech would be in the first person, as if Yahweh himself were speaking.

The divine question found in v. 5 can be read to imply that Yahweh does not oppose the idea of a house, only that David should build it: "Are *you* the one to build me a house to live in?" (or "Is it *you* who will build me a house?"). This question seems at odds with vv. 6-7, which suggest that Yahweh has no desire for a house at all, no matter who the sponsor. If David is understood as a representative human, however, v. 5 can be read as entirely opposed to the idea that any mortal should build a house for Yahweh: "Are *you* [a human being] going to build a house for *me* [God] to dwell in?" If there is to be any temple-building, it should come in response to divine initiative, not human presumption.

No matter how v. 5 is read, v. 6 stands at odds with the larger tradition. It quotes Yahweh as claiming that he (in the form of the ark, as Yahweh's representative symbol) had not dwelt in a house from the exodus period until David's day, but had always moved about freely in a tabernacle or tent. Yet there was a strong tradition of a temple in Shiloh (Judg 18:31; 1 Sam 1:7, 9, 24; 3:15) where the Elide priests had custody of the ark. This temple is called the "house (*bayit*) of the LORD" (1 Sam 1:7), where Eli could sit by the "doorpost" (1 Sam 1:9) and lie down in his "room" (1 Sam 3:2). Samuel is said to have slept "in the temple (*hêkal*), where the ark of God was" (1 Sam 3:3). The same tradition speaks of how Eli's worthless sons "lay with the women who served at the entrance to the tent of meeting" (*'ōhel mô'ēd*; 1 Sam 2:22), but the texts implying a solid structure are more prevalent. Jeremiah's prophecy implies that the ruins of the Shiloh temple still remained as a mute testimony in his own day (Jer 7:12, 14), suggesting a structure much more substantial than a tent.

In addition to the Shiloh temple, the tradition reports that the ark was sheltered in the "house" of Abinadab during its hiatus in Kiriath-jearim (1 Sam 7:1), and in the "house" of Obed-Edom during its brief quarantine after the Uzzah affair (2 Sam 6:11). These house-bound resting places were apparently considered insignificant in comparison to the wilderness and pre-settlement periods. Perhaps they were regarded as temporary or even illegitimate, so that they did not figure into Yahweh's assertion. In the early Samuel traditions, however, there is no indication that the worship of Hannah and Elkanah at Shiloh—or Eli's priesthood—was anything less than acceptable.

Whether Yahweh's ark had ever dwelt in a house is immaterial to v. 7, which emphasizes that Yahweh had never *asked* for a house from any previous leader of Israel. The question, "Why have you not built me a house of cedar?", connects the oracle to David's initial concern about living in a cedar house while Yahweh dwelt in a goatskin tent. [What Does Yahweh Ask?]

> **What Does Yahweh Ask?**
> Yahweh's claim that he never asked for a temple brings to mind the question of what God *does* ask of his followers. Mic 6:8 offers the classic answer, showing that Yahweh's desire is not for ritual splendor, but for righteous behavior.
>
> He has told you, O mortal, what is good;
> and what does the LORD require of you
> but to do justice, and to love kindness,
> and to walk humbly with your God?

The point of vv. 6-7 focuses on the theme of divine freedom. Yahweh will be free, not bound to a permanent house. In the exodus traditions, not only was the ark housed in a portable sanctuary, but it went at the head of the caravan as well. "Wherever I have moved about" in v. 7a indicates movement at God's initiative, not at the whims of humans. The ark had moved about at Yahweh's bidding in such a way that it led the people, including the great leaders Moses and Joshua. For David to bring the ark into his own city and ensconce it in a permanent sanctuary implies an attitude that Yahweh could be restricted, controlled, or manipulated through the enclosure of the ark in Jerusalem. Yahweh, however, refused to be maneuvered or misused—by David or anyone else.

The antitemple tenor of vv. 6-7 seems so different from the surrounding narrative that many scholars regard it as the work of a prophetic redactor during the time of the exile, when the demise of the temple led some religious leaders to presume that Yahweh had never wanted a temple to begin with. In the final redaction, however, the ambiguity of v. 6, along with the promise of v. 13a (endorsing David's son as the temple-builder), ameliorates the antitemple sentiment.

The second part of the oracle shifts from David's proposed gift for Yahweh to a review of Yahweh's past blessings on David and a promise of greater favors yet to come. Indeed, David's very ability to offer Yahweh a house came about as a result of Yahweh's history of gracious acts toward David. Verses 8-9 offer a brief reprise of David's rise to power, clearly attributed to Yahweh's initiative. David has come from the sheep's pasture to the prince's throne for one reason only: because the LORD desired it. The combination of personal pronouns and first-person verbs is emphatic: "*I* took you from the pasture [1 Sam 16:1-13] to become prince over my people. . . . *I* have been with you wherever you went [1 Sam 16:18; 17:37; 18:14, 28; 2 Sam 5:10]. . . . *I* have cut off your enemies from before you [2 Sam 5:6-9, 17-25]. . . . *I* will make for you a great name. . . . *I* will appoint a place for my people Israel. . . . *I* will plant them. . . . *I* will give you rest from all your enemies" (vv. 8-11a). [David the Prince]

David the Prince

AΩ The Hebrew word *nāgîd* is used to denote a person who has been designated for office, such as a crown prince (cf. 1 Sam 9:16). The term was commonly used by prophetic circles to indicate Yahweh's choice of someone to become king. The word is used of David in two earlier instances: in Samuel's oracle condemning Saul for his presumption in offering sacrifices (1 Sam 13:14), and in Abigail's speech praising David's accomplishments and looking toward his future (1 Sam 25:30).

David owed his position of power to Yahweh's constant presence and his prestigious reputation (great name) to Yahweh's preferential treatment, even as his people owed their secure place to Yahweh's willingness to fight for them. In David, Yahweh has brought a new day to Israel, a day in which they may dwell securely, for "evildoers shall afflict them no more, as formerly, from the time that I appointed judges over my people Israel" (vv. 10-11a).

The natural reading of these verses moves from past blessings to future promises, but some scholars press the verbal forms a bit, arguing that all should be interpreted as past tense. Indeed, to some extent, all of these promises had already been fulfilled. David's reputation was already extensive (1 Sam 18:7; 21:11; 29:5), and Israel's borders were secure (2 Sam 5:17-25): Yahweh already had granted David rest from all of his enemies (v.1). Thus, when God's gift of "rest" appears again in v. 11a, it acts as an inclusio, bracketing the ways in which Yahweh has already blessed David and preparing the way for a more significant promise that picks up the theme of David's dwelling in his house (also from v. 1), and carries it forward into new territory.

The narrator's artistry becomes evident in the wordplay marking this new thing that God is doing. David had offered to build a house for God, but Yahweh instructed Nathan to say, "Moreover the LORD declares to you that the LORD will make *you* a house" (v. 11b). Perhaps the dual use of "the LORD" (Yahweh) is intended to emphasize the unexpected extravagance of Yahweh's promise to build a house *for David*.

In this context, the word "house" refers not to David's home of wood and stone, but to his sons upon the throne. Yahweh promised to bestow his blessing upon an offspring of David ("who shall come forth from your body," v. 12), so that the throne would pass from father to son and a strong dynasty would be born in Israel. Saul's house had dissolved into weakness, but David's house would go from strength to greater strength, extending into perpetuity: "And I will establish the throne of his kingdom forever" (v. 13b). The phrase "who shall come forth from your body" does not necessarily exclude the sons whom David had already conceived, but it seems to hint that the divinely favored scion is yet to be born.

As mentioned above, v. 13a ("*He* shall build a house for my name") seems intrusive: the promise flows most naturally from v. 12 to v. 13b. It is likely that v. 13a was added by a later hand to soften Yahweh's opposition to temple-building in vv. 6-7, suggesting only that the time was not right. The Chronicler voiced a later tradition that David was not allowed to build the temple because he had shed too much blood, and was thus too defiled to construct a holy temple (1 Chr 22:8). Solomon, however, was to be known as a man of peace (the name "Solomon" [*šĕlōmō*] derives from the word *šalôm*, which can mean "peace"). Thus, Solomon was allowed to build the temple (1 Chr 22:9).

Whether David's son was allowed to build a house for Yahweh is beside the point for the present story, and the issue detracts attention from the central focus: Yahweh intends to build a dynastic house for David. As David had been a man after God's own heart, David's descendant would be like God's own child: "I will be a father to him, and he shall be a son to me" (v. 14). This terminology offers a dim echo of the common ancient Near Eastern concept that kings achieve divinity with their position and are incorporated into the national pantheon.

In Israel, the concept was a step removed: The king did not become divine, but was adopted by the Deity as a son of the gods, the earthly representative of divine rule. [Sons of the Gods] Thus, Israel's coronation hymns, such as Psalm 2, expressed the idea of divine adoption. In the litany of coronation, the king recited these words: "I will tell of the decree of the LORD: he

> **Sons of the Gods**
>
> AΩ A similar ideology was held by the Aramaean royalty of Damascus, Israel's neighbor. In the 9th century BC, shortly after Solomon's reign, kings of Damascus routinely bore the name "son of Hadad" (Hadad was the Syrians' chief god). This is obscured in the biblical text, where the name is simply translated as "Ben-hadad" from the Hebrew *ben-hădad*, meaning "son of Hadad" (e. g., 1 Kgs 15:18 = 2 Chr 16:12). In royal inscriptions from ancient Syria, the name is spelled *"bir hadad"* (cf. *bar*, the Aramaic word for "son").

said to me, 'You are my son; today I have begotten you. Ask of me, and I will make the nations your heritage, and the ends of the earth your possession' " (Ps 2:7-8; cf. Ps 89:26-27 [MT vv. 27-28]).

The amazing aspect of this divine grant is that David's dynasty is to rule "forever" (*ʿad ʿôlām*). [Does "Forever" Mean Forever?] This and related words occur no less than eight times in chapter 7, three times in Nathan's oracle (vv. 13, 16 [twice]), and five times in David's prayer (7:24, 25, 26, 29 [twice]). The strong concern for permanence is unmistakable.

Does "Forever" Mean Forever?

A promise in perpetuity is not necessarily irrevocable. For example, 1 Sam 2:30 asserts that Yahweh had promised to Eli that his descendants should serve as priests forever. Because of their rebellious behavior, however, the promise was annulled.

Yahweh had initially endorsed Saul's rule, but gave the kingdom to another when Saul disobeyed. Would David's descendants fare any better than Saul's? To forestall fears of divine desertion, the promise is qualified by vv. 14b-15: David's descendants might be punished for insubordination to Yahweh, but they would not be abandoned. Yahweh would not withdraw his steadfast love (*ḥesed*), as he had done with Saul. Later theologians interpreted Israel's defeat and exile at the hands of the Assyrians and Babylonians as Yahweh's well-deserved punishment "with a rod such as mortals use, with blows inflicted by human beings" (v. 14).

Thus, the Davidic ideology lived on, even in exile, on the presumption that David's descendants were down but not out, for Yahweh's promised kingdom was perpetual (v. 16). It was this same concept that certain prophetic circles transformed into an eschatological hope of a new Davidic messiah who would arise to rule with justice and restore the glory of Israel (Isa 9:7; 16:5; 22:22; Jer 23:5; 33:15, 17, 26; Ezek 34:23-24; 37:24). From the same oracular roots, the Christian community saw Jesus Christ as the final fulfillment of Yahweh's promise, a descendant of David who had been granted the throne and who would rule in righteousness forever (Matt 1:1; Luke 1:32; Acts 13:22-23; 2 Cor 6:16-18; Heb 1:5).

David's Grateful Prayer, 7:18-29

Yahweh's incredible promise to David is followed by an awestruck prayer of gratitude—and a demanding reminder that Yahweh must keep his promises. The prehistory or development of this prayer is widely debated. In its final form, at least, the prayer expresses a clearly Deuteronomistic ideology. [A Helpful Outline] Its repetitive insistence that Yahweh should keep the promises so graciously made may owe its fervor to a time of composition during the exile, when Israel longed for a return to the glory days of David.

In its present context, the prayer is set in the privacy of the tent shrine David had built to house the ark of the covenant. There, the king went in "before the LORD" to offer his prayer. The expression "went in and sat" is unusual. One might expect David to kneel

A Helpful Outline

Walter Brueggemann has suggested a helpful and artfully alliterated outline to highlight the structure of David's prayer (7:18-29). Notice how David moves from humble deference to glad doxology to persistent demand.

I. Deference (7:18-21)
II. Doxology (7:22-24)
III. Demand (7:25-29)

or prostrate himself before the ark; there are proper Hebrew words for those actions, but instead the ambiguous *yāšab* appears. The verb usually means "to dwell"; it is the word Yahweh uses to derisively ask, "Are *you* the one to build me a house to live in?" (v. 5). The common translation "sat" (NRSV, NIV, KJV) suggests only that David remained in the shrine as he prayed.

The vocabulary and recurring motifs of the prayer are notable. The term "Lord GOD" (*Adonai Yahweh*) appears no less than seven times in this prayer, but nowhere else in the Books of Samuel (though it occurs in 1 Kgs 2:26 and is characteristic of Ezekiel). [Lord GOD] The self-deprecating term "your servant" (cf. "my servant" in 7:5, 8) appears ten times, and there are seven references to the "house" Yahweh has promised to build for David.

> **Lord GOD**
>
> AΩ The appellative "Lord GOD" translates *Adonai Yahweh*. It appears in vv. 18, 19 (twice), 20, 22, 28, and 29. In addition, the name "LORD God" (*Yahweh Elohim*) occurs in v. 25. It is customary for Bible translations to spell the name Yahweh in all caps, usually as "LORD." When used in conjunction with *Adonai* (a generic term for "Lord" that can also apply to humans), the change is made. Observant readers will note that the NRSV has "LORD God" in v. 22. This is because some manuscripts have *Yahweh Elohim* in place of *Adonai Yahweh*, and the translators judged it to be the better reading.
>
> Other divine appellatives also appear in the text. Perhaps David's persistent repetition of God's name is a not-so-subtle reminder that God has a reputation to maintain (see 7:23).

Significantly, there are *no* allusions to the house (temple) that David had sought to build for Yahweh. It is also curious that David's petitions are all for things Yahweh has already promised. This odd combination of characteristics has led Kyle McCarter to propose that the earliest form of the prayer was associated with the ark narrative in chapter 6, rather than the dynastic oracle of chapter 7.[1]

In its current location, the prayer serves an important function, for it is the human response to divine grace. Yahweh has made a new and unconditional promise to David—and through David—to Israel. Although the ordinary trappings of a covenant ceremony are absent, David's prayer serves as his official acceptance of Yahweh's beneficent offer—and as a pointed reminder that he expects the LORD to keep his promises.

David's prayer begins with deferential amazement that Yahweh should have chosen him to become not only the king of Israel, but the founder of a perpetual dynasty (vv. 18-21). "Who am I?" was a standard expression of self-deprecation before a more powerful person (cf. 1 Sam 18:18; 1 Chr 29:14). The story of David's initial anointing had also emphasized the unlikelihood of God's choosing someone so socially insignificant as David (1 Sam 16). "That you have brought me thus far" refers to Yahweh's review of his divine activity in bringing David to the throne (7:8-9).

David's own rise, however impressive, was but a small thing in the light of Yahweh's promise that David's house should become a permanent dynasty (v. 19). "May this be instruction for the people" could be an editorial reminder of tendentious purpose, directing readers to respect the divine endorsement of David's house. The query of v. 20 ("And what more can David say to you?") implies that Yahweh's generosity has left David speechless, but the happy king's loquacity continues unabated.

The characteristic vocabulary of vv. 22-24 has led many scholars to propose that it is a Deuteronomistic composition, and its themes recur in other parts of the Hebrew Bible. In context, it is David's doxology to a God who is like none other (v. 22), who has called out a people and made them like none other (vv. 23-24). [Companion Themes to David's Doxology] [Companion Themes to the Covenant Motif]

In v. 9, Yahweh promised to make for David a great name; in v. 23 David expresses amazement at the way Yahweh has made a name for himself by means of the mighty things he has done for Israel. Thus, David, Israel, and Yahweh are all glorified together: The developing name and reputation of David and Israel also magnify the name of Yahweh, who is responsible for David/Israel's advancement and has promised their permanent establishment (v. 24).

Companion Themes to David's Doxology
Note these counterparts in other Old Testament texts:

2 Samuel 7:22-24
Therefore you are great, O LORD God; for there is no one like you, and there is no God besides you, according to all that we have heard with our ears. Who is like your people, like Israel? Is there another nation on earth whose God went to redeem it as a people, and to make a name for himself, doing great and awesome things for them, by driving out before his people nations and their gods? And you established your people Israel for yourself to be your people forever; and you, O LORD, became their God.

Deuteronomy 3:24
"O Lord GOD, you have only begun to show your servant your greatness and your might; what god in heaven or on earth can perform deeds and mighty acts like yours!

Deuteronomy 4:35
To you it was shown so that you would acknowledge that the LORD is God; there is no other besides him.

Psalm 86:8
There is none like you among the gods, O LORD, nor are there any works like yours.

Psalm 89:6 (MT v. 7)
For who in the skies can be compared to the LORD?
Who among the heavenly beings is like the LORD?

Psalm 113:5
Who is like the LORD our God,
who is seated on high?

Companion Themes to the Covenant Motif

The covenant motif of God's calling out Israel to be his special people is reminiscent of other passages from the Hebrew Bible:

Exod 6:7—"I will take you as my people, and I will be your God. You shall know that I am the LORD your God, who has freed you from the burdens of the Egyptians."

Lev 26:12—"And I will walk among you, and will be your God, and you shall be my people."

Ezek 11:20—"so that they may follow my statutes and keep my ordinances and obey them. Then they shall be my people, and I will be their God."

Ezek 37:27—"My dwelling place shall be with them; and I will be their God, and they shall be my people."

David's daring nature is not reserved for his dealings with humans alone. His humble words of acceptance and praise for God's blessings are followed by a series of piously wrought reminders that he expects Yahweh to live up to his promises. The adverbial conjunction "and now" (*wĕ'attâ*) typically introduces a present or future expectation based on the previous actions or conversation. David's prayer employs this expression no less than three times in five verses (vv. 25, 28, 29).

David's boldness would be shocking if it were anyone else but David: "And now, as for the word you have spoken . . . confirm it forever, do as you have promised!" (v. 25). The imperative verbs seem out of place in a prayer that begins with such deference, but David, by the very magnitude of his persona, successfully strikes a pose of both humility and demand.

The call for Yahweh to confirm his word and keep his promises is reinforced by a veiled threat: Fulfillment of the pledge would result in Yahweh's name being magnified forever in the byword "Yahweh of hosts is God over Israel" (v. 26). If the promises were not kept and Israel's reputation lapsed, it would be no great distinction to be known as God over Israel.

As Yahweh's personal repute was connected to Israel's continuing prosperity, so David's *chutzpah* to lift up such a prayer was intimately bound up with Yahweh's promises (v. 27). The implication is that David would not have dared to ask for such things on his own, but now that Yahweh had made the offer, David would make bold to hold him to it. Thus, the last two sentences share a common theme of Yahweh's identity as the true God who speaks true words (v. 28), for when God's words are spoken they cannot be broken (implied by v. 29). Yahweh has pledged "this good thing," and David (who repeatedly refers to himself as "your servant") expects to see it happen.

CONNECTIONS

This memorable story begins with a house and ends with a dynasty; what began as an act of personal piety and political power was transformed into a promise of divine and unconditional grace. Nathan's dynastic oracle in 2 Samuel 7 is the *turning point* not only of the Deuteronomistic History, but of the entire Old Testament. [The Significance of the Davidic Covenant in Biblical Theology]

This chapter, *this* text is the foundation of the theological bridge that leads from law to grace. *This* story of God and David is the first step on a new path that ultimately leads to the story of Jesus and all the "Davids" in the world. *This* account is at the root of all evangelical theology; it bears the seeds of the gospel.

To this point, God's relationship with Israel had been one of master and servant. It was a *conditional* relationship in which God was faithful, but his blessings were dependent on Israel's obedience,

---

The Significance of the Davidic Covenant in Biblical Theology

The importance of God's dynastic promise to David can hardly be overstated. Echoes of 2 Sam 7 reverberate throughout the Old Testament, early Judaism, and Christianity. Thus, Walter Breuggemann declares, "I judge this oracle with its unconditional promise to David to be the most crucial theological statement in the Old Testament." The significance of the text can be seen in several areas:

1. The text provided a basis for Israel's ideology of kingship, or royal theology (though not the only statement of that ideology; cf. Deut 17:14-20). God's election of the king is spoken of in 2 Sam 7 in language that echoes God's covenantal election of Israel ("I will be their God and they shall be my people" is roughly parallel to "I will be his father and he shall be my son"). Confidence in Yahweh's election led to the royal psalms' assurances to the king (see Pss 2; 89; 132).

2. Critical scholarship has shown that 2 Sam 7 is one of a series of key speeches in the Deuteronomistic History that marks crucial points or leadership transitions in Israel's history. See also Josh 1:11-15; 12:23; Judg 2:11-23; 1 Sam 12; 1 Kgs 8:14-61; 2 Kgs 17:7-23.

3. Hopes for a Davidic messiah also presuppose 2 Sam 7. Yahweh's promise is often cited in the Old Testament (Amos 9:11-15; Hos 3:4-5; Isa 9:1-7; Mic 5:1-6; Jer 23:5-

6; 30:1-9; 33:14-17; Ezek 34:23-24; 37:24-28). It is also a frequent subject in the literature of early Judaism (e.g., Psalms of Solomon 17; Sir 47:11, 22; 1 Macc 2:57). These strands of tradition do not all reflect the same understanding of the dynastic oracle, for messianic expectations were quite varied in early Judaism, and David played a negligible role in some of them. However, they all owe something to Yahweh's promise in 2 Sam 7.

4. The New Testament makes a point of establishing that Jesus is not just *any* Israelite, but a descendant of David— a fact never questioned by his family or his enemies. Matthew, more than any other New Testament source, emphasizes Jesus' Davidic ancestry (1:1, 6, 17, 20; 9:27; 12:23; 15:22; 20:30-31; 21:9; see also Mark 11:10; Luke 3:31; Rom 1:3; 2 Tim 2:8).

The expression of sonship in 2 Sam 7:14 (originally expressing the king's unique relationship to Yahweh), in conjunction with Ps 110, moved the early Christians to the christological affirmation that Jesus was not only the son of David but also the Son of God (Rom 1:3-4). The political, this-worldly kingdom promised in 2 Sam 7 also receives a new interpretation in the New Testament, where its meaning is spiritualized and applied to God's heavenly kingdom (Luke 1:32-33, 69-71; 3:31; Acts 13:16-41; 15:12-18).

Walter Brueggemann, *First and Second Samuel* (IBC; Louisville: John Knox Press, 1990), 259.

and the Israelites were no more inclined to obedience than anyone else. Deuteronomy, Joshua, Judges, and 1 Samuel tell the same story in different ways. When Israel is obedient, God's blessings are abundant. When Israel rebels, God is not to be found. The relationship between God and his people turns on the word *if.*

But now things are changing. With God's covenant promise to David, a new element enters the picture. It is the element of grace. In this covenant with David, God makes a promise that is not conditioned by his obedience or the obedience of his children. Rather, it is an *unconditional* promise of undeserved grace. Yahweh will bless David's house and establish his dynasty upon the throne. If David's descendants prove to be disobedient, God will allow them to experience the natural affects of their sin—"punishment with the rods of men" is the way he puts it—but God will never withdraw his steadfast covenant love (*ḥesed*).

When Saul disobeyed one time too many, God cut him off and withdrew his spirit. For David, God promises something new. "Disobedience will buy you trouble, but I will never cut you off. *Your house and your kingdom will endure forever before me; your throne will be established forever.*" The operative conjunction has been changed from *if* to *nevertheless.* God promised that his choice of David's descendants as the leaders and agents of salvation for Israel would never change.

Now, we know that the Davidic kingdom did not last forever, at least in Jerusalem. The kingdom of Judah lasted 150 years longer than the northern kingdom, but it too came to an end. In 587 BC, Jerusalem was burned to the ground, and the last descendant of David holding rights to the throne was carried in chains to Babylon. Yet God's promise was not violated. God's people became so corrupt that they fell prey to their own weakness, and they were chastised with the rods of men as Nathan had predicted. The men just happened to be Babylonians.

Still, God never left his people, never forgot them. The burning of God's temple and the capture of the ark had no effect at all on the presence of God with his people. The LORD went with his people into exile. God offered hope through the prophetic words of Jeremiah and Second Isaiah. After fifty years of exile, God used Cyrus the Persian as the agent of change who would conquer Babylon and allow the Jews to return to Jerusalem. Some did. Some did not. Yet God remained with all of them.

That was part of what the LORD wanted David to understand. God cannot be limited to one place, one king, one people. God cannot be housebroken, fenced in, or kept in a box, however beautiful. God will be free, or else he is not God at all.

Christians believe it was in God's freedom that he chose to enter our world in a new way, through the person of a man named Jesus, a descendant of David. In Jesus Christ, God completed the work of amazing grace that began in the Hebrew Bible and runs into the Christian Bible. Through the life, work, death, and resurrection of Jesus, God offers us salvation that is not predicated on our works or perfect obedience, but on the grace of God alone.

Our hope in God is not based on a human "if," but on a divine "nevertheless." Even though we are weak, even though we fail, even though we fall short of God's ideal, God loves us still. God forgives us still.

It is not up to us to build God a house in which to dwell. Rather, God's purpose is to build a house for us—a family of faith in which we may find forgiveness and acceptance and strength for every day. Paul spoke of how God's power works within us "to accomplish abundantly far more than all we can ask or imagine" (Eph 3:20). We also may sin and be subject to the earthly consequences of our sin, but that is not the end. God loves us *nevertheless*. The key to joyful and productive Christian living is found not in a legalistic gospel of how much we do for God, but in how much we allow God to do for us.

Now, just as God promised to David that his descendants would rule forever, so we believe that God in Christ rules forever and that his promises extend for all time. God has built a house for us. When the disciples mourned that Jesus was leaving them, he told them not to worry. *In my Father's house are many rooms,* he said. *I'm going to prepare a place for you* (John 14:1-3).

What an amazing kind of love and grace this is. When Nathan brought the word of God to David, the king was so overcome that he went straight to the tabernacle and seated himself before the ark of the covenant, where he believed the presence of God to be the strongest. There, he prayed (2 Sam 7:18-29), and in his prayer he concluded this:

> Because of your promise, and according to your own heart, you have wrought all this greatness, so that your servant may know it. Therefore, you are great, O LORD God; for there is none like you, and there is no God besides you.

God's great promise to David has implications even today. Those who know God best have learned that the divine/human relationship does not grow from building a house of good works in an attempt to please God, but through humbly accepting the house of grace and promise that God has already built.

NOTE

[1] P. Kyle McCarter, *II Samuel* (AB 9; Garden City: Doubleday, 1984), 240.

THE ESTABLISHMENT
OF THE EMPIRE

8:1-18

COMMENTARY

With chapter 8, the narrative returns to the mundane business of David's wars, which has been interrupted by the more theologically and ideologically exciting accounts of chapters 6–7, in which David seeks legitimation at his own initiative by bringing the ark to Jerusalem (ch. 6) and obtains divine endorsement for his dynasty at Yahweh's behest (ch. 7). There is an important shift in these chronicles of war, however. No longer limited to defensive battles (as in 5:17-25), David now mounts a series of offensives on many sides, with the apparent goal of expanding his territory and building an empire. [Expansion and Empire] David's territorial expansion goes beyond the promise of Yahweh in chapter 7, but is still attrib-

> **Expansion and Empire**
> David's conquests and alliances described in ch. 8 may be outlined as follows:
> I. The Philistines (8:1)
> II. The Moabites (8:2)
> III. The Arameans (8:3-8)
> IV. Hamath (8:9-10)
> V. The spoils (8:11-12)
> VI. The Edomites (8:13-14)

uted to Yahweh's blessing of David's agenda. Although David's military and political skills are at the forefront, it is twice said that "the LORD gave victory to David wherever he went" (8:6, 14). Even so, there arises an underlying tension between Yahweh's promise for Israel and David's desire for an empire.

The chapter falls into two parts: a description of David's conquests (8:1-14) and a brief look at David's developing administration (8:15-18).

David defeats his enemies, 8:1-14

The battle accounts found in this chapter seem to have been drawn from other sources and lumped together in an attempt to summarize how David advanced beyond the tenuous peace gained from the Philistines in 5:17-25 and rose to surpass the Egyptians as the strongest force in all the Levant. The collection is more concerned

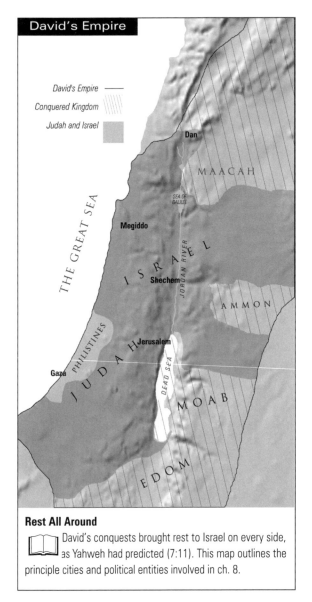

David's Empire

David's Empire ———
Conquered Kingdom
Judah and Israel

Dan

MAACAH

SEA OF GALILEE

THE GREAT SEA

Megiddo

I S R A E L

JORDAN RIVER

Shechem

AMMON

PHILISTINES

Jerusalem

Gaza

J U D A H

DEAD SEA

M O A B

E D O M

Rest All Around

David's conquests brought rest to Israel on every side, as Yahweh had predicted (7:11). This map outlines the principle cities and political entities involved in ch. 8.

with theology and ideology than with chronology; the battles probably did not occur in the quick succession (or even the order) in which they are presented.

According to the story, David first broke the supremacy of the Philistines (v. 1), securing his southwestern borders. The Moabites southeast of Jerusalem were an ancient enemy, and David also rendered them helpless (v. 2), along with the Edomites (vv. 13b-14) further to the south. The greatest threat to David's power was northward, where Hadadezer of Zobah apparently had forged a coalition of Aramean tribes and was aspiring to ascendancy. David's victory over the Arameans (vv. 3-8) was so impressive that King Toi of Hamath (even further to the north) sought a preemptive alliance with David (vv. 9-10). This left only the eastern and western flanks vulnerable. The Mediterranean Sea lay to the immediate west; across the Jordan, to the east, were the Ammonites, who had been weakened by their substantial defeat at Saul's hand (1 Sam 11). David dealt them the *coup de grace* in chapter 10. The narrator's clear intent is that the reader understand how Yahweh kept his promise by giving David rest from all his enemies (7:11; cf. 8:6, 14). The received text grants full accolades to David for these triumphs, not venturing to question whether the king had overstepped his charter. [Rest All Around]

The Philistines

"Some time afterward" probably refers to the previous chapter, but it may also connect this series of battles to David's two victories over the Philistines in 5:17-25. The conflict described in v. 1 probably is intended not as a reprise of 5:17-25 but as a new initiative intended not only to contain the Philistines, but to subjugate them. "David attacked the Philistines and subdued them" (v. 1a). This simple statement suggests that the once-awesome Philistines were no longer a menace to Israel.

The reference to Metheg-ammah is a puzzle. The NRSV and most modern translations translate it as place name, but there is no other evidence for such a place, which must have been significant given the context. The LXX translates it as "the common land," presumably an area that had been claimed and used by Israelites and Philistines alike, thus suggesting that David now claimed exclusive rights to the land for Israel. The Chronicler's synoptic passage is also different, as it has "Gath and its daughter villages" (1 Chr 18:1). H.W. Hertzberg's literal reading of the term as "reins of the forearm" is appealing. This interpretation suggests an ancient idiom meaning that David had taken the reins of power in Palestine from the Philistines and into his own hands.

The Moabites

David's defeat of Moab is notable only for its cruel aftermath. Nothing is told of the battle itself, but David reportedly slaughtered two-thirds of the captured Moabite soldiers. The method of apportioning the prisoners for life or death with lengths of cord is otherwise unattested in the ancient Near East.

David's ruthless treatment of the Moabites is surprising for two reasons. First, biblical traditions insist that David inherited Moabite blood from his grandmother Ruth (Ruth 4:21-22). Secondly, David's earlier relations with Moab were positive enough that he could sequester his family there during his lengthy flight from Saul (1 Sam 23:3-4). The reader must presume that something happened either before or during the battle to inspire David's brutal course of action. The Chronicler, perhaps finding the distasteful story unworthy of David, omits it from his account (1 Chr 18:2). The Moabites, suitably weakened, became a vassal state, paying annual tribute to Israel.

The Arameans

David's encounter with the Arameans poses another conundrum for the interpreter because vv. 3-8 suggest a decisive victory on David's part. Yet the same opponents later reappear in full fighting array (10:6-19), hardly characteristic of a force as decimated and crippled as the one David left in 8:3-8. Many scholars posit that the events of 10:6-19 must have preceded the account in 8:3-8, which has been placed among David's other victories for tendentious effect.

Just what initiated David's attack on Hadadezer of Zobah is a matter of uncertain interpretation. [Hadadezer of Zobah] Named for the Syrian deity Hadad ("Hadad is a help") and presumably a native of Beth-Rehob, the nascent king seems to have forged a coalition of various Aramean political entities, with the result that David's victory had significance beyond Zobah.

Hadadezer of Zobah

Appreciating David's defeat of Hadadezer of Zobah requires a brief geography lesson. About thirty miles north of the Sea of Galilee lie two mountain ranges that run parallel to each other on a diagonal to the northeast. The western range is called "the Lebanon," while the eastern mountains, lying opposite the rich valley between, are called the "Anti-Lebanon." The southern extremity of the Anti-Lebanon range is Mount Hermon, to the east of which lies Damascus. The southern end of the valley was called Beth-Rehob, while the northern end was called Zobah. The cities of Berothai, Cun, and Tebah were located in Zobah, and probably should be identified as its leading cities.

The problem lies in determining whether David or Hadadezer was journeying toward the river (presumably the Euphrates), and for what purpose. The MT's "the river" is often used to indicate the Euphrates. The LXX, 1 Chronicles 18:3, and a later gloss to the MT specify the Euphrates, though some argue for the Yarmuk or the Jordan. The western reaches of the Euphrates typically marked the easternmost border of Levantine hegemony, and it was customary for the principle sovereign of the area to erect a monument by the river to demarcate and celebrate his sphere of power. For example, the Egyptian kings Thutmosis I and Thutmosis III each erected a stela by the river near Carchemish to commemorate successful military campaigns.[1]

Thus, some interpreters argue that Hadadezer (or David) was en route to "erect a monument [lit., 'hand']" as a symbol of their supremacy. However, the verb for "erect" can mean either "cause to remain" or "restore" depending on the vowel pointing. The Masoretes added the vowel points for "restore," and the word *yad* ("hand") is used as a metaphor for power much more often than as a euphemism for a stela. Thus, most translations see Hadadezer as having traveled toward the river to "restore his power" over some eastern province that had proved troublesome. According to this scenario, David attacked the unsuspecting Arameans from the rear, winning a decisive victory over Hadadezer's well-equipped army (v. 3). The size of Hadadezer's army is uncertain since the various textual traditions disagree, and the MT seems to have suffered the loss of a few words. Comparison with 1 Chronicles 18:4 and the LXX suggests that the most likely size of the army was a thousand chariots, seven thousand charioteers (which seems excessive), and twenty thousand infantry. Whether the word "thousand" is to be interpreted literally or as a "platoon" of one dozen or so men is unclear. The former option is the most natural reading.

Another Hamstringing

To hamstring a horse is to render it crippled by severing the huge tendon at the back of the hock, which is called the "hamstring." The hamstringing of one leg would render the horse unfit for military service, but would not kill it.

This act seems to have been ordered by Yahweh in Josh 11:6-9, as Joshua attacked the Caananites at Hazor:

And the LORD said to Joshua, "Do not be afraid of them, for tomorrow at this time I will hand over all of them, slain, to Israel; you shall hamstring their horses, and burn their chariots with fire." So Joshua came suddenly upon them with all his fighting force, by the waters of Merom, and fell upon them. And the LORD handed them over to Israel, who attacked them and chased them as far as Great Sidon and Misrephoth-maim, and eastward as far as the Valley of Mizpeh. They struck them down, until they had left no one remaining. And Joshua did to them as the LORD commanded him; he hamstrung their horses, and burned their chariots with fire.

As with the Moabites, David's treatment of the enemy is often questioned as cruel. Why hamstring seven thousand good horses, saving only one hundred for his own use? Was it simply because David had not yet learned to make good use of horses and chariotry? There is an alternate interpretation, for the word for "horse" does not appear in the passage. The term for "chariot" appears, and is sometimes translated as "chariot horse" on the principle of metonymy. The verb translated as "hamstring" literally means "to uproot," "to tear loose," or "to mutilate." In Joshua 11:6-9, there is little doubt that it means "to hamstring." [Another Hamstringing] But since the object of the verb is the word for chariot ("horse" only by association), it is also possible that the narrator intends to say that David ordered the chariots to be stripped and torn apart. The following reference (vv. 7-8) to the goods David took from the Arameans reinforces this alternate reading.

Hadadezer's Aramean allies did not arrive in time to assist the king, but only to increase the scope of David's victory. When a contingent from Damascus joined the fray, David's army reportedly killed twenty-two thousand men (v. 5)—an astounding figure.

Because the newly conquered territory lay so far north of David's power base, he installed garrisons of soldiers to enforce the Arameans' new status as the unwilling vassals of Israel (v. 6). As trophies of war, David co-opted all precious metals belonging to the enemy force, including the "gold shields" (a better translation is "gold bow-cases") carried by Hadadezer's retinue—probably ceremonial garb of the king's personal honor guard. These were brought to Jerusalem, where they remained until they were captured during an Egyptian incursion against King Rehoboam. The Chronicler's memory of this event led him to add a further

An Additional Note

The LXX, OL, 4QSam^a, and Josephus all add comments to the effect that these golden trophies were later lost to Shoshenq, king of Egypt, "when he came up to Jerusalem in the days of Rehoboam, son of Solomon." This addition is based on 1 Kgs 14:25-26: "In the fifth year of King Rehoboam, King Shishak of Egypt came up against Jerusalem; he took away the treasures of the house of the LORD and the treasures of the king's house; he took everything. He also took away all the shields of gold that Solomon had made."

comment, which is also found in the LXX, the OL (Old Latin version), 4QSam^a, and Josephus. [An Additional Note] The comment that "Yahweh gave victory to David wherever he went" seems premature here. It may have marked the end of an early version of the battle accounts that was later expanded. The clearly theological claim is more appropriate as a summary statement in v. 14.

The city of Betah (MT) should probably be read as "Tebah," as found in 1 Chronicles 18:89, the LXX, and the Syriac version. Tebah was located at the northern extremity of Zobah; "Betah" is otherwise unknown. Berothai was in the southern part of Zobah. The naming of these two principle cities suggests that David's collection of bronze loot was taken from one end of Zobah to the other. First Chronicles 18:8 substitutes "Cun" for Berothai. Cun was a different city, located a few miles southwest of Tebah. The Chronicler's account (1 Chr 18:10), along with the LXX, the OL, and Josephus, adds a note identifying this captured bronze as the raw material for the bronze sea, pillars, and various utensils used in Solomon's temple (cf. 1 Kgs 7:13-47).

Hamath

David's crushing victory over the Arameans sent shock waves throughout the political landscape. King Toi, who ruled the Neo-Hittite state of Hamath, had long been troubled by Hadadezer (lit., "Hadadezer was a man-of-wars of Toi"). [Hamath] Rejoicing in Hadadezer's defeat, but perhaps fearing that David also had designs on Hamath, he sent a messenger to sue for peace. The seriousness of his gesture is seen in the use of his own son as an envoy (8:9-10).

Hamath

In David's day, Hamath was a Neo-Hittite kingdom whose capital of the same name was located by the Orontes River, about 120 miles north of Damascus. At that time, Hamath's borders reached from Zobah to the Euphrates River. The same city is now known as Hama.

The son is named Joram in the MT. This is quite curious, since Toi (Tou in 1 Chr 18:9) was a good Hurrian/Hittite name, while Joram was not only Semitic, but Yahwistic. "Joram" is an abbreviation of "*Yāhū-rām,*" meaning "Yahweh is exalted." In 1 Chronicles 18:10, the same son is called "Hadoram," probably an abbreviation of *haddu-rām,* meaning "Hadad (the storm god) is exalted." It is most likely that the son's original name honored Hadad, and was later changed to Joram as a sign of subservience toward David (compare Eliakim/Jehoiakim in 2 Kgs 23:34 and Mattaniah/Zedekiah in 2 Kgs 24:17). Whether the name was changed at Toi's initiative or at David's insistence is not stated.

Toi's expensive gifts of silver, gold, and bronze imply that he was offering an alliance with David, acknowledging David as the more powerful partner. Thus, while the land of Hamath did not come under direct Israelite control, it was included within David's sphere of influence. The Babylonians and Assyrians to the east were in a state of weakness during the tenth century BC, but in the event of a Mesopotamian resurgence, Hamath would have served as a strategic buffer zone—to Israel's benefit.

The Spoils

The reference to King Toi's tribute leads the narrator to note that David brought all the spoil of his victories back to Jerusalem, where it was consecrated to Yahweh (vv. 11-12), presumably for future use in the temple. It was typical of a holy war that all plunder should be devoted to God. This act and the statement in vv. 6 and 14 that "Yahweh gave victory to David wherever he went" suggest that David considered these wars of conquest to be wars of Yahweh. This ideology served David well, enabling him to build an empire with Yahweh's apparent endorsement.

The summary statement of v. 12 also mentions plunder taken from the Edomites, the Ammonites, and the Amalekites, though none of those conflicts have been described. A battle with Edom (vv. 13b-14) is next on the list, and an extended conflict with the Ammonites is recorded in chapter 10. Significantly, that battle involved Hadadezer as an ally of the Ammonites, adding to the presumption that the events of chapter 10 either preceded or should be considered in conjunction with the conquests of 8:1-14.

David's only recorded conflict with the Amalekites occurred before he became king, and there the resulting spoil was not consecrated to Yahweh but distributed among the towns of Judah (1 Sam 30:26-31).

The Edomites

Verse 13 begins as a summary statement, to which a further conflict with the Edomites is added, almost as an afterthought. "David won [lit., 'made'] a name for himself" can also be interpreted to suggest that David built a monument to memorialize his achievements (compare the discussion at v. 3). The apparent hubris of David's "making a name for himself" stands in some tension with the earlier prediction that *Yahweh* would make a name for David (7:9), and with the repeated assertion that *Yahweh* gave David his victories (vv. 6, 14). The narrator allows the tension to stand without comment.

While v. 13 attributes the crushing defeat of the Edomites to David, the Chronicler accords the victory to Abishai, the brother of Joab (1 Chr 18:12). Since Abishai, like the remainder of the army, served under David, the Deuteronomist could safely add the victory to David's roll call of conquests. As David had established garrisons in the northern territory of Aram because of its distance from Jerusalem, he also put garrisons throughout the far-flung southern reaches of Edom. The result was that David had vassals (lit. "servants") from the southern to the northern extremities of Palestine. David's kingdom had come to supplant Egypt as the dominant power in the Levant. Here, the explanation of David's incredible success is most appropriate: "Yahweh gave victory to David wherever he went" (v. 14).

David's Delegation of Duties, 8:15-18

From the military establishment of an empire in vv. 1-14, the narrator moves to the equally important institution of David's administrative cabinet. Only the highest officials are listed, but even their small number shows how far David has advanced over Saul's bumbling attempt at establishing a viable monarchy. This

---

The Just King

According to the prophets, the ideal king not only delivers his people from their enemies, but also judges them with equity and righteousness. Such equitable judgment is a reflection of Yahweh's rule: "Righteousness and justice are the foundation of your throne; steadfast love and faithfulness go before you" (Ps 89:14).

Jeremiah's advice to the last remnants of the Davidic dynasty in Jerusalem echoed this ideal:

Thus says the LORD: "Act with justice and righteousness, and deliver from the hand of the oppressor anyone who has been robbed. And do no wrong or violence to the alien, the orphan, and the widow, or shed innocent blood in this place." (Jer 22:3)

Both Isaiah and Jeremiah used similar terminology when they predicted the advent of an ideal king who was yet to come:

His authority shall grow continually,
and there shall be endless peace
for the throne of David and his
kingdom.
He will establish and uphold it
with justice and with righteousness
from this time onward and
forevermore.
The zeal of the Lord of hosts will do
this. (Isa 9:7)

The days are surely coming, says the LORD, when I will raise up for David a righteous Branch, and he shall reign as king and deal wisely, and shall execute justice and righteousness in the land. In his days Judah will be saved and Israel will live in safety. And this is the name by which he will be called: "The LORD is our righteousness." (Jer 23:5-6; cf. 33:15-16)

Christian believers see the description of an ideal king in these passages as a foreshadowing of Jesus Christ.

also shows how it was David—not Saul—who set in place the groundwork for the unpopular levies predicted by Samuel (1 Sam 8:10-18).

Verse 15 pictures David as the ideal king, one who "administered justice and equity to all his people." [The Just King] David is pictured as having taken over the role of "judge" that had belonged to Samuel, the last in a long line that began with Joshua. Thus, early in his rule, David was remembered as taking an active and caring role in the day-to-day affairs of his kingdom and his people. Later, he was accused of losing interest in dispensing justice. When David's son Absalom sought to usurp the throne, Absalom prepared the way by positioning himself at the city gate and insisting to all who brought complaints that David no longer cared about justice and would not even appoint a deputy to hear their cases. Absalom asserted that if only he were king, justice would be done (2 Sam 16:1-5). Absalom's success in gaining a following speaks to the need of a king to administer justice.

David's chief officers are divided into pairs, which may be significant, suggesting that he did not wish any one person to gain too much power. Each pair oversaw aspects of one of three governmental departments: military, administrative, and ecclesiastical.

The two military leaders were Joab, son of Zeruiah, who was over the Israelite levy and other fighting troops (v. 16), while Benaiah, son of Jehoiada, commanded David's mercenary bodyguard (v. 18). [The Cherethites and the Pelethites] Joab was a kinsman of David who had served as an army commander in Hebron (2 Sam 2:13-32). It was he who assassinated the Israelite general Abner, earning him David's public criticism and private thanks (2 Sam 3:22-31). When David conquered Jerusalem, he reportedly offered to make the first man who reached the city his general, and Joab was the man (1 Chr 11:6). Joab served David faithfully for many years, but ran afoul of the king when he killed the rebellious Absalom despite David's explicit instructions to spare his son (2 Sam 18). Benaiah

---

The Cherethites and the Pelethites

David's private bodyguard consisted of mercenary soldiers who owed their allegiance to him alone, not to Israel or Judah. Since non-Israelites could have little hope of gaining a following in Israel, this reduced the chance of a bloody *coup d'état*. Some of these soldiers may have been drawn from the band of loyal supporters who had followed David from the beginning (1 Sam 22:2), but others were strictly foreign mercenaries whose roots may have gone back to David's days in Ziklag (1 Sam 27–31). First

Sam 15:18 describes a contingent of loyal Gittites (Philistines from Gath) who followed David from Ziklag.

The "Negeb of the Cherethites" (1 Sam 30:14) was in the same vicinity as Ziklag. The Cherethites and Pelethites are usually presumed to have been descended of sea peoples who came from Crete, closely related (or perhaps identical) to the Philistines. The consonantal roots of "Philistine" and "Pelethite" are very similar. In time, "Cherethites and Pelethites" may have become an honorary title for David's bodyguard, regardless of its ethnic makeup.

would eventually supplant Joab (1 Kgs 2:35) as commander of the army.

Two civil servants are mentioned. Jehoshaphat, son of Ahilud, was David's recorder (v. 16), literally, his "rememberer." His function may have been to supervise the writing, storing, and reading of all official documents both to and from David's administration. By comparison to a similar Egyptian official, some scholars think he also served an important function as David's public spokesperson.

The other top civil officer was Seriah, called Shavsa in the Chronicler's version (1 Chr 18:16). A similar list in 2 Sam 20:23-26 names the official Sheva. Whatever the name, this person was David's royal scribe, sometimes described as his secretary of state. The secretary's specific functions are unknown, but his mention in this short list attests to the importance of his position. The Hebrew word translated "secretary" literally means "counter" or "enumerator." Thus, this official may have been responsible for financial affairs and the keeping of statistics related to the calling out of labor or military levies and the collection of taxes.

Two priests are listed by name in v. 17: Zadok, son of Ahitub, and Ahimelech, son of Abiathar. Zadok does not appear before David's arrival in Jerusalem. Many scholars have considered him to be a powerful Jebusite priest who was recruited by David to serve along with Abiathar, the lone survivor from the sanctuary at Nob, who had fled to David and served him throughout his early career (1 Sam 22:6-23). [Whence Zadok?] When David died, Abiathar was banished, and Zadok assumed the role of high priest alone (1 Kgs 2:26, 35). Eventually, only Zadok's descendants could serve in the Jerusalem temple, the rest being relegated to minor functionary positions.

The MT's identification of Zadok's counterpart as "Ahimelech son of Abiathar" is problematic since Abiathar was the son of Ahimelech (1 Sam 22:20; 23:6; 30:7). First Chronicles 18:16 also seems to have the patronymics reversed. It is clearly Abiathar who is associated with Zadok in 2 Samuel 15:24, 35; 19:11 (MT 19:12); and 1 Kings 4:4.

The list concludes with the surprising statement that "David's sons were priests" (*kōhănîm*). Some writers conjecture that the word for priest could have a different meaning when used in a civil setting; the priests of a king would then be court officials. There is

Whence Zadok?

While a strong tradition of scholarship asserts Zadok's Jerusalemite provenance, 1 Chr 5:29-34 (MT 6:3-8) claims that Zadok was descended of Eleazar, the son of Aaron. Many commentators believe this genealogy was manufactured to serve the Chronicler's own purposes, but F. M. Cross has supplied a tenable defense of Zadok's Aaronide ancestry, noting a Zadok among the group of Aaronide men who joined David's army in Hebron (1 Chr 12:28.)

F. M. Cross, *Canaanite Myth and Hebrew Epic* (Cambridge MA: Harvard University Press, 1973).

Another List

The list of officials in 8:15-18 may be compared to a very similar roll call of royal ministers in 20:23-26. The two lists differ in some ways and may reflect administrative changes as time passed. The second list adds two officers not found in the first: Adoniram, as head of all corvée labor, and Ira the Jairite as David's personal priest. Notice that the second list is arranged more logically, with the two military leaders listed together, then the three civil officials, and finally the three priestly figures. The list in 8:15-18 is more random in presentation.

---

little evidence, however, to support this view. David himself acted as a priest in the offering of sacrifices during the ark's installation (6:13, 17-18; see [The King as Priest]). In the Deuteronomistic ideology, the king was Yahweh's representative *par excellence*, and thus was qualified to perform sacerdotal duties. If David could function as a priest, it follows that his sons could also. Their priestly role may have been limited to the royal house rather than to public service. The list of officials in 20:23-26 does not mention David's sons, but it does name Ira the Jairite as "David's priest." [Another List]

The overall intent of chapter 8 is simple and straightforward, advised more by theology than chronology. Through this series of military victories, Yahweh has fulfilled his promise to give David rest from all his enemies (7:11) so that David's nation and throne might be secure. The list of David's administrative aides is a simple reminder of just how entrenched the kingdom had become. To the modern reader, David's activities may sound like questionable empire-building beyond the ken of Yahweh's bequest. For the ancient editor, however, that tension is secondary to the role of David's conquests in paving the way for the fulfillment of Yahweh's dynastic promise to David.

CONNECTIONS

How Much Is Enough?, 8:1-14

David's expansion of the kingdom went beyond defensive self-preservation, moving toward an offensive mode of self-aggrandizement. David's victories were impressive, but they also were bought at a price. No record of Israelite losses remains, but the enemy deaths reported were considerable, and there is evidence of extreme cruelty in the aftermath of some battles. The growth of an empire—whether military, political, or financial—virtually always comes at the expense of others.

In this chapter, David walks a fine line between what Yahweh has promised (to give rest from his enemies, 7:11) and what David wants (to rule over an empire). The narrator recognizes no disparity in David's deeds, however. He applauds David's every move and insists that it was Yahweh who gave victory to David "wherever he went" (8:6, 14). The editor sees David's success as the positive fulfillment of the Deuteronomistic tenet that God blesses the faithful, as well as the consummation of Yahweh's promise to give David rest from his enemies.

"A man after God's own heart," David was considered worthy to receive Yahweh's blessing, which included both security and fame. Yahweh had promised to make a great name for David (7:9). When the narrator described the realization of that promise, he blithely changes the vocabulary without comment: In 8:13 it is not Yahweh who gave David a great name, but *David made a name for himself*. As mentioned above, this phrase may imply that David erected a monument to commemorate his achievements and strike fear into his enemies.

All believers must struggle with similar issues. Our empires are more often related to finances, business, and influence than to military conquests. Yet, like David, we must also ask, "How much is enough?" At what point is God's promise to care for me fulfilled, and where do I step over the line into excessive self-enhancement? Does it require $20,000 for that—or $50,000 or $100,000? Is millionaire status necessarily a sign of God's blessing and favor?

There can be no pat answer that will fit every person. We each must deal with the question of where the boundaries are in God's desire for our lives. How much money, how much power do we need? Do our career and financial goals enhance our witness or detract from it? Can we prosper without bringing harm to others? Each person, in prayer and daily struggle, must deal with these issues. Success in making a name for ourselves is not necessarily a sign of divine endorsement.

Finding Good Leaders, 8:15-18

The description of David's cabinet is significant, for it shows how he was sensitive to a variety of needs within his kingdom. David himself headed the justice department (see [The Just King]). No one can rule well who is not in touch with ordinary people and committed to winning them equitable treatment. David's personal demise as king began when he deserted the cause of justice in favor of selfish goals.

David assigned military, administrative, and sacerdotal responsibilities to others who were well equipped for their tasks. He trusted them to do this work properly. No organization can be the domain of one person. Nations, municipalities, schools, volunteer fire departments, churches, and the like function best when there is a division of responsibility. As each person contributes their best gifts and trusts others to do their parts (Rom 12; 1 Cor 12), the organization develops its full strength.

The existence of leaders also implies the presence of followers. Wisdom is required to determine when we are called to lead and when we are called to follow.

NOTE

[1] James B. Pritchard, ed. *Ancient Near Eastern Texts Relating to the Old Testament*. 3rd ed. (Princeton: Princeton University Press), 239, 240.

DAVID SHOWS LOYALTY
TO SAUL'S HOUSE

9:1-13

Since the 1926 publication of Leonhard Rost's landmark study, it has been common to speak of chapter 9 as the beginning point of a consciously constructed narrative designed to explain how it was determined that Solomon would succeed David as king. Second Samuel 9–20 and 1 Kings 1–2 are usually given as the limits of this document, commonly called the "Succession Narrative" (SN). [The Succession Narrative]

In recent years, some scholars have acknowledged the basic outline of the narrative, while arguing that the document has a larger purpose than the question of succession. It describes, in short, the gradual decline and ultimate demise of David. The issue of his successor is a natural corollary to the story of David's denouement, not vice versa.

The Succession Narrative

Leonhard Rost's 1926 study, *Die Überlieferung von der Thronnachfolge Davids*, is available in translation as *The Succession to the Throne of David* (trans. M. D. Rutter and D. M. Gunn [Sheffield: Almond Press, 1982]). Earlier scholars had noted that 2 Sam 9–20 + 1 Kgs 1–2 bore a unifying literary theme related to the question of David's successor. Rost, however, approached the question more systematically and in far greater detail.

The precise limits of the SN are not entirely clear. For example, 2 Sam 9:1 is not a particularly good beginning for the narrative, and some see hints of an earlier beginning in 2 Sam 5:1. The narrative flow is interrupted by 2 Sam 21–24, probably as a result of the Deuteronomistic History's literary development. Early versions of Samuel and Kings were almost certainly a single scroll. Later, the account was broken into Samuel and Kings, and the miscellaneous materials found in 2 Sam 21–24 were added as appendices, leading to the separation of 1 Kgs 1–2 from the remainder of the SN.

The unifying literary theme related to the question of David's successor gives the SN a smoother narrative

continuity than the surrounding text. The SN also exhibits a common writing style and vocabulary. Whereas other parts of 1–2 Samuel are characterized by frequent dual accounts, these are largely absent from the SN.

The author writes as if he were an eyewitness to the events, leading some to suggest that the SN was first composed during Solomon's reign, perhaps as an apology for his accession to the throne. Not only is the SN one of the earliest examples of conscious history-writing in Israel, but also some regard the SN to be the finest historical narrative ever produced in ancient Israel.

For further reading, see P. R. Ackroyd, "The Succession Narrative (so-called)," *Interpretation* 35 (1981): 383-96; D. M. Gunn, *The Story of King David: Genre and Interpretation*, JSOTSup 6 (Sheffield: University of Sheffield, 1978); P. Kyle McCarter, " 'Plots True and False.' The Succession Narrative as Court Apologetic," *Interpretation* 35 (1981): 455-67; R. N. Whybray, *The Succession Narrative: A Study of 2 Samuel 9–20 and 1 Kings 1–2*, Studies in Biblical Theology 9, 2d ser. (London: SCM, 1968).

One distinguishing characteristic of this narrative is the way in which the editors have moved Yahweh's involvement to the background. While the Deuteronomists' theological agenda is laid out for all to see in earlier chapters, it is more subtle here. In the Succession Narrative, the exigencies of human reality are brought to the fore. David and his children are revealed to possess all the weaknesses and foibles that are common to the human race. Yahweh puts his work into the hands of humans and still manages to accomplish his purposes despite their stumbling ways and their persistent penchant for hurting each other.

COMMENTARY

In the narrative immediately preceding this chapter (ch. 8), David was tending to business on the international front, making war with other nations and expanding the borders of Israel in a spurt of virtual empire-building. With chapter 9, David turns briefly to domestic affairs, concluding his consolidation of power by moving to tie up a potentially dangerous "loose end" that remained from the previous administration. On the surface, it is a story about David's loyalty to his friend Jonathan. For the careful reader, it is also about David's amazing ability to honor a man and control him at the same time.

The very premise of the chapter—David's search for a descendant of Saul to whom he can show honor—creates a chronological difficulty. Only two descendants are found in chapter 9. The most prominent is a grandson of Saul and son of Jonathan. He is named Mephibosheth (or Meribaal; see comment at 2 Sam 4:4). The second is Mephiposheth's son, Mica. The problem is that a similar search in 2 Samuel 21 uncovered not only Mephibosheth, but also seven sons of Saul by his two concubines, Rizpah and Merab. David sacrificed those seven Saulide sons in a peace-making gesture toward the Gibeonites, ostensibly to repay an old debt incurred by Saul.

Obviously, the narrative would make better sense if chapter 21 preceded chapter 9, for the sons of Saul's concubines appear to be out of the picture when David begins his search for Saul's survivors. In the source documents containing original versions of these stories, the time frame was probably different. Some writers have postulated that chapters 9 and 21 once constituted a short "Mephibosheth cycle." If so, the Deuteronomists seem to have inserted the two episodes in separate places, out of chronological order, and with a few editorial changes.

For example, if chapter 9 had followed chapter 21 in an original document, there would really be no need for David to institute a search, for Mephibosheth is known in 21:7. The search motif is an important aspect of the story, however. It is quite possible that the reference to Mephibosheth in 21:7 was inserted by the editor in deference to the material already presented in chapter 9, along with 16:1-4 and 19:24-30.

The story in chapter 9 serves two purposes in its present position: It illustrates David's ingenuity in dealing with a thorny domestic issue, and it introduces two characters (Ziba and Mephibosheth) who will enter the story again (Ziba at 16:1-4; Mephibosheth at 19:24-30).

The gory scene of chapter 21 is likely to have occurred early in David's reign, but the narrator has been careful to portray David's rise in a completely positive light. The idea of turning over Saul's seven sons for a bloody execution seems unworthy of David; so the editor reserves it until later, when the flaws in David's character have already become evident and any questionable behavior is more acceptable.

The central theme of chapter 9 is loyalty: The word *ḥesed* appears in vv. 1, 3, and 7 [*Ḥesed*] David had once sworn an oath to Jonathan that, if David should become king, he would not eliminate Jonathan's descendants, but nurture them. [1 Samuel 18:3-4; 20:14-15, 23, 42] Having attained the throne, David made a public appeal for information concerning the whereabouts of Saul's descendants, that he might show kindness (*ḥesed*) to them "for Jonathan's sake."

> **Hesed**
>
> AΩ The word *ḥesed* has a rich history in Hebrew and defies translation into easy English equivalents. Its basic connotation has to do with covenant loyalty, but it could also refer to the lovingkindness that results from loyal relationships.
>
> *Ḥesed* is said to be a constant characteristic of Yahweh's relationship with Israel. When Moses asked to see God's glory (Exod 33:18), he received both a quick view of the divine afterglow as Yahweh passed by and the memory of God's self-revelation:
>
> > The LORD, the LORD,
> > a God merilul and gracious,
> > slow to anger,
> > abounding in steadfast love (*ḥesed*) and
> > faithfulness,
> > keeping steadfast love (*ḥesed*) to the
> > thousandth generation,
> > forgiving iniquity and transgression
> > and sin,
> > yet by no means clearing the guilty,
> > but visiting the iniquity of the parents
> > upon the children and the children's
> > children,
> > to the third and the fourth
> > generation. (Exod 34:6b-7)
>
> This text reveals Yahweh's nature as being one of mercy and grace, but one that is also bound by covenant love. Sometimes covenant commitments are expressed through steadfast love. At other times, covenant commitments require that persons experience the consequences they have brought upon themselves and their descendants.
>
> The image of Yahweh as a God of *ḥesed* became a signature description, and different versions of God's self-revelation are repeated often in the Scriptures (see Neh 9:17; Jonah 4:2; Joel 2:13; compare also Ps 108:4; Rom 2:4).

A prominent member of Saul's household staff was located. His name was Ziba, and he seemed to have served as Saul's steward. [Flexible Labels] The conversation between David and Ziba is straightforward, but marked by meaningful nuances. David's question

1 Samuel 18:3-4; 20:14-15, 23, 42

Jonathan's earlier covenant with David is illustrated in these verses. Note that the request for loyalty from David extended to Jonathan's descendants.

Then Jonathan made a covenant with David, because he loved him as his own soul. Jonathan stripped himself of the robe that he was wearing, and gave it to David, and his armor, and even his sword and his bow and his belt. (18:3-4)

"If I am still alive, show me the faithful love of the LORD; but if I die, never cut off your faithful love from my house, even if the LORD were to cut off every one of the enemies of David from the face of the earth." (20:14-15)

"As for the matter about which you and I have spoken, the LORD is witness between you and me forever." (20:23)

Then Jonathan said to David, "Go in peace, since both of us have sworn in the name of the LORD, saying, 'The LORD shall be between me and you, and between my descendants and your descendants, forever.' " He got up and left; and Jonathan went into the city. (20:42)

("Are you Ziba?") was answered with the self-abasing words "your servant" (some ancient versions have "I am your servant"). The NRSV's "at your service!" may be a bit more enthusiastic than intended.

David's query in v. 3 moves the issue of showing loyalty beyond David's pledge to Jonathan and into the arena of David's role as Yahweh's representative. "Is there anyone remaining . . . to whom I may show the kindness of God?" may have been intended to defuse Ziba's suspicions. If David meant harm to Saul's descendants, it is unlikely that he would have invoked God's name over it. David also shows himself to be loyal and kind, as Yahweh has demonstrated himself to be a God of steadfast love.

Ziba's answer reveals much by what it does and does not include. He acknowledges that a Saulide scion still lives, but does not mention his name. The salient facts are that the man in question is a son of Jonathan (which reminds David of his loyalty covenant with Jonathan), and he is crippled in both feet (which shows that he is no threat to David). The story of how the boy became lame is found in 2 Samuel 4:4.

Upon further interrogation, Ziba reveals that the lone survivor of Saul's house is to be found "in the house of Machir son of Amiel, at Lo-debar," but the man still goes unnamed. Ziba may have withheld the name as a means

Flexible Labels

AΩ Ziba is called a *na'ar* of Saul in 9:9, a *na'ar* of the house of Saul in 19:18 (cf. 9:2), and the *na'ar* of Mephibosheth in 16:1. The word is often translated as "boy" or "lad," but it could also mean "servant" (see 13:7, of household servants; and 1 Sam 9:3, 5, in reference to the servants of Kish who accompanied Saul in his search for the lost donkeys). The term sometimes indicated a person of high standing and responsibility. Ziba appears to be an older person who had a large family of his own and significant responsibilities for managing Saul's property. Thus, a word like "steward" is an appropriate translation.

of protection, but this seems unlikely since he had clearly divulged his location and the identifying mark of his lameness. More likely, the failure to name this son of Saul's house is a literary reminder of his political insignificance.

The person in question may not have been a threat *to* David, but he obviously felt threatened *by* David—which would be quite understandable, especially if the events of chapter 21 preceded this account. He no longer lived on his father's estate (which had presumably been appropriated by David), but in the Transjordan, with Machir of Lo-debar. [Machir of Lo-debar]

The precise location of Lo-debar is unknown, but it apparently was near Mahanaim, where Abner and Ish-bosheth had set up their rump government after Saul's death. Machir, presumably, was a strong enough supporter of Saul to have risked the danger of harboring the former king's grandson when David took the crown.

> **Machir of Lo-debar**
> The name Machir has a good pedigree in Israel. The tribe of Machir is mentioned in the Song of Deborah (12th century). In the genealogies of Genesis (50:23) and Numbers (26:29), Machir is presented as a son of Manasseh and the father of Gilead, namesake of the territory granted them by Moses (Num 32:39-40; Deut 3:15).

Saul's lone, lame descendent was duly summoned, and appeared before David. Finally, his name—Mephibosheth—is spoken for the first time by David. How David knows his name is not revealed, but Mephibosheth responded in an even more subservient manner than his steward, as he "fell on his face and did obeisance" (v. 6). "I am your servant" shows due respect to David as the acknowledged king and ruler, to whom Mephibosheth owes his continued existence. It was not uncommon for all members of the old royal house to be eradicated when a new king took office. David's offer to show kindness, then, was an exception to the rule.

David offered to do two things for Mephibosheth: to return to him the considerable estate that had belonged to Saul, and to invite him to reside in Jerusalem, where he would have the signal honor of eating at the king's table. [Eating at the King's Table] Saul's property, presumably, would have been in and around Gibeah. It must have been extensive, for David appointed Ziba and his substantial household (including fifteen sons and twenty servants, see 9:10) to care for it and send its produce to Mephibosheth. Thus, David offered to Mephibosheth an all-expense paid position as his royal guest, but also granted to him the ample income that Saul's estate would have produced.

It seems a bit strange that David would order Ziba to send produce to Mephibosheth in Jerusalem "so that he might have food to eat," while also insisting that Mephibosheth would be eating at the king's table. This implies that Mephibosheth would not need the

Eating at the King's Table

Sharing table fellowship carries symbolic meaning. This is true in the modern world and was even more evident in the ancient world. Since dining together can create or seal a bond between parties, a shared meal could signify the ratification of a covenant (Gen 26:26-31), even as wedding meals or corporate banquets celebrate relationships today. Dining together both creates and represents friendship, so much so that Plutarch spoke of the "friend-making character of the table" (*Quaest. Conv.* 614A-B).

Meals also mark social boundaries by including or excluding individuals. In her study of social "codes" embedded in meal customs, Mary Douglas has written, "Drinks are for strangers, acquaintances, workmen, and family. Meals are for family, close friends, honored guests. The grand operator of the system is the line between intimacy and distance. . . . The meal expresses close friendship."

These symbolic values are evident in the Old Testament narratives concerned with "eating at the king's table" (in addition to 2 Sam 9, see also 1 Sam 20; 1 Kgs 2:7; 18:19; 2 Kgs 25:27-30; along with the interesting theological variation in Ps 23:5). To be invited to the king's table was a mark of honor, signifying inclusion in the king's social realm Friendship between David and Mephibosheth is indicated b the thrice-repeated "show kindness" in 2 Sam 9. In 2 Kgs 25:27-30, the Babylonian monarch "spoke kind things" to the exiled King Jehoiakim, allowing him to eat at the royal table in Babylon.

Recent literary studies have pointed to an intertextual relationship between 1 Sam 20, 2 Sam 9, and 2 Kgs 25:27-30. The *hesed* shown by the house of Saul (via Jonathan) t David in 1 Sam 20 is reciprocated when David shows *hesed* to the house of Saul in 2 Sam 9 by being kind to Jonathan's crippled son Mephibosheth. This kind treatment of the crippled house of Saul in 2 Sam 9 then foreshadows and mirrors the treatment of the crippled house of David in 2 Kg 25:27-30.

Mary Douglas, "Deciphering a Meal," *Daedalus* 101 (Winter 1972): 66.

food that was to be sent to him. We are to understand, perhaps, that this food was to support Mephibosheth's family and servants who lived in Jerusalem with him, for the invitation to sit at the king's table was extended to Mephibosheth alone. Such an invitation may also have involved only ceremonial meals, and not everyday fare. Excess produce (of which there should have been much) could also be sold as a means of providing material income for the son of Jonathan.

The extent of Mephibosheth's surprise and gratitude is revealed by the depth of his self-abasement: "What is your servant, that you should look upon a dead dog such as I?" (v. 8). [Dead Dogs in Ancient Literature] The Israelites regarded dogs as pests, rather than pets. To speak of oneself as a dog is to acknowledge insignificance; a dead dog would be even more so.

David's royal grant of Saul's estate, combined with his appointment of Ziba to manage it and send the produce to Mephibosheth, effectively relegated Ziba and his household to the role of serving Mephibosheth (vv. 9-10), as they had served Saul. Ziba himself may have been an employee rather than an indentured servant or slave. The fact that Ziba had servants of his own suggests, at least, that he had lived as a free man after Saul's death. David's show of kindness to Mephibosheth, however, has also put Ziba under obligation (or provided him with a steady job, depending on the point of view).

Dead Dogs in Ancient Literature

The metaphor of a "dog" or "dead dog," when applied to a person, is an example of shaming by labeling (see [Shaming in the Ancient World] for more on public shaming). The metaphor was common in the ancient Near East and continues to find wide usage in the modern world. Like other labels, it could be used by an individual to refer to himself in a self-deprecating manner, or by one person as an invective against another.

Why should "dog" have such a negative connotation? Though dogs were probably the first animals to be domesticated, they were not welcome in all societies, including Hebrew culture. Some scholars hold that the ancients saw dogs as particularly vile and contemptible, while others see comparison to a dog as a comment on one's insignificance. Dogs were actually held in high esteem among the Philistines, as attested by archaeological discoveries of many burials that include entire dog skeletons. The popularity of canines among the hated (and "heathen") Philistines may have contributed to Israel's antipathy toward the animals.

The dog metaphor as a self-deprecation. In addition to 2 Sam 9:8, other biblical examples of the self-deprecating dog metaphor include Mephibosheth's obeisance in 2 Sam 5:8, Abner's remark to Ishbaal in 2 Sam 3:8, David's self-deprecation when confronting Saul in 1 Sam 24:14 (MT v. 15), and Hazael's response to Elisha's prophecy in 2 Kgs 8:13.

Extrabiblical texts reveal the same pattern. Among the Amarna letters, there is one in which one "Abdi-Asratu reported to the king: 'As I am a servant of the king and a dog of his house, I guard all Amurru for the king, my lord' " (Letter 60; see also 61).

Kyle McCarter cites a 14th century letter from Syria that asks: "Who am I, some dog?", as well as a 6th century letter from Lachish that asks, "Who is your servant, a dog, that my lord should have remembered his servant?" (Lachish ostracon 2.4).

The metaphor used as an invective. There is one biblical example, also found in 2 Samuel, in which David's nephew and military henchman Abishai said to the king, "Why should this dead dog curse my lord the king? Let me go over and take off his head" (2 Sam 16:9).

Extrabiblical examples include a reference from the royal archives at Mari: "What are they? Dogs!" (G. Dossin, *Archives royales de Mari*, I. no.27, I 28). Several examples appear in the Amarna letters, most in reference to one Abdi-Asirta, who is called "servant and dog" (Letter 71, 75, 85; see also 67).

The figure of a dog was used as a derogative in the New Testament period, as in Phil 3:2: "Beware of the dogs, beware of evil workers." Also, Rev 22:15 says, "Outside are the dogs and sorcerers and fornicators and murderers and idolaters, and everyone who loves and practices falsehood."

Amarna texts from William L. Moran, ed. and trans., *The Amarna Letters* (Baltimore: Johns Hopkins University Press, 1992).

P. Kyle McCarter, *II Samuel* (AB 9; Garden City: Doubleday, 1984), 261.

Mephibosheth's son Mica is mentioned in v. 12, but does not appear again in Samuel–Kings. First Chronicles 8:34-45 (cf. 9:40-41) reports that he became the father of four sons. The brief mention here of his existence reminds the reader that the future of Jonathan's house is now secure under David's loyal patronage.

The final verse of this account is a redundant addition intended to underscore Mephibosheth's privileged but limited position. He lived in Jerusalem by the king's grace (and under his watchful eye)—and as a dependent cripple who was unlikely to spark any sort of separatist movement. Thus, though David has demonstrated loyalty by preserving Jonathan's descendants, he has not weakened his own position by doing so.

CONNECTIONS

The story of David and Mephibosheth, for all of its possible political machinations, is a story about loyalty. The skeptical reader may find in David's actions a kind of self-service, but the author writes as if David's intent were singular and sincere: to live out the pledge of love he had made to Jonathan.

Loyalty is expressed in one way or another throughout this story. David desires to demonstrate loyalty to Jonathan by showing kindness to Jonathan's descendants. The earnest favor that David bestowed upon Mephibosheth inspired Saul's scion to turn his loyalty to David and led Ziba to show loyalty to both of them, serving both David and Mephibosheth.

Modern negotiators and business leaders are always looking for the proverbial "win/win" situation. Here is an ideal model: the mutual loyalty shown by David, Ziba, and Mephibosheth served to benefit all parties involved. David gained greater security in knowing that Mephibosheth would be no political threat, while the handicapped son of Jonathan gained the security of knowing that David meant him good, not harm. David gained the good will of the people through his kind treatment of a possible rival, while Mephibosheth gained an honored place and his family's land. In the process, Ziba won a royal appointment as the steward of Saul's considerable estate.

In a very subtle way, through a virtual slip of the tongue, the narrator reminds us that such loyalty as this has its roots in Yahweh. In v. 3, David asks if there is yet a survivor of Saul's house to whom he may show "the kindness of God." The history of Yahweh and his people was a history of Yahweh's continued faithfulness, even when Israel did not deserve it. The rich expression of Yahweh's love for Israel was colored by the multivalence of the term *ḥesed*, which can mean "lovingkindness" on the one hand and "loyalty" or "faithfulness" on the other.

This is the way God is, and this is the way God calls his people to be. When we are loyal to Yahweh, we will demonstrate our commitment through kindness to others. Our kindness, in turn, is a witness of God's love, leading others to respond with faith, trust, and loyalty of their own.

A significant sidelight of this story is David's faithfulness to his pledge despite radically changed circumstances. When David first pledged his loyalty to Jonathan's house (1 Sam 20:1-7; 23:18), Saul was very much in power, and David was living in the wilderness as a fugitive. Now David was in power, and the only surviving member of Saul's household was living in the Transjordan as a frightened fugitive. The tables were turned completely, and David could easily have foresworn his earlier pledge in the name of political expediency—but he did not.

Today, we also make promises: promises to God, promises to our spouses, promises to parents or friends or employers. In our society it has become all too acceptable to break promises on the basis of changing circumstances—that is, when it is no longer to our benefit to keep the promise. Yet promises are not made for our advantage alone; they do not lose their binding force when we lose the benefits.

The Scriptures often speak of the danger of swearing falsely (Lev 6:3; 19:12; Jer 5:2; 7:9; Mal 3:5; Matt 5:33). Those who swear are expected to keep their word, even when the circumstances are different and the expected gain is no longer evident. There is spiritual profit in standing by one's promises, even when the material benefit is no longer apparent. David could have ignored Mephibosheth or even had him killed, but he chose the better way. The loyalty of God calls us to choose the better way as well.

DAVID SHOWS LOYALTY—
AND A SWORD—TO AMMON

10:1-19

With chapter 10, the narrative pendulum swings back from domestic issues to foreign affairs, but there is a connection with the previous chapter: Both concern *loyalty*. In chapter 9, David was concerned with showing loyalty (*ḥesed*) to the house of Saul. In chapter 10, he desires to demonstrate *ḥesed* to the new king of Ammon. Whether domestically or internationally, David is presented as a man of loyalty.

Chronologically, the events in this chapter seem to have preceded the Aramean War described in 8:3-8 and may have followed the rebellion of Absalom in chapters 13–20 (note the assistance of Ammon in 17:24-29). [David's Ammonite-Aramean Wars] Why, then, are these military accounts placed here? The answer seems to be one of context. The chapter looks both backward and forward. It balances chapter 9 by showing that David's loyalty was true both within Israel and beyond its borders.

> **David's Ammonite-Aramean Wars**
>
> David's Ammonite-Aramean Wars seem to have fallen into three stages: the initial victory under Joab's command (10:6-14), David's victory over an army reinforced by additional Aramean mercenaries (10:15-18), and David's pursuit of the fleeing Arameans, extending his hegemony to the Euphrates River (8:3-8; 10:19). All of this was set in motion by a diplomatic blunder on the part of Ammon's new king (10:1-5).

More significantly, the chapter points forward to the infamous episode involving Bathsheba—a dark period in which David showed a *lack* of loyalty to his own family and to his faithful fighting men. Since the David-Bathsheba-Uriah cycle is set during the siege of the Ammonite capital Rabbah, chapter 10 sets the stage for David's internal fall while simultaneously acclaiming his external victories.

COMMENTARY

David's Diplomacy and Hanun's Mistake, 10:1-5

The narrator assumes a previous relationship of some sort between David and the Ammonites, though it is never mentioned in the text.

Some writers propose that David simply built upon Saul's defeat of Nahash (1 Sam 11), assuming that both Israelite kings had kept the Ammonites under continuous subjugation. Most, however, suspect the existence of a friendship treaty between David and Nahash, probably stemming from the days when David was seen as Saul's opponent or engaged in hostilities with Saul's successor Ish-bosheth. At that time, David himself was not a threat to the Ammonites, and Nahash would have found it advantageous to befriend anyone who stood against his enemies in Israel.

After David became king over Israel, the political situation changed, but his treaty with Ammon remained in effect throughout Nahash's tenure. On at least one occasion the house of Nahash offered succor to David (during his flight from Absalom, which may have preceded this account; see 17:24-29). Thus, when King Nahash died, David sent the expected diplomatic envoys to Rabbah, the Ammonite capital. Their mission was to express consolation to the Ammonites in their time of grief, and to reaffirm the covenant of cooperation between the two nations.

The narrator described David's diplomacy as an indication of his desire to show loyalty to Hanun, even as the new king's father Nahash had shown loyalty to David (vv. 1-2; cf. 17:27). Hanun and his advisors, however, cognizant that David had become a potential danger to them, rebuffed David's overtures. They accused the delegation of coming to spy out the city in preparation for a later attack. In a shocking violation of diplomatic immunity and respect, Hanun ordered that the envoys be publicly humiliated by cutting off their beards and the lower halves of their clothing. [A Symbolic Castration?]

The comment in v. 5 concerning David's initial reaction to this affront reminds the reader of how David was able to command such loyalty from his men. David did not express anger at the envoys for their failure in successfully renegotiating a friendly

---

A Symbolic Castration?

Ancient Hebrew men wore full beards as a public sign of their manhood. Hanun's shaving of the emissaries' beards was intended to cause acute embarrassment and shame (cf. Isa 15:2; Jer 41:5; 48:37). There is some question as to how much of the beard was removed. The MT says *half* the beard was shaved—presumably not the bottom half, but one complete side. The versions, however, tend to leave out the word "half," which may be a corruption stemming from the loss of the lower half of the men's clothing.

The cutting off of the men's garments ("in the middle at their hips") had only one purpose: to expose the men's genitals and buttocks and so add further insult to their public degradation (cf. Isa 20:4). Together, these two actions served as a sort of "symbolic castration," a temporary but embarrassing theft of the envoys' collective masculinity.

In some ancient Near Eastern folklore, there was a symbolic relationship between a man's eyes and his testicles. Since David's envoys had been accused of "spying out" the land, the Ammonite leaders may have intentionally punished them by exposing their lower set of "eyes."

ericho

Jericho is sometimes called the oldest city in the world, with an archaeological record extending over 6,000 years. Located in a depression (845 feet below sea level) near the northwestern extremity of the Dead Sea, it is so the *lowest* city in the world.

Jericho would have been on the main road leading from Jerusalem to Rabbah, crossing the Jordan just north of the Dead Sea. (Photo Credit: Mitchell G. Reddish)

alliance. His sensitivity in allowing the men to remain at the famous old city of Jericho until their beards had grown was a mark of his skill in personal and public relations. [Jericho]

Hanun and his advisors would have known that no self-respecting king could let this incident of public shaming pass without retribution, so their act was in fact a declaration of war against Israel. [Shaming in the Ancient World] Conflict was now a certainty; only the time and place remained to be determined.

David Defeats the Ammonites and Arameans, 10:6-19

The war itself took place in several stages, two of which are detailed in vv. 6-14 and 15-18. Because of their obvious affront, the Ammonites had "become odious to David"—literally, "they stunk with David." Knowing this, Hanun arranged a makeshift alliance with several Aramean leaders to assist him in waging war against David. [Israel, Judah, and the Arameans] Although the text says that the Arameans were "hired," it is unlikely that Ammon had the

Shaming in the Ancient World

To shame is to impute a sense of humiliation, inadequacy, or disgrace to an individual or group. Both shame and honor are social evaluations, molded by the customs and attitudes of a society. They are especially important in group-oriented societies where one's social standing is conferred by the group, unlike highly individualistic societies such as modern America.

Shaming may be accomplished in several ways, most of which are found in the books of Samuel. Shame may be conferred, for example, by labeling. Labels such as "unclean," "foolish," or "wicked" indicated shame (e.g., the interpretation of Nabal's name as "fool" in 1 Sam 25:25).

Shame could also be communicated through judicial sanctions. Deut 25:5-10 calls for one who refused the duties of the levirate to be spat upon and slapped with a sandal. The shame of the individual passed on to his family, as well. In this case, shaming is a form of social control, designed to encourage conformity to community expectations.

A third means of shaming is through political acts of humiliation. Prisoners taken in warfare were stripped naked and mocked (Isa 20), a practice designed to demoralize captives and render them psychologically defenseless.

Saul's fear that the Philistines would "make sport of me" (1 Sam 31:4) probably reflects his aversion to such shaming as well as to his fear of torture.

When Nahash the Ammonite announced a plan to gouge out the right eye of every inhabitant of Jabesh-gilead (1 Sam 11:1-4), he was also practicing a type of psychological warfare used to terrify and control weaker persons through shame.

The treatment of David's ambassadors to Hanun (2 Sam 10:1-6) reveals still another form of political disgrace. By cutting half of the emissaries' beards and robes, thus exposing their genitals (see [A Symbolic Castration?] on "symbolic castration"), the Ammonites made them look foolish. The Ammonites' purpose was status manipulation by this action, they humiliated not only the ambassadors, but David and Israel as well, thereby raising their own status relative to David (cf. Isa 3:17; 7:20).

The particular nuance of shame associated with defacing the beard is debated. Whether the beard was understood as a symbol of a man's sexual virility, masculinity, or seniority, however, the purpose in shearing it was clear: In ancient Near Eastern culture it made the individual appear to be less of a man, and thus less likely receive respect within the community.

wherewithal to retain the Aramean armies as pure mercenaries. Some symbolic payment or a promise of a share in the plunder may have been made, but most likely the Arameans would have recognized the advantage of making common cause with the Ammonites, for David was a growing threat to them, too.

The mercenaries from Beth-rehob and Zobah are the same armies mentioned in 8:3-8. Beth-rehob and Zobah were located north of the Sea of Galilee, between the Lebanon and anti-Lebanon mountains. The southern part of the valley was called Beth-rehob, the northern part Zobah. Since Beth-rehob is mentioned first, it may have held pride of place in the area. The most prominent leader in the area was Hadadezer of Zobah, but he was identified as a "son of Rehob" (8:3). Beth-rehob and Zobah were said to have contributed 20,000 men to the war effort, though the ambiguity of the term translated as "thousand" allows for a much smaller number.

Additional soldiers were recruited from the king of Maacah and the people of Tob (v. 6). Maacah occupied the northern part of what is now called the Golan, just east of the Sea of Galilee, south of Mount Hermon, and north of Geshur. The city-state of Geshur, which encompassed the southern part of the Golan, had allied itself

rael, Judah, and the Arameans

The Arameans were a people populating the northern and northwestern parts of the Fertile rescent; some Aramean kingdoms were reported in the ortheastern section of the same area, east of the Tigris ver and near Assur, as well as into Babylonia. In Old estament history, the Aramean kingdom of Syria = Aram) is most important.

After Israel's settlement of Canaan, relations between rael and the Aramean kingdom of Syria were frequent nd usually hostile. An early report is the hostility entioned in Judg 3:8-10. Saul is reported to have onquered Zobah, an Aramean kingdom in southern Syria Sam 14:47), while David and Joab are also said to have ained victory over Zobah (2 Sam 8:3, 5) and a larger oalition of Aramean states (10:6-19). Not all relationships ith the Arameans were hostile, however. David married he daughter of the king of Geshur, who became the other of Absalom. When Absalom fled after killing his alf-brother Amnon, he stayed for three years in that outhern Aramean state (2 Sam 13:37-39).

During the divided monarchy, relations between the rameans and the states of Israel and Judah were a onvoluted series of shifting alliances and intermittent varfare. In the early years of the 9th century BC, King Asa f Judah enticed Ben-hadad I of Syria to break his treaty vith Baasha of Israel and attack the latter (1 Kgs 15:17-0). Warfare continued between Syria and Israel (1 Kgs 0:1-30), and eventually Israel and Judah became allies

against Syria to recapture Ramoth-gilead (1 Kgs 22:1-4, 29-37). By the mid-9th century, however, Israel and Syria were allies again, along with other Aramean states, due to the threat posed by a greater enemy, Shalmaneser III of Assyria. After Shalmaneser's defeat at Qarqar in 853 BC, Israel and Syria quickly resumed their warfare against each other, with Syria sometimes the victor (2 Kgs 6:8; 6:24–7:8; 8:28-29; 10:32-33; 13:3-7, 22), and Israel prevailing at other times (2 Kgs 13:25; 14:25-28).

In 735 BC Israel and Syria again joined forces to oppose Assyria; they attempted, unsuccessfully, to force Ahaz of Judah to join their coalition (2 Kgs 15:37; 16:5-9). This coalition, unlike that at Qarqar, was crushed by the Assyrians. Syrian national identity was lost as Syria became a province of Assyria, and Aramean ethnic identity was diluted due to the Assyrian practice of deporting populations.

Despite the frequent hostilities, Israel's patriarchal traditions identified the nation's ancestors as Arameans. Abraham reportedly sent his servant to Aram-Naharaim to find a wife from "my country . . . and my kindred" for Isaac, and Rebekah's relatives are called "Arameans" (Gen 24:1-10; 25:20; 28:5; 31:20, 24). In a liturgical credo, Israel confessed, "A wandering Aramean was my ancestor" (Deut 26:5). This tradition probably reflects Israel's understanding that both her ancestors and the Arameans of Syria descended from the Northwest Semitic peoples of Upper Mesopotamia.

with David through marriage (2:9), but Maacah (which was closer to the Aramean strongholds to the north) chose to side against the Israelite king.

The land of Tob was a small state in the northern Transjordan. If it can properly be identified with modern El-aiyibeh, its center would have been about twelve miles southeast of the Sea of Galilee. Tob's ruler may not have held the title of king, for the MT refers to aid coming from the "man of Tob" (not *men* of Tob, as in NRSV). Maacah and Tob together added another twelve or thirteen thousand men to the martial equation.

Whether intended as a means of battle strategy or as a pointed way of saying that they served only themselves, the Aramean coalition camped in the open country north of Rabbah, while the Ammonite soldiers arrayed themselves at the gate of their city (v. 8). [Where Did the Arameans Camp?] Whatever the intention, this arrangement initially proved fortuitous to the anti-David forces, for David's general, Joab, led his armies across the Jordan just north of

---

Where Did the Arameans Camp?

The synoptic text in 1 Chr 19:6-7 includes additional information not found in the MT, but also appearing in a shorter form in 4QSam^a.

2 Samuel 10:6	1 Chronicles 19:6-7
(6) When the Ammonites saw that they had become odious to David, the Ammonites sent and hired the Arameans of Beth-rehob and the Arameans of Zobah, twenty thousand foot soldiers, as well as the king of Maacah, one thousand men, and the men of Tob, twelve thousand men.	(6) When the Ammonites say that they had made themselves odious to David, Hanun and the Ammonites sent a thousand talents of silver to hire chariots and cavalry from Mesopotamia, from Aram-maacah and from Zobah. (7) They hired thirty-two thousand chariots and the king of Maacah with his army, who came and camped before Medeba. And the Ammonites were mustered from their cities and came to battle.

The Chronicler's version shows clear signs of exaggeration. One thousand talents of silver could have bought 100,000 slaves! The assertion that the king of Maacah and his army camped before Medeba is problematic, because Medeba (some twenty miles south of Rabbah, over rugged terrain) seems too far south to offer the Ammonites much assistance, unless their purpose was to prevent an opportunistic Edomite invasion.

Jericho, where they found themselves caught between the Arameans to the north and the Ammonites to the south.

Joab's entrance to the battlefield may have been inopportune, but his quick-thinking tactics quickly turned the situation to his advantage. Splitting his forces into two camps and putting his brother Abishai in charge of the forces going against Rabbah, Joab devised a strategy in which each part of the army could watch the other's back and send reserves if necessary. Joab roused his troops with a stirring speech that called upon his men to save the "cities of our God" (v. 12), and he led them into battle with such fervor that the Arameans were quickly routed (v. 13). News of this unexpected development forced the Ammonites to withdraw into their city (v. 14). For some unexplained reason, Joab did not pursue his advantage, but presumably left enough soldiers to enforce a siege of Rabbah.

The flight of the Arameans proved to have been a strategic withdrawal, delaying the pitched battle until additional reinforcements could be brought in from "across the river" (vv. 15-16). Some scholars doubt the author intended the Euphrates, but there were many Arameans in northwestern Mesopotamia during this period, so there is no real reason to propose that the Jordan, the Yarmuk, or the Leontes Rivers were intended instead of the normal translation.

The newly strengthened Aramean armies then gathered for battle behind Hadadezer's general, Shobach, at a place called Helam, which seems to have been a general region located in the Transjordanian plateau. [Helam and Other Places: David's Battles with the Arameans]

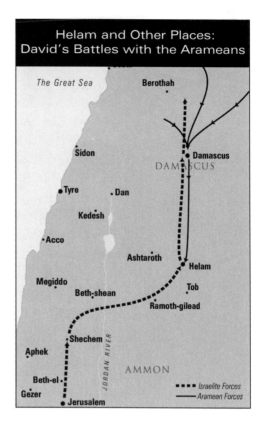

Helam and Other Places: David's Battles with the Arameans

There is no evidence that David had participated in the actual fighting of the first battle since Joab and Abishai are portrayed as Israel's military leaders. This time, however, David led his army into battle, crossing the Jordan further to the north than Joab had done. This avoided the entrapment Joab had experienced and also served to cut off the Arameans from any Ammonite assistance.

The text insists that the two armies fought and David won a great victory, killing huge numbers of the enemy, including the famed general Shobach (v. 18). The precise number and identification of enemies slain (footsoldiers vs. charioteers) varies widely in the versions, and all seem exaggerated.

The flight of the Arameans back to their homeland would have provided a fitting context for David's pursuing attack from the rear that eventually brought the Arameans under his rule (8:3-8). The summary statement of 10:19—that the Arameans sued for peace and became subject to David—is most logical in the aftermath of all the conflicts reported between David and the Aramean coalition.

There was yet unfinished business with the Ammonites, however. This will be the subject that introduces David's errant ways (11:1), provides the context for his heartless murder of Uriah (11:14-21), and finally is concluded in 12:26-31.

CONNECTIONS

Finding homiletical inspiration in these ancient war stories is like looking for kindness in a punch to the midsection, but there are some things of interest here. For example, the significance of these stories is found in what is *not* said as well as in what is said.

In several of David's earlier wars, the narrator made it clear that David piously sought divine permission to go into battle, and even received specific advice from Yahweh on how the battle should be fought (e.g., 2 Sam 5:17-25). Other stories say less about the divine endorsement of David's actions prior to battle, but still insist that "the LORD gave victory to David" (8:6, 14).

In chapter 10, the activity of Yahweh has moved to the background. There is no indication that David asked for or received God's endorsement before going into battle, nor is there any spoken claim that the resulting victories were due to Yahweh's intervention. Rather, the military activities of Joab, Abishai, David, and the armies of Israel are described. Success seems to come so quickly and easily that the reader may *presume* that Yahweh has a hand in it, but the narrator does not say so.

In chapter 10, Yahweh is mentioned only by Joab, who inspires his men to defend "the cities of our God," and who sends his men into battle with this blessing: "May the LORD do what seems good to him" (10:12). The battle's outcome suggests that it seemed good to the LORD to assist David and his men, but the reader must look between the lines to discover any theological claims.

This characteristic style of the Succession Narrative reminds believers that God often works unobserved in our lives, and not always through victory. Failure, tragedy, and sorrow will come to David's house soon enough; God will remain in the background, but always present. Even in this story, there is pain and humiliation for the envoys who were robbed of their visible signs of manhood.

Yet the reader has confidence that beneath the surface of the story, in high points and low, Yahweh's purposes were not thwarted and Yahweh's people were not deserted. Our lives contain success and failure, joy and sorrow, elation and depression. God's presence and activity are not always apparent to us. Yet the witness of Scripture suggests that God is always walking along beside us—hidden, perhaps, but available to hear our prayer and guide our steps.

DAVID COMMITS ADULTERY

11:1-27

David's War Within, 11:1–12:31

This memorable chapter marks the beginning of the end for David, for he finally meets an enemy he cannot defeat. Previous accounts have focused almost exclusively on David's dealings with other people: his wars with the enemies of Israel, his struggle to overcome conflicts within the newly united kingdom, and his efforts to make Jerusalem the center of Israel's religious as well as political life. With chapter 11, David's battles turn inward. The focus of his energy turns from foreign and domestic matters to truly *internal* affairs, for David's greatest enemy is now himself. [The Structure of the Story]

With few exceptions (such as 2 Sam 6:9, after the Uzzah incident), David has revealed little or no self-doubt. At no time—according to the text—has he exhibited any sign of personal weakness; even his loud lamentation for Saul (2 Sam 1) is portrayed as a sign of strength and fidelity. To this point, David's commitment to the path Yahweh has chosen for him is unquestioned, and his personal righteousness is portrayed as a glowing example to all Israel—to this point, but not after. David's fall from the pinnacle of power has begun, and there are few interruptions in his downhill slide.

> **The Structure of the Story**
>
> Following the introduction in v. 1, the narrative movement of 11:2-27 falls naturally into four sections:
>
> 1. David's affair with Uriah's wife (11:2-5)
> 2. David's attempt to cover his sin by duping Uriah (11:6-13)
> 3. David's attempt to cover his sin by killing Uriah (11:14-25)
> 4. David's marriage to Uriah's widow (11:26-27)

COMMENTARY

Some writers (notably Kyle McCarter) argue that chapters 11 and 12 are so different in tone that they did not originally belong to the surrounding text but were added later, perhaps by a "prophetic school" that would have remembered the works and words of Nathan. There is indeed an obvious shift in the way David is portrayed, for with chapter 11 his deepest and darkest weakness comes to the fore, virtually eclipsing the shining image of the righteous warrior that has dominated the earlier David stories.

The account, however, is not unrelated to its context. The previous chapter has set the stage for David's adultery in two ways: first by describing the Ammonite wars that provide the historical setting, and second by emphasizing the motif of David's covenant loyalty (*ḥesed*). An incredibly different David emerges in chapter 11; though he shows scrupulous loyalty in the political arena, he proves faithless in dealing with his family and his most valiant soldiers.

"In the spring of the year" literally means "at the turning of the year." This has traditionally been interpreted to mean the springtime, after the winter rains have ended, leaving dry conditions more conducive to field maneuvers. Thus, spring is "the time when kings go out to battle." The NRSV, like most translations, glosses over the article attached to "kings" in the MT. The intended meaning could be "when *the kings* marched out to battle," with the Aramean kings of chapter 10 as the intended referent (cf. 10:6; 1 Chr 19:9).

If McCarter's contention is correct, the siege of the Ammonite capital Rabbah would have begun one year after the initial conflict, which may well have been in the spring.[1] Of note in this particular conflict is that David did not lead his troops into the field. He is no longer the king Israel had asked for, who would "go out before us and fight our battles" (1 Sam 8:20). David had often led Israel's armies prior to this point, but now he sends Joab to fight for him, along with "his officers and all Israel." The MT has "his servants," but many translators assume that the term denotes David's personal band of mercenary soldiers as opposed to the national militia, described as "all Israel."

The most significant statement of v. 1 rings like a bell in the reader's mind: "But David remained in Jerusalem." For the king to remain removed from battle was not disgraceful in itself; as David grew older, his subordinates insisted that he avoid military conflict for his own safety (2 Sam 21:15-17). The disgrace David acquires does not derive from what he did not do on the battlefield, but from what he did while away from the battlefield.

David's decline began with an afternoon nap. The narrator's careful location of David "on his couch" in the late afternoon implies that David is giving less attention to his work and showing more regard for his personal pleasure. The text suggests that David had a patio suite prepared on the roof of his palace, complete with a shaded bed. Rooftop rooms were common in the ancient Near

East, as they tended to be cooler, catching the afternoon breeze.
[Rooftop Rooms]

The king's house, presumably, was taller than the surrounding homes, allowing David an open view of activities on other roofs and in courtyards below. Many homes in ancient Israel had rooms for sleeping, eating, and storage on four sides, surrounding an open courtyard that was used for cooking, bathing, and other activities.

Rooftop Rooms

Typical homes in the ancient Near East had flat roofs constructed of horizontal beams overlaid with clay or mud plaster to form a solid floor for an open-air second story, surrounded by a low bannister. In nicer homes, the roof was covered with clay tiles or thin slabs of stone. Several examples of these rooftop rooms are found in Scripture.

For example, when the Israelite judge outwitted and killed the Moabite king Eglon, he did so in Eglon's "cool roof chamber," which was equipped with a bathroom (Judg 3:20-25). Many years later, the prophet Jeremiah predicted a time when lamentation would arise from every housetop in Moab (Jer 48:38).

When Saul journeyed in search of his father's donkeys and was invited to spend the night with Samuel, he slept on the roof (1 Sam 9:25-26).

Interior of a 3rd century house.
(Illustration Credit: Barclay Burns)

David's own rooftop adventures are recorded in 2 Sam 11, while 2 Sam 16:22 describes his son Absalom's activities on the same roof. To demonstrate power over his father, Absalom ordered a canopy to be pitched on the palace roof, where he engaged in public intercourse with David's concubines.

The memorable story of Elijah's friendship with a Shunamite family begins with the wife's desire to provide regular hospitality to the itinerant prophet by constructing "a small roof chamber" for his use (2 Kgs 4:10).

King Ahaz of Judah had pagan altars constructed in his "upper chamber." These were dismantled and thrown into the Wadi Kidron during Josiah's reform movement (2 Kgs 23:12).

Nebuchadnezzar, king of Babylon, was known to take walks on the roof of the royal palace in Babylon (Dan 4:29).

Israel's sages noted that "it is better to live in a corner of the housetop than in a house shared with a contentious wife" (Prov 21:9; 25:24), and one sad psalmist described himself as a lonely bird on the housetop (Ps 102:7).

Since material culture changed little in the way of home construction during the New Testament period, it is not unexpected that Jesus would tell his disciples to proclaim his teachings from the housetops (Matt 10:27). In his apocalyptic teaching, Jesus warned that those who were dwelling on the roof when the end came should not bother going in the house to collect any belongings (Matt 24:17; Mark 13:15; Luke 17:31).

Finally, the Apostle Peter ate, prayed, and slept on the roof of Simon the tanner's home in Joppa (Acts 10:9-16).

Modern flat-roofed house in Israel. (Credit: Scott Nash)

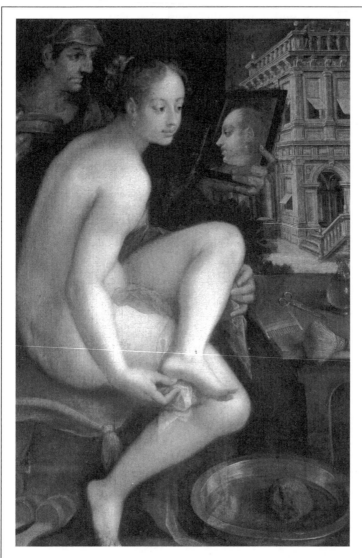

The Mysterious Bathsheba: A Popular Subject for Artists

Hans van Aachen, who takes his name from the city of his father, began his career around 1567. Like most Northern painters of this Mannerist period, he traveled to Rome and Florence for study. In 1592 he became a court painter to Emperor Rudolf II in Prague. He continued to work for the Emperor Matthais and painted another Bathsheba (1612-15, Ksthist. Museum Vienna), that, like this work, emphasized the nude body of the female figure. It is placed as the subject of the painting and has the elongated form that characterizes the Mannerist style internationally.

Francesco Hayez, an artist of the period known as Romanticism, also depicts the nude figure of Bathsheba. He places her slightly off center to enable the viewer to see past a room and through a doorway. There is a landscape visible out a window. This gives the painting a voyeuristic tone. We have surprised the nude Bathsheba as we arrive just outside her room.

(Left) Hans van Aachen (active 1567–1614). *Bathsheba in Her Bath.* 16th century. Louvre. Paris France. (Credit: Erich Lessing/Art Resource, NY)

(Right) Francesco Hayez (1832–83). *Bathsheba at Her Bath.* 16th century. Sotheby's, New York. (Credit: Cameraphoto/Art Resource, NY)

Nicer homes included multiple courtyards containing kitchens, wells, baths, and even shade trees. One would presume that homes built near the king's palace would belong to the upper class. Thus, when David spied a beautiful woman bathing, she was probably using a plastered bath dug into one of the courtyards of her home (cf. the apocryphal story of Susanna, who was spied upon while using a garden bath, Sus 1:15-27). [The Mysterious Bathsheba: A Popular Subject for Artists]

When David inquired about the woman, she was identified to him as "Bathsheba daughter of Eliam, the wife of Uriah the Hittite." The name Bathsheba could mean "daughter of Sheba," perhaps "daughter of an oath," or even "daughter of seven" (born

on the seventh day?). Of more importance are the other names
attached to Bathsheba. She is the daughter of Eliam and the wife of
Uriah the Hittite.

   According to the list in 2 Samuel 23:34-39, both Eliam the son
of Ahithophel the Gilonite *and* Uriah the Hittite belonged to
David's elite corps of loyal fighters known as "the thirty." [Uriah the
Hittite] While we cannot be certain that this is the same Eliam, there
is little question that Uriah was one of David's strongest and most
valiant supporters. The message is understated but clear. The adultery David is about to undertake involves not only Bathsheba
herself, but also the wife and daughter of men who had devoted
their lives to David's service.

Uriah the Hittite

Uriah's designation as a Hittite does not necessarily identify him as a first generation immigrant, though it does indicate his ethnic ancestry. The Hittite homeland in Central Anatolia was originally called "Hatti-land." A strong empire emerged there during the second millennium, but by 1200 BC it had degenerated into a series of small Neo-Hittite city-states surrounding the city of Carchemish, whose king still claimed to rule an empire. The Hittite states were largely overrun by the Arameans by the time David came on the scene, though small enclaves remained until the 8th century, when they were absorbed by Assyria.

Uriah's family may have emigrated south several generations before, perhaps settling into an aristocratic life in the Jebusite city of Jerusalem, then throwing their support to David when he conquered the city. Ezekiel may have preserved a tradition of Hittite influence in Jerusalem's founding when he said of the city, "Your father was an Amorite, your mother a Hittite" (Ezek 16:3). Uriah himself had a good Yahwistic name: "My light is Yahweh."

The nefarious action that led to David's decline is reported in the space of one short statement built on active verbs: "David sent messengers. . . . She came to him. . . . He lay with her. . . . Then she returned to her house" (v. 4). One would think that, as far as David was concerned, the illicit liaison was over, but the seeds of trouble had already been sown.

A parenthetical aside in v. 4 points out that Bathsheba was in the process of purifying herself after her menstrual cycle. [The Law of Purification] Some writers interpret the parenthesis to indicate that she had not completed her purification rites, thus compounding David's sin, since intercourse with a menstruating woman was forbidden. It is more likely, however, that the note is intended to indicate two things: first, that she could not possibly be pregnant by Uriah, and secondly, that she was at a point in her cycle that was favorable to conception.

With this parenthetical comment in mind, the reader is not surprised by v. 5, which notes that Bathsheba became pregnant and

---

The Law of Purification

The people of Israel, like other ancient neighbors, considered a woman to be ritually unclean during her menstrual period. A man was forbidden to have sexual intercourse or even to touch a woman during menstruation, lest he also become unclean. Thus, cultic regulations were developed to promote ritual purity.

Israel's rules regarding menstruation are found in Lev 15:19-24:

When a woman has a discharge of blood that is her regular discharge from her body, she shall be in her impurity for seven days, and whoever touches her shall be unclean until the evening. Everything upon which she lies during her impurity shall be unclean; everything also upon which she sits shall be unclean. Whoever touches her bed shall wash his clothes, and bathe in water, and be unclean until the evening. Whoever touches anything upon which she sits shall wash his clothes, and bathe in water, and be unclean until the evening; whether it is the bed or anything upon which she sits, when he touches it he shall be unclean until the evening. If any man lies with her, and her impurity falls on him, he shall be unclean seven days; and every bed on which he lies shall be unclean.

sent word of it to the king. David's dallying had now become a more serious matter. David had sufficient power and popularity that his political survival would have been assured even if he had forcibly taken Bathsheba from Uriah. Israel had strict laws concerning adultery, even calling for the death penalty for both parties (Lev 20:10; Deut 22:22), but it is unlikely that any court in Israel had enough authority to order the king's execution. Indeed, it seems that public shaming was a more common punishment for adultery in the preexilic period (Hos 2:2-13; Jer 3:6-14). David, however, had risen to power on the strength of his pure persona, and he did not want it tarnished; so he sought to conceal his sin. Unfortunately, David's effort to preserve the appearance of purity led to deeper and deeper internal corruption.

David's first attempt at a cover-up (vv. 6-13) crumbled before the loyalty and piety of his servant soldier Uriah. Brought home from the battlefield on the pretext of reporting news of the war to David (vv. 6-7), Uriah refused David's invitation to go home and "wash his feet" (v. 8), probably intended as a sexual innuendo common among bantering soldiers ("feet" was sometimes used as a euphemism for genitals; cf. Ezek 16:25). The narrator carefully has David ask after the "well-being" of Joab, the soldiers, and the war. Three times he uses the word *šalôm*, but the man who speaks of peace and welfare has adultery and murder on his mind.

Some scholars suggest that Uriah had heard enough court gossip to know about David's affair with Bathsheba. Thus, he was forcing David's hand by pretending ignorance and refusing to enter his own home. Uriah's public explanation, however, does not presume such knowledge. Uriah claims that he is only doing what good soldiers ought to do: He is keeping himself pure during a time of holy war (v. 11; cf. Deut 23:10-15; 23:9-14; Josh 3:5). [Troublesome Terminology] David had once been scrupulous about observing the same practice (1 Sam 21:5 [MT v. 6]), but now he stands condemned by a subordinate whose piety far outshines his leader.

The depth of Uriah's convictions is underscored by his oath: "As you live, and as your soul lives, I will not do such a thing." The form of this oath varies from the more common practice of calling first upon Yahweh's life, as well as the life of the person being addressed (cf. 1 Sam 20:3; 25:26; 2 Sam 15:21). Thus, some scholars avoid the anomalous tautology by emending the text to read, "As Yahweh lives, and as your soul lives." The force of the oath is clear in any case, and David's carefully cultivated image is eclipsed by the bright piety of Uriah the Hittite, whose name means "My light is Yahweh."

Troublesome Terminology

AΩ The specific intent of v. 11 is open to interpretation. Some assume that Uriah's claim that "the ark and Israel and Judah remain in booths" is a reference to the tents of their battle camp, presumably with the ark among them (cf. 1 Sam 4:3-11).

However, the word *sukkôt* routinely refers to booths made of branches, not to tents. Thus, some interpreters suggest that the action took place during the annual Feast of Tabernacles, when the Hebrews were expected to construct outdoor shelters made of branches and to dwell in them during the festival. This would have provided Uriah an additional reason to avoid entering his house.

This explanation seems unsatisfactory, however, as we know very little about how (or if) the Feast of Tabernacles was celebrated in the 10th century BC. So others propose to translate *sukkôt* as a proper noun for the place name Succoth. The Valley of Succoth appears to have been an important strategic forward base for David during his eastern and northern campaigns. However, if Succoth is to be located near Deir 'Allā, as commonly assumed, it would have been some twenty-five miles north of Rabbah, more than a day's march and probably too far away to serve effectively as a ready station for reserves.

Whatever the specific social background might have been, the implication is clear: Uriah is determined to do the right thing, and will not be influenced even by David's encouragement, presents, or deceptions.

Uriah's determination to abstain from sexual intercourse apparently did not extend to drinking wine. David invited him to stay a day longer and "made him drunk" in a last attempt to loosen Uriah's qualms about sleeping with his wife, but again he was unsuccessful; even inebriation did not alter Uriah's inhibitions (v. 12). A younger David had found little difficulty in defeating the Philistine giant Goliath or any army sent against him, but he could not defeat the will of unyielding Uriah.

The third episode of this sordid story reveals an ugly and desperate side of David, who determined that if he could not control Uriah, he would kill him. The motif of an unsuspecting messenger bearing his own death warrant is well known in ancient literature, but that does not necessarily imply that this story is contrived. [The Trusting Soldier] The text does not specify that the letter was sealed to prevent Uriah from reading it, but seals and wax were common in the ancient world and this clandestine letter would be an unlikely exception. Nor does the text reveal whether Uriah was literate, as both David and Joab apparently were. The narrator's point is built on the tremendous irony of the situation: David takes advantage of Uriah's sterling character to entrust him with the order for his own death.

The message was simple: Uriah was to be assigned to the front lines of the fiercest battle, then deserted by his compatriots and left

The Trusting Soldier

The motif of the trusting soldier who delivers his own death warrant is common in ancient literature. Of several examples, a story from the *Iliad* (6.168-190) is most illustrative. There, the Argive king Proteus suspects a young man named Bellerephon of having committed adultery with his wife, the queen. He contrives Bellerephon's death by having him carry a coded message to the king of Lycia (who just happens to be the queen's father). The message asks the king to execute Bellerephon.

as an easy target for the Ammonites. Joab followed the spirit of David's instructions, but not the letter. If he had adhered to David's plan, Joab's soldiers would have known that their leader had willingly betrayed one of his own best men. It would be difficult to regain their trust afterward. So Joab adopted a different strategy, simply sending Uriah's contingent of soldiers to a spot where the battle was so thick and the odds of survival so poor that he was bound to be killed sooner or later (vv. 14-17). The upside of this scheme is that Joab's purpose was not known to the other soldiers. The downside is that many other troops also died to cover Uriah's gallant fight to the finish.

Thus we begin another game of cover-up. To protect his own reputation, since he knew that the military tactics leading to Uriah's death were patently foolhardy, Joab fashioned his report to David so that the bad news was followed by a comment designed to soothe the king's ire: "Your servant Uriah the Hittite is dead too" (vv. 18-21).

Many writers have called this portion of the text into question, finding it preposterous to imagine that Joab would know exactly how David would respond. The LXX has a long addition after v. 22, containing roughly the same material found in the MT at vv. 20-21. Some writers presume that both should be present: Joab's anticipation of David's response and David's recitation of precisely the issue that Joab predicted. Others propose that something was lost from the MT, leading to the millstone story's being put in Joab's mouth, when it rightly belongs to David. [A Lesson from History] Thus, they would reorganize the text, moving vv. 20b-21 to follow v. 24.

A Lesson from History

By his own testimony, Joab knew the danger of pressing the battle too close to the wall. He also knew that David would recognize this tactical blunder of the most basic sort. Approaching too close to a defended city wall puts the invading army in easy reach of enemy archers, especially when the fighting is near the city gate (as in 2 Sam 11:23-24), where the walls are thickest and the fortified towers highest. Pressing the combat to the wall itself brings other potential enemies into play, persons who should never have the opportunity to strike a blow. In Israel, the proto-typical example of this unwarranted danger stemmed from a battle recorded in Judg 9:50-55:

Then Abimelech went to Thebez, and encamped against Thebez, and took it. But there was a strong tower within the city, and all the men and women and all the lords of the city fled to it and shut themselves in; and they went to the roof of the tower. Abimelech came to the tower, and fought against it, and came near to the entrance of the tower to burn it with fire. But a certain woman threw an upper millstone on Abimelech's head, and crushed his skull. Immediately he called to the young man who carried his armor and said to him, "Draw your sword and kill me, so people will not say about me, 'A woman killed him.' " So the young man thrust him through, and he died. When the Israelites saw that Abimelech was dead, they all went home.

Despite Abimelech's desire that he not be remembered for having met his death at the hands of a woman, that is precisely what happened. Whether the recitation of this historical excerpt belongs to Joab or David—or both—the message is clear.

Even with the textual confusion, the narrator's intent is apparent: Joab had the messenger hold back the news of Uriah's death until the end, knowing that it would assuage David's predictable anger over the needless loss of so many men (the LXX puts the number of casualties at eighteen). The report of the valiant Uriah's death would remind David that the other deaths were not needless, after all. The other soldiers' lives were spent in covering David's intentional elimination of Uriah.

The message had its intended effect. David instructed the messenger to repeat these words to Joab: "Do not let this matter trouble you, for the sword devours now one and now another; press your attack on the city, and overthrow it" (v. 25). In addition, David bade the messenger to encourage Joab. This note may suggest that the messenger in question was not a routine runner, but a close confidant of Joab; one who could be trusted to accurately convey Joab's message and who was close enough in stature to offer reassurance to the general.

David's comforting reply to Joab blames the loss of Uriah's life on the vicissitudes of war, in which "the sword devours now one and now another." The most telling phrase in David's response, however, is obscured by virtually all translations. "Do not let this matter trouble you" (NRSV) translates a phrase that literally means "Do not let this thing be evil in your eyes." David wanted to avoid thinking of himself or of Joab as having done anything evil in taking Uriah's life. He wanted it to appear that the death of Uriah was nothing more than business as usual in a time of war.

The final scene in this ignoble account is a brief summary of what happened in the aftermath of Uriah's death. Bathsheba mourned for her husband, and David unquestionably joined the public mourning for his "mighty man," even as he had led the mourning for Saul (2 Sam 1), for Abner (2 Sam 3:31-39), and presumably for Ishbaal (2 Sam 4:9-12). The typical mourning period was seven days (Gen 50:10; 1 Sam 31:13; 1 Chr 10:12; Jdt 16:24). The thirty-day mourning periods for Aaron and Moses (Num 20:29; Deut 34:8) were the exception rather than the rule.

As the account of David's affair with Bathsheba is told with an economy of language, so is the report of his marriage. Once the period of mourning was over, "David sent and brought her to his house, and she became his wife, and bore him a son" (v. 27a). To all outward appearances, David has succeeded with his cover-up. At least nine months have passed. He has gotten away with his reputation intact.

It is a plausible story: David's valiant friend Uriah is dead, he comforts the widow, they fall in love and are quickly married. All appears to be quiet and at peace, but the latter half of v. 27 shatters the apparent calm with a simple editorial observation: "But the thing that David had done displeased the LORD" (NRSV).

Some commentators append v. 27b to the following story, but from a literary perspective it is also appropriate to read it as the narrative conclusion of chapter 11, a brief insight into Yahweh's judgment of the matter. Grammatically, the phrase can be attached to the opening sentence of chapter 12, and it is clearly designed to serve as a transition between the two. As a transition statement, it belongs thematically to both units. From the perspective of chapter 11, this short statement is of special significance, as it clues the Hebrew reader to understand the significance of David's contention in v. 25 that Joab should not let Uriah's murder seem evil in his eyes.

Once again, most modern translations mask the sharpness of the narrator's literary skill, for the statement conveying divine displeasure literally says, "But the thing that David had done *was evil in the eyes of Yahweh.*" The proximity of this statement to v. 25 and the similarity of vocabulary make it evident that the author is drawing an intentional contrast: David may think what he has done is not evil, and he may tell Joab not to consider the thing to be evil, "but the thing that David had done was evil in the eyes of Yahweh." [Two Similar Statements]

With this closing reminder that Yahweh has not left the scene, though he remains in the narrative background, the reader is prepared for chapter 12, in which Nathan draws open the curtain on Yahweh's judgment of David's sin.

Two Similar Statements

AΩ A more literal translation of these two statements reveals the artistry of the Hebrew author.

David's Message to Joab	**Yahweh's View of the Matter**
(2 Sam 11:25)	(2 Sam 11:27b)
NRSV: "Do not let this matter trouble you."	NRSV: "But the thing David had done displeased the LORD."
Literal translation: "Do not let this thing be evil in your eyes."	Literal translation: "But the thing David had done was evil in the eyes of Yahweh."

CONNECTIONS

Maybe David's problem began with too much prosperity. With the beginning of chapter 11, he seems bored. David had worked long and hard to get to where he was as the king of all Israel. Second Samuel 3 tells how he was crowned king over the southern tribes, which he ruled from Hebron. Chapters 4–5 tell how he was finally crowned king of the northern tribes and how he conquered Jerusalem and made it his own personal city. Chapters 6–7 tell how he worked to make Jerusalem the governmental and religious center of the country and how the LORD promised to establish his descendants upon the throne.

David had arrived. There were still things to do, of course. Second Samuel 8 describes a series of wars in which David fought hard to consolidate his kingdom. Chapter 9 tells how he brought internal peace to Israel by showing kindness to Saul's descendants, and chapter 10 records other military victories that established an external peace.

David had set up his official state agencies with strong supporters to lead them. With the borders finally safe, he had turned over military operations to his nephew Joab, who was his chief general. David did not even go out to war any longer. At last, he could sit back and enjoy just being king, and that is where the trouble began. David seems to have become detached from his people, and detached from his personal relationship with God as well. A crisis was looming, but his state of political and personal ennui left him unawares and unprepared.

The spark that put his crisis into motion was the sight of a woman named Bathsheba, who just happened to be bathing in the late afternoon as David walked restlessly along the balconies of his palace. It was lust at first sight, but it was also more than that. David's interest in Bathsheba could not have been based on a need for companionship or sex alone, for he already had a sizeable harem of wives and concubines. According to the record, David had taken *seven wives* when he ruled in Hebron (2 Sam 3:2-5, 13-16), and he added "*more wives and concubines*" after establishing himself in Jerusalem (2 Sam 5:13-16). There is nothing about David's situation that modern readers could find acceptable; but in the ancient world, the size of a king's harem was a visible symbol of his power, and none of his wives or concubines could refuse him.

So it was not a frustrated libido that led David to send a messenger down the street to Bathsheba's house with instructions for her to come and visit him. Maybe it was the need for another conquest that drove him, or the need to exercise his power. Maybe

David, now in middle age, felt a personal need to prove that he could still win the heart of a beautiful young woman. Maybe it was romance he was after. We simply do not know for sure.

Nor do we know what Bathsheba was thinking that night. Did she come willingly to her illustrious neighbor, or out of fear and obedience to the great king? Was she tired of her husband Uriah's spending so much time away from home on the battlefield and ready to seek greener pastures for herself? Did she cooperate willingly with David, or was she the victim of a royal rape, a coercive abuse of power? The Bible suggests that Bathsheba did fall in love with David, that they had a fiery romance. Bathsheba became the love of David's life and his number-one wife. Of all David's wives, Bathsheba is the one who acts like a queen. [Bathsheba in Literature]

But this story is about the beginning of it all, about that first heart-in-your-throat night of mixed emotions and blinding desire

This illustration imagines that David was playing the harp, rather than napping, prior to his encounter with Bathsheba.

Julius Schnoor von Carolsfeld. *David and Bathsheba.* 19th century. Woodcut. *Das Buch der Bucher in Bilden.* (Credit: Dover Pictorial Archive Series)

Bathsheba in Literature

The Bathsheba motif became particularly popular during the Renaissance, with its positive attitude toward sensuality. Explorations of the story moved in several directions. Francis Sabie used the incident as a pretext for writing erotic poetry ("David and Bathsheba" 1596), while authors such as Remy Belleau (*Les Amours de David et de Bersabee*, 1572) and George Peele (*David and Fair Bethsabe*, 1599) reveled in her beauty. In Peele's play, Bathsheba warns of her own dangerous attractiveness:

> Let not my beauties fire,
> Enflame unstaied desire,
> Nor pierce any bright eye,
> That wandreth lightly (ll. 34-37).

Peele's play *David and Fair Bethsabe* also explored the seductiveness of sexuality and the effects of a father's sins on the children and, unlike many other works, did so without ponderous moralizing. In the Middle Ages, the David-Bathsheba incident had provided grist for a widespread moralistic, even "anti-woman," tradition, as the story was used to warn of the dangers of women. Marbod, bishop of Rennes (c. 1035–1123), for example, had written, "Countless are the traps which the scheming enemy has set throughout the world's paths and plains: but among them the greatest—and the one scarcely anyone can evade—Is woman. . . . Who led astray David the holy and who led wise Solomon astray with sweet charm to that one turned adulterer and the other committed sacrilege—who but seductive woman?" (*The Book with Ten Chapters*, III.1, 4).

In the 19th century the Bathsheba episode appeared indirectly in several notable literary works. Thomas Hardy alludes to her in *Tess of the D'Urbervilles* when Angel Clare, remembering Bathsheba's transition from adulteress to queen, regrets having deserted Tess because of her sexual relations. In Hardy's *Far From the Madding Crowd*, the heroine Bathsheba Everdene bears the shadow of her biblical namesake, as a woman who suffers horribly in ill-fated love affairs before finally finding redemption and happiness.

In the 20th century the Bathsheba story has been treated by French playwright Andre Gide in his *Bethsabe* (1908) and in Hungarian playwright Karoly Pap's *Batseba* (1940), while Gladys Schmitt's historical novel *David the King* explores the feelings of the powerless woman before the advances of her king. Modern Hebrew writer Moshe Shamir's novel *Kivsat harash* ("The Poor Man's Lamb," translated into English as *The Hittite Must Die*, 1964) tells the David-Bathsheba story from Uriah's point of view. Shamir used the biblical story to reflect on the abuse of power he saw in the state of Israel in the early 1950s.

and heavy breathing. David sent for beautiful Bathsheba, and she went to him. One thing led to another, and they wound up in bed together. One thing led to another, and a child was conceived (11:1-5).

When the message came from Bathsheba reporting her pregnancy, the implications were complex. Under normal circumstances, David's indiscretion might have gone unnoticed, but now Bathsheba was pregnant and her husband had been out of town for many weeks as he fought the king's war against the Ammonites. When the baby arrived, everyone would know it was not Uriah's. Palace insiders would know that the child belonged to David.

David was nothing if not a quick thinker. He developed a swift plan to recall Uriah and send him home to his wife, but the ship of David's plans foundered on the rocky promontory of Uriah's piety. Despite his constant labeling as a Hittite, Uriah had a name and a faith that belonged to Yahweh alone. Uriah was a man of such honor and principle that he did not think it was right for him to sleep with his wife while Israel was still in a state of war, while his colleagues were still encamped on the battlefield, endangering their lives (11:10-11).

David was well aware that the rules of holy war called for soldiers to avoid intercourse until the war was over. Early in his career, David had insisted that all his men remain celibate whenever they were on a military outing (1 Sam 21:5 [MT v. 6]). Now, however, David wants Uriah to break the rule. Both David's attempt to gain Uriah's cooperation and his effort to ply the loyal soldier with drink were unsuccessful in persuading Uriah to betray his convictions (11:12-13).

One would think that David might learn something from Uriah, that he would admit his mistakes and try to do the right thing. Instead, blinded by lust and power, David fell deeper and deeper into the pit of deception and darkness. He plotted Uriah's death and sent his orders by the innocent man's own hand (11:14-15). The dependable soldier delivered David's message, and then faithfully followed Joab's orders to a certain death (11:16-25).

Bathsheba lamented for her fallen husband, the narrator tells us, and as soon as the official period of mourning was over, David brought her to the palace and married her (11:26-27). And that was that, or so it seemed.

But all was not as it seemed. Though Yahweh is virtually absent from the story (except as the focus of Uriah's piety), he is not unaware of David's sin. The story closes with a pair of phrases that draw an intentional contrast between the way David sees himself and the way Yahweh sees him. David insisted to Joab that he should not let Joab's murder seem evil in his eyes (11:25), but "the thing that David did was evil in the eyes of Yahweh" (11:27b). The same David who once was famed as a man after God's own heart has now become so blinded by personal greed that he can no longer recognize evil when he sees it.

The prophets would later warn against such a decrepit spiritual condition, bemoaning Israel's inability to distinguish between good

---

Spiritual Blindness

Isaiah accused Israel of spiritual perversion with these words:

"Ah, you who call evil good and good evil,
who put darkness for light and light for darkness,
who put bitter for sweet and sweet for bitter!" (Isa 5:20)

Amos, a contemporary of Isaiah, broached the same subject in a call for faithfulness:

"Seek good and not evil,
    that you may live;
and so the LORD, the God of hosts, will be with you,
    just as you have said.
Hate evil and love good,
    and establish justice in the gate;
it may be that the LORD, the God of hosts,
    will be gracious to the remnant of Joseph." (Amos 5:14-15)

Micah, another 8th century prophet, spoke of those who "hate the good and love the evil, who tear the skin off my people, and the flesh off their bones" (Mic 3:2).

Jeremiah, who lived in Jerusalem just before the exile, had little hope that God's people would come to their senses:

"For my people are foolish,
    they do not know me;
they are stupid children,
    they have no understanding.
They are skilled in doing evil,
    but do not know how to do good." (Jer 4:22)

Later, in the postexilic period, the prophet Malachi charged the Israelites with being so obtuse that they accused God of having good and evil confused:

"You have wearied the LORD with your words. Yet you say, 'How have we wearied him?' By saying, 'All who do evil are good in the sight of the LORD, and he delights in them.' Or by asking, 'Where is the God of justice?' " (Mal 2:17).

The dichotomy of good and evil is also a frequent theme in the New Testament (see Matt 5:45; 7:11; 12:34-35; 13:38; Luke 6:45; 11:13; 16:25; John 5:29; Rom 3:8; 7:19, 21; 12:9, 21; 14:16; 16:19; 2 Cor 5:10; 1 Thess 5:15; Heb 5:14; 1 Pet 3:10-11, 17; 3 John 1:11).

and evil. [Spiritual Blindness] It is no wonder that McCarter and others would attribute this text to a "prophetic" source. Israel's people were not alone in their failure to follow God's way. Even the man after God's heart was subject to temptation and terrible deeds.

The most amazing thing about this troublesome tale is the fact that it exists in Scripture at all. The author doesn't have to tell this story (the Chronicler *did not*), but he lets us see both sides of David, warts and all. [Was It All David's Fault?] The same author has told us that David is a man after God's own heart (1 Sam 13:14), that God chose David to be king (1 Sam 16:1, 11-13), and that God has been with David in his life and work (1 Sam 16:18; 18:14; 2 Sam 5:10).

Now the narrator tells us that David has lost his way and is no longer following the LORD as he should. The first clue is in the first verse of chapter 11, where we are told that it is the time of year when kings go out to battle, *but David remained in Jerusalem.* Instead of leading his soldiers into battle, David led one soldier's wife to bed. When David summons the soldier home in hopes of disguising his actions, Uriah proves to have more character and devotion than David—and Uriah is not even an ethnic Israelite. The storyteller consistently tells us that Uriah was a Hittite. Yet he is the one who proves most faithful to the God of Israel.

Was It All David's Fault?

Who was guilty? Surprisingly, many rabbinical stories attempt to exonerate David of guilt. According to *Sanhedrin* 107a, God chose to test David to see if he was worthy of having prayers offered in his name. While Bathsheba was washing her hair behind a large vessel, Satan appeared to David in the guise of a bird. David shot at the bird, but his arrow shattered the vessel, exposing Bathsheba to David.

Some rabbis argue for David's innocence on the basis that Bathsheba was not technically married when he took her. This derives from a convoluted rationale based on 1 Sam 17:18 and used to claim that soldiers who went into battle left a bill of divorce with their wives (*Shabbat* 56a).

Yet others blame Uriah for David's uncomfortable predicament, since he disobeyed David's royal order to go home to his wife and was therefore guilty of treason (*Shabbat* 56a; *Qiddushin* 43a). These arguments fall into the same trap that ensnared David: They substitute human rationalization for God's law. Uriah (whose theophoric name testifies to the light of Yahweh) is the only shining example of righteousness in this story; he is clearly blameless. David is the guilty one. Any attempt to relieve David of responsibility is misguided at best.

One tradition admits David's guilt but assumes that he was *predestined* to commit adultery in order to teach others the way of repentance through his personal example and through writings such as Ps 51 (*Aboda Zara* 4a-5a; and the midrash to Ps 51:3).

Other traditions focus on David's guilt and the tragic consequences for his family. According to *Yoma* 22b, David paid for the Bathsheba incident with a series of tragedies involving not one but four children: the child conceived as a result of their adultery (who died shortly after birth), Tamar (who was raped by her half-brother), Amnon (murdered by Absalom for raping Tamar), and Absalom (killed by Joab—against David's wishes—in a failed coup).

An interesting tradition connects the Bathsheba incident to the construction of the temple. According to *Aggadas Bereishis* 38, David was sick and bedridden for thirteen years, during which time he wept so profusely over his adultery that his bedding had to be changed seven times daily. When he recovered, David stood up and transmitted to the people a scroll containing instructions for building the temple.

Both Joab and David reveal an ability to learn from history. They know, for example, the tactical foolishness of pressing a fight beneath a fortified wall that is crowned with archers; they learned this from the story of Abimelech. Yet they do not learn from the spiritual mistakes of Israel in the wilderness or during the period of the judges. They do not learn from Samson, or from Hophni and Phinehas, or from Saul—all of whom chose their ways over God's way, and all of whom met a bad end. David and Joab willingly learn military lessons but not spiritual ones, and when confronted by a master teacher, they kill him.

This dark story reminds modern readers that sin often takes root in idleness. An old saying suggests that "an idle mind is the devil's playground." If David had been doing what good kings were supposed to do, he would have been winning a war instead of wooing a woman who belonged to another.

The story also illustrates how one sin often leads to another. Just as one lie often requires another for cover, attempting to hide one sin will inevitably lead to another, sometimes greater sin. In David's case, the sin of lust led to the sin of adultery, which led to a wrongful attempt at deception and, ultimately, murder. When Jesus observed that one who lusted was also guilty of adultery (Matt 5:28), he knew that one sin would inevitably lead to the other.

Finally, this story insists that we can hide our sins from others, but not from God. When we fail, it is not a cover-up we need, but confession. Drunk with power, perhaps, and thinking that a king was entitled to whatever he wanted, David refused to confess his wrongdoing and to repent. He stopped being a giver and became a taker, as Samuel had predicted (1 Sam 8). David may have thought for a while that he had successfully painted over his sin, but the story's final words remind us that Yahweh knows, and the matter is not by any means finished. "The thing that David did was evil in the eyes of Yahweh." Thus, we are prepared to hear the prophet speak in chapter 12.

NOTE

[1] P. Kyle McCarter, *II Samuel* (AB 9; Garden City: Doubleday, 1984), 285.

NATHAN CONFRONTS THE KING

12:1-15a

COMMENTARY

The last phrase of chapter 11 ("But the thing that David did was evil in the eyes of Yahweh") serves also as a transition to chapter 12, for it is grammatically connected to the opening words of 12:1 ("And Yahweh sent Nathan to David"). Thus, many scholars draw a line after 11:27a and begin chapter 12 with 11:27b. It is helpful to remember that modern chapter divisions were unknown when these narratives were composed and edited; the editorial comment found in 11:27 serves as an artful transition between the story of David's sin and the account of his comeuppance. [Editorial Comments in the Succession Narrative] The reader is to understand that Yahweh's displeasure with David's actions in the Bathsheba-Uriah incident is the direct cause of Yahweh's actions in chapter 12 and beyond.

Editorial Comments in the Succession Narrative

In an influential essay on the Succession Narrative, Gerhard von Rad argued that 2 Sam 11:27b is one of only three comments to be found in the SN for which the Deuteronomistic editors were responsible. The others are found in 12:24 and 17:14. One classic characteristic of the SN is that Yahweh's activities and thoughts remain largely in the background. In these three brief comments, however, the narrator's perception of Yahweh's judgment is brought into the foreground.

2 Sam 11:27: "When the mourning was over, David sent and brought her to his house, and she became his wife, and bore him a son. *But the thing that David had done displeased the LORD.*"

2 Sam 12:24: "Then David consoled his wife Bathsheba, and went to her, and lay with her; and she bore a son, and he named him Solomon. *The LORD loved him.*"

2 Sam 17:14: Absalom and all the men of Israel said, "The counsel of Hushai the Archite is better than the counsel of Ahithophel." *For the LORD had ordained to defeat the good counsel of Ahithophel, so that the LORD might bring ruin on Absalom.*

Von Rad's observation spotlights the narrator's belief that Yahweh's sovereignty does not cease, even when his people are disobedient.

Gerhard von Rad *The Problem of the Hexateuch and Other Essays*, trans. E. W. Trueman Dicken, from 1958 German ed. (New York: McGraw-Hill, 1958).

Those actions are expressed through the prophet Nathan, who first appeared in chapter 7. There, he was the medium of Yahweh's landmark promise to David that he would begin a dynastic house destined to rule over Israel forever. One would assume, then, that Nathan was in good standing with the king, and would have relatively easy access to him.

Nathan's initial message to David takes the form of a parable. [Nathan's Strategy] The Talmud calls it a *māšāl,* a broad term that could encompass any sort of short story or riddle told for the purposes of instruction. Some question the use of the formal term "parable," but it is perhaps the best term we have. Some recent scholars prefer to categorize the story as a "juridical parable," since it is found in a legal context. Yahweh has put David on trial with Nathan as the prosecutor, though David does not know it at first. The purpose of the parable is to describe the guilty party's crime in parabolic fashion, so that the targeted hearer will pass judgment on the guilty and thus condemn himself. [Other Juridical Parables]

Two men are sharply contrasted. One is rich, powerful, and arrogant. The other is poor, helpless, and humble. The rich man has more animals in his flocks and herds than he can count, while the poor man has only one lamb, so precious that he loves it like one of his children. When the wealthy man was obligated to entertain a passing traveler, he stole the poor man's only lamb, slaughtered it, and fed it to his guest (vv. 2-4).

Nathan's Strategy

Nathan's strategy in confronting David's power takes the following approach:

1. The telling of a parable designed to arouse David's moral outrage over the rich and powerful taking what they want from the poor and innocent (12:1-4)
2. David's anticipated expression of anger, and his suggested sentence (12:5-6)
3. Nathan's identification of David as the guilty party, coupled with an oracle of Yahweh designed to clarify David's culpability and justify Yahweh's sentence (12:7-12)
4. David's confession of guilt, and Nathan's communication of Yahweh's response (12:13-14)

Other Juridical Parables

The Bible contains at least three other parables designed to elicit a response of self-judgment. In 2 Sam 14:1-20, David is again the intended target: After David banished Absalom for killing his brother Amnon, Joab persuaded a "wise woman of Tekoa" to come before David, pretending that she had a case for him to decide. Her story was that she had two sons, one of whom killed the other in a misunderstanding. Now the community sought her remaining son's life, and she pleaded with the king to restore him to her. When David agreed, the woman pointed out that David had not been so willing to restore his son Absalom.

In 1 Kgs 20:39-40, an unnamed prophet caught King Ahab's attention with a parable designed to criticize him for allowing Ben-hadad to go free after having taken him prisoner in a great victory over the Syrians. The parable asked the king's judgment on a soldier who had lost a prisoner through inattention.

The prophet Isaiah used a poetic parable with great effectiveness to lead his hearers to condemn themselves. I Isa 5:1-7, often referred to as "the song of the vineyard," Isaiah sang of a beloved friend who had devoted much energy, expense, and patience to preparing, planting, and cultivating a field of choice, importedgrapes. After much work, however, the vineyard produced only worthless fruit. The congregation joined Isaiah in passing judgment on this worthless vineyard before the prophet pulled the trigger, identifying the vintner as Yahweh and his unproductive vineyard as Israel.

The characters in this story are so clearly drawn and the rich man's behavior so contemptible that David responds with an oath formula ("As the LORD lives") and does not hesitate to declare the wealthy one to be patently guilty and worthy of punishment (v. 5). Unfortunately, the specific meaning of David's comments is not at all clear.

David called the guilty landowner "a son of death" (*ben-māwet*), which may have been intended as a strongly negative appellative, much like the modern invective "son of a bitch." Kyle McCarter opts for "fiend of hell," comparing this expression, along with "man of death" (*'iš-māwet*; 19:26), to the disparaging title "son of hell" or "man of hell" (*wĕiš habbĕlîyāʿal*) and *'îš bĕlîyaʿal*) in 16:7 and 20:1.[1] Most translations, including the NRSV, interpret "son of death" as one who "deserves to die," but there are no good parallels using "son of māwet" in a similar way.

Reading "son of death" as an invective seems most appropriate and allows us to avoid the difficult problem of David's passing two dissimilar sentences: one of death and the other of a relatively small financial penalty. The comment in v. 5 is not intended to label the rich man as worthy of death, but as a poor excuse for a human being. The judicial sentence is found in v. 6. There, David called for the guilty party to restore the stolen lamb fourfold (MT). Most versions of the LXX and several other versions have *seven*fold. Some writers suggest that the term "sevenfold" was original, suggesting a "perfect" or "complete" restitution, and perhaps even working into the verdict a veiled reference to Bathsheba's name ("Bathsheba" could mean "daughter of seven"). Those who take "sevenfold" as original assume that the MT was adjusted to correlate with the case law found in Exodus 22:1 (MT 21:37), where the penalty for stealing a sheep was the restitution of *four* sheep, not seven. [The Penalty for Sheep-Stealing] Some of the rabbis taught that David's fourfold payment was in the tragedies affecting four of his children: the first son of Bathsheba, his daughter Tamar, and his sons Amnon and Absalom (*Yoma* 22b).

The narrator carefully has David comment on the malefactor's character as well as his actions. He is a scoundrel and should be punished not only because of his action in stealing the sheep, but "because he had no pity."

The Penalty for Sheep-Stealing

According to the casuistic laws found in Exodus, the penalties for sheep-stealing could range from double restitution to a lifetime of slavery:

When someone steals an ox or a sheep, and slaughters it or sells it, the thief shall pay five oxen for an ox, and four sheep for a sheep. The thief shall make restitution, but if unable to do so, shall be sold for the theft. When the animal, whether ox or donkey or sheep, is found alive in the thief's possession, the thief shall pay double. (Exod 22:1)

It was at this point that David was prepared to *get* the point, probably at the end of Nathan's pointed finger: "*You are the man!*" With these two Hebrew words ("you [are] the-man"), David learned that the royal judge and the rich oppressor were one and the same. The crestfallen king's words of judgment now rested on his own head.

The narrator's literary artistry boldly highlights David's hypocrisy and ingratitude, contrasting Yahweh's benevolent actions with David's destructive deeds. If David was once a man after God's own heart, those days were past.

Following a formal marker of prophetic speech ("Thus says the LORD, the God of Israel"), the author details how Nathan spoke in the very name of Yahweh, using a striking combination of first-person and second-person verbs to remind David (who seems to have forgotten) of the shocking nature of his sin: "*I* anointed you. . . . *I* rescued you. . . . *I* gave you. . . . *I* would have added as much more" (vv. 7-8). In contrast, *you* despised the word of the LORD. . . . *You* have struck down Uriah. . . . *You* have taken his wife. . . . *You* have killed him (v. 9).

Yahweh's sentence is then introduced using a third-person verb to mark the transition from accusation to judgment: "The sword shall never depart from your house" (v. 10). That it is Yahweh who wields the punishing blade is clarified by another series of first-person verbs: "*I* will raise up trouble. . . . *I* will take your wives . . . and give them to your neighbor" (v. 11). David's sin was committed in secret, but his punishment would be a matter of public record (v. 12).

The reference to anointing probably points to the anticipatory anointing in 1 Samuel 16:13 more so than the two official ceremonies described in 2 Samuel 2:4 and 5:3. David's anointing at the hands of Samuel was clearly described as Yahweh's doing, while the others were primarily acts of the state. Also, Nathan's comment about Yahweh's anointing precedes his reminder of how Yahweh delivered David from Saul, suggesting that it is 1 Samuel 16:13 he has in mind.

The only textual evidence that David took Saul's small harem for himself is found in v. 8, where Saul's wives appear in a series of deific gifts arranged from lesser to greater as a way of emphasizing Yahweh's generosity. [Powerful Rhetoric] The overwhelming nature of this recitation of divine beneficence is also marked by the dual

[43.5] Powerful Rhetoric

AΩ Here is a rather literal translation of v. 8:

"And I gave to you the house of your master, and the women of your master into your bosom,
and I gave to you the house of Israel and Judah,
and if [that was] too little,
I would have added to you things like these
and [more] things like these."

mention of the word *house*, which hints at the dynastic promise of chapter 7. David was given the house of his master (Saul), along with leadership of the house of Israel and Judah. Yahweh had also promised to David a "house" of his own, an enduring dynasty in Jerusalem. The pointed failure of Nathan to mention that house (which he himself had predicted) may suggest that David's future is now in jeopardy.

The "word of the LORD" that David had despised (v. 9) refers to the law, which David had broken at several points, violating the commandments against coveting, adultery, theft, and murder. Enough time had passed for the child conceived in David's sin to be born. Enough time, perhaps, for the king to imagine that the Uriah affair was history. If David thought his despicable deeds would be forgotten, however, he was mistaken. Nathan's fiery charges target David's evil in no uncertain terms. The accusation of murder is unmistakable: Twice he accuses David of killing Uriah with the sword of the Ammonites. [A Sword or an Arrow?] David had not only committed adultery with Bathsheba, but had stolen her from Uriah. "[You] have taken *his* wife to be *your* wife."

Nathan advances the sword metaphor with a prediction that David, who previously had benefitted from God's blessings, is now destined to experience divine retribution (v. 10). "I will raise up trouble against you from within your own house" (v. 11a) may be seen as a prediction of all that is to come, culminating in Absalom's failed coup and early death. David's daughter Tamar was pierced by her half-brother Amnon's rape, Amnon was thrust through with the swords of Absalom's servants, and Absalom fell victim to the sharp weapons of Joab and his armor-bearers. David did not realize how prophetic was his callous comment on Uriah's death: "The sword devours now one, and now another" (11:25).

David's decline would be marked by public humiliation as well as personal sorrow. Just as Yahweh had given to David the wives of his predecessor, so he would give David's wives into the power of another, who would put David's weakness on display by sexually assaulting his wives in full public view (v. 11). [Troublesome Terms] This would be another example of retribution-in-kind—the difference being that David's concubines would be taken in public view, in

A Sword or an Arrow?

AΩ Nathan twice accuses David of murdering Uriah with the sword of the Ammonites, even though 11:24 clearly implies that Uriah was killed by archers shooting from the defended walls of Rabbah. The word "sword" is used metaphorically, not literally. Likewise David, when he heard the report that Uriah had been killed by archers, responded by saying, "The sword devours now one and now another" (11:25).

Nathan built upon the metaphor to show that one violent act begets others. He predicted that the sword would not depart from David's house, indicating the trouble and heartache that lay ahead.

Troublesome Terms

AΩ Nathan's prediction is fulfilled in 16:20-23. As the prophet Samuel told Saul that Yahweh would take the kingdom away and give it to "a neighbor" who was better than he (1 Sam 15:28), so now Nathan insists that Yahweh will give David's wives to "a neighbor," though there is no comment concerning the neighbor's worthiness. The word translated as "neighbor" technically refers to someone who is close by, whether related or not.

The story in 2 Sam 16:20-23 does not seem to match exactly, but this is a problem of terminology only. It seems that Nathan expects David's "neighbor" (who turns out to be his son Absalom) to have the run of David's entire harem, including his formal wives, but the account in 16:20-23 mentions only certain concubines who were left behind to keep house when David fled the city. The word used in 16:21-22 is a specific term for "concubines," while the term used by Nathan is the generic word for "woman," which could also mean "wife" or "concubine" in certain contexts. Thus, Nathan's broad prediction could be fulfilled in a more narrow way without calling his vocabulary into question.

One might also perceive a minor aberration in Nathan's claim that the "neighbor's" erotic activity would take place in broad daylight (12:11; lit., "before the eyes of this sun"), for the text says that Absalom had a tent pitched on the roof of the palace, beneath which he took his father's concubines as a sign that he also had taken the kingdom. Nathan's idiomatic intent is obviously that the thing be done in public view, as 16:22 expressly declares that the deed was done "in the sight of all Israel." Nathan's meaning is further clarified by v. 12, which contrasts David's secret sin with the public humiliation to be engineered by Yahweh.

The careful reader will also notice the irony involved: Absalom's crime against his father's wives will take place on the same roof where David stood when the seeds of his own misdeeds were planted.

---

contrast to the king's quiet liaison and secret plans carried out in the Bathsheba-Uriah affair.

Nathan's cutting words had their intended effect on David, though his response is downplayed so as not to take the spotlight from Nathan. "I have sinned against the LORD" is all David manages to say (but see [David's Plea] on Ps 51). The prophet's response is remarkable: He declares that Yahweh has put away David's sin. The grace David received, however, was not cheap. David's guilt did not simply disappear as a result of divine forbearance. He had "utterly scorned the LORD," and his sin could not be dismissed easily. [The Lord or His Enemies?] Rather than falling upon David, however, the death penalty David deserved was transferred to the innocent child of his adultery (v. 14). [A Dangerous Dalliance]

The Lord or His Enemies?

AΩ The MT and every other chief witness to the ancient text (including the LXX, the Old Latin, the Syriac, and the Targums) have a peculiar expression in v. 14. Although the NRSV translates Nathan's charge as "you have utterly scorned the LORD," a footnote points out that the Hebrew text says he "scorned the *enemies of the LORD*." Most scholars agree that this difficult expression must be a Hebrew euphemism along the lines of 1 Sam 25:22, where "the enemies of David" is substituted for the name of David alone. There is much less agreement about how this particular figure of speech developed, or why it was used here and not elsewhere.

With this stark prediction, the interview was over. Without entertaining questions or waiting to be dismissed, the sharp-tongued prophet departed. The narrator reports this with a straightforward "then Nathan went to his house" (12:15; cf. 1 Sam 24:22; 26:25).

A Dangerous Dalliance

According to the law as transmitted in Deuteronomy, adultery was punishable by death to both parties:

If a man is caught lying with the wife of another man, both of them shall die, the man who lay with the woman as well as the woman. So you shall purge the evil from Israel. If there is a young woman, a virgin already engaged to be married, and a man meets her in the town and lies with her, you shall bring both of them to the gate of that town and stone them to death, the young woman because she did not cry for help in the town and the man because he violated his neighbor's wife. So you shall purge the evil from your midst. (Deut 22:22-24)

CONNECTIONS

The reader who knows David's prior reputation is shocked to read chapter 11 and discover how obdurate the once-devoted king has become. Royalty apparently had a deleterious effect on David's spiritual life. Without apparent thought, he lusted after his neighbor's wife, committed adultery with her, begat a child, and had the husband killed in a poor effort to cover his sin. Despite the shining example of Uriah's dauntless devotion, David appeared unfazed by it all, unaware of the immensity of his sin, of how much trouble he was in.

That is why the LORD sent the prophet Nathan to David some months later. Nathan came to tell David a story, to shock him from his reverie. The last time we saw Nathan, he was predicting that God's blessing on David would continue through all generations and that one of David's descendants would rule forever.

Now Nathan came armed with a pointed story (and a pointed finger) and a prediction that the child David had conceived with Bathsheba would die (vv. 1-15). David got the point. He repented of his sin. He mourned and he prayed. He sought God's favor, and God forgave him. But the child still died. In this story we seem to have an amazing instance of atonement in the form of an innocent child's dying on behalf of a responsible adult's sin. It is a theme that will appear again—a glimpse, perhaps, into the heart of a God who will redeem his people at any cost.

1. *Israel's Story.* Now, what are we to make of this dark story? Is there anything to be learned, anything that will bring inspiration or help or hope to our lives?

One thing we learn is an obvious truth that is repeated in various ways throughout the Bible. *Sin hurts.* Sin is dangerous. The inevitable result of sin is death. There is little doubt that David's affair with Bathsheba was exciting for him. The fact that Bathsheba was married added an element of danger that only made it more thrilling. But David's initial step out of bounds led him further afield, until he finally got lost in the darkness. His initial lust flowered into adultery and bore the bitter fruit of murder. In all these things, David was a thief. He first stole Uriah's wife—then he stole Uriah's life! When the child born as a result of David's adultery also died, he lost a piece of himself, too.

There is no way to avoid the simple truth that sin is deadly. Paul put it in simple and memorable words when he said, "The wages of sin is death" (Rom 6:23). One thing leads to another. When we step onto the road of rebellion, we must know where the road is going. It leads to death, and not always for the sinner alone.

So, as we read David's story, we come to realize that the story is bigger than David. The person or persons who put together the books of Joshua through 2 Kings did so to make this point: Faithfulness leads to life. Sin leads to death. The Old Testament rules are there for all to read in the book of Deuteronomy (e.g., Deut 11; 28). The examples are there in the history that follows. Over and over again, the author tells us that David's story is Israel's story. We can read the accounts of the judges. We can study the stories of every king who came after David. The story never changes. One thing leads to another. God's way leads to life. Rebellion leads to death.

2. *Our Story.* When we read the New Testament, we discover that the story continues. David's story is not only Israel's story; it is *our* story. We, too, stand at a fork in the road every single day, sometimes many times a day. We are faced with choices between good or evil, life or death.

This is not to suggest that a person dies every time someone sins. But there is more than one way to die. There is more than one kind of death. Our sin can lead to the death of trust between friends or family members. It can lead to the death of relationships. It can lead to the death of hopes, plans, and dreams—ours or those of another. Sin can lead to the death of our financial health or our physical well-being. All too often, sin still leads to the conception of unwanted children, and sometimes to their death. One thing leads to another. The wages of sin is death.

But we can rejoice in knowing that this is not the end of the story. The gospel story tells us that God loved the world so much that he decided to break the cycle, at least in the ultimate sense. The wages of our sin led to the death of another innocent son, only this time it was the Son of God.

Somehow, some way beyond human understanding, Jesus' death put a crack in that eternal principle. In this world our sin may still bring death, in ways both big and small. But for those who trust in Jesus Christ, the end of the road is not death, but life.

"The wages of sin is death, but the free gift of God is eternal life through Jesus Christ our Lord" (Rom 6:23). So said the Apostle Paul. Because of the life and work, death, and resurrection of Jesus Christ, we may have faith that leads to life. Sin is always out there, lying in wait like an aggressive rattlesnake. There is evil in this world, and it will tempt us as long as we live. We may give in to it, and we will find that there are still consequences to be paid.

But the glorious news of the gospel is that God is ever loving, ever longing to hear our prayer of repentance—always wanting to forgive—anxiously waiting for the chance to bless us with life both abundant *and* eternal. It is certainly more than any rational person could ever hope for. The love of God in Christ is beyond our comprehension, but experiencing it still requires our *choice*.

NOTE

[1] P. Kyle McCarter, *II Samuel* (AB 9; Garden City: Doubleday, 1984), 299.

A DEATH, A BIRTH,
AND A VICTORY

12:15b-31

COMMENTARY

A Death, 12:15b-23

In this section, Nathan's funereal forecast (12:7-14) begins to unwind with his final word of judgment finding the first fulfillment. Nathan had prophesied that the son born as a result of David's illicit union with Bathsheba would die—not from any fault of its own, but as an atoning replacement for David, whose crime was worthy of death. The narrator amplifies the image of David's guilt in this affair by refusing to call Bathsheba by her own name. The doomed child is the one "that Uriah's wife bore to David."

Readers often assume the child was a newborn who was ill from birth and only lived seven days, but the slim evidence found in the text points to the contrary. The child's birth was recorded in 11:27, after which Nathan came to visit David. At some point following Nathan's prediction (as the narrator tells it), Yahweh "struck the child" so that he became very ill. For the infant suddenly to become ill suggests that he had enjoyed a previous period of health, however brief. Whether the baby was days or months old is immaterial to the story.

The author is unconcerned with sharing any details about the child, who functions mainly to inspire the curious and memorable response of his father. David knew *why* the child was ill. Perhaps he is the only one, besides Nathan, who knew that the child had not been afflicted by a disease alone, but by the deadly weight of his father's sin. Thus, David knew that if any healing came to the child, it would have to come from Yahweh. If healing were possible, it would have to result from his own confession and penance.

Thus, the narrator tells us that David *pleaded with God* for the child's life; David *fasted* before the LORD; David *went in and lay all night on the ground*, presumably by the child's bed (v. 16). [David's Plea]

David's Plea

The ancient traditions responsible for the superscriptions attached to certain psalms ascribed Ps 51 to David, describing the eloquent poem as David's prayer for forgiveness concerning his guilt in the Bathsheba-Uriah affair. The psalm does not mention a child, but is a poignant plea for a new beginning. Whether it truly derives from David is uncertain, and whether it grew from this dark period is a matter of speculation. Its words, however, do offer a glimpse into the kind of self-abasement and hope of healing that David experienced during these bleak days of waiting for the child to die and hoping that he would not. The superscription of the psalm reads: "To the leader. A Psalm of David, when the prophet Nathan came to him, after he had gone in to Bathsheba." The psalm itself is haunting in its beauty and depth of emotion, as these excerpts reveal:

> Have mercy on me, O God,
>   according to your steadfast love;
> according to your abundant mercy
>   blot out my transgressions.
> Wash me thoroughly from my iniquity,
>   and cleanse me from my sin.
> For I know my transgressions,
>   and my sin is ever before me. . . .
> Purge me with hyssop, and I shall be clean;
>   wash me, and I shall be whiter than snow.
> Let me hear joy and gladness;
>   let the bones that you have crushed rejoice.
> Hide your face from my sins,
>   and blot out all my iniquities.
> Create in me a clean heart, O God,
>   and put a new and right spirit within me.
> (Ps 51:1-3, 7-10)

David's abject sorrow was so apparent that his political counselors ("the elders of Israel") pleaded with him to get up from the ground and to comport himself in a more regal fashion, but he would not (v.17). David's refusal to return to the table and eat with them is a reminder not only that he declined to break his fast, but also that he remained aloof from matters of state and protocol (see comments and [Eating at the King's Table] at 2 Sam 9:7).

David knew what his advisors did not know: that the child's sickness and imminent death were David's own doing, and his constant beseeching of God's mercy was the only hope of its undoing. When David's prayer was not granted and the child died, however, David's demeanor changed. He had done all he could do, and it was not enough. He had begged for the child's life, without effect. With nothing remaining that he could do for the child, he returned to the everyday world of bathing and dressing, of taking his meals and looking after the matters of state (v. 20).

The storyteller portrays David as a living conundrum in the eyes of his royal household. He had wept over the child as long as the ailing infant lived—unleashing such depth of emotion that the servants were afraid to tell him when the child died (vv. 18-19)—yet David refused to join the official mourning after the boy's death. This aroused such consternation among observers that even his servants reproved him (v. 21). David responded with a rationalization that may have been real or may have been the best excuse he could think of (vv. 22-23).

In effect, David had spent himself emotionally before the child died. Though his weeklong period of fasting and prayer had focused on his own failure as much as the child's illness, it could be said that David had already finished his time of mourning, albeit proleptically. The normal period of grief in Israel was seven days (see comments at 11:27), and that is how long David had wept for the life of the little one.

Once his efforts had proven fruitless, David refused to mourn any longer. There is a certain appeal to this pragmatic approach, but David does not adopt it when faced with other deaths. Though some writers have suggested a change in David's approach to death, this refusal to mourn is not characteristic of David, either before or after this incident. In other situations, David joined in public mourning for the dead *post mortem* (for Saul and Jonathan in 1:17-27; for Abner in 3:31-35; for his son Amnon in 13:36-37; for Absalom in 18:33–19:4). In Absalom's case, David had also grieved for his son and sought to preserve his life before death occurred (13:39; 18:5).

In an interesting turnabout, David would later mourn so abjectly when his son Absalom was killed that David's general, Joab, had to castigate the king and urge him to minimize his deep grief for the traitorous Absalom, lest his loyal followers feel unappreciated. Thus, David also resumed his royal duties on the day that Absalom died, but his heart was not in it (19:5-8). The ironic contrast is that David's counselors questioned his love when he refused to continue in mourning for Bathsheba's baby, while Joab questioned his loyalty when he did not cease to mourn for Absalom! Once David abandoned Yahweh's way, he found new frustrations at every turn.

The difference in David's approach to the death of Bathsheba's infant son is to be accounted for by the simple fact that David knew the child's blood was on his hands. Despite natural public suspicions, David was not culpable in the deaths of Saul, Jonathan, Abner, or Absalom. Indeed, some writers propose that his vocal expression of bereavement for Saul and Abner was carefully calculated to allay possible public distrust. David's week of fasting for the child of Bathsheba was an effort to absolve his sin and to save the child. Only he and Nathan understood what that struggle meant and why he faced it. Once the child was dead, David seemed to have made his peace with Yahweh and was ready to get on with life.

David's visit to the "house of Yahweh" (v. 20) is problematic, for the narrator has been very careful to insist that David was not allowed to construct a temple in Jerusalem—that the ark of God remained in a tent. Some writers have suggested that a former Jebusite sanctuary had been taken over and modified to serve as a Yahwistic temple, but the simplest explanation is to regard the phrase as anachronistic. If Kyle McCarter is correct, chapters 10–12 are later than the surrounding material, bearing the marks of a prophetic writer who may have worked as late as the eighth century BC. The account of David's sin and its aftermath was later inserted into the framework of the Succession Narrative, which could have originated during Solomon's reign. The prophetic writer (or editor) was so familiar with the presence of the temple in Jerusalem that it was an easy mistake for him to say "house of Yahweh," even though David would actually have visited a tent shrine, if anything.[1]

A Birth, 12:24-25

The birth of Solomon appears as a surprise. The reader knows that Solomon will be blessed by God and become the future king, so it is somewhat unsettling to find his birth story emerging from the shadow of Nathan's curse. Perhaps the narrator wants to emphasize that although Yahweh did not answer David's plea to save the first child of Bathsheba, his grace was expressed in the granting of another son. Later readers would need to hear that there is hope, even in the midst of darkness. Thus, it is not only David's words or actions that bring consolation to Bathsheba, but the gift of another child.

Solomon does not face the same stigma as his unfortunate brother, for his parents' union is no longer illicit. When David consoles Bathsheba, it is "his wife" that he lays with, and God's blessings seem to be upon their marriage, for the LORD's love is clearly upon the child. The text states simply but forcefully: "The LORD loved him," presumably in contrast to his older sibling, who may have been loved by Yahweh but who also fell victim to God's wrath.

The naming of the child is both significant and confusing. Naming children seems to have been the mother's prerogative in this period (note Hannah's choice of Samuel, 1 Sam 1:20; and the story of Phinehas' widow, who named her child Ichabod, 1 Sam 4:21). Bathsheba named him Solomon, which is derived from the word that is often translated "peace." [Solomon] First Chronicles 22:9 pointedly connects Solomon's name to the motif of peace, but some modern scholars argue with some merit that in this context it may mean "replacement" (cf. 1 Chr 22:9).

Even more curious is the *second* name given to the child, reportedly by Yahweh himself, through the agency of the prophet Nathan. "Jedidiah" (*yĕdîdyāh*) literally means "Beloved One of Yahweh." One would think such a memorable name would prove popular, but it does not appear again in the Bible. Some writers have suggested that "Solomon" was used as the future king's personal name and "Jedidiah" as his throne name. The argument is appealing, but if it is accurate, one would have expected to see the name again, at least in connection with Solomon's coronation.

> **Solomon**
>
> AΩ First Chr 22:9 says that Yahweh had spoken to David when he sought to build the temple, predicting that a son would be born to him who would be "a man of peace," for God would give to that son peace (*šālôm*) from his enemies on every side. God's reputed message to David predicted that the child would be named Solomon, or *šĕlōmōh*. This suggests an ancient tradition that Solomon's name was a comment on the age of peace to come under his rule.
>
> Modern scholarship has suggested many alternative explanations, some of dubious value. The most successful suggestion connects the name to a verbal form of the same root: *šillēm* means "to make complete" and can be used in the sense of "to make amends" or "to restore." Thus, *šĕlōmōh* could mean "replacement." This would be a fitting name for Bathsheba to give the child, understanding Solomon to be a replacement for the child who was lost.

Solomon's birth story is surprisingly brief, given his later significance, but the brevity of his story sharpens the contrast between him and his ill-fated brother, placing him clearly in the bright (if small) spotlight. The first son of Bathsheba was both unnamed and unfortunate, cursed by Yahweh with his father's sin. In contrast, Solomon is twice-named and clearly blessed by Yahweh, whose love for the child is stated by the narrator, announced by the prophet Nathan, and signified by the name Jedidiah.

A Victory, 12:26-31

Having completed the sad story of David's fall, his judgment, and the beginning of its tragic aftermath, the author neatly closes the narrative unit in chapters 11–12 by reporting on the conclusion of the seige of Rabbah, whose beginning had set the stage for David's initial encounter with Bathsheba. The account of the victory (vv. 26-31) is placed here as a narrative marker, not as a chronological note. As the text now stands, it suggests that the siege of Rabbah extended for at least two years, lasting through two entire pregnancies plus the indefinite time before, after, and in between. It is unlikely, however, that the campaign would have extended beyond one season. The victory is recorded at the end of chapter 12 as a convenient bookend corresponding to 11:1, enclosing the bitter story of David's sin and the hopeful account of Solomon's birth. As mentioned above, 11:1 and 12:26-31 should also be read in conjunction with 10:1-19 and 8:3-8 to get the full picture of David's conflict with the Ammonites and Arameans.

The actual conquest story in 12:26-31 is remarkable for the uncharacteristic self-effacement of Joab, whom David had set in charge of the campaign. Having achieved such a superior position that victory was assured, Joab sent word for David to come to the battlefield and take credit for the victory, lest the acclaim go to his general (vv. 26-28).

Joab's message that he had taken "the royal city" and "the water city" is a bit of a puzzle. The different terms probably refer to the same place, most likely a heavily fortified section of the city that housed the royal palace and also guarded the water supply (compare the "city of David," which was one part of greater Jerusalem). If this part of the city was conquered, all that remained for David was the task of mopping up.

David did not hesitate to seize the opportunity, but mustered the reserves and marched with them to Rabbah, where they stormed the city and took it (v. 29). David celebrated the victory by taking the "crown of Milcom from his head" (v. 30). The consonantal text (*mlkm*) could also be read as "their king" (presumably Hanun still reigned), but the better reading is Milcom, patron god of the Ammonites (1 Kgs 11:33; Jer 49:1, 3; Zeph 1:5). The jeweled crown that David lifted from the chief image in Rabbah's national temple reportedly contained a full talent of gold. Estimated equivalents for a talent range from sixty-six to seventy-five pounds, so it was almost certainly the precious stone(s) that David later wore, not the crown itself. The word for "stone" appears in the singular but also could be understood as a collective.

The golden crown of Milcom was only the beginning of the spoil that David took from the Ammonites. After stripping their city of valuables, he set its inhabitants to work dismantling the city's vaunted fortifications to assure future cooperation. The text and translation of v. 31 is difficult. Some commentators have judged that David tortured the populace in a grisly rite of sawing them into pieces and pressing them through a brick mold. The intended meaning, however, is almost certainly that he set the captives to work with saws and picks, demolishing the defenses of their own city and perhaps working on new construction projects for David.

It is worth noting once again that David was allowed to take spoil from the city, apparently with Yahweh's blessing, and this despite the fact that Uriah, at least, considered the campaign to be a holy war. Saul was cursed for doing the same thing (1 Sam 15) although Samuel had expressly forbidden him in advance from collecting loot, a prohibition apparently not extended to David.

"This he did to all the cities of the Ammonites" suggests an extended but probably rapid campaign in which all other Ammonite cities were brought under Israelite control. Since Rabbah was the strongest city, and the best fighters from other towns had been brought in for the defense of the capital, this final phase of the operation was probably accomplished in short order, bringing the entire nation of the Ammonites into the sphere of David's growing empire.

CONNECTIONS

A Death

David's behavior during his child's sickness and in the aftermath of the baby's death foreshadows Qoheleth's comment that there is a proper time for everything (Eccl 3:2-8). Since David had hopes that his abject prayer and period of fasting might win Yahweh's favor and save the child, it was appropriate for him to pour out his heart and soul before the LORD. Once the child died, however, David felt no obligation to continue in the posture of mourning.

David's advisors did not understand him. Perhaps they considered David's behavior during the child's illness to be a sign of weakness or unnecessary sentimentality. The infant mortality rate was high in those days, and birth control was nonexistent. Many children were born, and there were many who did not live. Why should David (who, after all, had many wives and several children), be so affected by the sickness of this one child?

David explained to his advisors that his earlier prayer had been for Yahweh to show mercy and save the child's life. David's question lies at the heart of every petitionary prayer: "Who knows? The LORD may be gracious to me" (v. 22). [The Problem of Petitionary Prayer] Once the child died, however, there was no need to continue: "But now he is dead; why should I fast? Can I bring him back again? I

The Problem of Petitionary Prayer

Qoheleth, the skeptical author of Ecclesiastes, was fond of asking the question "Who knows?" (Eccl 2:19; 3:21; 6:12; 8:1; 10:14), but not in the context of prayer. David's hopeful but plaintive plea is echoed, however, in two texts from the prophets. Jonah explained that he had first refused to prophecy in Nineveh for fear that God might turn his wrath away and let the Assyrians live after all: *Who knows? God may relent and change his mind; he may turn from his fierce anger, so that we do not perish* (Jonah 3:9). The prophet Joel expressed the same thought, but in a more hopeful vein, as he encouraged Israel to repent and change in hopes that God might bring a blessing rather than punishment to the recalcitrant nation:

Who knows whether he will not turn and relent,
   and leave a blessing behind him,
a grain offering and a drink offering
   for the LORD, your God? (Joel 2:14)

As with David's prayer, both of these texts are in the context of people who have sinned and are threatened with divine retribution. The prayer of repentance asks God to relent and is offered in hope, but without guarantees. Who knows what God might do?

---

shall go to him, but he will not return to me." [An Ancient Hebrew View of the Afterlife]

There is some logic to David's argument, though many would argue that David still owed it to his wife and to the baby's memory to mourn the child's passing, however impractical it may have seemed. David's actions remind us, however, that there comes a time to let go. David may have let go more quickly than others were prepared to accept, but they did not know what he had been through already, so perhaps he could be excused for his behavior.

David's actions seemed precipitous, but he seemed intent on putting the death (and his sin?) behind him, letting go of the grief, and moving forward. All persons who experience loss must do this sooner or later, or else death will truly be the victor. The loss of a child is especially traumatic, for it violates our expectations that parents will die first. Persons who have lost children know that the empty place left behind is not soon filled or easily forgotten. Even for those who are emotionally stable

2 Samuel 12:15-23—Who can tell? David prayed and wept while the child lived, hoping that God might be gracious and grant life.

Julius Schnoor von Carolsfeld. *David and Bathsheba's Child Dies.* 19th century. Woodcut. *Das Buch der Bucher in Bilden.* (Credit: Dover Pictorial Archive Series)

and spiritually mature, years may go by before they begin to feel "normal" again, ready to get on with life and to hope again for the future.

One might surmise that David's abrupt departure from mourning was not as complete as it might appear. David apparently internalized his grief. He seemed determined to channel the energy behind it into a more positive direction. David was not done with grieving, however.

A Birth

David's strategy for resuming a normal life included encouraging his wife Bathsheba to find solace in him and in the possibility of new life. At least one writer has suggested—based on the presumption that the first child lived only seven days—that Solomon was conceived just one week after his unfortunate brother was born. This is unlikely, but the text does suggest that Bathsheba's second pregnancy began rather soon after the first infant's death.

Solomon figures so prominently into Israel's history that it seems strange to find his birth story limited to two verses, and those told within the shadow of his father's sin and his brother's death. The story's brevity belies its significance, however. Nowhere else in the Hebrew Bible is God's love so clearly expressed toward a child. The narrator tells us that "the LORD loved him," and insists that Yahweh was not satisfied for Bathsheba alone to name the child, sending Nathan to pronounce a second name, Jedidiah, meaning "Beloved One of Yahweh." This name was given, the author reminds us, "because of the LORD." Some recent scholars argue that this phrase should be translated "by the grace of the LORD." [Comparative Linguistics]

An Ancient Hebrew View of the Afterlife

The ancient Hebrews, like many of their neighbors, believed that the dead persisted as disembodied shades who retained a measure of consciousness and lived in a place called Sheol, thought to be located beneath the surface of the earth. In the Hebrew understanding of the afterlife prevalent during David's time, there was a continuing connection between the spirit of the dead and his or her earthly remains, thus the careful disposition of dead bodies.

Bodies were typically buried in family tombs, often cut into rock, with one or two shelves cut as a resting place for the recent dead. Hebrews did not embalm the dead, and their tombs were rarely air tight. In the dry climate of Palestine, bodies desiccated and deteriorated quickly, leaving only the bones. Periodically, a family member would go to the tomb, gather the bones of the most recently deceased, and add them to a growing collection of other bones stored in a cavity that was often cut into the rock beneath the shelf. Thus, the bones of many generations might be mingled together, giving rise to the expression "being gathered to one's fathers" (Gen 49:29; Judg 2:10).

David believed that in one way or another he would join his infant son in the land of the dead, but he knew that the child could not return to join him in life, for Sheol was a place from which there was no return (Job 7:9; 10:21); instances such as 1 Sam 28 are rare and temporary exceptions. Thus, David pragmatically refused to add seven more days of mourning to the seven days he had already spent in prayer and self-abasement. What was the point?

A Victory

The fierce warrior Joab is depicted as David's right-hand man, always willing to serve the country's (if not David's) best interests, even when it required doing things that David did not desire (such

Comparative Linguistics

AΩ Enigmatic Hebrew words or phrases can often be elucidated by comparing them to analogous phrases in other ancient languages. All languages belonging to the Northwest Semitic family were very similar. A set of Phoenician inscriptions from the late 8th century BC found in the ancient city of Karatepe (in the southeastern part of modern Turkey) contain several equivalent expressions in a context that seems to mean something like "by the grace of DN" (DN = "Divine Name"). The phrase in 2 Sam 12:25 is *baʿăbûr yahweh*, while the corresponding phrase from the Karatepe inscriptions is *bʿbr.* (H. Donner and W. Röllig, *Kanaanäische und aramäische Inschriften* [Wiesbaden: Harrassowitz, 1962-1964], 26.I.8; II.6,11-12; III. 11). Thus, the Hebrew phrase could mean not only "with respect to Yahweh," but "by the grace of Yahweh."

as the murder of Abner, 2 Sam 2:27-28; the killing of Absalom, 2 Sam 18:14-15; and the murder of Amasa, whom David had appointed in Joab's place, 2 Sam 20:9-10). Joab was a strong-willed man, but he *was* devoted to David.

That devotion is evident in this story of the fall of Rabbah, but in a more positive fashion. Joab and his trained troops had besieged the city and brought it to the very brink of defeat. Rather than striking the final blow himself, however, Joab sent word to David so that the king could come, bringing the national militia with him, and claim the victory for himself and for Israel. This was an unselfish act on Joab's part, done for the good of the king and the good of the nation.

The work of the church or other organizations would be so much easier if more of us adopted Joab's attitude—if more persons were more concerned with the life, health, and growth of the whole than with gaining individual credit for their contributions. David's hired mercenaries and professional troops undoubtedly played a lead role in conquering Rabbah, but Joab's actions allowed not only David, but also the Israelite soldiers drawn from all over the country to experience the victory and feel a part of it. Many churches or other organizations have suffered from the megalomania of a pastor or other leader who sought to take credit for every advance. The best accomplishments are those that are won and shared by all.

2 Samuel 12:27-28—Joab practiced uncharacteristic self-effacement in calling for David to come and take credit for the final victory over Rabbah, the Ammonite capital.

Gustave Doré (1832–83). *David Punishing the Ammonites.* 19th century. Engraving. (Credit: Dover Pictoral Archive Series)

NOTE

[1] P. Kyle McCarter, *II Samuel* (AB 9; Garden City: Doubleday, 1984), 302.

RAPE, REVENGE, AND EXILE

13:1-39

David's Troublesome Children, 13:1–18:33

Second Samuel 13 begins an extended literary unit devoted to the greatest political crisis of David's career—the rebellion led by his own son Absalom. [Outline of 2 Samuel 13–20] As the story unfolds with all of its attendant ugliness, the heavy weight of Nathan's portentous prophecy falls upon David's shoulders. "Thus says the LORD," Nathan had said, "I will raise up trouble against you from within your own house." (12:11a). The word "trouble" is a mild characterization of what awaited David: the Hebrew word (*rāʿâ*) is the classic term for depicting that which is evil or bad. It is often used as the opposite of good. There was nothing good about what David's children had in store for him, and little good in the way he responded to their strongly negative behavior.

These chapters are not about trouble alone, however, for they deal with the heart of the Succession Narrative's primary theme, the question of who would succeed David as king. Would it be, as expected, one of his children? And if so, which one?

COMMENTARY

Amnon Rapes His Sister Tamar, 13:1-22

The story of Tamar's rape and Amnon's murder provides important background information for the ensuing chapters, helping the reader to gain some insight into Absalom's abiding anger that led him not only to kill his brother, but to rebel against his father. It was not simply political ambition that set Absalom on the course of mutiny, but an outraged sense of justice.

The narrator's approach to the story of Amnon and Tamar is telling: it begins with a notice that "David's son *Absalom* had a beautiful sister whose name was Tamar." Absalom will not re-enter the picture until later, but his appearance in 13:1 overshadows all that

---

Outline of 2 Samuel 13–20

📖 The common factor binding these chapters into a large unit within the Succession Narrative is the presence and activity of Absalom, whose growing anger and ambition find their genesis in ch. 13, and lead him to rebellion and an early death in ch. 18. Even the events of chs. 19–20 (and to a lesser degree, 1 Kgs 1–2) are portrayed as eddies and currents associated with the receding flood of Absalom's insurrection. Once the dam of resistance to Davidic rule had broken, others would naturally follow in Absalom's wake.

I. David's Troublesome Children (13:1–18:33)
   A. Rape, Revenge, and Exile (13:1-39)
      1. Amnon rapes his sister Tamar (13:1-22)
      2. Brother Absalom gets revenge (13:23-39)
   B. Joab's Love for Father and Son (14:1-33)
      1. The woman of Tekoa tells a story (14:1-20)
      2. Absalom returns to Jerusalem (14:21-24)
      3. Absalom returns to the palace (14:25-33)
   C. Absalom's Rebellion (15:1–18:33)
      1. A false vow and a threatening conspiracy (15:1-12)
      2. David "flees"—and sets a trap (15:13-37)
      3. Parting shots from Saul's house (16:1-14)
      4. Absalom in Jerusalem (16:15-23)
      5. Absalom's competing counselors (17:1-23)
      6. David's strategy and Absalom's unwanted death (17:24–18:18)
      7. David mourns for his son (18:19-33)
II. David Diminished and a Discontented Nation (19:1–20:26)
   A. David returns to Jerusalem, but not in triumph (19:1-43)
      1. Joab's anger and Israel's question (19:1-10)
      2. David reaffirmed by Judah (19:11-40)
      3. David reaffirmed by Israel (19:41-43)
   B. David deals with internal dissent (20:1-26)
      1. Sheba's revolt (20:1-3)
      2. Joab and Amasa (20:4-13)
      3. Sheba's end: the wise woman of Abel (20:14-22)
      4. The roll of the faithful (20:23-26)

---

follows, for he *will* be the main player before it is over. [Tamar and Her Namesake]

The word "sister," in this context, denotes Tamar's relationship to Absalom as a full sister: they both were children of David and his wife Maacah, a royal princess from Geshur who had probably been married to David to seal a political alliance (cf. 2 Sam 3:3). Amnon, on the other hand, was the son of Ahinoam of Jezreel, and half-brother to both (1 Sam 25:43; 2 Sam 3:2).

Amnon was David's firstborn son. His name is derived from the verbal root *'āman*, which means "to be faithful," but his character and his name were a poor match. Amnon first appears as a frustrated man who lusts after his half-sister Tamar, convinced that he

Tamar and Her Namesake

Tamar may have been named for a woman reputed to be one of David's ancestors through her son Perez (Ruth 4:18-22; 1 Chr 2:3-5, 9-15; Matt 1:3-6). The elder Tamar's story, told in Gen 38, is an interesting counterpart to the story of David's daughter. Tamar became a daughter-in-law of the patriarch Judah, having married his sons Er and Onan consecutively. Both died without begetting children, and according to the rules of Levitical marriage, the next brother (Shelah) should also have married her so that she could conceive a son and so be assured that someone would care for her in her old age.

Having observed the fates of his first two sons, Judah refused to allow Shelah to marry Tamar when he came of age. In retaliation, Tamar disguised herself as a prostitute, lured Judah himself to sample her wares, and conceived twin sons, Perez and Zerah.

The irony of comparing the stories is that the elder Tamar cleverly used her sexuality in order to correct what she perceived as an injustice, making Judah the victim of her scheme. In contrast, Amnon perpetrated a grave injustice against the younger Tamar, exploiting her sexuality and making her the victim of his misguided lust. It was then left up to her brother Absalom to recenter the balance of justice.

For further reading, see Phyllis Trible, *Texts of Terror* (Philadelphia: Fortress, 1984).

---

is in love with her. Indeed, the passionate Amnon claims to have been made sick by his infatuation for Tamar and his inability to reach her: virgin daughters of the king were probably confined to a special section of the palace and guarded closely. [A Lovesick Man]

Even royal daughters had little freedom to direct their own lives. They held great value to the king as potential brides for foreign princes, the living expressions of friendship between nations (and immediate hostages if international amity soured). Apparently even Amnon's status as a son of the king did not give him the run of palace: "it seemed impossible to Amnon to do anything to her" (v. 2b).

An intriguing character enters the picture to counsel the enamored Amnon. His name is Jonadab, and he is described as Amnon's "friend." Some commentators suggest that Jonadab held some official position as matchmaker for the court, but the evidence is scanty. Jonadab is identified as a first cousin, the son of David's brother Shimeah. He seems to have been one friend among others in Amnon's circle of intimates. Noting Amnon's lovesickness, Jonadab cleverly suggested that Amnon feign a physical illness and request that Tamar come to nurse him back to health by emerging from her isolation to cook a special dish and feed it to him. [What Did Tamar Cook?]

Some scholars postulate an ancient belief that the bland but hearty food in question would have stronger curative powers when prepared and served by the hands of a virgin. If so, Amnon's

A Lovesick Man

Lovesickness was a motif common to Egyptian love poetry, especially when connected to the absence of one's lover. A similar theme appears in the Song of Solomon, which is a beautiful example of a Hebrew love song. In Cant 5:8, the woman speaks of her mate in this way:

> I adjure you, O daughters of Jerusalem,
>   if you find my beloved,
> tell him this:
>   I am faint with love!

What Did Tamar Cook?

AΩ Most modern translations render the medicinal dish as "cakes" that are baked, but the MT, followed by the versions, clearly says that the dish was boiled. Dough that is mixed, kneaded, and then boiled produces a dish best described by the word "dumpling." The actual Hebrew word (*lĕbībôt*) may suggest that they were heart-shaped (*lēbāb* means "heart"), but it may also refer to the dish's hearty nature (the verb *libbēb* means "to enhearten" or "give strength").

request would have carried greater weight. In any case, Jonadab's crafty plan succeeded, for David sent Tamar to Amnon's house with instructions to cook the medicinal repast for him (v. 7).

Tamar carried out the assignment without complaint. When the dish was prepared and presented, however, Amnon refused to eat it—revealing that he had called for Tamar under false pretenses. Amnon's order for all to leave has been described as "courtly," but carries much force. He was determined to be alone with the object of his affection—and without witnesses. As with Bathsheba, the reader is left in the dark with regard to Tamar's personal feelings or level of comfort with the initial stages of their encounter.

When Amnon's sexual intentions surfaced, however, Tamar's alarm and her displeasure became evident. Tamar pleaded with Amnon to show respect to her, to himself, and to the traditions of Israel. Carefully calling him "my brother," she pointed to the odious nature of his proposition: "No, my brother, do not force me, for such a thing is not done in Israel; do not do anything so vile!" (v. 12). [The Literary Motif of Brother-Sister Sex] Tamar's concern for the vileness of Amnon's intent derives more from its being forced than from the consanguinity involved. Sex between siblings was expressly forbidden by the law (Lev 18:9, 11; 20:7; Deut 27:22), but these regulations may not have been in force during the tenth century, at least with regard to children of different mothers. Tamar's language is reminiscent of Genesis 34:7, where the rape of Dinah is called "a sacrilege in Israel." When Tamar asked Amnon to consider the shame that would fall to her and the scandalous reputation that would devolve to him, the primary issue was rape, not incest.

Tamar's attempt to forestall Amnon's assault by suggesting that he ask David for her hand in marriage offers a troubling puzzle. Did she really want to marry Amnon, or was her request a failed ploy to dissuade Amnon from pursuing his plan? In either case, the reader is forced to imagine either that the Levitical regulations opposing sibling marriage were not in force in Jerusalem, or that David would have been willing to violate the law by allowing such a marriage.

The Literary Motif of Brother-Sister Sex

Biblical evidence regarding marriage or sexual relations between brothers and sisters is ambiguous. Lev 18:9 and Deut 27:22 prohibit sibling relations of any sort, while Gen 20:12 and 2 Sam 13:13 suggest conditions in which they were acceptable. Abraham insisted that Sarah was his paternal sister, the daughter of his father, but not of his mother. The same case would have held with Amnon and Tamar, a situation in which Tamar implies that marriage would be possible.

This relationship found some measure of approval from the rabbis, as well. The extensive discussion in bSanhedrein 58a seems to allow marriage to a paternal sister, but not between maternal siblings.

Evidence from other ancient Near Eastern cultures is divergent. The Code of Hammurabi seems ambivalent. It expressly forbids several types of incest (father-daughter or daughter-in-law, son-mother or foster mother), but it does not mention relations between siblings (CH 154-158). Royal marriage among siblings in ancient Egypt is rather well known, and there is some evidence that sibling marriages were practiced among commoners into the first three centuries AD (Keith Hopkins, "Brother-Sister Marriage in Ancient Egypt," *Comparative Studies in Society and History* 22 [1980]: 303-54).

Among the Hittites, however, there is at least one royal text that roundly condemns sibling marriage. A letter from King Suppiluliumas (14th century BC) to an Armenian vassal named Huqqanas includes these instructions:

> Furthermore, my sister whom I, the Sun, have given you in matrimony has many sisters of different degrees; and you have acquired these (as sisters) too since you have taken their sister (as wife). But in the land of the Hittites there is an important rule: a brother does not take his own sister or cousin (as a wife); it is not permitted. Whosoever does this sort of thing shall not remain alive in Hattusas; he shall die. Now since your land is barbaric, (the people) therein are retarded (?); a brother does take his own sister or cousin (in marriage); but in Hattusas this is not permitted.

(Translated in Samuel Greengus, "Sisterhood Adoption at Nuzi and the 'Wife-Sister' Motif in Genesis," HUCA 46 [1975]: 9).

Roland de Vaux (*Ancient Israel: Its Life and Institutions*. Trans. John McHugh [Grand Rapids: Eerdmans, 1997], 19-20) noted that many scholars follow Robertson Smith's conclusion that the early Semitic family was matriarchal, in which a child's lineage is traced through the mother, not the father. Thus, since Amnon and Tamar were born of different mothers, they would not have been considered related, and their sexual relationship would not have been considered incest. This relies on speculation, however: if a matriarchate ever existed, we have little evidence for it.

Tamar's words—as the narrator has given them to us—were eloquent and heartfelt, but her rational argument was designed to appeal to the mind, and in that moment Amnon was not thinking with his mind. Exercising his greater physical strength, he forced his sister to submit, and raped her (v. 14).

Thus, Tamar entered the record as one of the most tragic victims of the Bible, even as Amnon established himself as a most memorable boor. Having raped his sister, his reputed love turned to loathing. [Love, Hate, and Rape] He took her, but would not keep her. The appalling scene is described in such detail that the reader staggers with incomprehension at Amnon's insensitive brutality. As Tamar had pleaded with him not to assault her, so now she pleads with him not to send her away, since there would be less shame in being violated and then married than in rape and rejection. According to Exodus 22:16 (MT v. 15) and Deuteronomy 22:28, a man who raped a virgin was obligated to marry her. Thus, Amnon's subsequent rejection only added to Tamar's shame. The word she used for "send away" is the same word used to describe a divorce.

Love, Hate, and Rape

📖 The hatred Amnon expressed for Tamar after raping her has been explained in several ways. One possibility is the psychological phenomenon known as ambivalence, in which both love and hate are felt for an intimate partner. Geraldine K. Piorkowski explained it this way:

> Ambivalence is a common psychological phenomenon in intimacy that poses problems for both partners. For the possessor, ambivalence feels like an unnatural and disturbed state much like schizophrenia. However, rather than facing a split personality, in ambivalence we are faced with divided and contrasting feelings. One moment we love our intimate partners, and the next moment we are filled with hatred. . . . The rapid shifts in feeling-tone occur because positive feelings are anxiety-arousing (e.g., we worry that if we love someone, they will not reciprocate or that once we get involved, we will be sitting ducks for criticism).

> (Geraldine K. Piorkowski, *Too Close for Comfort: Exploring the Risks of Intimacy* [New York: Plenum Press, 1994], 22).

Kyle McCarter cites related statements: one by Tacitus, who said, "It is human nature to hate those whom you have injured," and the other by Max Meerbohm, who opined that "of all the objects of hatred, a woman once loved is the most hateful."

The incestual nature of the relationship may also have been a factor. Amnon may have been afraid of being found out, or he may have taken out his own self-recrimination upon his victimized sister. Psychologists note that this often happens in families where incest occurs, at least where father-daughter relations are involved. The victim is often blamed for the perpetrator's actions, becoming a family scapegoat (George Thorman, *Incestuous Families* [Springfield IL: Charles C. Thomas, 1983], 71-72).

Amnon's hatred may also be explained by the realization of what he had done—and its consequences. Not only did Amnon know that he had committed an evil against his sister, but he also knew that she had a legitimate and life-long marriage claim against him. With her own words, Tamar had told Amnon what a despicable character he would become if he forced her, and she reminded him of the marriage option as well. Having sated his lust for power, Amnon wanted nothing more to do with Tamar: the existence of her claims against him would be a continuing burr to his personal sense of well-being. Her voiced criticism prior to the act left him feeling scorned afterward. The only way to salvage his pride was to order her from his house because her very presence was a standing allegation against him.

The rabbis produced at least one solution that should be mentioned if for nothing more than its high score on the absurdity scale: Sanh 21a suggests that Amnon's love turned to hate because, during the rape, he injured himself by becoming entangled in her pubic hair.

Again, however, the uncouth Amnon refused to listen. He spoke harshly—as if she was the one who brought shame on him—and had her forcibly thrown from the house (vv. 15-17). The modern reader might imagine that Amnon's own sense of shame finally overwhelmed him, but in his immaturity he directed it toward Tamar rather than toward himself.

A brief parenthesis explains Tamar's dress, though its appearance still remains enigmatic. The descriptive term is used only here and in Genesis 37, where it describes Joseph's "many-colored" or "long-sleeved" coat. The Hebrew word behind the expression "in earlier times" (*měʿîlîm*) is also unusual and may mean "from puberty" instead (deriving from *ʿalmâ* rather than *ʿôlam*). The author emphasizes Amnon's serious violation of Israel's cultural taboos and the depth of his sin against Tamar by carefully depicting Tamar's abject state of mourning, symbolized by her torn clothing, ash-strewn hair, and loud wails (vv. 18-19). [Symbols of Mourning in Ancient Israel] She laments the loss of her virginity (and future marriage prospects) in the same way that a widow grieves the loss of her husband.

When Tamar carried her grief to her brother Absalom, she was in need of more than consolation. Having been sexually violated, she no longer had the status of a young virgin in the king's house or the prestige of a potential political bride. No longer would Tamar be allowed to dwell with her other unmarried sisters, and she might not have trusted David's protection under any circumstances. So it was that she sought out her brother Absalom, who was grown and apparently had his own house in Jerusalem (see also 14:24).

Perhaps Tamar sensed that David would offer her no comfort or justice and that her full brother Absalom was the only man she could trust to stand up for her. Indeed, the narrator is careful to point out that when David learned of Amnon's crime, he was

---

Symbols of Mourning in Ancient Israel

Various mourning rites were practiced in ancient Israel, varying little from public expressions of grief to be found among neighboring peoples such as the Egyptians and Mesopotamians. These rites frequently occur in the books of Samuel and seem to be a recurring motif within the extended description of David's sin and its aftermath. Bathsheba mourned for her husband Uriah after David engineered his death (11:26) and later undoubtedly mourned the death of her infant son (12:24). David was criticized for adopting a posture of mourning before the child died (12:15-19) and for refusing to do so after the child's demise (12:20-23). Tamar mourned the loss of her virginity and marriage prospects following Amnon's rape (13:19), and David grieved deeply when he thought Absalom had killed all his sons (13:31). The woman of Tekoa appeared before David in mourning dress (14:2), pretending that one of her sons had killed the other. The whole country mourned as David and his entourage left Jerusalem during Absalom's revolt (15:23), and David also wept as he walked barefoot up the Mount of Olives (15:30). There he was met by Hushai, who had torn his clothes and put dirt on his head (15:32). David's poignant expression of grief over Absalom's death

(18:33-19:4), like his plaintive elegy for Saul and Jonathan (1:19-27), is legendary.

Mourning rites could involve special things that were done: Special mourning clothes were sometimes worn (2 Sam 14:2), or normal clothes could be ripped as an expression of grief (2 Sam 13:19, 31; 15:32). Ashes, or dirt, were also commonly imposed upon the head as a sign of sorrow (13:19; 15:32). David went barefoot as he wept on his way out of Jerusalem (15:30) and lay prostrate upon the ground while pleading for his infant son (12:16) and bemoaning the supposed loss of his other sons (13:31).

Various forms of self-abnegation also expressed mourning. Normal practices of life, such as eating, bathing, and personal hygiene, might be eschewed as public signs of grief. Joab told the woman of Tekoa to avoid anointing herself with oil (14:2), even as David ended his period of mourning by bathing, changing his clothes, anointing himself, and eating (12:20).

Public mourning typically began on the day of death and lasted for seven days (Gen 50:10; 1 Sam 31:13; 1 Chr 10:12; Job 2:12-13). The thirty-day periods of mourning for Aaron and Moses (Num 20:29; Deut 34:8) were the exception rather than the rule. Jacob was mourned for seventy days, in accordance with Egyptian custom (Gen 50:3).

paralyzed by his own conflicting emotions. He did nothing *to* Amnon, and nothing *for* Tamar. David's actions are those of a sentimental father whose love (for sons, at least) leads to leniency and ultimately to lawlessness. David was very angry, the text says (lit., "he burned greatly against him"). Even so, he refused to punish Amnon, "because he loved him, for he was his firstborn" (v. 21).

The entire comment about David's refusal to punish Amnon because of his love is missing from the MT, but may be recovered from the LXX. Its loss can be explained as a result of haplography, the scribe's eye skipping from a word at the beginning of the lost text to an identical word at the beginning of v. 22.

David offered Tamar nothing, but Absalom consoled his sister and allowed her to live in his house, where she dwelt as a "desolate woman." Tamar's desolation was so severe because Amnon's assault and subsequent spurning had taken not only her virginity, but also her future prospects of marriage. Her status was equivalent to that of an unwanted divorcee.

The narrator's picture of Absalom is one of a complex man whose mind works on many levels. Even as Absalom comforted his violated sister and urged her not to "take it to heart," he ignored his own advice and inwardly swore vengeance against his half-brother Amnon. "Absalom spoke to Amnon neither good nor bad" (v. 22) could mean that Absalom did not speak to Amnon at all, but more likely suggests that he bided his time, masking the depth of his anger over Amnon's affront.

Absalom's wait, according to the text, lasted two years. When the king and father did not act to punish his criminal son or to aid his violated daughter, Absalom sought the right moment to take his own action.

Brother Absalom Gets Revenge, 13:23-39

The propitious opportunity arose when Absalom planned a great celebration surrounding the shearing of the sheep on his estate in Baal-hazor. [Baal-hazor] His invitation to David (who declined, v. 24) helped to alleviate any suspicion, as well as to absolve David of any implication in the following events. It is surprising, however, that Absalom would ask specifically for Amnon to attend since he had already invited "all the king's sons" to the festal meal (v. 23), and this special request would draw attention to the bringing of Absalom and Amnon together.

Baal-hazor

AΩ Baal-hazor is identified in the MT as being "near Ephraim." In this context, Ephraim does not refer to the tribal boundaries of the Ephraim clan, but to a particular town. Other witnesses to the text identify the town as *ʿoprâ* (see also Josh 18:23) or *ʿeprôn* (see 2 Chr 13:19). Perhaps Ephraim was a later name deriving from the earlier ones. Some have related it with the town called Ephraim in John 11:54.

David's excuse for not attending was "let us not all go, or else we will be burdensome to you" (v. 25a). The reader must presume that David had suggested keeping some of the other sons behind, too. Thus, Absalom "pressed him" (13:27a), until David agreed to allow all of his sons, including Amnon, to make the journey to Baal-hazor. The NRSV says David "*let* Amnon and all the king's sons go with him." The Hebrew verb, however, means "sent" (*šālaḥ*): Amnon may not have gone of his own volition, but at his father's behest.

A short phrase missing from the MT but present in the LXX, OL, and probably 4QSamª suggests that the celebration itself was so elaborate that it was "like a king's feast" (v. 27b; cf. 1 Sam 25:36). Though "feast" is a common translation, the Greek word *poton* reflects the underlying Hebrew word *mišteh*, which describes a drinking bout.

Drinking bouts commonly lead to excess, which figured into Absalom's plan. Once Amnon was deep into his cups, he would also be off his guard, allowing Absalom's servants to make easy work of his execution-style slaying (vv. 28-29a). Absalom's encouragement to his servants ("be courageous and valiant") is ironic. In other biblical contexts, similar words inspire positive behavior that brings glory to God, not death to a brother (cf. 2 Sam 10:12 = 1 Chr 19:13; 1 Kgs 2:2; 1 cf. Macc 2:64; 3:58).

Absalom's vengeful act was not a private matter only. The breadth of its political overtones is seen in the ensuing melee, when all other royal sons jumped on their mules and fled for their lives, fearing that Absalom had lured them all to their deaths so that he would have no rivals for king. [Mules] Indeed, the first garbled reports that reached David insisted that all the king's sons were dead, leading to a court-wide outpouring of grief (vv. 30-31).

With a large stroke of irony, the narrator describes how the same slick-tongued Jonadab who had helped Amnon in plotting Tamar's

---

Mules

In David's time, the mule seems to have been the chosen mode of transportation for royalty. Camels, ...ses, horses, and chariots would have been available for ...rsons of royal means (note Absalom and Adonijah's use of ...ariots), but the humble mule seems to have served the ...veryday purpose of getting individual members of the king's ...usehold from place to place. Despite his use of a chariot ...r show, Absalom rode a mule into his final battle (2 Sam ...:19). Later, the saddle used on David's mule was officially ...esented to Solomon as a sign of his succession to the ...rone (1 Kgs 1:33, 38, 44).

It is often suggested that mules (the hybrid offspring of a male donkey and a female horse) would have been imported since the law forbade cross-breeding. We have no way of knowing, however, whether the regulations of Lev 19:19 were widely known or observed during this period. Indigenous Canaanites and many persons of other nationalities lived within the borders of Israel, and they would not have been encumbered by the Hebrew purity laws, so a local supply of mules may have been available.

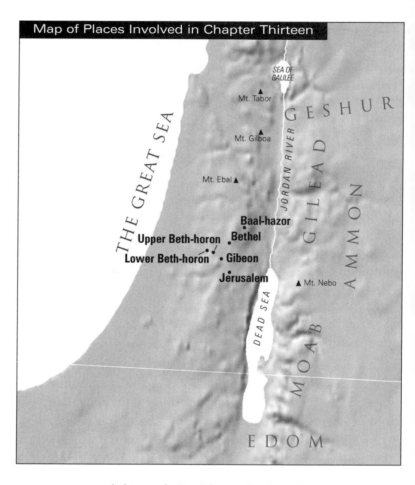

Map of Places Involved in Chapter Thirteen

rape now counsels his uncle David, assuring him that Amnon alone had fallen victim to Absalom's plot since he was the only one who deserved death (vv. 32-33). Thus, Jonadab interprets the event as the outworking of a personal grudge, rather than a bold play for the throne.

Verse 34 opens with a reference to Absalom's flight that seems out of place because it interrupts the story of how David learned the fate of his other sons. Some scholars suggest that it might derive from a marginal note on v. 38 that was mistakenly copied into the text at an early stage since it appears in all witnesses. It is possible, however, that the narrator wanted the reader to be cognizant of Absalom's escape as he told the story of the other brothers' return.

The Horonaim road mentioned in v. 34 derived its name from Upper and Lower Beth Horon (in Hebrew, the suffix *ayîm* indicates a dual number). [Map of Places Involved in Chapter 13] The two Horons are now called Beit 'Ur el-Foqa and Beit 'Ur el-Tata, and they exist a couple of miles apart at a point ten to twelve miles northwest of Jerusalem. The returning party presumably traveled through Bethel (about five miles southwest of Baal-hazor) to Gibeon (another seven or eight miles southwest), where they picked up the Horonaim road to Jerusalem. This may not have been the most direct route but probably offered the best road for a band of significantly impaired mule riders traveling by night.

Once David's watchman announced the party's approach, Jonadab took the opportunity to remind the king of his prescient assurance (v. 35). On the one hand, this note casts an aspersion of conceit on Jonadab. It serves a larger purpose, however, reminding the reader that David had no complicity in the death of Amnon—even the reason for his murder had to be explained to David.

The return of David's sons should have brought some relief to the grieving court (v. 31), but the reunion of the royal family only intensified their weeping (v. 36). The mourning in Jerusalem was not only for the death of Amnon and the flight of Absalom, but for a certain loss of trust and innocence. Whether Absalom intended it or not, the issue of throne succession and its attendant dangers had now been brought into the open. From this point, relationships within the king's family would always be touched by mistrust and paranoia.

The announcement of Absalom's destination explains to the reader why he had chosen Baal-hazor to stage his attack on Amnon: it was sufficiently north of Jerusalem to give him a good head start on any pursuit as he made his way north and east to the region of Geshur, located just east of the Sea of Galilee, in the region now called the Golan. There he found sanctuary in the home of his maternal grandfather Talmai, the king of Geshur (v. 37).

It is not clear that Absalom really needed any sort of political asylum, for David seemed as reticent to punish Absalom as he had been loath to discipline Amnon. When the narrator notes that "David mourned for his son day after day" (v. 37b), the reader is left to wonder if David was mourning for his dead son or his missing one. The reference is almost certainly to Amnon, but the ambiguity adds an artistic element of doubt.

Many commentators assign vv. 38-39 to the following narrative (ch. 14), which explains how it was that Absalom returned to Jerusalem and into David's good graces, at least in a public sense. However, the account of Joab's intercession seems a natural beginning point for that story. Verses 38-39 do not really belong to the preceding story of Amnon's murder, but they serve as an effective transition to the next section, reminding the reader of an extended interim between chapters 13 and 14. Absalom remained in exile for a full three years before his return could be considered.

With v. 39 the author offers a daring view of David's interior feelings and motives, though his precise intention is as muddled as the text. A common translation (as in the NRSV) imagines that David's spirit or heart "went out" to Absalom, yearning for him. A different tradition in the LXX, supported in part by 4QSamᵃ, leads to an entirely different interpretation, namely that the king's enthusiasm for going after Absalom to capture him had cooled after three years so that careful steps toward reconciliation could begin. If David was truly "pining away" for Absalom (as the NJPS suggests), Joab's intervention would hardly have been necessary, and David's treatment of Absalom in 14:24 would be incongruous.

The comment that David "was now consoled over the death of Amnon" seems abrupt, but the reader must remember that three years had passed since Amnon's death. There had been time for healing with regard to Amnon's loss, and the hope of healing David's breach with Absalom was now a possibility.

CONNECTIONS

1. *The sins of the parents.* If the death of Bathsheba's firstborn to David began the fulfillment of Nathan's dark prophecy, the actions of Amnon and Absalom brought it to a full flowering that would ultimately bear even more bitter fruit in Absalom's revolt. Nathan had predicted that Yahweh would raise up adversity for David out of his own house (12:11) and that David's secret sins would be reproved in the light (12:12). Kenneth Chafin has pointed out the way in which Amnon and Absalom fulfilled this forecast by reenacting David's own sins: Amnon's rape of Tamar reflected David's sexual aggression in taking Bathsheba, while Absalom's cold-blooded plot against Amnon replicated David's calculated killing of Bathsheba's husband, Uriah.[1] David's knowledge of this may have impacted his inability to punish Amnon: it was not only his love of Amnon as his eldest son that stayed David's hand, but the awareness that he was also guilty of a similar deed and had set a poor example for his son. It is difficult to punish children for imitating their parents' behavior.

One way in which the sins of the fathers are visited upon subsequent generations (Exod 34:7; Jer 31:29) is that God allows children to observe and learn from their parents, and many learn negative lessons rather than positive ones. Amnon and Absalom had learned about unbridled passion and premeditated murder from their father—and the victims of their crimes were their own sister and brother. Thus, trouble rose up within David's own house, and he could not avoid the knowledge that the responsibility lay at his own feet.

The names of David's two troublesome children border on the prophetic. "Amnon" means "faithful one," but he proved as unfaithful to his sister as David had been unfaithful to his own family. "Absalom" means something like "the father is peace," but it was violence that David's son learned from his father. This observation brings to mind an important question for believers in Jesus Christ, who are called by the name "Christians." This name suggests a meaning such as "Christlike ones." Those who bear the name should practice a periodic self-examination to see if they are living up to it.

2. *Dangerous emotions.* The reader cannot miss the difference in Absalom's response to Amnon and that of his father David. According to the narrator, David "was very angry" (13:21) with his prurient son, but Absalom "*hated* Amnon" (13:22). David was angry, but his anger was tempered by love. Absalom's anger had no such leavening influence. As Tamar remained desolate in Absalom's house, his anger turned to hatred, and the more he nurtured it, the darker it became. Eventually, it led him to plan a cold-blooded killing.

Emotions are dangerous things, especially the negative feelings of anger and hatred. Anger is a natural reaction, but harbored anger leads to discord and the dissolution of relationships. Jesus pointed out that murder, like adultery, begins in the heart (Matt 5:21-22). Marriages may also die as a result of anger or grudges that could have been dealt with early on but grew out of control because they were nurtured over a long period of time.

3. *Family favoritism.* One of David's problems is that his favoritism for certain children was obvious. Especially telling is the note that he did not punish his dissolute son Amnon, "because he loved him, for he was his firstborn" (13:21). Did David not love his daughter Tamar? As far as the text is concerned, David gave no more thought to his daughter, who was now useless to him as a potentially valuable candidate for a political marriage. The reader would like to think that David *did* care, but there is no evidence that he demonstrated any special concern for his violated daughter, while his sentimental attitude toward her rapist led to complete leniency.

Parental partiality will always lead to trouble of one sort or another. Children learn to resent their parents as well as each other.

The seeds of discord are sown, and the harvest is virtually certain. One thing leads to another.

4. *Time helps.* Time may not heal all wounds, but it helps to make them less noticeable. After Amnon's death, it took David three years to reach a point of readiness for renewing his relationship with Absalom. [Does Time Heal?] The time is glossed over quickly in the text, so David's consolation over Amnon's death may seem abrupt to the reader. It may be helpful to recall what is involved in the passing of three years: the number of birthdays, holidays, seasons of the year that occur in the annual cycle, then appear again and again. One mark of David's unique and powerful personality was his ability to feel things deeply but not be paralyzed by his feelings. He could express profound emotion but then move on to practical tasks (cf. 12:15-25; 19:1-8). Amnon was dead, and Absalom was in exile. Nothing David could do would bring Amnon back from the grave. Absalom still lived, however, and the possibility of restoration remained. As the narrative transitions from chapter 13 to chapter 14, the time for mourning had passed, and the time for renewal was at hand.

Does Time Heal?

Grief counselors and persons with experience know that for most people one's response to loss changes over time. The loss of a child is especially painful, for it seems to violate the natural order of the way things should be. One does not "get over" the loss of a child, but emotionally healthy persons do learn to "get through it."

The first year after the death of a loved one is bitter and lonely, as every holiday, birthday, or anniversary comes fraught with a resurgence of pain. The second year is more tolerable, for the passing of time dulls the edge of loss, and the bereaved has learned to anticipate the sharper pain of special days. Many persons find that they begin to feel like themselves again after two or three years. The loss is still present in mind and heart, but it no longer dominates the emotions and thinking process. That David was consoled for his son Amnon after a period of three years fits well with the life experiences of others who have suffered the death of a child.

NOTE

[1] Kenneth L. Chafin, *1, 2 Samuel* (CC; Dallas: Word Books, 1989), 312-19.

JOAB'S LOVE FOR FATHER AND SON

14:1-33

Chapters 13 and 14 describe the background events leading up to Absalom's rebellion against David. Chapter 13 explains two things: (1) the roots of Absalom's disillusionment with his father, and (2) how Absalom found himself in exile, further alienated from David. Absalom's dismay grew from David's failure to administer justice to Amnon, who had raped Absalom's sister Tamar. His exile derived from his decision to take matters of justice into his own hands, resulting in Amnon's death. Chapter 14 begins after an interval of three years, during which Absalom has remained with his maternal grandparents in Geshur, while David refused to make any overtures for good or bad.

COMMENTARY

There appears to be a serious textual misplacement in chapter 14, unless the author has intentionally convoluted his story for literary effect. If so, the confusion of the present order far outweighs the intended purpose. Verses 15-17 obviously belong with the woman's original tale, taking up the story where v. 7 leaves off and before David responded in v. 8. The narrator may have intended for the present order to stand, with vv. 15-17 representing the woman's attempt to return to her dissimulation even after David had found her out, which would be pointless. Suggested reasons for creating the present literary order are not convincing, while any logical explanation for a textual transposition—which occurs in all witnesses—is lacking. The meaning or intent of the story does not change in either case, but it makes most sense when read in this order: vv. 1-7, 15-17, 8-14, 18-33.

The Wise Woman of Tekoa

Tekoa was a rustic farming village, located in the desolate hills of Judea, some ten miles south of Jerusalem. It was a dry, sparse place to live. Occasional voices suggest that Tekoa was also home to a strong wisdom tradition, but the evidence is limited to two things: (1) Joab enlisted a "wise woman of Tekoa" to act out a parable before David (2 Sam 14:2), and (2) the 8th century prophet Amos had some connections with Tekoa. It is usually assumed that Tekoa was Amos' home town, but the text says nothing more than that the words of Amos were known among the shepherds of Tekoa (Amos 1:1). It is just as possible that Amos settled in Tekoa after his northern ministry, and his teachings were remembered and recorded there. Scholars often note the influence of wisdom traditions in Amos' writing, but there is no other evidence to put Tekoa on the map as a center of Hebrew wisdom.

The Woman of Tekoa Tells a Story, 14:1-20

The closing verses of chapter 13 suggested that David's thoughts had turned toward Absalom, though the particular tenor of his thinking is unclear. Most translations suggest that "his heart went out to Absalom," though the text can also be interpreted to mean that David's enthusiasm for going out to capture Absalom had subsided. David's exact attitude may remain a mystery to the reader, but the perceptive Joab understood that "the king's mind was on Absalom" (v. 1) and that David would never be at peace until the Absalom issue was resolved. This must be why the faithful aide chose to intervene with the king, masterminding a risky ruse intended to force David's hand.

Joab is pictured throughout the books of Samuel as a man of action who gets things done. How Joab knew of the wise woman from Tekoa is unspoken. [The Wise Woman of Tekoa] Some writers suggest that she was a well-known and influential personage, like the wise woman of Abel who wielded such apparent power in 2 Samuel 20:16-22. If so, however, she would certainly have been recognized by some in the court, unless her mourning dress doubled as an effective disguise. Tekoa, an agricultural village, was located about ten miles south of Jerusalem in the desert hills of Judea. The Hebrew word for "wisdom" (*ḥokmâ*) has many connotations, including the gifts of being skilled in speech, quick-witted, and capable of performing a task. Joab was in need of an actress who could think on her feet, not a living repository of Hebrew traditions.

Putting Words in Others' Mouths

In modern speech, we sometimes say, "You took the words right out of my mouth." This depicts the reverse of Joab's actions, which were to put words into another's mouth. This expression also appears in other biblical texts. In Exod 4:15, Yahweh told the reticent Moses how Aaron would speak for him: "You shall speak to him and put the words in his mouth; and I will be with your mouth and with his mouth, and will teach you what you shall do." Likewise, the pagan prophet Balaam insisted to King Balak of Moab that God had put words in his mouth, and he had no choice but to speak the words he had been given: "I have come to you now, but do I have power to say just anything? The word God puts in my mouth, that is what I must say" (Num 22:38). Though obscured in most English translations, Ezra's instructions to a courier in Ezra 8:17 were described by the same idiom: Ezra put words into his mouth.

Two Sons, a Field, and a Fight

It is often noted that the woman's account calls to mind the story of Cain and Abel (Gen 4:1-16). Cain reportedly killed his brother while in the field and then fled into exile, from which he never returned. The stories are different in other ways, however. Cain's murder of Abel was premeditated and one-sided, an ambush rather than a fair fight. In contrast, the woman of Tekoa suggested that her sons fought in the heat of the moment, and one was killed only because no one was present to separate them. The story of Cain and Abel is actually closer to the truth of David's situation, however, since Amnon's murder was also carefully planned and executed.

The narrator insists that the plan is Joab's from the beginning (vv. 2-3). He gives detailed instructions for what the woman is to wear, to do, and to say; the text graphically notes that "Joab put the words in her mouth." [Putting Words in Others' Mouths] The reader may note how the motif of mourning has appeared again, as it did in 13:19 and 31 (see [Symbols of Mourning in Ancient Israel]). The same motif will recur at 15:23, 30, 32, and 18:33–19:4. This frequent reference to mourning behavior reminds the reader that Absalom's story is filled with grief from beginning to end.

The reader wonders if Joab took his inspiration from Nathan, whose sharp juridical parable was so effective in convincing David of his guilt in the Bathsheba-Uriah affair. The woman comes before David dressed in the mourning clothes of a widow doubly bereaved, and falls to her face in the most obsequious, pitiful posture, crying out for help (v. 5). At David's invitation, she poured out her story. The reader knows that her histrionics are an act and that her story is pure dissembling. But David does not know.

The woman relates a pitiable tale. Not only has her husband died, but one of the two sons who remained to support her in her old age has killed the other in an impulsive altercation. [Two Sons, a Field, and a Fight] Now, other family members feel compelled to extract blood vengeance against her son, which would deprive the poor woman of all that remained to her, and cut off her family from Israel's future. [The Avenger of Blood] She asks David, in effect, to issue a pardon for her remaining son and to guarantee his safety, even though he is admittedly guilty and though such a pardon would fly in the face of the law. He is her "last remaining ember" (v. 7), the only one left to care for her, the only one who could maintain the position of her husband's family within "the heritage of God" (v. 16).

The Avenger of Blood

ΑΩ In v. 7, the woman states that her extended family has risen against her, and in v. 15 it is "the people" who give her concern. In v. 11, however, her fears concern the "avenger of blood" (gōʾēl haddām, lit., the "redeemer of blood"). Technically, the avenger of blood was the closest male relative of the slain kinsman, obligated by ancient custom to carry out a vendetta of death against the murderer (see Gen 9:6). Hebrew law allowed persons who killed without intent to find refuge in certain sanctuary cities until their case could be heard (Num 35:9-28; Deut 19:4-13; Josh 20:1-9). If convicted, the guilty party was to be surrendered to the blood avenger for summary execution.

The woman's story (*Joab's* story!) suggests that there are times when legalism must give way to grace, when justice must be tempered with mercy, when different solutions must be found. Joab knew that David would be susceptible to such thinking because he already practiced it: he had not enforced the law against Amnon, nor had he actively sought for Absalom's apprehension. Thus, he had instructed the woman to flatter David by insisting that he should recognize such aberrant cases when he saw them, for he was "like the angel of God, discerning good and evil" (v. 17; see also v. 20 and 19:28). [Like an Angel?]

Like an Angel?

David's comportment in the preceding years would certainly not predispose one to imagine that he behaved like an angel. The word translated as "angel" means "messenger" or "envoy." Some argue that the appellation suggests an Israelite theology of kingship in which the king was considered to be semi-divine (cf. Ps 2). Whenever this particular expression is used, however, it is on the lips of someone trying to ingratiate themselves to King David. Also, it is limited to the arena of justice. The woman claims that David is "like the angel of God, discerning good and evil." Good and evil are not to be interpreted as a merismus (suggesting royal omniscience), but as indicators of the king's astute judgment in legal matters.

David's first response is ambiguous ("I will give orders concerning you," v. 8), leading the woman to press for an official judgment in her favor. She offers to accept any blame upon herself if the judgment should prove to be in error (v. 9) and implies that David should call Yahweh to mind in conjunction with his decision (v. 11). David seems to have accepted her appeal for clemency under the extenuating circumstances described. He promised to offer his protection (v. 10), swearing by Yahweh: "As the LORD lives, not one hair of your son shall fall to the ground" (v. 12).

Having brought the king around to her way of thinking, the woman commenced her risky foray into the king's business. More tactfully than Nathan, but with less force, she asks permission to speak a further word to the king (v. 12). She implies that David, by his own judgment, has convicted himself of being a wrongful avenger of blood, in that he has not brought home "the banished one" (v. 13). Her argument in v. 14 is convoluted, but clear. Amnon is dead: like water spilled on the ground, he cannot be recovered. Absalom, however, still lives. Renewal is possible. God wants Absalom restored and has devised this plan to accomplish the goal.

The reader should know that there are several points of dissimilarity between the woman's story and David's situation. The woman's reputed son was killed in an unintentional, impulsive act, but Absalom's murder of Amnon was coldly premeditated. In addition, the woman's argument about having only one son left to carry on does not apply to David, who had many sons, none of whom had a destitute widow for a mother. Finally, her story implies that David had been seeking Absalom's death, while the text insists that

Absalom was in no immediate danger. The parable was not so crisp or straightforward as Nathan's tale (12:1-6), but the woman did not have the same right to come before the king and tell him someone else's story. She had to pretend it was her own tale, and the included elements were necessary to gain David's sympathy.

Despite the disparities, however, the basic principle was the same. One son had killed his brother, but there were mitigating circumstances to consider. There were many who considered Amnon's murder a justifiable homicide, and David himself was culpable in the circumstances leading to it. The woman complains that David's failure to restore Absalom is an intentional affront to the people of God (v. 13)—implying that Joab is only one of many who longs for the exile's return.

Once David saw through the woman's ruse, he immediately suspected Joab of complicity and demanded that the woman come clean. She then gave up the masquerade and honestly reported that Joab had planned the entire scheme "to change the course of affairs" (vv. 18-20). The woman's quick wit is seen in her continued use of fawning flattery, speaking again of David as the wise angel of God who knows all and thus decides rightly.

Absalom Returns to Jerusalem, 14:21-24

David was now faced with the difficult task of bringing Absalom home while pretending that it was his own decision. The text implies that Joab was standing by David even as the woman spoke so that David turned immediately to Joab and said, "Very well, I grant this [lit., "I will do this thing"]; go, bring back the young man Absalom" (v. 21). Joab's immediate and obeisant prostration before David must have grown from relief over his personal safety as much as the success of his ruse (v. 22). David could have punished Joab severely for his daring effrontery, but he chose to accept the rebuke with good grace and to allow Absalom's return.

The story does not lead to the expected happy ending, however. Though Joab immediately traveled to Geshur and brought Absalom back to Jerusalem (v. 23), David refused to see his son. "Let him go to his own house," the king said, "he is not to come into my presence" (v. 24). Thus, while Joab found favor with David, Absalom had not, but the text does not say why. Had David's emotional feelings for Absalom cooled after the encounter with the Tekoite woman? Had other advisors stepped in during Joab's absence to question David's decision? Was the king simply having second thoughts, or was he afraid of what he might do when he saw Absalom again? The reader is left to speculate while Absalom and his father remain alienated for another two full years.

Absalom Returns to the Palace, 14:25-33

Verses 25-27 offer the reader a parenthetical aside, probably a secondary insertion, but drawn from long-standing traditions. It was designed to explain why Absalom was so popular with the people. Earlier, the narrator had warned against judging potential kings based on their appearance (1 Sam 16:7), though he could not refrain from gushing over David's beauty (1 Sam 16:12). Absalom is the only one of David's sons to be described as handsome, and no biblical personage is accorded such a fawning picture of physical attractiveness (v. 25). Absalom's practice of shaving his head once per year led the rabbis to postulate that he was a Nazirite (*Nazir* 4b), but there is no other evidence for that view. The hair from his annual shave reportedly weighed 200 shekels, roughly four to five pounds (the LXX has a more realistic 100 shekels).

The mention of Absalom's hair may serve several purposes. It may be intended, as with Samson, to be a sign of personal virility and strength. It may look backward to David's oath that he would not let one hair of the guilty son's head fall to the ground. Or it may even foreshadow the account of Absalom's death, since interpreters from the time of Josephus have postulated that it was his luxuriant locks that became entangled in the tree.

The report that Absalom had three sons is a puzzle because 18:18 insists that Absalom built a monument to himself because he had *no sons* to carry forward his memory. It has often been suggested that there were indeed three sons, all of whom died young. Perhaps that is why their names are not given. Absalom's one daughter was named Tamar, perhaps in honor of her desolate aunt. Commentators have occasionally argued that it was Absalom's daughter and not his sister who was the victim of rape. Both are described as "beautiful women" and both are related to Absalom, but there is no other reason to confuse their identities or to suggest there was only one Tamar.

For the modern reader, it may seem difficult to imagine Absalom living in Jerusalem for a full two years without once being invited to the palace (v. 28). Perhaps David was convinced by his royal counselors—or his other royal sons—that he should keep Absalom at a distance and not effect a full reconciliation. Even Joab, apparently, was in agreement with the king's position since he made no further moves to intercede for Absalom.

He made no further moves, that is, until Absalom forced the issue. After Joab refused the requests to come and meet with him (v. 29), Absalom ordered his servants to set fire to Joab's barley fields, which happened to adjoin one of Absalom's estates (v. 30). [Absalom's Dirty Work] The reader is not to imagine that these fields were in Jerusalem, connected to the houses in which Absalom and Joab lived, making them neighbors in the ordinary sense. Wealthy people who lived in the city generally had estates in the countryside that were supervised by trusted employees and farmed by servants.

> ### Absalom's Dirty Work
>
> Absalom is routinely portrayed as a forceful and determined man, but it is interesting to note that he tended to have others do his dirty work for him. Absalom planned his brother Amnon's murder, but ordered his servants to commit the actual crime (13:28-29). When Absalom could not get Joab's attention by conventional means, he schemed to burn Joab's fields, but again he ordered his servants to do the deed (14:30).
>
> The narrator will turn this practice back upon Absalom at his death. While hanging helplessly in a tree, he was accosted by Joab, who struck the first blow and apparently knocked him from the tree (see comments at 18:14-15) but then allowed ten of his aides to finish the job.

Like his famous hair, Absalom's audacity in burning Joab's fields reminds the reader of the impetuous Samson, who reputedly burned the Philistines' harvest by catching 300 foxes, attaching burning firebrands to their tails, and releasing them amid the standing grain (Judg 15:1-8). Absalom's methods were more prosaic, but just as effective, for Joab immediately stormed into Absalom's house to demand an explanation (v. 31).

Absalom's explanation reveals the depth of his despair—or of his cunning. He had to burn Joab's fields to get his attention, and he had to get Joab's attention because Joab was the only one who could intercede with him for David, and his continued existence was pointless if there could be no reconciliation with the king. Absalom insists that he was better off living in Geshur than in limbo, and declares his preference for death over continuing as a nonentity in Jerusalem (v. 32). It had been five years since the death of Amnon. Absalom, almost certainly, already had designs on the throne, but his options for currying support were limited as long as he remained *persona non grata* with the king. The narrator suggests that Absalom's patience had worn through: he seemed determined to obtain an official pardon or to die trying.

Absalom succeeded in gaining Joab's attention, if not his respect. The ease with which Joab arranged an audience for Absalom is surprising, considering the difficulty of engineering his earlier return to Jerusalem. The narrator's brevity in describing the long-awaited meeting suggests that the occasion was more political than personal, a public gesture that meant more to Absalom than to David. The son approached his father in the manner of a servant or courtier, prostrating himself before the king. [An Intriguing Motif]

An Intriguing Motif

AΩ It is surprising to note how often the motif of falling upon the ground plays into the account of Absalom's rebellion. In some instances, the prostration relates to mourning: In 13:31, David laid on the ground in mourning for Amnon, as he had done for the child of Bathsheba (12:16). Presumably, David did the same for Absalom. David's mourning for Absalom is described in detail, though without specific reference to laying on the ground. When Joab rebuked David, however, he covered his face, and when David agreed to end his public display, he "got up" (18:33–19:8), suggesting a prior position of prostration.

Physical prostration also accompanied obeisance before the king: the woman of Tekoa (14:4), Joab (14:22), Absalom (14:33), Ziba (16:4), and Ahimaaz (18:28) all showed such respect before David. The narrator carefully points out that during Absalom's ploy to steal the hearts of Israel, he posed as the righteous judge that people would

like to have. Suppliants genuflected before him, after which he would kiss them according to custom (15:5).

Other references to falling to the ground relate to violence. David promised the Tekoite woman that not on[e] hair of her son's head would fall to the ground (14:11). A[s] Absalom planned his assault upon David, Hushai's intentionally bad advice spoke of how the troops would f[all] upon David as the dew fell upon the ground (17:12). Wh[en] Absalom died, he was not only knocked from the tree tha[t] had caught him, but his body was thrown into a pit and covered with stones (18:17).

These frequent references to falling upon the ground, accompanied by the recurring motif of mourning (13:19, 31; 14:2; 15:23, 30, 32; 18:33–19:8), give to the narrati[ve] a dark and somber cast. There is no joy for David here. Because of his sin, the good that lay before him had bee[n] turned to evil, the light to darkness, and the sharpest blo[w] came from within his own house (12:11). (See also [Bowing and Scraping].)

Nothing is recorded of what Absalom said or of what David may have replied. David's eloquent weeping for Absalom in 18:33 finds no foreshadowing here. There are no embraces, no tears, no warm words of contrition or forgiveness. Only this—that Absalom fell on his face before the throne, and "the king kissed him."

Some scholars imagine that David's kiss was a sign of acceptance and restoration, as if the prodigal had come home and been forgiven. [The Prodigal] Others suggest that David's kiss imparted to Absalom the seal of approval as his heir apparent. One should be careful, however, not to read too much into David's gesture. In the Old Testament, a kiss was ordinarily a sign of affection or greeting (Gen 27:26-27; 31:28, 55; 20:9; 1 Kgs 19:20), though it was sometimes accompanied by much emotion (Gen 29:11, 13; 33:4; 45:15; 48:10; 50:1). It is surprising that, outside of Genesis, kisses are rarely mentioned. The narrator's restraint in describing the encounter between David and Absalom suggests that Absalom's obeisance was decorous rather than deferential, and David's kiss was more perfunctory than purposeful.

The Prodigal

AΩ The reader may find value in comparing the results of this story with Jesus' account of the prodigal son and the openly forgiving father, as recorded in Luke 15:11-32. Jesus came as a son of David who would be greater than David. He was certainly more willing to forgive than his illustrious ancestor. David may have been an expert in repentance (if Ps 51 may truly be accorded to him), but he knew little of grace.

Absalom had obtained David's public acceptance, but not his approval. Nor had David gained any greater respect from his son. Once the "press conference" was done and Absalom had been officially welcomed home, the royal son immediately set out to displace his father.

CONNECTIONS

Telling Stories, 14:1-20

The power of a good story is an amazing thing. Both Nathan and Joab used stories for the express purpose of helping David to see things in a different way and thus to change. Jesus later adopted the same practice in his teaching, telling parables that were designed to make people think about things in a different way and hopefully to change their living in response to their new understanding.

Unfortunately, the power of a story can work for good or for bad. Evidently, Joab saw the handsome, charming, and popular Absalom as the best candidate among David's sons to succeed him as king. [Absalom] He understood that it was important to plan ahead and to be prepared, lest the king's death initiate a period of weakness and upheaval as various candidates vied for the throne. David's seeming unconcern made his chief aide uneasy. Joab's own tendency was to deal with his enemies by killing them (Abner, Absalom, Amasa), so he may have admired Absalom for his decisive role in eliminating Amnon. Absalom, like Joab, was a man of faithfulness and action. When no one else would avenge Tamar, Absalom took matters into his own hands.

So it was probably with the country's best interest in mind that Joab interceded for Absalom, writing and producing a play to be performed by the woman from Tekoa. He succeeded in persuading David to allow Absalom's return to Jerusalem, though not to the palace. In time, Joab learned that Absalom's foibles outweighed his strengths. The arson Absalom inflicted on Joab's fields was a clue that the young man was too angry and impulsive to be an effective leader.

Absalom
(Illustration Credit: Barclay Burns)

By that time, however, it was too late. Once Absalom received his father's public blessing, he quickly stole the hearts of the people and turned them against David. The character flaws that surfaced make it clear that Absalom would not have been a good king. In the end, David fled the city before Absalom's advance, and it was left up to Joab himself to correct his earlier mistake and eliminate the same young man he had once championed.

Choosing good leaders is crucial to the health and well-being of all nations, municipalities, businesses, and organizations. Poor or mismatched leaders can bring much grief. This is as true of churches as of any other organization. For example, many congregations have grieved because they called a pastor or staff member whose appearance and references were good, but whose personal character, theological views, or political activities proved antagonistic to the people who had called him or her to lead them. Sometimes the persons or committee who were instrumental in the call must pursue the distasteful task of dismissing the troublesome leader.

When choosing leaders of any type, we must beware of being swayed by good stories, impressive speeches, or effective public relations campaigns. Joab and his proxy believed they were the instruments of God's plan when they facilitated Absalom's return (14:14). If Absalom's return was God's design, however, it was a plan for punishment, and not for good.

Coming Home, 14:21-33

When David allowed his son to return, he refused to see him! What an amazing thing. For three years Absalom had lived in exile. For two more years he dwelt in Jerusalem, but under virtual house arrest. David and Absalom were each the most important person in the other's life, yet they did not speak. As a result, there was no healing. David's heart seemed to grow more distant, while Absalom's heart burned ever hotter with anger and a desire for revenge. The reader is left to wonder how things would have turned out if David and Absalom had simply talked and listened to each other.

There is no future for relationships that do not involve constant communication. Persons might remain related by blood or history or the ties of official ceremony, but when spouses, sisters, brothers, or friends do not communicate, their relationships cannot survive. Mutual rapport becomes twisted by misunderstanding, wrongful presumptions, needless anger, and harbored grudges. Without effective communication, relationships will die.

Communication does not begin until some person takes the initiative of approaching the other. Joab took the initiative to facilitate communication between David and Absalom. If he had succeeded, perhaps Israel's history would have been different. Instead, the story of David and his son was a tragedy from beginning to end. The reader is encouraged to review his or her own stories and relationships, and ask, "Who do I need to call today?"

A FALSE VOW AND A
THREATENING CONSPIRACY

15:1-12

Absalom's Rebellion, 15:1–19:8a

With chapters 13–14, the reader has been privy to the personal and somewhat private factors leading up to Absalom's play for the throne. Chapters 15–18 carry the reader beyond the palace walls and into the public arena, as Absalom carries his campaign to the people. [A Chiastic Campaign?] These stories describe Absalom's years of political activity in Jerusalem (15:1-6), followed by the consolidation of his conspiracy in Hebron (15:7-12), a popular march on Jerusalem (15:13–16:23), and the planning of actual war against David, which fails miserably (17:1–18:33).

In all of this, David is conspicuously withdrawn. He freely allows Absalom to sow dissension in Jerusalem and to organize his revolt in Hebron. He flees from Jerusalem before Absalom's advance. After planning an effective military strategy to defend the crown, he pleads with his own soldiers to "deal gently for my sake with the young man Absalom" (18:5). When they kill the rebel leader instead, David mourns more loudly than he had done for any of his other sons (18:31–19:8a). It is the same pattern of behavior that David followed after his son Amnon raped his daughter Tamar: he was clearly distraught, but patently unable to take any effective action regarding his own children, even when their machinations extended far beyond the royal household. If the narrator's intent is to portray David as a weak

---

A Chiastic Campaign?

AΩ A.A. Anderson (*2 Samuel*, 202), who follows C. Conroy (*Absalom*, 89) with some modifications, finds a chiastic structure in the account of Absalom's rebellion, extending through the end of ch. 20:

A. The beginning of the revolt—15:1-12
  B. David's flight (meeting scenes)—15:13–16:14
    C. Confrontation of counselors—16:15–17:23
    C´. Confrontation of armies—17:24–19:8a
  B´. David's return (meeting scenes)—19:8b-41
A´. The end of the rebellion and its aftermath—19:41–20:22

and broken man in the aftermath of his blatant adultery and Nathan's bleak prophecy, he has succeeded.

COMMENTARY

Absalom's ceremonial reconciliation with David (14:33) released him from his *persona non grata* status and allowed him to express in public fashion his growing megalomania and obvious designs on the throne. This brief section describes how Absalom duped the people who came to Jerusalem in search of justice (15:1-6), how Absalom duped the king into allowing his departure from the city (15:7-9), and finally, how Absalom duped the people of Hebron and elsewhere, with the result being that "the conspiracy grew in strength, and the people with Absalom kept increasing" (15:12b).

The narrator leaves no doubt about Absalom's intentions. First, he obtained a chariot and fifty bodyguards, an ostentatious sign of royal pretension (v. 1). Some years later, his brother Adonijah would do the same thing to announce his own regnal ambitions (1 Kgs 1:5). Whether the fifty men were intended more for public display or as the nucleus of a potential army is uncertain. Moses reportedly divided Israel into administrative units of thousands, hundreds, fifties, and tens (Exod 18:21; Deut 1:15). These numbers may have served for military divisions, also. Some writers have proposed that the chariot and bodyguards were granted by the king to the heir apparent, but the evidence that Absalom was so designated is missing. The text makes it clear that both Absalom and Adonijah took the initiative in obtaining their accouterments of royalty.

A carefully designed series of verbs designed to show habitual behavior carries the action in vv. 2-6. Thus, Absalom's practice of standing beside the city gate and interviewing all who came seeking a royal hearing is presented as a daily habit. The young pretender routinely acknowledged that the litigants' claims were just, and bemoaned the lack of anyone appointed by the king to hear their case. If it were up to *him*, Absalom insisted, *he* would bring justice to the land. In this way, Absalom subverted the loyalty of the people and guided prospective litigants away from the palace before they could learn whether his claims were true.

It is often suggested that Absalom simply exploited a real situation in which David's growing senility or declining interest in government had led to an inadequate or ineffective system of justice in the kingdom. Thus, Absalom would have been fanning the flames of preexisting discontent. This may be true, but is not a necessary assumption. David does not appear to be incapacitated so much as distant. Also, the alleged unhappy state of justice in the land is always described *in Absalom's words* and at Absalom's initiative. He would *get up early* in the morning, *station himself* by the gate with his regal panoply, and actively *call out* to those who came seeking justice. It is obvious that Absalom intended to draw attention to himself and to prejudice the people's opinion of David, thus circumventing the normal channels of appeal.

If the king cared nothing for justice, it is surprising that Joab's ruse of 14:5-11 was so successful, for it depended on an unwashed widow from tiny Tekoa successfully gaining access to the king himself and obtaining a favorable judgment. The implication is that Absalom interposed himself upon claimants at the city gate, because had they proceeded, they *would* have found a hearing. For Absalom's plan to succeed, he had to turn them away at the gate. The young pretender's claim that there was not one person appointed to handle legal claims seems highly exaggerated, though necessary to give proper force to Absalom's constant and vocal wish: "If only *I* were judge in the land!" (v. 4).

---

owing and Scraping

AΩ The image of "falling to the ground" is a recurring motif in the account of David's personal suffering nd decline in the aftermath of the Bathsheba affair. The notif is developed around two *Leitwörter*, or frequently epeated terms. They are *nāfal*, meaning "to fall" (14:4, 11, 2; 17:11), and *šāḥah*, which indicates bowing down or rostrating oneself to pay homage (14:4, 22, 33; 15:5; 16:4; 8:21, 28). Twice, the word *nāšaq* ("to kiss") is associated vith the latter word (14:33; 15:5).

Many writers have pointed to the highly stylized nature of Sam 13–20, but the motif of "falling down" has rarely been oticed. The woman of Tekoa, sent by Joab, falls to the round (*nāpal*) and pays homage to David (*šāḥah*, 14:4) efore relating her story to the king. After achieving the esired result, Joab concludes the interview by doing the ame (14:22). When Absalom is finally brought before the ng, he also bows with his face to the ground (*šāḥah*) efore receiving the king's kiss of public affirmation (14:33).

The motif carries into the following chapter, where bsalom sets himself up as a pseudo-king who would hear he cases of litigants who have come in search of justice. Vhen the populace would bow down and pay homage to im, Absalom would grant them the royal kiss (15:5).

A related theme of "falling" has to do with violence. Vhen David heard the Tekoite woman's faux suit, he swore

that not one hair of her son's head would fall to the ground (14:11). This may be an ironic foreshadowing of ch. 18, where David's own son Absalom (who corresponds to the Tekoite woman's putative progeny) will die, perhaps as a partial consequence of his luxuriant hair! The word for "falling" is not used of Absalom in ch. 18, but the young pretender and all of his hair not only fell *to* the earth, but *into* the earth.

The account of how the news of Absalom's death is brought to David also employs a series of prostrations. There were probably four, though only two are mentioned in the text. The Cushite runner bowed before Joab as he received his assignment (18:21). Ahimaaz also received an assignment, but there is no comment about his bowing (18:22-23). Ahimaaz reached David first and prostrated himself before the king (18:28). When the Cushite messenger arrived, he also presumably bowed before David, though the text does not record it (18:31).

An element of ironic inversion touches on this motif. In 17:11, the trusted counselor Ahithophel recommends a plan to attack David in which Absalom's army would steal upon him and fall upon him like the dew. In reality, it is Absalom's army who will be fallen upon and destroyed by David's seasoned troops.

The reader will note the recurring motif of bowing or doing obeisance, accompanied here (as in 14:33) by royal kissing as a sign of public acceptance, if not affection. [Bowing and Scraping] It is this persuasive play of accepting obeisance and offering royal affection, repeated time after time, that enabled the charming but deceptive Absalom to *steal* (*wayĕgannēb*)—not "win over"—the hearts (or loyalty) of Israel's impressionable populace. The narrator's bold irony is unmistakable: the one who speaks so loudly of justice is a thief!

Absalom's machinations won him wide acclaim throughout the kingdom, and it would be naive to assume that David was unaware of his son's actions. Yet he made no moves to forestall him. As Absalom prepared for the next step in his coronation, however, he needed to find another venue where there would be greater freedom to pursue his plot without interference from Joab or other officials who might persuade David to take action.

Apparently, even royal princes needed permission from the king to travel very far. Not only did Absalom want to journey all the way to Hebron, but he wished to take a large party with him. The reader knows by now that Absalom's earlier desire to be reunited with David was only a ruse to return to Jerusalem in official favor and to win a broader base of support. David, however, acts as if he does not know this. The narrator portrays him as being ruled by a sentimental love for Absalom that causes him to be overly trustful, always hoping for the best.

Thus, when Absalom comes to David after four years of biding his time (v.7), David seems ignorant of his son's intentions. This strikes the reader as incredible. Could Absalom parade around with a chariot and fifty bodyguards, openly promoting himself and subverting the king, without David hearing about it? Would David's love for Absalom have blinded him to the obvious? Whatever the case, Absalom takes no chances, and designs a pretext for his journey to Hebron that cannot be denied: the payment of a sacred vow. [Making and Paying Vows]

As Absalom approaches the king with his request, the careful reader will remember that once before he had come to the king with hidden motives, requesting leave to host a festal occasion. In 13:23-38, Absalom had asked David's permission for the other royal sons to attend the annual festivities surrounding the

Making and Paying Vows

Old Testament vows, by definition, involve conditional promises attached to particular requests. Thus, Absalom pledges to offer special worship in Hebron, but *only if* Yahweh should bring him back safely to Jerusalem (cf. Num 21:1-3; Gen 28:20-22; Judg 11:3-40; see discussion of vow-making at 1 Sam 1:1-11).

One might promise a material gift to God or some act of personal service and devotion. Vows were often accompanied by sacrifices as a final element of closure to the bargain. The meat from the sacrifices was shared by the priests and the person making the sacrifice, but had to be eaten within two days. Thus, the payment of vows was often accompanied by a feast, to which family and friends might be invited.

shearing of his sheep, using the affair as a ruse to arrange Amnon's murder. Now, Absalom comes again, begging leave to go to Hebron, taking with him a large number of unsuspecting guests to participate in the festal meal accompanying the sacrifices he would offer in payment of his vow.

How could David be taken in again? Only because of the unique qualities of Absalom's crafty artifice: the vow was a sacred obligation that had to be honored. If the customs found in Numbers 30 were current in David's (or the narrator's) time, fathers could cancel the vows of their daughters, but not of their sons. Thus, David may wonder why Absalom has waited for four (or possibly six) years to fulfill his vow, and he may suspect that his son has ulterior motives in claiming to have made this vow, but he cannot deny him the privilege of fulfilling it.

> **Yahweh in Hebron**
>
> ΑΩ Interpreters are divided on the issue of whether this phrase means that Absalom promised to go to Hebron to worship Yahweh or whether he pledged worship to Yahweh-in-Hebron, a presumed local manifestation of Yahweh. There is some epigraphic evidence from Kuntillet ʿAjrūd that should be considered: inscribed pithoi from the 8th century BC bear the titles "Yahweh of Samaria" and "Yahweh of Teman." Even so, the more natural sense is to read the phrase as an adverbial construction, though admittedly in an ambiguous position. The addition of a comma clarifies this view: "Please let me go and pay my vow which I have vowed to Yahweh, in Hebron."

"At the end of four years" (v. 7) is generally thought to mean four years after Absalom's public reconciliation with David, and thus six years after his return to Jerusalem. Absalom claims to have made a vow while still living in Geshur, promising that if God would bring about his return to Jerusalem, he would offer worship to Yahweh in Hebron (v. 8). [Yahweh in Hebron] Since David had expressed a desire to establish a temple in Jerusalem, Absalom's request to pay his vow through offering sacrifices in Hebron serves to further distance father and son. Hebron was David's capital when he was crowned king over Judah, prior to the uniting of the kingdom. According to 2 Samuel 3:3, Absalom was born there.

The description of Absalom's audience with the king is significant: The narrator has arranged Absalom's quotation of his vow in such a way as to underscore the irony of the situation: "For your *servant* vowed a vow . . . saying, 'If Yahweh will surely return me to Jerusalem, then *I will serve* Yahweh' " (v. 8). In v. 2, Absalom had delighted in having others call themselves "your servant" while bowing before him. He does anything but "serve" David while undermining his father's popular support, and his promised "service" to Yahweh seems just as fraudulent. The very vagueness of the pledge, in contrast to the specific promises made in other biblical vows, underscores the specious nature of his purported vow. Absalom has no intention of being anyone's servant. [Absalom and Jacob]

Absalom and Jacob

The account of Absalom's vow suggests an implicit comparison between the vows of Absalom and Jacob, another strong-willed swindler (cf. Gen 28:20-22). Both Absalom and Jacob prayed for a safe return to their home. Characteristically, they also both tended to seek the upper hand at any cost and were willing to use even the sacred institution of vow-making to further their own interests.

It is inconceivable that David would not have had serious misgivings about Absalom's request, but the narrative reveals nothing of it. David sent Absalom away with his blessing: "Go in peace" (v. 9).

[Speaking Peace Where There Is No Peace]

Vows were often paid in conjunction with annual festivals (see 1 Sam 1:21), so an approaching celebration may have facilitated Absalom's ruse, which involved two hundred men from Jerusalem who were invited guests. Perhaps Absalom took them with him for cover: the narrator insists that they went "in their innocence, knowing nothing of the matter" (v. 11). As he traveled from Jerusalem, Absalom's furtive emissaries were spreading through the land ("to all the tribes of Israel"), preparing his supporters for action. "The sound of the trumpet" refers to the piercing wail of the shofar a wind instrument made from a ram's horn. The high squeal of the shofar can be heard for great distances, but obviously not throughout Israel unless some sort of relay network was in place.

The narrator underscores the depth of Absalom's deception by insisting that even in the midst of the sacred act of offering the sacrifices promised by his reputed vow (v. 12), he was sending messages in support of the insurgence. As he maintained the festal charade, Absalom sent for Ahithophel the Gilonite, a covert

---

Speaking Peace Where There Is No Peace

The careful reader will note the development of an ironic theme played out through an intricate wordplay on the stem *šlm*. Cognates of *šlm* can suggest "peace," "wholeness," or "well-being." In the present context, the motif of peace seems to be most evident.

Absalom's very name is built from the stem *šlm*: *ʾabšālôm* could mean "the [heavenly] father is peace," or perhaps, "my father is peace." But neither Absalom nor his father is a man of peace: their lives are characterized by violence and bloodshed. Absalom asks leave to go and *fulfill* his vow, which is denoted by the verbal form *šallēm*. The intensive verbal form of *šlm* can mean "to pay" or "complete"—a good way to keep peace with creditors. In Absalom's purported vow, he had prayed for a safe return to *Jerusalem* (*yĕrûšālaim*), a city whose name might mean "city of peace"

(though some say it means "foundation of Shalem," with *šalem* being the name of a local god). A reader who is familiar with the vow of Jacob (Gen 28:20-22), which specifically requests a return home "in peace" (*bĕšālôm*), might expect to find the same adverbial modifier here. In a sense, this gap where the word is expected serves to emphasize the impact of David's terse reply: *lēk bĕšālôm*, "Go in peace." David, who had perhaps entertained hopes peace when he first spoke his son's name, continues to ho for peace as he sends Absalom away with the last words h will ever speak to him in life: "Go in peace." But Absalom is going to war, and his father will be his foe. For further reading, see Tony W. Cartledge, *Vows in the Hebrew Bible and the Ancient Near East*, JSOT Supplement Series 147 (Sheffield: JSOT Press, 1992), 193-98.

Ahithophel the Gilonite

Some writers have suggested that this name may be a deliberate distortion of the original, a nickname given after the fashion of the Ishbosheth/Ishbaal substitution (see discussion at 2 Sam 2:8). *ʾAḥî* means "my brother," but the element *tōpel* does not appear in any other Hebrew name. *Tōpel* seems to mean something like "foolishness." Thus, "Ahithophel" would mean "my brother is foolishness," an astonishing moniker for the man whose counsel was considered to be "the oracle of God" (2 Sam 16:23). It is possible, then, that the official's original name is lost to us but was deliberately distorted by later writers as a satirical jab at the traitorous counselor. Some have suggested an original name such as "Ahiphelet," reflecting a rearrangement of the consonants (compare the name "Eliphelet," 2 Sam 5:16 and 23:34), while others have opted for "Ahibaal," on the model of Ishbaal/Ishbosheth (2 Sam 2:8).

The city or town of Gilo is listed in Josh 15:48-51 as one of eleven towns located south of Hebron in the hill country of Judah. Its current site is unknown.

Ahithophel had a son named Eliam who was renowned as one of David's "mighty men" (23:34). Since Bathsheba's father was named Eliam (11:3), some have suggested that Ahithophel was her grandfather-in-law. It is just as likely, however, that there were two different men named Eliam.

Ahithophel offered Absalom wise counsel on more than one occasion, but his last bit of advice was not heeded. When Ahithophel's good counsel to Absalom regarding the attempted capture of David was frustrated by Hushai's deliberately bad advice, he knew that Absalom's uprising would fail and that his treasonable actions would bring him a swift execution. So he went home to Gilo, put his affairs in order, and hanged himself (18:23).

co-conspirator who had continued to serve David's counselor. [Ahithophel the Gilonite]

The arrival of Ahithophel and other confederates in Hebron bolstered Absalom's cause, so the narrator could summarize that "the conspiracy grew in strength, and the people with Absalom kept increasing" (v. 12). [Why the Revolt?] The language is reminiscent of 3:1; while David had ruled as king in Hebron, "David grew stronger and stronger, while the house of Saul became weaker and weaker." The author has not spoken as plainly of David's weakness in contrast to Absalom's strength (in Hebron!), but the implication is clear.

The ironic motif of this section deserves a summary reprise: Absalom speaks of justice while stealing the people's loyalty from his father. Absalom, who will be no one's servant, claims to serve both David and Yahweh. Absalom, who claims to have made a sacred vow, takes Yahweh's name in vain. Absalom, whose name may reflect a father's wish for peace, seeks public peace with his father, is granted a blessing of peace, and then goes out to prepare for war against the one who had blessed him.

Why the Revolt?

The reader is left largely in the dark concerning the real issues underlying the great surge in support for Absalom, though the account in 15:1-6 contains two clues that bear exploration. Absalom's devious methods suggest that he contributed to the blooming disaffection by telling supplicants that there was no justice to be found in the court of the king.

A second element, generally overlooked, is that Absalom would commonly ask of disgruntled claimants, "From what city are you?" When the person said, "Your servant is of such and such a tribe in Israel," *then* Absalom would say, "See, your claims are good and right" (15:2b-3a). The establishment of one's ethnic identity as an Israelite provided sufficient evidence for Absalom to say "your claims are good and right." This suggests the possibility of an increasing resentment against foreign influence in Israel, especially in leadership positions.

David had put his capital in a Jebusite city and then quickly appointed Zadok (widely presumed to be a Jebusite priest) to serve alongside Abiathar as co-high priest in Israel. David's own army included mercenaries from other nations, including the Philistines. Uriah the Hittite and Ittai the Gittite are only two of many foreigners who had gained positions of power and prestige under David's administration. Uriah lived within easy sight of David's palace (11:2-3), an obvious sign of royal favor. Ittai commanded 600 Gittites who served faithfully in David's defense, joining the "Cherethites and the Pelethites" as stalwarts of David's army. David's outward attempt to forestall Ittai from accompanying his retreat ("for you are foreigner," 15:19) may suggest an awareness of disconte as much as a test of loyalty.

Thus, despite Absalom's own multiethnic background (his mother was a princess from Geshur, 3:3), he may ha tapped into a burgeoning nationalistic sentiment to fuel h own ambitions. He sympathizes with the injustice given t native Israelites; he has himself proclaimed king in the former capital of Hebron; he draws his support from families of long-standing in Israel and Judah. Rather than playing on a rivalry between the northern and southern tribes, Absalom seems to have united the ethnic core of Israel and Judah against the influence of immigrants. The growth of protectionist and nationalist sentiment in mode Western nations such as America—even in times of grea prosperity—illustrates how easy it is to tap into popular fear and resentment of persons who are of different ethni or national backgrounds.

CONNECTIONS

Theft Protection for the Heart, 15:1-12

The early stages of Absalom's rebellion are filled with contrasts and rife with irony. By stationing himself at the gate with his princely entourage and royal trappings, Absalom made himself appear to be king, though he was not. He shrewdly fanned the flames of discontent with the monarchy, ingratiating himself to the people of Israel and promising a better life if only he were king. Over a period of time, Absalom managed to dupe both common people and leaders of the land, acquiring a sizeable following in Israel. The narrator uses a forceful verb to say that Absalom "stole the hearts" of the people.

The reader quickly becomes aware that the narrator's sympathies do not lie with Absalom. Despite David's own failures, he portrays David as the good king and Absalom as the wicked usurper. David, though imperfect, is God's man, but Absalom seeks to overthrow him by fraudulent means.

Absalom's techniques in "stealing" the hearts of Israel are remarkably similar to the serpent's strategy for persuading Eve to turn against God (whether this tradition was known to Absalom is moot; it was apparently familiar ground for the narrator). The serpent had craftily suggested that God was holding back the knowledge that would grant divine wisdom, thus planting seeds of distrust and leading Eve to accept the tempter's choice of action (Gen 3:1-7). Likewise, Absalom led persons to believe that King David was withholding the justice they deserved and desired, cultivating distrust in the current regime and winning their loyalty for his insurrection.

Modern readers who seek the word of God in this story may profit from putting themselves in the place of those who came to Jerusalem seeking justice and were led astray by Absalom's smooth deception. What voices in our world lead us to doubt the goodness or justice of God by leading us to seek personal excitement or immediate gratification through channels that are antagonistic to God's way? How quickly and thoroughly are we duped by television commercials and print advertisements that promise greater joy through buying, wearing, drinking, or smoking certain wares? How easily are we deceived by the spoken and unspoken pressures of our peer group?

The world is such that there will always be those who employ craft and deceit to sway people toward their own purposes. Mature believers learn to recognize such manipulative mendacity and to trust the goodness of the true God even when tempted by other gods who are more appealing.

David's early response to Absalom's sedition suggests another lesson—one having to do with the danger of allowing evil to go unchecked. David could not have been so naive that he did not notice Absalom's chariot and his fifty runners. He could not have been so uninformed that he was unaware of his son's subversive activities at the gate. Having been led astray by Absalom's deceit prior to the murder of Amnon, David could not have been unsuspecting when his conniving son hid behind the cloak of piety and requested permission to fulfill his reputed vow in Hebron.

Yet the narrator implies that David did nothing. He sent Absalom away with a wish for peace. [Peace Saying and Peace Making] It is as if he hoped the threat would go away if only he ignored it long enough. Modern believers cannot be unaware of the many encroachments evil has made into our culture. Immorality and the "reasonable" use of alcohol or controlled substances are considered acceptable in our society. Abortion is widely embraced as nothing

Peace Saying and Peace Making

AΩ Both Jeremiah and Ezekiel pointed to the dangers of trying to maintain the appearance of tranquility while failing to confront the demons of disharmony within. Jeremiah spoke of those who say "Peace, peace" when there is no peace (6:14; 8:11). Ezekiel spoke of false prophets who misled God's people by "saying 'Peace,' when there is no peace" (13:10; compare 13:16).

Whether individually or collectively, our desire to avoid conflict and to maintain the status quo is both natural and dangerous. By glossing over problems in relationships, marriages fall so deeply into trouble that they never recover. By avoiding issues of genuine disagreement, churches allow the seeds of resentment and factionalism to grow past the point of healing.

David wished a blessing of peace upon his son (whose name meant "My father is peace") even though Absalom had no intention of doing anything peacefully. The last words David said to Absalom were "Go in peace." When Absalom returned, however, it would be for war.

The dynamics of relationships have not changed. David's hard lesson suggests that those who are wise will not ignore conflict, but confront it, even when it is difficult, even when mediation is required. Peace does not come by *saying* "Peace" where there is no peace, but by working hard to make peace a reality. Jesus did not say "Blessed are the peacesayers," but "Blessed are the peace*makers*" (Matt 5:9).

---

more than an alternative means of birth control. The exploiting of the poor in third-world countries is sanctioned or overlooked—so long as it keeps the prices of our new clothes in check. We may know of children or spouses who experience abuse within their families, but we hold our peace and do not intervene. These and many other issues threaten the peace and stability of individuals, of communities, of an entire culture. Christian believers must ask themselves if it is appropriate to keep our heads in the sand, hoping that such deceptive influences will disappear of their own accord.

Believers may well debate how best to influence society, and there will be differences of opinion about how the issues described above (along with many others) can best be approached. The story of David and Absalom offers no advice for holding such dangerous forces in check because David did nothing. Perhaps it is enough to recognize that simple truth and to affirm that we will not just stand by and "watch the world go to hell in a handbasket." As God leads, we will find ways to be light and salt in our world, and we will make a difference.

DAVID'S RETREAT FROM JERUSALEM

15:13–16:14

COMMENTARY

David "Flees"—and Sets a Trap, 15:13-37

The time required for Absalom to consolidate his revolutionary party, like the reasons for Israel's discontent, is glossed over by the narrative. Absalom's specific actions in Hebron—beyond paying his vow and summoning Ahithophel—remain a mystery. There is no account of how the disaffected factions were united under Absalom's leadership, nor of how the rebel army was organized. The fate of the 200 unsuspecting friends who traveled with Absalom to Hebron "in their innocence" (15:11) is not revealed: Did they join the rebellion since they were already implicated? Were they kept as hostages? The narrator does not say. Likewise, Absalom's secret message that the shofar would be blown as a rallying signal for his cause (15:10) is left hanging. The reader must assume that something similar has happened, the dissident troops have mustered, and Absalom has begun his march on Jerusalem.

The messenger who came to David (v. 13) could have been an emissary from Absalom, but was probably a supporter of the king, perhaps a member of his own intelligence network. "The hearts of Israel have gone after Absalom" recalls the earlier note that "Absalom *stole* the hearts of the people of Israel." Modern commentators often suggest that disgruntled factions within Israel shrewdly used Absalom as their figurehead, but in the narrator's mind Absalom was the manipulator, cozening the unwitting people into joining his movement.

David's alarmed response in 15:14 seems entirely overdone unless the reader presumes that the messenger brought additional news concerning the movements of Absalom's army. The reader must wonder why David would choose to flee Jerusalem rather than make a stand in the city that was famed for its strong defenses. Perhaps David wanted the conflict to be fought on another battlefield, one that would not leave obvious scars for the public to see in years to come. Perhaps the hasty evacuation suggests that Absalom's forces were truly massive or that reinforcements awaited in the direction of David's flight. Since the Cherethites and Pelethites, along with 600 Gittites, all fled with the king (v. 18), the reader knows that David was not without military support. Evidently he did not think it was enough.

A brief note in 15:15 reminds the reader that those who remained close to David were truly loyal and willing to follow his leadership, while the comment about the concubines in 15:16 foreshadows Absalom's assault upon them in 16:20-23. The "last house" (or "Far House") where David stopped to review his departing troops and take note of those who remained faithful (v. 17) may have been a well-known landmark at the time, the last (or first) house on the road leading into Jerusalem from the east, opposite the Mount of Olives.

With David's pause on the outskirts of Jerusalem, the narrator skillfully changes the pace of the story. Absalom's actions leading to the revolt are related in quick fashion, like a videotape on fast forward. David's immediate response to the threat also seems frantic and hurried (v. 14). Once the evacuation begins, however, the tempo shifts to a virtual crawl, like slow motion. This change of pace is conveyed by a series of five "meeting scenes" in which David engages friends and foes alike. [Meeting Scenes] Each encounter will have implications that will be resolved later in the story.

Meeting Scenes

AΩ The five meeting scenes involve Ittai the Gittite (15:19-22), Zadok and Abiathar (15:24-29), Hushai the Archite (15:32-36), Ziba the steward of Mephibosheth (16:1-4), and Shimei of Bahurim (16:5-13). When David reenters the city in ch. 19, he will engage in three meeting scenes, including Shimei of Bahurim (again), Mephibosheth (who will counter Ziba's earlier claims), and Barzillai, a strong supporter from Mahanaim.

On the surface, the evacuation suggests royal weakness, but through this series of exchanges the narrator carefully portrays David as a shrewd leader who still has his wits about him and who acts with resolute skill to protect his kingdom and defend himself against the insurgents. David's review of his supporters allows the reader to observe that his family and a cadre of royal officials are with him, defended by his personal bodyguards and professional army, the "Cherethites and Pelethites" (see note at 8:18) along with 600 Gittites. These faithful soldiers had apparently been with David from the time of his service to Achish, the Philistine ruler of Gath (1 Sam 27:1-12). The reader may wonder what has happened to David's personal band of 600 men who had joined him prior to his collusion with the Philistines. Kyle McCarter argues that the 600 soldiers in v. 18 should be understood as David's original force (also numbered as 600 in 1 Sam 23:13; 27:2; 30:9), rather than a count of the Gittites.[1] Both the MT and the LXX show definite signs of corruption in vv. 17-18, and McCarter's view (supported in the main by the Syriac) is a viable alternative.

David's first conversation is with Ittai the Gittite (15:19-22), apparently a recent arrival in Jerusalem, though David's reference to "yesterday" is probably a figure of speech. Some writers see David's conversation as a test of Ittai's loyalty, but the narrator portrays the king as being sincerely concerned for Ittai's future, granting his mercenary supporter permission to pursue other options with no hard feelings. David's invitation to "Go back and stay with the king" strikes the reader with the strange anomaly of the situation, for "the king" of which David speaks is the pretender Absalom. Ittai was already an exile from his native land. Would he become an exile once again by following David into the wilderness?

The exchange between David and Ittai bears remarkable similarities to Naomi's farewell exchange with Ruth and Orpah. There, Naomi urges her daughters-in-law to remain in Moab, and offers the blessing "May Yahweh deal kindly with you" (lit., "do *ḥesed*," Ruth 1:8). David offers a similar blessing to Ittai: "May Yahweh show steadfast love (*ḥesed*) and faithfulness to you" (v. 20). But Ittai, like Ruth, refuses to leave, and pledges in "Ruthesque" terms to remain with David, following him faithfully whether to death or to life (v. 21).

The "little ones" who journeyed with the company should probably be understood to include women and the elderly as well as children, the natural meaning of the term. The point is that Ittai and the Gittites, like the other evacuees, brought their dependents with them.

The effect of David's flight on those who remained in Jerusalem is depicted with an exaggerated reference (or a possible personification) of "the whole land" weeping as the royal entourage left the city (v. 23). The Wadi Kidron refers to the deep valley separating Jerusalem from the Mount of Olives. It served as a natural border for the limits of the city. Having passed over, the king was on his way into the wilderness.

David's second encounter is with the two high priests, Abiathar and Zadok (vv. 24-29). Knowing how important the ark was to David, they had brought it with them to accompany the king on his retreat. Many commentators regard the phrase "with all the Levites" as a gloss since the Levitical office was not fully organized until long after David's reign.

Here I Am

AΩ David's assent to God's will recalls the words of the young Samuel when he first heard God's voice (1 Sam 3:4, 5, 6, 8, 16), and of Isaiah when he heard God's call and the question "Whom shall I send, and who will go for us?" (Isa 6:8). The phrase translates a single compound word in Hebrew (*hinněnî*), literally, "Behold, me!"

A closer study reveals that the phrase appears frequently in the Old Testament, often in the context of expressing one's availability to God. When "tested" to sacrifice his son, Abraham responded "Here I am" to the call of God and to the angel's command to cease (Gen 22:1, 11), as well as to his son Isaac's questioning (Gen 22:7). Jacob responded in the same way when confronted by the angel of God (Gen 31:11; 46:2), and Moses answered God's address with "Here I am!" when he stood before the burning bush (Exod 3:4). In a psalm attributed to David, the hymn writer expressed his identity as one to whom God gives life with the same phrase (Ps 40:7).

An intriguing pair of usages is found in Isaiah, where the prophet predicts that Yahweh will respond to the prayers of his people by saying "Here I am" (Isa 58:9), then bemoans the fact that God cries out "Here I am, here I am" to a people who refuse to call on him (Isa 65:1).

Even in the New Testament, pious Hebrews respond to God's call with the Greek equivalent of *hinněnî* (*idou* + 1st person pronoun). Both Mary (Luke 1:38) and Ananias (Acts 9:10) accepted God's call by saying "Here I am" (= "Behold, me!).

The phrase could also be used in other contexts. In speeches to Israel, both Joshua (Josh 14:10) and Samuel (1 Sam 12:3) expressed their continued availability to God with the phrase "Here I am." Several times, the same phrase is used in self-defense, in the context of an oath or solemn statement before God (Jonathan to Saul, 1 Sam 14:43; Ahimelech to Saul, 1 Sam 22:12; Jeremiah to the royal officials of Judah, Jer 26:14).

Finally, the phrase also appears in discussion between persons, though still characteristically in solemn or significant discourse (Esau to Isaac, Gen 27:1; Isaac to Jacob, Gen 27:18; Joseph to Jacob, Gen 37:13; Paul to the Corinthians, 2 Cor 12:14).

David's response to Zadok and Abiathar is a surprising amalgam of faith and realism. On the one hand, David expresses humble trust by refusing to take the ark with him. He will not presume upon God but will throw himself upon divine mercy, trusting that if he found favor in Yahweh's eyes, God would return him to Jerusalem, where the ark would await him (v. 25). An element of fatalism seems to creep into 15:26 as David concedes that the response might be negative. "Here I am," David said. "Let him do to me what seems good to him." [Here I Am]

David may be willing to accept what Yahweh has in store, but he has no intention of sitting idly by and waiting for it to happen. He has been a man of action for too long. Employing an ancient version of the philosophy that "God helps those who help themselves," David puts himself into God's hands and then sets his own hand to the task of self-preservation. He instructs Zadok and Abiathar to remain in Jerusalem with their sons, to gather intelligence while he waits by the Jordan. If the priests learn anything useful, they are to send either Jonathan or Ahimaaz to warn him (15:27-28).

The text of this account is difficult. At times, David seems to be speaking only to Zadok, and there are signs that Abiathar was added to the text at a later date. Other differences exist between the MT and the LXX. For example, the NRSV chooses the LXX

Covered or Not?

AΩ The NRSV follows the traditional interpretation, saying that David's head was covered. Traditional mourning posture, however, left the head bare, covered with only ashes or dust (2 Sam 13:19; 15:32; Neh 9:1; Job 2:12). For example, God's instruction to Ezekiel that he should disguise his grief instructs him to wear his turban, implying that going bareheaded was a sign of mourning (Ezek 24:17, 23). Thus, it seems strange that David and his companions covered their heads and bared their feet, unless we are to assume that their heads were covered with ashes, dust, sackcloth, or some other token of grief.

Kyle McCarter translates that David's "head was bare," as were the heads of those who accompanied him, but he does not explain how he arrived at this translation in either the textual notes or the commentary that follows. The LXX, to which McCarter often appeals, also has "covered." The matter of David's head could be explained by the assumption that *lô* ("to him," or "his") has replaced the homonym *lōʾ* ("not"), as frequently presumed to be the case in Ps 100:3. Thus, "his head covered" might have been "head not covered." This is an appealing argument; unfortunately, it does not apply in the case of David's companions, who also "covered their heads" before tearfully ascending the Mount of Olives.

There seems to be more support for the understanding that David's head was covered as a sign of mourning. Customs in Ezekiel's time could have changed.

P. Kyle McCarter, *II Samuel* (AB 9; Garden City: Doubleday, 1984), 361.

---

reading of David's instruction, beginning with "Look, go back." The MT introduces David's remarks with a question that could be translated as "Are you a seer?" but probably means something like "Are you not an observant man?"[2] This appropriately leads in to the undercover role David has in mind for the priests. They are to observe and to report.

David's encounter with Zadok and Abiathar is revealing. David will not attempt to manipulate Yahweh by means of the ark, which he recognizes as a dangerous game (cf. 2 Sam 6:6-11). Rather, he will entrust his future to God's will and his own wits, believing that life with Yahweh is a cooperative venture.

The series of meeting scenes is interrupted by an observation revealing that David is not dispassionate or uncaring about his future. As he climbed the familiar path up the Mount of Olives, he assumed a mourning posture, with tears on his cheeks, a covering over his head, and nothing on his feet (v. 30). [Covered or Not?] The reader must know that David does not leave the city lightly or easily, but freighted with grief and burdened by a heavy heart.

As David and his weeping companions made their way up the steep path, the word of Ahithophel's collusion came to them, and David received it as the blow it was. Ahithophel had been a valued counselor—one whose word was like the oracle of God (16:23)—and his advice would be a powerful weapon in Absalom's cause. Thus, David prayed for help. Note again that David has committed his future to God's care, but he has not stopped caring or acting in his own behalf. He prays specifically, asking Yahweh to frustrate the inevitably wise counsel of Ahithophel by making it appear foolish. Ironically, the name Ahithophel may mean "My brother is foolishness" (see [Ahithophel the Gilonite]). David seems to have so much confidence in Ahithophel that he expects only good counsel: his only hope is that Ahithophel's genius would not be recognized.

David's hopes were fulfilled when he reached the crown of the Mount of Olives, at a site "where God was worshiped." [Where God Was Worshiped?] There, David met the answer to his prayer in the form of Hushai the Archite, another high official who had come to express his loyalty and to demonstrate his own grief (compare Hushai's mourning posture in v. 32 with Tamar's in 13:19). The Archites were a Benjaminite clan (Josh 16:2). Hushai sought to make common cause with David on his journey to exile, but David saw the opportunity to have a loyal plant in the very center of Absalom's war council. He begged Hushai to return to Jerusalem and feign allegiance to Absalom for the express purpose of countering the wise counsel of Ahithophel. His mission would be dangerous but invaluable. Together with Zadok and Abiathar, they would form the nucleus of a small but well-placed intelligence and disinformation network, with the priestly sons serving as messengers (vv. 32-36).

Hushai, who will prove to be a master of doublespeak, accepted the challenge. The narrator skillfully uses his compliance to remind the reader that Absalom's forces were entering the city even as David's party disappeared over the crest of the Mount of Olives.

Parting Shots from Saul's House, 16:1-14

The initial three meeting scenes dealt with persons who would play important roles in the resolution of Absalom's rebellion against his father: Ittai would command one third of David's troops in the battle at the forest of Ephraim (15:19-23; 18:2). Zadok and Abiathar were deployed to set up an intelligence network in Jerusalem so that David would be cognizant of Absalom's plans (15:24-29; 17:15-22). Hushai was commissioned as a secret agent,

Where God Was Worshiped?

AΩ The reference to a worship site on the Mount of Olives has puzzled interpreters for years, for there is no other biblical reference to such a place. Sanctuaries were often built on the heights, so it would be no surprise to learn that the middle summit of the Mount of Olives had once hosted a worship site, perhaps during the early monarchical period or even before. Some scholars have speculated that the central summit may have been the locus of the priestly city of Nob (1 Sam 22:19).

It may be significant that the text does not say "Yahweh" was once worshiped there, but "Elohim," a divine epithet that can also be translated as "gods." Thus, the text may refer to the worship of Canaanite or Jebusite gods. Second Kgs 23:13 describes how other gods were worshiped on the Mount of Olives at the instigation of Solomon's foreign wives, but this was probably located at the southern summit, while David's path to Bahurim would have led him over the central peak.

a pro-David plant in the inner circles of Absalom's counselors, with the stated mission of sabotaging Ahithophel's sage advice (15:32-37; 17:5-14). The narrator has cleverly arranged their respective audiences with David in chiastic form, a reverse order of their later appearance in the narrative: Ittai → Zadok/Abiathar → Hushai, then Hushai → Zadok/Abiathar → Ittai.

The next two meeting scenes involve people who confront David with material support (Ziba, vv. 1-4) and a curse (Shimei, vv. 5-14). Ziba will reenter the picture at 19:24-30, Shimei at 19:18-23. Once again, the narrator has reversed the order of their appearance: Ziba → Shimei before the battle, Shimei → Ziba afterward.

Ziba is familiar to the reader as the former steward of Saul and caretaker of Saul's crippled grandson, Mephibosheth. Despite his pedigree as a Saulide, David had granted Mephibosheth the royal favor of living in Jerusalem and eating at the king's table, while Ziba and his sons were put in charge of Saul's estate (9:1-3). Ziba comes to David in a show of support, reportedly against Mephibosheth's wishes. Thus, he does not meet David within sight of Jerusalem, but only after David has crested the summit of the Mount of Olives. Knowing of the king's hasty retreat, Ziba comes bearing the gift of provisions for the journey— the fruit of the land that David had entrusted him to administer. [Provisions for the Journey]

David had instructed Ziba to bring the land's produce to Mephibosheth for his material support (9:10), but in this instance the steward has brought it to David instead. This prompted David's question: "Why have you brought these?" (16:2), meaning, "Why have you brought these *to me*?" Ziba's noncommittal reply is an exercise in the obvious: "The donkeys are for the king's household to ride, the bread and summer fruit for the young men to eat, and the wine is for those to drink who faint in the wilderness."

David ignored Ziba's nonanswer by pressing the issue. The gift of provisions was obviously a declaration of support, but from whom? From Ziba, or from Mephibosheth? Thus, when David asks "And where is your master's son?", he is not concerned about Mephibosheth's physical location but his political allegiance (v. 3). Whose side was he on? David's careful use of the phrase "your master's son" reminds Ziba that he was once loyal to the one who

> **Provisions for the Journey**
>
> AΩ According to the NRSV, Ziba brought two saddled donkeys bearing 200 loaves of bread, 100 bunches of raisins, 100 summer fruits, and one skin of wine. Some Greek versions read "ephah" in place of "100" for the raisins and summer fruits. The description of the summer fruit is enigmatic, for the text says "100 of summer fruits," as if a word like "baskets" or "cakes" was omitted. The LXX translates the word for "summer fruit" (*qî*) as "date cakes," but figs or pomegranates are just as likely.
>
> Ziba's gift calls to mind the present brought by Abigail while David was in southern Judah avoiding Saul's pursuit. Abigail brought 200 loaves of bread, two skins of wine, five dressed sheep, five measures of parched grain, 100 clusters of raisins, and 200 fig cakes (1 Sam 25:18).

became David's enemy. Thus, the conversation is a test of loyalty for both Ziba and Mephibosheth.

Ziba's answer surprises the reader. He claims that Mephibosheth is joyfully awaiting Absalom's arrival, in hopes that the "house of Israel" will restore to him his grandfather's throne. Any anticipation that the ambitious Absalom would gain the kingdom only to turn it over to the crippled son of Jonathan was patently ridiculous, of course, and Mephibosheth would later claim to be an innocent victim of Ziba's lying slander (19:27-29). Nevertheless, David chose to believe Ziba, and issued an immediate decree that Ziba would become not only the steward, but also the *owner* of Mephibosheth's inherited estate (vv. 3-4a). If Ziba's intention had been to ingratiate himself to the king (as his flowery obeisance in v. 4b indicates), he had surely succeeded.

The final encounter during David's flight from Jerusalem occurred as David passed through the village of Bahurim, a few miles northeast of Jerusalem. Shimei, son of Gera, who was a resident there, emerged to vent his considerable rage at David and his party. [Shimei, Son of Gera] Shimei was a relative of Saul, and apparently held David to be guilty in the death of some, if not all Saulides who had been killed. The narrator's careful effort to dissociate David from the deaths of Saul, Jonathan, Ishbosheth, and Abner (2 Sam 1–3) suggests that there was popular sentiment to the contrary. Commentators often presume, however, that Shimei's venomous wrath was inspired by David's willing surrender to the Gibeonites of seven sons of Saul by his concubines. The Gibeonites publicly executed them in humiliating fashion as vengeance for crimes that Saul had committed against Gibeon. This story does not appear until 21:1-14, but many scholars suspect that it actually occurred early in David's reign and occupies its present position in the narrative for literary, not historical, reasons.

Whatever his motivation, Shimei came out pelting David with both curses and stones, kicking up dust as if he wanted to cover David with it (v. 5). David was surrounded by many traveling companions as well as his bodyguard of "mighty men" (v. 6), but he could not escape the painful rain of curses and stones. Shimei's vituperative demeanor toward the king shocks the reader, who has just reviewed a series of supportive encounters between David and his humble courtesans. In particular, Ziba's humble obeisance and request to "find favor in your sight, my lord the king" still hums in

Shimei, Son of Gera

Shimei's patronymic has troubled some readers since Saul was of the Matrite clan, while Gera is also known as a Benjaminite clan (Gen 46:21). Gera, however, was a common Northwest Semitic name that occurs in Egyptian and Phoenician records in addition to biblical usage. There is no reason to assume that the name Gera was limited to the clan of Gera or that it signifies anything other than the name of Shimei's father, who would have been a Matrite, like Saul.

Murderer! Scoundrel!

AΩ "Murderer" and "scoundrel" are literally "man of blood" and "man of belial." One can be a man of blood without being a murderer. Some suggest that Shimei was accusing David of being a bloodthirsty criminal (cf. Pss 5:6 [MT v. 6]; 26:9; 55:23 [MT v. 24]; Prov 29:10). The word "belial" is sometimes translated as "worthlessness" on the assumption that it is compounded of *bĕlî* (meaning "not" or "without") and * yaʿal* (meaning "worth" or "use"). McCarter argues that the latter element could also mean "coming up." The combination "place of not-coming-up" would suggest Sheol, from which the dead do not return. In 22:5, the same word is clearly used in poetic parallel to death and Sheol. Thus, McCarter translates it as "hellfiend," a more colorful and serious accusation than indicated by the English term "scoundrel."

P. Kyle McCarter, *II Samuel* (AB 9; Garden City: Doubleday, 1984), 373.

the reader's mind as Shimei begins his shocking counterpose with sharp rocks and sharp words: "Out! Out! Murderer! Scoundrel!" [Murderer! Scoundrel!]

David's attitude toward Shimei is just as surprising as Shimei's public affront to the king. Abishai, David's cousin and a military stalwart, offered to go over and remove Shimei's head since his voiced fury was technically treasonous (v. 8; cf. Exod 22:28). Abishai, like his brother Joab, saw few problems that could not be solved with a swift execution (cf. 1 Sam 26:8-11; 2 Sam 19:21-23; 21:17). He saw Shimei as nothing more than a bothersome odor, a dead dog on the side of the road (see note at 9:8).

David, on the other hand, took Shimei's words to heart. He accepted at face value Shimei's claim (v. 8) that his present difficulties had been engineered by God as punishment for his sins. "What have I to do with you?" is an enigmatic idiom (lit., "What to me and to you?") that may mean "What do we have in common?" or "What is there between us?" (cf. Judg 11:12; 1 Kgs 17:18; 2 Chr 35:21). In this context, as in 19:23, it seems to imply "What do you have against me?", as if David knew that following Abishai's advice would cause only greater trouble.

Indeed, taking immediate vengeance on Shimei would not have been astute. Running from his own son, the last thing David needed was to make more enemies and push the Saulides further into Absalom's camp. Since Bahurim would have been home to Shimei's kinsmen, some may have come to defend him if swords were brought into play, and David could not afford the time to pause for an armed altercation.

This is not why David told Abishai to hold his peace, however. David acknowledged that he had lived under a curse ever since Nathan predicted trouble as a result of his sin with Bathsheba (12:10-11). Shimei had only given voice to the curse that Yahweh had already set into motion (v. 10b). Shimei's grievance was not the

Stones

📖 This terrain is typical of the hills David passed on his way from Jerusalem to the Jordan. One can readily see how Shimei could have scrambled along a roughly parallel course, high enough to lob the ubiquitous stones into David's procession.

(Right) Julius Schnoor von Carolsfeld. *Shimei's Blasphemy.* 19th century. Woodcut. *Das Buch der Bucher in Bilden.* (Credit: Dover Pictorial Archive Series)

(Below) Judean Hills near Jerusalem. (Credit: Mitchell G. Reddish)

same as Yahweh's, but David thought it not inappropriate that God might instruct a kinsman of Saul to fill the air with vocal curses to illustrate the cloud under which David lived. For David, the curses of a Benjaminite hardly compared to his own son's attempt to unseat and kill his father (v. 11).

David had confessed his sin, sought forgiveness, and put his life into God's hands (15:25-26). There were no guarantees that he would once again know the taste of divine favor, but he could still hope that Yahweh would have mercy and bring some good result from his extended period of misery. With nothing more than his hope to sustain him, David and his company traveled on beneath Shimei's fusillade of curses and stones until they arrived, with great weariness, at the river crossing (15:28; 17:16). [Stones] "At the Jordan" is missing from the text, which says only that he arrived weary, but the context seems to require a place name. Suggestions such as "at the Jordan," "at the fords of the wilderness," or "at the water" are equally feasible. It was a place for stopping, resting, and refreshing oneself from the hard march out of Jerusalem. [A Marching Song]

A Marching Song

The scribes responsible for the superscriptions preceding many of the psalms remembered an ancient tradition that attributed Ps 3 to David, "when he fled from his son Absalom." The attribution may be imaginary, but the words are appropriate.

> O LORD, how many are my foes!
>   Many are rising against me;
> many are saying to me,
>   "There is no help for you in
>   God." Selah. . . .
> Rise up, O LORD!
>   Deliver me, O my God!
> For you strike all my enemies on the
>   cheek;
>   you break the teeth of the wicked.
> Deliverance belongs to the LORD;
>   may your blessing be on your
>   people! Selah.

CONNECTIONS

The People We Meet, 15:13–16:14

David's orderly retreat from Jerusalem is a reminder that sometimes we can only go forward by first stepping back. By the time Absalom marched on the capital, David had given up his apparent hope that the rebellion would evaporate on its own. Once the die was clearly cast, the king seems to have regained his composure. He knew that his best chance of victory was in leaving the city and allowing Absalom to hang himself.

As David left Jerusalem, the narrator carefully describes a series of five meeting scenes between David and others who both supported and criticized him. [A Lesson in Relationships] David responded to each person with what appears to be wisdom and care, accepting what that person had to offer and giving what he had in return.

David first met Ittai, a mercenary soldier and leader of a small army from Gath who had voluntarily attached themselves to David. David offered Ittai the gift of accepting his loyalty. Many people have difficulty allowing others to make free choices or in accepting the love and loyalty that others might offer. Perhaps they lack sufficient self-worth to think themselves deserving of another's care. David had learned the value and the mutual benefit of granting liberty and accepting freely given love.

David's second meeting was with Zadok and Abiathar, the two high priests who were among his strongest supporters. David

---

A Lesson in Relationships

David's five encounters during his retreat from Jerusalem could be used as an outline, or as discussion starters, for a study on good relationship skills. Take note of the five meetings and the distinctive themes related to each:

David meets:	*The encounter involves:*
Ittai the Gittite	The ability to grant others freedom and to accept their loyalty when offered.
Zadok and Abiathar, the high priests	The ability to sense others' need to be of service and to allow them that opportunity.
Hushai the Archite	The ability to see the hand of God at work in others and to accept it as a gift.
Ziba, steward of Mephibosheth	The ability to accept support when it is offered appropriately, even from unlikely sources.
Shimei of Bahurim	The ability to accept criticism with grace and to learn even from our antagonists.

---

accepted their service and gave them something positive to do by setting up an intelligence network in the capital.

David's actions here also suggest an important lesson regarding the pragmatic side of faith: David openly expressed his trust in God for the future, then immediately took personal action to set up a spy system in support of his cause. At his best, David knew that true faith is neither an abstract belief *in* God nor a fatalistic surrender *to* God, but a cooperative venture *with* God. As James would later point out, faith without works is dead (2:17). We trust in God for the eventual outcome, but we do not ask God to do for us what we can do for ourselves. Faith that works is not ethereal and empty, but pragmatic and cooperative.

When David met Hushai, he had the spiritual insight to recognize that his faithful counselor was an answer to prayer. He dared to ask his friend to take on the hazardous role of an undercover agent in Absalom's court. Prayers to God are often answered by human hands, words, and deeds. David was wise enough to recognize that truth and accept the gift.

As David crested the Mount of Olives and lost sight of Jerusalem, he was met by Ziba, whom he had appointed as managing steward of the property belonging to Mephibosheth, Saul's grandson. Ziba had come bearing a gift of provisions for David and his army. David had no way of knowing whether Ziba's intentions were pure.

Yet he acted on the information available to him, accepted the offer of support, and was strengthened by it. We also may find friendship or support in unexpected places and should be careful not to overlook such unanticipated blessings.

David's last meeting was with Shimei, who attacked David as he traveled through the village of Bahurim, Shimei's hometown. Shimei accused David of murder (perhaps in relation to the Saulides turned over to Gibeon, ch. 21) and unleashed a vitriolic barrage of curses and stones. As David had accepted good from the others he had met, so he accepted the harsh words of Shimei. Indeed, David agreed that there was truth in Shimei's words, and accepted the rebuke as having come from Yahweh himself. There are times when we need to hear the truth that none of our friends will speak. There are times when our enemies reveal what we most need to know. Accepting such words requires discernment and grace: discernment to separate the truth from the acrimonious chaff, grace to hear hard words without retaliating in kind. A later Son of David would also demonstrate a remarkable ability not only to endure the insults of those who opposed him, but to turn the other cheek (Matt 5:39).

NOTES

[1] P. Kyle McCarter, *II Samuel* (AB 9; Garden City: Doubleday, 1984), 363-64.

[2] A. A. Anderson, *2 Samuel* (WBC 11; Waco: Word Books, 1989), 204.

ABSALOM'S TRIUMPH

16:15–17:23

COMMENTARY

Absalom in Jerusalem, 16:15-23

Absalom has been waiting offstage as the narrator focused on David, appearing only in the brief reference that Absalom entered Jerusalem just as Hushai arrived there following his interview with David (15:37). Now the plot returns to that moment, as Absalom takes center stage, sharing the spotlight with the influential Ahithophel (v. 15). The leader of the coup seems taken aback when Hushai (whom the narrator reminds us is David's friend) presents himself with the surprising salute: "Long live the king! Long live the king!" (v. 16). The expression (lit., "May the king live!") is not just a wish for life, but an acknowledgment of authority.

The reader may note Hushai's careful choice of words. He does not say *which* king (cf. 1 Kgs 1:25, 31, 34, 39). The reader knows that Hushai speaks to King Absalom, but secretly serves King David. Absalom's expected test of loyalty twice makes a point of using the term "friend" (*rĕ'eh*). "Friend of David" may have been an official title for David's intimate counselor, as well as a mark of their personal feelings of fraternity.

The word translated "loyalty" is *ḥesed*, a mark of covenant loyalty that David held in high esteem. Absalom wants to know why such a close friend of the king should prove so disloyal as to desert to his opponent (v. 17). Hushai is a master of doublespeak. He insists that his greatest loyalty is not to the person on the throne, but to the institution of kingship. If God and the people of Israel had chosen a new king, then Hushai would serve the new king, even as he had served the old (v. 18-19). In this way Hushai persuaded Absalom to accept his service as a royal counselor and friend of the new king.

Once Hushai had successfully insinuated himself into Absalom's court, the stage was set for a battle of the minds between the two competing counselors. Ahithophel, whose counsel was thought to be

The Conquest of the Concubines

Absalom's taking of David's concubines is an example of a political act of public humiliation, comparable to Hunan's offense in 10:1-6. The king's concubines—his harem—were tokens of royal authority, evidence of the king's virility. Some scholars speak of an ancient notion that kings who were sexually impotent were also considered to be politically incapacitated. Absalom's rape of his father's concubines was a political ploy, a deliberate stratagem intended to shame David. Ahithophel's comment that this would make Absalom "stink" with his father underscores this interpretation, as the verb "to stink" belongs to the literary context of public shaming (cf. 10:6; 1 Sam 27:12; Prov 13:5).

In *The Social World of Ancient Israel 1250–587 BCE*, Victor Matthews and Don Benjamin have argued that "sexual relationships were a measure of the honor and shame of the households to which these men and women belonged. To test the stability or honor of a household, a man from another household attempted to rape one of its women."

For other examples of taking a king's concubine, see 2 Sam 3:7-8; 1 Kgs 2:13-22; and compare Nathan's prediction in 2 Sam 12:8. Some scholars argue that taking the king's concubines was a direct claim to the throne, an expected action when one king succeeded another. Others hold that Absalom's action was designed mainly to show his followers that the rebellion was past the point of no return because of the great breach it would cause between Absalom and David.

Victor H. Matthews and Don C. Benjamin, *The Social World of Ancient Israel 1250–587 BCE* (Peabody MA: Hendrickson, 1993), 180.

"like the oracle of God" (v. 23), willingly serves Absalom. Hushai, who truly has God in his corner (17:14), waits patiently for an opening to unleash a rhetorical barrage.

Absalom seeks counsel first from Ahithophel, who advises the rebel leader to seal his break with David by publicly cavorting with the king's concubines (vv. 20-21), and then to send a strong leader (namely, Ahithophel himself) with an overwhelming force designed to intimidate David's army and make short work of the king (17:1-4). Hushai's opinion was not asked in the matter of the concubines, and he says nothing, apparently biding his time for a more strategic opportunity, which quickly arrives (17:5-14).

The taking of a former king's concubines was a public symbol that the new sovereign had assumed full control, though the act itself granted no particular legitimacy to the king (cf. 3:7; 12:8). [The Conquest of the Concubines] Ahithophel's reasoning was that such a blatant act would bring about an obvious and irreversible breach between Absalom and David. Absalom's assault on the concubines would make him "become odious" to his father (lit., "stink with his father"; cf. 1 Sam 13:3-4; 2 Sam 10:6). Ahithophel reasoned that the act would galvanize Absalom's support because it would demonstrate that there was no going back.

The pitching of the (bridal?) canopy on the palace roof may give to Absalom's actions the sense of a royal wedding (cf. Ps 19:4-5 [MT, vv. 5-6]; Joel 2:16), as he takes David's concubines for his own (on the relationship of the concubine as a wife of lower rank, see [The Custom of Concubinage] at 2 Sam 3:7). Absalom's cohabitation with David's concubines, however, was a direct violation of the law, which prohibited a son from taking his father's wife, at least while he was alive (see Lev 18:8; 20:11; Deut 22:30 [MT 23:1]; 27:20). Thus, A.A. Anderson, following K. Budde, has suggested that Absalom was leading the people to believe that David was not just on the run, but already dead.[1] This view does not fit the context, however. Ahithophel advised Absalom's atrocity for the purpose of alienating David, not as a declaration of his death.

The reader knows, however, that this act is not merely a measure of Ahithophel's mental agility or Absalom's sexual prowess. Both men have become tools in the hands of Yahweh, whose punishment of David was not yet fulfilled. Nathan had predicted that David's secret tryst with Bathsheba would be repaid by one of his sons taking his own wives in public view (12:11-12).

The narrator deftly breaks the action in preparation for the competing counsel over battle plans by reminding the reader of the high esteem accorded to Ahithophel's counsel by both David and Absalom. In his early career, David had often instructed his priest to seek an oracle from God, presumably through the medium of the Urim and Thummim. As a settled monarch, he had apparently come to rely upon the wisdom of professional counselors, but Ahithophel's reputation was such that his counsel "was as if one consulted the oracle of God" (v. 23). This accolade for Ahithophel serves to increase tension for the reader. If Ahithophel's wisdom is so sound and well regarded, how can Hushai possibly thwart it? The following chapter is devoted to that subject.

Absalom's Competing Counselors, 17:1-23

Several elements are involved in Ahithophel's proposed plan for eliminating David. The first is the selection of a task force that is unmatched in quality ("let me choose"), impressive in size (12,000 men, as opposed to the hundreds who accompanied David from Jerusalem), and led by a brilliant strategist. (Ahithophel himself). The second element is surprise: an immediate pursuit and attack in the night, while David is still weary, unsuspecting, and lacking in reinforcements. The third element is a promise that there would be no divisive war at all. David's small army would panic and flee, leaving Ahithophel free to dispense with the former king and lead "all the people" (David's companions?) back to Absalom "as a bride comes home to her husband" (vv. 1-3). Perhaps Ahithophel chose the bridal terminology deliberately. His earlier advice had led Absalom to take David's concubines for his own. Now, Ahithophel's military strategy promised to deliver David's former supporters into Absalom's power, if not his heart.

Ahithophel's strategy was worthy of his reputation. By following his scheme, bloodshed would be averted for all but David, preserving the peace and bringing the kingdom fully under Absalom's control. Naturally, the advice delighted not only Absalom, but "all the elders of Israel" (v. 4). Nevertheless, Absalom did not accept Ahithophel's counsel without due consideration, but summoned Hushai to add his own analysis (vv. 5-6).

This was the opportunity Hushai had waited for, but refuting Ahithophel's plan would demand all his rhetorical skills. Hushai began by suggesting that Ahithophel's perfect record had come to an end: "*This time* the counsel Ahithophel has given is not good" (v. 7). Hushai spoke the truth, but again he invoked doublespeak. Ahithophel's counsel was in fact not good—for David! It would have been very good for Absalom. Nevertheless, Hushai found clever ways to rebut Ahithophel's plan point by point.

Ahithophel had suggested that David's men would turn and run in the face of overpowering odds, but Hushai plants strong seeds of doubt that it would be so easy. Using careful language designed to magnify the threat of David's army, Hushai appeals to common knowledge: "You know that your father and his men are warriors, and that they are enraged, like a bear robbed of her cubs in the field" (v. 8a). [What Do Bears and Pigs Have in Common?] Furthermore, Hushai scoffs at the notion that David could be so easily found: he was not so naive as to sleep openly with the troops, but would have his own secure retreat in some hard-to-find place (vv. 8b-9a). Thus, even if Ahithophel's army did manage to defeat David's troops, there was no guarantee they would find David, and much blood would be shed for nothing. Hushai imagined that success in battle was unlikely even so. Absalom's troops were not so seasoned as David's. He predicted that the first casualties among them would lead to a panicked outcry: "There has been a slaughter among the

What Do Bears and Pigs Have in Common?

Hushai's suggestion that David and his crack troops would fight like cornered animals uses the familiar illustration of a female bear bereft of her cubs (cf. Hos 13:8; Prov 17:12). A major Greek witness includes another phrase that may have fallen out of the Hebrew text because of haplography since both phrases end with the same words. The LXX[B] has "like a bear bereft in the wild or a sow snared in the wild" (McCarter's translation, *II Samuel* [AB 9; Garden

City: Doubleday, 1984], 379). Wild pigs were known in Israel, though not permissible as food. The ferocious ravaging of wild boars was used as a description of Israel as "God's vine" falling to its enemies in Ps 80:13 [MT, v. 14]). The reference to a sow is probably original. It is easier to see how it might have dropped out—either by haplography or from a scribe's distaste for describing David's warriors as sows—than to imagine why it would be added later.

troops who follow Absalom!" (v. 9b). He then reinforced the mental image already planted by affirming that "all Israel knows that your father is a warrior, and that those who are with him are valiant warriors" (v. 10).

Hushai's own advice would appear ridiculous if not for the power of his rhetoric and his charismatic ability to appeal to the war council's emotions rather than to logic. To engage David's ferocious troops, 12,000 men would not be enough; the militia should be called in "from Dan to Beer-sheba," a common idiom describing the whole of Israel. [From Dan to Beer-sheba] Only when his army was like the sand of the sea could he hope to defeat David (v. 11). Furthermore, this massive army should not be led by Ahithophel, but by Absalom himself. Israel's first call for a king had been so the king could go before them and lead them to victory over their enemies (1 Sam 8:20). Having stroked Absalom's ego, Hushai suggested that David could be located at their leisure. Once found, Absalom and his massive army would fall upon David and his troops as uniformly and inevitably as dew (or fog) envelopes the land. Thus would David and all of his troops be annihilated (vv. 11-12). Hushai capped his speech with a theatrical flight of rhetorical fancy, painting an image of Absalom's victorious troops tying ropes to the walls of any city that gave David sanctuary, pulling it into the nearest deep wadi and obliterating it from the face of the earth (v. 13).

> **From Dan to Beer-sheba**
>
> AΩ This idiom was used as a merismus, a figure of speech intended to describe the whole by means of two opposite parts. For example, in Gen 3:5, the serpent's suggestion that Adam and Eve would know "good and evil" by eating from the tree is probably a merismatic way of saying that they would know everything.
>
> Since Dan was in the far north of Israel, and Beer-sheba in the southern extremity of Judah, the expression "from Dan to Beer-sheba" was commonly employed to describe all Israel, including other instances in the books of Samuel (1 Sam 3:20; 2 Sam 3:10; 24:2, 15). Its usage here adds further weight to the argument that Absalom's rebellion was a nationwide movement, rather than a tribal conflict.

Absalom and his counselors, as Hushai hoped, were swept up in the emotional torrent of his highly charged pep talk. They concluded that Hushai's counsel was better than that of Ahithophel. The editor, however, is not content to leave it at that. He wants the reader to know that Hushai's victory was not his alone. There was another persuasive force at work in the hearts and minds of Absalom and his council. It was the pervasive will of God: "For the LORD had ordained to defeat the good counsel of Ahithophel, so that the LORD might bring ruin on Absalom" (v. 14). This is the last of three explicit editorial comments in the Succession Narrative that Gerhard von Rad attributed to the Deuteronomistic redactors' intention to underscore the appropriate theological interpretation.[2] The others are found at 11:27 and 12:24.

The foresight of David's establishment of an intelligence network becomes clear in 17:15-27 as Hushai employs it to advise David.

Several writers have suggested that Hushai's advice does not follow logically from the outcome of the war council. Although his counsel of delay and strength in numbers was accepted, he still urges David to cross the river without delay and find a place of safety. Some scholars use this evidence to support a view that Hushai's involvement was not a part of the original story, but added by a pro-David redactor to underscore the favor shown to David by Yahweh.

There is no need to invoke such an explanation, however. Hushai does counsel haste, but it is still his plan, by and large, that Absalom follows. He does not pursue David immediately, as Ahithophel had counseled, nor does he agree to let Ahithophel lead the troops. Absalom's army delays for an unspecified period of time, and when they come out, it is Absalom who leads them in keeping with Hushai's pep-rally style counsel of bravado. None of this impinges on the need for David to make haste in leading his considerable entourage across the Jordan. Absalom could change his mind and begin the pursuit at any time, and David could not afford to brook any delay. We learn from 18:1 that David not only attained the safety of Mahanaim's walls, but had sufficient time to marshal his forces and set his defense plan. This was the gift bought by the undercover work of Yahweh and his agent Hushai.

According to the narrator, Hushai reported to Zadok and Abiathar, as planned, summarizing for them Ahithophel's counsel and his own competing proposal (v. 15). In hearing Ahithophel's counsel, David would recognize that Ahithophel had identified his weaknesses, and thus would see the wisdom of Hushai's recommendation that he cross the fords immediately. Should Absalom think things through and change his mind—or if the young schemer had only pretended to accept Hushai's counsel, thinking to double-cross David's espionage—he would be in immediate danger. The phrase "will be swallowed up" is of uncertain translation because the verb could derive from one of two identical Hebrew stems (*blʿ*), which hark back to different precedents. Kyle McCarter has gone to great lengths to derive the meaning "or else disaster will befall the king,"[3] but the result differs little from the traditional and more obvious translation, "be swallowed up."

There is a clear implication that this was not the first message transmitted to David via the two priests and their sons, Jonathan and Ahimaaz. The two young men were waiting at En-rogel, where the appointed servant girl *used to go and tell them, and they would go and tell King David.* [En-rogel] The verb forms imply repetitive

En-rogel

En-rogel was the name of a well-known spring (Hebrew *ʿēn* means "spring") not far from Jerusalem, just beyond the juncture of the Kidron and Hinnom Valleys. In the ancient world it was remembered as a traditional boundary marker between the tribal lands of Benjamin and Judah (Josh 15:7; 18:16). In the modern world, it is called Bîr Ayyûb, meaning "Job's Well."

Surprisingly, En-rogel was almost due south of Jerusalem, nearly opposite the northeast heading which David and his entourage had taken to Bahurim and beyond. Perhaps this site was chosen precisely because it was out of the way and thus less conspicuous. It had the disadvantage, however, of leaving the messengers a longer trek before reaching with David. Apparently, there was no convenient shortcut through the desert since the messengers also passed through Bahurim (17:18-19).

---

actions, suggesting that regular communications were maintained between David and his informants in the city.

The text notes that Ahimaaz and Jonathan were detected by a sharp-eyed boy, presumably after they had left En-rogel, but before reaching Shimei's town of Bahurim, where they sought refuge with a Davidic sympathizer, who allowed them to hide in his well while his wife disguised the opening (vv. 18-19). The motif of two spies being hidden by a woman calls to mind the story of Rahab, who once hid two Israelite spies who had been sent out by Joshua. Rahab instructed the men to lie down on her roof, then covered them with stalks of flax (Josh 2:6). In the present text, David's agents are concealed in a well whose opening is covered with a cloth or skin and then spread over with groats, or possibly sand. [What Kind of Grains?] As in the story of Rahab (Josh 2:3-5), the unnamed heroine boldly faced those who sought her secretive guests, and deceptively led the searchers to believe the men had already left (v. 20).

This part of the story serves to remind the reader that Ahimaaz and Jonathan were no mere pages running messages from place to place, but courageous agents involved in a high stakes game of

---

What Kind of Grains?

How was the spies' hiding place concealed? The MT suggests that a covering was spread over the aperture, then sprinkled with some form of grain (NRSV). The word *hărîpôt* is used only here and in Prov 27:22, where it seems to describe something crushed with a mortar and pestle. The ancients often ground and cooked barley, then used it to produce a coarse kind of cereal called "groats," very different from modern grits. The text, then, would suggest that the woman pretended to be drying groats, when in fact she was hiding spies.

Other scholars propose a slight emendation to *hărîpôt*, which could mean "grains of sand." This reading implies that the woman completely disguised the well opening by covering it over, then spreading enough sand on top to match the surrounding earth. This argument seems weak for several reasons in addition to the necessity of changing the text. First of all, domestic courtyards would have been well traveled, and their surfaces would tend to be hard-packed, rather than loose sand. Secondly, such courtyards were not very large. An unwary visitor, in his search, could easily fall through the covering and stumble upon the hidden spies.

The image of a drying cloth covered with grain in some stage of preparation offers the most likely scenario for the woman's clandestine activity.

espionage. The information they carried had the potential of saving King David's life—or of costing them their own.

The informants' report to David is sharply abridged in the text. Some scholars see 17:21 as evidence that the original story did not include Hushai since only Ahithophel is mentioned and his counsel is cited as the reason for urging David to ford the Jordan without delay. However, the details of the competing counselors have already been given (vv. 1-14). They were reduced in Hushai's espionage report to (v. 15) "thus has Ahithophel counseled" and "thus have I counseled." The narrator repeats only the salient features of the conversation involving David; the reader may presume that a full report was given after the most crucial part of the message had been delivered.

In modern times, Israeli irrigation projects have reduced the Jordan River to the volume of a healthy stream, but in ancient times it was a much larger river, presenting a formidable barrier to those who wished to cross it (cf. Josh 3). [The Jordan River] The river's course was marked by several rocky fords, however, where intrepid travelers could cross in relative safety. Even a well-known ford,

The Jordan River

 The once mighty Jordan has now been reduced to a trickle by massive irrigation projects that have turned desert land into productive farmland for the enterprising Israelis.

(Credit: Mitchell G. Reddish)

however, could become treacherous in the dark. Nevertheless, David acted quickly upon the messengers' advice, leading his entire entourage to safe harbor on the east bank before daybreak (v. 22).

The suicide of Ahithophel brings a somber note to the narrative, while also serving as a spacer to allow for the passing of an uncertain amount of time between David's escape and Absalom's pursuit. A surface reading suggests that Ahithophel was prideful and petulant, choosing to kill himself rather than to live with the shame of having his renowned counsel rejected. His motives almost certainly grew from a deeper logic, however. Ahithophel had erred in choosing Absalom over David, but his wisdom was not diminished, and his party would have had the upper hand had his counsel been followed. When Absalom took the bait and chose crafty Hushai's counsel, Ahithophel was wise enough to know that the rebellion was doomed. A swift strike might have defeated David, but the delay engineered by Hushai's interference would swing the advantage back to David, who would certainly make the most of it. Ahithophel's treachery was widely known: when David returned to power, he would certainly be executed. Thus, Ahithophel's careful suicide was not an act of desperation or petulance; it was the only opportunity Ahithophel would have to meet death on his own terms. The narrator does not condemn Ahithophel for this action, and the note that he was buried in the family tomb suggests that suicide carried no major negative stigma during this period, at least under the circumstances described. [The Stigma of Suicide]

---

e Stigma of Suicide

Many modern believers, especially within the Roman Catholic Church, fear that suicide is an forgivable sin since it involves murder (albeit of oneself) th no opportunity to repent and seek forgiveness. The ole has little to say about the issue of suicide, though the achings against killing are quite clear. In the Old stament, however, persons who are in extreme situations d near death find no condemnation for their actions. Saul's oice of falling on his own sword rather than submitting to e predations and humiliations of the Philistines is portrayed a courageous rather than cowardly or sinful act (1 Sam :1-5; cf. Abimelech, Judg 9:54; and Zimri, 1 Kgs 16:18; ong with 2 Macc 14:41-46).

During the Jewish rebellion against Rome in the early 70s , the Jews who had held out against a lengthy siege at asada chose mass suicide over submitting to the Romans, guing that death with liberty was better than lives of very. This event is fondly remembered in Hebrew circles as an act of valor, not as something shameful. Likewise, Ahithophel's decision to hang himself is objectively presented as a matter of fact, with no value judgments offered (2 Sam 17:23).

Many scholars have noted certain similarities between the suicides of Ahithophel and Judas. Both were traitors: one to David and one to the "Son of David." David was on the path leading over the Mount of Olives when he learned of Ahithophel's conspiracy. Likewise, Jesus was in the garden of Gethsemane (located on the slopes of the Mount of Olives) when Judas identified him for the authorities. Any literary dependence, of course, would lie with the latter tradition. There are two versions of Judas' death, and the account in Acts 1:18-20 implies an accidental or physical cause for the former apostle's demise. This has led some scholars to propose that the suicide story found in Matt 27:5 was a literary fabrication, loosely based on the example of Ahithophel.

CONNECTIONS

Competing Counselors, 16:15–17:23

The intriguing story of how Hushai contrived to counter Ahithophel's sage advice is built around two types of arguments, both of which can be very persuasive. Ahithophel's advice was rational, logical, left-brained. David should be pursued and eliminated immediately, before he had a chance to reach a safe haven, organize his troops, and set his defenses.

Hushai's advice was rhetorical, emotional, right-brained. He planted seeds of fear by referring to David and his troops as dangerous warriors who would fight like cornered beasts. By appealing to the emotions of fear, uncertainty, and pride, Hushai persuaded the war council to withdraw their endorsement of Ahithophel's sound plan and to sign on to his self-defeating strategy. The narrator insists that Absalom chose Hushai's plan because God had willed it, but this does not diminish the importance of Hushai's visceral appeal.

Does this suggest that choices should always be made on the basis of pure logic, rather than intuition? Of course not. Neuroscientists and cognitive behavioralists have learned that no two people learn to think in the same way. Our brains are not preprogrammed at birth; we each must learn to think in our own way, laying down favored means of thought that become chemically hardened over time and are very difficult to change. Some of us are more at home with front-brain, cognitive thinking, while others feel more at ease operating from perceptions that originate in the sensory centers located in the back part of the brain. The logic-oriented, language-making left side of the brain seems natural to many persons, while others prefer the intuitive, creative, feeling-based right brain for making decisions.

There were people who followed David because of their hearts and not because of the logical appeal of retreating with a weakened king. There were people who made common cause with Absalom, not because they had good feelings about the would-be king, but because his massive level of support made him the rational choice.

We make better choices when we give credence to both logic and feeling, with a sufficient awareness of our own personal preference that we are not unduly swayed by one or the other. We make our best choices when we allow ourselves to be guided by the will of God, who cares what we do and who desires our good.

NOTES

[1] A. A. Anderson, *2 Samuel* (WBC 11; Waco: Word Books, 1989), 214.

[2] Gerhard von Rad, *The Problem of the Hexateuch and Other Essays*, trans. E. W. Trueman Dicken, from 1958 German ed. (New York: McGraw-Hill, 1958),199-200.

[3] P. Kyle McCarter, *II* Samuel (AB 9; Garden City: Doubleday, 1984), 388.

DAVID'S VICTORY AND GRIEF

17:24–19:8a

COMMENTARY

David's Strategy and Absalom's Unwanted Death, 17:24–18:18

Mahanaim was roughly a day's journey east of the Jordan, possibly more for David and his retinue since we do not know where they crossed the river. The NRSV translation of 17:24 implies that David's arrival in Mahanaim and Absalom's crossing of the Jordan were virtually simultaneous. The larger context, however, favors the view that David had already attained the safety of Mahanaim's walls before Absalom and his army ("all the men of Israel") gained the east bank of the Jordan.

It is both ironic and surprising that David should seek and find safe haven in Mahanaim, the same city to which Saul's son Ishbaal had retreated during his tenure as Saul's putative successor to the throne of Israel (2 Sam 2:8-10). Some commentators suggest that David had little choice in the direction of his flight since even his former capital of Hebron had turned against him. David may have won support from cities of the east bank because of his aggressive military stance designed to restrain the advances of Ammon to the south and the Arameans to the north (8:1-14; 10:1-19; 11:1; 12:26-31). In addition, David's sizable mercenary force could have inspired a warmer welcome than David might normally receive.

Some scholars regard 17:25 as secondary since it seems to interrupt the narrative and seems to serve primarily to foreshadow later stories about Amasa (19:13; 20:4-12). Whether secondary or not, the verse is problematic because the description of Amasa's kinship ties flatly contradicts other biblical traditions regarding David's family. [Confused Relations]

The content of 17:26 belongs with 17:24. The region east of the Jordan, roughly centered between the Sea of Galilee and the Dead Sea, was called Gilead. That, of course, is where the present narrative takes place. Though largely bare now, in David's day the area

Confused Relations

AΩ Amasa's family connections, as described in the MT, raise several problem issues. Here are some points of interest:

1. Amasa is here identified as the son of "Ithra the Ishmaelite." The same man is called "Jether" in 1 Chr 2:17, but this is not a large problem; the names Ithra and Jether are much more similar in Hebrew than in English and could have been longer and shorter forms of the same name. The gentilic "Ishmaelite" is unusual, but not unknown in Hebrew.

2. Ithra, it is said, had "gone to" (*not* "married," as in NRSV) a woman named Abigail, who is identified as the sister of Zeruiah (Joab's mother) and the daughter of Nahash. The Chronicler's record is also careful not to name Ithra and Abigail as husband and wife. This may imply that Ithra was the product of an illegitimate relationship, while others have proposed that Abigail and Ithra shared a type of loose marriage known as *ṣadiqa* among the Arabs, in which the woman dwelt with her parents but received periodic visits from her partner (cf. Samson's marriage relationship with the Philistine woman of Timnah, Judg 14).

3. Zeruiah, the mother of David's stalwarts Joab and Abishai, is clearly named as the daughter of Jesse (1 Chr 2:16) and thus the sister of David. How, then, could she be called the daughter of Nahash? It is possible that the appearance of "Nahash" is nothing more than a scribal error, accidentally picked up from the phrase "son of Nahash" in 17:27. If so, the error would have occurred ver early since it is repeated in all witnesses. The Nahash mentioned in 17:27 was the king of Ammon and an ally of David. The name (from the root meaning "serpent") was not unique to the Ammonites, however. The similar name "Nahshon" was also known in Judah (Ruth 4:20; 1 Chr 2:10, 11).

If the appearance of Nahash is not a textual corruption, how could Abigail be the sister of Zeruiah but not the daughter of Zeruiah's father Jesse? One possibility is that Nahash was her mother's name, but the identification by a matronymic would be highly unusual. Another potential explanation is that Jesse's unnamed wife had been previously married to a man named Nahash. This presume that she bore Abigail and was widowed before marrying Jesse and bearing at least nine children (eight sons + Zeruiah) to him.

4. It seems a bit strange that there are only two women in the Bible named Abigail, one of which is David's sister, and the other his wife (1 Sam 25). Some scholars argue that the two are identical, remembered differently in variant traditions. There is no additional evidence to support this proposal, however.

included dense forests. The word order "Israel and Absalom" is surprising since one would expect "Absalom and Israel." Some suppose the narrator reversed the order as an insult to Absalom. Others suggest that only "Israel" or "Absalom" was present in the early traditions, with the second name being added by a later hand.

David's warm welcome in Mahanaim comes at the hands of three disparate men who join forces to provide comfortable bedding and useful utensils for David and his family, along with ample field rations for those who traveled with him. [Food for the Troops] Shobi, "son of Nahash from Rabbah of the Ammonites," is mentioned only here. Some presume that David had appointed Shobi to rule Rabbah after crushing the Ammonite revolt led by his brother Hanun (12:26-31). Others argue that the chronology is confused and that the events related in chapter 10 and in 12:26-31 did not occur until later. In that scenario, Shobi would not have come on his own, but as his father Nahash's representative. David and Nahash reportedly had congenial relations. Politically, it would have been in Ammon's best interests to support David's minority position and thus encourage Israel's internal dissension.

Machir, son of Ammiel of Lo-debar, had once provided housing for Saul's grandson Mephibosheth (see 2 Sam 9:4). Thus, he had been (presumably) a loyal supporter of Saul, and it is surprising to see him offer such generous aid to David. Perhaps David had won Machir over by his kind treatment of Mephibosheth, providing the unfortunate Saulide a home in Jerusalem and relieving Machir of a very expensive house guest.

Barzillai the Gileadite from Rogelim first appears in this instance. "Gilead" normally refers to a geographic region rather than to a kinship group or ethnic unit, but it is also used in that sense in Judges 5:17. The location of Rogelim is unknown. After the war, David remembered Barzillai's kindness by inviting him to live in Jerusalem under royal patronage. Barzillai declined because of his own advanced age (80) and his desire to remain at home, but his sons later joined Solomon's court (2 Sam 19:31-39; 1 Kgs 2:7).

Food for the Troops

The supplies provided for David and company are largely self-explanatory, though there are a few textual issues. The LXX describes the MT's "beds" as "sleeping couches with embroidered covers," apparently more fit for a king. Some textual traditions count ten such beds.

The last food items mentioned are not entirely clear. "Curds, sheep, and cheese from the herd" (NRSV) appears in Hebrew as "curds of the sheep and cheese of the herd." The word translated "cheese" is *hapax legomenon*, occurring only here in the biblical record. In later Hebrew, the verbal form refers to a straining process in which liquid is poured off to leave a sediment behind. In a dairy context, this suggests some product similar to cheese, as supported by the parallel reference to "curds."

Absalom's revolt had been years in the making, but it came to an end in the space of a single battle on a single day. The first few verses are designed to stress David's active direction of the war effort while also explaining his absence from the combat itself. David used the time granted him by Hushai's canny counsel to muster his army of trained professionals and to develop a careful battle plan. The organization of troops into battalions or platoons of "thousands" and "hundreds" goes back to Mosaic times (Exod 18:21; Deut 1:15). As explained above (see [Counting Soldiers] at 1 Sam 4:2), "thousands" and "hundreds" may have been used as technical terms for military units rather than as literal head counts. The term "thousand" (*'elep*) is sometimes described as a "platoon" consisting of from five to fourteen men.

The division of an army into three parts was a frequent strategy in Israelite warfare (cf. Judg 7:16; 9:43; 1 Sam 11:11; 13:17). Joab, Abishai, and Ittai were appointed to lead the three units. Joab and Abishai were the sons of David's sister Zeruiah. At this point in the narrative, it seems superfluous for the narrator to point out that Abishai was Joab's brother, unless he was looking for every opportunity to draw attention to Joab. Ittai's appointment as head of the third group is not surprising since he had brought 600 Gittite soldiers with him. It is likely that this group formed one of the three units.

David was implicitly criticized in 11:1 for not going to war with his army, but here his absence is explicated in a way that brings no shame to David. He volunteered to lead the army, the storyteller says, but "his men" deferentially persuaded him to stay behind since the king's safety was not only paramount, but the entire point of the battle. "You are worth ten thousand of us" (18:3) is an obvious hyperbole, but the importance of David's life was indeed crucial. Without David, his supporters would have nothing to defend—the rebellion would have succeeded. David's greatest contribution would be to remain alive and send encouragement from the safety of Mahanaim.

David accepted the counsel of his troops with uncharacteristic humility ("Whatever seems best to you I will do," 18:4), suggesting that hard experience had taught him to acknowledge that his own judgment was not always most propitious. Accepting his role with grace, the king stood by the gate and reviewed his troops as they marched from the city. "At the side of the gate" (NRSV; most translations) literally means "at the hand of the gate," but *yad* was commonly used with the meaning "side." Kyle McCarter translates "atop the gate," but with no explanation.[1]

David's command in 18:5 sounds more like a plea: it is intended to absolve the king from any blame in the death of Absalom. As previously, David is portrayed as an indulgent father ruled more by sentimentality than reason when his children were involved. Unfortunately, "Deal gently for my sake with the young man Absalom" made for an ineffective motivational speech. [This Is Motivation?]

The account of the combat is so abbreviated that it seems like no battle at all. It is fought on a field of David's choosing, between two poorly matched armies. Absalom had taken over the national militia of conscripts, to which he would have added many new recruits if he followed Hushai's deceptive counsel. He may have had numbers on his side, but David's tripartite army was composed of seasoned professionals, mercenary men and military volunteers who had fought for David over a long period of time.

This Is Motivation?

Army generals and sports coaches know the strategic value of sending their troops/teams out with an inspiring motivational speech. Vince Lombardi, long-time coach of the NFL Green Bay Packers, was famed for the inspirational pre-game orations he gave to his football team. Imagine the team's confusion if a coach should say: "Fight hard, use your head, sacrifice your body if need be, and give it all you've got. I want you to go out and demolish the other team—just don't touch their quarterback, okay?"

Imagine the inner turmoil of David's soldiers when he sends them out to risk their very lives in battle, but prohibits them from attacking the enemy commander. Any inspirational value would have been overcome by David's ambivalence.

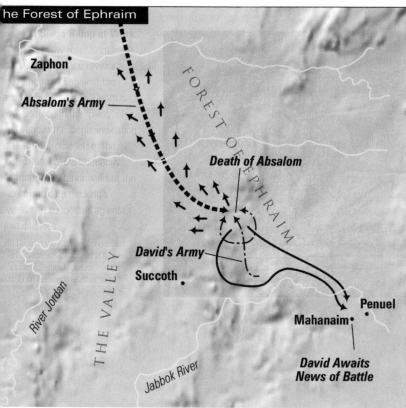

The Forest of Ephraim

Zaphon

Absalom's Army

FOREST OF EPHRAIM

Death of Absalom

David's Army

Succoth

THE VALLEY

River Jordan

Penuel

Mahanaim

David Awaits
News of Battle

Jabbok River

...e desert-like terrain of Gilead (now in the country of Jordan) was once so densely wooded that ...emiah and Zechariah both compared it to the deeply forested Lebanon (Jer 22:6; Zech 10:10). The name "forest of Ephraim" has occasioned some comment because it seems strange that a ...ographical feature on the east bank of the Jordan would be named for a tribal group that lived ...the western side of the river. It is sometimes suggested that certain elements of Ephraim had ...ginally settled the area, but supportive evidence is lacking.

The dense forest of Ephraim offered few difficulties to David's experienced warriors, but posed significant problems to Absalom's untrained troops. [The Forest of Ephraim] The text says little about David's specific strategy, but an army of three parts probably would have been deployed in a flanking movement, pushing Absalom's forces deeper into the dangerous forest from three sides, with flight to the rear the only option when the battle tide turned in David's favor.

The narrator takes some delight in reporting simply that Absalom's massive army ("the men of Israel") was soundly defeated by "the servants of David" (18:6). Indeed, it was more of a slaughter than a battle, as twenty thousand men (presumably of Israel) fell. Even if "thousand" is taken as "platoon" rather than a literal number, Absalom's losses would have been significant. The author also conveys his amusement by means of the pithy comment that "the forest claimed more victims that day than the sword" (18:8). The Hebrew phrase could be translated literally as "the forest ate more people than the sword ate." The image of trees swallowing soldiers sounds like hyperbole—until the reader learns that one of those swallowed up by a tree was Absalom.

The account of Absalom's death (18:9-15) is more than three times as long as the report of his army's defeat and the deaths of twenty "thousands" of soldiers (18:6-8). This reminds the reader that the story is really about Absalom and David. The civil war is only an effective backdrop against which the classic father-son struggle is played out.

The MT suggests that Absalom and certain soldiers of David met by chance in the forest, but the LXX^L says Absalom "was far ahead of the servants of David," implying that he was trying to escape on his mule when unexpectedly detained by the low-hanging branches of a large oak (= "terebinth") tree. Interpreters from the time of Josephus and the rabbis have presumed that Absalom was snared by his luxurious locks, finding an ironic moral in the young man's victimization by the very object of his apparent pride. The text, however, says nothing about his hair: only that "his head" was caught fast by the oak, a picture more amenable to being caught by the throat in a forked branch.

Of more significance is the image of Absalom hanging in the air because he has become unmuled. The mule was the favored mode of transportation for royalty in David's day (see [Mules] at 2 Sam 13:29). C. Conroy has noted the symbolic effect: in losing his mule, Absalom also has lost his kingdom.[2]

The conversation between Joab and the unnamed soldier who reported Absalom's plight depicts Joab as a bloodthirsty man who was driven to eliminate Absalom's threat by eliminating Absalom, and it profiles the messenger as a quick thinker who finds himself in a classic "Catch 22" situation (18:10-13). [Catch 22] The soldier

---

Catch 22

The phrase "Catch 22" was made popular by author Joseph Heller in a book by the same name (New York: Simon and Schuster, 1961). It described a situation prevailing among the crewmen who flew dangerous bombing missions over Germany during World War II. The only way to avoid the hazardous duty was to demonstrate serious injury or insanity. The catch was that any person who sought leave by claiming to be insane was turned down because nobody in their right mind would want to be flying in harm's way. Thus, the desire to opt out was considered proof of sanity: an airman was condemned to keep flying whether he acted insane or not.

The messenger who reported Absalom's predicament 1 Joab probably knew the general would be angry that he h not dispatched the rebel leader. The soldier assumed, however, that if he had killed Absalom, Joab might finger him as the culprit who killed Absalom and thus preserve h own good standing with David. Despite Joab's protestatic to the contrary, the quick-thinking soldier knew that he wa in a no-win situation: David would have condemned him whether he killed Absalom or not. Thus, it was an easy choice for the infantryman to observe David's well-known command to "deal gently" with Absalom.

saw through Joab's claim that he would have rewarded Absalom's slayer with ten pieces of silver and a belt. He presumed that Joab would not have supported him had he killed Absalom, but would have "stood aloof" when David found out and left the poor man to face David's wrath alone (18:13). The provocative words attributed to the messenger in 18:12—repeating David's command to protect Absalom—offer clear evidence that Joab has lost favor with the narrator because his first loyalty is not to David, but to his own ideas about what is best for the country. The lone soldier would not have disobeyed David's command even for a thousand pieces of silver. Joab disobeyed for no greater price than the cost of his own opinion. The time would come when Joab would pay dearly, however (19:12-13; 1 Kgs 2:5-6, 28-35).

Joab's declaration that he would no longer "waste time like this" with the messenger (lit., "tarry here before you") reveals his distaste for ethical quibbles (18:14a). Joab was a man of action, and he immediately took action with regard to Absalom. The traditional view that Joab first stabbed Absalom with three spears (or javelins, or darts) grows from translators' difficulty with the Hebrew word *šĕbāṭîm*, which means "sticks" or "rods." Some would emend the term slightly to a word that means "darts," but this is really unnecessary. The Hebrew phrase translated "thrust them into the heart" could also be rendered as "struck them against the chest" (18:14b). The impression, then, is that Joab picked up a handful of stout limbs and used them to strike Absalom across the chest, knocking him from the tree, whereupon Joab's retainers closed in for the kill.

The preference for this interpretation is made clear by the action in 18:15. If Absalom already had three spears, javelins, or even darts "in his heart," it hardly would have been necessary for Joab's companions to surround Absalom and smite him so that he died. [Violent Words] Since David had so clearly commanded that Absalom be spared, one presumes that Joab might have deliberately contrived the scenario so that no one person would bear the blame for Absalom's death. As with modern firing squads or executioners who throw multiple switches, the killing blow could not be traced to any one person. This did not, however, remove any of the responsibility from Joab's head. The narrator has

Violent Words

AΩ The word used to describe Joab's striking Absalom on the chest (or in the heart) is *tāqa*, meaning "to thrust," "to clap," "to give a blow," or even "to blow a horn." It was used in Judg 3:21 for Ehud's thrusting of his sword into Eglon's belly, but more commonly refers to the driving of tent pegs into the ground (Gen 31:25; Isa 22:23, 25; Jer 6:3) or even into a person's head (see the story of Jael and Sisera, Judg 4:21).

The term that depicts the fatal blows administered by Joab's armor bearers is from the root *nākā*, meaning "to smite." This word is frequently used to describe striking with deadly force, as David did against Goliath (1 Sam 17:49), as Saul attempted to do with his spear to David (1 Sam 18:11; 19:10), and as Abishai wished to do to Saul (1 Sam 26:8). The narrator's preference for this word as a term for a fatal thrust reinforces the view that Joab only struck the first blow, allowing his men to finish the job. This did not, however, absolve Joab of responsibility for Absalom's death.

2 Samuel: 18:9-17—Tradition holds that Absalom's famous locks were his downfall, but the text says only that his head was caught in a tree, leading the loss of his mule and his life.

Julius Schnoor von Carolsfeld. *Absalom's Death*. 19th century. Woodcut. *Das Buch der Bucher in Bilden*. (Credit: Dover Pictorial Archive Series)

carefully designed the story to demonstrate that Joab alone was guilty of orchestrating Absalom's demise.

Joab's restraint of the troops in 18:16 is somewhat ironic since he had shown no restraint in the pursuit and slaying of Absalom. Once the rebel leader was dead, however, his following evaporated and the revolt was finished. There was no further need for Israelites to die. The burial of Absalom in a deep forest pit—as the vanquished king's supporters "fled to their homes" (lit., "tents")—seems to be a further attempt on Joab's part to distance David from his son. Perhaps he thought that if David did not see Absalom's mangled body or cradle his dead son in his arms, his personal pain and anger at Joab would be less. If so, he was wrong.

Some writers have suggested a more politically and theologically apt motivation, proposing that Joab chose Absalom's burial place as a final insult, on the model of previous enemies of the state. After being stoned to death for the sacrilege of taking spoils during a "holy war," Achan was buried under a large pile of stones (Josh 7:26). In the same narrative, the king of Ai is first hanged from a tree, then cast into a pit and covered with a large pile of stones (Josh 8:29). Likewise, in Joshua 10:27, five enemy kings are executed, hung from trees, and thrown into a cave whose mouth is then sealed with large stones. Thus, Absalom's encounter with the tree, his execution, and his burial in a pit covered with stones suggest that he, too, is considered an accursed enemy of Israel.

The description of the great cairn that was raised over Absalom's grave may be an etiology for a well-known landmark, and it leads the narrator (or a later redactor) to mention another monumental construction associated with Absalom. Before his death, Absalom had reportedly raised a monolith in the "King's Valley" as a memorial to himself since he had no son to carry on his name. [The King's Valley] This statement seems to be in conflict with 14:27, which states that Absalom had three sons in addition to his beautiful daughter Tamar. Since none of the sons are named, some writers presume that they all died young. Thus, though sons had been

The King's Valley

The precise location of "The King's Valley" is uncertain, though the Kidron Valley, especially near its junction with the Hinnom Valley, is often suggested as a possibility. Gen 14:17-18 reports that, following Abram's defeat of Chedorlaomer's coalition, the patriarch met with the king of Sodom, and Melchizedek, the king of Salem, "at the Valley of Shaveh (that is, The King's Valley)." The parenthesis was probably a later gloss for readers who were familiar with the location of The King's Valley. The site preserved in folk tradition is directly east of the City of David, at the foot of the Mount of Olives, where the so-called "Tomb of Absalom" (dating from late Hellenistic or possibly Roman times) is located.

"Absalom's Tomb" is one of many traditional but unauthenticated pilgrim sites in Israel.
Francis Frith. *Absalom's Tomb*. 1857. Albumen Print. (Credit: Courtesy George Eastman House)

born to Absalom, he truthfully could say that he had no sons to carry on his name. "It is called Absalom's Monument to this day" refers to the day in which the redactional comment was added to the story. Neither the stone cairn over Absalom's grave nor Absalom's Monument should be confused with the late Hellenistic structure in the Kidron Valley, remembered in popular tradition as the "Tomb of Absalom."

David Mourns for His Son, 18:19–19:7 (MT 19:8a)

The account of how David learned of his son's death is told with great pathos and in considerable detail. Like the death of Absalom, the account of its report to David is considerably longer than the story of the battle itself.

Ahimaaz, the son of Zadok who had served with Jonathan as David's primary communication link with Jerusalem, requested the honor of proclaiming victory to the king. Joab's reticence has been explained in several ways. Perhaps he feared that Ahimaaz knew David too well to present the complete picture, including Absalom's death, as good news. Or he may have been concerned that David would not take the news of Absalom's death well. On more than one occasion, persons who thought they were bringing good tidings to David had met a bad end (although those messengers were also implicated in the deaths they were reporting, 2 Sam 1:1-16; 4:5-12). Ahimaaz was a significant and well-known person (note 17:17-18), the son of the high priest, and Joab could not risk the political damage that might result if David brought him harm.

"You are not to carry tidings today" (18:20) means, literally, "You will not be a man of good news this day." The only reason given is "because the king's son is dead," a factor that supports the view that Joab feared for the messenger's safety. The Cushite who is recruited in 18:20 was probably from Ethiopia or Nubia, the geographic area designated by the old term "Cush." [The Cushite] Some interpreters suggest that the Cushite's black skin would have signaled to David that he brought bad news, but this can hardly be the case since the tidings are presented in a most positive fashion.

Joab's instruction for the Cushite to go and "tell the king what you have seen" (18:21) may imply that the Cushite had been present when Absalom died, in contrast to Ahimaaz, who later testified that he only "saw a great tumult" that he could not identify. This provided Ahimaaz a convenient excuse for sidestepping the issue of reporting Absalom's death.

Once the Cushite had bowed before his superior officer and left, Ahimaaz returned to plead his case again. We are not told why Ahimaaz was so set on declaring the news, unless he considered

The Cushite

AΩ Readers may find it interesting to note that the second appearance of the term in the MT lacks the article, as if it were a proper name, "Cushi." Though the article returns throughout the MT, it is wholly lacking in the LXX, the Syriac, the Vulgate, and the Targums, all of which treat the term as a personal name throughout the narrative.

The superscription to Ps 7 is often noted: "A Shiggaion of David, which he sang to the LORD concerning Cush, a Benjaminite." It is not impossible that a man of Benjamin could have taken an Ethiopian or Nubian wife, whose children would be dark-skinned but full-fledged members of the tribe of Benjamin. One of them could have been named (or nicknamed) "Cush" or "Cushi."

himself to be David's personal messenger and took offense at being passed over. Joab implied that Ahimaaz was greedy for the reward that was presumably given to those who bore good news. Knowing that David would not rejoice at the report of Absalom's death, Joab insisted that there would be no reward in store (v. 22). Ahimaaz would not be deterred, however, pressing his case nearly to the point of insubordination: "Come what may, I will run" (v. 23). Joab's surrender is expressed in a single word: "Run."

The narrator's lengthy account of how Ahimaaz outran the Cushite and came first to the king serves to build suspense for the reader. The episode is related through a series of exchanges between a sentinel, who was perched atop the gate of Mahanaim, and King David, who pointedly sat "between the two gates," presumably in the middle of the road (18:24). David's position reveals his anxiety for Absalom: he is determined that no news should pass him by.

The conversation is almost inane. Parts of it must have been included for the benefit of the reader, who already knows that there are two runners and that Ahimaaz left last but will arrive first (18:23). [The Way of the Plain] At the watchman's first report of a single runner, David comments—as if an experienced sentinel would not know—that a single runner coming from battle was apt to be a messenger (18:25); multiple runners might indicate a retreat. The sentinel's announcement of a second runner trailing behind leads to a similar response from David, who seems to be making small talk to relieve his agitation and help the awkward time go by. "He is also bringing tidings." The NRSV, following the MT, has the sentinel's second announcement directed "to the gatekeeper," which makes no sense. The better reading is preserved by the LXX, which has "atop the gate."

The Way of the Plain

The Cushite's route is not described, but most commentators presume he took the most direct path to Mahanaim, a relatively straight but difficult track through steep and rugged terrain. Ahimaaz was apparently more familiar with the countryside and chose a longer but smoother route "by the way of the plain." This enabled him to bypass the Cushite and to arrive first, foiling Joab's intention.

The sentinel's familiarity with Ahimaaz's distinctive gait suggests that he was one of David's aides, rather than a man of Mahanaim. Ahimaaz had served David well as a clandestine messenger before losing his cover (17:17-18) and apparently choosing to remain with David's forces. David's comment that Ahimaaz was "a good man" and therefore must bear good tidings sounds more hopeful than certain (18:27). Joab would hardly have entrusted any tidings to a man who was not reliable and loyal, that is, "a good man."

The narrator notes that Ahimaaz prostrated himself before David, continuing a running motif previously discussed in [An Intriguing Motif] at 2 Samuel 14:4. His first statement ("All is well!") is intended to relieve the king's tension, but it does not. Ahimaaz's next statement, according to custom, attributes the victory to Yahweh: "Blessed be the LORD your God, who has delivered up the men who raised their hand against my lord the king." The reader may note that this is the first time Yahweh has been mentioned since Hushai's pledge in 16:18, except for the redactional comment in 17:24. Yahweh is given credit for winning the victory but is mentioned only in the stereotyped messenger report.

It quickly becomes clear that David cares little about the battle as a whole; he is concerned with only one soldier in the midst of the deadly fray: "Is it well with the young man Absalom?" (v. 29a). Surprisingly, Ahimaaz—who had been so eager to run with the news—demurs. He does not tell what he knows, hiding behind a small truth that he "saw a great tumult" but could not discern the details (18:29b). Knowing that another messenger was on his way, and perhaps desiring confirmation of one report against the other, David did not release the exhausted Ahimaaz to go and refresh himself, or even to sit down and rest, insisting that he "turn aside and stand here" (18:30).

The Cushite's initial announcement differed in vocabulary, but not in content from the message of Ahimaaz: both began by declaring good news, then praised Yahweh for delivering David from his enemy. [Two Speeches: Same Story, Sharper Emphasis] The Cushite's words are slightly less tactful: he adds the theme of vindication for David (18:31) and notes Yahweh's deliverance from "*all* who rose up against you," a number which must include Absalom.

David's interest has not changed: his query about Absalom leads to the devastating news that his son is dead, as expressed by a circumlocution: "May the enemies of my lord the king, and all who rise up to do you harm, be like that young man." The Cushite has couched the news of Absalom's death as gently as possible, reminding David that Absalom was indeed an enemy of the king, one whom loyal supporters of David would wish to have removed from the picture.

David is not comforted by the Cushite's diplomatic finesse. Indeed, he is utterly inconsolable. Even David's plaintive elegy for Saul and his friend Jonathan (2 Sam 1) seems bland compared to the king's ragged, visceral, tearful cry. The depth of David's emotion is conveyed by his retreat to the guard chamber above the gate and by his persistent repetition of the name "Absalom," and the words "my son" (*běnî*): "O my son Absalom, my son, my son Absalom! Would I had died instead of you, O Absalom, my son,

o Speeches: Same Story, Sharper Emphasis

Note how similar are the encounters between David and the two messengers in regard to form, but how different in their outcome:

ory Element	Ahimaaz (18:28-30)	The Cushite (18:31-33)
lutation of good tidings	Then Ahimaaz cried out to the king, "All is well!"	Then the Cushite came; and the Cushite said, "Good tidings for my lord the king!"
ostration before the king	He prostrated himself before the king with his face to the ground,	
rmulaic praise to Yahweh	and said, "Blessed be the LORD your God, who has delivered up the men who raised their hand against my lord the king."	"For the LORD has vindicated you this day, delivering you from the power of all who rose up against you."
avid's question	The king said, "Is it well with the young man Absalom?"	The king said to the Cushite, "Is it well with the young man Absalom?"
ne messenger's reply	Ahimaaz answered, "When Joab sent your servant, I saw a great tumult, but I do not know what it was."	The Cushite answered, "May the enemies of my lord the king, and all who rise up to do you harm, be like that young man."
avid's response	The king said, "Turn aside, and stand here."	The king was deeply moved, and went up to the chamber over the gate, and wept; and as he went, he said, "O my son Absalom, my son, my son Absalom! Would I had died instead of you, O Absalom, my son, my son!"

my son!" (18:33 [MT 19:1]). The narrator's implication is that David did not utter these words just once, but many times.

David's grief, in fact, was so profound that he wept unabated even as his victorious troops returned from battle (19:4 [MT 19:5]), expecting a welcome befitting of heroes, but finding a king who cared only for the enemy they had defeated. Thus, "the victory that day was turned into mourning," and the troops "stole into the city that day as soldiers steal in who are ashamed when they flee in battle" (19:1-3 [MT 19:2-4]). Joab, of course, was livid. Shoving the king's grief aside as childlike whimpering, David's general berated him for ignoring the emotional needs of the brave men who had risked their own lives to save David and his family from death. His words were harsh. He accused David of loving those who hated him and hating those who loved him, of caring more for his one rebellious son than for all of his loyal supporters (19:5-6 [MT 19:6-7]).

Joab finally forced David's hand by predicting that the broken king's attitude would cost him the loss of every adherent he had left. Joab called on the name of Yahweh with a powerful oath, challenging David to pick himself up and go out to review his troops, lest he be left with no troops to review (19:7 [MT 19:8]). The soldiers had won the victory for David; now David's grief had crushed their spirits and filled them with resentful shame. Only David could instill new pride and restore their loyalty. Joab's implication was that if David did not act, he would personally lead the troops in a mass desertion. David knew that the bold general had the ability to follow through on his threat, and he never forgave Joab for the affront, however justified and pragmatic it was.

Thus, David dried his tears and took his seat in the gate to review the troops, who readily came to accept his diffident congratulations and praise. The story of Absalom's rebellion began with the young aspirant to the throne avidly stationing himself in the gate of Jerusalem, where he offered deceptive words that would enable him to "steal" the hearts of Israel. The account of the revolt ends with David reluctantly sitting in the gate of Mahanaim, forcing himself to say the words that regain for him the loyalty of his closest supporters. These two accounts form a neat inclusio, marking the beginning and the end of the insurrection and the continuation of David's decline from his once lofty position.

CONNECTIONS

Decisions for Good and Evil, 17:24–18:18

What are we to do with this difficult text? How do we hear the word of God in this story of battle and blood and decisions good and bad? The clearest lessons grow from the protagonist's decisions.

Absalom's choices were consistently selfish and foolish. He had everything in his favor. He was the highest born and best-looking man in the kingdom. He was well spoken and popular. But Absalom's pride and resentment engendered choices that led to an ugly rebellion and an early death. The rabbis made much of

Absalom's good looks, finding it ironic and fitting that his own handsome head (specifically his hair) became his downfall, leading Absalom unmuled and hung in a tree.

David's choices leading up to the battle were choices made on the basis of what it takes to survive with the least possible family conflict. Unfortunately, that is not always possible. When conflict is present, it needs to be brought into the open and dealt with before it grows in upon itself and reaches the point where people start killing each other.

Joab was a pragmatic man. He chose to do what needed to be done for the good of all and to use whatever means were at his disposal to accomplish his goals. It was not the first time he had killed someone that David wanted alive, and it would not be the last. Joab's violence overshadows all of his other choices.

The unnamed warrior chose to stay out of trouble. When he saw a difficult situation in which he could not win, he chose to avoid it. That soldier's ability to recognize trouble ahead of time and the wisdom he demonstrated in avoiding it are worth remembering.

Ahimaaz wanted to be in the center of things. He was filled with excitement and wanted to tell the good news, but at the moment of truth he was so afraid of rejection that he backed away and pretended that he did not know anything. He calls to mind someone who thinks witnessing for Christ is a good idea—for someone else to do.

One thing all these decisions have in common is that God is not involved in any of them. In fact, God is wholly absent from this chapter except for two references, when Ahimaaz and the Cushite use the standard formula of praising God for the good news when they report it to the king. There is no evidence that God was consulted in the making of any of these decisions.

David was once known as a man after God's heart, but when he coveted Bathsheba, he chose to follow his own heart, and that is what left him with so many difficult choices later.

Absalom was never known for his piety. He once claimed to have made a vow to God (15:7-8), but it was only a ruse to get him out of town to sow the seeds of his rebellion.

Joab based his decisions on the belief that you do what you have to do to eliminate your enemies, and Joab did not know anything else to do but kill people. There is no evidence that Joab ever consulted God in the matter.

The unnamed warrior and Ahimaaz were both acting out of their own desires for self-survival or self-promotion. Their decisions may have been good or bad, but they were human decisions only.

There are many areas of life in which God expects us to use our own minds and make good decisions based on the information we have and the love in our hearts, but always within the context of the things he has taught us. When we make our decisions without reference to God's will for our lives, we are asking for trouble. If we remember to keep our decision-making within the context of prayer for God's direction, there is a good chance that we will make better choices.

All of us are faced in life with hard choices. We must decide between good and evil, between obedience and rebellion, between our way and God's way, between selfishness and service. Perhaps this ugly story may inspire us to think more clearly, to pray more fervently, and to make better decisions.

When All Seems Lost, 18:19–19:7 (MT 19:8a)

David's outpouring of grief over Absalom was interpreted by his men as treachery from the top down. They had risked their lives to save David and his family and were made to feel like villains. None of them, however, knew what David knew or felt what David felt. Most people have seen news reports or read articles about men or women who have perpetrated acts of obvious evil, yet their dazed parents declare that their violent and murderous progeny are really good kids who are misunderstood and must have been provoked. Parental love is like that.

The king's emotional outburst seems not limited to the loss of Absalom alone. David is also grieving the death of Bathsheba's son, the rape of Tamar, the murder of Amnon, his loss of the people's trust, and, ultimately, the knowledge that he is the one to blame. The prophet Nathan had declared to David that the sword would not depart from his house and that his own family would rise up against him (12:10-12). David's appeal for Absalom's life had been one last hope that Nathan's word might *not* come true, but it did. The prophet had been devastatingly correct: David's own sin had brought the king to his knees, his kingdom to the ground, and his son(s) to the grave. David's bitter tears and plaintive wails are not an expression of loss only, but an acknowledgment of his own failure. [David's Sorrow]

It was Joab who shook David out of his self-directed pity and recrimination, reminding him that there were still many persons who looked to him for leadership and who depended on him for support. *There was still a life ahead for David.* All was not lost. Joab would certainly not have considered himself to be a channel of

id's Sorrow

d's grief was palable and obvious to all, leading Joab to accuse the king of having no concern for his
ful army.

ave Doré (1832–83). *David Mourning the Death of Absalom* from the *Illustrated Bible*. 19th century. Engraving.
it: Dover Pictoral Archive Series)

grace, but his challenge became grace to David. The king dried his
tears, picked himself up, and went out to pay his troops the respect
and regard they were due. The past was painful, and even ugly, but
the future remained. As David had demonstrated this truth by his
own behavior after the death of Bathsheba's first son, so now he
accepted Joab's rebuke and made the hard choice to leave the past
behind and get on with the future.

Every person who lives long enough will face times of grief and
trial, and some of our troubles can be traced to our own mistakes.

We can spend our lives in brutal self-recrimination, or we can learn to accept the grace of God, who forgives our sin and offers us another chance (Rom 6:23). Grief must be acknowledged and worked through: it was not wrong for David to grieve the loss of his son, nor may we assume that his grief-work was done when he acceded to Joab and went out to review the troops. Sorrow and loss are very real, and they must be experienced, but they do not mark the end of life, only a new beginning. With faith and courage and grace born of God, believers can learn to face even the deepest agony of grief with hope and to let that sorrow become strength for days yet to come.

NOTES

[1] P. Kyle McCarter, *II Samuel* (AB 9; Garden City: Doubleday, 1984), 396.

[2] C. Conroy, *Absalom! Absalom! Narrative and Language in 2 Sam. 13–20* (Rome: Biblical Institute Press, 1978), 60.

DAVID RETURNS TO JERUSALEM, BUT NOT IN TRIUMPH

19:8b-43

David Diminished and a Discontented Nation, 19:8b–20:26

The immediate aftermath of Absalom's rebellion is played out in 19:8b–20:26. (All Hebrew verse numbers are +1 in ch. 19, but for simplicity's sake will not be indicated in the remainder of the discussion.) David's return to Jerusalem was not as simple as one might think, for he had been deposed by Absalom and could not return to the throne without the support of both Israel and Judah. The careful negotiations leading to David's restoration form the basis of 19:8b-43. Much of the narrative describing David's return to Jerusalem is devoted to three meeting scenes that echo in some ways the five meeting scenes that had earlier marked the king's departure. [More Meeting Scenes]

The narrator does little to hide the intense rivalry between Judah and Israel. David exploited this tribal envy to hasten his return to the throne, but sowed the seeds of further dissension in the process, leading to Sheba's short-lived separatist movement (ch. 20). The brief roll call of David's inner cabinet in 20:23-26 marks David's successful return to power and the reestablishment of his authority. David is diminished and chastened, but Yahweh's promise that he and his descendants will occupy the throne remains in force.

COMMENTARY

The Royal Vacuum, 19:8b-10

The death of Absalom brought an end to his rebellion, but it did not automatically restore David to the throne. The people of Israel had crowned him as king, effectively deposing David, who had surrendered the capital without a fight and gone into exile. Absalom's

---

More Meeting Scenes

The two sets of meeting scenes form an inner inclusio within the literary unit describing the causes and the consequences of Absalom's revolt (2 Sam 13–20). The meeting scenes are compared in the following chart. Notes in italics point to other encounters with the characters involved that are significant to the story, but not depicted as meeting scenes.

Meetings on David's departure	*Meetings on David's return*
Ittai the Gittite (15:19-22)	Zadok and Abiathar the priests (15:24-29) *David sends a message for Zadok and Abiathar to begin negotiations with Judah (19:11-15)*
Hushai the Archite (15:32-36)	
Ziba the steward of Mephibosheth (16:1-4)	*Ziba, with an entourage, arrives with Shimei (19:17b-18a). He assists in David's crossing, but has no conversation with the king.*
Ziba tells David that Mephibosheth remained in Jerusalem by choice.	Mephibosheth (19:24-30)
Shimei of Bahurim (16:5-13)	Shimei of Bahurim (19:16-17a, 18b-23)
Barzillai the Gileadite met David in Mahanaim and provided material support (17:27-29)	Barzillai the Gileadite (19:31-40)

---

attempt to bring about David's death led to his own demise, but it did not change the fact that David had been dethroned. This led to a power vacuum in Israel, an unsettling void that only David could fill.

"All the Israelites had fled to their homes" (lit., "tents") builds on a standard cliché for the dismantling of an army (Judg 7:8; 20:8; 1 Sam 13:2; 2 Sam 20:1 [cf. 2 Chr 10:16]), especially in defeat (1 Sam 4:10; 2 Sam 18:17, 22; 2 Kgs 14:12 [= 2 Chr 25:22]). The reference here points to the demobilization of Absalom's army after the rebel leader's death (2 Sam 18:17).

The NRSV's "All the people were disputing throughout all the tribes of Israel" (v. 9) is a typical translation, suggesting a widespread debate concerning the nation's political future. Kyle McCarter has argued that "all the people" refers mainly to the popular militia, who brought their complaints to the "staff-bearers" (a revocalization of the word for "tribes") or elders of Israel.[1] McCarter's interpretation makes specific an assumption that the disputants sought recourse from tribal elders. Either reading results in the same scenario: the populace has grown accustomed to the monarchy and feels lost without a leader. Many persons (whether

My Bone and My Flesh

AΩ While modern English readers normally trace family "bloodlines" and speak of being "blood relatives," the Hebrews saw their connection with kinspeople in terms of "flesh and bone," a euphemism for the physical body (Job 2:5). For example, in the creation account found in Gen 2, the first man says of the first woman, "This at last is bone of my bones and flesh of my flesh" (Gen 2:23). In similar fashion, Laban spoke of his nephew Jacob as "my bone and my flesh" (Gen 29:14). Among the traditions preserved in Judges, Abimelech sought support from his mother's extended family, bracing his appeal with the reminder that "I am your bone and your flesh" (Judg 9:2).

David uses this expression of kinship twice in 2 Sam 19, first regarding the elders of Judah (19:12), then with reference to Amasa (19:13). David was of the tribe of Judah, as was Amasa. There is no information beyond this to suggest that Amasa was closely related to David, as were Joab and Abishai. David uses the metaphor to underscore his kinship ties with Judah (as opposed to the northern tribes of Israel) in hopes that the elders will take the lead in returning him to the throne.

Ironically, when the elders of Israel had petitioned David to become their king the first time, they argued on the basis of the wider kinship shared by all the tribes: "Look, we are your bone and flesh" (2 Sam 5:1 [= 1 Chr 11:1]).

---

military or not) recall how David had brought stability by delivering Israel from its enemies, notably the Philistines. David had departed because of Absalom's rebellion, but now Absalom was dead. "Why do you say nothing about bringing the king back?" suggests a popular outcry for the elders to unite in seeking David's return to the throne.

David Reaffirmed by Judah, 19:11-40

The narrative beginning with v. 11 presumes that representatives from the northern tribes had made their wishes known to David, but similar backing from the southern tribes was not forthcoming. Thus, David turned again to his agents Zadok and Abiathar, urging them to use their priestly influence to shame the Judahites for their recalcitrance. As David's closest kin (v. 12), should they not be the first to call for his return, rather than lagging behind Israel? [My Bone and My Flesh]

David negotiated by offering the elders of Judah additional influence within his court in return for their enthusiastic welcome. Specifically, David brought to the table one of the most powerful positions in his cabinet: control of the national militia. Amasa, who had led Absalom's volunteer army against David, was apparently a man of great power and influence in Judah. David recognized him as a key player in the negotiations. At the considerable cost of swallowing personal pride and demoting the stalwart Joab, David offered the position to Amasa in return for his support (v. 13).

David's judgment was not misplaced: "Amasa swayed the hearts of all the people of Judah as one, and they sent word to the king, 'Return, both you and all your servants' " (v. 14). Armed with this official invitation, David and his supporters marched southwest from Mahanaim on a direct course for Jerusalem, pausing at the fords of the Jordan near Gilgal to await a formal escort. Gilgal, an ancient sanctuary site, was apparently used as a staging area for the homecoming (v. 15). [Gilgal] A renewed anointing and coronation celebration is not mentioned in the text, though it is implied, and probably occurred here.

David's return is marked by three meeting scenes, the first of which involves the last person to meet him on his departure from Jerusalem: Shimei of Bahurim. Shimei's Benjaminite heritage is mentioned (v. 16), as his kinship to Saul was noted earlier (16:5). On that previous occasion, Shimei had come out to vent his wrath on the deposed David, showering the royal entourage with strong curses and solid stones. Now, seeing that David's return is inevitable, Shimei has come to seek the king's pardon.

Shimei does not come alone, however. He also relies on the bargaining power of public influence, bringing with him a thousand people from Benjamin. Among those Benjaminites was Ziba, former steward of Saul and of Mephibosheth, who had also conversed with David during his flight from Jerusalem. The text notes that Ziba, along with fifteen sons and twenty servants, took the initiative of offering themselves in David's service. They ferried David's people and baggage across the shallow portage (vv. 17-18), but no conversation is recorded between Ziba and the returning king.

Shimei, on the other hand, becomes quite verbose when he reaches David on the far side of the Jordan (v. 18). He makes no excuses for his earlier behavior, but speaks with great deference and apparent contrition: "For your servant knows that I have sinned" (v. 19). His plea for forgiveness seems grounded completely in the show of support he has brought as "the first of all the house of Joseph to come down to meet my lord the king" (v. 20). Technically, the "house of Joseph" was limited to the tribes of Ephraim and Manasseh, but those tribes (Ephraim especially) were so large that the prophets often used "Ephraim" as a moniker for all Israel. Evidently, Shimei is also claiming the wider kinship.

Gilgal

Gilgal was a minor city whose exact whereabouts are now uncertain. It was, however, the home of an important shrine that played an important role in Israel's history, especially for the Benjaminites. Samuel included Gilgal on his yearly circuit of places visited (1 Sam 7:16), and several early traditions about Saul are centered at Gilgal. Saul was first affirmed as king at Gilgal (1 Sam 11:14-15), but it was also at Gilgal that Samuel pronounced Yahweh's withdrawal of support for Saul's reign. Perhaps David is intentionally drawing on these traditions when he returns to Israel at Gilgal. The text does not state, but implies that the crown was ceremonially returned to him at the ancient site.

Two Similar Conversations

Compare the two stories, as follows:

2 Samuel 16:9-10	*2 Samuel 19:21-22*
Then Abishai son of Zeruiah said to the king,	Abishai son of Zeruiah answered,
"Why should this dead dog curse my lord the king? Let me go over and take off his head."	"Shall not Shimei be put to death for this, because he cursed the LORD's anointed?"
But the king said, "What have I to do with you, you sons of Zeruiah?"	But David said, "What have I to do with you, you sons of Zeruiah, that you should today become an adversary to me?"
"If he is cursing because the LORD has said to him, 'Curse David,' who then shall say, 'Why have you done so?' "	"Shall anyone be put to death in Israel this day? For do I not know that I am this day king over Israel?"

As in the prior meeting, David's militant nephew Abishai sought permission to slay Shimei for having cursed the king, and David's similar response to Abishai suggests a stylistic repetition on the part of the narrator (see comments at 16:9-12). [Two Similar Conversations] When David asks why Abishai should become an "adversary" to (or for) him, the word is *śāṭān*, which can also mean "accuser." David seems to be suggesting that he does not need Abishai to act as his district attorney, implying that the bringing of charges is inappropriate on such a day of celebration, the day of the king's enthronement (v. 22). Some writers speculate that there was a general amnesty on a king's inauguration day.

The end result is that David offers a pardon, swearing an oath that "You shall not die" (v. 23). In 1 Kings 2:8, as David gives his parting advice to Solomon, he remembers his oath to Shimei differently, as "*I* will not put you to death with the sword." He feels no compunction, however, to place such an obligation on his son, trusting Solomon to "bring his gray head down with blood to Sheol" (1 Kgs 2:9). Solomon contrived a different pretext to order Shimei's execution so that David's oath would not be violated (1 Kgs 2:36-46).

The second meeting scene involves Mephibosheth, the son of Jonathan and grandson of Saul. On his departure from Jerusalem, David was told by Ziba that Mephibosheth had remained in the city with high hopes that the kingdom would be restored to the house of Saul. Spontaneously, David had granted to Ziba all of Mephibosheth's property (16:3-4). Now, however, Mephibosheth responds to David's test of loyalty (v. 25) by claiming that Ziba had slandered him grievously, having taken advantage of his physical disability by refusing to saddle a donkey so that Mephibosheth could follow David from Jerusalem (vv. 26-27). Mephibosheth's claim is bolstered by his appearance: he had not "taken care of his feet" (cut his toenails?), trimmed his beard (lit., "moustache"), or washed his clothes from the day of David's departure (v. 24).

By these longterm acts of public contrition—which could hardly be faked—Mephibosheth presents the evidence that he had been wronged. To one who might accuse him of only recently returning his allegiance to David, he could point to his long toenails, to the moustache growing over his lips, to the obvious and odorous soiling of his clothes. Mephibosheth's appeal bordered on groveling as he lauded David as an "angel of God" for saving him alive when all of Saul's family was certainly worthy of death (v. 28: lit., they were "men of death," though see discussion at 12:5). David appeared to have tired of Mephibosheth's bootlicking and the aggravation of trying to discover the real truth. More important matters demanded his attention. "Why speak any more of your affairs?" is a not-too-polite instruction for Mephibosheth to be silent. Uncertain about whom to believe and not wanting to trouble himself with such a matter on the day of his return to the throne, David pronounced that Mephibosheth and Ziba would share the estate that he had first appropriated from Saul, then awarded to Mephibosheth (9:7), and later given to Ziba alone (16:4). Mephibosheth's final show of fealty ("Let him take it all, since my lord the king has arrived home safely," v. 30) seems to have been ignored as David moved on to other business.

The final meeting scene involves Barzillai, an aged and wealthy patron from Gilead who had assisted David and his entourage during their stay in Mahanaim (vv. 31-32). David's offer to honor Barzillai by having him accompany the procession to Jerusalem and live as a royal guest was not entirely unselfish. If Barzillai was as wealthy and influential as the text suggests, his presence would have served David's cause as a continuing endorsement of David's reign (v. 33). Barzillai declined David's proposal, deferring to his great age (vv. 34-35). [Signs of Aging] He did, however,

Signs of Aging

Barzillai was reportedly eighty years old, considered more than a ripe old age in biblical times. Ps 90:10 observes that:

The days of our life are seventy years,
or perhaps eighty, if we are strong;
even then their span is only toil and trouble;
they are soon gone, and we fly away.

Barzillai mentioned several signs of his advancing age that would make the sumptuous life of David's court meaningless to him. "Can I discern what is pleasant and what is not?" is, literally, "Can I tell good from evil?", but the referent is clearly sensory versus moral. Perhaps Barzillai is suggesting that he could no longer experience sexual or physical pleasure. His sensory losses also included an inability to taste food and drink, along with hardness of hearing. A similar, though highly metaphorical, list of the vagaries of old age is found in Eccl 12:1-8.

offer to travel with David far enough to demonstrate his support and to send a man named Chimham—presumably his son—to march into Jerusalem with David and to remain in the royal court as an emblem of Barzillai's political support (vv. 36-38). [An Unusual Name]

Having set the stage for David's return to power through these three meeting scenes, the narrator swiftly describes David's crossing of the river, accompanied by "all the people" who had come with him from Mahanaim, as well as any others who had come across the Jordan to welcome him. As promised, Barzillai joined David in the river crossing, but soon departed for his own home, accepting David's final blessing and leaving behind his son Chimham (v. 38). "The king went on to Gilgal" implies that the procession stopped in the ancient city, where it is likely that David was anointed once again and officially reestablished as king over Israel.

An Unusual Name

AΩ Chimham is not mentioned elsewhere, even in 1 Kgs 2:26, when David commends the faithful "sons of Barzillai" to Solomon, asking that they be retained at the king's table. The most reasonable interpretation, however, is that Chimham was Barzillai's son, perhaps the oldest. The name "Chimham" is unusual. Some relate it to the Arabic *kamiha*, meaning "to change complexion" or "to become pale." Thus, Kyle McCarter nicknames him "Paleface."

P. Kyle McCarter, *II Samuel* (AB 9; Garden City: Doubleday, 1984), 422.

The census of those who accompanied David creates a bit of a conundrum. "All the people of Judah" is certainly a hyperbole, though not at all unusual. It may refer primarily to the armies of Judah who had come to welcome the king home. Since David had returned at the behest of the elders of Judah (albeit a contrived invitation), the appearance of "all the people of Judah" is not unexpected. What is surprising is the claim that "half the people of Israel" were also present. Shimei and his thousand Benjaminites are the only people from Israel to be named in the immediate context, although the tribes of Israel had been the first to call for David's return (vv. 9-10).

Perhaps the reader is to assume that Israel had sent representatives who are not otherwise mentioned. Gilgal was in the territory claimed by Israel (specifically, in Benjamin), so David's arrival would not have been unknown in Israel. The fraction "one half" is probably not to be taken literally; it may indicate nothing more than that "some," but not all, of the people from Israel followed David. The point of v. 40 becomes clear in the closing verses of the chapter: the representation of Judah and Israel is disproportionate with regard to their relative size and to their previous level of support for David. Naturally, this inequity leads to conflict.

Israel Claims David, Too, 19:41-43

The narrative leads the reader to assume that the confrontation in vv. 41-43 took place in Gilgal, before David's return to Jerusalem (see also 20:2). Although only "half" the people of Israel accompanied David to Gilgal, "all the people of Israel" (lit., "every man of Israel") then came to complain that the Judahites had overstepped their bounds and assumed too much responsibility for David's return (v. 41). They regard it as an affront that David has allowed the men of Judah to meet and escort him on his return to the throne. Their natural—and probably correct—assumption is that David would give greater rewards and positions of prestige to those who led in his return, as he had already done for Amasa.

Curiously, the narrator's picture of David in this scene is reminiscent of a rag doll being pulled back and forth between two bickering children. David does not speak or defend himself. When the men of Israel charge David with showing favoritism to Judah, it is the *men of Judah* who respond. They claim that it is only right for them to escort the king since they are closer kinsmen to David, a Judahite by birth. The men of Judah insist that they have taken no special favors from the king: they have neither lived on his patronage or accepted any special favors from him (v. 42).

The placating words of the Judahites have little effect, however. The Israelite representatives insist that, though Judah may be closer kin, they have *more* kin: "We have *ten shares* in the king, and in David also we have more than you" (v. 43a). Ten shares is a clear reference to the ten tribes who later made up the northern kingdom, as opposed to the two tribes (Judah and Simeon) of the south. "In David also we have more than you" seems to imply closer kinship, but that point can hardly be argued. The phrase is probably intended as a contention that they had shown stronger support for David. Judah had been the first to accept Absalom and the last to reaffirm David. Why should they presume pride of place in escorting David home?

The men of Judah responded, but the content of their answer is lost in the strident volume of their rebuttal. The narrator notes only that "the words of the people of Judah were fiercer than the words of the people of Israel" (v. 43b). Thus, Israel's charges were laced with anger (v. 42), and Judah's response took the form of ferocity (v. 43). By this not-too-subtle use of language, the narrator identifies the genesis of a conflict that will not be resolved easily, even with David's skill. David managed to preserve a tenuous unity during the remainder of his reign, as did Solomon, but when the

...ess politically astute Rehoboam came to the throne, the northern
...nd southern tribes went their separate ways.

CONNECTIONS

1. *The longing for leadership.* Israel's quick call for David's return
speaks to the human need for leadership. The same people who
had deserted David in favor of Absalom now clamor for his return,
suggesting that they are less concerned with *who* leads them than
with *how* they lead. David seems to have distanced himself from
the populace prior to Absalom's rebellion: his son succeeded in
winning popular support because he went out among the people
and acted like a leader, while David apparently kept mainly to the
palace. When stories of the failed rebellion were told, it became evident that David was reasserting his command, so the people did
not hesitate to call for his reinstatement as king.

Why do we hunger for leadership? Often it is because strong
leaders promise to bring order from the chaos of our lives. Even
leaders who have a malign agenda can often find a following
because they offer a vision that makes sense to people and brings
some sense of meaning or direction to their lives. The persistence of
tyrannical regimes in many parts of the world suggests that many
people would prefer to have a bad leader than no leader at all. The
apparent ease with which various cult leaders recruit followers
points to the inner need that many people have
to be included in something greater than themselves even when it makes no rational sense. The
intense popularity of leadership seminars in the
business world demonstrates the centrality of
good leadership as an ingredient for corporate
success. [Followership?]

While ancient Israel found their ideal leader
in David, Christian believers find their ultimate
leader in Jesus Christ, who offers a sense of personal healing and a purposeful life that extends
both into and beyond this world. The universal hunger for such
leadership should prompt believers to gladly share the good news
that there is an eternal king who is not only strong and purposeful,
but also loving and good. The reality of this yearning for direction
should also warn us, however, of the need to choose good leaders
who have good motives, rather than allowing primary leadership to

Followership?

Corporate culture tends to stress
success through good leadership, often
to the neglect of *followership*. Within the church,
we must not forget that Christian leadership
begins with *following* Christ. In this sense, the
best leaders are also the best followers—and the
most faithful in serving others. When Jesus'
closest followers argued over who would be
leader among them, he said, "Whoever wants to
be first must be last of all and servant of all"
(Mark 9:35, see also Matt 20:27).

fall into the hands of those who have the loudest voices or the biggest axes to grind.

2. *Practical, personal politics.* The return of David is marked by the impressive exercise of his adroit relational skills—and by a clear pointer to the danger of relying too heavily on political manipulations for building a base of power. These things are revealed through a series of negotiations and personal encounters.

Assured of the northern tribes' support, David sought to strengthen his backing among the people of Judah by playing one constituency against the other. By challenging the Judahites to take the initiative in bringing back the king, David forced their hand by offering them greater influence in his cabinet than the tribes' relative size would imply. The northern tribes were much more numerous than their southern neighbors. Not only were there ten tribes to two (only Judah and Simon in the south), but several of the northern tribes (notably Ephraim and Manasseh) had significantly larger populations than most other tribal units.

David came from the south, however, and most of his political insiders had been southern allies, including several family members or loyal foreigners who had attached themselves to his court. David's offer to make Amasa (who had served as Absalom's general) the commander of the popular militia would have stung his old ally Joab, but it also won him significant support in Judah, where Amasa had great influence.

David's encounter with Shimei is an example of both personal discipline and political agility. Shimei had cursed David on his departure from Jerusalem, but now he comes to beg David's forgiveness. The reader might like to think that David freely offered a pardon from the goodness of his heart, but the fact that Shimei was accompanied by 1,000 Benjaminites cannot be overlooked. Even if David did not fear the possibility of battle with Shimei's allies, he could not risk alienating such a significant segment of his support. So his public oath not to harm Shimei came under some obvious duress. It was, however, an astute move. David was able to put aside his personal affront for the sake of a larger goal.

David's meeting with Mephibosheth tested his patience as well as his wisdom. As Solomon would later be challenged to choose between two women with competing stories (and no DNA testing to discern the truth), David was faced with two men who told opposing tales: Ziba had insisted that Mephibosheth remained in Jerusalem when David fled because he had hoped that Absalom would return the throne to the house of Saul. [Two Hard Cases]

Two Hard Cases

The similarities in these two cases are notable, though they are rarely mentioned. The memorable plot twist from Solomon's judgment is lacking in David's encounter with Ziba and Mephibosheth, but several other elements are present.

David and the Two Saulides (2 Samuel 16:1-4; 19:24-30)	Solomon and the Two Women (1 Kings 3:16-28)
Two men make competing claims about Mephibosheth's loyalty to David, with his inherited estate in the balance.	Two women make competing claims about the identity of their babies, one of whom is dead, with the life of the survivor in the balance.
David decides to split the estate, awarding half to Mephibosheth (Saul's grandson) and half to Ziba, the steward.	Solomon decrees that the living child should be cut in half with a sword and divided between the women.
Mephibosheth declares that he would be just as pleased if Ziba took all the land, as he cared only for David's survival and safe return.	The true mother declared that she would prefer the lying woman to have the child, so long as it survived and remained safe.
David's response to Mephibosheth, if any, is not recorded	Solomon pronounced his judgment that the woman who was willing to surrender the child must be the true mother, and awarded custody to her.

Mephibosheth, on the other hand, now came to claim that he stayed in Jerusalem only because he was crippled and the treacherous Ziba had refused to saddle his mount. Mephibosheth had carefully neglected his personal hygiene as evidence of his betrayal. David had granted to Ziba all of Mephibosheth's estate in their earlier exchange, but now he was uncertain what to do. Unable to decide between them and unwilling to devote more time to a peripheral matter, David pronounced that Ziba and Mephibosheth should split the land.

Barzillai had supported David during his flight from Absalom, proving himself faithful under adverse circumstances. David invited Barzillai to accompany him to Jerusalem and live there at his expense as a reward for his generosity. The reader suspects an underlying motive as well: Barzillai was an influential man in the Transjordan, and his presence with David would carry considerable weight as a sign of support from that region. Barzillai declined David's invitation, but sent his son as his representative, an arrangement that benefitted both David and Barzillai.

David's impressive series of public relations victories ran aground, however, on the shoals of intertribal jealousy. His desire to build support in the south by offering political plums and by choosing the people of Judah to "bring back the king" led to intense resentment from the north, as evidenced in vv. 41-43. David's strategy to curry southern favor succeeded, but only at the cost of losing similar support among the northern tribes.

Through this series of encounters, the narrator portrays David as a man who succeeds because of his savvy machinations and his willingness to manipulate other people for his own benefit. God is notably absent from this text that describes David's return to the throne, in sharp contrast to the obvious work of God in initially bringing David to his position as king of all Israel. [Different Paths] The resulting image portrays a man who has exchanged his life-changing trust in God for a mixed bag of manipulative relationship skills that roughly amount to a mess of political pottage.

Different Paths

David's initial path to the throne was marked by several instances of divine intervention and David's careful dependence upon Yahweh's favor. These are seen, for example, in Yahweh's decision to anoint David (1 Sam 16:1-13), in the statement that Yahweh was with David (1 Sam 18:28), in Yahweh's initiative in sending a message through the prophet Gad (1 Sam 22:5), in God's apparent engineering of a Philistine attack that fortuitously diverted Saul from catching David in the open (1 Sam 23:27-28), and in Yahweh's declaration of covenant loyalty toward David (2 Sam 7).

David's dependence on Yahweh is shown in his affirmation of trust before the battle with Goliath (1 Sam 17:37) and in his desire to seek God's direction before taking action in a number of instances (before rescuing Keilah, 1 Sam 23:2; fleeing Keilah, 1 Sam 23:9-12; pursuing the Amalekites who had destroyed Ziklag, 1 Sam 30:7-8; going up to Hebron in view of becoming king, 2 Sam 2:1; attacking the Philistines, 5:19). David's desire to honor Yahweh is also seen in his desire to bring the ark to Jerusalem (2 Sam 6) and to build a shrine to house it (2 Sam 7:1-2).

In contrast, David's return to the throne after Absalom' rebellion is largely devoid of any reference to God. There i the editorial note in 2 Sam 17:14 that the LORD had ordained to defeat the good counsel of Ahithophel, but even that event is also described as a part of David's own strategy. According to the narrator, David never consults Yahweh for guidance on his return path to the throne. When he consults with the priests Abiathar and Zadok, it not to seek an oracle from God, but to instruct them in some manner of clandestine subterfuge or political persuasion.

All of this relates to the narrator's desire to show how David has changed; he is no longer the humble shepherd-king who seeks to serve God and his people; he is now a shrewd manipulator who will do what it takes to remain o top.

As modern readers, we would do well to look at these two pictures of David and consider which one is more characteristic of our own lives: Do we depend on God and seek divine guidance for our living, or do we prefer to take (and keep) matters in our own hands?

NOTE

[1] P. Kyle McCarter, *II Samuel* (Garden City: Doubleday, 1984), 412, 419-20.

DAVID DEALS WITH
INTERNAL DISSENT

20:1-26

COMMENTARY

Sheba's Revolt, 20:1-3

The beginning of chapter 20 is grammatically and contextually linked to the closing verse of chapter 19, which describes the fierce argument between Israel and Judah over who should have priority in returning David to the throne. Neither side wished to back down. With tensions high and no diplomatic intervention from David, an eruption of factionalism was inevitable. A Benjaminite named Sheba, identified as the son of Bichri, provided the spark that led to a very loud, if ineffectual, explosion of discontent among the northern tribes.

Sheba is otherwise unknown, though the rabbis identified him as none other than Nebat, the father of Jeroboam, who would later lead a lasting separatist movement between Judah and Israel (the same source, *Sanhedrin* 101a, also claims other aliases for Sheba). Some scholars suggest that Sheba was related to Saul, assuming that the name "Bichri" may be related to "Becorath," the name of Saul's great-great-grandfather (1 Sam 9:1). This connection remains speculative, but the text is clear in identifying Sheba as a member of Saul's tribal unit, the Benjaminites.

The narrator describes Sheba as a "scoundrel"—literally, as a "son of Belial" or "son of worthlessness" (see discussion of this term as a pejorative appellative at 2 Sam 16:7). The narrator's note that Sheba just "happened to be there" underscores Sheba's relative unimportance in Israel, suggesting that he represented no one but himself. Scoundrel or not, however, Sheba turned the tide of emotion against David with a rousing blast on the shofar and the instigation of a chant: "We have no portion in David, no share in the son of Jesse! Everyone to your tents, O Israel!" This same refrain would be

Similar Slogans

The similarity of the two rallying cries is illustrated below:

2 Samuel 20:2	*1 Kings 16:7*
Now a scoundrel named Sheba son of Bichri, a Benjaminite, happened to be there. He sounded the trumpet and cried out,	When all Israel saw that the king would not listen to them, the people answered the king,
"We have no portion in David, no share in the son of Jesse! Everyone to your tents, O Israel!"	"What share do we have in David? We have no inheritance in the son of Jesse. To your tents, O Israel! Look now to your own house, O David."

repeated when Israel joined Jeroboam in revolting against Solomon's son Rehoboam (1 Kgs 12:16). [Similar Slogans]

The text (v. 2) implies that the Israelite militia followed Sheba in the beginning of a second revolt. The army does not seem to have gathered *to* Sheba, however, so much as it withdrew *from* David. "To your tents" implies a demobilization of the army (see discussion at 19:8b) rather than a mustering for active rebellion. Sheba seems to have gained more sympathy than support, but David regarded the movement as a threat that could do more potential damage than Absalom's revolt.

As Sheba and his sympathizers withdrew from David, his southern supporters showed intensified allegiance as "the people of Judah followed their king steadfastly from the Jordan to Jerusalem." The narrator uses the expression "their king" in regard to the Judahites, but not the northern tribes. "Followed . . . steadfastly" translates a single verb that means "to cling."

A brief interlude in v. 3 completes the unfinished business of the concubines whom David had left in the city and who had been publicly assaulted by Absalom (16:20-23). It is not a pretty picture even for those unaffected by contemporary egalitarianism. Because the concubines had been physically compromised by Absalom, David alienated himself from them. In doing so, he also separated them from everyone else, putting them under lock and key for the remainder of their lives. Thus, Absalom's crime and David's pride conspired to rob the innocent women of their future. David provided for the women's material needs but forced them to spend the rest of their days "living as if in widowhood," literally, "widows alive." The expression may refer to their living as widows despite having a living husband (David), though the interpretation found in the NRSV is more common.

Joab and Amasa, 20:4-13

The interruption of v. 3 serves the added function of suggesting that some time had passed between David's arrival in Jerusalem and his disposition of the Sheba affair. David seems uncertain of Sheba's strength, but clearly perceives the divisive potential of the northern unrest. He must act quickly to reaffirm his reign over all of the tribes.

Although Sheba seems to have very little military support, David takes no chances. He will not rely on his mercenary army alone, but dispatches Amasa to muster the militia in Judah and report back within three days. For a time in which travel was by foot or beast of burden, three days was a remarkably brief period to allow for a national call-to-arms, even in a small country. Amasa failed to meet the deadline (vv. 4-5), and there are some who suppose that David intentionally set up his new general for failure, providing a convenient excuse to replace him without alienating his supporters in Judah.

When Amasa failed to appear on schedule, David ordered Abishai to lead the mercenary army ("your lord's servants") in pursuit of Sheba, hoping to capture the rebel leader before he could gather supporters and establish himself within a walled city (v. 6). The NRSV's "escape from us" means, literally, "to put a shadow over our eyes," that is, "to hide from us."

The remarkable thing about the quelling of Sheba's revolt is that the only blow struck by David's army was against itself, as Joab solved the problem of his demotion by murdering yet another rival (cf. 2 Sam 3:26-27; 18:14-15). How Joab came to be included in the army at all is problematic: v. 7 is textually difficult and the major witnesses disagree. The inclusion of "Joab's men," however, implies the presence of Joab as well. He had captained the mercenaries before and would not be left behind now, even if his brother Abishai was officially in charge.

Precisely what happened when Amasa finally arrived (v. 8) is a matter of debate, except for the obvious fact that it ended with Amasa writhing in a pool of blood and excrement as Joab stood over him with a dripping sword. The eventful meeting took place at "the large stone that is in Gibeon." [Landmarks] The problematic text takes pains to describe Joab's clothing, implying that it will play an important role in the narrative. "A soldier's garment" (NRSV) translates "girded in his tunic, his clothing," which is

Landmarks

AΩ The "large stone that is in Gibeon" may be identical with the "principal (lit., "great") high place" in Gibeon mentioned in 1 Kgs 3:4 or possibly with the large rolling stone used by Saul as an altar (1 Sam 14:33). This, like other landmarks, was apparently so well known to the author that he did not bother to explain further.

awkwardly redundant. A sword belt was fastened over the tunic, according to custom.

The text is clear in suggesting that the sword fell from its sheath as Joab went forward to greet Amasa with a deceptive kiss, but there is no explanation for how it came to be in Joab's hand, allowing him to disembowel Amasa without having aroused his suspicions. Some interpreters assume the sword fell to the ground, giving Joab a convenient excuse to pick it up and have it in his hand, but surely this would have put Amasa on his guard. Others suppose that the sword fell from its sheath and into a fold of Joab's garment, where it was easily retrieved. This would have been difficult, however. Israel's battle swords were much shorter than the long swords characteristic of later ages but were still distinguished from daggers by their length. Some interpreters speculate that Joab had a dagger hidden in his tunic (the "two sword hypothesis"), but there is no textual evidence for that view. In the Syriac version, the sword did not fall from the sheath, but Joab's hand fell over the sword, concealing and retrieving it at the same time.

The point that seems universally overlooked in these discussions is that Joab did his sword work with his *left* hand, which is why it was unsuspected. He "took Amasa by the beard *with his right hand* to kiss him." Soldiers normally wore their swords on the left hip to allow for easier access by the right hand (cf. the story of left-handed Ehud, whose eighteen-inch sword was undiscovered because he wore it on the right side, Judg 3:12-23). [A Similar Story] Drawing one's sword with the left hand would be awkward, unless it just happened to be tipped up and falling out of its sheath as Joab drew close to Amasa, as the text implies. Amasa paid attention only to Joab's sword hand, which was grasping his beard. As Ehud's thrust to Eglon's stomach was described as being so deep that the excrement came out, Joab's slicing blow was so massive that Amasa's "entrails poured out on the ground."

The text is careful to note that Amasa died without Joab having to strike a second blow—but also that he did not die immediately. The impression is that the vengeful Joab left Amasa to suffer and die slowly and ignominiously beside the road, leaving a trusted aide to stand watch while he and Abishai took up the pursuit of Sheba (presumably with the mercenary army in tow).

Amasa's assignment had been to bring the Judahite militia, but many of them balked at the macabre sight of their murdered leader. Joab's lieutenant challenged the volunteer soldiers to follow Joab as a sign of their loyalty to David (v. 11), but "all the people were stopping" when they came to the site of Amasa's final struggle

imilar Story

The account of Ehud's secretive strike against King Eglon bears several similarities to the present account, not in the setting so much as in the account of the blow and its aftermath. Others seem to have overlooked the parallel ments of these stories, but they are worth noting:

t Elements	Judges 3:15-16, 20-26	2 Samuel 20:8-13
e setting	But when the Israelites cried out to the LORD, the LORD raised up for them a deliverer, Ehud son of Gera, the Benjaminite, a left-handed man. The Israelites sent tribute by him to King Eglon of Moab.	[8] When they were at the large stone that is in Gibeon, Amasa came to meet them.
othing and naments	[16] Ehud made for himself a sword with two edges, a cubit in length; and he fastened it on his right thigh under his clothes. . . .	Now Joab was wearing a soldier's garment and over it was a belt with a sword in its sheath fastened at his waist; as he went forward it fell out.
e deceptive eeting	[20] Ehud came to him, while he was sitting alone in his cool roof chamber, and said, "I have a message from God for you." So he rose from his seat.	[9] Joab said to Amasa, "Is it well with you, my brother?"
e left-handed rust to the belly xcrement/ entrails w	[21] Then Ehud reached with his left hand, took the sword from his right thigh, and thrust it into Eglon's belly; [22] the hilt also went in after the blade, and the fat closed over the blade, for he did not draw the sword out of his belly; and the dirt came out. [23] Then Ehud went out into the vestibule, and closed the doors of the roof chamber on him, and locked them.	And Joab took Amasa by the beard with his right hand to kiss him. [10] But Amasa did not notice the sword in Joab's hand; Joab struck him in the belly so that his entrails poured out on the ground, and he died. He did not strike a second blow. Then Joab and his brother Abishai pursued Sheba son of Bichri.
he murderer aves he aftermath: onfusion	[24] After he had gone, the servants came. When they saw that the doors of the roof chamber were locked, they thought, "He must be relieving himself in the cool chamber." [25] So they waited until they were embarrassed. When he still did not open the doors of the roof chamber, they took the key and opened them. There was their lord lying dead on the floor. [26] Ehud escaped while they delayed, and passed beyond the sculptured stones, and escaped to Seirah.	[11] And one of Joab's men took his stand by Amasa, and said, "Whoever favors Joab, and whoever is for David, let him follow Joab." [12] Amasa lay wallowing in his blood on the highway, and the man saw that all the people were stopping. Since he saw that all who came by him were stopping, he carried Amasa from the highway into a field, and threw a garment over him. [13] Once he was removed from the highway, all the people went on after Joab to pursue Sheba son of Bichri.

(v. 12). Finally, the aide removed Amasa from the highway, secluding his corpse in a field and covering it with a garment. Once Amasa's body was removed, the soldiers joined the chase (v. 13), suggesting that they had been motivated more by curiosity than loyalty in pausing to stand by the dying general.

Abel of Beth-maacah

This city (modern Tell Abil or *Abil el-Qam*), located some twelve miles north of Lake Huleh and only a few miles from Dan, was at the northernmost extremity of Israel. Its significance is not measured by the wise woman's claim alone, but also by the frequency with which it was targeted by ancient enemies. Citing Albright, Kyle McCarter has suggested that it may be the same as the city called *'u-bi-ra* that was conquered by Thutmosis III in the 15th century BC. This would give the city a long heritage that would accord with its reputation as "a mother in Israel." Abel was conquered by Ben-hadad I of Damascus early in the 9th century BC when Baasha was king of Israel (1 Kgs 15:20 = 2 Chr 16:4). It also appears in a list of cities taken by the Assyrian Tiglath-Pileser III (who called it *Abilakka*) in the 8th century BC (*ANET*, 253; compare 1 Kgs 15:29).

The connection of the city to Beth-maacah—the "House of Maacah"—is unique to 2 Sam 20:15. It might suggest some clan connection to the kingdom of Maacah, which was located just to the east of Abel, south of Mount Hermon and east of the Jordan's northern reaches. Maacah was the home of Absalom's mother and the site of Absalom's retreat after the murder of Amnon. If Abel had collaborative connections with Maacah (and thus with Absalom), it would have been a likely place to seek support for another rebellion as well.

P. Kyle McCarter, *II Samuel* (AB 9; Garden City: Doubleday, 1984), 430.

The reader may wonder why the story devotes so much detail to Joab's treacherous murder of Amasa when the revolt of Sheba seems to be more significant. The purpose seems to be apologetic. As with the earlier deaths of Saul, Abner, Ishbosheth, and Absalom, the narrator takes extra pains to insist that David had nothing to do with the killing, however circumstantially fortuitous it seemed in furthering his cause.

Sheba's End: The Wise Woman of Abel, 20:14-22

The account of Sheba's demise and the end of his rebellion is told in quick fashion as if to discount its seriousness. The story is designed, however, to heap shame upon Sheba's head through the emphasis given to the manner of his death. The narrator depicts Sheba as a man on the run, not as the leader of a significant rebellion. He "passed through all the tribes of Israel" but apparently found no tangible support to speak of until he attained the city called Abel of Beth-maacah, at the northernmost extremity of Israel. [Abel of Beth-maacah]

The reference to Abel as belonging to Beth-maacah suggests a connection with the kingdom of Maacah, the home of Absalom's mother. If the region had supported Absalom, it might potentially support another rebellion as well. Sheba was allowed to enter the city, along with his supporters, who seem limited to his fellow "Bichrites."

A Siege Ramp at Work
This low relief from an
Syrian king's palace reveals a
ge ramp raised against the
elite city of Lachish. Depth is
nveyed through the "piling" of
ects above the siege, indicating
t they are to the left of the
ect. These reliefs frequently
corated the exterior walls of the
ace to indicate the king's
wess and successes against
midable foes.

ght) Detail of the Assyrian conquest of
hish. Palace of Sennacherib at Niniveh,
sopotamia. British Museum, London.
edit: Erich Lessing/Art Resource, NY)

Siege ramp at Lachish. (Credit: Mitchell G. Reddish)

The narrator portrays Joab in typical fashion, throwing his army against the city with no attempt at negotiation, bent on victory through violence. Walled cities were difficult to overthrow. A common strategy involved building a huge siege ramp against the fortified wall; if the besieging army could survive long enough to build the ramp, they would have ready access to the city. [A Siege Ramp at Work] The note that Joab's forces were "battering the wall to break it down" may suggest a second line of attack (battering rams were also popular), or it may imply that the soldiers were dismantling the top sections of the wall.

Victory appeared imminent for Joab when a certain "wise woman" from Abel called for a parley. [The Wise Woman of Abel] The woman apparently acted as a spokesperson for the entire city. The

The Wise Woman of Abel

The "wise," along with priests and prophets, served as religious and political leaders in Israel. The adjective "wise" had various connotations and could be attributed to a skilled administrator, such as Joseph (Gen 41:8, 33, 39), to a royal advisor (Isa 19:11, 12; Esth 6:13), or to a craftsman skilled in handiwork (1 Kgs 7:14).

Both men and women are numbered among the wise. In 1 Sam 14, the wise woman of Tekoa shows rhetorical skill and psychological insight in her conversation with David; she is not merely parroting words placed in her mouth by Joab. The wise woman of Abel displays recognized authority as she negotiates with Joab and persuades her townspeople to accept her plan. Both women intervene in the political matters of the state, both command the respect of male leaders, and both are successful in turning male leaders to their position. Judith was another example of such persuasive influence (see especially Jdt 8:29).

Recent scholars argue that these "wise women" were not merely exceptional individuals, but were representative of a professional social institution, the "wise women," having authority and status similar to that of the "wise" or elders. These wise women, along with numerous prophetesses in Israel, show that women's authority m[ ] extend well beyond the household.

Women skilled in a craft might also be called "wise," such as the professional mourning women of Jer 9:17-[ ] and the weavers of cloth in Exod 35:25-26, just as male craftsmen were called "wise" or skilled (Exod 28:3 and among others).

Some helpful studies for further reading: Athalya Bre[ ] *The Israelite Woman: Social Role and Literary Type in Bi[ ] Narrative*, The Biblical Seminar (Sheffield: JSOT Press, 1985); Claudia Camp, "The Wise Women of 2 Samuel: [ ] Role Model for Women in Early Israel?" *CBQ* 43 (Januar[ ] 1981): 14-29; and Grace Emmerson, "Women in Ancien[ ] Israel," *The World of Ancient Israel: Sociological, Anthropological and Political Perspectives*, ed. R. E. Clements (Cambridge: Cambridge University Press, 198[ ] 371-94.

source of her authority remains a mystery, but the power of her influence is readily apparent. She chided Joab for threatening to bring total ruin upon a metropolis whose ancient reputation as a seat of wisdom and justice was well known, a city of such antiquity and distinction that it was known as "a mother in Israel" (vv. 18-19). "I am peaceable and faithful," she declares, apparently speaking for herself and for the city. Thus, she suggests that the spirit of Israel's founding fathers (and mothers) lives on in Abel, and questions how Joab can consider erasing such a venerable heritage from the land by "seeking to cause the death of the city, a mother in Israel, and by swallowing up the heritage of Yahweh" (a literal translation). The reader wonders, however, why a city of such wisdom and reasonableness did not press for negotiations earlier in the siege.

Joab's reply echoes much of the wise woman's own vocabulary as he denies any desire to "swallow up or destroy" (v. 20). The repetition of "far be it" (*ḥālîlâ*) in the MT may be due to dittography. [Distant or Damned?] Joab identifies his intended target as a solitary man, a daring rebel whose surrender would lead to an immediate withdrawal. The description of Sheba as a "man of the hill country of Ephraim" seems to contradict the malcontent's earlier designation as a Benjaminite. "Ephraim," however, was sometimes used as a generic name for the territory occupied by the northern tribes, including the Benjaminite highlands.

Acting either from inherent authority or from supreme confidence, the woman promised to deliver Sheba's head to Joab and then convinced the city's residents to comply with her "wise plan" (lit., "her wisdom"). Once Sheba's head was separated from his body and dispatched over the wall, Joab proved true to his word and withdrew. The narrator's comment that Joab blew the trumpet and "all went to their homes" (lit., "tents") serves as a neat inclusio bracketing the account of Sheba's revolt, for the dissident had marked the beginning of his insurrection by blowing a shofar and shouting, "Everyone to your tents, O Israel" (v. 1).

Joab's return to Jerusalem is related as a simple fact, with no comment regarding David's reaction to his murder of Amasa. The following roll call of David's cabinet includes Joab as commander of the popular militia, suggesting that the king took no punitive action against his stalwart defender and sometimes foe. The account of David's last words to Solomon, however, suggests that David did not forget. He instructed Solomon to bring a bloody end to Joab's life, citing the unwarranted murders of Abner and Amasa as just cause (1 Kgs 2:5-6).

Distant or Damned?

AΩ Virtually all modern translations render the phrase *ḥālîlâ lî* as "Far be it from me!" The exclamation is common in the Old Testament (see Gen 18:24; 44:7; 1 Sam 14:45; 20:2, 9; 22:15; Josh 24:16, and others). The Hebrew root actually has nothing to do with distance. *ḥālal* means "to profane" or "to curse." Like other curses, the expression is routinely used in conjunction with the word for "if." Thus, "Far be it from me" is a polite circumlocution for "May I be cursed if I do (such and such)!"

McCarter accords the phrase its more colorful heritage, translating it as "I'll be damned if I'm going to afflict anything or destroy anything!"

P. Kyle McCarter, *II Samuel* (AB 9; Garden City: Doubleday, 1984), 426, 429.

The Roll of the Faithful, 20:23-26

The roster of David's inner council recorded in vv. 23-26 serves to mark the end of the large narrative unit that began with chapter 13 and concerned itself mainly with the events leading up to Absalom's rebellion, the revolt itself, and the proceedings related to David's reestablishment of his authority. The cabinet is little

Why Two Lists?

One scholarly speculation regarding the two lists of officials follows the reasoning described in the commentary; it served as a literary marker denoting the end of a large narrative section (chs. 13–20). In its current position, it also functions to update David's cabinet, which is appropriate since he has been deposed and reinstated as king. It is the cabinet of his "second term" as it were. Some changes should be expected.

Another proposed reason for the dual lists relates to the subsequent material in ch. 21, which seems to have been misplaced from its more logical position earlier in David's rule.

One hypothesis suggests that the events in ch. 21 originally preceded 9:1-13 but were transposed to a later position for literary or tendentious purposes. In the process, the preceding roster of David's cabinet (8:16-18) was also transferred, then updated to suit the literary context of its secondary position. While it does seem likely that ch. 21 is out of place, the argument that it dragged the list of David's officers along with it has little to support it. If 8:16-18 had been moved as a unit with the material in ch. 21, it should have disappeared from the earlier context, as did the account of David and the surrender of Saul's seven sons.

changed from the earlier list found in 8:15-18 (see comments there and in [Another List]). [Why Two Lists?] There are some minor changes: Sheva is listed as secretary rather than Seraiah, but these may be two names for the same individual. More notably, Ira the Jairite is named as "David's priest," and David's sons are no longer assigned the role of "priest." David's difficulty with his sons Amnon and Absalom may explain the change, though the responsibilities of this position remain mysterious.

The most significant change is the addition of Adoram as head of the conscripted labor force. He is probably the same person as the Adoniram who appears as the official in charge of forced labor under Solomon (1 Kgs 4:6) and Rehoboam (1 Kgs 12:18). "Adoniram" means "the LORD is exalted." It may be a variant of Adoram or possibly an intentional change to avoid the theophoric element *ʿad/had,* common among the Syrians, changing it to the more acceptable *ʾadonî.* The forced levy seems originally to have been composed of non-Israelites (1 Kgs 9:21 = 2 Chr 8:8); Adoram himself may have been a foreigner.

CONNECTIONS

Sheba's Revolt

Sheba was one man with little real support, which came mostly from his family. He represented no constituency other than his own small band of disgruntled partisans, yet he was able to create a crisis of leadership for David and of unity in Israel. It seems that very few Israelites spoke out or acted openly to support Sheba, but their withdrawal of support for David was damaging nevertheless.

Modern organizations sometimes experience similar crises of leadership and unity. A single person or family may find fault with the leadership and create enough unpleasantness to foster considerable disunity in the church. Open support for the dissident is often minimal, but other disgruntled members may also reduce or retract their personal participation or financial support. David's military solution is certainly inappropriate in the context of contemporary organizations, but it does point to the importance of confronting troublesome issues rather than ignoring dissent, and of dealing directly with those who oppose, rather than leaving the membership to try and resolve problems through passive-aggressive power games.

Using and Abusing the Innocent

The brief reference to David's confinement of the concubines abused by Absalom is a sad commentary on the inevitable result of treating people as objects. The women who composed David's harem probably had little or no choice in the matter. They were used by the king as a symbol of his power, a sign of his sexual prowess, and a salve for his ego. It is for this reason that Absalom took the concubines for himself, using and abusing them for his own political purposes. When David returned, he no longer had relations with the women since they had been "defiled" by Absalom. Neither, however, would he set them free to marry anyone else or have lives of their own. The innocent victims of Israel's kings spent the remainder of their lives locked away in the palace, robbed of their future.

The practice of keeping concubines is no longer an institution, at least among Western cultures. This does not mean, however, that people—especially women—are no longer used for purposes that have more to do with power and ego needs than with any intent of developing a meaningful or lasting relationship. When persons are molested as children, victimized as adolescents, or abused as adults, something of their future is taken away. When an irresponsible young man leaves behind a pregnant teenager to struggle alone with her dilemma or when an older man leaves behind his wife and children in search of a younger woman to fulfill his mid-life crisis, he is not so much different from David or Absalom, and the affected women are not unlike those who lost their reputations, their positions, and their futures to the pride and power of Israel's royalty.

Who Needs Enemies?

Joab was David's staunchest ally and also the biggest thorn in his side. Joab wanted to serve David, but only on his own terms. He could not see the broad picture that David envisioned, but maintained a narrow line of sight that was painted in black and white. David sought to solve problems through diplomacy, while Joab trusted in violence alone. More than once, David's careful negotiations fell victim to Joab's penchant for taking matters into his own hands. With both Abner and Amasa, Joab feigned friendliness while preparing to deliver a killing blow. In doing so, Joab's efforts to aid David actually undermined the king. In some cases, David's success was not because of Joab, but in spite of him.

Those who claim to serve Christ with the same allegiance that Joab professed for David might do well to ask themselves if their devotion is shaped by the teachings and the will of Jesus or by their own distorted view of reality. How else can we explain the "Christian" Knights of the Ku Klux Klan or the self-righteous Aryan movements that demean other races in the name of Christ? How else can we explain parents who beat their children and claim they are only being biblical? How else can we explain the vast numbers of people who call themselves Christians but live hypocritical lifestyles that reveal no apparent reference to the teachings of Christ?

Sometimes we are led to think that if the church succeeds, it will not be because of many who claim to support it, but in spite of them.

Using One's Head

The wise woman of Abel offers a textbook illustration of someone who solved a problem by using their head—albeit *someone else's head.* The woman confronted Joab with a challenge to be reasonable and to avoid widespread bloodshed through rational negotiation. Together, they concluded that the best course of wisdom was the sacrifice of one for the sake of the many. Thus, Joab and the wise woman put their heads together, and as a result Sheba lost his head in a terminal fashion. One cannot commend the same solution for other disputes, of course. Sheba's disposition could also have been resolved by delivering him alive.

The story suggests that much senseless violence could be avoided if only people were willing to communicate with one another, to use their heads in peaceable fashion to reach reasonable solutions when disputes arise. Conflict is inevitable; violence is not. Whether the issue involves husbands and wives or Israelis and Palestinians, peaceable negotiation is always preferable to physical aggression. "Blessed are the peacemakers," Jesus said, "for they will be called the children of God" (Matt 5:9).

DAVID DEALS WITH A FAMINE AND THE PHILISTINES

21:1-22

David Remembered, 21:1–24:5

Scholars generally regard 2 Kings 1–2 as a direct continuation of 2 Samuel 20, with 2 Samuel 21–24 being a later insertion into the narrative flow. These chapters contain an artistically arranged series of appendices that collect and present miscellaneous memories of David that are displaced from their historical context. [A Chiastic Collection] As such, they add little to the historical understanding of David's rule; their function is to add color and flesh to our understanding of David, his times, and his supporters. Each of the six units that make up this section stands alone, related to its neighbors only by the chiastic arrangement.

A Chiastic Collection

The elements found in these appendices are arranged in chiastic form, like a multi-layer sandwich in which each element has a correspondent. The following diagram reveals the chiastic pattern:

    A narrative about David, involving divine punishment (21:1-14)
      A list concerning David's men and their exploits (21:15-22)
        A song celebrating David's relationship with God (22:1-51)
        A song celebrating David's relationship with God (23:1-7)
      A list concerning David's men and their exploits (23:8-39)
    A narrative about David, involving divine punishment (24:1-24)

This artistic arrangement could have happened by chance, but most scholars who have observed it regard it as intentional.

COMMENTARY

The Slaughter of the Saulides, 21:1-14

The affair involving David, the Gibeonites, and the Saulide scions has been a subject of discussion at several points. It is often conjectured that the story belongs chronologically between chapters 8 and

9. Since the story casts David in something of a bad light and interrupts the smooth flow of David's rise to power, it seems to have
been excised from its original setting and repositioned as an
appendix. Thus, though this bloody story is related near the end of
David's reign, it most likely took place during the early years of his
kingship, shortly after the establishment of Jerusalem as David's
city and the center of Israel's government.

The traditional interpretation takes this narrative at face value as
a story designed to show how David perceptively determined the
cause of a famine that plagued Israel and how he made the daring
but necessary decision to sacrifice Saul's descendants in order to satisfy the bloodguilt that had led to divine displeasure, expressed as a
famine in Israel. Thus, though David is not as heroic as in other
stories, he is still portrayed as a good king who is faithful to God
and to his nation.

Walter Brueggemann has offered an alternate view, regarding the
narrative as a fabrication intended to undermine the positive view
of David and to portray him as a bloodthirsty and power-hungry
man who manufactured a religiously expedient excuse to rid himself of potential political rivals. Brueggemann has based his
argument on the lack of corroborating evidence that Saul had tried
to exterminate the Gibeonites and on the presumption that David's
oracular explanation for the famine was mere propaganda.[1]

One may counter this argument by observing that there are
many events that are only reported once and that there is no textual
evidence to suggest that Yahweh's revelation was less than genuine.
If the author had truly wanted to portray David as an unscrupulous
politician who would gladly sacrifice his rivals, he could have made
his point much more clearly.

There is no chronological referent for the story, except for three
possible lines of evidence. First, seven Saulide scions are known to
exist, which is no longer the case at the beginning of chapter 9.
Thus, it is likely that this event preceded the story of David's kindness to Mephibosheth in 9:1-13, which would have occurred early
in David's reign over the united kingdom. Second, David
responded to a time of crisis by seeking Yahweh's guidance, which
is quite characteristic of his early years, but not of the period following the Bathsheba incident (2 Sam 11). Third, Shimei's vitriolic
rage in 16:5-14 accuses David of wantonly shedding Saulide blood,
which has no known referent aside from the Gibeonite incident.

A famine is said to have plagued the land for three years. This is
the only reference to such a famine. Other early stories concerned
themselves primarily with David's military conflicts and political

machinations. As he had done on several previous occasions of uncertainty (1 Sam 23:2, 9-12; 30:7-8; 2 Sam 2:1; 5:19), David sought divine guidance. Literally, "David sought the face of Yahweh."

To "seek the face" of Yahweh was to request an audience or hearing for the purpose of obtaining divine counsel or aid (cf. Hos 5:15; 2 Chr 7:14). The phrase may suggest that David came before the ark of the covenant in hopes of gaining God's advice. David's earlier efforts to discern God's will generally came via a priestly oracle. Such oracles used the sacred lots (the *Urim* and the *Thummim*), which were capable of yes/no and either/or answers only. Obtaining the detailed information that Israel's misfortune was divine retribution for Saul's oath-breaking attack on the Gibeonites would have required an extensive and inventive pattern of questioning. [A Possible Scenario]

David was also the recipient of prophetic oracles (1 Sam 22:5; 2 Sam 12:1-15; 24:11-18), though not at his own initiative. Whether composed as the summary statement of a priestly oracle or as a divinely inspired prophetic oracle, the word of Yahweh declared the existence of bloodguilt upon Saul's house because of his treacherous act toward the Gibeonites, which is parenthetically explained in v. 2.

The Gibeonites dwelt in a tetrapolis that included the cities of Gibeon, Chepirah, Beeroth, and Kiriath-jearim (Josh 9:17). They were reportedly of Amorite extraction, an ethnic group who had avoided death or displacement during Israel's invasion of Canaan by cleverly pretending to be tired travelers from a distant land. They used this ruse to persuade Joshua and the elders of Israel to negotiate a sworn agreement that no harm should come to their people (Josh 9:1-15). When the Israelites learned of the Gibeonites' trickery—that they were not travelers from afar, but close neighbors—there was a popular outcry, and armed forces prepared to attack (Josh 9:16-18). The tribal leaders forestalled them, however, pointedly insisting

A Possible Scenario

Here is a suggestion for how David and his priest(s) could have arrived at the information utilizing nothing more than yes/no or either/or questions:

Question One (based on Israel's traditional theology): "Is the famine due to some sin on Israel's part?"

Answer One: "Yes."

Question Two (after the pattern demonstrated in 1 Sam 14:40): "Does the sin lie with the royal house or with the people?"

Answer Two: "With the royal house."

Question Three (based on the fact that there had been two royal houses): "Did the sin originate with Saul or with David?"

Answer Three: "With Saul."

Question Four (beginning a series of questions based on acts of Saul that might have offended God): "Was it the sacrifice at Gilgal that Samuel condemned?" (1 Sam 13:11-14).

Answer Four: "No."

Question Five: "Was it Saul's mistreatment of Jonathan that the people opposed?" (1 Sam 14).

Answer Five: "No."

Question Six: "Was it Saul's failure to enforce the ban against the Amalekites that Samuel also condemned?" (1 Sam 15).

Answer Six: "No."

Question Seven: "Was it Saul's mistreatment of David?" (1 Sam 18–27).

Answer Seven: "No."

Question Eight: "Was it Saul's visit to the illegal spirit medium of Endor?" (1 Sam 28)

Answer Eight: "No."

Question Nine or a subsequent query (among other possible offenses not otherwise mentioned in Scripture): "Was it Saul's slaughter of the Gibeonites, to whom Joshua had sworn safe haven?"

Answer Nine: "Yes."

May God Do Thus and More to Me!

Oaths in ancient Israel held to a specific literary form that routinely included a curse upon oneself if he or she should happen to violate the oath. The typical form is this: "Thus and more may God do to me/you, if I/you do/do not so and so."

The full form may occur, as in Eli's adjuration to Samuel: "May God do so to you and more also, if you hide anything from me of all that he told you!" (1 Sam 3:17). Likewise, when Israel's king swore to do away with Elijah in 2 Kgs 6:31, he used this typical form: "So may God do to me, and more, if the head of Elisha son of Shaphat stays on his shoulders today."

Thus, the anticipation of divine wrath toward oath breakers is an inherent form of the oath itself, and any oath made by Joshua and Israel's tribal elders would have shared this same basic format. David, then, would not be surprised to learn that Israel's plight was connected to the breaking of an oath; that is the way oaths work.

The specific punishment to be received is rarely stated in an oath: "May God do thus and so to me/you" was quite sufficient to motivate faithfulness in most instances.

---

that the sworn oath should be honored "so that wrath may not come upon us, because of the oath that we swore to them" (Josh 9:19-20).

As part of the treaty, the Gibeonites had agreed to serve the Israelites, so they were put to work as "hewers of wood and drawers of water for the congregation" (Josh 9:21), usually thought to mean that they provided the menial labor that supported Israel's cultic rituals associated with sacrifices and the upkeep of the temple. Some scholars have drawn on this bit of information as a possible referent for the event in question, assuming that Gibeonites would have been associated with the temple at Nob and thus included in Saul's wholesale slaughter of the city (1 Sam 22:6-22). The explanation in v. 2, however, insists that Saul had massacred the Gibeonites "in his zeal for the people of Israel and Judah." Whether this reflects an expansionist effort to bring the city of Gibeon under greater control or an act of racial genocide is left unsaid.

Whether Saul was aware of it or not, his attack on the Gibeonites violated the ancient oath. [May God Do Thus and More to Me!] Thus, it was not the shedding of blood (Saul shed the blood of many peoples), but the breaking of the oath that engendered "bloodguilt" upon Saul's house.

Once David had learned the catalyst of Yahweh's anger, he took the initiative in consulting with Gibeonite leaders concerning some appropriate act of propitiation (v. 3). [Placating the Storm God] Their response in v. 4 reveals the dilemma in which they have found themselves. As resident aliens, they had rights to financial redress when wronged by a citizen, but no authority to seek blood vengeance. "Silver and gold" was not an issue, and blood vengeance

...ating the Storm God

Documents from some of Israel's ancient neighbors reveal a common view that the violation of treaty oaths would occasion divine displeasure and necessitate ...ective action. The most famous example is found in the Hittite "Plague Prayers" of ...silis (or Muršiliš), a 14th century king of "Hatti land." After an unspecified plague ...afflicted the land for twenty years, Mursilis discovered a tablet describing an oath ...ather had made—and violated—before the Storm God. Here is an excerpt, from ...echt Goetze's translation in *ANET* (pp. 394-96):

... The second tablet concerned Kurustama. When the Hattian Storm-god had ...rought people of Kurustama to the country of Egypt and had made an agreement ...oncerning them with the Hattian Storm-god, the Hattians ignored their ...bligations; the Hattians promply broke the oath of the gods. My father sent foot ...oldiers and charioteers who attacked the country of Amka, Egyptian territory . . . ...vhen they brought back to the Hatti land the prisoners which they had taken a ...lague broke out among the prisoners and they began to die.

...Mursilis sought an oracle to determine if this was the root cause of the gods' ...er and the resultant plague, receiving an affirmative answer. Later, Mursilis ...fesses:

...]. Hattian Storm-god, my lord, [and] yet gods, my lords! It is only too true that ...man is sinful. My father sinned and transgressed against the word of the Hattian ...Storm-god, my lord. But I have not sinned in any respect. It is only too true, ...however, that the father's sin falls upon the son. So, my father's sin has fallen ...upon me.

...Mursilis went on to insist that he had given large (but unspecified) offerings as ...titution for the sins of his father, praying humbly that his life and the lives of his ...ople should be spared.

The god Baal, mounted on a horned altar, marches forward brandishing a mace. Leaves burst forth from his spear, symbolizing the effects of Baal's storm.

Baal with Thunderbolt. 1700–1300 BC. Bas-relief on limestone stele. From Ugarit Syria. Louvre, Paris. (Credit: Erich Lessing/Art Resource, NY)

was not an option; thus, the Gibeonites had no means of legal recourse for the wrong that had been done to them.

The Gibeonites' request for seven descendants of Saul may be symbolic of all who had died, rather than an indication that Saul had killed only seven Gibeonites. It may also suggest that they sought to kill all of Saul's descendants, even as they accused Saul of seeking to "consume us" and "destroy us" (v. 5).

The verb of execution in v. 6 is of uncertain interpretation and has given rise to much comment. It is the causative form of a verb (*yāqa'*) that has to do with dislocation or tearing apart. In the simple *qal* stem it is used to denote the dislocation of Jacob's thigh (Gen 32:26). An Arabic cognate means "to fall." There is no question that the causative stem, as used here, describes some solemn means of execution. The precise method of causing the deaths is uncertain.

Or Else!

The best interpretation of the mode of execution may be the concept of ritual dismemberment, which is also supported by other biblical terminology associated with treaty covenants. For example, the tradition of God's covenant with Abraham in Gen 15:10-18 involved the cutting of several animals into two parts, which were placed opposite each other. The treaty parties would pass between the dismembered animals as if to say "so may it happen to one who violates this covenant." This implication is spelled out in Jer 34:18-20, where Yahweh threatens to punish the covenant breakers in Israel as follows:

> And those who transgressed my covenant and did not keep the terms of the covenant that they made before me, I will make like the calf when they cut it in two and passed between its parts: the officials of Judah, the officials of Jerusalem, the eunuchs, the priests, and all the people of the land who passed between the parts of the calf shall be handed over to their enemies and to those who seek their lives. Their corpses shall become food for the birds of the air and the wild animals of the earth.

Note that this text also includes the ritual exposure of the dismembered bodies to the elements, which seems to have been an important aspect of the Gibeonites' action against Saul's descendants.

Some scholars rely on the Arabic cognate and the note in v. 9 that they "fell together" to suggest that they may have been cast down from the "Mountain of Yahweh" so that they died in the fall. The LXX translation suggests some sort of crucifixion in the sun, and the rabbis generally took it to mean "hang." The NRSV chooses the verb "impale" while Kyle McCarter opts for "crucify,"[2] and A.A. Anderson prefers the more generic word "execute."[3] Others rely on the basic meaning of the verb and the implications of treaty oaths to presume that the seven sons were ritually dismembered in accordance with the original covenant stipulations. [Or Else!] This seems to be the most likely fate of the unfortunate Saulides.

David offers to hand over the Saulide descendants, with the exception of Mephibosheth. Many scholars regard v. 7 as a harmonizing insertion, presuming that the narrative originally preceded chapter 9, in which David discovers Mephibosheth for the first time. By pointing out how David spared Mephibosheth, the editors also insist that David was *faithful* to his covenant with Jonathan, while also correcting the failure of Jonathan's father to honor Israel's covenant with the Gibeonites.

The "sons" of Saul that David surrendered actually included two sons and five grandsons. The sons belonged to Saul's concubine Rizpah, a wife of secondary status, the same woman who had been such a bone of contention between Saul's son Ishbaal and his general Abner (2 Sam 3:7-8). Presumably, Rizpah's son Mephibosheth s to be distinguished from the son of Jonathan who is ascribed the same name. Since it is likely that this is a pious revision of the original name (Meribaal or Mippibaal) in both cases, confusion could naturally occur (see comment on Ishbaal's name at 3:7).

The MT contains a rather obvious error with regard to the mother of the other five sons. She is called "Michal" in the MT, but 1 Samuel 18:19 makes it clear that it was Merab who married Adriel from Meholah. The text is clear in stating that Michal, who had been married to both David and Paltiel (1 Sam 18:18-29; 2 Sam 3:15), had no children at all (2 Sam 6:23). Scholars presume that "Michal" was a scribal mistake; it was corrected in most of the early versions.

Adriel's father is named "Barzillai the Meholathite." Those who presume this is that same well-known Barzillai of Rogelim, who had assisted David during Absalom's rebellion (17:27; 19:31-40), find the text problematic, and rightly so. Barzillai would hardly have been so kind to a man who had handed over five of his grandsons for execution. Both Rogelim and Abel-meholah were located in Gilead, but they were presumably different cities, and it is reasonable to assume that the stories involve two separate men named Barzillai.

The comment in v. 8 that the Saulides were killed on the mountain "before the LORD" (lit., "before the face of Yahweh") lends religious overtones to the killings but does not necessarily bring them into the category of a sacrifice, as some suggest. Rather, since Yahweh would have been invoked as a witness in the original covenant, the LORD's presence is also sought as witness to the punishment accorded to treaty violators.

The "first days of harvest, at the beginning of barley harvest" would have occurred in April, during the month called Ziv in the old Canaanite calendar. This seems a bit strange since the narrative began with a note that there was a famine. Time was measured by the seasons of planting and harvest, however, whether there was anything to be harvested or not.

Rizpah, the mother of Armoni and Mephibosheth, is presented as a woman of courage and honor. The king refused to protect her sons, handing them over for execution. She could not prevent that act, but she took it upon herself to singlehandedly protect the bodies of the dead from the predations of scavengers. As mentioned in [Or Else!] above, the exposure of dismembered bodies to the elements, the birds, and the wild animals was an integral aspect of the ritual punishment.

Rizpah's spreading of sackcloth on a rock implies that she camped out beside the bodies, exposing her own body to the elements in a feeble but loving effort to bestow some measure of honor and dignity upon the slain. This effort continued for some time: "from the beginning of harvest until rain fell on them from the heavens" (v. 10). This does not necessarily mean that Rizpah's vigil lasted from April until the return of regular rains in November (though the remains of the slain are referred to as "bones" when David's agents collected them). Perhaps the reference is to an unseasonable rain in late spring or summer, marking the end of the drought (though v. 14 implies that God did not heed "supplications for the land" until after the bones were buried).

When Rizpah's determined effort came to David's attention, he was inspired to give the bodies a decent burial (and to get Rizpah out of the spotlight), hoping to bring closure to the incident. In addition to the slain scions, David also had the remains of Saul and Jonathan exhumed from their resting place in Jabesh-gilead (see comments at 1 Sam 31:11-13) and installed in the family tomb of Saul's father, Kish. In doing so, David showed honor to the Saulide family even though he was also responsible for several of their deaths (which, the narrator would remind us, they actually brought upon themselves). As in the case of Abner (3:31-37) and Ishbaal (4:9-11), David found it expedient to show that he bore no personal animosity toward the dead, or personal responsibility for their deaths.

The text mentions only the bones of Saul and Jonathan in the burial account, but since the remains of the executed men were also gathered up, one presumes that they were also given an honorable interment in the family burial place. "Zela" (v. 14) is listed as a town in Benjamin in Joshua 18:28, but its location is unknown, as is its relation to Saul's family—Saul's hometown was Gibeah. Some scholars take the word to mean a "chamber" of the tomb, rather than as a place name.

The Exploits of David's Men, 21:15-22

This piece of flotsam amid the larger text has the outward form of a narrative, but it is really a list of several heroes who served under David, their stories briefly told in narrative format. These stories may derive from ancient archival material, and they concern four memorable champions whose deeds have earned them a place in Israel's collective memory. [The Giant Killers]

The Giant Killers

Here is a brief outline of the pericope:

1. Abishai killed Ishbi-benob, saving David's life (21:15-17)
2. Sibbecai the Hushathite slew Saph at Gob (21:18)
3. Elhanan, son of Jaare-oregim, defeated Goliath the Gittite (21:19)
4. Jonathan, son of Shimeah, killed the six-fingered giant (21:20-21)
5. Summary statement (21:22)

No historical context is given for the stories except that each takes place in battle with the Philistines, and the named opponent in each case is a "descendant of the giants." This may or may not indicate that the proper context is 5:17-25, where David's Philistine wars are recorded. The story of David becoming exhausted and in danger, leading his men to insist that he no longer accompany them to the front, is more reminiscent of his later years (cf. 18:3).

Of more interest is the description of each opponent as a "descendent of the giants" (*yělîdê hārāpâ*), presuming the traditional interpretation is correct. The verb *yālad* means "to bear" or "beget," and the noun form typically refers to children. *Hārāpâ*, though singular in form, appears to be related to the legendary inhabitants of Canaan called the Rephaim, a term that sometimes refers to giants, and sometimes to ghostly shades. [Rephaim]

Other scholars reject the traditional view, taking the root *yld* to mean "devotee," rather than descendant (cf. Gen 14:14), and reading "Harapha" as the name of a deity, "Rapha." This deity has parallels in Ugaritic, where he is called *rp'u*, "The Healthy One." This is an ironic title, since *rp'u* is generally considered to be a cthonic deity, a god of the shades who inhabit the underworld. By this interpretation, the four mighty adversaries conquered by the Hebrew heroes were not necessarily giants, but members of an elite military troop devoted to the god Rapha, thus "the votaries of Rapha."[4]

The first encounter describes a difficult battle with the Philistines in which David himself became extremely weary and was in danger of being overcome by a Philistine named Ishbi-benob. The name is unusual and may be corrupt, but that is a minor issue. The weight of the Philistine's spear (or possibly his helmet), was 300 shekels, or about seven and a half pounds—a heavy weight to manipulate in either case. The

Rephaim

The Bible actually speaks of the "Rephaim" in three different contexts. The shades who inhabit Sheol are called Rephaim (Ps 88:10; Prov 9:18). An ethnic group who lived in the Transjordan prior to the Israelite settlement are named Rephaim (Gen 14:5; Deut 2:10-11). And a race of giants who lived among the Philistines also are labeled as Rephaim (1 Chr 20:4, 6, 8; 2 Sam 21:16, 18, 20). In the present context, the meaning "giants" seems most appropriate since the warriors' huge weaponry is described. Curiously, however, the plural "*Rephaim*" is not used, but the singular form, prefaced by the definite article: "*Harapha*."

expression translated as "fitted out with new weapons" may indicate that he had just achieved warrior status.

Nothing is said of the battle in which Abishai came to David's aid and killed Ishbi-benob. Greater attention is paid to the issue of David's potential death. Israel had desired a king to fight its wars (1 Sam 9:16), and David had often done that, but his men insisted that he was more valuable to them alive, even if he was not in the forefront of battle (see comment at 18:3). The metaphor of the king as the "lamp of Israel" that should not go out is unique, though the reader is reminded of the perpetually burning lamp in the temple (Exod 27:20). The burning lamp as a metaphor for life is sometimes used in the wisdom literature, always in terms of a threat that the lamp of the wicked will go out (Job 21:17; Prov 20:20; 24:20). Perhaps David is to be thought of as a light to the people, as the representative of Yahweh, who is the source of Israel's life.

The city of "Gob," mentioned as the site of battles in vv. 18 and 19, is unknown. It was presumably somewhere near the frequently contested border between Israel and territory controlled by the Philistine hegemony. One "Sibbecai the Hushathite" defeated Saph in the first duel, and Elhanan, son of Jaareoregim, reportedly killed Goliath the Gittite in the second. Sibbecai may have been one of David's mighty men (Mebunnai the Hushathite in 1 Sam 23:7 is named Sibbecai the Hushathite in the parallel text of 1 Chr 11:29).

Readers tend to be far more concerned with the second encounter, involving the giant named Goliath. Elhanan's patronymics are difficult. The MT has "Jaare-oregim," which is an unusual construction. A man called "Elhanan, son of Dodo of Bethlehem" is named as one of David's mighty men in 23:24 and may be the same person. But who killed Goliath: David (1 Sam 17) or Elhanan (2 Sam 21:19)? The Chronicler claims that Elhanan, son of Jair, killed *Lahmi, the brother of Goliath* (1 Chr 20:5). This is widely regarded as a harmonizing attempt to avoid the difficulty of assigning Goliath's death to two different men.

The rabbis solved the problem by insisting that Elhanan was simply an alternate name for David. Another postulated view is that perhaps Elhanan was David's given name, while "David" was a throne name whose popularity eclipsed the use of his personal name.[5] A.M. Honeyman has avoided the difference in patronymics by emending "Jaare" to "Jesse."

It is possible that there were two giants from Gath who were named Goliath, though it seems unlikely that both should be remembered as carrying a spear whose shaft was "like a weaver's beam" (1 Sam 17:7; 2 Sam 21:19). Some writers have suggested that later traditions ascribed Elhanan's achievement to David as a means of magnifying the king. The great detail of 1 Samuel 17 and the treasured significance of David's altercation with the giant make this unlikely, however.

The last battle involved an unnamed giant who was renowned for having an extra digit on each extremity. He reportedly taunted Israel (as Goliath had done, 1 Sam 17:8-10), but was felled by Jonathan, the son of David's brother Shimei.

The closing summary (v. 22) pointedly reminds the reader that these Philistine champions were worthy adversaries, having been descended from the giants. Notably, though David had no part in any of the killings, the narrator notes that "they fell by the hands of David and his servants." The heroism of his fighting men contributed to the aura of power and invincibility that surrounded David, but the reader knows (from vv. 15-17) that David's heroic supporters meant more to his success than commonly acknowledged.

CONNECTIONS

Breaking Oaths, 21:1-9

The story of how David brought an end to Israel's famine by sacrificing the seven Saulides is an ugly, brutal account of how justice was perceived in the ancient world. The story involves more than blood-vengeance, however. Its primary significance has to do with the importance of keeping promises, especially in a corporate sense.

The making of a treaty in Israel inherently invoked Yahweh as witness to the covenant and potential executor of punishment for violators. The weather was always attributed to divine favor or displeasure, so it came as no real surprise to learn that Israel was paying the price for Saul's violation of the longstanding treaty with the Gibeonites.

Modern believers are less likely to attribute misfortune to divine punishment, but it remains true that consequences for good or ill are built into the fabric of covenant making. For example, the marriage of two persons involves the making of vows, promises to be faithful "till death do us part." Violation of those vows inevitably leads to heartache and suffering, especially where children are involved. The tragedy of broken relationships leaves deep and lasting scars. Many persons suffered in the famine during David's day who had nothing to do with Saul's transgression of the ancient oath. Saul's children and grandchildren suffered more than any other.

Newspapers carry, almost daily, stories of outrageous acts of terrorism or genocide, sometimes between differing states, sometimes between ethnic groups within a single country. Cease-fires are declared and truces are called, but the killing never stops. Whether one regards the result as divine punishment or not, the act of betrayal always brings consequences for the victim and the perpetrator alike. The ramifications may be as obvious as a troubled teen or a starving infant, or they may be as hidden as a bitter spirit and a lost soul. Such suffering does not bring expiation in itself. It does not make the act right; it only brings it to a natural conclusion.

The seven scions of Israel's former king did not go willingly to their deaths, yet the story indicates that their deaths paid the necessary price for Saul's sin, leading to a break in the famine and a cessation of divine punishment. The New Testament gospel declares that Jesus Christ was the innocent and only son of the King of the Universe, yet he freely suffered and died on behalf of an entire world of people who seem inherently unable to live in covenant obedience to God.

Those who hear and understand the gospel may choose to reject Christ's work and to remain on a spiritual starvation diet. Or they may accept the promise of divine grace and find that famine no longer holds their spirits captive.

Loyal Love, 21:10-14

The most inspirational aspect of this bloody and unhappy story is the courageous love of Rizpah, who risked her own life and health to defend her sons' broken bodies against the common scavengers of the earth. The mode of execution for treaty breakers called for the bodies of the slain to remain exposed to the elements as a way of bringing greater shame upon the guilty and of warning observers that violating a covenant is serious business.

Rizpah could not protect her sons from death; their fate was in the hands of others more powerful than she. Yet Rizpah did what she could to express her love. She stationed herself on a rocky crag, nearly as exposed to the elements as her slain sons, and defended after death the bodies of those she could not keep alive. It was Rizpah's determined effort to restore dignity to her sons that inspired David to give all the Saulides, including Saul and onathan, an honorable burial in the family omb.

Rizpah is somewhat reminiscent of the woman t Bethany who anointed Jesus with expensive perfume (Mark 14:3-9). [Unselfish Love] Though criticized for her extravagant display of love, Jesus connected her act of compassion to his coming death. She could not save him from that death, but "she has done what she could," Jesus said.

None of us can solve the great problems of the world. Racial hatred, ethnic genocide, world hunger, widespread poverty—these are stubborn issues that remind us of Jesus' comment that "you always have the poor with you" (Mark 14:7a). This, however, does not relieve us of doing what we can to bring hope and life to those who are within our reach. Jesus also said, "You can show kindness to them whenever you wish" (Mark 14:7b). The world is desperately in need of more persons like Rizpah—like the woman of Bethany—like Mother Teresa—like uncelebrated men and women around the world who give themselves to others every day—people who know they cannot solve every problem but who are determined to do what they can.

2 Samuel 21:10—Unselfish Love.
Gustave Doré (1832–83). *Rizpah's Kindness Unto the Dead* from the *Illustrated Bible*. 19th century. Engraving. (Credit: Dover Pictoral Archive Series)

Giant Killing, 21:15-22.

These brief stories relating the heroics of David's military men are significant because they remind us that David did not reach his place of influence and authority alone. David was always loved by

---

selfish Love

The story, as found in Mark 14:3-9, is as follows:

While he was at Bethany in the house of Simon the leper, as he sat at the table, a woman came with an alabaster jar of very costly ointment of nard, and she broke open the jar and poured the ointment on his head. But some were there who said to one another in anger, "Why was the ointment wasted in this way? For this ointment could have been sold for more than three hundred denarii, and the money given to the poor." And they scolded her. But Jesus said, "Let her alone; why do you trouble her? She has performed a good service for me. For you always have the poor with you, and you can show kindness to them whenever you wish; but you will not always have me. She has done what she could; she has anointed my body beforehand for its burial. Truly I tell you, wherever the good news is proclaimed in the whole world, what she has done will be told in remembrance of her."

others: by Saul (1 Sam 16:21), by Jonathan (1 Sam 18:1), by the populace (1 Sam 18:7), by Michal (1 Sam 18:20), by Abigail (1 Sam 25:39-41), and others. David's outlaw band (1 Sam 22:1-2) was fiercely loyal to him, as were the mercenaries who attached themselves to him (2 Sam 15:17-23). David's nephews Joab and Abishai devoted their own lives to furthering David's cause even though they sometimes disagreed about the best way to pursue it.

The love of David's men for their leader is made especially evident in 21:15-17, where Abishai comes to David's rescue and saves him from death at the hands of the Philistine Ishbi-benob. "There David's men swore to him, 'You shall not go out with us to battle any longer, so that you do not quench the lamp of Israel' " (21:17) David's supporters knew that their love for David also benefitted the kingdom as a whole. David, like a beautiful oil lamp, managed to bring the light of God's hope for Israel into focus as no one had before. Their service to David was also a service to God.

The crucial importance of leadership cannot be overestimated, but there are no leaders without willing followers. The kingdom grows best when leaders and supporters work together in humility and love for the good of all. When such cohesive harmony exists, even giants may fall. No obstacle is too great when God's people unite in behalf of kingdom growth and health.

NOTES

[1] Walter Brueggemann, *First and Second Samuel* (IBC; Louisville: John Knox, 1990), 337-38.

[2] P. Kyle McCarter, *II Samuel* (AB 9; Garden City: Doubleday, 1984), 436, 442.

[3] A. A. Anderson, *2 Samuel* (WBC; Waco: Word Books, 1989), 246, 249.

[4] See McCarter, *II Samuel*, 449-50.

[5] A. M. Honeyman, "The Evidence for Regnal Names among the Hebrews," *JBL* 67 (1948): 23-24.

DAVID'S PSALM OF PRAISE

22:1-51

COMMENTARY

The narrator's portrayal of David to this point has focused on his military and political heroics. Aside from the brief mention of his skill with the lyre (in a context fraught with military terminology, 1 Sam 16:18-23) and the quotation of his elegies for Saul, Jonathan, and Abner (2 Sam 1:19-27; 3:33-34), David's artistic side has remained unexplored, and no attention has been given to his popular reputation as a poet. Perhaps in an effort to offer a more balanced picture of David, the editors included in the appendices two psalms attributed to David. The first, 2 Samuel 22:1-51, is identical to Psalm 18 except for minor textual discrepancies.

Some scholars see in the psalm a deeper purpose than the adding of color to David's biographical portrait. [The Song of Hannah and the Psalm of David] They note similarities to the Song of Hannah, which comes

---

Song of Hannah and the Psalm of David

Interpreters have long recognized the similarity of these two songs in which God is a rock of refuge e righteous who overwhelms the wicked and lifts up eek with the same mighty power. Likewise, scholars noted the likelihood that both songs were inserted by ditor(s) who shaped the books of 1 and 2 Samuel as a arge building block in the overall Deuteronomistic ry. If this is true, the poetic bookends intentionally the internal narrative. The questions, then, are "Why?" What purpose do they serve?"

veral notable scholars argue that the two songs provide eneutical insight for the whole history in the books of uel. For example, Brevard Childs has argued that the s function as "an interpretive key for this history which ove all, to be understood from a theocentric ective."

'alter Brueggemann has advanced a similar view on the songs as an inclusio, arguing that the two hymns serve ving the spotlight away from human action and toward since both insist that there is no human

accomplishment without divine accompaniment (see also "1 Samuel 1: A Sense of Beginning," ZAW 102 [1990]: 33-48, where Brueggeman also finds similarity in the prose beginning and ending of the books of Samuel). Randall Bailey has added an intriguing suggestion that the poems function not only to *magnify* Yahweh, but also to *defend* Yahweh's actions, which sometimes appear questionable within the narrative.

Thus, as modern believers struggle with the incongruities of life yet find comfort in the elevation of God through the poetic liturgy of the church, the Deuteronomists' first audience probably felt more in common with the narratives of 1 and 2 Samuel, but may have found more comfort through the poetic lacework that framed it.

Brevard Childs, *Introduction to the Old Testament as Scripture* (Philadelphia: Fortress, 1979), 273.

Walter Brueggemann, *First and Second Samuel* (IBC; Louisville: John Knox, 1990), 339-40.

Randall Bailey, "The Redemption of YHWH: A Literary Critical Function of the Songs of Hannah and David," *Biblical Interpretation* 3 (June 1995): 213-31.

near the beginning of 1 and 2 Samuel (1 Sam 2:1-10). These two psalms, they hold, form a poetic inclusio that serves as a framework for understanding the narrative within, functioning to ameliorate the less-than-perfect images of both David and Yahweh as portrayed in the material bracketed by the psalms. In the Songs of Hannah and David, Yahweh is consummately wise, a strong and sure deliverer, while David is so faithful that he can say "I was blameless before him" (v. 24).

The unifying theme of God's dependable and delivering power runs throughout this psalm, but underlying counter-themes suggest that it may have begun as two separate thanksgiving psalms (vv. 2-20 and vv. 29-51) that were connected by an interlude extolling the traditional theology in vv. 21-28. In any case, the psalm raises eyebrows since it portrays David as "blameless" before God, when the reader knows better. Those who accept Davidic authorship for the poem can avoid the dilemma by assuming that he wrote it prior to the Bathsheba/Uriah affair, when he might still be considered "blameless" before God. [Did David Write This Psalm? Scholars who read the text as a later composition that was attributed to David must ascribe a certain amount of poetic license or metaphoric quality to the claims of Davidic purity.

The narrative introduction of v. 1 connects the psalm with an event in David's life, much like the superscriptions of Psalms 3, 7, 18 (= 2 Sam 22), 34, 51, 52, 54, 56, 57, 59, 60, 63, and 142. These are generally regarded as secondary. Unlike some of the other superscriptions (such as Ps 51, identifying the psalm with David's penitence after the Bathsheba incident), this introduction cannot be related to any specific moment in David's life.

Did David Write This Psalm?

The narrative introduction of 22:1 asserts that "David spoke to Yahweh the words of this song," a more pointed claim than the ambiguous *lĕdawîd* ("to," "for," or "of" David) that heads many of the psalms. Still, the introduction clearly belongs to the narrator, who is passing along an ancient hymn that tradition ascribed to David. The narrator no doubt believed that David wrote the psalm. Modern scholars tend to be more skeptical.

There are some orthographic oddities and vocabulary choices that suggest the psalm is of great antiquity, perhaps dating to the 9th or 10th century BC, at least (the early spelling irregularities are smoothed over in Ps 18). There are also elements that appear to be later additions, such as the Deuteronomistically flavored claims of vv. 21-25 and the wisdom sayings of vv. 26-28. As mentioned in the commentary, some writers regard the psalm as deriving from two older hymns of thanksgiving, spliced together with the later material in vv. 21-28.

The subtle evolutionary changes of Ps 18 over the primitive text of 2 Sam 22 serve as a reminder that the ancient texts were not static, but changing, as they were copied, edited, and adapted for different situations in life. More skeptical scholars might insist that David's putative penchant for poetry is a tendentious fabrication designed to magnify the memory of Israel's first great king. Others will note that the tradition seems too strong, too wide, and too deep to have no substance behind it. If the psalms are truly Davidic, one would expect those embedded in a narrative about David to be among them. Certain elements of this psalm may well go back to David's time, if not to David himself, though he may not have recognized it in its final form.

Other materials in chapters 21–24 are unattached from their historical context, and there is likewise no need to assume that this
psalm portrays David at the end of his life. The
intention of v. 1 must be to suggest a time early
in David's reign when David has been delivered
"from the hand of all his enemies, *and from the
hand of Saul.*" Saul was hardly a factor in David's
later life, but his relentless pursuit of the younger
David could have inspired the distress of vv. 5-7.
Mitchell Dahood's translation of *šāʾûl* as "Sheol"
(cf. 22:6) rather than "Saul" is unconvincing.[1]

The terminology of v. 1 is similar to 2 Samuel
7:1, which says that "the king was settled in his
house, and the LORD had given him rest from all his enemies
around him." David would battle other enemies after this point,
but generally on the offensive rather than the defensive, and thus
not in need of deliverance. In the context of chapter 7, David is
mindful of Yahweh's blessing, and sets his mind on building a
house for Yahweh. This period of David's life also has the advantage
of occurring before his fall from the pedestal of piety in chapter 11.
Perhaps the editor had such a time frame in mind.

> **Hendiadys**
>
> AΩ A hendiadys is a literary construction, a
> figure of speech in which two things are
> named with the intent that the first should
> modify the second; hence, the NRSV's "my rock,
> my fortress" would become "my rocky fortress."
> McCarter, who prefers other terms, has
> translated the same phrase as "my cliffside
> stronghold." In similar fashion, he has rendered
> "my God, my rock" (NRSV) as "my divine crag."
>
> P. Kyle McCarter, *II Samuel* (AB 9;Garden City: Doubleday,
> 1984), 464.

A Psalm of Deliverance, 22:2-20

The psalm begins with a series of common metaphors for God,
expressed in pairs and intended to celebrate Yahweh's mighty
strength as a refuge and his power to deliver (vv. 2-4). Kyle
McCarter interprets the paired words as examples of hendiadys, but
has few followers. [Hendiadys] For the characteristics of Hebrew
poetry in general and parallelism in particular, see [Singing Women] at
1 Samuel 2:1, in conjunction with the Song of Hannah.

The poet likens Yahweh to a strong cliffside fortress where one
could find a secure retreat. [Masada] The image of God as a rock (or
"crag") is quite common in the Bible. [God as a Rock]

> **as a Rock**
>
> The word translated as "rock" in v. 4 is *ṣûr*, which
> describes a rocky mountain peak or outcropping.
> word has a long history of use as a metaphor for
> ty, perhaps going back to the common practice of
> ciating deities with mountains. The Song of Moses in
> 32 describes God as "the Rock" (vv. 4, 15, 18),
> ribing his beneficence as "honey from the crags" and
> rom the flinty rock" (v. 13).
> ahweh is called the "Rock of Israel" (2 Sam 23:3; Isa
> 9), and in other texts "Rock" is a virtual synonym for the
> y (1 Sam 2:2; 2 Sam 22:3, 32, 47; Pss 18:2, 31, 46;
>
> 42:9; 62:7; 78:35; 89:26; 94:22; Isa 17:10; 26:4; 44:8; Hab
> 1:12). These texts often connect the idea of God as a rock
> with the theme of refuge or safety.
> The epithet "Shaddai" (usually as "El Shaddai," often
> translated as "God Almighty") also derives from a word that
> means mountain (Gen 17:1; 28:3; 35:11; 43:14; 48:3; Exod
> 6:3; Ezek 10:5).
> Even in contemporary urban society, the image of God as
> a strong and dependable rock remains a popular element in
> Christian worship, especially through contemporary choruses
> and praise songs.

Yahweh's strength is firm but not static; it is evident in his delivering, saving power. The expression "horn of my salvation" derives from the horn as a symbol of power in ancient Near Eastern iconography, where gods are typically depicted with horns. It may also refer to the horns that adorned each of the four corners of the altar. These horns were symbolic of Israel's security in Yahweh, and they supposedly granted sanctuary to one who grasped them (though, see 1 Kgs 2:28-34). The author writes as a testimony of his personal experience. He has called upon Yahweh, "who is worthy to be praised," and experienced deliverance from his enemies (v. 4; cf. 22:1).

Having introduced his theme, the writer moves to describe his time of distress from which Yahweh had saved him. He does so metaphorically (vv. 6-7). The "waves of death" and "snares of Sheol" call to mind Psalm 116:3 and perhaps Jonah 2:5-6a (MT 2:6-7a). "Torrents of perdition" translates "torrents of Belial" or possibly "torrents of hell." For a discussion of *bĕlîyaʿal*, see [Murderer! Scoundrel!] at 2 Samuel 16:7. The writer's deep distress was like falling into the fearsome, chaotic sea, sinking down to a certain death and an underwater admission to Sheol. The sea was a common symbol of distress in the ancient world where few people learned to swim, ships were primitive, and long distance sailing was always chancy. In Job 38:16-17, the "gates of death" are associated with the "recesses of the deep."

Again (as in v. 4), David recalls his cry to the LORD, who heard from "his temple" (v. 7; cf. Jonah 2:7 [MT 2:8], where God hears from "his holy temple"). The word for "temple" is *hêkāl*, poetically used for God's dwelling place in the heavens, as shown by the parallelism of Psalm 11:4: "The LORD is in his holy temple; the LORD's throne is in heaven." Thus, the psalmist celebrates Yahweh's ability to sit in the celestial throne room and still hear the cry of one who is lost in the bottom of the sea—and to do something about it.

The writer describes his deliverance in the classic terminology of theophany (vv. 8-16), through metaphors no less hyperbolic than in vv. 5-6. The cosmic quaking described in v. 8 frequently accompanies the divine presence in theophanies (cf. Ps 77:18 [MT 77:19]; Isa 5:25; 24:18). In Judges 5:4-5 and Psalm 68:8 (MT 68:9), the earthquake is also accompanied by heavy rain, as in v. 12 below.

God's anger is introduced in the third stich of v. 8 ("and quaked, because he was angry"). It is then described with physical metaphors in v. 9, where the divine appearance is likened to a fire-breathing dragon. In Job 41:18-21, the great sea monster Leviathan is described in similar terms. [The Dragon Lord] Other texts from the Hebrew Bible also associated divine wrath with the image of Yahweh bringing fire or smoke to bear, though not always from his nostrils (Deut 29:20 [MT 29:19]; Ps 74:1; Isa 65:5; 66:15; Ezek 21:31 [MT 21:36]; 22:31; 38:19).

In the ancients' mindset, such manifestations of fire and smoke may have been related to natural disasters such as volcanoes, even as earthquakes were also related to theophanic appearances. Earthquakes were and are common in Palestine, for the Jordan Rift Valley is part of a deep fault line. Volcanoes would have been far more rare, but the lightning associated with thunderstorms—and the smoking of forest fires set ablaze by such lightning—would

---

The Dragon Lord

Compare the theophanic image of God in 2 Sam 22:9, 13 (Ps 18:8, 12) with the intimidating portrait of Leviathan in Job 41:18-21:

2 Samuel 22:9, 13	*Psalm 18:8, 12 (MT 18:9, 13)*	*Job 41:18-21*
Smoke went up from his nostrils, and devouring fire from his mouth; glowing coals flamed forth from him. . . .	Smoke went up from his nostrils, and devouring fire from his mouth; glowing coals flamed forth from him. . . .	Its sneezes flash forth light, and its eyes are like the eyelids of the dawn. From its mouth go flaming torches; sparks of fire leap out.
Out of the brightness before him coals of fire flamed forth.	Out of the brightness before him there broke through his clouds hailstones and coals of fire.	Out of its nostrils comes smoke, as from a boiling pot and burning rushes. Its breath kindles coals, and a flame comes out of its mouth.

How Did Yahweh Get Through?

A Ω The NRSV prefaces Yahweh's cosmic appearance with the phrase "He bowed the heavens" (KJV and NASB take similar tracks). The NIV has "He parted the heavens," consistent with the reasoning of McCarter, Anderson, and others. The Hebrew verb is ambiguous, appearing in this context only here and in Ps 144:5. It may mean "to spread out," "to stretch out," "to bend," or "to incline." It is hard to get a handle on the image conveyed by "bending" or "bowing the heavens," unless one imagines that Yahweh pressed down upon the dome-like firmament thought to cover the earth in the ancient three-storied cosmology. At some point, even if the heavens were "bowed," Yahweh would need to break through.

A similar passage in Isa 63:19 speaks of God "tearing open" the sky to come down to the earth. There, the verb clearly means "to rend." Here, the sense of spreading out or stretching can carry the thought of Yahweh splitting the heavens or stretching the fabric of the sky to the breaking point as preface to his impressive entrance upon the storm clouds.

---

have been well known. Israel attributed control of the weather to Yahweh, and virtually all polytheistic societies had their own storm-god. Impressive thunderstorms, with their high winds, hard rain, crashing thunder, and frightening lightning, were inevitably associated with the expression of divine wrath. In vv. 13-15, "brightness" and "flaming coals of fire" will be clearly related to the LORD thundering from heaven and sending forth arrows of lightning.

The signs of Yahweh's approaching power finally give way to the approaching Deity, who splits the heavens and soars through the sky as he comes to his supplicant's aid. [How Did Yahweh Get Through?] Yahweh is also depicted as a "sky rider" in Psalm 68:33 (MT 68:34), as Baal is called "cloud rider" in Ugaritic texts. In Psalm 104:3 and Isaiah 19:1, the LORD rides a cloud chariot through the heavens. In the present text, Yahweh's appearance is described in at least three different ways. First, God surfs across the sky with thick darkness (presumably storm clouds) under his feet (v. 10b). Then he rides on the wings of a cherub, "and he flew" (v. 11a). [Cherubim] Whether "and he flew" refers to the cherub's flight or to Yahweh's unassisted aerial maneuvers is ambiguous. Finally, Yahweh is seen floating, as it were, "upon the wings of the wind" (v. 11b).

The plethora of images used to describe God's heavenly arrival demonstrates the poet's inability to capture Yahweh's awesome appearance in human words. He stretches the imagination to the breaking point yet fails to arrive at a single image that does justice to the thought of Yahweh's personal and perceivable descent through the sky. Multiple metaphors will have to do.

The images of Yahweh coming on thick darkness (v. 10b) and "upon the wings of the wind" (v. 11b) lead into the picture of a fierce thunderstorm, which the psalmist develops further in vv. 12-15. Yahweh arrives, cloaked in a "canopy" or "covert" which consists of rain clouds. "A gathering of water" (NRSV) is literally "the sieve of the waters" (v. 12). The image apparently derives from the "sifting" of the waters above the firmament into raindrops before they hit the ground.

Out of the gathering storm clouds, Yahweh vents his wrath, speaking in thunder and acting by hurling arrows of lightning (vv. 13-15). The LXX and Psalm 18:12 (MT 18:13) add hailstones to the dangerous mixture of stormy ingredients; the MT is apparently defective at this point. The NRSV reading suggests these actions are taken against Yahweh's enemies, throwing "them" into a total rout (v. 15), but the verb could also suggest that the thunderbolts themselves scattered in confusing patterns through the sky. The psalmist's enemies do not appear until v. 18.

Thunder as the voice of the storm-god is also known from Ugaritic tablets recovered at Ras-Shamra (Baal), and Akkadian tablets from Tell Amarna (Adad), as well as other biblical references, both in poetry (Job 37:4; Pss 29:3-9; 46:6 [MT 46:7]; 68:33 [MT 68:34]; 77:17-18 [MT 77:18-19]; 104:7; Isa 30:30-31; Jer 10:13 = 51:16; Joel 3:16 [MT 4:16]; Amos 1:2), and in prose

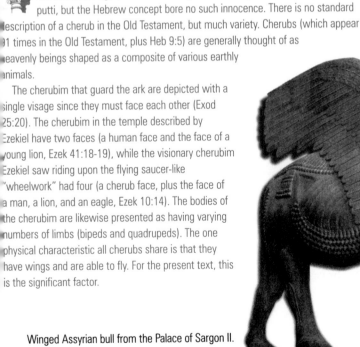

Cherubim

The modern image of a "cherub" conjures the thought of Michelangelo's angelic putti, but the Hebrew concept bore no such innocence. There is no standard description of a cherub in the Old Testament, but much variety. Cherubs (which appear 91 times in the Old Testament, plus Heb 9:5) are generally thought of as heavenly beings shaped as a composite of various earthly animals.

The cherubim that guard the ark are depicted with a single visage since they must face each other (Exod 25:20). The cherubim in the temple described by Ezekiel have two faces (a human face and the face of a young lion, Ezek 41:18-19), while the visionary cherubim Ezekiel saw riding upon the flying saucer-like "wheelwork" had four (a cherub face, plus the face of a man, a lion, and an eagle, Ezek 10:14). The bodies of the cherubim are likewise presented as having varying numbers of limbs (bipeds and quadrupeds). The one physical characteristic all cherubs share is that they have wings and are able to fly. For the present text, this is the significant factor.

Winged Assyrian bull from the Palace of Sargon II.
(Credit: Mitchell G. Reddish)

(Exod 9:22-35; 1 Sam 7:9-10). [The Storm God] Likewise, the Greek god Zeus and the Canaanite Baal joined Yahweh in throwing lightning bolts at those who opposed them (Pss 77:18 [MT 77:19]; 97:4; 144:6; Hab 3:11).

The tempestuous signs of Yahweh's appearance finally focus on the reason for the theophany: the rescue of the poet, who is metaphorically trapped at the bottom of the sea, wrapped in seaweed and floundering at the gates of Sheol (see vv. 5-6). As a strong wind had cleared a path through the sea for the Israelites to escape Pharaoh's clutches (Exod 14:21), so now the divine storm wind lays bare the very floor of the sea, at the lowest foundation of the world (22:16), where the distressed psalmist awaits Yahweh's answer to his call for help.

The act of deliverance is related in vv. 17-20 as Yahweh reached down from on high and drew the wretched psalmist from the "mighty waters," representative of the forces that opposed him. When the poet claims that Yahweh "took me, he drew me out," he uses the unusual verb *māšâ*, the same root that gave rise to the name "Moses"("because I drew him out of the water," Exod 2:10). This may be an intentional echo of the Mosaic birth/rescue story, but the comparison should not be stressed too heavily.

Once the author emerges from the "mighty waters," the metaphor falls aside, and his distress is now attributed to a "strong enemy . . . those who hated me . . . were too mighty for me" (vv. 17-18)." There is no evidence to identify these enemies except that, for a while, they held the upper hand over the psalmist, be he David or some other poet. The thought would have been appropriate for David on several occasions, such as when he survived narrow escapes from Saul (1 Sam 19:10-18; 24:26-29), from the people of Gath (1 Sam 21:10-15), from the ungrateful inhabitants of Keilah (1 Sam 23:12-13), from the dilemma of fighting his own people (1 Sam 29), from the potential attack of his son Absalom (2 Sam 17), and from specific battlefield dangers, such as the incident mentioned in 2 Samuel 22:15-17.

The psalmist's relief in being rescued is expressed in spatial terms. In "the day of . . . calamity," he had felt that he was drowning beneath the pressure of his enemies, hemmed into a tight spot with no place to go. Now, however, Yahweh has brought him "into a broad place" (v. 19a), a place of safety and peace (cf. Ps 31:8 [MT 31:9]). There, the psalmist can breathe easily and move freely,

The Storm God

Brought to the palace of Nebuchadnezzar II, this stele shows the storm god of the Hittites with his arms raised holding a thunderbolt in one hand and an axe in the other.

Hittite basalt relief depicting the strom god Hadad of Aleppo. Late Hittite Period. 9th C. BC. Museum of the Ancient Orient. Istanbul, Turkey. (Credit: Mitchell G. Reddish)

relieved of the cramped and confining stress of danger, safe in the care of Yahweh.

The latter half of v. 20 serves as an artful transition to the next section, in which the author (probably a later editor) offers interpretive comments designed to bolster the Deuteronomist's basic theological presupposition. In vv. 21-25, he will argue that Yahweh heard and answered the psalmist's prayer for one reason only: because the supplicant was obedient and blameless before God.

Theological Interlude, 22:21-28

The material in this section falls into two parts that may or may not be original to the psalm, or even from the same hand: vv. 21-25 reprise the works-righteousness theology supported by the Deuteronomist, while vv. 26-28 make the same point but in the form of talionic wisdom sayings asserting that God's attitude toward any person is entirely dependent on that person's attitude toward God.

The last line of vv. 2-20 is either a skillful transition by the original poet or an opportune opening for a later editor: "He delivered me, because he delighted in me" (22:20b). The reader naturally wonders *why* Yahweh delighted in the psalmist so much that he was willing to appear in fearsome theophany and deliver him. The answer is found in vv. 21-25: It is because the poet was righteous and obedient to God. This purity of heart is expressed poetically through no less than five paired premises, as the author justifies Yahweh's beneficence to him. He has been rewarded (vv. 21, 25) for these reasons:

"according to my righteousness" / "according to the cleanness of my hands" (v. 21),
"for I have kept the ways of Yahweh" / "and have not departed wickedly from my God" (v. 22),
"for all his ordinances were before me" / "and from his statutes I did not turn aside" (v. 23),
"I was blameless before him" / "I kept myself from guilt" (v. 24),
"according to my righteousness" / "according to my cleanness in his sight" (v. 25).

Righteousness, then, is defined entirely by behavior: cleanness of hands, obedience to the ways (ordinances, statutes) of Yahweh. It is this that makes one blameless and innocent before God, whose blessings are reserved precisely for those persons who exhibit such piety. John Durham has argued, from the perspective of Psalm 18:23 (MT 18:24), that the word *tāmîm* (whose root meaning is "complete" or "whole") should be translated as "honest" rather than "blameless."[2] That is, the psalmist claims to have maintained his integrity by being honest, without claiming to be perfect. Even if this is allowed, however, the overwhelming number of parallel claims regarding the psalmist's spiritual state clearly points to an assertion of innocence.

It is possible that the original psalmist desired to express his own faith in the traditional theological system, but it seems more likely that a later hand has interpreted the poet's original experience. As mentioned above, the reader knows that David himself is certainly not so innocent, at least after the Bathsheba/Uriah affair. One could argue, for that matter, that no one could boast so eloquently about his own humble piety without revealing a thick layer of pride. Proclaiming and illustrating the principles of Israel's "old-time religion" was the primary agenda underlying the entire Deuteronomistic History's promulgation; it is reasonable to suppose that these verses came from the same school.

With vv. 26-28, the personal pronouns shift from "I" to "you" as the psalmist (or his editor) moves from celebrating his own right-eousness to celebrating God's faithfulness—and predictability. [Is God Really So Predictable?] This gnomic quatrain insists that God can be all things to all people: loyal to the loyal, blameless toward the blameless, pure toward the pure—but *perverse* (lit., "making himself twisted") in dealing with those who are crooked (vv. 26-27)! These verses celebrate a God with whom you get what you pay for: Those who invest humility get deliverance, while those who lay up haughtiness are asking for a fall (v. 28).

The reader knows that David's life was a prime example of this principle, for the narrator has stressed the manifold ways in which Yahweh blessed the young and devout David, who was a man after God's own heart, while insisting that David's later fall from power, family problems, and resulting life of misery were due entirely to his presumption in committing adultery with Bathsheba and killing her husband, Uriah (2 Sam 11). David's pathway leads unerringly upward from 1 Samuel 16 to 2 Samuel 10, but winds through a desolate and downward road from 2 Samuel 12 to 2 Kings 2.

To the modern reader, it may seem strange to see David (presumably, pre-Bathsheba) portrayed as composing a psalm extolling the very principles that led to his own downfall. For the Deuteronomistic editors, however, it made perfect sense, because in

the books of Samuel, David is "Exhibit A" in convincing the jury
(Israel in exile) that they must renew their commitment to the God
(as expressed by the traditional theology) if they are to have any

---

Is God Really So Predictable?

The Deuteronomists' intense defense of the traditional theology was fueled in part by the common recognition that it did not always work; sometimes the wicked prospered and the righteous suffered. This awareness led to the creation of more skeptical literary works such as the book of Job (which has ancient analogues in Mesopotamia and Egypt) and the book of Ecclesiastes. The purpose of these books was nothing less than to call the traditional theology into question.

In the book of Job, for example, Job is portrayed as a most righteous man (1:1), yet he suffers terribly as the result of heavenly machinations. Job's friends presume that Job's misfortune betrays some secret sin, but Job insists throughout that he is innocent (for example, see 6:8-9, 24; 9:20-21; 12:2-3; 13:1-3). Job complains bitterly and cries out to God for an answer, or at least an audience (ch. 23).

Robert Frost captured the essence of Job's message in a poem called "A Masque of Reason." In the following excerpt, set long after Job's earthly life, Job and God are engaged in friendly conversation. Job has just asked God to explain something about heaven, and this is how God responds:

Yes, by and by. But first a larger matter.
I've had you on my mind a thousand years
To thank you someday for the way you helped me
Establish once for all the principle
There's no connection a man can reason out
Between his just desserts and what he gets.
Virtue may fail and wickedness succeed.
'Twas a great demonstration we put on. . . .
Too long I've owed you this apology
For the apparently unmeaning sorrow
You were afflicted with in those old days.
But it was of the essence of the trial
You shouldn't understand it at the time.
It had to seem unmeaning to have meaning.
And it came out all right. I have no doubt
You realize by now the part you played
To stultify the Deuteronomist
And change the tenor of religious thought.
My thanks are to you for releasing me
From moral bondage to the human race.
The only free will there at first was man's,
Who could do good or evil as he chose.
I had no choice but I must follow him
With forfeits and rewards he understood—
Unless I like to suffer loss of worship.
I had to prosper good and punish evil.
You changed all that. You set me free to reign.

Robert Frost, "A Masque of Reason" (New York: Henry Holt, 1945); citation from reprint in Edward Latham, *The Poetry of Robert Frost* (New York: Holt, Rinehart, and Winston, 1969), 475-76.

hope of being delivered, like the psalmist, from their suffocating distress.

A Royal Psalm of Victory, 22:29-51

The connective material in vv. 21-28 may continue into v. 29, which smoothly shifts into the celebrative song of victory that concludes the chapter. Some scholars include v. 29 with the interpretive material, while others read it as the introductory image of the following psalm.

When the image of a lamp appears in the wisdom literature as a symbol of life, it is usually an assertion that the lamp of the wicked is destined to go out (Job 18:6; Prov 20:20; 24:20). In Psalm 119, often attributed to the wisdom school, God's word is "a lamp to my feet and a light to my path" (Ps 119:105). In the present verse, God himself is a lamp who brightens the darkness. Whether the psalmist is thinking of spiritual illumination or emotional inspiration is unclear, though the latter seems more likely in light of the following verses. David himself was called the "lamp of Israel" (2 Sam 21:17), perhaps as a mediator of God's presence.

Yahweh's empowering presence enables the psalmist to perform superhuman acts: to "crush a troop" or to "leap over a wall." The translation itself is difficult, though the intent is clear. The verb taken as "crush" by the NRSV is literally "I can run," as in "I can run at [charge] a whole troop!" The alternate translation "crush" must presuppose an unusual derivation from a similar verb. The courage to charge an entire squadron of the enemy or the capacity to surmount the wall of a defended city would both be helpful capacities in a time of war.

There are also translational difficulties with v. 31. The tricola is unusual in a poem consisting mostly of couplets, and the second two lines are very similar to Proverbs 30:5 ("Every word of God proves true; he is a shield to those who take refuge in him"). The MT is awkward, as reflected in the NRSV's translation: "This God—his way is perfect." Literally, it is "*The* god" (*ha'ēl*), using god in a generic sense. The word rendered as "his way" can also mean "his dominion" in certain contexts, and the word behind "perfect" carries the connotation of "complete." The verb is unstated in the phrase, which is not unusual with verbs of being, leaving the interpreter to decide where it should go. Thus, McCarter's translation, "The god whose dominion is complete," while giving an entirely different sense, is just as legitimate.[3]

McCarter also has argued that the second line is intrusive, a scribal insertion based on Proverbs 30:5. Hebrew has no designated word for "promise" in the English sense: the word here means "utterance" or "speaking." Any word of Yahweh, however, can be considered a promise. The verbal form translated as "proves true" means "refined," commonly used to describe pure silver.

The word "shield" derives from a verb meaning "to cover" or "to defend." It also can be used in a figurative sense to mean "ruler" or "sovereign." The psalmist attests that Yahweh is a defender who offers refuge to all who seek him.

The image of God as a sure defense leads back to the rock metaphor (v. 32b), as in vv. 2-3. The poet uses two rhetorical questions to praise the incomparability of Yahweh (cf. 1 Sam 2:2; 2 Sam 7:22; Isa 43:11; 44:7-8; 45:21). "Who is God (*ʾēl*), but Yahweh?" builds on the previous verse, which describes Yahweh as "the god who is complete." This sentiment, if not entirely monotheistic, is leading in that direction. There are others who are called gods, but in the psalmist's experience Yahweh is the only one who lives up to the name. Because of the strongly monotheistic content, many scholars regard this verse as a later insertion, but it fits well into the poetic flow.

Verses 33-37 offer practical illustrations of the theological affirmation in v. 32. David claims that Yahweh is the *real* God, the one who has strengthened him and widened his path (v. 33), given him skill and confidence to travel high and precarious paths (v. 34), enhanced his offensive prowess in time of war (v. 35), defended him like a divine shield (v. 36a), and made his stride long and sure (v. 37). [Strengthened or Created?] The result is that God's greatness is introduced to the human arena, for the psalmist claims, "Your help has made me great" (v. 36b). Modern readers might read this as pompous narcissism, but the psalmist intends it as a humble testimony to the care and the power of God. His claim of greatness is not a personal affectation, but a reflection of the greatness of God at work in his life.

This greatness is further illustrated in vv. 38-43, where the psalmist takes the role of a strong military leader who has accomplished great things at God's behest and with God's help. This is a fitting image of David, especially during his early years. The verbs are first person as the psalmist salutes his accomplishments in

Strengthened or Created?

AΩ McCarter takes an interesting approach to vv. 34-36. Unpacking the difficult terminology in the light of Arabic, Ugaritic, Akkadian, and Aramaic analogues, he arrives at a colorful translation, which describes the psalmist's divinely inspired creation as a fighting man:

Stationing my legs like tree trunks, he made me stand upright; programming my hands for fighting, he shaped the bows of my arms.

P. Kyle McCarter, *II Samuel* (AB 9; Garden City: Doubleday, 1984), 454, 470-71.

Yahweh's behalf. Active verbs predominate in vv. 38-39, where the psalmist *pursued, destroyed, consumed,* and *struck down* his enemies, who were *consumed, fell,* and *did not rise.* The spotlight swings to Yahweh in vv. 40-41, again through verbal action. Yahweh girded the psalmist with strength while making his assailants "sink" beneath him and turn their backs to run.

Thus, David's success is due to divine favor. When his enemies cried for help, they also tried calling upon Yahweh, but without avail (v. 41). This may reflect David's struggles with fellow Yahwists like Saul, Absalom, or Sheba and their supporters, but it seems unusual that he would take such delight in treating fellow Hebrews the way he does in v. 43: beating them into dust and stamping them into the mud. Such intense language points beyond the totality of defeat to the prospect of annihilation. Perhaps the author means to suggest that even foreign enemies deserted their own gods and called on Yahweh but found it too late to avoid destruction.

The psalmist takes on a truly royal persona in vv. 44-46, a role that David played well. During David's rule, he may have been as powerful as any surrounding king, though he hardly ruled an empire. He claims to have overcome "strife with the peoples" to become "the head of the nations," ruling even over "people whom I had not known" (v. 44). David's military might and political skills led some foreign neighbors to sue for peace, though probably not as abjectly as vv. 45-46 would indicate.

The unifying conclusion of the psalm returns to the theme expressed at the beginning of the victory song (v. 32), as well as the previous song of deliverance (22:2-3). "Yahweh *lives!*" declares the poet's conviction that Yahweh, unlike other gods, truly lives and has the power to act in behalf of his people (cf. 22:32). Yahweh's life and Yahweh's commitment to Israel are as sure as stone; thus, Yahweh is "my rock." "The rock of my salvation" calls to mind David's experience in the wilderness of Maon, where Saul's pursuit had come so close that only the rocky top of a mountain separated them. When Saul was forced to call off the chase and deal with an (in)opportune Philistine invasion, David was delivered, and the site was named the "Rock of Escape" (1 Sam 23:28).

The focus of Yahweh's delivering power is expressed in vv. 48-49 by verbs, prepositions, and adverbs that indicate direction. Yahweh brought *down* peoples to be *under* the psalmist, even as he brought the king *out from* his enemies and exalted (*lifted up*) him *above* his adversaries, *away from* the violent.

In glad appreciation for all the beneficence of Yahweh as expressed in the preceding verses, the poet gives thanks and praise to God (v. 50), a common theme in the psalms. Scholars have long suggested that v. 51, or at least the final line, must be an addition intended to identify the psalm more closely with David. It is also possible that the verse could be original if we presume that the psalm (in part, at least) did in fact originate in the Jerusalem court. The language of v. 51 echoes the conclusion of Nathan's oracle in 2 Samuel 7:12-16, where Yahweh promises to show *steadfast love* to David's *descendants* so that his house will be established *forever*.

In review, 2 Samuel 22 probably comprises two poems (vv. 2-20 and 29-50 [with the possible exception of 22:32]) of high antiquity—perhaps as old as David himself. Orthographic evidence suggests that they may have originated in northern Israel, but they were prized in Judah as well. The two psalms celebrate deliverance from enemies and royal conquests, two themes that were commonly associated with David, as were the psalms themselves. It is likely that the Deuteronomist(s) combined these psalms by means of the material in vv. 21-28, then wrapped up the package with a prose introduction (22:1) and a poetic conclusion (22:51) designed to give the resulting unit a clearly Davidic stamp.

CONNECTIONS

God as a Rock, 22:2-3, 32, 47

The metaphor of God as a rock stems in part from the obvious strength, stability, and solidity of stone, but also from the majestic beauty of the rocky crags that dominate the landscape in the hill country of Judea, and especially in the area bordering the Dead Sea. Readers who are fortunate enough to have seen the Grand Canyon or other impressive rock formations of the American West have some appreciation of the awestruck respect ancients had of the great rocky mountains in whose shadow they lived.

To think of God as a rock is to celebrate God's *solidity*. [Rock of Ages] For the believer, Yahweh is no vacuous creation of the human psyche, like the new age concept of "God" being something that one finds within oneself. Israel's belief in the solid reality of Yahweh

---

Rock of Ages

The metaphor of God as a rock has an enduring appeal, as evidenced by our music. Christian hymnody celebrates the image of God as a rock in a wide variety of traditional hymns, spiritual songs, and contemporary praise choruses, from "Rock of Ages" to "The Solid Rock," from "I Go to the Rock" to "Jesus Is My Rock."

grew from the personal experience of divine deliverance, an act so impressive that it is still celebrated today in the age old way, as Jews relive the exodus event through observing Passover. Christian belief in the reality of God also grows from an event, and the Christ event is likewise celebrated again and again through the observance of the Lord's Supper, a new Passover that celebrates spiritual as well as physical deliverance.

To think of God as a rock is to celebrate God's *stability*. Believers trust that God is dependable and faithful even when we are not. Israel believed that Yahweh was a God who maintained steadfast love and kept his covenants (Exod 34:6-7; Num 14:18; Neh 9:17, 31; Ps 103:8; Jer 32:18; Jonah 4:2). Christians confess that God in Christ is faithful (1 Cor 1:9; 2 Cor 1:18), can be trusted to care for his own (John 10), and will endure for eternity (Rev 1:8; 21:6; 22:13).

To think of God as a rock is to celebrate God's *strength*. David believed that Yahweh had the ability to deliver him from every enemy and to empower him to overcome every obstacle (1 Sam 17:37, 46-47, for example). Christians see evidence of God's strength in the enduring nature of the church. That strength was seen in the Apostle Peter (whose name means "Rock"), to whom Jesus said, "On this rock I will build my church" (Matt 16:18). That strength is seen in believers who take Jesus' advice to build their spiritual homes upon the rock of faith in Christ, rather than the shifting sands of unbelief or worldly ways (Matt 7:24-27).

God as a Deliverer, 22:2-20

The poet described Yahweh's coming to deliver in terms of a catastrophic celestial theophany, complete with fire, smoke, storm clouds, wind, and cosmic quaking. Such a description of God's appearance depends heavily on metaphor and the human imagination of what God's literal appearance must be like. Other theophanies echo similar elements (Exod 19:16; Judg 5:4-5; Pss 29:3-9; 68:7-35; Hab 3:3-15; Mic 1:3-4).

God does not always appear in such overwhelming fashion, however. When Yahweh spoke to Elijah, it was not through the mighty wind, earthquake, or fire, but through a "still, small voice" (1 Kgs 19:11-12, KJV), perhaps better translated as "sheer silence" (NRSV).

While many Christians look forward to an impressive cosmic return at the *parousia* (Matt 24:39-41), God's most significant appearance took the form of a helpless human baby in a nameless manger near Bethlehem (Luke 2:1-20). In the weeks preceding our commemoration of Christ's birth, we celebrate his incarnational theophany through a season called "Advent," which means "Coming."

Jesus' great power and relationship with God were declared by John the Baptizer and demonstrated by Jesus' own mighty works and words, but his eternal immensity was normally cloaked by his humanity and humility. Paul's use of the old hymnic description of Jesus' appearance (Phil 2:5-8) describes Christ as one who "emptied himself," "taking the form of a slave, being born in human likeness . . . he humbled himself and became obedient to the point of death—even death on a cross."

Today's culture seems obsessed with the idea that God (or an authorized representative) may appear at any moment to save the day when we are in trouble or to teach the evil and the stubborn needed lessons about the folly of their ways. Angels are all the fashion. What most of us have seen of God, however, has come through the loving touch of persons who are human, as Christ was, and who are willing to give of themselves for others, as Christ did.

The important thing is not *how* God comes, but *that* God comes to those who cry out for deliverance, trusting that God's grace will always be sufficient.

God as a Deal-Maker, 22:21-28

The interlude in vv. 21-28 brings Deuteronomistic theology and traditional wisdom sayings to bear in support of the view that Yahweh's delight in the psalmist—and resultant deliverance—was due to his personal righteousness:

> "The LORD rewarded me according to my righteousness; according to the cleanness of my hands he recompensed me." (v. 21; cf. 22:25)

This righteousness results from action: the poet has "kept the ways" of Yahweh without departing from them (v. 22), and remained true to God's ordinances and statutes (v. 23) with the result that he was blameless and without guilt (v. 24), thus deserving of Yahweh's redeeming recompense (v. 25).

The skeptic might ask: "If he's so blameless, and if God always rewards obedience, why does God not prevent him from getting into such a stressful situation to begin with?" The situation of distress, metaphorically described in vv. 5-6, suggests a time of deep anguish and genuine uncertainty. If the psalmist had been so righteous and worthy of rewards, why did Yahweh allow him to experience such suffocating suffering before finally coming to his rescue?

Texts such as this, while not approaching Job's theodicy or Qoheleth's skepticism, do offer an insight that is sometimes overlooked: The traditional theology, for all its emphasis on righteousness and reward, does not promise a life free from struggle and pain. What it does offer is ultimate deliverance. There are no extant psalms declaring:

> He makes me to lie down in beds of roses,
>   sweet of smell and without thorns,
> He has filled my soul with manifold delights
>   throughout my long and happy life,
> For I was blameless and pure through every day,
>   my feet did not wander from the paths of righteousness.

None of Israel's great heroes of the faith was without struggle. Abraham, Isaac, and Jacob struggled. Joseph is described as being exceptionally obedient, yet the pitfalls he faced on the way to joining Egypt's elite are well known. Moses gave Israel the Law and walked so closely with Yahweh that his face shone from the contact (Exod 34:29-35), yet his life was so hard that he prayed to die (Num 11:15). Faithful Joshua faced difficult days, as did Gideon, Deborah, and all the heroic judges exalted by the Deuteronomist. The psalmist here claims to have been obedient in every way but also attests that he nearly drowned in a sea of enemies. If we are to attribute this part of the poem to the Deuteronomist, we must recognize that even he was aware that bad things happen to good people. The righteous are not exempt from trial; the difference between them and the wicked is that God's faithful ones have the hope of ultimate redemption and vindication from their suffering.

The wisdom sayings found in vv. 26-27 are another story, unless we regard the context as a toning down of their original intent. According to these gnomic claims, God always responds to humankind in "tit-for-tat" fashion, with an eye for an eye and a tooth for a tooth. He is loyal to the loyal, blameless toward the blameless, pure with the pure. When confronted by the crooked, he twists himself to match their own deviousness. The intent of these sayings is laudable in that they encourage persons to follow God's way. The problem with their approach is that there is no grace in them; we only get what we deserve, for good or ill.

This is why the New Testament message of grace is so welcome: "But God proves his love for us in that *while we still were sinners*

Christ died for us" (Rom 5:8). "For the wages of sin is death, but *the free gift of God* is eternal life in Christ Jesus our Lord" (Rom 6:23). The New Testament does not remove the issue of obedience from the table but makes it clear that our basic acceptability to God does not derive from our perfectionist piety, but from God's amazing grace.

God as a Warrior and Great-Maker, 22:29-43

The terminology of these verses describes God as a divine warrior who outfits and trains his faithful one in the art of smashing his enemies. Some modern readers will find the metaphor repulsive while others will take delight in designating themselves as "prayer warriors." As always, context is crucial. With these verses, the psalm takes on a decidedly "royal" cast. If the psalm was not written by David or another king, it was written by someone who spoke of himself in that way.

Israel's first purpose in calling for a king was a military one: that he would fight their battles and defeat their enemies (1 Sam 8:20). David surely fulfilled this role, at least in the early part of his reign. The question for modern readers is not "What size armor should I order?" but "What enemy of goodness is God calling me to fight—and how?" Is it world hunger? Racial prejudice? Misguided materialism? Ethical emptiness? AIDS? Poverty? Substance abuse? All of these are adversarial to God's good way for his people.

Our biggest failure is in thinking that we cannot do anything—that we are too small, too weak, too helpless. The psalmist has an opinion on that matter. His words in v. 36b seem presumptuous and proud at first: "Your help has made me great." David (or his speech writer) recognized that he had been gifted by God in ways that are not inappropriately called "great." His admission that such greatness comes from God is also an acknowledgment that God's gifts are to be used for God's purpose. God can indeed make us great—not for our own personal benefit—so we can do great things for God.

Great things for God rarely happen through violence or even through combative and unloving speech. We can trust God's Spirit both to guide and to empower us in accomplishing the divine will. As Zechariah declared to Zerubbabel: "Not by might, nor by power, but by my spirit, says the LORD of hosts" (Zech 4:6).

NOTES

[1] Mitchell Dahood, *Psalms I:1–50* (AB 16; Garden City: Doubleday, 1965), 104.

[2] John I Durham, "Psalms" (BBC 4; Nashville: Broadman, 1971), 204.

[3] P. Kyle McCarter, *II Samuel* (AB 9; Garden City: Doubleday, 1984), 454, 469.

DAVID'S LAST WORDS

23:1-7

COMMENTARY

This poetic oracle is self-designated as "the last words of David," but there is no other reason to assume that the wisdom it conveys should be associated with the latter part of his life. Indeed, the content suggests a time nearer to 2 Samuel 7 and Nathan's oracle declaring Yahweh's choice of David's house to become an everlasting dynasty in Israel.

David's last words recorded in the biblical narrative are found in 2 Kings 2:1-9, a biting text in which David first blesses Solomon as his successor, then instructs his son to engineer untimely deaths for Joab and Shimei. David bore grudges against both of those ill-fated men, but could not afford to take vengeance during his own lifetime. Perhaps the final editors of the Deuteronomistic History did not wish for David to be remembered by this vindictive and callous counsel. Thus, they may have titled this intensely positive poem "The Last Words of David" as a way of encouraging readers to think more favorably of David's final days.

The remark identifying the text as David's last words is clearly editorial, and the remainder of v. 1 serves as an introduction to the remainder of the text. These introductory words are strongly reminiscent of the formula that begins Balaam's oracles in Numbers 24:3 and 15. [Balaam's Oracles] The great antiquity of the Balaam texts is widely accepted; thus, the similarities argue in favor of a very old date for this oracle of David. Many scholars are confident enough to assign the text to David's era, if not to David himself.

Balaam's Oracles

AΩ Compare the introductory words to the oracles of Balaam and David:

Numbers 24:3 (= 24:15)	*2 Samuel 23:1*
The oracle of Balaam son of Beor, the oracle of the man whose eye is clear	The oracle of David, son of Jesse, the oracle of the man whom God exalted

Three Impressive Titles

AΩ The text of 23:1 is difficult and the translation suspect at several points. "The man whom God exalted" assumes an emendation to the text, changing the MT's *ʿal* to *ʾēl*, the generic word for god. The word *ʿal* is ordinarily a preposition meaning "upon," "for," "toward," or the like, but it can also act as a substantive meaning, "height." It sometimes appears as an abbreviation of the divine appellative *ʾelyôn*, meaning "The Most High." Thus, alternate readings are "the man who was exalted on high" or "the man exalted by the Most High." Neither changes the sense substantially.

The title "anointed of the God of Jacob" relies on the LXX[L] and OL. The MT has "Israel" in place of Jacob. "Israel" originated as a new name for "Jacob" (Gen 32:28).

The most notable problem of interpretation in this verse is reflected in "The favorite of the Strong One of Israel"

(NRSV), which is radically different than the traditional rendering as "the sweet psalmist of Israel" (KJV, RSV, ▮ NIV has "Israel's singer of songs"). The familiar translat▮ quite defensible on textual or grammatical grounds, bu▮ seems out of place from a poetic standpoint. The expre▮ is parallel to "the anointed of the God of Jacob," so one▮ would expect a corresponding phrase describing David'▮ relationship to God. A comment on David's reputation a▮ composer or performing artist seems out of place.

Scholars who noticed this discrepancy have excavate▮ number of Semitic cognates for the word *zimrat* (traditi▮ rendered as "psalmist") and have found several similar words, most having to do with strength or power. Thus, propose that *zimrat* should be considered a divine epith▮ "The Strong One" or "The Stronghold" of Israel.

The use of the word *nĕʾūm* is remarkable, as it belongs to the specialized vocabulary of prophetic pronouncements. The basic meaning is "utterance," but its prophetic associations are so strong that it is often translated as "oracle." This is the first scriptural suggestion that David ever acted as a prophet. As such, it is highly unexpected, suggesting that it may have been preserved in different circles than the narrative traditions. The tradition that David was a prophet emerged rather late, when many of the psalms were being read with prophetic import. By New Testament times, David's reputation as a prophet was firmly entrenched (Acts 2:30).

The introduction consists of four parallel lines that assign to David three impressive titles in addition to his designation as "son of Jesse." David is "the man whom God exalted," "the anointed of the God of Jacob," and "the favorite of the Strong One of Israel" (v. 1). [Three Impressive Titles]

Many scholars regard v. 2 as a later insertion designed to bolster David's prophetic image. As McCarter pointed out, the only evidence of late vocabulary is found here in the word *millâtô* (from *millâ*), probably of Aramaic derivation, as a synonym for *dābār*, or "word" (the word also appears in Pss 19:4 [MT 19:5]; 139:4; Prov 23:9; and the poetry of Job).[1]

In the books of Samuel, the coming of "the spirit of the LORD" or "the spirit of God" is usually associated with ecstatic experiences (1 Sam 10:6, 10) or the temporary fervor and power reminiscent of the Judges (1 Sam 11:6; 16:13; cf. Judg 3:10; 6:34; 11:29; 13:25; 14:6, 19; 15:14). Here, however, it expressly relates to prophetic

n Overwrought Introduction

The reader may notice that there are no less than three introductions to the oracle (v. 1, v. 2, and v. 3b), each capable of standing alone. The earliest is probably v. 3b, e latest v. 2. These expansions were intended to bolster the poem's reputation as a ophetic oracle since the text would not have born the identification otherwise. David's ords in vv. 3b-4 have the form of a wisdom saying, a *māšāl*, rather than that of a typical ophetic oracle.

---

spiration, as in 1 Kings 18:12; 22:24; 1 Chronicles 12:18; Isaiah 1:1; Ezekiel 11:5; Micah 3:8.

As noted above, v. 2 may be a late insertion, and it is also super-uous, for v. 3b provides yet another introduction to the oracle self, which is found in vv. 3b-4. [An Overwrought Introduction] In Iebrew, both lines begin with the verb: *'āmar* ("has spoken") and *ibber* ("has said"). The "rock of Israel" as a divine epithet recalls milar imagery in 2 Samuel 22:3, 32, and 47.

The surprising thing about the "oracle" is that it takes the form f a wisdom saying, or *māšāl*. It consists of a proverb concerning ne ideal king (vv. 3b-4), to which is attached an asseveration that David fits the bill (v. 5a) and a contrasting observation concerning ne expected fates of the righteous and the wicked (vv. 5b-7). The ext is often difficult (a sign of its antiquity?), but the writer's intent clear.

To rule justly is to have one's actions guided by "the fear of God" v. 3b). As in Proverbs 9:10 and Psalm 111:10 ("the fear of the ORD is the beginning of wisdom"), to "fear" the divine denotes nore than a sense of awe before the Almighty; it suggests a general

---

A Troublesome Translation

AΩ Much of this ancient poetic text is difficult to translate. For example, in this passage there are no active verbs or verbs of being except for those that are implied. The sampling of differing translations offered below helps to illustrate the difficulty. Parentheses or italics indicate words (usually verbs) that must be supplied:

(Author) "(He is) like the light of morning at sunrise,
(like) a morning without clouds
(when) from the rain (there comes) grass from the earth"

(NRSV) "like the light of morning,
like the sun rising on a cloudless morning,
gleaming from the rain on the grassy land.

(NASB) "Is as the light of the morning *when* the sun rises,
a morning without clouds,
When the tender grass *springs* out of the earth,
Through sunshine after rain."

(McCarter) "is like the light of a morning at sunrise,
a morning too bright for clouds,
when because of a rain there is verdure from the earth."

attitude of religious devotion that includes obedience to God's way
Such behavior is the foundation of a good king's just or righteou
(*ṣadîq*) reign.

The people's delight in this just king is characterized through a
extended metaphor in v. 4. The translation is troublesome, but th
general thrust is clear: the just king's rule is like a bright and cloud
less morning after rain, when the fields gleam with growth. [
Troublesome Translation] Thus, the king who reigns with justice bring
light, freshness, and increase to his people. The metaphor implies
kingdom characterized by peaceful productivity. The motif of a
nation's king as the sun of his people is also common in the roya
ideology of other ancient Near Eastern cultures, especially among
the Egyptians and the Hittites. [The Sun King]

The poet asserts that David's rule merits just such praise: "Is no
my house like this with God?" (v. 5a). The theme then moves to
God's "everlasting covenant" with David's house. Whether the
righteous reign *resulted from* the everlasting covenant, or whether
the everlasting covenant was a *reward for* David's just rule is left fo
the reader to judge. The implication is that the two are not unrelated. This everlasting covenant is almost certainly a reference to
2 Samuel 7, in which Yahweh promised David that he would
"establish the throne of his kingdom forever" (2 Sam 7:13;
cf. 7:16).

The phrase "everlasting covenant" (*běrît ʿôlam*) is not used elsewhere of the Davidic covenant, though it describes divine
covenants with Noah (Gen 9:16), with Abraham (Gen 17:7, 13,
19), with Jacob/Israel (1 Chr 16:17; Ps 105:10), and with the

---

The Sun King

The just king of vv. 3b-4 is described as one who brings morning light and rain-fresh growth to his people. This image does not identify the king as the sun *per se*, for it includes the whole scene of a bright new morning after rain on the fertile fields.

The "sun king" metaphor is rare in Hebrew literature, but Israel's neighbors made frequent and specific use of the solar image. For example, the king of the Hittites was commonly addressed by the title "Sun." A treaty between the Hittite king Mursilis and Duppi-Tessub of Amurru begins with "These are the words of the Sun Mursilis, the great king, the king of Hatti land." A reference to his victory over the Amurru says "And the Sun destroyed them." Later paragraphs begin with "When I, the Sun, sought after you" and "As I, the Sun, am loyal to you" (*ANET³*, 203-204).

In Egypt, the king was like a solar god who facilitated the growth and health of plants and humans alike. Kyle McCarter

noted the strong similarity of themes between the meta
of 2 Sam 23:3b-4 and a Middle Kingdom hymn to Amor
which addresses the king in the following manner:

The lord of rays, who makes brilliance . . .
Who extends his arms to him whom he loves,
(But) his enemy is consumed by a flame. (ANET³, 365
cited by McCarter, *II Samuel*, 484).

The Babylonians also employed the metaphor, as seen
the prologue to the famed Code of Hammurabi, which
predated David by at least eight centuries. There, the kin
said "to rise like the sun over the black-headed (people),
light up the land" ("black-headed people" was a descript
self-designation used by the Babylonians, referring to hai
color). Likewise, the king is "the sun of Babylon, who cau
light to go forth over the lands of Sumer and Akkad" (AN
164-65).

arth's population in general (Isa 24:5). It is also the subject of
rophetic promises (Isa 61:8; Jer 32:40; 50:5; Ezek 16:20; 37:26).
he concept of the Davidic covenant as an eternal arrangement
ppears, though in different words, in later literature (2 Chr 13:5;
1:7; Pss 89:19-37 [MT 89:20-38]; 132:12; Isa 55:3; Jer 33:17,
0-22).

Because David is a just king who has been granted an everlasting
ovenant with Yahweh, it follows that God will bring prosperity
nd security to his reign (v. 5c) so that it will truly be remembered
s a bright day after a refreshing rain.

Some writers regard v. 5 as a parenthesis since it precedes the
xpected negative contrast (vv. 6-7) to the positive promise of
v. 3b-4. A righteous ruler shines like the golden sun, but the god-
ess ones (or "evil men") are like worthless thorns deserving of
nstant immolation. "Godless" translates *bĕlîyaʿal*, which usually
neans "worthless" (1 Sam 1:16; 25:25; 30:22), but also may be
sed as a derogatory reference to residents of the underworld
2 Sam 16:7). Either meaning would be an appropriate designation
or the antithesis to the righteous ruler of vv. 3b-4.

The translation of vv. 6-7 is subject to some differences in inter-
retation, but none that are significant to the meaning. The just
ing brings light and life to the land, but the wicked are like thorns
hat are not only useless ("thorns that are thrown away") but
armful to life ("for they cannot be picked up with the hand / to
ouch them one uses an iron bar / or the shaft of a spear").

The precise identity of the wicked cannot be determined.
ypical wisdom poetry (cf. Ps 1; Jer 17:5-8) speaks in generalities:
the righteous" and "the wicked" are abstract constructs, not spe-
ific persons. Since 2 Samuel 23 identifies the positive person as a
ust king, namely David or a Davidic descendant, some scholars
magine that the evil men of vv. 6-7 should be identified as David's
wn enemies or as the northern kings who later stood juxtaposed
o the Davidic dynasty. Fortunately, the point of the comparison
oes not depend on the identity of the polar parties.

The fate of the wicked is destruction, here by incineration.
cholars have occasionally noted the thematic similarity between
2 Samuel 23:3b-7 and Malachi 4:1-3 (MT 3:19-21). [Similar Themes]
The major difference is that 2 Samuel 23 speaks to a particular,
resent situation, while Malachi's prophecy looks toward the judg-
nent-bringing "day of the LORD."

Similar Themes

Compare the thematic similarities between these disparate texts, largely in reverse order: the wicked are destroyed by burning, but those who fear God are blessed by the sun of righteousness.

2 Samuel 23:3b-7

3One who rules over people justly,
ruling in the fear of God,
4is like the light of morning,
like the sun rising on a cloudless morning,
gleaming from the rain on the grassy
land. 5Is not my house like this with God?
For he has made with me an everlasting
covenant,
ordered in all things and secure.
Will he not cause to prosper
all my help and my desire?
6But the godless are all like thorns that
are thrown away;
for they cannot be picked up with the
hand;
7to touch them one uses an iron bar
or the shaft of a spear.
And they are entirely consumed in fire on
the spot.

Malachi 4:1-3 (MT 3:19-21)

1See, the day is coming, burning like an
oven, when all the arrogant and all
evildoers will be stubble; the day that
comes shall burn them up, says the LORD
of hosts, so that it will leave them neither
root nor branch. 2But for you who revere
my name the sun of righteousness shall
rise, with healing in its wings. You shall
go out leaping like calves from the stall.
3And you shall tread down the wicked,
for they will be ashes under the soles of
your feet, on the day when I act, says the
LORD of hosts.

Few scholars have noticed, however, that one of Jesus' teachings also echoes the same themes. In explaining the parable of the weeds among the wheat (Matt 13:24-30),

37He answered, "The one who sows the good seed is the Son of Man; 38the field is the world, and the good seed are the children of the kingdom; the weeds are the children of the evil one, 39and the enemy who sowed them is the devil; the harvest is the end of the age, and the reapers are angels. 40Just as the weeds are collected and burned up with fire, so will it be at the end of the age. 41The Son of Man will send his angels, and they will collect out of his kingdom all causes of sin and all evildoers, 42and they will throw them into the furnace of fire, where there will be weeping and gnashing of teeth. 43Then the righteous will shine like the sun in the kingdom of their Father. Let anyone with ears listen!

Again, the same motifs are evident: the wicked are like useless weeds fit only for burning, but the righteous shine like the sun.

CONNECTIONS

David's Legacy, 23:1-3a

These verses are called "the last words of David," perhaps in hopes that they would be remembered as his legacy to those who followed him. The first verse reminds the reader that David had humble beginnings as the shepherd-boy son of Jesse from Bethlehem, but was anointed by God and raised up to sit on the throne of Israel by Yahweh's power, not his own. David owes everything to the LORD. Even these "last words of David" are in reality the words of Yahweh:

> *2 The spirit of the LORD speaks through me,*
> *his word is upon my tongue.*
> *3 The God of Israel has spoken,*
> *the Rock of Israel has said to me.*

Thus, both David's rise and the positive aspects of David's legacy are described as the gifts of God. So it is with all who acknowledge that our lives, our abilities, and even our opportunities should be perceived as the gifts of a loving and generous God. The preceding narrative has shown that David tarnished his reputation and left a dark shadow over his legacy because he chose to follow his own desires rather than trusting in Yahweh's continued leadership. As a result, any reader who knows David's story will take these "last words" with a large grain of salt. The wisdom saying represents the *ideal* king, not the *real* king that David was. David's failure to live up to his calling as the bright morning of Israel leaves the reader longing to find a truly just king who is not so impeachable. The Christian believer finds in Jesus Christ the one ruler who is truly righteous and worthy to be described by the metaphor that follows in vv. 3b-4.

David's identification as a prophet also brings to mind the person of Christ, because of the multiple roles they both played. David the king had taken on a priestly role in offering sacrifices to accompany the ark's introduction to Jerusalem (2 Sam 6:13). With the addition of the prophetic title to his résumé, David assumes the model aura of one who is prophet, priest, and king, roles later ascribed in hymnody to Jesus Christ.

[Prophet, Priest, and King]

Prophet, Priest, and King

The multiple roles fulfilled by Jesus are celebrated in v. 3 of the familiar hymn by Fanny J. Crosby, "Praise Him! Praise Him!":

Praise Him! praise Him! Jesus, our blessed Redeemer!
Heav'nly portals loud with hosannas ring!
Jesus, Savior, reigneth forever and ever;
Crown Him! crown Him! prophet and priest and King!

The Joy of a Just King, 23:3b-5

The likeness of the just king to the bright sun of morning calls to mind eschatological images of Christ as one who shines like (or brighter than) the sun (Matt 17:2; Acts 25:13; Rev 1:16; 10:1; 21:23). Jesus spoke of himself as "the light of the world" (John 8:12; 9:5), but also described his followers in the same way (Matt 5:14). Drawing on the very same motifs found in 2 Samuel 23:3b-7, Jesus described the coming judgment by insisting that the wicked were like useless weeds that were destined for burning, while "the righteous will shine like the sun" (Matt 13:43).

The metaphor also serves as a reminder that all people bearing leadership responsibilities face the same dichotomy expressed in the poem. Good leaders are like a beacon that brings both guidance and growth to their organizations or to the people who look to them for direction. Leaders who think only of themselves or who compromise their position with wrongdoing become worse than worthless. Not only do they fail to lead in the right direction, but they may actually bring harm to those who depend on them. They do not deserve to retain their leadership position.

People expect much of their leaders, and rightly so. The last three decades of the twentieth century saw leaders fall on every level, from county sheriff to television evangelist to President of the United States. In some way, injustice is done, people are hurt, and carefully constructed towers of power bite the dust. The shared shame of such public failures is not limited to the fallen leaders, for when people in authority abuse their position, they are not the only ones who suffer consequences.

Every person has the potential to be a leader on some level. The measure of our authority, however, is far less important than the measure of our faithfulness.

The Fate of the Wicked, 23:6-7

Old Testament texts such as 2 Samuel 23:6-7 and Malachi 4:1-3 (MT 3:19-21), along with Isaiah 66:24, probably played some role in the later development of the doctrine of hell as a place of damnation where punishment takes the form of fire. The concept is found in Jewish writings from the third century BC, which speak of places where evil spirits and the wicked dead are punished by fire (*1 En.* 18:11-16; 108:3-7, 15; 2 Esdr 7:36-38). Jesus exploited this commonly known concept by referring to a place where the wicked are punished by fire (Matt 3:10-12; 5:22; 7:19; 13:40-42, 50; 18:8-9; 25:41; plus parallels). Other New Testament writings echo the thought, including 2 Thessalonians 1:8; Hebrews 10:27; 2 Peter 3:7; Jude 7; Revelation 19:20; 20:14-15; 21:8.

For many Christians, a firm belief in a fiery place of torment is essential to proper faith, and Jesus' apparent endorsement of the doctrine seals the issue. If Jesus talked about a burning hell, the argument goes, then there must be a literal place of blazing punishment for the wicked. This view does not allow for the possibility that Jesus could have employed a familiar metaphor out of deference to a concept already held by most of his hearers. This is not the only New Testament witness concerning the afterlife of the unrighteous. The prospects of the wicked are also described in terms of a final death as opposed to eternal life (John 8:51-52; Rev 2:11, 20:6; 21:8), and as utter darkness (Matt 8:12; 22:13; 25:30; Jude 13).

The point, in every case, is that the wicked have no good future, by their own choice. The metaphor of fire offers up a mental image of how something might cease to exist by being reduced to ashes; it need not be considered any more than that. Eternal life is not a given, but a gift. Those who die in Christ are granted eternal life so that they *might not* perish (John 3:16). Those who choose to live in darkness *will.*

NOTE

[1] P. Kyle McCarter, *II Samuel* (AB 9; Garden City: Doubleday, 1984), 480-81.

DAVID'S MIGHTY MEN

23:8-39

COMMENTARY

This collection of military lists, like 21:15-21, adds color to the background in the editors' portrait of David. The martial exploits of these mighty men are memorable, in some instances outshining even David's reputation for courage in battle and consummate fighting skill. Nevertheless, they are incidental to the story of David's rise, and would have drawn attention away from David if mentioned earlier. Thus, they are relegated to the appendices, too important to omit but too distracting to be included earlier.

The larger text falls naturally into four sections. [A List of Lists] The impressive accomplishments of the "Three" are found in vv. 8-12, followed by the account of a courageous act of gallantry credited to three unnamed members of the "Thirty" (vv. 13-17). This is followed by an account detailing the fearless feats of Abishai and Benaiah (vv. 18-23) and a roster of the Thirty from early in David's career (vv. 24-39a). A confusing editorial comment concludes the chapter (v. 39b). Some scholars argue that vv. 13-17a are a poorly placed secondary insertion so that v. 17b should be regarded as a continuation of vv. 8-12. The same expression "the three warriors" occurs in both v. 16 and v. 17, however, suggesting that v. 17b concludes the account in vv. 13-17, rather than vv. 8-12.

The text, unfortunately, is not as straightforward as it seems. There are a number of difficulties, including many variants between 2 Samuel 23:8-39 and the Chronicler's expanded version in 1 Chronicles 11. Added to this there are textual difficulties relating to the pointing of a root word (*šlš*) that can mean three, thirty, or third, among other things. [Threes, Thirties, and Thirds] There are many textual difficulties, including discrepancies between the *Kethib* (a scribal note

> **A List of Lists**
> Here is a brief outline of 23:8-39:
> I. Heroic Acts of the Three (v. 8-12)
> II. A Gallant Deed by Three Members of the Thirty (v. 13-17)
> III. The Prowess of Abishai and Benaiah (v. 18-23)
> IV. A Roster of the Thirty (v. 24-39a)

Threes, Thirties, and Thirds

AΩ The variant pointings and spellings are illustrated by the following table (keep in mind that the original text had no vowel points, only the consonants, leaving some words open to question):

Spelling/pointing	Meaning	Appears in 2 Sam 23:8-39 at:
šālôš, šĕlōšâ	three	23:9 (*bišĕlōšâ*, "among the three")
		23:13 (*šĕlōšâ*, "three")
		23:16 (*šĕlōšet*, "three of")
		23:17 (*šĕlōšet*, "three of")
		23:18 (*haššĕlōšâ*, usually read as "the thirty")
		23:18 (*ʿal-šĕlōš mēʾôt*, "over three hundred")
		23:18 (*baššĕlōšâ*, "in" or "by the three")
		23:19 (*min-haššĕlōšâ*, "of the three," often emended to "of the thirty")
		23:19 (*šĕlōšâ*, "three")
		23:23 (*ʾel-haššĕlōšâ*, "to the three")
šĕlîšî, šĕlīšî	third	23:13 (*mēhaššĕlīšîm*, but usually read as "from the thirty")
šĕlōšîm	thirty	23:23 (*min-haššĕlīšîm*, "among the thirty")
		23:24 (*baššĕlōšîm*, "among the thirty")
		23:39 (*šĕlōšîm wĕšibʿâ*, "thirty-seven")
šālîš, plural *šālîšîm*	third man in a chariot, adjutant, officer	23:8 (*haššūlīšî*, usually emended to "the Three")

indicating "what is written") and the *Qere* (a note that an alternate spelling or pointing should be read).

Some scholars view this text as little more than a collection of archaic hero stories that have become attached to David's story. Others find in it a key to understanding how David's military hierarchy was structured. At the heart of the debate is whether we are to imagine an informal group of thirty warriors, an administrative cadre of select officers, or something else entirely. [Who Were the Three and the Thirty?]

The immediate question that comes to mind is this: "Where is *Joab?*" Joab, David's close kinsman and loyal supporter, frequently appears in the larger narrative as David's foremost military leader. His name occurs no less than 96 times in 2 Samuel, but appears in this list of heroes only as the brother of Abishai (23:18) and Asahel (23:24), and as the man for whom Naharai of Beeroth served as armor bearer (23:37). Since Joab is so conspicuous elsewhere and is

Who Were the Three and the Thirty?

Here are three suggested interpretations:

he most popular interpretation posits two groups of
surrounding David: the Three and the Thirty. The
Josheb-basshebeth, Eleazar, and Shammah; 2 Sam
) were the highest-ranking officers, and the Thirty
23:24-39) were of lesser rank. The fact that more
rty warriors are listed is testimony to the fluid nature
roup, which was subject to change as soldiers died
e or retired from active service.

seems to be the approach taken by the NRSV, NIV,
d NEB. Kurt Elliger was an early proponent of the
n ("Die dreissig Helden Davids," *Palästina-Jahrbuch*
35): 29-75), and has been followed by many
uent scholars, including Hertzberg (*1 and 2 Samuel*,
McCarter (*II Samuel*, 499-501), and Bright (*A History of*
207).

Another view holds that there was no such institution
Thirty and that the lists in 2 Sam 23 and 1 Chr 11
be regarded as a record of David's officer corps, the
. Nadav Na'aman argued that *šālîšîm* originally
ed in 2 Sam 23:8, 13, 19a, 23, and 24, rather than

šělîšîm ("The List of David's Officers [*salasim*]," *VT* 38
[January 1988]:71- 79). The term, he argued, always refers
to a military officer and should be translated as captain,
lieutenant, or adjutant. Josheb-basshebeth is to be
understood as chief of the officers, followed by Eleazar,
Shammah, and Abishai, each of whom commanded a sub-
unit of soldiers. Benaiah, commander of the king's royal
bodyguard is named next, followed by the rest of the
officers.

(3) Most recently, Donald Schley proposed an alternate
understanding of the term *šālîšîm*, arguing that they were
the special forces units of ancient Israel—three-man squads
of elite warriors who carried out special assignments for the
king and answered directly to him ("The *Salisim*: Officers or
Special Three-Man Squads?" *VT* 40 [July 1990]: 321-26).
The exploits of one such team are narrated in 2 Sam 23:13-
17 (compare 2 Kgs 9:25 and 10:25 for other examples).
Thus, the names in 2 Sam 23:24-39 include the men who
had served at some point on a three-man commando unit,
with no apparent attempt to categorize them into specific
teams.

---

he subject of several stories, it appears that the reader should
nderstand it as a given that Joab was chief of the armed forces.
The fact that other people are identified by their relationship to
oab proves that he could not have been forgotten. Above the
Three (Josheb-basshebeth, Eleazar, Shammah),
he Two (Abishai and Benaiah), and the Thirty,
23:24-39) was the One: Joab.

Heroic Acts of the Three, 23:8-12

"These are the names of the warriors whom
David had" introduces not only the Three, but
also the other lists that follow. The first of the
Three is Josheb-basshebeth, who appears only
here and in 1 Chronicles 11:11, where he is
called "Jashobeam." His real name may have
been Yeshbaal, as preserved in the LXX^L.
[Problematic Pagan Names] The patronymic "a
Tahchemonite" may be an error for
"Hachmonite"; the witnesses preserve several
variants. According to 1 Chronicles 11:11 and
27:2, he was the son of Zabdiel, a descendant of
Perez, and also the officer in charge of the first

Problematic Pagan Names

AΩ The name Josheb-basshebeth is so
strange that it begs for some
explanation. In 1 Chr 11:11, the same man is
called Jashobeam, while the LXX^L preserves what
may be the original, *iesbaal*, which in Hebrew
would be *yešba'al*, meaning "Baal exists." As
with Saul's son Ishbaal ("Man of Baal"), whose
name was piously corrected to
"Ishbosheth"("Man of Shame") (see [Ishvi,
Ishbaal, Eshbaal, or Ishbosheth?] at 2 Sam 2:8),
Yeshbaal's name might have been subject to a
scribal change to *yešbōšet* (Yeshbosheth), which
suffered textual corruption, resulting in the
ungainly moniker Josheb-basshebeth.

As noted in previous discussions dealing with
similar name changes, it is entirely possible that
Yeshbaal's family worshiped the Canaanite Ba'al,
but also conceivable that the title Ba'al was an
accepted designation for Yahweh during that
period.

The Chronicler's Twelve Divisions

According to 1 Chr 27, David's military forces were organized into twelve divisions of 24,000 troops, each assigned to active duty one month of the year, and commanded by a single officer. These officers also appear in the list of warriors found in 2 Sam 23 but with no hint of the Chronicler's divisions, and in a different order.

The officers in charge of the twelve divisions, by month, are listed as:
1. Jashobeam, son of Zabdiel (v. 2; 2 Sam 23:8)
2. Dodai the Ahohite (v. 4; 2 Sam 23:9-10 [Dodo, son of Ahohi])
3. Benaiah, son of the priest Jehoiada (v. 5; 2 Sam 23:20-23)
4. Asahel, brother of Joab (v. 7; 2 Sam 23:24a)
5. Shamhuth the Izrahite (v. 8; not listed in 2 Sam 23, unless corrupted from Shammah of Harad, 2 Sam 23:25a)
6. Ira, son of Ikkesh the Tekoite (v. 9; 2 Sam 23:26b)
7. Helez the Pelonite (v. 10; 2 Sam 23:26a)
8. Sibbecai the Hushathite (v. 11; 2 Sam 23:27b, if "Mebunnai" is an error for Sibbecai)
9. Abiezer of Anathoth (v. 12; 2 Sam 23:27a)
10. Maharai of Netophah (v. 13; 2 Sam 23:28b)
11. Benaiah of Pirathon (v. 14; 2 Sam 23:30a)
12. Heldai the Netophathite (v. 15; probably original for "Heleb" in 2 Sam 23:29a)

month's division of David's army, according to the Chronicler's scheme. [The Chronicler's Twelve Divisions]

Why Josheb-basshebeth should be considered "chief of the Three" is unstated, unless it is because his memorable act of heroism involved the most enemies slain in a single encounter. Reportedly, "when he was chief of the Three; he wielded his spear against eight hundred whom he killed at one time." The translation "wielded his spear" is actually adopted from the version in 1 Chronicles 11:11 because the MT is garbled at this point in 2 Samuel 23:8. Some translators have found in the MT's difficult string of consonants another proper name ("Adeno the Eznite" [KJV, NASB, NJPS]), usually rendering it as an alternate name for Josheb-basshebeth, then adding the Chronicler's note that he "brandished his spear" against the eight hundred.

No context or clue is given to identify the incompetent enemies who apparently threw themselves on Josheb-basshebeth's spear. The text implies that he killed all 800 single-handedly, and on a single occasion, but most commentators presume that the number is exaggerated or that he was assisted by the troop under his command. The lack of evidence precludes a firm judgment, but the general thrust of these stories seems to be focused on personal heroism through single combat. Whether a modern reader chooses to believe it or not, the ancient author credited Josheb-basshebeth with 800 kills in one battle. The parallel text in 1 Chronicles 11:11 gives the number as 300; Josephus remembered it as 900.[1] This is

ot the highest number attributed to an Israelite hero; Samson was
eputed to have slain 1,000 Philistines with the jawbone of an ass
1 a single encounter (Judg 15:9-19).

Eleazar, son of Dodo, son of Ahohi, is listed second among the
'hree. [The Ahohite] His exploits are clearly associated with the
'hilistine wars, perhaps preceding 2 Samuel 5. The MT provides
10 location for Eleazar's exploits, but 1 Chronicles 11:13 says it was
t Pas-dammim, a reading also preserved in the
XX^L. It is quite possible that the place name
ell out of the MT in the transmission process,
possibly by haplography, when the scribe's eye
kipped from the first occurrence of
'Philistines" to the second. Pas-dammim is
probably to be identified with the Ephes-
lammim of 1 Samuel 17:1, the site of David's memorable
confrontation with Goliath, when both Israel and the Philistines
vere also "gathered there for battle."

> **The Ahohite**
>
> The MT's "son of Ahohi" is "the Ahohite"
> in 1 Chr 11:12. Apparently this identifies
> him as a member of the Ahohite clan, descended
> from Ahoah, the son of Benjamin's oldest son
> Bela (1 Chr 8:4). One of the Thirty, named Zalmon,
> was also called an Ahohite (2 Sam 23:28).

Eleazar is credited with standing alone when his fellow soldiers
fell back, smiting Philistines until his sword arm cramped and he
could no longer stretch his fingers to release his weapon. The
NRSV says he fought "until his arm grew weary, though his hand
clung to the sword" (v. 10). The translation "arm" and the addition
of "though" are attempts to make better sense of the text, which literally says "until his *hand* grew weary and his hand stuck (or clung)
to the sword." These changes are unnecessary, however. Anyone
who has operated a chain saw or swung a hammer for any significant length of time knows what it is to have such cramps in one's
"business hand" that the fingers must be pried away from the tool.

The narrative insists that Eleazar's compatriots eventually
returned, but not to his aid. They ventured back to the field only to
strip the dead and profit from a battle they did not fight. The
theme of one man standing alone against overwhelming odds while
the army of Israel cringed in the background is reminiscent of
1 Samuel 17, when David reportedly stood against Goliath in the
same place.

The comment that "the LORD brought about a great victory that
day" (v. 11) is almost certainly an editorial insertion to the original,
archival text. It is no less accurate for that, however. Eleazar's feats
in the fields of Pas-dammim are no less impressive than David's,
which were also attributed to the power of Yahweh.

The third member of the Three was Shammah, the son of Agee,
a Hararite. Some scholars identify the Hararites with an obscure
city named *a-ra-ru*, one of several cities in the Golan that rebelled

against the Egyptian king Akhenaton[2], while others imagine a connection with the Transjordanian city of Aroer (2 Sam 24:5), and yet others see in the Hararites a clan not known from other sources.

Shammah's heroics also involved the Philistines, and would have taken place before David became king, or early in his reign. Lehi is the same place mentioned in Judges 15:9-19, where Samson reportedly was surprised by the Philistines and responded by killing 1,000 of them with an impromptu weapon, the jawbone of a skeletal ass. The parallel version in 1 Chronicles 11:13-14 is there confused with Eleazar's mighty deeds, and Shammah is not mentioned by name.

Shammah also distinguished himself through single combat against overwhelming odds. Shammah's devotion was such that he risked his life to defend nothing more than a plot of ground sown in lentils (1 Chr 11:13 says it was barley). [Lentils] As with Eleazar, his fellow soldiers (lit., "the people") fled, but he bravely fought on so that once again the editors could add "and the LORD brought about a great victory" (v. 12).

> **Lentils**
>
> Lentils were a common crop in the ancient Near East. Lentils belong to the family of legumes, and their characteristic lens-shaped seeds gave rise to the scientific name *Lens culinaris*. The nutritious seeds could be used as the base for a red soup or stew (Gen 25:29-34). According to Ezek 4:9, lentils could also be ground into flour and used for baking bread. Lentils, along with other legumes such as beans, were among the provisions brought to David and his entourage when he fled Jerusalem in the face of Absalom's revolt (2 Sam 17:28).

A Gallant Deed by Three Members of the Thirty, 23:13-17

The devoted trio whose valiant service to David is described in vv. 13-17 are identified only as members of the Thirty (v. 13). In the MT, as reflected in the NRSV, the word for "head" or "chief" is added to the number thirty, resulting in translations such as "the thirty chiefs." This is one bit of evidence for the theory that the Thirty were leading officers in David's military administration.

This story appears to be set long before David became king, when he was still on the run from Saul and using the fortress-cave at Adullam as his base of operations (1 Sam 22:1). Adullam (also mentioned in Josh 15:33-35 and 2 Chr 11:7) was about sixteen miles southeast of Jerusalem. The beginning of harvest time is typically a dry season, conducive to military field campaigns. The text does not suggest that David's men and the Philistines were engaged in active combat—only that the Philistines were encamped between David's stronghold and his hometown of Bethlehem.

David and his men were almost certainly not without water. David was a shrewd military commander and would hardly have chosen a site without access to water for his headquarters. The water, however, may have been collected during rare rains and kept

ter Storage

Towns or villages having no natural springs nearby often collected rainwater during
equent showers, sometimes by means of an
enious network of gutters. Public cisterns could
huge underground affairs containing millions of
ons, as in the temple area of Jerusalem, and at
giddo. Private homes also had smaller cisterns
structed to meet the needs of families (2 Kgs
31; Prov 5:15; Isa 36:16); these are frequently
nd in archaeological excavations. Water was
wn by using a pottery jar attached to a length of
e.
Smaller cisterns were usually pear- or bottle-
ped, with an elongated neck and a small

The Cistern in Shiloh. Shiloh, Israel. (Credit: Erich Lessing/Art Resource, NY)

ening at the top that could be sealed to reduce evaporation, prevent unauthorized use, and ward against accidental falls
od 21:33-34). The inner walls were sealed with limestone plaster to prevent the water from seeping away into the
ous stone from which the cisterns were carved. Jeremiah spoke of Israel's spiritual desolation by the metaphor of a
cked cistern that could hold no water (Jer 2:13) or a cistern that was dry for lack of rain (Jer 14:3).
Both Joseph (Gen 37:22) and Jeremiah (Jer 38:6-13) were imprisoned in pits such as these, for their depth and shape
vented escape without outside help. Cisterns occasionally needed to be cleaned of collected mud in the bottom, and
eir plaster walls needed periodic replenishment. In such cases, access was gained by means of a rope and one or more
mpanions above ground.

in cisterns, causing it to be brackish. [Water Storage] Thus, David's spoken desire for a drink from the well by the gate at Bethlehem probably was prompted more by nostalgia for the good-tasting water of Bethlehem's well than by real thirst.

The story suggests a time when David had few of the trappings of officialdom. He lived a life in close contact with his men and was willing to share even his inner longings with them. For David's retainers, who were fiercely loyal to him, the leader's wish was their command. At great risk to themselves, they "broke through" the Philistine cordon, a description that implies more than a secretive slipping through the lines. Having drawn attention to themselves, they attained the well, drew water, and then made their way back through the Philistine gauntlet to David, bringing the water he had longed for (v. 16a).

David's response is one that puzzles the casual reader and amazes the careful student; he poured the hard-won water onto the ground! A surface reading suggests that David's action was ungrateful, rendering his men's valiant efforts meaningless. A deeper examination, however, reveals that David's action consecrated the soldiers' feat as nothing less than sacred before God. Knowing that his warriors had imperiled their lives and risked the shedding of their blood to obtain the precious liquid, David identified the water they brought with the very blood they chanced in order to gain it: "Can I drink the blood of the men who went at the risk of their lives?" (v. 17). As such, it could not be drunk by humans, for blood was holy and belonged only to God. The sacramental act of pouring blood upon the ground was a means of offering it to God, as Israel's religious laws required (Lev 17:10-13; Deut 12:23-24).

The three warriors may not have understood David's actions immediately. The text says nothing about their reaction to David's words and deeds. In time, however, they would have realized the special nature of the moment. Their accomplishment was more than a military errand; it was a daring quest growing from love rather than necessity. To use the metaphor of another age, the men left as common soldiers, but returned as knights. It was this deed that earned the men a lasting place on the royal list of David's heroes.

The Prowess of Abishai and Benaiah, 23:18-23

Abishai and Benaiah appear in an unusual position. They are beside the Three, but not equal to them (vv. 19, 23)—among the Thirty, but listed separately from them. The story of both men follows a similar pattern: the narrator describes their exploits, notes their renown among the Thirty, names their specific command, and comments that despite all this, they did not achieve the same status as the Three.

Abishai is well known as the brother of Joab and cousin of David, a stalwart supporter who seemed to believe that the solution to most political problems was a well-placed blade (cf. 1 Sam 26:8; 2 Sam 3:30; 16:9; 19:21). Abishai commanded large segments of David's army during the Ammonite/Aramaean wars (2 Sam 10:10, 14) and during the revolts of Absalom (2 Sam 18:2) and Sheba (2 Sam 20:6).

The present text recounts a battle in which Abishai reportedly killed 300 of the enemy (v. 18). The text does not specify that all 300 fell in a single battle, but the context (cf. v. 8) implies it. Abishai's exploits won him honor above the Thirty, and he is called their commander (v. 19).

Benaiah is also known from other contexts. According to 2 Samuel 8:18 and 20:23, he commanded the Cherethites and the Pelethites, a mercenary army drawn from troops who were probably related to the Philistines. During the power struggles of

muel 23:18—Abishai, the brother of Joab, was one of David's most valorous supporters.
ve Doré (1832–83). *Abishai Saves the Life of David* from the *Illustrated Bible*. 19th century. Engraving.
t: Dover Pictoral Archive Series)

David's last days, Benaiah wisely sided with David's son Solomon (as opposed to Joab, who supported Adonijah; see 1 Kgs 1). After Solomon attained the throne, Benaiah became his chief executioner and military aide (1 Kgs 2).

The list of David's heroes provides additional information about Benaiah, "a valiant warror from Kabzeel." Kabzeel is mentioned in Joshua 15:21 as a town belonging to the tribe of Judah. It was located in the extreme south, in the vicinity of Beer-sheba, the traditional southern boundary of Israel. Benaiah is called "a doer of great deeds." A literal translation would be "of great doings." Some would read the phrase to mean "chief of the workers" (that is, the forced labor). The grammar would allow this interpretation, but the context does not. The emphasis is on Benaiah's great deeds, some of which are listed.

The deeds themselves contain more than one puzzle. According to the MT, he smote "two *Ariel* of Moab." The word *'ări'ēl* is apparently compounded of the words for "lion" (*'ări*) and for "god" (*'ēl*). The result could mean "lion of God," "mighty lion," or possibly "lionlike man." It is also possible that "Ariel" is a proper name. The NRSV, NASB, and others assume that "sons" has fallen out. Benaiah killed two sons of Ariel, who presumably would have been known to ancient readers. The KJV says he killed "two lionlike men of Moab." The RSV makes no attempt to translate rendering the phrase as "he smote two ariels of Moab" and leaving the reader to wonder what an "ariel" might be. The NIV's "two of Moab's best men" is unquestioned by some writers[3].

The lion motif is also present in the second deed, which may have led to some confusion in the first. Benaiah reportedly ventured into a pit to face a lion on a memorable, snowy day and was victorious (v. 20).

Benaiah's defeat of an Egyptian champion also contains troublesome elements. In describing the Egyptian, the NRSV follows the MT: "a handsome man" translates a phrase meaning "a man of appearance," which is probably corrupted from an original word meaning "giant," as in 1 Chronicles 11:23. Or one can imagine that "a man of appearance" implies an imposing figure. The emphasis, in any case, is upon the Egyptian's apparent military might, not his finely cut features. 2 Samuel 23:20 mentions the Egyptian's spear only as a foil for Benaiah's staff, but 2 Chronicles 11:23 adds "like a weaver's beam" (cf. 1 Sam 17:7; 2 Sam 21:19). The point of the story is that Benaiah appeared to be overmatched and underarmed, but he valiantly strode into the fray and surprised everyone by defeating an apparently superior opponent.

As with Abishai, the narrator notes that Benaiah had greater renown than the Thirty, and was compared to the Three, but not included among them. As mentioned above, David appointed Benaiah as chief of his royal bodyguard, the mercenary Cherethites and Pelethites. The reader may notice that greater attention is given to Benaiah than the other heroes, and more specific exploits are recorded. At least one scholar took this emphatic treatment of Benaiah as a clue that the archive was first composed during the reign of Solomon, when Benaiah was the chief military commander.[4]

A Roster of the Thirty, 23:24-39a

The remainder of the Thirty are listed by name and lineage, gener-ally with no other comment. The reader will note that those listed early in the list (including those already named) are uniformly from the south, beginning near Bethlehem and spreading outward. This suggests that people attached themselves to David over a long period of time, reflecting his growing influence in far-ranging parts of the kingdom and beyond. The list is also given in the Chronicler's record, with a variety of differences in the names included and their spellings. [A Convenient Comparison]

The inclusion of Asahel (v. 24a) suggests that the list could not postdate David's transition from king of Judah to king of all Israel, for Asahel died during that period. The geographic evidence implies, however, that the list grew over time. It includes more than thirty names, suggesting that new heroes were added as others died or retired. Like Abishai, Asahel was a brother of Joab and close kinsman of David. He was renowned for his swiftness and tena-ciousness, both of which contributed to his death (2 Sam 2:18-23).

Elhanan, son of Dodo of Bethlehem (v. 24b), is probably to be identified with the Elhanan of 2 Samuel 21:19, who is credited with killing a giant named Goliath (see discussion at that point). There he is called a Jearite.

Shammah (v. 25a) may be another name for Shamhuth the Izrahite, mentioned in 1 Chronicles 27:8. Like Elika (v. 25b), he is from an obscure place called Harod. Some have associated this location with the Spring of Harod near Jezreel (Judg 7:1), but the modern consensus is that it points to a village a few miles southeast of Jerusalem, near Bethlehem. Now called Khirbet el-Ḥarēdān, it was known as Beth Harudu in Roman times. Elika does not appear in the Chronicler's list where it would be expected at 1 Chronicles 11:27. He is probably the victim of an inadvertent scribal omission.

Helez the Paltite (v. 26a) may have been from Beth-pelet, far in the south of Judah, near Beer-sheba. The Paltites were named for Pelet (1 Chr 2:47), a descendant of Caleb.

Ira, son of Ikkesh (v. 26b), was from Tekoa, the same tiny agri-cultural village which gave rise to the wise woman who confronted David (2 Sam 14) and which sheltered the prophet Amos for at least part of his life (Amos 1:1).

Anathoth was the home of Abiezer (v. 27a), as it was of the prophet Jeremiah (Jer 1:1). Anathoth was located about three miles northeast of Jerusalem in the territory of Benjamin, and was desig-nated as a priestly city (Josh 21:18). After the high priest Abiathar

A Convenient Comparison

The wide disparity between the Chronicler's list and that in 2 Sam 23 reveals the difficulty of accurately preserv[ing] ancient documents, even official archives.

2 Samuel 23:24-39	*1 Chronicles 11:26-47*
24Among the Thirty were	26The warriors of the armies were
Asahel brother of Joab;	Asahel brother of Joab,
Elhanan son of Dodo of Bethlehem;	Elhanan son of Dodo of Bethlehem,
25Shammah of Harod;	27Shammoth of Harod,
Elika of Harod;	Helez the Pelonite,
26Helez the Paltite;	28Ira son of Ikkesh of Tekoa,
Ira son of Ikkesh of Tekoa;	Abiezer of Anathoth,
27Abiezer of Anathoth;	29Sibbecai the Hushathite,
Mebunnai the Hushathite;	Ilai the Ahohite,
28Zalmon the Ahohite;	30Maharai of Netophah,
Maharai of Netophah;	Heled son of Baanah of Netophah,
29Heleb son of Baanah of Netophah;	31Ithai son of Ribai of Gibeah of the Benjaminites,
Ittai son of Ribai of Gibeah of the Benjaminites;	Benaiah of Pirathon,
30Benaiah of Pirathon;	32Hurai of the wadis of Gaash,
Hiddai of the torrents of Gaash;	Abiel the Arbathite,
31Abi-albon the Arbathite;	33Azmaveth of Baharum,
Azmaveth of Bahurim;	Eliahba of Shaalbon,
32Eliahba of Shaalbon;	34Hashem the Gizonite,
the sons of Jashen:	Jonathan son of Shagee the Hararite,
Jonathan 33son of Shammah the Hararite; Ahiam son of	35Ahiam son of Sachar the Hararite,
Sharar the Hararite;	Eliphal son of Ur,
34Eliphelet son of Ahasbai of Maacah;	36Hepher the Mecherathite,
Eliam son of Ahithophel the Gilonite;	Ahijah the Pelonite,
35Hezro of Carmel;	37Hezro of Carmel,
Paarai the Arbite;	Naarai son of Ezbai,
36Igal son of Nathan of Zobah;	38Joel the brother of Nathan,
Bani the Gadite;	Mibhar son of Hagri,
37Zelek the Ammonite;	39Zelek the Ammonite,
Naharai of Beeroth, the armor-bearer of Joab son of	Naharai of Beeroth, the armor-bearer of Joab son of
Zeruiah;	Zeruiah,
38Ira the Ithrite;	40Ira the Ithrite,
Gareb the Ithrite;	Gareb the Ithrite,
39Uriah the Hittite:	41Uriah the Hittite,
thirty-seven in all.	Zabad son of Ahlai,
	42Adina son of Shiza the Reubenite, a leader of the
	Reubenites, and thirty with him,
	43Hanan son of Maacah,
	and Joshaphat the Mithnite,
	44Uzzia the Ashterathite,
	Shama and Jeiel sons of Hotham the Aroerite, 45Jediael
	son of Shimri,
	and his brother Joha the Tizite,
	46Eliel the Mahavite,
	and Jeribai and Joshaviah sons of Elnaam,
	and Ithmah the Moabite,
	47Eliel, and Obed,
	and Jaasiel the Mezobaite.

pported Solomon's rival Adonijah in his bid for the throne, the
ccessful Solomon banished Abiathar to the city of Anathoth.

As mentioned in conjunction with 2 Samuel 21:18, Mebunnai
e Hushathite (v. 27b) is probably to be identified with Sibbecai,
ho slew the warrior Saph, reportedly descended from the giants.
Chronicles 27:11 places him in the clan that traced its descent to
erah, one of the sons of Judah (Num 26:20; 1 Chr 2:6). Husha
nodern Ḥûsān) is just southwest of Bethlehem.

Zalmon (v. 28a), like Eleazar (23:9), is called an Ahohite, prob-
bly indicating descent from Ahoah, a grandson of Benjamin
1 Chr 8:4; see [The Ahohite] at v. 9).

Netophah, the home of Maharai (v. 28b) and Heleb, son of
aanah (v. 29a), was most likely not far from Bethlehem, to the
outheast. A spring there retains the name ʿAin en-Nāṭûf. Kyle
IcCarter argued that Heleb is a graphically confused version of
Heldai," who was a descendant of the judge Othniel (1 Chr 4:13;
f. Josh 15:15-19; Judg 1:11-15; 2:7-11) and who had charge of
David's military division during the twelfth month (1 Chr
:7:27:15).[5]

Ittai's identity is given in more detail than most (v. 29b). Perhaps
he emphatic note that he was "son of Ribai of Gibeah of the
Benjaminites" was intended to set him apart from Ittai the Gittite,
vho led a band of mercenaries from Gath in support of David
2 Sam 15:19-23; 18:2). It may also be a clue that the list of heroes
s about to venture away from David's homeland, for the next warrior cited is from Ephraim.

Benaiah of Pirathon (v. 30a) should not be confused with the
more famous Benaiah of Kabzeel (vv. 20-23). Pirathon was located
within the tribal boundaries of Ephraim, about thirty miles north
of Jerusalem. It was the home of Abdon, one of the so-called
"minor" judges (Judg 12:13-15).

The "torrents of Gaash" must have been close to Mount Gaash,
about fifteen miles northwest of Jerusalem and a similar distance
southwest of Shechem. This was the home of Hiddai (v. 30b). The
translation "torrents" is unfortunate, as it suggests a permanent
waterfall, which is unlikely. The Hebrew word means "wadis," normally dry valleys that channel "torrents" of water only after the
seasonal rains.

Abi-albon the Arbathite may reflect a corruption of an original
that read "Abial the Beth-arabathite."[6] Some of the Greek texts
have "Abiēl son of the Arabathite." The name Abi-albon makes
little sense, but the other options would mean "My father is ʾal " or
"My father is ʾel." Both ʾal (meaning "the high one") and ʾel

(generic for "god") could be used as divine appellatives. The tow
of Beth-arabah is mentioned in Joshua 15:6 and 18:18 as a tow
on the border between Judah and Benjamin.

Azmaveth's unusual name (v. 31b) means "death is strong." Som
writers surmise that the reference is to a god named death (*Mot*), a
with "Ahimot" in 1 Chronicles 6:10. Bahurim was just north o
Jerusalem, on the road David traveled when he retreated befor
Absalom (2 Sam 16:5). Shimei, who cursed David, was also from
the Benjaminite city of Bahurim.

Eliahba ('*elyaĕbâ*, v. 32a) was from Shaalbon, probably identica
to the Shaalbim of Judges 1:35 and 1 Kings 4:19 and the Shaalbi
of Joshua 19:41-42. It was probably about sixteen miles wes
northwest of Jerusalem, near Gezer. Eliahba may mean "Goo
hides."

The latter part of v. 32 is probably corrupt and has led to much
discussion. The NRSV's translation is a literal rendering of the sur
viving Hebrew text: "the sons of Jashen: Jonathan." The
consonantal form of the phrase "son of" (*bny*) is identical to the
last three letters of "the Shaalbonite" and may have been inadvertently copied twice (dittography). If this is the case, Jashen i
missing a patronymic, which some scholars supply from the parallel text in 1 Chronicles 11:34, where Jashen is called "the
Gizonite." Translations that follow the MT must assume that "sons
of Jashen" was a sort of title, as in 1 Chronicles 11:34, where a
slight consonantal change renders "sons of the name," a reference
to men who had made a name for themselves. If this is the proper
interpretation, the beginning of the notable list is evident, but there
is no way to determine where the roster ends.

Jonathan (v. 32b) was the son of Shammah the Hararite (v. 33a),
who is called Shagee in 1 Chronicles 11:34. The Chronicler's
spelling is probably a corrupt form of "Shammah son of Agee."
Jonathan's father should probably be understood as the Shammah,
son of Agee the Hararite, who was one of the Three. His exploits
are detailed in vv. 11-12 (see discussion of "Hararite" at that point).
Ahiam, son of Sharar (v. 33b), was also called a Hararite, though
the text may be confused; the LXX has "the Urite."

Eliphelet, son of Ahasbai (v. 34a), was either from a place named
Maacah or descended from the clan of Maacah. In the MT he is
called a "Macaathite." This probably does not refer to the small
kingdom of Maacah, the Aramaean home of Absalom's mother
(2 Sam 10:6), or to the northern town of Beth-Maacah (2 Sam
20:14-15), but to the Macaathite clan who lived in southern Judah,
probably near Hebron (1 Chr 4:19).

Eliam, son of Ahithophel the Gilonite (v. 34b), was almost certainly the son of David's counselor who deserted him in favor of Absalom (15:12, 31; 16:20-17:4; 17:23). Some have speculated that Eliam might also be the father of Bathsheba, who is called "the daughter of Eliam" in 2 Samuel 11:3.

Hezro of Carmel (v. 35a), like David's wife Abigail (1 Sam 25), was a Judahite from the southern city of Carmel, which was located several miles south southeast of Hebron. The more renowned Carmel, located on the northern coast of Palestine, is a far less likely candidate.

Paari (v. 35b) may have been an Arbite (MT) or an Archite (some Hebrew manuscripts, LXX). 1 Chronicles 11:37 has confused both his name and the patronymic, reading "Naarai son of Ezbai." The Arbites are otherwise unknown; the Archite clan occupied an area south of Bethel in the territory of Benjamin. David's faithful counselor Hushai was also an Archite (2 Sam 15:32).

Zobah, cited as the home of Igal the son of Nathan (v. 36a), may refer to the Aramaean kingdom whose conflicts with Israel are recorded in 2 Samuel 8:3 and 10:6-14. McCarter, however, judged that the text is corrupt at several points. Instead of "from Zobah, Bani the Gadite," he read "commander of the army of the Hagrites."[7] Since the Hagrites were a nomadic population living east of the Jordan, McCarter presumed that Igal was the leader of a band of mercenaries much like that of Ittai and the Gittites who followed him (2 Sam 15:3).

Whether Bani the Gadite (v. 36b) was a man to be counted among the Thirty or a reference to the "sons of Hagri" depends on the accuracy of McCarter's reconstruction. The consonants in "Bani" usually mean "son(s) of," but the name Bani is fairly common in biblical Hebrew (see 1 Chr 6:46; 9:4; Ezra 2:10; 8:10; 10:29, 34; Neh 3:17).

The appearance of Zelek the Ammonite (v. 37a) is most unusual, given the intense hostility between David and the Ammonites following the accession of Hanun (2 Sam 10:1-14; 12:26-31). Perhaps Zelek came into David's service during the reign of Nahash, when friendlier relations persisted (2 Sam 10:2).

Naharai of Beeroth (v. 37b) was from the same town mentioned in 2 Samuel 4:2-3 as the home of the sons of Rimmon, who had led raiding parties in the service of Saul. They sought to curry favor with David by bringing him Ishbaal's head, with disastrous results for their own heads (2 Sam 4:5-12). Beeroth was a Benjaminite town whose Hebrew spelling (but not location) is identical to modern Beirut. Naharai is named as the armor bearer of Joab, son of Zeruaiah. This is striking since Joab himself does not appear anywhere in the lists of David's heroes. Apparently Joab's fame was such that he stood above even the Three and the Thirty and so was not included among them.

Ira and Gareb (v. 38) are both called Ithrites. Their home may have been Kiriath-jearim, for in 1 Chronicles 2:53 the Ithrites were listed first among the leading families of that city. Along with the other clans listed in 1 Chronicles 2:53, the Ithrites were indigenous to the area before the Israelites appeared. Some scholars propose that they, like the people of Beeroth, were descended from the Hivites.

The final name on the list is devastating to the memory of David. The last named of his mighty men—probably listed there for greater emphasis—was Uriah the Hittite, the unfortunate husband of Bathsheba (v. 39a; 2 Sam 11). It is a not-so-subtle reminder that David was fortunate to have men who served him with a loyalty that far surpassed his own.

A concluding note, probably a later addendum, states that there were thirty-seven names in all. This number has led to considerable head-scratching, for the names in 23:8-39 listed do not add up to thirty-seven [Do the Numbers Add Up?] Only 35 names are clear (the Three, Abishai and Benaiah and the Thirty). The many corruptions that have crept into the text are probably to blame for the apparent miscalculation. As noted above, the text can be read in different ways at several points, allowing for more or less proper names.

📖 Do the Numbers Add Up?

Here is an attempt to achieve the sum of 37 men:

The Three = 3
Abishai and Benaiah = 2
The Thirty = 30
Total = 35

Where are the two missing men? The reader may recall that the MT has "Adino the Ezenite" (23:8) in place of the LXX's "brandished his spear." If the editor who made the note had read this name and subconsciously added Joab, the total would be 37. This, however, is speculative, as are various other schemes that have been proposed.

CONNECTIONS

The truths inherent in this rather mundane text are not so much spiritual as practical. The careful list of David's warriors reminds the reader that David did not achieve his lofty position alone. He had help, not only from God, but also from others. His three cousins Joab, Abishai, and Asahel were with him from the first. A band of outlaw warriors attached themselves to him soon after his break with Saul, and many of them remained with him. Some of the stories in 2 Samuel 23:8-39 may go back to those early days. Whether it was the Three, the Thirty, or the Cherethites and Pelethites, David was aided by loyal supporters and encouragers.

throughout his career. To David's credit, he was the kind of man who inspired loyalty and dedication from those who followed him. To the narrator's credit, these stalwart and devoted men are not forgotten.

The love and loyalty that drove these heroic men to devote their lives to David's service are best evidenced by the anonymous trio who risked their lives to bring David a drink of water from Bethlehem's well (23:13-17). On a whim, David had expressed a longing for the water he had known as a youth, but his men interpreted David's nostalgic desire as a veritable command, and they put their own lives on the line to fulfill it. David recognized the sacred character of their noble gift.

The list as we have it seems to have originated early in David's reign. Unfortunately, as David grew in power and age, he apparently began to take the sacrifices of his men for granted. Uriah the Hittite was one of David's devoted, mighty men (v. 39a). David not only took Uriah's willingness to die for granted, but he also counted on it as a means to gain Uriah's wife for himself (2 Sam 11).

Like his ancestor David, Jesus knew better than to make a career of going it alone. He understood the importance of finding strength in others. Even as Jesus taught his disciples and called them to faith and faithfulness, he also depended on them for support. He sent them out on mission, and he relied on them to build on what they had learned to give form to the emerging church. Even though Jesus' three closest friends were prone to let him down (they went to sleep during his moment of greatest sorrow, Mark 14:32-41), they grew to the point of being willing to surrender their own lives for Jesus' sake. [Asleep on the Job]

Although it is difficult to work out precisely from the text, David's warriors seem to have been organized for maximum effectiveness. Each knew his place and his part in the larger scheme, working willingly together for the good of the king and the kingdom. Paul spoke of the church as the body of Christ, in which each person has a different role, but contributes joyfully to the good of the whole (1 Cor 12:12-31; compare Eph 4:11-13). The loyal warriors of 2 Samuel 23:8-39 served King David selflessly and seem to have considered it a privilege. Contemporary believers continue to serve an even greater king, the Son of David, and it is an even greater privilege.

Asleep on the Job

Unlike the three companions of David who risked their lives to bring him refreshing water from Bethlehem, Jesus' three closest disciples could not remain awake to offer him the comfort of their company in the dark night of Gethsemane. The good news about Peter, James, and John—and the great challenge for contemporary believers—is that Christ's resurrection woke them from their stupor and sent them on a lifelong mission to carry the water of life into the world.

Fra Angelico was a Florentine painter of the 15th century who painted in tempera and fresco. His figures were copied when artists needed models for subjects in contemplation, elegant drapery styles and naturalistic scenes.

Fra Angelico (c.1395–1455). *Prayer in the Garden of Gethsemane.* Pinacoteca. (Credit: Scala/Art Resource, NY)

NOTES

[1] Josephus, *Ant.* 7. 308.

[2] James B. Pritchard, ed., ANET (3d ed., Princeton: Princeton University Press, 1969), 486.

[3] Robert Bergen, *1, 2 Samuel* (NAC; Broadman and Holman, 1996).

[4] A. Zeron, "Der Platz Benajahus in der Heldenliste Davids [II Sam 23:20-23]," ZAW 90 (1978): 20-28.

[5] P. Kyle McCarter, *II Samuel* (AB 9; Garden City: Doubleday, 1984), 492.

[6] Ibid., 493-94, 499.

[7] Ibid., 492, 498.

DAVID'S MISTAKE
AND GOD'S JUDGMENT

24:1-25

COMMENTARY

This account of David's census, God's response, and the building of an altar in Jerusalem is paralleled by a similar story in 1 Chronicles 21. The Chronicler's version contains both additions to and deletions from the Deuteronomistic account in 2 Samuel, along with one blatant contradiction. [Who Inspired the Census?] These issues, along with a host of internal inconsistencies in 2 Samuel 24, have led scholars to postulate any number of potential literary histories leading up to the received text. [Internal Inconsistencies]

Was this originally a story about a plague that was later explained by the account of the census and expanded by the purchase of Araunah's threshing floor? Was the census itself the beginning point for the story, which attracted the other elements and grew by the process of accretion? Or did the account begin as an etiology for the establishment of the altar in Jerusalem, which called for additional explanations? Is it possible that the story was a unified narrative from the beginning, related in three movements, but confused by later

---

Internal Inconsistencies

The story abounds in apparent contradictions. Here is a representative sampling:

Is Yahweh responsible for the census (24:1)	Or is David responsible? (24:10)
Did Yahweh stop the plague before it reached Jerusalem, as v. 16a claims,	or did it continue in Jerusalem, as vv. 16b-17 suggest?
Did the plague cease because Yahweh had mercy (24:16),	or because David erected an altar, offered sacrifices, and prayed for relief (24:25)?
Was David motivated to build the altar by his vision of the destroying angel (24:16b),	or by the instruction of the prophet Gad (24:18-19)?

Who Inspired the Census?

Compare the very different versions of the Deuteronomist and the Chronicler:

2 Samuel 24:1	**1 Chronicles 21:1**
Again the anger of the LORD was kindled against Israel, and he incited David against them, saying, "Go, count the people of Israel and Judah."	Satan stood up against Israel, and incited David to count the people of Israel.

To these opposing explanations, we should also add the words of 2 Sam 24:10, in which David himself assumes full responsibility for making the decision to conduct a census: "But afterward, David was stricken to the heart because he had numbered the people. David said to the LORD, 'I have sinned greatly in what I have done. But now, O LORD, I pray you, take away the guilt of your servant; for I have done very foolishly' " (compare also 24:17).

What is clear is that David took a census. It is likely that he decided to do this on his own because it was good governmental policy. To Israel's theological historians, however, it was poor sacerdotal policy, a violation of trust in Yahweh. The Deuteronomistic editors begin the story with Yahweh's anger at some unnamed sin (or collection of sins) in Israel. Such sin cried out for punishment, but for the judgment to be understood as coming from Yahweh, a more focused catalytic event was needed. Thus, the Deuteronomist credited Yahweh with inciting David to order the census for the express purpose of provoking punishment (cf. Yahweh's hardening Pharaoh's heart in Exod 7–9 or the divine disinformation given the prophets of Ahab in 1 Kgs 22:19-23).

The Chronicler was no longer comfortable with the idea that God might incite someone to sin in order to set them up as a public illustration of the Deuteronomistic claim that wickedness must be punished. So the Chronicler insists that it was not Yahweh, but Satan, who inspired David to take a census (1 Chr 21:1). The word *śāṭān* is the same as in the book of Job, except that in 1 Chr 21:1 it has no definite article, as it characteristically does in Job 1:6-12; 2:1-6. Thus, while Job uses *haśśāṭān* as a title for a heavenly district attorney ("The Accuser"), in Chronicles "Satan" seems to have become a proper name for one who leads humankind into evil. This concept continued to develop in the postexilic period and was popularly accepted in the New Testament.

Thus, the theological and historical perspectives of the tradents have influenced their opinion of whether Yahweh or Satan incited David to number Israel. The most likely scenario is that David made the decision on his own, while later interpreters debated whether he did so under divine or demonic inspiration.

---

editorial insertions? Any of these options—plus several others—can be found in the secondary literature.

The story's location in the narrative is easier to explain than its literary history. Chronologically, chapter 24 probably belongs rather early in David's rule, not long after he had established Jerusalem as his capital. The first verse "And again the anger of the LORD was kindled against Israel" is an editorial introduction intended to connect the account to 2 Samuel 21, another displaced

story from early in David's reign. Both 2 Samuel 21 and 24 involve
the theme of Yahweh's anger and resulting judgment upon Israel,
counterposed with David's daring strategy for appeasing God's
anger and ameliorating Israel's distress. As argued above, chapter 21
probably followed chapter 8 in the original narrative before being
displaced for reasons discussed in the commentary at that point.

The present chapter also derives from early in David's reign, perhaps even preceding the events now found in chapter 21. The
cultic emphasis involved in the construction of an altar on the site
later used for Solomon's temple suggests that it may have originally
fit into the general context of David's introduction of the ark to
Jerusalem (2 Sam 6). The prophetic themes in 2 Samuel 7, however, insist that David was not allowed to build a temple for
Yahweh in Jerusalem. This task was deferred until the reign of
David's son Solomon. Thus, the chapter was probably moved to
the very end of 2 Samuel because it helps to set the stage for the
construction of Solomon's temple (1 Kgs 6). The Deuteronomist's
account does not locate Solomon's temple on the site of Araunah's
threshing floor, but the Chronicler's version does (2 Chr 3:1).

The story itself follows a straightforward pattern, beginning with
the census (vv. 1-9), moving to the account of the plague (vv. 10-
17), and concluding with David's acquisition of Araunah's
threshing floor as a place for sacrifice (vv. 18-25).

The story itself begins with the most obvious incongruity of all,
the amazing assertion that Yahweh was angry at Israel and that he
incited David to commit a flagrant sin as a public pretext to the
punishment Israel already deserved because of the unnamed prior
sin (v. 1). As mentioned above, v. 1 is tailored as a transitional verse
between 2 Samuel 21 and 24. There must have been a time when
the two stood side by side. The cause of Yahweh's anger is not
named as it was in chapter 21, where Saul's affront to the
Gibeonites had wrought an injustice.

Two issues beg for further explanation: the source of David's
inspiration to take a census and the question of why a census
should be considered such a bad thing.

The second sidebar in this chapter [Who Inspired the Census?] explores
the issue of David's inspiration. 2 Samuel 24:1 is not the first
account in which Yahweh is credited with contributing to a
human's sin. In Exodus 7–9, Yahweh continually "hardened
Pharaoh's heart" so that the Egyptian king brought plagues of
increasing severity upon himself and his people. Interpreters often
suggest that it was already in Pharaoh's heart to resist the divine will
and that Yahweh simply strengthened Pharaoh's resolve to do what

he already wanted to do. Presuming the assertion in v. 1 is correct, a similar argument could be made for David in 2 Samuel 24. David may have desired to take a census long before he sensed, in some fashion, a divine endorsement to carry it out.

The second issue regards the census itself. What is so sinful about a census? Why does David regard his action as a wicked thing before God even before the prophet Gad pointed it out to him? Some commentators argue that the sin was in the innovation; David was taking entirely too many things into his own hands and failing to honor the traditional channels of theocracy which left such matters in God's hands. There is something appealing about this argument, though the innovative aspect of the census seems overplayed. David is surely not the first king to have counted his subjects.

The most obvious problem with the census was its purpose. Although David asks only for "a census of the people" (v. 2), the number reported to him counts only males of fighting age (v. 9). The census, then, was taken for the purpose of establishing a bureaucratic database to assist in the military draft or possibly in the recruitment of corvee labor. This suggests a lack of trust in Yahweh, an oversupply of self-reliance, a failure to factor Yahweh into Israel's military aims (despite claims such as those in 1 Sam 14:6).

Another possible affront resulting from the census has to do with cultic purity. The Pentateuch gave instructions for a census in which each person registered was expected to pay a half-shekel tax to the temple as a kind of "redemption price" (Exod 30:11-16). This suggests that the taking of a census was regarded as a dangerous thing, requiring a ransom for each person counted as a means of preserving their safety. The expected ransom price also gives a cultic meaning to the institution of the census, one that was apparently ignored in 2 Samuel 24. People who were registered but who failed to pay the tax prescribed in Exodus 30 (whether they were asked for it is immaterial) would have become subject to judgment or at least ritually unclean. It is possible that this widespread impurity contributed to the sense of offense in the eyes of God.

The Census, 24:1-9

As mentioned above, the phrase "*again* the anger of the LORD was kindled" is an editorial transition, probably intended to recall a similar situation of divine displeasure from chapter 21. The stories take quite different tracks, however. In 2 Samuel 21, the land ndures three years of famine as punishment for Yahweh's anger before David seeks to learn the cause of God's vexation (Saul's earlier pogrom against the Gibeonites). In 2 Samuel 24, the initial cause of Yahweh's vexation is not named. Perhaps it related to a more general apostasy, as the prophets often condemned, rather than to a specific political event.

Perhaps because of the nonspecific nature of Israel's offense, the author gives the impression that Yahweh inspired David to undertake the census for the express purpose of creating a pretext to give public legitimation to his already-existent anger and to the consequent punishment.

David's part in the census is described in vv. 2-4a. He called Joab "and the commanders of the army" (lit., "the princes of the mighty men"), entrusting them with the task of numbering Israel "from Dan to Beer-sheba," the traditional extremes of Israelite territory. David makes his purpose clear: "so that I may know how many there are." The reader soon learns, however, that David is not interested in a population count, but a roster for the military draft.

Joab did not take the assignment eagerly. For once, hot-headed Joab is the one who speaks with the voice of reason. He offers a blessing to David and expresses a desire to see the population grow exponentially under the king's leadership, but then asks a question tinged with the fear and apparent amazement of one who knows that census-taking is anathema: *But why does my lord the king want to do this?* (v. 3b).

No answer is given. David does not explain his actions and certainly does not claim to be acting on Yahweh's instructions. Joab's voice of reason had turned David about when he was mired in grief following Absalom's death (2 Sam 19:1-8), but not here. The text records only that "the king's word prevailed against Joab and the commanders of the army" (v. 4a). The word for "prevailed" usually means "to be strong or firm." Both aspects may be present here. David's word was stronger by virtue of his position and apparently undergirded by a firmness of determination that his officers could not match.

The kingdom-wide compass of the census is described in vv. 4b-7. The account of the census-takers' itinerary is not included in the Chronicler's work, suggesting that it may have been a later addition to the text. It describes the officials' travel through the outer limits of the kingdom, beginning in the southeast corner, moving north, then west, and finally down to the southernmost extreme. Most scholars assume that the territories within this circuitous route were also polled, though at least one argued that David only counted the

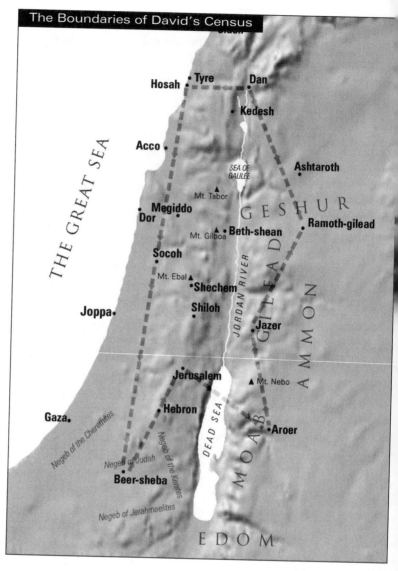

The Boundaries of David's Census

recently conquered outlying regions to see how many potential soldiers they added to the smaller population he inherited from Saul.[1] Since the tally is reported in terms of people from Judah and from Israel, however, it seems more reasonable to presume that the entire country was canvassed.

The precise route is difficult to trace because of several textual irregularities. [The Boundaries of David's Census] Most commentators assume that "Aroer" refers to a Transjordanian city now known as ʿArâʿir. It sat on the north bank of the Arnon River, at about the midpoint of the Dead Sea. The biblical tradition asserts that the Israelites took Aroer from Sihon, an Amorite king, during the early stages of the conquest (Deut 4:48; Josh 12:12). Aroer represented Israel's southern boundary east of the Jordan. There was another

Aroer located west of the Jordan, near Beersheba (1 Sam 30:28), but v. 5 insists that the officials first crossed the Jordan before reaching their starting point.

The NRSV translation "and from the city that is in the middle of the valley" suggests that the census had two starting points, from which the officials moved northward toward the territory of Gad and the city of Jazer. It is grammatically possible for "toward Gad and on to Jazer" to be read as identifying modifiers for the unnamed second starting point of the census: McCarter translated "the city in the wadi of the Gadites near Jazir."[2] It seems unlikely, however, that the two starting points would be so far apart. The unnamed city was probably near Aroer. Perhaps both groups worked their way north from that point, their direction being indicated by the track toward the territory of Gad and the city of Jazer. The tribal territory of Gad was located east of the Jordan, north of the Dead Sea, and south of the Sea of Galilee. Jazer was in the south-central part of Gad, on the border between Israel and the traditional territory of the Ammonites. Its ancient site was about twelve miles west of modern Amman, Jordan.

The route continued north (v. 6) through Gilead (the northern part of Gad), but the next point of the itinerary is textually uncertain. The NRSV follows the MT, which has "Kadesh of the Hittites." There was a Kadesh in the tribal lands of Naphthali (east of the Sea of Galilee and stretching northward to Dan), but it seems too far west for the indicated route and has no known association with the Hittites. There was also a Kadesh located on the Orontes River, but it was almost certainly too far north. Several scholars favor a view that assumes an unusual textual corruption, suggesting that the original reading was "beneath Hermon." Mount Hermon was just above Dan, the northernmost extremity of David's kingdom and the natural turning point for Joab's census takers. The distance from Aroer to Mount Hermon also appears in other texts as a traditional means of describing the extent of Israel's possessions east of the Jordan (cf. Deut 3:8; 4:48).

The officials traveled around toward the northern city-state of Sidon, apparently skirting its borders before turning south along the border with the city of Tyre. [Tyre and Sidon] "The fortress of Tyre" is an unusual expression, probably used to indicate that the emissaries did not go into the region of Tyre itself, but travelled past a Tyrian fortress located on the border.

The Hivites are unknown outside of the Old Testament. At times, they seem to be equivalent to the Horites, known extrabiblically as Hurrians. Both they and the Canaanites predated the

Tyre and Sidon

Both Tyre and Sidon were located on the Mediterranean coast in the region now occupied by Lebanon. The mountainous area was renowned for its cedar trees and its craftsmanship. Tyre is remembered as the home of King Hiram, who assisted in the building of both David's palace and Solomon's temple (2 Sam 5:11; 1 Kgs 5:1; 7:13-14; 9:11). Jezebel, the Baal-worshiping wife of King Ahab, was a Sidonian (1 Kgs 16:31).

In prophetic writings, Tyre and Sidon are often mentioned together as twin city-states who were a source of temptation to Israel (Jer 25:22; 27:3; 47:4; Joel 3:4; Zech 9:2). Jesus sometimes retreated to the area near Tyre and Sidon (Matt 15:21; Mark 7:31). He once referred to Tyre and Sidon as cities known for their wickedness, but who were more likely to repent than the Israelite cities of Bethsaida and Chorazin (Matt 11:21-22; cf. Luke 10:13-14).

Israelites in Palestine and maintained many ethnic enclaves within Israel.

Beersheba, the traditional southern border of Israel, was the ending point for the census. The Negeb is the desert-like area that comprises southern Judah in and about Beersheba.

According to v. 8, the taking of the census required nine months and twenty days, and resulted in a count of 800,000 potential soldiers from Israel, and 500,000 from Judah. Each person counted was called a "man of valor, drawing the sword" (a literal translation). [Brave Soldiers] The expression is intended to convey the number of men whose age, health, or ability rendered them capable of "drawing the sword" in battle.

The results of the census are considerably different in the variant traditions. The LXX[L] has the same total, but in the proportions of 900,000 and 400,000. The Chronicler's reckoning is much larger, as he lists 1,100,000 from Israel and 470,000 from Judah (1 Chr 21:5). All of these numbers seem too high for an ancient population occupying an area no larger than that found in Israel. They suggest a total population exceeding five million. Even today, with modern cultivation methods and a supply network that allows much denser settlement patterns, Israel's population hovers around six million.

Some scholars explain the problem by presuming that the numbers originally included women, children, and the aged, while others suspect a textual corruption. A third possibility is one mentioned on several previous occasions, that the term translated "thousand" (*'elep*) could also refer to a platoon of soldiers numbering from five to fourteen men (see comments at 1 Sam 4:2, 10). Using these figures, one computes an available army of less than 20,000 available draftees, which seems much more reasonable.

Brave Soldiers

AΩ The phrase *'îš ḥayil* originally meant "man of valor" in the sense of a strong and respectable person (like Saul's father Kish, 1 Sam 9:1; David, 1 Sam 16:18; Jeroboam, 1 Kgs 11:28; and others). In certain contexts, however, *ḥayil* could mean "army" (Exod 14:4, 9, 17, 28; 15:4; 1 Sam 17:20; 2 Sam 8:9; and others), so the expression could refer to any soldier.

he Plague, 24:10-17

he reader is surprised when David is suddenly stricken with pangs f guilt for ordering the census. Perhaps there was something about earing his people quantified in numbers that led him to recognize he non-spiritual nature of his enterprise. Perhaps it was the spirit f God. In any case, v. 10 is an account of David's prayer of deep ontrition. David acknowledged that he had "sinned greatly" and done very foolishly." He prayed for Yahweh to "take away the guilt f your servant."

As if in response to David's prayer, the prophet Gad appears to offer David a choice between three punishments as a means of atoning for his sin (24:11-13). [Pestilence, Sword, and Famine] This is Gad's first appearance since 1 Samuel 22:5, where he emerged as a companion of David who gives strategic advice to aid David in his flight from Saul. Gad seems to have held an official position; the Chronicler (2 Chr 29:25) refers to him as David's "royal seer" (*ḥōzēh-hammelek*), as opposed to Nathan, who is called simply "the prophet" (*hannābîʾ*).

The opportunity to choose one's punishment is most unusual in Scripture, making the story even more memorable. The three options before David may have been equally severe in their result, but were quite different in their duration. They are presented in descending order, from the longest to the shortest: three *years* of famine (the LXX and 1 Chr 21:12; MT has seven), three *months* of military defeat, or three *days* of pestilence. David had personal experience with Yahweh's ability to produce a famine (ch. 21), and Israel's traditions contained many examples of Yahweh's punishing power through pestilence and military defeat.

The ultimate source of either option would be Yahweh, but only one would be purely at Yahweh's pleasure—the plague. During a time of famine, the wealthy inevitably eat at the expense of the poor, so the resulting death and sorrow have a human element to them. During a time of war, it is humans who press to kill more or less, and by means of varying cruelty. When a deadly plague strikes in the ancient world, however, it affects both rich and poor, and its extent is measured only by the mercy of God, for there is no human recourse to defend against it. Thus, David's choice is the

Pestilence, Sword, and Famine

The death-dealing trio of pestilence, sword, and famine frequently appears together in Scripture, especially in the prophecies of Jeremiah and Ezekiel. Both prophets commonly predicted that Yahweh would send punishment upon Israel in the form of pestilence, sword, and famine. For example, Jeremiah threatened the population of Judah who remained under Zedekiah, saying "And I will send sword, famine, and pestilence upon them, until they are utterly destroyed from the land that I gave to them and their ancestors" (Jer 24:10; see also Jer 14:12; 15:2; 18:21; 21:7, 9; 27:8, 13; 29:17-18; 32:24, 36; 34:17; 38:2; 42:17, 22; 44:13).

Ezekiel declared against Jerusalem that "One third of you shall die of pestilence or be consumed by famine among you; one third shall fall by the sword around you; and one third I will scatter to every wind and will unsheathe the sword after them" (Ezek 5:12; see also Ezek 5:17; 6:11-12; 7:15; 12:16; 14:21).

In the light of these dire predictions, it seems a mercy that David was given the chance to choose only one member of the lethal trio.

only one he could have made that would maximize an appeal t
God's mercy: he chose the pestilence.

Some readers see an element of selfishness on David's part for no
choosing to have his enemies pursue him. David knew, howeve
that enemies would hardly pursue the king without also defeatin
his army, ravaging the countryside, and killing many people. An
option chosen would have affected a large element of the popula
tion, not David alone. Whether or not physical harm came t
David, his reputation would be damaged by the death whic
occurred under his leadership and apparently as the result of hi
errant choice. David does not speak the word "pestilence" but pray
only to fall into the hands of Yahweh, rather than humans (th
LXX adds an interpretive expansion in v. 15, stating that Davi
named the pestilence as his choice and that it came during the tim
of the wheat harvest).

In Scripture, the expression "hand of Yahweh" commonly refer
to the bringing of plagues. For example, when the ark was capture
and taken to the Philistine temple of Dagon, "the hand of th
LORD was heavy upon the people of Ashdod, and he terrified then
and struck them with tumors" (2 Sam 5:6; similarly vv. 7, 9, 11).

The pestilence itself is unnamed and undescribed except for th
fact that it apparently worked very quickly, killing 70,000 people
There is some confusion in the story about how the plague came t
an end, suggesting some combination of sources or heavy editoria
work. Depending on how the text is read, v. 15 may imply that th
plague lasted for only one day. The MT has "So the LORD sent a
pestilence on Israel from that morning until the appointed time"
(NRSV, v. 15a), which seems to indicate the full three days indi
cated by v. 13. The LXX, however, has "until dinner time"
(preferred by AB, NEB), which would reflect a Hebrew exempla
only one letter removed from the present text.

If "until dinner time" is correct, then the scourge lasted only fo
part of one day and was suspended early at Yahweh's initiative, ful
filling David's hope that the LORD would show mercy. In contrast
the reading "until the appointed time" suggests that the pestilenc
ravaged Israel for the designated three-day period. If that is th
case, the scene with the destroying angel at the threshing floor o
Araunah seems pointless, for the predicted period of plague woul
have been completed and there would have been no need fo
Yahweh to "relent concerning the evil" or for David to build a
altar to appease Yahweh's anger and bring an end to the plague
Thus, the larger context supports the LXX as the preferred reading

Destroyer

Yahweh's agent of destruction is described in v. 16 as "the angel" (*hammalʾāk*), as "the angel who was [do]ing destruction among the people" (*hammalʾāk [ha]mašḥît bāʿām*) and as "the angel of Yahweh" (*malʾāk [YH]WH*). *Malʾāk* is the Hebrew word for "messenger" or [env]oy." The Greek translation is *angelos*, leading to the [mod]ern translation as "angel." The envoy of Yahweh was a [heav]enly being sent to do the work of Yahweh—in this case [de]structive work. A similar agent of divine destruction [app]ears in the story of the death of the firstborn in Exod [12:]3. There the heavenly envoy is called "the destroyer" [(ha]mašḥît).

[S]ome recent interpreters relate the account to an ancient [deity] associated with a non-Israelite god such as Resheph, [a] Canaanite god of pestilence. The Mesopotamians also [had] such a god (Nergal), and the Greeks assigned destructive functions to Apollo. The name Resheph may be derived from the word for "fire," presumably because of the fevers associated with many illnesses associated with plague. Numerous written sources from ancient Mesopotamia (3rd millennium BC) and later from the Ugaritic city of Ras-Shamra testify to the popularity of the cult of Resheph. There is evidence that the cult also existed in Egypt during the eighteenth dynasty (1546–1310 BC). Israel was thus surrounded by and intermingled with populations who worshiped Resheph. In 1 Chr 7:25, an Israelite is named Resheph, and in Deut 32:24 and Ps 78:48, the word *rešep* is used with the meaning "pestilence."

These factors suggest a familiarity with the cult of Resheph in Israel, but the association of the avenging angel with Yahweh is too strong to presume that a Resheph tradition underlies the present story, where Yahweh is emphatically in control from beginning to end.

The agent of the plague is an envoy of Yahweh, a destroying angel similar to the one who caused the death of the firstborn in Exodus 12:23. [The Destroyer] The account seems awkward since the first reference to the divine envoy bears no explanation. The reader is simply told that "the angel" pointed his destructive hand toward Jerusalem, as if he has been introduced previously. Perhaps we are to understand that ancient readers would have presumed that any plague resulted from the work of a deific executioner, so no introduction was needed. As explained further in the adjacent box, certain gods of the ancient world were closely associated with pestilence.

The most theologically significant phrase in this text is the remarkable assertion that "the LORD relented concerning the evil" and ordered the angel to cease and desist. "Relented" reflects a Hebrew verb stem (*nḥm*) that is commonly used in the passive form to mean "to be sorry," "to have compassion," or "to be moved to pity." It can also carry the sense of repenting for one's actions, leading one to relent and reverse course. [Can Yahweh Repent?] David had hoped that Yahweh would be merciful, and his hopes were well founded. Having seen the sorrow and death left in the wake of the avenging angel, Yahweh called a halt at the edge of Jerusalem, saying "It is enough."

As the story is told, David is not convinced (or does not know) that the plague has been halted. He sees the destroying angel hovering over Araunah's threshing floor (the Chronicler says, "and in his hand a drawn sword stretched out over Jerusalem," 1 Chr 21:6). Threshing floors were often associated with theophanies or

---

Can Yahweh Repent?

AΩ The word "repent" may reflect one of two Hebrew verbs. The word *šub* means "to turn around, reverse course," and it is commonly used for human repentance made necessary by human sin. The word *niham* means "to be sorry" and can carry the sense of "repent" only as a change in behavior moved by pity. The Bible frequently refers to God as being sorry he had done something (such as creating man, Gen 6:6-7; or making Saul king, 1 Sam 15:1). Sometimes, such divine regret led Yahweh to change course.

The only time *šub* is associated with Yahweh is in Jonah 3:9, where the "King of Nineveh" expressed hope that God would relent and change his mind about the promised destruction of the city. The word *šub* is used twice, translated first as "relent," then as "turn." *Niham* appears in the same verse, translated as "change his mind." The next verse, which shows that the king's hopes were not in vain, uses *niham* to say that God had indeed changed his mind.

The impression is that Yahweh may repent or change, but only because he has been moved by compassion, not

because God has been guilty of doing wrong. In the pre[s] text (2 Sam 24:16), Yahweh calls the destroying angel t[o] halt because of his compassion for the suffering people, saying "it is enough." God may even repent "of evil," as [in] this text, but only in the sense that the deserved judgme[nt] from God's hand can be understood as an untoward eve[nt] for the recipient, not that Yahweh was wrong in sending [it] (compare also Amos 7:3, 6).

The prophets frequently foresaw judgment in Israel's future, but also declared the mercy of God, holding out t[he] hope that if humans would *repent*, Yahweh might *relent* [of] the intended judgment.

There is a limit to God's patience, however. Jeremiah speaks of a time when Yahweh will grow weary of relenting (15:6).

Thus, the biblical evidence suggests that God may indeed change his mind and relent concerning certain judgments he had planned for humankind. This change, however, is always motivated by divine mercy or human repentance, not an awareness of moral error on God's pa[rt]

---

visitations from God (Judg 6:37; 2 Sam 6:6). Assuming that the plague is still in force, David repents yet again. Arguing that he alone is guilty, and likening his subjects to innocent sheep, David pleads for Yahweh to spare the people and direct any further punishment toward himself and his own family (v. 17; in the LXX, David refers to himself as "the shepherd").

The Altar, 24:18-25

David's repentance serves as a transition to vv. 18-25, which seem to have originated separately from the previous story. Thus far the text implies that Yahweh alone called a halt to the plague just as the angel reached "the threshing floor of Araunah the Jebusite" (v. 16b). The remainder of the chapter, however, relates a different story in which David repents and responds to God's word through the prophet Gad by building an altar and offering sacrifices as an appeasement to God so that *"the LORD answered his supplication for the land, and the plague was averted from Israel"* (v. 25b).

This same story, with additional details about the angel's appearance and David's repentance, is found in the Chronicler's work (1 Chr 21:16-27). [David and the Angel in 2 Samuel and 1 Chronicles] It is likely that this section originated independently as an etiology intended to explain the location of Solomon's temple and to connect its purchase with David. Both stories may have arisen in

David and the Angel in 2 Samuel and 1 Chronicles

The account of David's encounter with the destroying angel is given fuller treatment in 1 Chronicles. The Chronicler's version appears to be supported by the Qumran text of Samuel (4QSamᵃ) and could be closer to the original. Here are the two for easy comparison:

2 Samuel 24:17

When David saw the angel who was destroying the people, he said to the LORD, "I alone have sinned, and I alone have done wickedly; but these sheep, what have they done? Let your hand, I pray, be against me and against my father's house."

1 Chronicles 21:16-17

David looked up and saw the angel of the LORD standing between earth and heaven, and in his hand a drawn sword stretched out over Jerusalem. Then David and the elders, clothed in sackcloth, fell on their faces. And David said to God, "Was it not I who gave the command to count the people? It is I who have sinned and done very wickedly. But these sheep, what have they done? Let your hand, I pray, O LORD my God, be against me and against my father's house; but do not let your people be plagued!"

The Chronicler's added detail sharpens the fearsome image of the angel and also the depth of David's repentance. Although the Deuteronomist and the Chronicler assign the incitement of the census to Yahweh and Satan, respectively, both versions report that David accepted the guilt as his own.

---

association with the same plague, but the difference in approach suggests that they experienced a period of separate development. At some point, they were spliced together with little or no attempt to resolve the apparent contradiction between v. 16 and vv. 18-25.

The name Araunah ("Ornan" in the Chronicler's version) is so unusual that it has given rise to much comment. It seems to be non-Semitic and has often been linked to a Hurrian root that means "lord" or "king." In its first appearance in the MT (24:16), it has a definite article, as if it is a title: "*The* Araunah." This word form, along with a jumbled reading in v. 23 that could be read as "Araunah the king," has led many scholars to see Araunah not just as an indigenous landowner, but as the pre-Israelite king of Jerusalem. The word "Araunah" is otherwise anarthrous, however, clearly used as a personal name and not a title. There is little real evidence to suggest that Araunah is anyone other than a respected and probably well-known landowner in Jerusalem, whose residence there predated David's arrival.

As in v. 11, David's penitent prayer is followed immediately by a visit from the prophet Gad, who appears as if he has been sent by Yahweh with the answer to David's prayer. Gad advised David to build an altar on the site. No further instructions are given, but David clearly understood the implication that he should also offer appeasing sacrifices to Yahweh once the altar was built.

David's immediate response in v. 19 is surprising, not because David obeyed, but because he appears to have received the message at some distance from the threshing floor. The text insists that David had seen the destroying angel personally (24:17), leading the reader to presume that he had been nearby. When David prepared to purchase Araunah's threshing floor, however, he "went up" while Araunah "looked down" to see the king and his retinue approaching (v. 20a). The storyteller's implication is either that David first saw the angel from a distance or that he had left the area prior to receiving Gad's message later in the day.

Araunah responded to David's approach with obeisance fitting the king that David had become (v. 20b). The negotiations that follow are reminiscent of Abraham's purchase of a burial plot from the Hittites (Gen 23:3-16). The seller couches his comments in extremely polite language that borders on being obsequious. He claims to be in the buyer's debt and offers to give the desired property freely, whereupon the buyer insists that a price must be paid for the transaction to have meaning. This deferential repartee was a customary manner of bargaining among many ancient oriental peoples.

David's response to Araunah's initial query makes it clear that his intention in buying the threshing floor is to build an altar and offer sacrifices for the purpose of bringing the plague to an end (v. 21). Although Yahweh has already called the pestilence to heel (24:16), David does not know. Araunah is just as anxious as David to avoid the plague, so his offer to give the land is accompanied by a generous proposal to freely give the oxen, along with their wooden yokes and threshing sledges, to serve as the sacrificial offering and the fire (vv. 22-23a). Araunah adds to his offer a word of blessing, a voiced hope that David's sacrifice will be successful in averting the plague (v. 23b).

David's reply has inspired readers time and time again. "No, but I will buy them from you for a price; I will not offer burnt offerings to the LORD my God that cost me nothing" (v. 24a). David knew that there was a price to be paid for sin. The plague was already exacting a terrible price, which David hoped to stanch through the agency of an appeasing sacrifice. Yet David knew that for his own sacrifice to have meaning, it must cost him something. If he had accepted Araunah's offer, it would have been Araunah's sacrifice, and not David's. Since David accepted responsibility for the sin

hich had brought on the plague, he knew that he must also
houlder the expense of the propitiatory sacrifices designed to
ssuage Yahweh's anger.

The precise cost to David is uncertain because of variant tradi-
ons. The present text says that he bought the threshing floor and
he oxen for fifty shekels of silver, while the parallel story in
Chronicles 21:25 insists that David paid *600 shekels of gold* for
he land alone, with no mention of the oxen. There is little hope of
esolving the wide discrepancy. The Jewish exegete Rashi argued
hat David paid to Araunah fifty shekels for each of the twelve
ribes (a total of 600), but this does not explain the shift from silver
o gold.

The story concludes with a brief account of David's altar-
uilding and his offering of two types of sacrifice: "burnt offerings"
nd "offerings of well-being." The "burnt offering" ('ōlâ), also
:alled a "holocaust offering," was completely consumed by the fire
;o that it ascended to God in the resulting smoke. It sometimes had
in expiatory function (Lev 9:7; 14:20; Job 1:5; 42:8) and was asso-
:iated with petitions to God (1 Sam 13:12; 2 Sam 24:25).

"Offerings of well-being" (šĕlāmîm), sometimes called "peace
offerings," functioned to maintain good relations between God and
those who worshiped him. The šĕlāmîm was a shared offering in
which the blood and visceral fat were burned on the altar, while the
remainder of the meat was shared by the priests and people (Lev
7:16-17, 28-34; 10:14-15; 22:18-23). The inclusion of šĕlāmîm
offerings in this context suggests that David sponsored it as a community event in which others participated.

The result of David's sacrifice is succinctly stated: "and the plague
was averted from Israel" (24:25b). This implies that both Yahweh's
mercy (24:16) and David's acts of penitence (24:17-25) played
roles in the cessation of the plague. In the prophetic books, divine
mercy and the reversal of fortunes are often promised, but only
after the offending people repent. It is significant that in this text,
God's grace comes first. When David offered his sacrifice he was
apparently unaware that Yahweh had halted the angel. David's personal penitence and public worship, however, reinforced Yahweh's
decision to bring the plague to an end. Divine mercy is freely given
because it is an integral part of Yahweh's character. Justice, however,
is another facet of God's character. Human penitence confirms that
judgment has fulfilled its function, facilitating the expression of
divine mercy.

CONNECTIONS

The account of David's experience with the census is almo[t]
certainly out of place chronologically, but it serves an importa[nt]
function in its present position as the last chapter of 1 an[d]
2 Samuel. From a literary as well as a cultic standpoint, it functio[ns]
as a bridge from the rule of David to the rule of Solomon, demo[n]
strating how the great temple of Solomon had its roots in the wo[rk]
of David, whose last action in 2 Samuel is to purchase the site lat[er]
used for Solomon's temple, to build an altar, and to offer sacrific[e]
to God. Thus, there is continuity between the work of the grea[t]
king David and his famous son Solomon.

The chapter also serves an additional function that is generall[y]
overlooked in favor of the literary/critical/historical issues. There i[s]
a prophetic, almost gospel-like cast to this chapter. If we think the[o]
ologically, the general outline of the story makes these assertions:

(1) Human sinfulness leads to divine anger.
(2) There is a price to be paid for sin.
(3) God's sense of justice is great, but his sense of compassion is even
greater.
(4) God offers grace to those who repent.

When God Gets Angry 24:1-9

The Bible often speaks of the wrath of God. God's anger generally
arises from some provocation on the part of his people (Deut 9:7;
Jer 7:19-20). Cultic offenses such as touching the ark could provoke God's anger (2 Sam 6:7), as could an act of injustice such as
Saul's pogrom against the Gibeonites (2 Sam 21). More often,
however, it is idol worship (1 Kgs 16:13; Ps 78:59; among many
others) or apostasy in general ("forsaking God," Ezra 8:22) that
sparks Yahweh's wrath. God's passionate desire is that his people
should follow his way and enjoy his blessings. God's passionate
anger is aroused when his own people forsake his way for a life of
idolatry, whether the idol is a material image or a self-centered
lifestyle.

In later years, prophets like Isaiah, Jeremiah, Amos, Micah, and
Hosea would roam the countryside and preach in the cities,
declaring Israel's corporate sin and predicting dire punishment for
the unrepentant. In 2 Samuel 24, God's message is not proclaimed
through an influential prophet, but through an action of the king.
People who were living without reference to God may not have
connected a famine or plague with their own behavior, but people

---

Root of All Evil

All sin, in one way or another, reflects a lack of trust in God, a prideful belief that we know better ⌐God. This is illustrated by the classic story of how sin ⌐ed the world (Gen 3). The serpent succeeded in ⌐ting Eve to eat of the forbidden tree by convincing her ⌐God was holding back and refusing to share all the ⌐ings of life. Eve took matters into her own hands and ⌐d the fruit, not because she was hungry, but because ⌐no longer trusted God to fulfill her needs.

⌐very intentional sin grows from a belief that the choices ⌐make for ourselves are better than the choices God ⌐d have us to make. The result of trusting self rather ⌐God is self-evident. Jeremiah put it this way in ch. 17:

⌐hus says the LORD:
⌐ursed are those who trust in mere mortals
   and make mere flesh their strength,
   whose hearts turn away from the LORD.

6They shall be like a shrub in the desert,
   and shall not see when relief comes.
They shall live in the parched places of the wilderness,
   in an uninhabited salt land.
7Blessed are those who trust in the LORD,
   whose trust is the LORD.
8They shall be like a tree planted by water,
   sending out its roots by the stream.
It shall not fear when heat comes,
   and its leaves shall stay green;
in the year of drought it is not anxious,
   and it does not cease to bear fruit.

Jeremiah's poem is reminiscent of Israel's wisdom school (cf. also Ps 1), who taught that the fear of the LORD was the beginning of wisdom (Job 28:28; Ps 111:10; Prov 1:7; 9:10). Yahweh's action against Israel was designed to heighten the nation's awareness of sin and to encourage all to put their trust in Yahweh.

---

who experienced severe trial immediately following a national census would be more likely to make the connection.

It may be helpful to think of David's census as a magnifying glass held in the sun, a single provocation that focused the nation's widespread sin into an easily identifiable beam. The sin in the census was a lack of trust in Yahweh to protect and provide for his people. The widespread but unnamed sin of v. 1, like every other sin, would have had its roots in a lack of trust in God as well. [The Root of All Evil]

The Powerful Potential of Choice, 24:10-17

The text does not question Yahweh's right to be angry or to punish those who provoke him. The remarkable thing about this story is that David is given the opportunity to choose his poison. Yahweh's offer through the prophet Gad reminds David that his earlier choice had elicited the current situation; his present choice would impact the future. The three options were probably intended to be relatively equal in severity, differing primarily in duration. David saw that they also varied in the extent to which humans would be involved in effecting the punishment.

When David was given a choice, he chose the only option that put his future wholly in the hands of God. A famine could lead to more suffering or less, depending on how those affected react to their deprivation. Oppression by one's adversary could result in greater or lesser tribulation and death, depending on the cruelty of the enemy. A plague, however, was God's doing alone. By choosing the option of a pestilence, David also put his faith and hope in the possibility of divine mercy.

Every person is faced with many choices in every day. Some choices are amoral. Whether we wear the red shirt or the blue shirt is lacking in spiritual implications, unless we know that one of the shirts was manufactured under oppressive conditions. Every day we choose how we will treat the people in our families and our work-place. Every day we decide whether we will go out of our way to help another. Every day we choose behaviors that are characteristic of the narrow way to life or the broad way to destruction.

The ability to make choices for ourselves is both liberating and dangerous. It is also what makes us human. If God had not granted to humankind the freedom to choose our own way, we would be nothing more than incredibly intricate biological robots. As long as we live, choices lay before us. As long as there are choices, there is hope.

David's choices for both good and evil had far-reaching consequences, as do ours. The text reminds us that the wise will choose the way of God.

The Painful Price of Mercy, 24:18-25

David's purchase of Araunah's threshing floor has great literary and historical significance, but the theological truth behind it carries far more power. Acting on Gad's advice, David acquired the threshing floor of Araunah, a level place in an elevated part of Jerusalem that would serve as an ideal place for an altar devoted to the worship of God.

Araunah offered to give the field to David, along with the oxen and their wooden sledges and yokes for the sacrifice. David demurred, with words that ring clear and true through the years: "I will not offer burnt offerings to the LORD my God that cost me nothing" (24:24b). David understood that a sacrifice without cost is no sacrifice at all. The meaning of the sacrifice is found in the cost it exacts from the one who gives it.

David paid a price from his own pocket to purchase the sacrifices designed to appease God's wrath and bring an end to the plague. God responded with grace, and Jerusalem was saved. Before taking action to buy the land and offer the sacrifices, David accepted responsibility for the sin that had prompted Yahweh's judgment.

sing the image of a shepherd who cares for his sheep, David leaded with God to impose the penalty upon his house alone, ranting life to his "innocent sheep" (24:17). The reader remembers that Yahweh was already angry *at Israel* before David called for census, and that at Yahweh's instigation (24:1). There is a sense, hen, in which David has taken upon himself the guilt of the ation.

Christian readers may see in this a foreshadowing of the coming on of David who would also speak of himself as the shepherd of he sheep (John 10), one who would take the sin of the people upon himself and pay the price for their salvation. The story of David, the man after God's own heart, ends with David making a personal sacrifice so that others might live another day on the earth. The story of David's descendant ends with Jesus making the ultimate sacrifice so that all who trusted him might live in eternity John 3:16).

The final form of the books of Samuel grew out of the bleak period of the exile, when Israel had little hope of new life. The Samuel scroll begins with the sacrifice of Hannah, ends with the sacrifice of David, and unknowingly sets the stage for the sacrifice of Israel's long-awaited Messiah, who would offer a hope not yet envisioned by the ancient authors.

NOTES

[1] S. Herrmann, *A History of Israel in Old Testament Times*, (London/Philadelphia: SCM Press/Fortress Press, 1975), 157.

[2] P. Kyle McCarter, *II Samuel* (AB 9; Garden City: Doubleday, 1984), 502, 510.

BIBLIOGRAPHY

BIBLICAL COMMENTARIES

Anderson, A. A. *2 Samuel.* Word Bible Commentary 11. Waco: Word Books, 1989.

Baldwin, Joyce. *1 & 2 Samuel: An Introduction and Commentary.* Tyndale Old Testament Commentaries. Leicester, England: Intervarsity Press, 1988.

Bergen, Robert D. *1, 2 Samuel.* The New American Commentary. Nashville: Broadman & Holman, 1996.

Budde, K. *Die Bücher Samuel.* Kürzer Handkommentar zum alten Testament 8. Tübingen: Mohr, 1902.

Brueggemann, Walter. *First and Second Samuel.* Interpretation: A Bible Commentary for Teaching and Preaching. Louisville: John Knox Press, 1990.

Caspari, W. *Die Samuel Bücher.* Leipzig: Deichertsche, 1926.

Chafin, Kenneth L. *1, 2 Samuel.* The Communicator's Commentary. Dallas: Word Books, 1989.

Dhorme, R. *Les livres de Samuel.* Etudes bibliques 9. Paris: Gabalda, 1910.

Driver, S. R. *Notes on the Hebrew Text and the Topography of the Book of Samuel,* 2d. ed. Oxford: Clarendon Press, 1913.

Hertzberg, H. W. *I and II Samuel.* Philadelphia: Westminster Press, 1964.

Keil, C. F., and F. Delitzch. *Commentary on the Old Testament in Ten Volumes, II.* Repr., Grand Rapids: Eerdmans, 1971.

Klein, Ralph W. *1 Samuel.* Word Biblical Commentary 10. Waco: Word Books, 1983.

McCarter, P. Kyle. *1 Samuel.* The Anchor Bible 8. New York: Doubleday, 1980.

McCarter, P. Kyle. *2 Samuel.* The Anchor Bible 9. New York: Doubleday, 1984.

Philbeck, Ben. "1-2 Samuel." Pages 1-145 in *The Broadman Bible Commentary* 3. Nashville: Broadman Press, 1970.

Robinson, Gnanna. *1 & 2 Samuel: Let Us Be Like the Nations.* International Theological Commentary. Grand Rapids: Eerdmanns, 1993.

Smith, Henry Preserved. *A Critical and Exegetical Commentary on the Books of Samuel.* International Critical Commentary. Edinburgh: T. & T. Clark, 1899.

IER RELATED BOOKS

Robert. *The Art of Biblical* Poetry. New York: Basic Books, 1985.

Marcus J. *Jesus: A New Vision.* San Francisco: HarperSanFrancisco, 1987.

. *Meeting Jesus Again for the First Time.* San Francisco: HarperSanFrancisco, 1994.

nach, Sarah Ban. *The Simple Abundance Journal of Gratitude.* New York: Time rner, 1996.

er, Athalya. *The Israelite Woman: Social Role and Literary Type in Biblical Narrative,* Biblical Seminar. Sheffield: JSOT Press, 1985.

gemann, Walter and Hans Walter Wolff. *The Vitality of Old Testament Traditions,* 2d Atlanta: John Knox, 1982.

ner, Frederick. *Wishful Thinking: A Theological* ABC. New York: Harper & Row, 3.

dge, Tony W. *Vows in the Hebrew Bible and the Ancient Near East.* JSOT plement Series, No. 147. Sheffield: JSOT Press, 1992.

y, C. *Absalom! Absalom! Narrative and Language in 2 Sam. 13-20.* Rome: Biblical itute Press, 1978.

e, Peter. *The Problem of War in the Old Testament.* Grand Rapids, Eerdmans, 1978.

Frank Moore. *Canaanite Myths and Hebrew Epic.* Cambridge, MA: Harvard versity Press, 1973.

ello, Anthony. *Taking Flight.* New York: Doubleday, 1988. p. 32.

x, Roland. *Ancient Israel: Its Life and Institutions.* Translated by J. McHugh. 2 vols.; don: Daughton, Norman, & Todd, 1961.

er, H. and W. Rollig. *Kanaanische und aramaische Inschriften.* 3 vols.; Wiesbaden: rassowitz, 1962-64.

dt, Otto. *Die Komposition der Samuelis-b cher.* Leipzig: Hinrichs, 1931.

er, Lyle. *Kingship of God in Crisis: A Close Reading of 1 Samuel 1-12.* Sheffield: ond Press, 1985.

stein, Israel and Nadav Na'aman. *From Nomadism to Monarchy: Archaeological and orical Aspects of Early Israel.* Washington: Biblical Archaeology Society, 1994.

im, Terrence. *The Deuteronomistic History.* Nashville:Abingdon, 1983.

in, Raymond Jean and Jan Wojcik, eds. *The David Myth in Western Literature.* due University Press, 1980.

mann, Jan P. *Narrative Art and Poetry in the Books of Samuel, II, King David.* Assen: Gorcum, 1981.

. *The Crossing Fates.* Assen: van Gorcum, 1986.

a, J. C. L. *Textbook of Syrian Semitic Inscriptions,* vol. 1. Oxford:Clarendon Press, 1-82.

ald, Norman K. *The Tribes of Yahweh: A Sociology of the Religion of Liberated Israel, 0-1050 B.C.E.* Maryknoll, NY: Orbis Books, 1979.

, R. K. *The Dream Theophany of Samuel: Its Structure in Relation to Ancient Near ern Dreams and its Theological Significance.* PhD diss., Vanderbilt University, 1980.

Gunn, D. M. *The Story of King David, Genre and Interpretation.* JSOT Supplement 6. Sheffield: JSOT Press, 1978.

Horner, Tom. *Jonathan Loved David: Homosexuality in Biblical Times.* Philadelphia: Westminster Press, 1978.

Hylander, I. *Der literarische Samuel-Saul Komplex (1 Sam. 1-15) traditionsgeschichtlic Untersucht.* Uppsala: Almqvist & Wiksell, 1932.

Ishida, Tomoo. *The Royal Dynasties in Ancient Israel: A Study on the Formation and Development of Royal-Dynastic Ideology.* BZAW 142. New York: Walter de Gruyter 1977.

Jeffrey, David Lyle, ed., *A Dictionary of Biblical Tradition in English Literature.* Grand Rapids: Eerdmans, 1992.

Lehmann, Arthur C. and James E. Myers, *Magic, Witchcraft, and Religion: An Anthropological Study of the Supernatural.* Palo Alto, CA: Mayfield Publishing Company, 1985.

Lindblom, J. *Prophecy in Ancient Israel.* Philadelphia: Fortress Press, 1962.

Matthews, Victor H. and Don C. Benjamin. *The Social World of Ancient Israel 1250- BCE.* Peabody, MA: Hendrickson, 1993

Miller, J. M. and J. M. Hayes. *Israelite and Judean History.* London: SCM Press, 1990

Miller, Patrick D. and J. J. M. Roberts, *The Hand of the Lord: A Reassessment of the "A Narrative" of 1 Samuel.* The Johns Hopkins Near Eastern Studies. Baltimore: Johns Hopkins, 1977.

Miscall, P. *I Samuel: A Literary Reading.* Bloomington, IN.: Indiana University Press, 1986.

Noth, Martin. *Überlieferungsgeschichtliche Studien,* 1943. Translation *The Deuteronom History,* 2ᵈ ed., JSOT Supplement Series No. 15. Sheffield: Sheffield Academic Pres 1991.

Piorkowski, Geraldine K. *Too Close for Comfort: Exploring the Risks of Intimacy.* New Y Plenum Press, 1994.

Pritchard, James, Editor. *Ancient Near Eastern Texts Relating to the Old Testament.* 3ᵈ e Princeton: Princeton University Press, 1969.

Rost, L. *The Succession to the Throne of David,* trans. of *Überlieferung von derThronnachfolge Davids* (1926) by M. D. Rutter and D. M. Gunn. Sheffield: Almond Press, 1982.

Roux, Georges. *Ancient Iraq,* 2ᵈ ed. Harmondsworth, England: Penguin Books, 1980.

Smend, Rudolph. *Yahweh War & Tribal Confederation.* Translated by Max G. Rogers Nashville: Abington, 1970.

Sternberg, Meir. *The Poetics of Biblical Narrative: Ideological Literature and the Drama Reading*. Bloomington: Indiana University Press, 1987.

Thorman, George. *Incestuous Families.* Springfield, IL:Charles C. Thomas, 1983.

Tigay, Jeffrey. *The Evolution of the Gilgamesh Epic.* Philadelphia: University of Pennsylvania Press, 1982.

Trible, Phyllis. *Texts of Terror.* Philadelphia: Fortress Press, 1984.

von Rad, Gerhard. *Holy War in Ancient Israel.* Translated by Marva Dawn. Grand Rapi Eerdmans, 1991.

_. *The Problem of the Hexateuch and Other Essays.* Translated E. W. Trueman Dicken,
·m 1958 German Edition. New York: McGraw-Hill, 1958.

1am, George. *The Book of Leviticus.* NICOT. Grand Rapids, Eerdmans. 1979.

·bray, R. N. *The Succession Narrative: A Study of II Samuel 9-20 and I Kings 1-2.*
ndon: SCM Press, 1968.

ams, Michael E., ed. *Judges-Kings.* The Storyteller's Companion to the Bible, Vol. 3.
ashville, Abingdon Press, 1992.

·n, Robert R. *Prophecy and Society in Ancient Israel.* Philadelphia: Fortress Press,
·80.

·hwein, E. *Der Erzählung von der Thronfolge Davids—theologische oder politische
·schicts-schreibung?* Theologische Studien, 115. Zurich: Theologische Verlag, 1974.

_. *The Text of the Old Testament.* Grand Rapids, Eerdmans, 1979.

JRNALS AND OTHER ARTICLES

·yd, Peter. "The Succession Narrative (so-called)." *Interpretation* 35 (1981): 383-96.

·ght, W. F. "The Israelite Conquest of Canaan in the Light of Archaeology." *BASOR*
·039)74:11-23.

·ews, Stephen J. "Molech." Pages 580-01 in *MDB.* Edited by Roger Bullard, Joel F.
·inkard, Jr., Walter Harrelson, and Edgar V. McKnight. Macon: Mercer University
·ss, 1990.

·3arak, Zafrira. "The Legal Background to the Restoration of Michal to David."
·*Sup* 30 (1979): 15-29.

·rd, Roger. "Texts/Manuscripts/Versions." Pages 890-96 in *MDB.* Edited by Roger
·llard, Joel F. Drinkard, Jr., Walter Harrelson, and Edgar V. McKnight. Macon GA:
·rcer University Press, 1990.

·, Claudia. "The Wise Women of 2 Samuel: A Role Model for Women in Early
·ael?" *CBQ* 43 (January 1981): 14-29.

·dge, Tony W. "The Nazirites." *The Biblical Illustrator* 19 (Oct.-Dec. 1992): 54-58.

_. "Sacrifice." Pages 783-84 in *MDB.* Edited by Roger Bullard, Joel F. Drinkard, Jr.,
·lter Harrelson, and Edgar V. McKnight. Macon GA: Mercer University Press, 1990.

_. "Vows." Pages 998-99 in vol. 4 of *The International Standard Bible Encyclopedia.*
·ited by G. W. Bromiley. 4 vols. Grand Rapids: Eerdmans, 1979-1988.

_. "Were Nazirite Vows Unconditional?" Pages 409-22 in *CBQ* 51 (1989).

·n, Kenneth I. "King Saul, A Bungler from the Beginning." *BibRev* 10 (October
·94).

·hill, C. H. "Ein elohistischer Berich Über die Entstehung des israelistischen
·nigtums in 1 Samuelis 1-15 aufgezeight." Pages 130-31 in *Zeitschrift für kirchliche
·ssenschaft und kirchliches Leben* 6 (1885).

·berg, Bruce. "Vengeance/Avenger." Pages 947-48 in *MDB.* Edited by Roger Bullard,
·l F. Drinkard, Jr., Walter Harrelson, and Edgar V. McKnight. Macon: Mercer
·iversity Press, 1990.

·at, L. "Tendenz und Theologie der David-Solomon Erzählung." Pages 26-36 in *Das
·ne und nahe Wort*, BZAW 105. Berlin: de Gruyter, 1967.

Douglas, Mary. "Deciphering a Meal." *Daedalus* 101 (Winter 1972): 66.

Driver, G. R. "Ugaritic and Hebrew Words." *Ugaritica* 6(1969): 181-86.

Dus, J. "Die Geburtslegende Samuel I Sam. 1: Eine traditionsgeschichtliche Untersuchung zu 1 Sam. 1-3." Pages 163-94 in *Revista degli study orientali* 43 (196⟨

Emmerson, Grace. "Women in Ancient Israel." Pages 371-94 in *The World of Ancient Israel: Sociological, Anthropological and Political Perspectives*, ed. R. E. Clements. Cambridge: Cambridge University Press, 1989.

Fokkelman, Jan P. "Saul and David: Crossed Fates." *BibRev* 5 (June 1989):20-32.

Fritz, Volkmar. "Conquest or Settlement? The Early Iron Age in Palestine." *BA* (1987):84-100.

Galling, K. "Goliath und seine Rüstung." Pages 150-69 in *Volume du Congrès: Genève* VTSup 15. Leiden: E. J. Brill, 1966.

Greenberg, Moshe. "Avenger of Blood." *IDB*. 4 vols. New York: Abingdon, 1962.

Greengus, Samuel. "Sisterhood Adoption at Nuzi and the 'Wife-Sister' Motif in Gen⟨ HUCA 46 (1975): 9.

Halpern, Bruce. "The Political Import of David's Marriages," *JBL* 99 (1980): 507-18⟨

Hinz, W. "Persia, c. 2400-1800 B.C." *CAH* I, 2: 644-80.

Hoffner, H. A. " *'Ûbh*," *TDOT* I: 130-34.

Hoftijzer, J. "Das sogannte Feueropfer," *Hebraische Wortforschung*. Leiden: E. J. Brill, 1967. 114-34.

Hopkins, Keith. "Brother-Sister Marriage in Ancient Egypt," *Comparative Studies in Society and* History 22 (1980): 303-54.

Jastrow, Morris. "The Name Samuel and the Stem *ö'l.*" *JBL* 19 (1900): 82-105.

Jeremias, J. "*poimen*," *TDOT*, 6:485-502.

Knight, Douglas A. "Family." Pages 295-96 in *MDB*. Edited by Roger Bullard, Joel F⟨ Drinkard, Jr., Walter Harrelson, and Edgar V. McKnight. Macon: Mercer Universi⟨ Press, 1990.

Lambert, W. G. "Enmeduranki and Related Matters." *JCS* 21 (1967): 126-138.

Levinson, J. D. "1 Samuel 25 as Literature and as History." *CBQ* 40 (1978): 11-28.

_____. "1 Samuel 25 as Literature and as History." *Literary Interpretations of Biblical Narratives*, vol. 2. Ed. K. R. R. Gros Louis. Nashville: Abingdon, 1982.

Lust, J. "On Wizards and Prophets." *Studies in Prophecy*, VTSup 26 (Leiden: E. J. Bri⟨ 1974): 133-42.

Mattingly, Gerald. "Ammon/Ammonites." Pages 23-24 in *MDB*. Edited by Roger Bullard, Joel F. Drinkard, Jr., Walter Harrelson, and Edgar V. McKnight. Macon: Mercer University Press, 1990.

McCarter, P. Kyle. "'Plots True and False.' The Succession Narrative as Court Apologetic." *Interpretation* 35 (1981): 455-67.

Mendelsohn, I. "Samuel's Denunciation of Kingship in the Light of the Accadian Documents from Ugarit." *BASOR* 143 (1956): 17-22.

Mendenhall, George. "The Census Lists of Numbers 1 and 26." *JBL* 77 (1958): 52-⟨

_____. "The Hebrew Conquest of Palestine." *BA* (1962) 25:66-87.

rs, Carol. "David as Temple Builder." *Ancient Israelite Religion: Essays in Honor of ank Moore Cross.* Edited by Patrick D. Miller, Jr., Paul D. Hanson, and S. Dean cBride. Philadelphia: Fortress Press, 1987.

, R. "Der Prophet Samuel: Eine traditionsgeschichtliche Untersuchung." *ZAW* 56 936): 177-225.

ks, Hershel. "I Climbed Warren's Shaft (But Joab Never Did)." *BAR* (Nov.-Dec. 99): 30-35.

nbs, L. E. "War, Ideas of." Pages 796-801 in *IDB*, Vol. 4. New York: Abingdon, 62.

aux, Roland. "Single Combat in the Old Testament." Pages 122-135 in *The Bible and e Ancient Near East.* Garden City, NY: Doubleday, 1971.

ers, Stanley. "Hannah and Anna: The Greek and Hebrew Texts of I Sam. 1." *JBL* 07(1988): 385-412.

is, J. T. "Function of Comprehensive Anticipatory Redactional Joints in 1 Samuel 16-8." *ZAW* 85 (1973): 294-314.

is, T. "An Anti-Elide Narrative Tradition from a Prophetic Circle at the Ramah anctuary." *JBL* 30 (1971): 288-308.

___. "Cultic Elements in the Story of Samuel's Birth and Dedication." *Studia heologica* 26 (1972): 32-61.

___. "Samuel versus Eli." *TZ* 35 (1979): 201-212.

son, Johnny. "Holy War." Pages 385-86 in *MDB*. Edited by Roger Bullard, Joel F.)rinkard, Jr., Walter Harrelson, and Edgar V. McKnight. Macon: Mercer University ress, 1990.

INDEX OF MODERN AUTHORS

1 SAMUEL
INDEX OF SIDEBARS

Illustration Sidebars

2 SAMUEL
INDEX OF SIDEBARS

Illustration Sidebars

INDEX OF SCRIPTURES

INDEX OF TOPICS